EDUCATING STUDENTS WITH AUTISM SPECTRUM DISORDERS

Similar to a handbook in its comprehensive description of the theory and research supporting current practices in the treatment of autism spectrum disorders, this interdisciplinary text shows how the existing knowledge base can be used to explore promising new possibilities related to the field's many unanswered questions. Key features include the following:

Comprehensive—This is the first text to consider the history and current state of autism as a field in transition, to cover its varied approaches and philosophies, and to describe the interventions used throughout the developmental cycle.

Cross Disciplinary—Serving students with autism necessitates communication and collaboration among professionals from several disciplines as well as family members. The editors have, therefore, brought together divergent perspectives, theories and philosophies in order to demonstrate that scientific evidence, rather than educational orientation, must determine which practices should be selected for use in particular situations.

Research Based—Whereas many existing texts advocate a particular type of treatment, this one recognizes that interventions must be selected and evaluated based on the scientific evidence of their effectiveness.

Integrated Methodology—Chapter authors consider findings from studies that employ single-subject designs, experimental large-scale studies, and qualitative methodology. The inter-relatedness of therapies and disciplines will be highlighted throughout.

Expertise—The volume editors are all highly visible researchers in autism and developmental disabilities. Likewise, each chapter is directed by a senior, highly accomplished author who is nationally recognized for his/her work in the topic being addressed.

This book is appropriate for practicing professionals in education and psychology and for speech/language therapists and other clinicians. It is also suitable as a graduate level text in these fields.

Dianne Zager is Michael C. Koffler Professor in Autism at Pace University.

Michael L. Wehmeyer is Gene A. Budig Teaching Professor of Special Education at the University of Kansas.

Richard L. Simpson is Professor of Special Education at the University of Kansas.

EDUCATING STUDENTS WITH AUTISM SPECTRUM DISORDERS

Research-Based Principles and Practices

Edited by Dianne Zager, Michael L. Wehmeyer, and Richard L. Simpson

Routledge
Taylor & Francis Group

LONDON AND NEW YORK

First published 2012 by Routledge
2 Park Square, Milton Park, Abingdon, Oxon OX14 4RN
52 Vanderbilt Avenue, New York, NY 10017

Routledge is an imprint of the Taylor & Francis Group, an informa business

© 2012 Taylor & Francis

Library of Congress Cataloging in Publication Data
Educating students with autism spectrum disorders / edited by Dianne Zager, Michael L. Wehmeyer, and Richard L. Simpson.
   p. cm.
   Includes bibliographical references and index.
   1. Autistic children—Education. 2. Autism. 3. Inclusive education. I. Berkell Zager, Dianne
II. Wehmeyer, Michael L. III. Simpson, Richard L.
LC4717.E36 2011
371.94—dc22
2011000891

ISBN13: 978-0-415-87756-5 (hbk)
ISBN13: 978-0-415-87757-2 (pbk)

Typeset in Bembo and Gill Sans by
EvS Communication Networx, Inc.

This book is dedicated to members of CEC's Division on Autism and Developmental Disabilities and all professionals who contribute to the education of students with autism and developmental disabilities.

CONTENTS

PREFACE

The increased prevalence of autism diagnoses over the past decade has led to heightened demand for information on autism spectrum disorders (ASD). In the special education arena, autism has become a major concern. With issues related to etiology and treatment still receiving frequent media coverage, autism has been, and continues to be the focus of extensive study, debate, and frequently controversy.

When we were approached by Lane Akers, Senior Editor at Routledge/Taylor & Francis Publishing and asked to produce a text on research-based practices to support the education of learners with ASD, we agreed to do so because we recognized the need to objectively examine the extant database underlying current practices in ASD. Royalties from the sale of this text will be contributed to the Division on Autism and Developmental Disabilities (DADD) of the Council for Exceptional Children in the hope that the text will contribute knowledge by providing a vehicle through which to share research-based information. Proceeds will help DADD to continue its important work of advocating for people with developmental disabilities and the professionals that support them.

This text considers the needs of people with ASD at various stages in their development from different perspectives. While people on the autism spectrum share basic characteristics, such as communication challenges and restricted interests, they may also have a wide array of diverse abilities and support needs. The thrust of the book is to examine the research base for a variety of current, widely employed practices in the field.

In each chapter, the evidence (or limitations to that evidence base) to support particular methods is explored. Not surprisingly, as the contributing authors, all of whom are leading experts in their disciplines, wrote their respective chapters, several contacted us to express difficulty in finding high quality evidence to support methods they were describing. In the midst of the process, in appreciation of the state of the science of autism intervention; we changed the text's original title of *evidence-based* to *research-based*. This decision was grounded in recognition of the lack of indisputable evidence to support certain principles and practices employed today. This is not to say that the methods are not worthy, but to reaffirm the need to conduct high quality research, both quantitative and qualitative, on which we can make sound educational decisions. We are comfortable that the information provided represents what is best practice in the field at this point in time. The lack of an evidence base for any particular strategy or intervention does not speak directly to the potential efficacy of that strategy or intervention, it speaks only to the need to conduct and disseminate more rigorous research to test (and, in many cases, we're certain, confirm) the intervention's efficacy. It is our hope that in future editions of texts such as this, there will be a stronger evidence base upon which to make instructional decisions for students with ASD.

The text is divided into four sections. Section I provides an overview of the field of ASD, beginning with an examination of historical perspectives and legislation by Tom Smith, Robert Stodden, David Smith, and Mary White. In chapter 2, Joel Bregman and Claudine Higdon present a comprehensive discussion of characteristics of children with ASD. Catherine Lord,

Constanza Colombi, So Hyun Kim, and Alayna Schrier take us through the identification and into diagnosis of autism spectrum disorders in the third chapter.

Section II covers widely held philosophies and current practices in ASD. Applied behavior analysis is reviewed by Jack Scott and Kyle Bennett, followed by a chapter on the developmental individual relationship model by Serena Wieder. Structured teaching and the TEACCH model are presented by Gary Mesibov, Victoria Shea, and Stephanie McCaskill. Academic development through integrated behavioral experiential teaching is presented by Dianne Zager and Francine Dreyfus to highlight a model of instruction dedicated to math and literacy. The Zaggurat model is described in the final chapter of Section II by Brenda Smith Myles, Barry Grossman, Ruth Aspy, Shawn Henry, and Sheila Smith.

In Section III, educational needs are considered from different developmental and cultural standpoints. Cultural and linguistic diversity, as they affect children with ASD, are addressed by Elizabeth West and Pei-Yu Chen. Amanda Boutot and Jennifer Walberg's chapter deals with early intervention and early childhood education. Juane Heflin and Jackie Isbell cover instructional issues for school-age children and adolescents. Social skills and interaction are addressed in depth by Richard Simpson, Jeni Ganz, and Rose Mason. Michael Wehmeyer and Tom Smith provide a chapter that addresses both self-determination and social interaction, which is followed by Michael Wehmeyer and James Patton's presentation of an overview of transition to employment, postsecondary education, and adult living. Section III closes with a discussion of family support and involvement written by Teresa Doughty and Emily Bouck.

The interrelatedness of disciplines to the practice of educating students with ASD is addressed in Section IV. Approaches and models used to enhance language and communication development in students with ASD is presented by Carol Alpern. Kim Spence-Cochran and Cynthia Pearl describe assistive technology for the classroom. The text closes with a discussion of consultation and collaboration for system-wide change by Jack Hourcade and Gardner Umbarger.

This text has brought together several of the nation's leading experts to examine current principles and practices in the education of students with autism spectrum disorders. The authors have integrated historical and current perspectives to help us understand how we have arrived at current approaches and where we need to focus our attention as the field continues to mature. In short, the main emphasis of the text is directed toward examination of the research base and theory underlying current models and practices in the education of students with autism spectrum disorders.

CONTRIBUTORS

Carol Alpern, Ph.D., Professor and Program Director of the Communication Sciences and Disorders Program, Pace University, 41 Park Row, New York, NY 10038, calpern@pace.edu

Ruth Aspy, Ph.D., Licensed Psychologist, The Ziggurat Group, 5232 Village Creek Drive, Suite 200, Plano, TX 75093, www.texasautism.com

Kyle Bennett, Ed.D, BCBA, Director of the Center for Autism and Related Disabilities at Florida Atlantic University, Boca Raton, Florida, kbennett@fau.edu

Emily Bouck, Ph.D., Assistant Professor of Special Education, Special Education Program, Department of Educational Studies, College of Education, Purdue University, Steven C. Beering Hall of Liberal Arts & Education, 100 N. University Street, West Lafayette, IN, 47907-2098, bouck@purdue.com

E. Amanda Boutot, Ph.D., Associate Professor, Texas State University-San Marcos, Department of Curriculum and Instruction, 601 University Drive, San Marcos TX 78666, eb15@txstate.edu

Joel D. Bregman, MD, Executive Director, Thompson Center for Autism and Neurodevelopmental Disorders, Endowed Chair of Child Health, Professor of Clinical Psychiatry, University of Missouri 205 Portland Street, Columbia, MO 65211, bregmanj@health.missouri.edu

Pei-Yu Chen, Ph.D., BCBA-D., Department of Special Education, National Taipei University of Education, No. 134, Sec.2, Heping E. Rd., Da-an District, Taipei City 106, Taiwan, pychen@tea.ntue.edu.tw

Constanza Colombi, Ph.D., Research Senior Supervisor, University of Michigan Autism and Communication Disorders Center (UMACC), 1111 East Catherine, Ann Arbor, MI 48109-2054, ccolombi@umich.edu

Francine Dreyfus, Ed.D., Education Director, Bronx Early Learning Center-Volunteers of America, Greater NY, 1887 Bathgate Avenue, Bronx, NY 10457 and Adjunct Assistant Professor, Center for Teaching and Research in Autism, Pace University, fld1997@aol.com

Jennifer B. Ganz, Ph.D., BCBA-D, Associate Professor of Special Education, Department of Educational Psychology, 4225 TAMU, Texas A&M University in College Station, College Station, TX 77843-4225Texas. jeniganz@tamu.edu

Barry G. Grossman, Ph.D., Licensed Psychologist, The Ziggurat Group, 5232 Village Creek Drive, Suite 200, Plano, TX 75093, www.texasautism.com

Claudine Higdon, M.D., Zucker-Hillside Hospital, North Shore-LIJ Health System, 75-59 263rd St., Glen Oaks, NY 11004

Jack Hourcade, Ph.D., Professor, Department of Special Education and Early Childhood Studies, MS 1725, Boise State University, Boise ID 83725, jhourca@boisestate.edu

L. Juane Heflin, Ph.D., Associate Professor, Department of Educational Psychology and Special Education, Georgia State University, P.O. Box 3979, Atlanta, GA 30302-3979, jheflin@gsu.edu

Shawn A. Henry, MS, 2536 Westmont Blvd, Upper Arlington, OH, 43221 shawn_henry@mac.com

Jackie S. Isbell, MA, Urban Graduate Research Collaborative, Department of Educational Psychology and Special Education, Georgia State University, P.O. Box 3979 Atlanta, GA 30302-3979, jisbell1@student.gsu.edu

So Hyun Kim, M.A., TLLP, Doctoral Candidate in Clinical Psychology, University of Michigan University of Michigan Autism and Communication Disorders Center (UMACC), 1111 East Catherine Ann Arbor, MI 48109-2054, sohkim@umich.edu

Catherine Lord, Ph.D., Senior Research Scientist and Director, University of Michigan Autism and Communication Disorders Center, Professor of Psychology and Psychiatry, University of Michigan Center for Human Growth and Development, 300 North Ingalls, 10th Floor, Ann Arbor, MI 48109-5406, celord@umich.edu

Rose A. Mason, M.S., Licensed Specialist in School Psychology and doctoral candidate, Texas A & M University in College Station, Texas, address: 4225 TAMU, Department of Educational Psychology, College Station, TX 77843-4225, rosemason519@neo.tamu.edu

Stephanie McCaskill, MS.Ed, Network Leader, School District Administration, 400 First Avenue – 4th floor, New York, NY 10010, smccaskill@schools.nyc.gov

Gary B. Mesibov, Ph.D., Professor Emeritus of Psychology, Frank Porter Graham Child Development Center, CB# 8040, University of North Carolina, Chapel Hill, NC 27599-8040, gary_mesibov@med.unc.edu

Brenda Smith Myles, Ph.D., 7881 Folkstone Road, Upper Arlington, OH 43220, brenda_myles@mac.com

James R. D. Patton, Ed.D., Educational Consultant, 1406 Thaddeus Cove, Austin TX 78746, jpatton@austin.rr.com

Cynthia Pearl, Ph.D., Project Director, University of Central Florida; Department of Child, Family and Community Sciences; College of Education P.O. Box 161250, Orlando, FL 32816-1250, cpearl@mail.ucf.edu

Alayna Schreier, B.A., University of Michigan Autism and Communication Disorders Center (UMACC), 1111 East Catherine, Ann Arbor, MI 48109-2054, aschreie@umich.edu

Jack Scott, PhD, BCBA-D, Associate Professor of Exceptional Student Education and Executive Director of the Center for Autism & Related Disabilities at Florida Atlantic University, Boca Raton, Florida.jscott@fau.edu

Victoria Shea, Ph.D., Adjunct Associate Professor, Dept of Psychiatry, University of North Carolina at Chapel Hill, 1506 E. Franklin Street, Suite 202, Chapel Hill, NC 27514, victoria. shea@yahoo.com

Richard L. Simpson, Ed.D., Professor of Special Education, Department of Special Education, University of Kansas, Joseph R. Pearson Hall, 1122 W. Campus Drive, Lawrence, KS 66045, richsimp@ku.edu

J. David Smith, Ph.D., Professor, Department of Specialized Education Services, University of North Carolina-Greensboro, 212A Ferguson Building, P.O. Box 26170, Greensboro, NC 27402-6170, jdsmi24@umcg.edu

Tom E. C. Smith, Ed.D., Dean, University Professor of Special Education, College of Education and Health Professions, University of Arkansas, 324 Graduate Education Building, Fayetteville, Arkansas 72701, tecsmith@uark.edu

Sheila M. Smith, Ph.D., Assistant Director, Ohio Center for Autism and Low Incidence (OCALI), 470 Glenmont Avenue, Columbus, OH 43214, sheilasmith@mac.com

Kim Spence-Cochran, Ph.D., Coordinator of Educational & Training Programs, Center for Autism and Related Disabilities, University of Central Florida, P.O. Box 162202, Orlando, FL 32816-2202, kcochran@mail.ucf.edu

Robert Stodden, Ph.D., Director and Professor, Center on Disability Studies, College of Education, University of Hawaii at Manoa, 1776 University Avenue, UA 4-6, Honolulu, HI 96822, stodden@hawaii.edu

Teresa Taber Doughty, Ph.D., Associate Professor of Special Education, Special Education Program, Department of Educational Studies, College of Education, Purdue University, Steven C. Beering Hall of Liberal Arts & Education, 100 N. University Street, West Lafayette, IN, 47907-2098, tabert@purdue.edu

Garner Umbarger, 111, Ph.D. Associate Professor, Department of Teacher Education, Saginaw Valley State University, 7400 Bay Road, University Center MI 48710,gumbarger@woh.rr.com

Jennifer Loncola Walberg, Ph.D., Associate Professor, DePaul University, School of Education, 2320 North Kenmore, Chicago, Il 60614

Elizabeth West, Ph.D., Assistant Professor, College of Education, Area of Special Education,102 H. Miller, Box 353600,Seattle, Washington 98195-3600, eawest@u.washington.edu

Michael L. Wehmeyer, Ph.D., Professor and Director, Department of Special Education, University of Kansas, 1200 Sunnyside Ave., Room 3136, Lawrence, KS 66045, Wehmeyer@ ku.edu

Serena Wieder, Ph.D., Clinical Psychologist, Founder of Interdisciplinary Council of Developmental and Learning Disorders and DIR Institute, 140 Riverside Drive, New York, New York 10024, serenawieder@gmail.com

Mary L. White, Graduate Student, Department of Specialized Education Services, University of North Carolina-Greensboro, 212 Ferguson Building, Greensboro, NC 27402

Dianne Zager, Ph.D., Director, Center for Teaching & Research in Autism and OASIS College Support Program, Michael C. Koffler Professor in Autism, Pace University, 163 William Street, 16th Floor, New York, NY 10038, dzager@pace.edu

SECTION I

Knowledge of the Field of Autism

1

AUTISM SPECTRUM DISORDERS

Historical, Legislative, and Current Perspectives

Mary L. White and J. David Smith
UNIVERSITY OF NORTH CAROLINA AT GREENSBORO

Tom E. C. Smith
UNIVERSITY OF ARKANSAS

Robert Stodden
UNIVERSITY OF HAWAII

Congress designated autism as a separate disability category within the Individuals with Disabilities Education Act in 1990. Children with autism spectrum disorders (ASD) have quickly become one of the most challenging groups for educators to effectively teach. There are several reasons for this, which include the rapid growth in the number of children identified with ASD over the past 10 years; the lack of definitive criteria for identifying children as having ASD; and the limited research on best practices for serving this group of children. The dramatic increase in the number of children identified as having ASD brought a sense of urgency to school districts responsible for identifying children in this group and developing and implementing appropriate educational services (Iovannone, Dunlop, Huber, & Kincaid, 2003; Simpson, 2005; Simpson et al., 2005; Weatherly, 2005). The history of education for children with ASD describes confusion about identification, etiology, and appropriate interventions. This chapter will provide a history of the disorder, legislative actions related to autism, and current perspectives.

History of Autism Spectrum Disorders

Although they were not described until the 20th century, it is likely that ASDs have impacted individuals throughout human history. Some historians believe that Victor, the wild boy described by the French physician, Itard, could have had ASD (cited in Scheuermann & Webber, 2002). Regardless of these early instances, the word *autism* has only been used for approximately 100 years. In 1911, the Swiss psychiatrist Eugen Bleuler used the term to describe children with emotional or social disorders (WebMD, 2010). Autism did not receive *modern* attention until Leo Kanner, a psychologist at Johns Hopkins University, first identified the condition in 1943 when he published the results of a study of 11 children with severe language delays. In his paper, "Autistic Disturbances of Affective Contact," Kanner described a group of children who had normal intelligence, did not have any indicators of neurological impairments, and were from parents in higher social classes (Kanner cited in Mesibov, Shea, & Adams, 2001). Kanner emphasized the role of biology as the likely cause of autism and was careful to differentiate between autism and schizophrenia. He developed the term, *early infantile autism* and described it as the inability to relate as a feature of the developmental context (Volkmar & Lord, 1998).

During the same period Hans Asperger studied 200 German children who had similar characteristics to those in Kanner's study, with the exception of severe language delays. While Asperger's study was later credited with identifying children with Asperger syndrome, the term was not used in the literature to describe this condition until 1981 (Volkmar & Lord, 1998). Asperger referred to the problems experienced by this group of children as "autistic psychopathy of childhood" (Wolff, 2004, p. 204).

Kanner and Asperger were both born in Austria and received their professional training in Vienna. Kanner, who became the head of the Child Psychiatric Clinic at Johns Hopkins University, and Asperger, who became the Chair of Pediatrics at the University of Vienna (Mesibov et al., 2001), noted social difficulties, communication problems, and repetitive and restricted activities among the children they studied, although both researchers distinguished the children's characteristics from those of childhood schizophrenia (Wing, 1997).

Another early researcher in autism was Bruno Bettelheim, an Austrian physician. In numerous articles published in the 1950s and 1960s, Bettelheim created the idea that children with autism were the victims of "refrigerator mothers." Best known in this area for his book *The Empty Fortress: Infantile Autism and the Birth of Self* (1967), he compared children with autism to prisoners in concentration camps while their parents were portrayed as the guards (cited in Mesibov et al., 2001). Unfortunately, this assertion created significant problems for parents and the field of autism. Already dealing with children with serious problems, Bettelheim's theory added a professional basis for parental guilt that took many years to overcome.

There was no definitive research in the field of autism at that time, and many professionals accepted the idea of the refrigerator mom. Even though Bernard Rimland (1964) emphasized that autism was not an emotional illness but was due to a neurodevelopmental disorder, the idea of the refrigerator mom was the popular theory underlying autism. Rimland's book, *Infantile Autism: The Syndrome and Its Implications for a Neural Theory of Behavior,* is credited with changing the perception of what causes autism. Rimland, a psychologist and parent of a son with autism, argued for the biological basis of autism and advocated for biomedical and behavioral therapies for treatment (Rimland, 1964; Volkmar & Lord, 1998). He developed a diagnostic checklist, which is considered one of the "earliest attempts to prove a truly operational approach to diagnosis" (Volkmar & Lord, 1998, p. 14). In addition, he established the Autism Research Institute (ARI) as a research center and biomedical clearinghouse and the Autism Society of America in 1965 (Maugh, 2006). All of these organizations made significant contributions to a better understanding of autism spectrum disorders.

Educational programs for students with autism did not begin to develop until the 1960s. In the United Kingdom, Sybil Elgar is known as the first teacher to work only with children with autism. In 1964 she formed the Society for Autistic Children, which is now the National Autistic Society. Ten years later Elgar founded Britain's first residential community for adults with autism. She was widely recognized as a gifted teacher and pioneer for students with autism. During the period when she was teaching, diagnosis of children with autism was limited and there were no specific teaching methods for her to adopt. As a result, she developed her own approaches, many of which are still used today (Wing, 2007).

In 1968 Dr. Ruth Sullivan became the first elected president of the Autism Society. The mother of a son with autism, Sullivan was told by four psychiatrists that she was responsible for her son's autism because of her lack of bonding during his infancy—refrigerator mother. At this time there were very few school programs for children with autism. The family moved to Cabell County Schools in Huntington, West Virginia, so that her son could attend a classroom for children with autism (Darst, 2007). In 2003, Dr. Sullivan founded the Autism Services Center in Huntington, and was one of six experts selected for the initial Autism Summit Conference supported by the U. S. Department of Education and the U.S. Department of Health and Human Services.

Emerging Interventions: Ivar Lovaas and the Creation of TEACCH

In 1965, Ivar Lovaas and other researchers at the University of California in Los Angeles began using Skinner's experimental behavior analysis for older children with autism. With the early results being mixed, he refocused his efforts on younger children. His treatment was based on the ideas of rewarding children when they were adaptive and punishing behaviors that were maladaptive. Lovaas's (1988) treatment was considered controversial due to the ongoing use of punishers. His study, published in the *Journal of Consulting and Clinical Psychology* concluded that nearly half of the children who were provided with intensive weekly sessions that incorporated methods derived from ABA showed few characteristics of autism after 2 years of treatment. The study affirmed a place for ABA as what was considered the first popular treatment for autism, despite the fact that his sample size was so small that the results were statistically unreliable (Metz, Mulick, & Butter, 2005; Tutt, Powell, & Thorton, 2006).

Eric Shopler and Richard Reichler started the Child Research Program at the University of North Carolina School of Medicine in 1968. Shopler had been influenced by early experiences in pre–World War II Germany and his work with Bruno Bettelheim. He viewed parents differently from Bettelheim, however, and rejected the idea that poor parenting caused autism. He also believed that autism was neurologically based and was not a mental illness. The initial project, supported by a 5-year grant from the National Institute of Mental Health, was later expanded into a teaching model still used today, TEACCH or Treatment and Education of Autistic and related Communication Handicapped Children. In 1972, TEACCH was endorsed by the North Carolina General Assembly as a statewide program to help people with autism across the life span, and shortly afterwards the first demonstration class opened. By 1976 TEACCH supported 10 demonstration classrooms.

While there were gains in the field in the 1960s, there were also some setbacks. In 1967 the International Statistical Classification of Disease and Related Health Problems listed "infantile autism" as a form of schizophrenia. During the 1950s and 1960s schizophrenia was considered widespread, particularly in the United States, and children with autism included in the category often received expensive psychotherapy as the primary treatment approach (Wolff, 2004). This belief, in conjunction with the release of Bettelheim's *The Empty Fortress* (1967), emphasized the role of the mother in causing autism and resulted in a period of many years when professionals were misdirected in their efforts to determine the underlying cause of autism and appropriate interventions.

Autism was added to the third edition of the *Diagnostic and Statistical Manual of Mental Disorders* (*DSM-III;* American Psychiatric Association, 1980) after more evidence indicated there was a neurological basis to the disorder. In 1990 it was added as a separate category under the Individuals with Disabilities Education Act (IDEA). During this time autism was still considered rare, with the Centers for Disease Control (CDC) reporting that autism impacted 44 out of every 100,000 children (CDC, 2008). An estimate of the prevalence of autism at the time of writing is approximately one in 100, making it one of the major disability categories for children today.

As a better understanding of autism developed, publications steadily increased in number. Two of the most notable were Lovaas's *The Me Book*, a guide for parents, and Lorna Wing's 1981 seminal paper describing Asperger syndrome. Wing was a British researcher, mother of a child with autism, and founder of the National Autistic Society in the United Kingdom. Her paper was credited with introducing Asperger syndrome in the United States and Britain and drawing attention to the autism spectrum (Wolff, 2004). New interest in this form of high-functioning autism also prompted the translation into English of Hans Asperger's study (Shopler, 2001). Language skills were typically an area of relative strength for individuals with Asperger syndrome, although the differential in diagnosis was historically considered controversial until guidelines were established for clinicians (Volkmar & Lord, 1998). During the 1980s, Christopher Gillberg also made significant contributions to the field with publications in epidemiology, genetics, outcomes, and clinical management of children on the autism spectrum (Wing, 1997; Wolff, 2004). His work also clarified the features of Asperger syndrome as part of a range of disorders that was later used for diagnosis.

Even with the increase in research publications, the popular perception of autism in the eighties was established almost exclusively by the 1988 release of the movie *Rain Man*. For the public, Dustin Hoffman's portrayal of a man with autism in *Rain Man* initiated a demand for more information about the condition (Mesibov et al., 2001). The public became fascinated with what was considered a rare disorder characterized by impairments in socialization and communication, and restricted interests. Unfortunately, the new interest was founded on a characterization that is not necessarily representative of the majority of people with autism. Still, it brought a great deal of attention to the disorder which in turn resulted in more professional work in the field.

What Are Autism Spectrum Disorders?

While there has been a significant increase in professional interest in children with ASD, there are still major questions about the true nature of autism. Generally speaking, autism can be described as a neurological disorder that manifests itself in significant behavior and communication differences. The *DSM-IV-TR* (2000) includes autistic disorder and Asperger syndrome as two different disorders under the umbrella of pervasive developmental disorders, which are disorders "characterized by severe and pervasive impairment in several areas of development: reciprocal social interaction skills, communication skills, or the presence of stereotyped behavior, interests, and activities" (p. 69). Autism is described as a disorder in which there are markedly abnormal or impaired social and communication skills, and restricted interests and activities. The impaired social skills can be manifested in several ways, including impairments in:

- Use of nonverbal behaviors
- Developing peer relationships and friendships
- Seeking peers to share enjoyment, interests, and achievements
- Social and emotional reciprocity
- Understanding the needs of others

With regard to communication, people with autistic disorder may have delayed or total lack of communication; difficulty initiating or sustaining conversations; stereotyped or repetitive language; and abnormal pitch, intonation, rate, and rhythm when speaking (*DSM-IV-TR*, 2000).

The *DSM-IV-TR* describes children with Asperger syndrome as having "severe and sustained impairment in social interaction and the development of restricted, repetitive patterns of behavior, interests, and activities" (p. 80). Children with Asperger syndrome typically have good oral communication skills, the characteristic that sets them apart from their peers classified as having autism. While the assumption is that autism spectrum disorders have a neurological base, they are defined using behavioral terms (Heflin & Alaimo, 2007).

All of the disorders in the spectrum share common characteristics of impairments in social and communication skills, as well as stereotypical behaviors. There are, however, some distinct differences among these disorders. For example, the primary difference between children classified as having autistic disorder and those with Asperger syndrome is language. Children with Asperger syndrome do not have a delay or deviance in early language development. Rett syndrome primarily occurs in females, while autistic disorder is more prevalent in males. Children with Rett syndrome also experience a deceleration of head growth and lose purposeful hand and body movements. Childhood disintegrative disorder differs from autistic disorder in that it is usually associated with severe mental retardation and seizure activity. These are a few examples of the differences found among the major disorders listed under the pervasive developmental disorder group.

Diagnosis of children with ASD is accomplished using the *DSM-IV-TR* diagnostic criteria. In order to be classified as having these disorders, individuals are required to display a minimal number of behaviors within broad behavioral categories. For example, to be classified as having autism, an individual must exhibit six or more items from three different categories of behaviors, with at least two from the first category (impairments in social interactions) and one each from the other two categories (impairments in communication and repetitive and stereotyped patterns of behavior). Diagnosis of children with Asperger syndrome is accomplished using a similar model. A problem with this sort of diagnosis is the unclear definitions of certain behaviors; behaviors are not described in quantifiable terms, making diagnosis difficult (Shapiro, Menon, & Accardo, 2009).

The Individuals with Disabilities Education Act (IDEA; 1990), federal legislation mandating special education services, defines autism as

> a developmental disability significantly affecting verbal and nonverbal communication and social interaction, generally evident before age three, that adversely affects a child's educational performance. Other characteristics often associated with autism are engagement in repetitive activities and stereotyped movements, resistance to environmental change or change in daily routines, and unusual responses to sensory experiences. (34CFR300.7)

Unfortunately, definitions of autism, Asperger syndrome, and autism spectrum disorders are not particularly clear. Diagnostic procedures are primarily focused on behavioral manifestations. There is no autism diagnostic test that can be given to a child with the result being a score that would rule a child as having or not having autism. Until more sophisticated measures are developed, school personnel, medical specialists, and psychologists will have to use their professional judgment when applying the behavior criteria included in the *DSM-IV-TR* when diagnosing this disorder.

Legislation and Students with Autism Spectrum Disorders

Like students with a wide range of disabilities, students with ASD received few services prior to the 1970s. Autism was not a separate category under Public Law 94-142, which established the requirements for the provision for special education services; however, it was included under the category of serious emotional disturbance until 1981. At that time the category was moved to the *other health impaired* group, a change that was very much in line with then–current research into autism (Zabel, 1988). In 1990 Congress reauthorized the law and included autism as a separate disability category (Smith, Polloway, Patton, & Dowdy, 2008). This marked a major milestone in the recognition of autism as a major disability for children and a source of major problems for their families. It was strongly supported by professionals whose focus was on this disorder.

As a result of children with autism being included as a separate category of disabilities under IDEA, the number of students identified as having autism and the need for programs grew considerably. One result of this growth was the increase in the number of disagreements between parents and schools regarding appropriate services for this group of students. Slater and Norlin (2007) summarized more than 200 court cases and impartial hearings that related to students with autism. A few of these cases are summarized below:

- Federal court rules that schools should consider areas such as communication, in addition to how well a child performs in classrooms, when determining eligibility.
- A New York school district did not have to provide special education and related services to a student diagnosed with Asperger syndrome because the student was doing well academically and had no other specific problems.
- A hearing officer ruled that a California district did not deny a student a free appropriate public education by mislabeling the student because it did provide an appropriate individualized education plan (IEP) for the student.
- A judge ruled in favor of the school when the parents claimed that the school had not met their child's educational needs when it denied provision of home-based ABA services for the 4-year-old.
- A school district did not have to reimburse a parent for placing a child in a private school because the program it offered was individually developed for that child.

These decisions show the wide range of cases dealing with students with autism vis-à-vis public school programs. Schools must primarily follow due process procedures when identifying, evaluating, and implementing individual programming for students with autism, similar to how they provide appropriate services to students with other disabilities. IDEA mandates that schools are responsible for providing a free appropriate public education for students with autism and all other students eligible under IDEA.

Educators recognized the importance of utilizing research-based practices and methods and to continually evaluate the services provided because of the number of disputed IEPs for students with ASD (Helfin & Simpson, 1998). The IDEA was important in the evolution of services for students with ASD. It not only provided a mandate for delivery of these services, but also a substantial funding opportunity for states and local school districts. The designation of autism as a separate disability category in 1990 provided the impetus for schools to identify and develop appropriate programs for this growing number of students.

In recognition of the rapid growth in the number of children diagnosed with autism, President George W. Bush signed The Combating Autism Act of 2006 (Public Law 109-416), which authorized an expansion of actions for research, prevention, and treatment through 2011. Currently the United States has more than 1.5 million individuals with autism and the prevalence rates continue to increase rapidly (MMWR, 2009).

In addition to IDEA, the No Child Left Behind Act (NCLB; a 2001 reauthorization of the Elementary and Secondary Education Act [ESEA]) has forced school districts to consider the academic progress of individual students with disabilities, including those with autism, with accountability measures being in place for the first time. NCLB (2001) placed emphasis on teacher preparation, academic accountability, and research-based teaching methodology

(Yell, Drasgow, & Lowrey, 2005). The 2004 amendments to IDEA addressed the importance of academic progress and research-based methodologies, while taking steps in defining what is considered an appropriate education. The increase in debates over instructional strategies and what constitutes an appropriate education for students with ASD makes choosing intervention and treatment strategies more difficult. School districts must consider legal mandates from IDEA and ESEA as well as court decisions when making such determinations (Mesibov et al., 2001). Part D of IDEA supports the development and expansion of teacher preparation programs specific to educating students with ASD (Yell, 2006), and the relatively new emphasis on research and teacher preparation will benefit students with ASD because educators are better equipped to meet the needs of students who have struggled to make progress.

Some children diagnosed with ASD may not be eligible for special education services under IDEA because they may not need special education. In all categories, IDEA requires documentation of the need for special education services. Many of these children are likely eligible for protections and services, however, under Section 504 and the Americans with Disabilities Act (1991, ADA). These two laws, basically civil rights legislation for individuals with disabilities, provide a broader definition of disability than does IDEA. As a result, some children not eligible under IDEA may still be eligible under these laws, which do not require students to need specially designed instruction. To be eligible under 504 or the ADA, the impairment must only substantially limit a major life activity, which does not have to be academic learning (Smith et al., 2008).

Issues in Autism Spectrum Disorders

The identification of research-based curricula and methodologies remains a challenge in practice for teachers, particularly for teachers of students with ASD (Simpson, 2005). The factors that make this task difficult include the range of skills, unique behavioral characteristics, variety of interventions, and the publicity surrounding treatment options for students on the autism spectrum. Contradictory findings in research among interventions and treatments have resulted in state and local educational agencies taking the responsibility for determining appropriate levels of services. Decisions from case law have consistently shown that when students are making educational progress, the court will leave methodology decisions up to the district (Yell, 2006). Unfortunately students with ASD often progress slower than some students with other disabilities.

Due to the significant increase in prevalence, funding for research in treatment and interventions has increased significantly over the past 10 years. In 2000, the National Institutes of Health and the 26 universities collaborating with the National Institute on Child Health and Development developed public policy regarding best practices for students with autism spectrum disorders (Feinberg & Vacca, 2000). Effective practices identified by the National Research Council (2001) include:

- early intervention,
- instructional programming equivalent to the school day over the course of the year,
- parent involvement,
- utilization of deliberate teaching,
- small-group or one-to-one instruction, and
- a communication-rich environment.

Iovannone et al. (2003) identified six core elements of effective practices for students with autism spectrum disorders. These include: individualized supports and services for students and families, systematic instruction, comprehensible/structured learning environments, specialized curriculum content, functional approaches to problem behavior, and family involvement.

In 2005, Simpson identified 33 intervention and treatment methods for students with ASD and evaluated them based on scientific research-based principles. Interventions were categorized as (a) scientifically based practices, (b) practices that show potential, (c) practices with limited support, and (d) practices that are not recommended for use. Several interventions were identified as showing potential for skills-based information, including the picture exchange communication system, incidental teaching, structured teaching, or TEACCH, argumentative alternative communication, assistive technology, and joint action routines. For the development of cognitive-based skills, Simpson (2005) identified cognitive behavior therapy, cognitive learning strategies, social stories, and social decision-making strategies as having potential. For the area of interpersonal relationship building play-oriented strategies are recommended. Sensory integration is considered promising for the physiological/biological, neurological area.

Seventeen approaches are categorized as having limited support information for practice. These include the Son-Rise program, Floor Time, Irlen Lenses, Power Cards, and the Feingold diet. Holding therapy and facilitated communication are the only two treatments that are not recommended (Simpson, 2005; Simpson et al., 2005).

The promise of new interventions for autism, combined with families desperate to help their children, has provided an open door for the creation of treatment fads. *Autism: A Late-20th-Century Fad* (Metz et al., 2005) suggested that few conditions other than autism have experienced the same level of controversial and unsupported treatments. The number of proposed interventions, most of which are promoted commercially, range from biomedical or psychosocial to mechanical. Few of these interventions have been subjected to impartial scientific study and, as Simpson pointed out in his review, many treatments that have been evaluated only have limited support or may not even be recommended. Yet parents and professionals alike continue to explore interventions that promise to cure autism (Simpson, 2001). Feinberg and Vacca (2000) emphasized that a conflict exists among families and professionals over the data used to support treatments and the ability to use the data for decision-making purposes given the wide range of each child's individual needs.

Autism remains a controversial topic within education, medical, and parent circles and is fueled by continual publicity in the media. The increase in prevalence combined with students' unique needs provide educators with challenges in determining appropriate educational services. School districts are responding to the increased demand for services for this group of children by seeking qualified experts and in some cases creating teacher leader positions within schools. Siegel (2003) has noted that for every student who makes significant progress using a particular methodology there will be one who makes comparable gains with a different methodology.

The controversy surrounding autism goes well beyond intervention strategies. Some groups believe that autism is preventable and curable, while others advocate accepting autism as a condition that results in some people displaying different characteristics from others. The belief that autism can be cured is strongly supported by the group, Autism Speaks. The Autism Speaks Web site (n.d.) notes that the organization "is dedicated to facilitating global research into the causes, treatments, prevention and an eventual cure for autism."

Supporting the notion that autism is merely a group of characteristics that result in individual differences is The Autistic Self Advocacy Network (ASAN, n.d.), a nonprofit organization that is "run by and for Autistic people." In its mission statement, ASAN notes that it "seeks to advance the idea of neurological diversity, putting forward the concept that the goal of autism advocacy should not be a world without Autistic people. Instead, it should be a world in which Autistic people enjoy the same access, rights and opportunities as all other citizens."

Implications for the Future

As researchers continue to focus on the etiology and efficacy of interventions, educators will need the skills to not only provide newly identified interventions but also evaluate the effectiveness of interventions and individual student growth. Teacher preparation programs have begun adding classes or programs to meet the growing need for teachers in the area. The Network of Training and Technical Assistance Programs (NATTAP) held its first annual conference in September 2007 and created a draft for National Teacher Standards for teachers of students with ASD. The draft was reviewed and accepted by the Division on Autism and Developmental Disabilities of the Council for Exceptional Children. The Standards provide guidance for future teacher preparation programs, future teachers, and students with autism spectrum disorders. The question remains as to how much impact these standards will have on future fads in treatment. Understanding the history of educational decisions for students with autism provides a foundation for identifying issues in the educational context and beyond.

The autism journey over the past 65 years only recently received widespread recognition as the number of children diagnosed with ASD has sharply increased. In the beginning, the etiology and treatment of autism was a mystery even to professionals in the area. Children with autism in the 1950s and 1960s who received formal education worked with teachers who relied on their intuition to serve them. As educational services slowly evolved in the 1970s and 1980s, states began to create programs and classrooms specific to students with ASD. Since 1990, individuals, families, and professionals have benefited from increased awareness and funding; however, the prevalence has increased at such a rate that many educational agencies are searching for methods of expanding appropriate services. Major advances in understanding the facets of autism and the focus of research provide hope for the future.

As a result of the rapid growth of autism spectrum disorders in schools, educators, researchers, and parents have expended a great deal of effort on determining the underlying causes of these disorders as well as appropriate educational interventions. While there are numerous interventions and claims that are unsupported with research, more and better research is beginning to identify some of the underlying causes of autism as well as evidenced-based interventions.

References

Americans With Disabilities Act of 1990, Pub. L. No. 101-336, § 2; 104 Stat. 328 (1991).

American Psychiatric Association. (1980). *Diagnostic and statistical manual of mental disorders* (3rd ed.). Washington, DC: Author.

American Psychiatric Association. (1994). *Diagnostic and statistical manual of mental disorders* (4rd ed.). Washington, DC: Author.

American Psychiatric Association. (2000). *Diagnostic and statistical manual of mental disorders* (Text rev., 4th ed.). Washington, DC: Author.

Autistic Self Advocacy Network. (n.d.). Retrieved from http:// www.autisticadvocacy.org

Autism Speaks. (n.d.). Retrieved from http://www.autismspeaks.org

Centers for Disease Control and Prevention. (2006). *How common are autism spectrum disorders (ASD)?* Retrieved from http:www.cdc.gov/ncbdd/autism/asd_common.htm

Centers for Disease Control and Prevention (CDC). (2008). *MMR vaccine and autism fact sheet.* Retrieved from http:// www.cdc.gov/vaccinesafety/concerns/mmr_autism_factsheet.htm

Darst, P. (2007, November 1). Autism center founder hands over reins. *The State Journal—News for West Virginia's Leaders.* Retrieved from http://www.statejournal.com/story.cfm?func=viewstoryid=30916&

Feinberg, E., & Vacca, J. (2000). The drama and trauma of creating policies on autism: Critical issues to consider in the new millennium. *Focus on Autism and Other Developmental Disabilities, 15,* 130–137.

Heflin, L. J., & Alaimo, D. F. (2007). *Students with autism spectrum disorders.* Upper Saddle River, NJ: Merrill/Prentice Hall.

Heflin, L. J., & Simpson, R. L. (1998). Interventions for children and youth with autism: Prudent choices in a world of exaggerated claims and empty promises. Part II: Legal/policy analysis and recommendations for selecting interventions and treatments. *Focus on Autism and Other Developmental Disabilities, 13*, 212–220.

Individuals with Disabilities Education Act of 1990, 20 U.S.C. § 1400 et seq. (1990).

Individuals with Disabilities Education Improvement Act of 2004, 20 U.S.C. § 1400 et seq. (2004).

Iovannone, R., Dunlop, G., Huber, H., & Kincaid, D. (2003). Effective educational practices for students with autism spectrum disorder. *Focus on Autism and Other Developmental Disabilities, 18*, 150–165.

Lovaas, O. I. (1988). Behavioral treatment and normal educational and Interventions functioning in young autistic children. *Journal of Consulting and Clinical Psychology, 55*, 3–9.

Maugh, R. H. (2006, November 26). Bernard Rimland, 78; author was the father of modern autism research. *LA Times*. Retrieved from http://www.autism.com/ari/rimland/rimlandlatimesobit.htm

Mesibov, G. (2006). A tribute to Eric Shopler. *Journal of Autism and Developmental Disorders, 36*, 967–970.

Mesibov, G., Shea, V., & Adams, L. (2001). *Understanding Asperger syndrome and high functioning autism*. New York: Kluwer.

Metz, B., Mulick, J. A., & Butter, E. M. (2005). Autism: A late-20th century fad. In J. W. Jacobson, R. M. Foxx, M. Richard, & J. A. Mulick (Eds.), *Controversial therapies for developmental disabilities: Fad, fashion and science in professional practice* (pp. 237–263). Mahwah, NJ: Erlbaum.

MMWR Surveillance Summaries. (2009). *Prevalence of autism spectrum disorders – Autism and developmental disabilities monitoring network, United States*. Washington, DC: Ceners for Disease Control and Prevention.

National Research Council. (2001). *Educating children with autism*. Washington, DC: National Academy Press.

Network of Training and Technical Assistance Programs. (2007, September). *National Teacher Standards*. Retrieved from http://www.autismsociety-nc.org/html/for_teachers_.html

No Child Left Behind Act of 2001. 20 U.S.C. 70 § 6301 et seq. (2002).

Rimland, B. (1964). *Infantile autism: The syndrome and its implications for a neural theory of behavior*. New York: Appleton-Century-Crofts.

Scheuermann, B., & Webber, J. (2002). *Autism: Teaching does make a difference*. Stamford, CT: Wadsworth.

Shapiro, B. K., Menon, D. U., & Accardo, P. J. (2009). Clinical overview of the Autism Spectrum. In B. K. Shapiro & D. U. Menon (Eds.), *Autism frontiers* (pp. 1–20). Baltimore, MD: Brookes.

Shopler, E. (2001). Treatment for autism. In E. Shopler, N. Yirmiya, C. Shulman, & L. Marcus (Eds.), *The research basis for autism intervention* (pp. 9–24). New York: Kluwer Academic/Plenum.

Siegel, B. (2003). *Helping children with autism learn: Treatment approaches for parents and professionals*. New York: Oxford University Press.

Simpson, R. L. (2001). ABA and students with autism spectrum disorders: Issues and considerations for effective practice. *Focus on Autism and Other Developmental Disabilities, 1*, 68–71.

Simpson, R. L. (2005). Evidence-based practices and students with autism spectrum disorders. *Focus on Autism and Other Developmental Disabilities, 20*, 140–149.

Simpson, R. L., de Boer-Ott, S. R., Griswald, D. E., Myles, B. S., Byrd, S. E., Ganz, J. B., et al. (2005). *Autism spectrum disorders: Interventions and treatments for children and youth*. Thousand Oaks, CA: Corwin Press.

Slater, A. E., & Norlin, J. W. (2007). *Autism case law: A desktop reference to key decisions*. Horsham, PA: LRP.

Smith, T. E. C., Polloway, E. A., Patton, J. R., & Dowdy, C. A. (2008). *Teaching students with special needs in inclusive settings* (5th ed.). Boston: Allyn & Bacon.

Tutt, R., Powell, S., & Thorton, M. (2006). Educational approaches in autism: What we know about what we do. *Educational Psychology in Practice, 22*, 69–81.

Volkmar, F. R., & Lord, C. (1998). Diagnosis and definition of autism and other pervasive developmental disorders. In F. Volkmar (Ed.), *Autism and pervasive developmental disorders* (pp. 1–25). Cambridge, UK: Cambridge University Press.

Weatherly, J. (2005). *Autism programs and services: Lessons from the law*. Mobile, AL: LRP.

WebMD. (2010). Retrieved from http://www.webmd.com

Wing, L. (1997). *The history of ideas on autism: Legends, myths and reality*. London: The National Autistic Society.

Wing, L. (2007, January 24). Sybil Elgar: Pioneer in teaching and care of autistic people. *The Guardian*. Retrieved from http://www.guardian.co.uk/news/2007/jan/24/guardianobituaries.obituaries2

Wolff, S. (2004). The history of autism. *European Child & Adolescent Psychiatry, 13*(4), 201–208.

Yell, M. L. (2006). *The law and special education*. Columbus, OH: Merrill.

Yell, M. L., Drasgow, E., & Lowrey K. A. (2005). No Child Left Behind and students with autism spectrum disorders. *Focus on Autism and Other Developmental Disabilities, 20*, 130–140.

Zabel, R. H. (1988). How are "emotional disturbances" defined? *ERIC Digest, 454*, 1–5.

2

DEFINITIONS AND CLINICAL CHARACTERISTICS OF AUTISM SPECTRUM DISORDERS

Joel D. Bregman

FEINSTEIN INSTITUTE FOR MEDICAL RESEARCH, NORTH SHORE-LIJ HEALTH SYSTEM

Claudine Higdon

ZUCKER-HILLSIDE HOSPITAL, NORTH SHORE-LIJ HEALTH SYSTEM

Overview of the Autism Spectrum

Conception of the Autism Spectrum

Autism and the pervasive developmental disorders (PDDs) are highly complex and variable in their clinical presentation and manifestations; symptoms and characteristics change with developmental maturity and vary with the degree of associated cognitive impairment (Filipek et al., 1999a). This evolving pattern of clinical features can make the differential diagnostic process very difficult in some cases. Nonetheless, the defining feature of autism is the presence of a distinctive impairment in the nature and quality of social and communicative development, which is influenced by the specific biological and environmental circumstances of the individual. It is this impairment that distinguishes autism from other neurodevelopmental conditions such as intellectual disability (previously termed mental retardation), developmental language disorders, or specific learning disabilities. Whereas intellectual disability is characterized by a pervasive developmental delay, autism is characterized by a distinctive impairment in the nature of social–communicative development. The prognostic significance of this autistic social dysfunction is underscored by preliminary studies that report a negative correlation between the severity of this social impairment and treatment responsiveness, at least with regard to social and linguistic growth following intensive, behaviorally based early intervention (Ingersoll, Schreibman, & Stahmer, 2001). Additional complexity in the differential diagnosis of autism and related PDDs results from a wide range of accompanying abnormalities within cognitive, adaptive, affective, and behavioral domains of development, including mental retardation (Volkmar, Cook, Jr., Pomeroy, Realmuto, & Tanguay, 1999; Volkmar & Klin, 1999); deficits in executive functions (Liss, Fein et al., 2001; Ozonoff, 1995, 1997; Pennington et al., 1997); limitations in adaptive skills (especially in socialization and functional communication; Liss, Harel, et al., 2001); learning disabilities (e.g., nonverbal learning disability; Rourke, 1995, p. 518); mood instability (Di Martino & Tuchman, 2001; Hellings, 1999; Hollander, Dolgoff-Kaspar, Cartwright, Rawitt, &

Novotny, 2001); stereotypic and self-injurious behaviors (King, 2000); anxiety disorders (Kim, Szatmari, Bryson, Streiner, & Wilson, 2000); and aggression (Hollander et al., 2001; King, 2000).

The Broader Autism Spectrum

The reported prevalence of autism-related conditions has risen markedly since the mid-1990s (Bryson, Clark, & Smith, 1988; Fombonne, Du Mazaubrun, Cans, & Grandjean, 1997; Fombonne, Simmons, Ford, Meltzer, & Goodman, 2001; Wing & Potter, 2002; Yeargin-Allsopp et al., 2003). The most recent prevalence data (from the U.S. Centers for Disease Control [CDC] and UK) indicate that ASD occurs in 1 in every 80 to 100 children (Baron-Cohen et al., 2009; Kogan et al., 2009). Prevalence is higher in boys compared to girls by a ratio of 4:1, a finding that is consistent in many studies (Kogan et al., 2009). Some clinical studies report increased prevalence with advanced paternal age (Kolevzon et al., 2007). This increase is, in part, the result of a broadening of the diagnostic concept to include milder and more atypical variants. This has led to the increasingly frequent use of the term *autism spectrum disorder* (ASD) within clinical and educational settings (Filipek et al., 1999b), consistent with prior conceptions of autism, including the broader autistic spectrum (Wing & Gould, 1979) and ASD (Allen, 1988). Recent genetic studies lend support to this concept because it appears that the heritable factor in autism is not the specifically defined disorder itself, but rather, subtle weaknesses in social interaction and interpersonal discourse (Bailey, Palferman, Heavey, & Le Couteur, 1998; Le Couteur et al., 1996). The literature suggests that the genetic liability for autism may be associated with limited interest in social interaction, few close confiding friendships, impaired socioemotional responsivity (a less robust finding), language delays, conversational impairments, problems in communication planning, and possibly anxiety and rigidity (Bailey et al., 1998). The boundaries of the behavioral phenotype for autism have been examined in same-sex twin pairs (28 monozygotic [MZ] and 20 dizygotic [DZ]), one of whom had autism (Le Couteur et al., 1996). Among the discordant co-twins (those *without* autism), findings included language impairments in childhood and social deficits persisting into adulthood. This broader phenotype was much more common among MZ pairs than DZ pairs, indicating a strong genetic influence. Behavioral and cognitive characteristics of autism appear to be less genetically based because no differences were found within and between MZ twin pairs.

Family and case control studies of community-ascertained probands with autism support the broader autism phenotype (BAP) concept (Folstein et al., 1999). These investigators identified a subset of autism family members manifesting a language component of the BAP (separate from the social component). This is consistent with the hypothesis that several independently segregating genes (i.e., those that have distinguishable manifestations) interact to cause autism (Folstein et al., 1999). Dawson and colleagues propose that the identification of autism susceptibility genes will be strongly influenced by success in characterizing dimensional attributes of broader phenotype autism traits (Dawson et al., 2002). These investigators have hypothesized that six traits characterize this broader phenotype, namely, (a) face processing, (b) social affiliation or responsiveness to social reinforcement, (c) motor imitation, (d) memory for social–emotional stimuli, (e) executive functioning (e.g., planning and flexibility), and (f) language ability (e.g., phonology).

However, in considering the BAP, it is important to keep in mind that this is not synonymous with the diagnostic entity of autism or ASD itself. Rather, it represents a genetically determined set of personal characteristics that increases the susceptibility of offspring to the development of the clinical syndrome. This is similar to a large number of clinical conditions that are influenced by susceptibility genes, such as certain types of malignancies, cardiovascular disease, and so forth. The presence of these susceptibility genes does not automatically result in the actual disorder; rather, it increases the likelihood that future generations will develop the clinical condition. Therefore, a "carrier" of these susceptibility genes should not be diagnosed as manifesting autism or ASD.

Several methodological issues are present both within and across studies of the BAP that complicate the interpretation of reported findings (Bailey et al., 1998). For example, there is a good deal of heterogeneity among probands with regard to PDD subtype; that is, autistic disorder vs. Asperger syndrome (AS) vs. PDD not otherwise specified (NOS), diagnostic criteria (i.e. edition of *DSM* or *ICD* used), and the presence of known medical and comorbid neuropsychiatric conditions. In addition, there are differences across studies with regard to the subject ascertainment procedures employed (e.g., epidemiological or consecutive case); the nature of control subjects, if any (e.g., other genetic conditions or developmental disabilities); and the relatives that were studied (e.g., siblings, parents, and cousins) (Bailey et al., 1998).

Historical Perspective

Current conceptions of the clinical syndrome of autism are direct extensions of the work of Leo Kanner, Hans Asperger, and Michael Rutter. Classic autism (or Kanner syndrome) is the prototypical ASD, representing the PDD subtype that involves the most severe social–communicative impairments and the greatest number and range of clinical characteristics. The essential features of Kanner syndrome are most closely captured by the *DSM-IV* (American Psychiatric Association, 1994) and *ICD-10* (World Health Organization, 1992, 1993) PDD subtypes of autistic disorder and childhood autism, respectively.

In his seminal paper published in 1943, Leo Kanner carefully described a unique neurodevelopmental condition (which he termed *early infantile autism*) that appeared to result from a congenital inability to form close affective ties with others and to tolerate minor changes in the environment and in daily routines (Kanner, 1943) . He also described what he considered to be secondary characteristics, including speech and language abnormalities (e.g., delays, unusual intonation, echolalia, pronominal reversal, and perseveration), uneven cognitive development, repetitive behaviors, and unusual sensitivities. Kanner was struck by the unique nature of the social and affective impairments manifested by his cohort of patients with autism, viewing them as fundamentally different from the problems in social and emotional functioning experienced by his patients with more common neuropsychiatric conditions.

A year later, in 1944, Hans Asperger, a Viennese physician, published a paper in the German literature in which he described four children who also manifested a striking impairment in social relatedness, yet who had sophisticated linguistic skills, good problem-solving abilities, and intense yet restricted patterns of interest (Asperger, 1944). However, knowledge of Asperger's work did not become widespread until the 1980s, following the publication of Wing's case studies and discussions of the syndrome (Burgoine & Wing, 1983; Wing, 1981).

Despite knowledge and clinical experience, a diagnostic category for autism and related disorders was not introduced until publication of the third edition of the *Diagnostic and Statistical Manual* (*DSM-III*; American Psychiatric Association, 1980). Until that time, autism was classified under the psychotic conditions, most notably childhood schizophrenia. By the end of the 1970s, it had become clear that autism was a unique condition, separate from schizophrenia in terms of genetics, clinical manifestations, and course. The diagnostic criteria that were adopted in the *DSM-III* reflected those identified originally by Kanner and expanded by Rutter in the mid- to late 1970s (Rutter, 1974, 1978, 1979), which highlighted an early onset, impairments in social relatedness, atypical language forms and usage, as well as unusual resistance to change, and stereotyped, ritualistic patterns of behavior. Thus, the first diagnostic category for autism reflected the classical early concept. As such, it was highly specific and overly narrow.

In the *DSM-III*, two other categories were included under the pervasive developmental disorder label (a diagnostic term coined to indicate what are now considered to be ASDs), including childhood onset pervasive developmental disorder (which was soon dropped because of questionable validity), as well as an atypical category (which included cases of autistic social dysfunction that did not meet full criteria for autistic disorder). A growing recognition that the *DSM-III* conception of autism was overly narrow resulted in a modification of the PDD criteria, which were field tested in the mid-1980s. This culminated in the publication of a revised edition in 1987 (*DSM-III-R*). This edition of the *DSM* included two PDDs, namely, autistic disorder and PDDNOS. However, it soon became obvious that the *DSM-III-R* criteria were overly inclusive, blurring the boundaries between autism and other conditions that shared some clinical features but differed from autism regarding the nature of the social and communicative impairment. Therefore, the criteria were revised and field tested again, culminating in the publication of the fourth edition of the *DSM* in 1994 (*DSM-IV*). A major advance at that time included the adoption of a highly similar set of criteria by both the *DSM-IV* and the International Classification of Diseases (*ICD-10*; World Health Organization, 1992, 1993).

Based on current conceptions, the primary clinical symptomatology of the PDDs (i.e., ASDs) falls within three major categories, namely: (a) qualitative impairment in social interaction; (b) impairments in communication; and (c) restricted, repetitive, stereotyped behavior, interests, and activities. The following discussion of clinical characteristics is based on the prototypical ASD—autistic disorder (*DSM-IV*, 1994)/childhood autism (*ICD-10*, 1992, 1993). For the purpose of this discussion, the terms *autistic disorder* and *autism* are used synonymously. The unique features of the other recognized PDDs are discussed in a following section.

Clinical Characteristics

Qualitative Impairments in Social Interaction

Within the social domain, the central features of autism include impairments in social reciprocity (the give and take of social interaction); the integration of verbal with nonverbal aspects of social discourse; the development of selective friendships; and the sharing of excitement, interests, and enjoyment with others (Filipek, Accardo, Ashwal, et al., 2000; Volkmar, Cook, Pomeroy, Realmuto, & Tanguay, 1999; Volkmar & Klin, 1999). From the first months of life, impairments are present in social reciprocity and social communication. Infants and toddlers with autism make meaningful eye contact and attend to the voices and faces of others less often than their typically developing peers. Responsive smiling may be absent, and social imitative games (e.g., peek-a-boo, so big, and pat-a-cake) may be largely one sided. In addition, toddlers with autism engage less often in social referencing and joint attention, rarely sharing observations, excitement, and achievements with others in a reciprocal fashion through the integration of speech, vocalizations, reciprocal eye contact, pointing, facial expressions, and gestures. Although they may label or point out something of interest, they typically do not utilize this as a springboard for a give-and-take interaction with others. They may not make reciprocal eye contact as they point and vocalize; monitor the reactions of others to gauge interest, enthusiasm, and approval; or demonstrate curiosity about the interests, preferences, opinions, and experiences of others. When in the midst of stimulating social activity, they may prefer to explore their inanimate environment or engage in a perseverative interest or behavior.

Evidence supporting the presence of early social deficits is accruing from studies of home videotape recordings filmed prior to the recognition of autism (Bernabei, Camaioni, & Levi, 1998; Osterling, Dawson, & Munson, 2002), as well as from prospective studies of very young children using standardized assessment tools (Baron-Cohen, Cox, Baird, Sweettenham, & Nightingale, 1996; Lord, 1995). For example, in a study of 1-year-olds, raters "blind" to subject group membership found that children later identified as manifesting ASD looked at others and oriented to their names less frequently than did infants with mental retardation and typical social development (Osterling et al., 2002). This represented a finding specific for autism, because the groups with ASD and mental retardation did not differ from each other with regard to the presence of other behaviors (e.g., gesturing and looking at objects held by others, engaging in repetitive motor actions), although both groups *did* differ from their typically developing peers. In another study, the absence of social smiling and appropriate facial expressions by 1 year of age were predictive of autism (Adrien et al., 1993).

Bernabei et al. (1998) conducted a videotape study that utilized an observational checklist targeting social interaction, communication, and both functional and symbolic play. The investigators reported that 1.8- to 4.6-year-old infants and toddlers who were later diagnosed with autism/PDD rarely made communicative gestures, played imaginatively, or participated in conventional social games (Bernabei et al., 1998). However, they did demonstrate mutual attention, attachment behaviors, emotional reactions, and vocalizations, although the degree of reciprocity with which they did so is unclear.

Baranek (1999) analyzed videotapes retrospectively and found that 9- to 12-month-olds later diagnosed with autism exhibited impairments in visual orientation, sensitivity to tactile stimulation, and limited responsiveness to name, in contrast with typically developing children and those with developmental delays (Baranek, 1999).

In a prospective study, 16,000 18-month-olds were screened by primary care clinicians using the Checklist for Autism in Toddlers (CHAT). Eighty-three percent (83.3%) of the 12 toddlers who failed the items of protodeclarative pointing, gaze-monitoring, and pretend play were later diagnosed with autism (confirmed on reassessment at 3½ years of age) (Baron-Cohen et al., 1996). Protodeclarative gestures are used for the purpose of sharing observations and experiences with others, whereas protoimperative gestures are used to direct the behavior of others (generally to fulfill requests or needs). In a longitudinal study, Lord (1995) found that 2-year-old children who failed to make appropriate gains in social skills and who engaged in repetitive behaviors were at significant risk for the development of autism by 3 years of age. Utilizing valid and reliable interview and observational instruments, Lord found that deficits in two specific social–communicative areas were highly predictive of autism, namely, showing behavior (joint attention) and responsiveness to one's name being called.

Children with autism observe, imitate, approach, and interact with their age-mates less often than do typically developing peers. In social settings (e.g., play groups, infant–toddler programs, preschool classes, and family gatherings), they tend to remain on the periphery of social activity, respond solely to adults, or engage other children in one-sided physical or highly scripted play (in which they direct the action). They may exhibit a precocious aptitude for early academic tasks and an avid interest in exploring the details of the inanimate world around them, yet fail to understand or derive pleasure from imaginative and interactive play. When older, they generally prefer spending their time amassing factual knowledge on narrow, esoteric topics rather than playing creatively with other children, participating in social events, or joining clubs and athletic teams. Their interests often revolve around taxonomy, classification, and categorization. Although they may enjoy participating in chess tournaments, *Star Wars* memorabilia auctions, or Pokémon and Magic Card swaps, they typically do not enjoy "hanging out" with peers, discussing favorite teams, music, and clothing, or attending sports events or concerts. Studies that have examined gender preferences in play have found differences between children with autism and their typically developing peers. For example, among typically developing children, boys exhibit more interest in mechanical, transportational, and constructional play, whereas girls are more likely to choose play with dolls, kitchen supplies, or toy animals (Knickmeyer, Wheelright, & Baron-Cohen, 2008). However, girls with autism do not exhibit the play preferences of their typically developing counterparts.

Adolescents and young adults with autism may fail to demonstrate basic social etiquette; understand social intent; appreciate subtle emotional states within themselves and others; or predict the thoughts, feelings, and behavior of others even in relatively straightforward social situations. They may ask unusual, overly personal, or rhetorical questions in order to obtain factual information related to an esoteric interest; seek repeated reassurance over a minor issue; or awkwardly attempt to demonstrate friendliness. Statements may be made that are experienced by others as highly provocative, curt, or insensitive, when this is not the intent. Highly literal and concrete problem solving can lead to socially inappropriate comments and behavior, with little appreciation of the need to consider extenuating circumstances, exceptions to the rule, or the unique needs and preferences of others. Research studies have documented impairments among those with autism on tests of social cognition (e.g., empathy, emotion perception, inference), such as the Social Stories Questionnaire (Lawson, Baron-Cohen, & Wheelwright, 2004), the Reading the Mind in the Eyes task (Baron-Cohen, Jolliffe, Mortimore, & Robertson 1997), and the recognition of "faux pas" in short stories (Baron-Cohen, O'Riordan, Stone, Jones, & Plaisted, 1999). In addition, compared with typically developing children, those with autism scored significantly lower on the children's version of the Empathy Quotient (EQ-C) and significantly higher on the Systemizing Quotient (SQ-C), which assesses a preference to analyze, explore, and construct (Auyeung et al., 2009).

Recent studies reveal neurobiological abnormalities which may underlie impairments in these areas of social development. For example, in comparison with age and IQ-matched neurotypical controls, preadolescents with autism exhibited reduced activity in Broca's area during an fMRI social imitation task, a finding that correlated with the severity of impairments on the social subscales of the Autism Diagnostic Interview-Revised and the Autism Observation Schedule-Generic (Williams, 2008). Impairments in imitation and social cognition have also been linked to abnormalities in the mirror neuron system (MNS), which is comprised of premotor and parietal cells that are activated during the performance and observation of motor actions.

Qualitative Impairments in Communication

Within the communication domain, impairments are present in a number of linguistic and nonverbal areas, the most fundamental of which are pragmatics and semantics (i.e., the social usage and explicit or implicit meaning of language and gestures). Although linguistic capability varies greatly across the spectrum (from a total absence of speech to highly sophisticated and erudite language), significant impairments in pragmatics and semantics are universal among individuals with ASD. They communicate primarily to express needs, desires, and preferences, rather than to convey sincere interest in others, or to share experiences, excitement, and feelings. Even among those possessing highly sophisticated and complex language, compliments, words of empathy, and expressions of joy in the good fortune of others are very rare. There is little reciprocity, mutuality, or shared purpose in discussions. In addition, speech and gestural forms of communication are poorly integrated, often resulting in awkward and uncomfortable social interactions. Implicit, subtle, and indirect communications are neither used nor perceived. Expressive communication tends to be explicit, direct, and concrete. During discussions, persons with autism often fail to prepare their speaking partners for conversational transitions, new topics, or personal associations. This can result in digressive, circumstantial, and tangential comments and discussions. It would appear as though persons with autism assume that others are implicitly aware of their experiences, viewpoints, attitudes, and thoughts.

The fashion in which these deficits are manifest is influenced by age, overall cognitive level, temperament, and the presence of sensory or physical limitations. In toddlers, for example, impaired pragmatics may be manifested by significant limitations in reciprocal eye contact, *responsive* smiling, joint attention (mutual sharing of interests and excitement), and social imitative play. In addition, socially directed facial expressions, instrumental and emphatic gestures, and modulation of speech prosody (intonation, cadence, and rate) are rarely used to complement speech, communicate feelings and attitudes, or moderate social discourse. Among preschool children, impairments in symbolic functioning (e.g., language) are accompanied by serious limitations in pretense (e.g. symbolic, imaginative, creative, and interactive play). In contrast, pragmatic impairments among adolescents with Asperger syndrome may be manifested by one-sided, pedantic discussions, with no attempt to involve speaking partners by acknowledging and integrating *their* experiences, ideas, and viewpoints into conversations. Sincere attempts by others to engage in reciprocal conversations may be met with a lack of acknowledgment, annoyance, and disinterest. Comments or questions that are "snuck in" by the listener may be experienced as rude interruptions, prompting the directive, "Wait! I'm not done talking yet." The result is a monologue or lecture that often includes abrupt changes of topic and the introduction of unexplained personal associations. This lack of conversational reciprocity suggests that persons with AS high-functioning autism (or HFA) inherently assume that the listener is implicitly aware of their own experiences, viewpoints, and intent.

Because the relaying of factual and concrete information is the primary goal of "social" dialog among those with ASD, the communication of subtle attitudes, viewpoints, and emotions (particularly secondary emotions, such as embarrassment, guilt, and envy) are largely irrelevant and superfluous. Therefore, emphatic gestures, informative facial expressions, and vocal modulation lack essential meaning for them. The result is that persons with autism generally disregard nonverbal cues and fail to incorporate them into their own discussions. Because this component of social communication often conveys essential information regarding feelings, attitudes, and opinions, an inability to identify, interpret, and produce nonverbal cues can have a highly detrimental effect on social interactions and relationships. Given these impairments, it is not surprising that verbal and nonverbal aspects of communication are poorly integrated, and that subtlety and nuance are rarely conveyed.

Figurative and inferential language is another area of communication that is impaired in autism, largely due to a combination of deficits in abstract and conceptual thought, social reciprocity, and appreciation of the subtleties of social communication. Persons with ASD are highly literal and concrete in their language and thought processing, typically failing to understand metaphor, irony, sarcasm, and facetiousness. As a result, comments are often misinterpreted and discussions misunderstood. In addition, in an effort to remain true to the facts, comments and questions are often presented in an overly direct, straightforward, and "brutally honest" manner, lacking appropriate tact and sensitivity. This can cause embarrassment and distress for the listener and confusion for the speaker with AS or HFA. Both may become angry and resentful; the listener, because of emotional distress and perceived mistreatment; the speaker, because of the seemingly unjustifiable overreaction and negative attitude displayed by the listener. From the perspective of the person with AS or HFA, the listener responded in a rude and ungrateful manner to comments that were intended to be informative, useful, and corrective. The emotional distress, embarrassment, and attack on self-esteem experienced by the listener are relatively foreign to the individual with autism. Interestingly, principles, rules, and codes of behavior can be interpreted in a highly concrete and rigid manner. This can result in insensitive and hurtful comments and behavior, because exceptions to the rule, adjustments to unexpected social contingencies, and appreciation for the spirit (not simply the letter) of the law are relatively foreign to those with autism. There is little awareness that rigid adherence to unavoidably flawed rules can result in a situation that is antithetical to the underlying intent of the rule itself. For example, someone with AS might argue that in order to respect and honor flag and country, persons with paralyses should be barred from attending public events that include the singing of the national anthem, because they would be unable to stand respectfully, as generally expected.

Abnormalities in other aspects of speech and language are also influenced by the social deficits of autism. For example, modulation of speech prosody (e.g., intonation, inflection, and cadence) can be very powerful in conveying feelings, attitudes, and impressions. However, because emotions, social self-esteem, and admiration are not fully appreciated or experienced by those with ASD, it is not surprising that the social modulation of speech prosody is either absent or so exaggerated that insincerity and disdain are conveyed (even when this is not the intent). In addition, a lack of appreciation for reciprocity, mutuality, and the distinction between statements and questions may contribute to such features of autism as echolalia, scripted phrases, and a questionlike intonation when making comments. (What better way to accurately relate data and factual information than to produce an exact duplicate of the statements and writings of others, replete with the faithful preservation of pronouns, tenses, and intonation.)

Restricted, Repetitive, and Stereotyped Patterns of Behavior, Interests, and Activities

Within the sensory and behavioral domains, developmentally immature and atypical perceptions, reactions, and behaviors occur. For example, many children with autism continue to experience the proximal senses of touch, taste, and smell as highly salient long after they have become overshadowed by the distal senses of sight and hearing among typically developing children. This might account for the predominance of olfactory, tactile, and oral forms of exploration among some children and adolescents with autism. In some cases, the salience of proximal sensation persists well into adulthood.

Another sensory feature is hypersensitivity to various stimuli (auditory, tactile, visual, and olfactory). Even low-intensity exposures can result in distress, agitation, and discomfort. Such unexpected reactions may convey the impression of physical pain or a marked overload of the central nervous system pathways responsible for modulating and neutralizing excessive stimulation (both negative and positive).

One of the defining features of autism and Asperger syndrome (as conceived by Kanner and Asperger) is that of rigidity and inflexibility in response to minor change and transition in the environment and daily routines. This insistence on sameness and invariance can be highly impairing, because the precipitants of these reactions often are of little social significance and do not disturb the smooth functioning of the social world. It is as though persons with autism depend on these inanimate markers of space and time because the social priorities that typically direct schedules and routines have little meaning and significance for them.

A range of repetitive stereotyped, compulsive, and ritualistic behaviors occurs in autism, although no one behavioral symptom or symptom cluster is present among the majority of individuals. Compulsive behaviors include ordering and rearranging, ritualistic patterns of walking and pacing, repetitive actions (e.g., turning lights, mechanical devices, and electronic equipment on and off), and insistence on keeping all doors or cabinets closed. Stereotypic movements also occur in ASD (particularly among those with classic autism accompanied by significant cognitive impairment). A variety of different movements can be present, such as hand and arm flapping, toe walking, repetitive jumping, head shaking and weaving, and side-to-side rocking.

Restricted repetitive behaviors (RRBs) present in ASD are heterogeneous in their nature. Research suggests that age and level of functioning are associated with variations in the manifestation of RRBs in individuals with ASD. Stereotyped movements and restricted interests appear to be less frequent among older individuals, self-injurious behaviors and compulsive behaviors appear comparable across age groups, and ritualistic behavior/insistence on sameness appears to be more frequent among older individuals (Lam & Aman, 2007). Furthermore, younger children are more likely to engage in motor and sensory-based stereotypies, whereas older children are more likely to engage in complex repetitive behaviors (Militerni, Bravaccio, Falco, Fico, & Palermo,, 2002). In a study of 712 individuals with ASD who were between 2 and 62 years of age, Esbensen, Seltzer, Lam, and Bodfish (2009) found that adults displayed fewer repetitive behaviors than did children even when controlling for sex, a comorbid diagnosis of ID, and prescription of psychotropic medications. They also reported that individuals with comorbid ID exhibited more persistent repetitive behaviors, more frequent self-injury, and more severe stereotyped movements (particularly females). However, they were less likely than those without ID to exhibit ritualistic behavior. This pattern was not present for insistence on sameness, compulsions, and restricted interests (Esbensen et al., 2009).

There may be changes in the frequency and pattern of RRBs over time. In a 4.5-year prospective study of 241 adolescents and adults with an ASD (10–52 years of age), Shattuck et al. (2007) reported declines in core and maladaptive behavioral symptoms in the majority of individuals, particularly within the domain of repetitive behaviors and interests. However, impairments in social reciprocity and nonverbal communication (core features of autism) were the most persistent.

Interests and preferred activities are generally narrow and restricted. Among those with more classic forms of autism, a great deal of sensory exploration may occur, often involving minor details or parts of toys and objects. Often there is a fascination with subtle physical characteristics of toys and objects, such as texture, shading, and hue. The relationship among the parts of objects may also be of interest, such as the manner in which moving parts rub against one another or the distance that objects maintain from one another when they are spun independently. Exploration using combined senses also occurs, such as the intense visual scrutiny of light diffraction patterns as a prismlike stone is twirled in the sunlight. There also appears to be an apparent dissociation between the parts and the whole. Children and adults with autism often seem to be unaware of the significance and relevance of the whole toy or object (functional, symbolic, and emotional). Individuals with AS (less often with HFA) pursue highly restricted, nonfunctional, and often unusual interests, pastimes, and preoccupations. Factual information, concrete perceptions, and the processes of classification, categorization, and taxonomy are of particular interest and importance. Depending on the cognitive level, reading ability, and motivation of the individual, these interests can involve complex, detailed topics on which a great deal of time is spent memorizing facts, numbers, and visual patterns. In AS, these intense preoccupying interests can include such topics as the exhaustive categorization of water heaters, downspouts, highway guardrails, meteorological forecasts, television program ratings, architectural styles and details, and battle formations over the centuries. Such individuals literally can become world experts on such topics, yet resist suggestions to transform this interest and knowledge into functional, meaningful, or marketable skills. The sole appeal seems to be the very process of memorization, categorization, and classification.

Sex Differences in Symptom Presentation

Epidemiological studies of ASD have demonstrated a male to female ratio of approximately 3–4:1 (Centers for Disease Control and Prevention [CDC], 2007; Fombonne, 2003). Sex differences are influenced by the degree of intellectual impairment. Among those with moderate to severe intellectual disability, the male to female ratio is 2:1, whereas among those with average intellectual functioning, it is approximately 5–6:1 (Holtmann, Bolte, & Poustka, 2007). Studies of older children with ASD report that girls are more likely to have intellectual disability in the severe to profound range when compared to boys (Hartley & Sikora, 2009). Among younger children with ASD, several studies suggest that there is a similar pattern of relative developmental strengths, such that both boys and girls perform better on visual reception and fine motor tasks than on gross motor and language tasks (Carter et al., 2007; Hartley & Sikora, 2009; Joseph, Tager-Flusberg, & Lord, 2002; Lincoln, Allen, & Kilman, 1995). In a sample of 22 girls and 68 boys with ASD aged 18 to 33 months, Carter et al. (2007) found that when controlling for visual reception, boys had better developed language, motor, and social-competence ratings. When controlling for language, girls had better visual reception abilities.

Research that examined sex differences in the phenotypic expression of ASD (i.e., autism-symptom presentation and comorbid behavioral disturbances) has yielded inconsistent findings. Some studies report that girls have more appropriate interests (Kopp & Gillberg, 1992; Wolff & McGuire, 1995) and less unusual motor movements and abnormal use of their body and objects (Lord, Schopler, & Revicki, 1982; Tsi, Stewart, & August, 1981; Volkmar et al., 1988). In contrast, other studies report no sex differences in symptom presentation (Baron-Cohen et al., 2006; Baron-Cohen et al., 2001; Volkmar, Szatmari, & Sparrow, 1993; Wakabayashi et al., 2007; Wakabayashi, Baron-Cohen, & Wheelwright, 2006; Wing & Gould, 1979). However, these studies did not control for intellectual functioning, which is negatively correlated with the severity of autistic features. Two more recent studies report no sex differences on diagnostic features when age and IQ are controlled (Holtmann, Bolte, & Poustka, 2007; Pilowsky, Yirmiya, Shulman, & Dover, 1998). In contrast with these findings, three studies have found significant sex differences in autistic symptomatology. Controlling for IQ, higher rates of restricted and repetitive behavior were reported for males aged 3 to 8 years of age (Lord et al., 1982) and 6 to 26 years of age (McLennan, Lord, & Schopler, 1993). Carter et al. (2007) found a trend for girls to have greater communication impairment than boys on the Autism Diagnostic Observation Schedule-Generic (ADOS-G). Hartley and Sikora (2009) studied 157 boys and 42 girls 1.5 to 3.9 years of age on developmental profiles using the Mullen Scales of Early Learning, features of autism using the ADOS-G, and comorbid behavioral problems using the Child Behavior Checklist (CBCL). Girls with ASD exhibited more communication deficits, sleep problems, anxiety, and dysphoria, whereas boys exhibited more restricted, repetitive, and stereotyped behaviors. The most consistent finding across studies is a higher rate of stereotyped and restricted behaviors among boys. Further research on the phenotypic differences in autistic symptoms between boys and girls should contribute to the development of improved assessment measures and treatments.

Diagnosis and Classification

Overview

The process of accurate diagnosis and classification is an essential endeavor in medicine, for it is key to ensuring validity and reliability, thereby enabling etiological research, and identifying effective methods of treatment. Although ASDs are not medical illnesses in the classical sense, they do result from neurodevelopmental abnormalities that affect social, communicative, and behavioral functioning in fundamental ways. Our current state of knowledge indicates that autism is not a unitary condition with a single etiology, pathogenesis, clinical presentation, and treatment approach; rather, it is a group of related conditions that share many clinical features and underlying social–communicative impairments. The fundamental purpose of arriving at an accurate diagnosis is to promote meaningful research that will eventually lead to effective treatment and an ultimate cure. Accurate diagnosis also enables investigators, clinicians, educators, and parents to communicate clearly, effectively, and efficiently. Ideally, a valid and reliable diagnosis should convey a great deal of information about developmental strengths and weaknesses, short- and long-term prognosis, and treatments that are most likely to be effective. Both basic and applied research endeavors are enhanced by improvements in diagnosis and classification. Unfortunately, some would argue that categorical diagnosis results in stigmatization, reductionistic thinking, and in some cases, discriminatory practices. However, this need not be the case.

Early Screening and Diagnosis

In recent years, efforts have been made to identify ASD as early in life as possible, in order to begin implementing educational and treatment interventions; providing families with education, support, and community resources; and reducing the stress and anxiety families experience as a result of incorrect or misleading diagnoses (Filipek et al., 1999b). The importance of an early diagnosis is supported by findings of improved linguistic, cognitive, and adaptive functioning as a result of intensive early intervention (Harris & Delmolino, 2002; Pelios & Lund, 2001; Rogers, 1998; Schreibman, 2000).

Studies have begun to appear in the research literature assessing the reliability and stability of autism diagnoses made during the early preschool years. Experienced clinical investigators have demonstrated that an accurate diagnosis of autism can be made in the second and third years of life. However, accuracy depends on the completion of a comprehensive, interdisciplinary assessment, one that includes the use of standardized diagnostic instruments in conjunction with clinical expertise (Charman & Baird, 2002). Nonetheless, even among experienced clinicians and investigators, false positive and false negative diagnoses are sometimes made. Within this age group, the most difficult diagnostic distinction is between autism and developmental language disorders (Charman & Baird, 2002). Diagnosis of the broader range of ASD is less reliable, as has been found for older samples (Klin, Lang, Cicchetti, & Volkmar, 2000; Mahoney et al., 1998; Volkmar et al., 1994). In particular, less severe ASD presentations may be misdiagnosed as developmental or language delays in very young children.

Investigators have begun to examine clinical variables that may be predictive of treatment response and general prognosis. For example, Ingersoll et al. (2001) found that preschool children with autism who exhibited low baseline levels of social avoidance experienced significantly more social and linguistic progress than did their high-avoidance counterparts following 6 months of intensive incidental teaching and pivotal response training (provided in an inclusive setting).

Pervasive Developmental Disorder Subtypes

Although the field of autism has not lacked for controversy regarding diagnostic criteria and the boundaries of autism and related disorders, these conditions are among the most reliably diagnosed and validated conditions in all of neurodevelopment and psychiatry. With that said, there is much to be learned about this spectrum, given its enormous complexity.

During the past several decades, a great deal of progress has been made in the area of diagnosis and classification of autism and related pervasive developmental disorders. This has been the result of intellectual curiosity, clinical dedication, and the ever-increasing sophistication of biomedical research, clinical practice, and education. In the specialty of neuropsychiatry, much progress has been made in the area of differential diagnosis. With the publication of *DSM-IV* (American Psychiatric Association, 1994) and ICD-10 (World Health Organization, 1992, 1993), the process of reliable and valid diagnosis was begun. A major accomplishment of *DSM-IV* and *ICD-10* has been general agreement regarding the subtypes and criteria for the pervasive developmental disorders. Although some differences are present in the number and nature of PDD subtypes included under these two diagnostic systems, criteria for the autism proper, Asperger syndrome or disorder, Rett's syndrome or disorder, and childhood disintegrative disorder are essentially identical. This represents a major advance, because the international community can communicate using similar diagnostic criteria and conducting collaborative research investigations. The characteristics of autistic disorder have been described previously. In this section, the other officially recognized PDD subtypes are discussed, in addition to disorders and syndromes that share some clinical features of PDD but do not involve a true autistic social dysfunction.

Asperger Disorder.   The validity of Asperger disorder (AS) as a diagnostic entity distinct from HFA remains unproven (Klin & Volkmar, 2003; Klin, Volkmar, Sparrow, Cicchetti, & Rourke, 1995; Ozonoff & Griffith, 2000). Although some investigators have presented data in support of this diagnostic distinction (Klin et al., 1995; Lincoln, Courchesne, Kilman, Elmasian, & Allen, 1988), others have not (Miller & Ozonoff, 2000; Szatmari, Archer, Fisman, Streiner, & Wilson, 1995). The lack of consensus is due, in part, to disagreement regarding the clinical characteristics that define AS; a subject of ongoing debate and research. As described by Asperger, the central clinical feature of the condition he named *autistic psychopathy* is a serious qualitative impairment in social reciprocity, manifested by either social isolation or atypical, one-sided interactions that lack fluidity, sensitivity, and adequate awareness of the unique viewpoints, feelings, and attitudes of others (Asperger, 1944). Those with AS fail to appreciate the significance of non-verbal social cues, social intent, the depth and range of feeling states, and the emotional impact that comments and behavior can have on others (Klin, Schultz, Rubin, Bronen, & Volkmar, 2001; Shamay-Tsoory, Tomer, Yaniv, & Aharon-Peretz, 2002). Although less socially withdrawn and avoidant than children and adults with classic autism, their social interactions are one sided and lacking in adequate reciprocity.

According to *DSM-IV* criteria, the diagnosis of AS cannot be made in someone with a history of *delays* in speech and language development. Currently, there is much debate regarding the validity of this criterion. However, *impairments* in language and nonverbal communication are present, including poorly modulated prosody (intonation, volume, and rate); impoverished or exaggerated nonverbal communication (e.g., gestures and facial expressions); a formal, pedantic, and long-winded linguistic style; and the use of erudite phrases and terminology that are developmentally uncharacteristic and inappropriate for the particular social circumstances. Discussions often are one sided, incessant, circumstantial, and tangential (largely due to a lack of preparation of the listener for topic changes and personal associations). Another key feature of AS is the presence of intense, preoccupying interests that generally are unusual in nature and highly restricted and narrow in scope and breadth. An impressive store of factual knowledge is accrued on relatively esoteric topics; however, this knowledge is rarely utilized for functional, socially meaningful purposes. Rather, factual knowledge is pursued for its own intrinsic value to the AS individual. In addition, children and adults with AS tend to be physically awkward, uncoordinated, and poor in judging visual–spatial perspective (often failing to maintain comfortable interpersonal space during social interactions).

With regard to neuropsychological functioning, verbal abilities are generally much better developed than are nonverbal abilities (e.g., perceptual motor, visual-spatial). In some cases, this pattern appears to be indicative of a nonverbal learning disability (Gunter, Ghaziuddin, & Ellis, 2002; Klin et al., 1995; Rourke & Tsatsanis, 2000; Volkmar & Klin, 1998). In a majority of cases impairments are present in executive functions, including working memory, organization, and cognitive-set flexibility (Miller & Ozonoff, 2000; Ozonoff & Griffith, 2000).

A complementary strategy for assessing the validity of AS vis-à-vis HFA is to examine the pattern of associated symptomatology. In this regard, a study investigated emotional and behavioral disturbance (psychopathology) in 4- to 18-year-olds with HFA and AS (Einfeld & Tonge, 1995). The Developmental Behaviour Checklist (DBC), an informant-based instrument completed by parents and teachers, was used to assess psychopathology. The DBC contains the following six subscales: disruptive, self-absorbed, communication disturbance, anxiety, antisocial, and autistic relating. Its psychometric properties are satisfactory (Einfeld & Tonge, 1991, 1995). After controlling for the effects of age and cognitive level, children and adolescents with AS exhibited higher levels of psychopathology than those with HFA, particularly disruptive behavior, anxiety, and problems with social relationships (Tonge, Brereton, Gray, & Einfeld, 1999).

Rett's Disorder.   Rett's disorder is one of the two PDD syndromes in that there is a marked deterioration in global functioning. First described by Andreas Rett in 1966, the syndrome that bears his name has been linked to mutations of the MECP2 gene on chromosome Xq28 (Amir et al., 1999; Ellaway & Christdoulou, 1999b; Gura, 1999; Van den Veyver & Zoghbi, 2002). The disorder is far more common in females, although aided by recent genetic findings an increasing number of males have been identified (Moog et al., 2003; Zeev et al., 2002).

Following 6 to 12 months of apparently normal development, a significant developmental regression occurs, affecting a range of developmental domains. Although head circumference is normal at birth (with no clear indications of perinatal abnormalities), a deceleration in head growth ensues. In addition, purposeful hand use declines as an apparent motor apraxia develops (affecting both gait and functional hand use). Over the next months, severe to profound mental retardation becomes apparent, as well as marked impairments in speech and language development and in social relatedness and reciprocity. In addition, a distinctive pattern of motor stereotypy develops, namely, midline hand-wringing movements (except among some affected males). In a high percentage of cases unusual breathing patterns (e.g., periods of hyperventilation) and bruxism (tooth grinding) are present. Additional features include the development of seizures and musculoskeletal abnormalities (scoliosis, peripheral muscle wasting, and hypotonia) (Hagberg, 2002; Hagberg, Hanefeld, Percy, & Skjeldal, 2002; The Rett Syndrome Diagnostic Criteria Work Group, 1988). These clinical features reach a plateau in late adolescence and early adulthood. Although the prognosis in Rett's disorder is quite poor, some stabilization of functioning often occurs, particularly with regard to social interactions and relatedness. Some clinical investigators have reported a somewhat reduced life expectancy; however, this is not significant as long as rigorous medical care and supervision are provided.

Childhood Disintegrative Disorder.   The other regressive form of PDD recognized by *DSM-IV* and *ICD-10* is termed *childhood disintegrative disorder* (CDD; Volkmar, 1992, 1996; Volkmar

& Rutter, 1995). Originally described as disintegrative psychosis (or dementia infantilis) by Heller in the early 1900s, the condition is very rare, perhaps 1/10 as common as autism (Volkmar, Klin, Marans, & Cohen, 1997). It differs from autistic disorder primarily in its distinctive onset and course. Following at least 2 years (typically 3 to 4 years) of what appears to be perfectly normal development, children with CDD experience a dramatic developmental deterioration (either abrupt—days or weeks; or gradual—weeks or months). The loss of skills involves at least two of the following areas: language, social skills, play, motor skills, and toileting. In addition, atypical patterns of development arise within at least two developmental domains involved in autism (e.g., social reciprocity, pragmatic communication, behavioral atypicality). In some cases, this dramatic deterioration is heralded by an identified neurobiological insult; however, in the significant majority of cases the etiology remains unknown. It is important to note that the developmental regression is significant and follows a normal period of development, including age-appropriate phrase and sentence speech, imaginative and early interactive play, and social interest and participation. The regression is not limited to the loss of several words or short phrases and decreased interest in social interaction, as often occurs between 18 and 24 months of age among children diagnosed with autism.

Once established, the clinical syndrome of CDD is consistent with that of an ASD (in terms of social and communicative functioning). In a comparison between cases of autistic disorder (AD) and CDD ascertained during the *DSM-IV* field trials, significant differences were found (Volkmar & Rutter, 1995). The CDD cases had a significantly older age of onset (38 months versus 12.5 months for the AD cases) and were more likely to be mute, severely cognitively impaired, and living in residential placements. In general, the prognosis for those with CDD is less optimistic than for those with AD (Volkmar et al., 1997). Approximately 75% of the children experience a significant developmental and behavioral deterioration, following which a functional plateau is reached. In a relatively small percentage of cases, language and adaptive skills improve; however, a significant recovery is uncommon. Unless a progressive, degenerative neurobiological condition is responsible for the regression, further deterioration does not typically occur.

Pervasive Developmental Disorder Not Otherwise Specified (PDDNOS). The diagnostic category of PDDNOS is very complex, largely undefined, and highly variable (Towbin, 1997; Volkmar et al., 1994). It is included as a subtype within the *DSM* and *ICD* diagnostic categories of PDDs for several reasons. First, in keeping with all other diagnostic categories, a NOS subtype was added to capture cases that embody a symptom profile (and presumed pathogenesis) that is consistent with the general diagnostic concept of the category, yet for a variety of reasons does not meet full algorithm-defined criteria for one of the recognized and reliably diagnosed subtypes. The algorithms were determined by setting cut-off scores (for the total category and for symptom domains), such that the most acceptable balance was achieved among key psychometric variables, including specificity, sensitivity, positive predictive value, and negative predictive value. Second, the PDDNOS classification is meant to include cases in which there is a strong suspicion that the general condition is present, yet because of insufficient information (e.g., developmental and family history, neuropsychological test scores, and age of onset and developmental trajectory), diagnostic confirmation or linkage with a more specific subtype is not possible. Third, some professionals use the category to include cases in which the social–communicative impairment is less severe than expected for someone with the prototypical condition (in this case, AD). Because no specific guidelines are provided, this becomes a subjective judgment. Fourth, cases are included that meet criteria for AS, except for a history of modest delays in language development or mild impairments in cognitive functioning. Fifth, some clinicians and investigators include "unofficial" clinical diagnostic entities within the PDDNOS category on the basis of shared clinical features. These conditions include atypical development, atypical autism, multiplex developmental disorder, semantic–pragmatic disorder, and schizoid or schizotypal disorder.

The only specified criterion for this category involves the presence of a disorder with similarities to autism, in which there are impairments in social relatedness and in some aspects of communicative or behavioral development and functioning. Given the largely undefined nature of this diagnostic category and the many different (but acceptable) ways in which this category is used, there is a lack of clinical consistency and homogeneity within and across the subject populations reported in research studies. This seriously hampers attempts to compare and contrast findings across studies and to draw valid and reliable conclusions from analyses of clinical data. An additional complication that was present in the original *DSM-IV* criteria was rectified in 2000 (Volkmar, Shaffer, & First, 2000). In order to maintain consistency across all diagnostic categories, the 1994 release of the *DSM-IV* stipulated that satisfaction of the criteria for any one of the three clinical domains of PDD could qualify for a diagnosis. This allowed for the diagnosis of PDD in the absence of the essential underlying clinical feature, namely, a distinctive impairment in social interaction and reciprocity. In view of the seriousness of this oversight, an amendment was added to the criteria that required the presence of autistic social dysfunction (Volkmar et al., 2000).

Given the lack of diagnostic specificity inherent in the PDDNOS category, and the resultant subject heterogeneity, it is not surprising that relatively poor interrater reliability has been reported for the distinction between autism and the other PDDs, including PDDNOS (Mahoney et al., 1998; Volkmar et al., 1994). This stands in contrast with high reliability figures for the distinction between autism or PDD and non-PDD conditions (Mahoney et al., 1998; Volkmar et al., 1994).

Despite these difficulties, several studies have reported clinical features that are characteristic of PDDNOS, as well as symptoms that appear to distinguish PDDNOS from autism. In a study of emotional role taking, children diagnosed with PDDNOS performed similarly to typically developing children in their ability to infer other people's emotions on structured role-taking tasks (Serra, Minderaa, van Geert, & Jackson, 1999). However, on a task involving free person descriptions, personal, psychological characteristics were used less frequently by children with PDDNOS to describe their peers (Serra et al., 1999). In comparison with autism, PDDNOS is associated with less impaired cognitive, communicative, and social functioning (Cohen, Paul, & Volkmar, 1986). In addition, interests are less restricted, play is more imaginative, nonverbal communication is better developed, and the disorder is recognized at an older age (Buitelaar, Van der Gaag, Klin, & Volkmar, 1999).

Most experienced clinicians and clinical investigators would agree that the PDD diagnostic category should be reserved for persons who meet clinical criteria for a true autism-related condition (i.e., the presence of qualitative impairments in social reciprocity and pragmatic communication), yet whose developmental profile does not satisfy criteria for a specific PDD subtype (for the reasons discussed previously). However, with the recent broadening of the diagnostic concept of autism and the complexities of integrating dimensional and categorical approaches to diagnosis that are inherent in the PDD concept (i.e., adoption of the term autism spectrum), some professionals have become overly inclusive with the PDD designation. There is an increasing tendency to diagnose some children and adults with autism or AS or PDD, whose clinical profile is more accurately conceptualized as social phobia and secondary withdrawal, a nonverbal learning disability complicated by secondary depression, and a developmental language disorder in the presence of an attention deficit hyperactivity disorder (ADHD). Because optimal educational and treatment programming and ultimate prognosis differ significantly for those with ASD versus those with these other conditions, it is incumbent on professionals to strive for an accurate diagnosis. Although there does appear to be an autistic spectrum within the PDD diagnostic category, it cannot be assumed that this spectrum is contiguous with the social distribution for the general population. It appears more likely that a categorical distinction exists between autism or PDD and the upper end of the normal distribution for self-sufficiency, individualism, and the pursuit of personal interests. Given our current state of knowledge, there appears to be a premature blurring of these boundaries.

Studies are being conducted to validate PDDNOS and to distinguish it from non-PDD conditions that share some clinical features. For example, PDDNOS has been distinguished from developmental language disorders by the presence of social impairments, such as deficits in ToM as assessed by false belief tasks (Sicotte & Stemberger, 1999). This holds true when sex and verbal mental age are held constant.

Among the clinical entities that are often categorized within the PDD rubric, schizoid disorder, multiplex developmental disorder, and semantic–pragmatic disorder warrant some discussion. The concept of schizoid personality disorder bears similarities to PDDNOS and AS, particularly with regard to symptoms of social isolation or withdrawal, a lack of social adroitness, a preference to engage in solitary activities, and restricted interests (Chick, Waterhouse, & Wolff, 1979; Wolff, 2000; Wolff & Barlow, 1979; Wolff & Chick, 1980). However, social understanding is often better developed and interpersonal interactions and relationships are often less impaired than they are in autism, at least in structured situations (Volkmar et al., 1999; Wolff, 2000b).

PDD-Related Disorders

Multiplex Developmental Disorder.   Multiple complex developmental disorder or multiplex developmental disorder (MCDD) is a diagnostic concept closely related to PDDNOS (Cohen, Towbin, Mayes, & Volkmar, 1994; Demb & Noskin, 2001; Klin, Mayes, Volkmar, & Cohen, 1995; Paul, Cohen, Klin, & Volkmar, 1999; Scheeringa, 2001; Zalsman & Cohen, 1998). MCDD has been defined as a developmental disorder in which deficits are present in affective regulation and modulation, social relatedness and sensitivity, attachment, and thought stability (Cohen et al., 1986; Cohen et al., 1994; Zalsman & Cohen, 1998). Specific criteria have been developed and exhibit good interrater reliability (Towbin, Dykens, Pearson, & Cohen, 1993). In a study of 15 children diagnosed as manifesting MCDD (applying the criteria of Towbin et al., 1993), the following symptoms were most common: disturbed attachments (82%), idiosyncratic anxiety reactions (64%), episodes of behavioral disorganization (64%), and wide emotional variability (54%) (Demb & Noskin, 2001). The data also suggested the presence of two distinct behavioral clusters, with one similar to so-called borderline syndromes and the other similar to PDD. The social impairment present in MCDD is less severe, and interest in developing and maintaining relationships is greater than that in autism, and perhaps in the majority of children diagnosed with PDDNOS.

Semantic–Pragmatic Disorder (SPD) or Pragmatic Language Impairment (PLI).   Semantic-pragmatic disorder (SPD; Bishop & Rosenbloom, 1987), more recently termed *pragmatic language impairment* (PLI; Bishop & Norbury, 2002), has received increasing attention, particularly regarding its relationship to ASD. SPD or PLI includes the following clinical features: a verbose linguistic style; difficulties understanding and constructing clear, meaningful, and sequentially related conversations; as well as atypical language forms and content, such as tangential, stereotyped, or socially inappropriate phrases and comments. Some investigators report findings supporting the viewpoint that SPD or PLI may be a subtype of HFA (Shields, Varley, Broks, & Simpson, 1996a, 1996b), because subjects with PLI perform more similarly to those with autism and to those with specific language impairment (SLI) on measures of social cognition and neuropsychological functioning. In contrast, other investigators (Bishop, 1998, 2000; Bishop & Adams, 1989) have asserted that PLI falls on a continuum between SLI and autism. They have found that only some children with PLI meet full or partial diagnostic criteria for ASD (Bishop, 1998). In a 1998 study, the Children's Communication Checklist (CCC) was used for assessing language structure (speech and syntax), pragmatics, and nonlinguistic characteristics of autism. A subgroup of children with "pure" SPD did not differ from children with SLI in the quality of their social relationships or in the nature of their preferred interests (Bishop, 1998). With the obvious exception of impairments in language pragmatics and semantics, children in this pure SPD group exhibited none of the social or behavioral features of autism.

In a follow-up study (Bishop & Norbury, 2002), the relationship between PLI and autism or PDD was investigated in greater detail among children 6 to 9 years of age. The following hypotheses were studied: PLI is a subtype of autistic disorder, PLI is a subtype of autism or a related PDD, or PLI and autism or PDD are distinct conditions (with the possibility of different underlying semantic and pragmatic impairments); however, some children may manifest both conditions. Subjects received a general speech and language assessment and were separated into SLI and PLI groups on the basis of results from the CCC. Additional comparison groups included subjects with autistic disorder and those with typical development. Diagnostic instruments for autism or PDD were administered, including the Autism Screening Questionnaire (ASQ), the Autism Diagnostic Interview-Revised (Lord et al., 1997; Lord, Rutter, & Le Couteur, 1994; Lord, Storoschuk, Rutter, & Pickles, 1993), and the Autism Diagnostic Observation Schedule-Generic (Lord et al., 2000). Within the total PLI group, 16% met criteria for AD, and among 13 children with PLI in the first of two study phases, an additional 15% met criteria for PDDNOS. However, a subset of children with pragmatic impairments was not diagnosed as manifesting ASD, presenting as sociable, communicative, and normal in their use of nonverbal communication, and free from other features of autism.

Shields (1991) found that adults who had sustained right hemispheric lesions exhibited similar speech and language abnormalities as children diagnosed with semantic–pragmatic language disorder, including fluent and complex language; atypical prosody; poor comprehension of metaphor, humor, inferential meaning, and paralinguistic features; and limited sensitivity regarding the appropriate choice of language for varying social contexts. Similar findings were reported for a group of children with high level autism (in contrast with children manifesting phonologic–syntactic language impairments and those with normal development) (Shields et al., 1996a). The authors hypothesized that the impairments in communication and cognition present among those with SPD and autism may reflect underlying right hemispheric dysfunction. In another study by the same investigators (Shields et al., 1996b), children with SPD exhibited similar deficits on tests of social cognition (theory of mind, social comprehension, and detection of eye direction) as children with high-level autism. The performance of both of these groups was inferior to that of comparison groups of children with phonologic–syntactic language impairment and normal development. The authors conjectured that semantic–pragmatic language disorder may lie on the autistic spectrum (Shields et al., 1996b).

Associated and Comorbid Conditions. Frequently, the PDDs are accompanied by associated symptom clusters. Whether these should be considered part of the syndrome of autism itself or designated as independent, comorbid disorders remains controversial. Approximately 70 to

75% of individuals with autistic disorder also have mental retardation (appropriately considered a comorbid condition; Volkmar et al., 1999; Volkmar & Klin, 1999). In addition, a significant number of those with PDD engage in stereotyped and self-stimulatory mannerisms and behaviors. However, this symptom cluster should be considered part of the autism syndrome and not a separate stereotyped movement disorder. In a small percentage of autism cases, motor and phonic tics develop, suggesting comorbidity with Tourette's syndrome. However, it is important to distinguish tics from motor stereotypy. In addition, many individuals with autism exhibit signs and symptoms suggestive of an ADHD (e.g., overactivity, selective attentional weaknesses, distractibility, and impulsivity). However, rather than reflecting the presence of a comorbid ADHD, these symptoms may reflect underlying neuropsychological and behavioral features of autism. In many cases, inattention and distractibility are secondary to confusion, limited motivation, and the relatively low reinforcement value of attention and praise, rather than to a separate neurophysiological abnormality. However, in some cases, particularly those with AS or PDDNOS, a comorbid ADHD diagnosis may be justified.

Sturm, Fernell, and Gillberg (2004) reviewed the records of 101 children with AS, PDDNOS, and high-functioning autism, and identified attentional problems in 95%, motor difficulties in 75%, problems regulating activity level in 86%, and impulsivity in 50%.

Symptoms of anxiety occur frequently among those with pervasive developmental disorders and often become increasingly prominent as individuals with AS and PDDNOS mature. In the clinical setting, anxiety-related concerns are among the most common presenting problems for school-age children and adolescents with ASD (Ghaziuddin, 2002). A review of the prevalence of anxiety symptoms in youth with autism and related disorders indicates that between 11 and 84% of children with ASD experience some degree of impairing anxiety (White, Oswald, Ollendick, & Scahill, 2009). Anxiety symptoms experienced by children with ASD have been shown to be similar to those experienced by non-ASD clinical samples (Weisbrot, Gadow, DeVincent, & Pomeroy, 2005; White et al., 2009). Age and cognitive functioning have been shown to affect the degree of anxiety symptoms in children and adolescents with ASD, with younger children experiencing milder anxiety and cognitively higher functioning children experiencing more anxiety (Sukhodolsky et al., 2008; White et al., 2009). Weisbrot et al. (2005) found that anxiety problems were more evident in children with AS than in those with AD, possibly reflecting higher cognitive and linguistic abilities within the AS group.

A broad range of anxiety symptoms can arise, including phobias, social anxiety, generalized anxiety symptoms, paniclike episodes, and compulsivelike behavioral patterns. Highly ritualistic ordering and rearranging behavior, marked intolerance for minor changes in the environment and daily routines, a preoccupation with order and symmetry, and in some cases, distressingly intense compulsive rituals can occur. Although the continuity of these symptoms with obsessive–compulsive disorder (OCD) remains uncertain, anxiety and distress often are clearly present. For individuals with ASD who experience highly distressing, ego-dystonic symptoms, a comorbid diagnosis of OCD may be appropriate. However, for others, the repetitive thoughts and behaviors appear to represent pleasurable preoccupations, and, hence, may bear a closer relationship to impulse control disorders that to OCD.

Similar to typically developing youth, specific phobias may be more common in younger children with ASD, while disorders such as social phobia and OCD become more common in adolescence (Farrugia & Hudson, 2006; Ollendick, King, & Muris, 2004; White et al., 2009). Simonoff et al. (2008) assessed the prevalence of comorbid psychiatric disorders in a population-derived sample of children ages 10 to 14 with confirmed ASD diagnoses (50 with PDDNOS and 62 with AD) and found that the most prevalent psychiatric disorder was social anxiety disorder in 29.2% of the sample, followed by generalized anxiety disorder in 13.4%, and panic disorder in 10.1%. Adolescents may be more vulnerable to anxiety since they exhibit a greater awareness of being different from their peers. Kuusikko et al. (2008) found that children with HFA/AS reported an increase in social anxiety with age in contrast with typically developing children who reported a decrease in social and performance anxiety. Physiological hyperarousal and impaired social skills contribute to increased self-reports of social anxiety among adolescents with ASD (Bellini, 2006). Anxiety may compound the core social deficits of autism (White et al., 2009). For example, ASD children with anxiety may further retreat from social situations and experience additional stress during peer interactions. Further research is needed to: (a) identify the risk factors for anxiety in ASD; (b) develop more accurate assessment tools for making a definitive comorbid diagnosis of anxiety in youth with ASD; and (c) clarify how anxiety interacts with the core impairments seen in ASD.

Among those with AS and HFA, depression can sometimes occur in adolescence and young adulthood, often in response to social failure and marginalization. There have been reports of mood disorders, such as bipolar disorder, in persons with autism and family members (DeLong & Dwyer, 1988); however, a definitive association has not been established.

In approximately 20% of autism cases, a seizure disorder develops (not uncommonly during adolescence) (Tuchman, 2000; Volkmar, 2000). The rare condition, acquired developmental aphasia with epilepsy (Landau-Kleffner syndrome), should be included in the differential diagnosis of PDD for cases with a later onset, significant regression in speech and language functioning, and relative preservation of social interest or relatedness and nonverbal communication. A distinctive EEG pattern is often present, although rigorous electroencephalographic efforts are sometimes necessary to document this.

Differential Diagnosis of Non-PDD Disorders

There are a number of clinical similarities between ASD and the prodromal and nonpsychotic phases of early-onset schizophrenia (EOS), including social discomfort and isolation, reduced eye contact, social awkwardness, unusual language patterns (e.g., indirect, and metaphorical), perseverative behaviors, restricted interests, misinterpretation of subtle social cues, overly concrete thought processing, and so-called negative symptoms (e.g., blunted or inappropriate affect, reticence, reduced motivation, and apathy). Another similarity is the presumed developmental nature of both conditions. Recent findings suggest that schizophrenia (similar to autism) may be a neurodevelopmental disorder, with origins early in life (Hakak et al., 2001). In fact, early conceptions of autism included a continuity with schizophrenia and related psychotic disorders (Volkmar et al., 1999; Volkmar & Klin, 1999). During the past several decades, autism and schizophrenia have been shown to be distinct disorders genetically, developmentally, and symptomatically. Despite some apparent behavioral similarities, EOS is associated with better social reciprocity and understanding and the capacity to maintain interpersonal relationships that include mutuality. Despite several case reports suggesting that children with autism may be at increased risk for the development of comorbid schizophrenia, systematic studies have negated this suggestion (Volkmar & Cohen, 1991).

Although the initial social impairments exhibited by children with reactive attachment disorders (RAD) may resemble those present in ASD, marked improvement occurs once adequate care and nurturance are provided (Richters & Volkmar, 1994; Volkmar et al., 1999). The quality of social interactions and the ability to infer mental states (thoughts, feelings, attitudes, and intentions) in others are better developed among those with RAD; however, lower levels of social functioning are present than observed in other clinical disorders (Boris, Zeanah, Larrieu, Scheeringa, & Heller, 1998). In addition, there are suggestions that a reliable diagnosis of attachment disorder can be made in the absence of unequivocal evidence of early "pathogenic" care (Boris et al., 1998).

Standardized Diagnostic Instruments

Preschool Measures

In view of the complexity of differential diagnosis among preschoolers, clinical investigators have been working toward the development of screening tools capable of identifying young children at risk for the development of ASDs. Among the most promising tools are CHAT (Baird et al., 2000; Baron-Cohenet al., 1996; Baron-Cohen et al., 2000), the Modified-Checklist for Autism in Toddlers (M-CHAT; Charman et al., 2001a, 2001b; Robins, Fein, Barton, & Green, 2001), and the Screening Test for Autism in Two-Year-Olds (STAT; Stone, Coonrod, & Ousley, 2000). Preliminary studies of these instruments indicate good psychometric properties (e.g., discriminant validity and interrater and intratest item reliability, sensitivity, specificity, positive predictive value, and negative predictive value). Increasing numbers of studies are being designed to assess the usefulness of these measures both as screening instruments within the general preschool population and as diagnostic instruments among children suspected of manifesting an ASD. However, it is important to keep in mind that these three instruments were developed with different objectives. The CHAT was designed solely as a general population screening instrument for use by primary care practitioners in their routine well-childcare roles (particularly for toddlers 18 months of age). It is intended to identify young children who may be at risk for ASD and who should be referred for a more comprehensive assessment (or series of assessments that increase in specificity, as clinically indicated). The M-CHAT was conceived to improve the sensitivity of the CHAT by adding items to accommodate a slightly older population (18 to 24 months) and to adapt it for use in the United States and other countries in which home healthcare practitioners do not routinely screen the general childhood population. Although ostensibly designed as a population-screening instrument, the M-CHAT also has been used by its developers as a second-level screen among preschool children (18 to 30 months of age) already identified as being at risk for a developmental disorder by early intervention professionals. In contrast, the STAT was developed as a second-level screen for use as a source of diagnostic information in the assessment process.

The CHAT is a brief, 14-item checklist developed to screen for early social–communicative behaviors, particularly joint attention and imaginative play, within the general childhood population. Nine items are completed during a brief parental interview by the primary care physician, and five items are completed by a home health visitor (the CHAT was developed for use in Britain). The items found to be the most strongly associated with autism included protodeclarative pointing (pointing to share an observation or interest), gaze monitoring, and imaginative play. The CHAT has been studied in large populations as a screening instrument to detect early signs of atypical development that may signify the presence of ASD (Baird et al., 2000; Baron-Cohen et al., 1996). In a longitudinal study, 16,235 toddlers 18 months of age were screened by their primary care clinicians (Baird et al., 2000). Cases were reevaluated when the children were 3, 5, and 7 years of age in order to assess the sensitivity, specificity, and positive predictive value of the CHAT in diagnosing childhood autism. At 18 months, 19 of the toddlers were identified by the CHAT as being at risk for autism. At follow-up, 50 of the children met criteria for autism when all sources of information were considered. On this basis, the CHAT exhibited a sensitivity of 38% and a specificity of 98%. When maximized by repeat screening at 1 month, the positive predictive value was 75% but the sensitivity declined to 20%, and the specificity rose close to 100%. In addition to autism, the screen also was successful in identifying cases of PDD and other developmental disorders (e.g., language). The authors concluded that the CHAT can be used to identify cases of autism and PDD at 18 months of age. Given its relatively low sensitivity, it should not be considered an adequate screen to rule out potential cases of autism; however, in view of its high specificity, it is quite useful in distinguishing autism from other developmental conditions. It is of interest that Scambler, Rogers, and Wehner (2001) achieved a sensitivity of 85% and a specificity of close to 100% by slightly altering the original CHAT criteria.

The M-CHAT is a 23-item scale that is scored dichotomously (with yes or no responses; Robins et al., 2001). It was adapted and expanded from the CHAT to serve as a screening instrument within the health care environment of the United States. It includes the nine parent report items from the CHAT, in addition to items derived from previous research and clinical experience that involve developmental domains affected in autism, including language, arousal modulation, sensory responsiveness, theory of mind, motor functions, and social and emotional development, among others. Following a preliminary analysis the original 30 items were reduced to 22 and an additional item was added (social referencing deficits). Six items were found to be particularly salient on discriminant function analysis, including pointing to express interest, responsiveness to his or her name, interest in other children, showing behavior, response to joint attention, and social imitation. Internal reliability was judged to be adequate, with Cronbach's alpha coefficients of 0.85 and 0.83 for the entire checklist and the critical items, respectively. The sensitivity, specificity, positive predictive power (PPP), and negative predictive power (NPP) for the 23-item scale and the six best items, were as follows: sensitivity, 0.97 and 0.95, respectively; specificity, 0.99 and 0.98, respectively; PPP, 0.68 and 0.79, respectively; and NPP, 0.99 and 0.99, respectively. The population for which psychometric data were collected included 1,122 18- to 24-month-olds screened by primary care physicians during well-childcare visits and 171 18- to 30-month-olds screened through early intervention service providers. Therefore, the sample included both nonreferred and "high-risk" populations and constitutes a combined first- and second-stage screen.

STAT is a 12-item, clinician-scored interactive, second-stage screening instrument for preschool children between 24 and 35 months of age (Stone et al., 2000). It was developed to differentiate children with ASD from those with other developmental disorders. It is administered within the context of a playlike interaction. The items of the STAT were derived from measures of play, imitation, and social communication. In a validation sample of 32 preschool children, the sensitivity of the instrument was 0.83 and the specificity was 0.86.

Informant-Based Measures

Over the years, a number of informant-based questionnaires and checklists have been developed in order to assist in the diagnosis of autism and related PDDs. The earlier instruments tended to focus on behavioral symptoms common among those with classic autistic disorders, such as the Rimland E-2 Scale (Deckner, Soraci, Deckner, & Blanton, 1982) and the Autism Behavior Checklist (ABC; Krug, Arick, & Almond, 1980). More recently developed instruments have focused on symptomatology common among those with HFA, AS, and PDDNOS (Baron-Cohen et al., 2001).

The ABC (Krug et al., 1980) is a 57-item screening questionnaire for autism, designed for completion by teachers (with parental assistance). The developers of the ABC grouped the items into five subscales: sensory, relating, body or object use, language, and social or self-help. Although responses are dichotomous, the items are weighted (in a manner determined by prior statistical analyses of the scale). Based on summary scores, the presence of autism is determined to be unlikely, questionable, or probable. Recent reanalyses of the psychometric properties of the scale have identified a factor structure different from that originally proposed. In one case, a 3-factor model was suggested (Wadden, Bryson, & Rodger, 1991), and in another, a (different) 5-factor model was suggested (Miranda-Linne & Melin, 2002). Investigators have reported fair to good accuracy discriminating autistic from nonautistic developmentally impaired children (Volkmar et al., 1988; Wadden et al., 1991).

The Autism Screening Questionnaire (ASQ) is a 40-item parent checklist that was derived from the clinician-based semistructured interview, the Autism Diagnostic Interview-R (ADI-R; Berument, Rutter, Lord, Pickles, & Bailey, 1999). The objective was to devise a valid and reliable screening instrument that included items from three areas of functioning known to be impaired in ASD, namely, reciprocal social interaction, language and communication, and repetitive and stereotyped patterns of behavior. The items were modified from the ADI-R in order to make them more understandable to caregivers. The ASQ has two versions: one for children under 6 years of age and one for those 6 and over. In a study of 200 subjects (160 with PDD and 40 with non-PDD diagnoses), 33 of 39 scored items succeeded in statistically differentiating the populations. Correlations between the ASQ and the ADI were highly significant for all three major symptom domains.

Discriminative validity also has been calculated (Berument et al., 1999). The following scores have been reported: PDD versus non-PDD, 0.88; autism versus mental retardation, 0.93; and autism versus other PDDs, 0.73. These scores were very similar to those derived from the ADI. With a cut-off score of 15 (the maximum score is 39), the ASQ exhibited the following psychometric qualities for differentiating PDD from non-PDD conditions: sensitivity, 0.85; specificity, 0.75; positive predictive value, 0.93; and negative predictive value, 0.55. Discriminating autistic disorder proper from other diagnoses resulted in improved discriminatory values, including a sensitivity of 0.96 and a specificity of 0.67. These reported properties of the ASQ may be overestimated, because a majority of the participating families had been interviewed with the ADI-R sometime in the past. Although the ASQ was quite accurate in differentiating PDD and autism from non-PDD conditions, it was decidedly less effective in differentiating autism from other subtypes of PDD. In this regard, it is not dissimilar to other screening questionnaires. The finer points of differential diagnosis are better addressed by more comprehensive assessments, including standardized investigator–clinician diagnostic interviews.

A 29-item subscale of the Developmental Behaviour Checklist has been developed, the Autism Screening Algorithm (DBC-ASA). The DBC-ASA was piloted in a sample of 180 children with *DSM-IV*-diagnosed autism and 180 controls matched for age, sex, and IQ range (Brereton, Tonge, Mackinnon, & Einfeld, 2002). The DBC–ASA was found to have good discriminant validity across a wide range of IQ (normal to severe mental retardation) and of age (4–18 years). The DBC is the parent and teacher questionnaire from which the DBC-ASA was abstracted. The DBC was developed to assess signs of affective and behavioral problems in children and adolescents with a range of developmental disabilities (Einfeld & Tonge, 1995). It contains 96 items and is patterned after a questionnaire commonly used within the general population (CBC). It includes a three-level rating format for each item. The DBC contains six subscales: disruptive, self-absorbed, communication disturbance, anxiety, antisocial, and autistic relating. Its psychometric features are satisfactory, including internal consistency and interobserver agreement (Einfeld & Tonge, 1991, 1995; Tonge et al., 1996).

The Autism Spectrum Screening Questionnaire (ASSQ) is another recently developed screening instrument for HFA or AS (Ehlers, Gillberg, & Wing, 1999). It is a 27-item checklist designed for completion by parents and teachers of children and adolescents suspected of manifesting an ASD and who have IQs at or above the level of mild mental retardation. A 3-point rating scale results in a total score range between 0 and 54. The study population included the following subject groups: ASDs, disruptive behavior disorders (DBD), learning disorders, as well as an AS validation sample. The ASSQ was successful in distinguishing subjects with ASD from those with DBD. Good test–retest and interrater reliabilities were reported, as well as good agreement between parent and teacher ratings. Cut-off scores of 19 for parents and 21 for teachers resulted in true-positive and false-positive rates of 62 and 10%, and 70 and 9%, respectively.

The Autism Spectrum Quotient-Children's Version (for ages 4–11 years) (Auyeung, Baron-Cohen, Wheelwright, & Allison, 2008) and the Adolescent Autism Spectrum Quotient (ages 12–16 years) (Baron-Cohen et al., 2006) are recently developed parent questionnaires designed for the higher-functioning ASD population.

Self-Report Measure. A new screening questionnaire, the Autism-Spectrum Quotient (AQ), has been developed for use by adults of average intelligence who are suspected of having traits that fall along the autistic continuum (Baron-Cohen et al., 2001). This self-report measure consists of 50 questions (piloted among adults with HFA, AS, and age-matched controls) that are grouped into five categories, including social skill, attention switching, attention-to-detail, communication, and imagination. Responses indicating atypicality receive 1 point, resulting in a sum scoring range between 0 and 50. A cutoff score of 32+ resulted in an 80% true-positive identification rate among HFA or AS subjects and a 2% false-positive identification rate among controls (a random community sample and a Cambridge University student sample). The mean AQ total score of adults with AS or HFA was significantly higher than that of the community controls. Within the AS or HFA group, male and female scores did not differ significantly. Test–retest and interrater reliability of the AQ was good. The developers concluded that the AQ appears to be a valuable screening instrument for estimating where on the continuum from autism to normality adults with average cognitive ability lie.

Investigator- and Clinician-Based Instruments. In an effort to standardize the process of diagnosis, particularly for research purposes, clinical investigators have developed diagnostic rating instruments and semistructured diagnostic interviews. Clinician-based rating scales were the first to be developed, including the Behavioral Rating Instrument for Autistic and Other Atypical Children (BRIAAC) (Ruttenberg, Dratman, Fraknoi, & Wenar, 1966; Ruttenberg, Wolf-Schein, & Wenar, 1991) and the Childhood Autism Rating Scale (CARS) (Schopler, Reichler, DeVellis, & Daly, 1980).

The CARS is a commonly used clinician-based rating instrument that is completed following a period of observation (typically a clinical evaluation). The CARS consists of 15 scales, labeled: Relating to People; Imitation; Emotional Response; Body Use; Object Use; Adaptation to Change; Visual Response; Listening Response; Taste, Smell, and Touch Response and Use; Fear or Nervousness; Verbal Communication; Nonverbal Communication; Activity Level; Level and Consistency of Intellectual Response; and General Impressions. The rating of each scale is based on a 7-level ordinal structure (accompanied by anchor-point descriptions). Ratings are made from 1 to 4 in half-point increments. The total sum score range (15 to 60) has been divided into three diagnostic categories (based on previous studies), namely, Nonautistic, Mildly–Moderately Autistic, and Severely Autistic. Final scoring is based on where along this 45-point continuum the individual's total sum score falls.

Two factor analytic studies of the CARS have been conducted. In the first, three factors were identified with moderate to good internal consistency: Social Impairment (SI), Negative Emotionality (NE), and Distorted Sensory Response (DSR) (DiLalla & Rogers, 1994). Scores on the SI factor distinguished subjects with autism from those with PDDNOS and non–PDD developmental impairments with 78% accuracy. SI scores improved over time equally across the three subject groups. NE scores were the most responsive, whereas DSR scores were the least responsive to treatment interventions. The second study involved children and adolescents with either autism or PDDNOS (Stella, Mundy, & Tuchman, 1999). Five factors were identified that accounted for 64% of the variance in total CARS scores. The factors were labeled as follows: Social Communication, Emotional Reactivity, Social Orienting, Cognitive and Behavioral Consistency, and Odd Sensory Exploration. Factor-based scales developed during the study distinguished the subject groups (autism, PDDNOS, and nonautistic controls). The results supported the presence of a "partially independent" social impairment domain among the PDD subjects (Stella et al., 1999).

The most systematically investigated and widely used diagnostic interview is the Autism Diagnostic Interview-Revised (ADI-R), a semistructured, investigator-based interview for those caring for children and adults who are suspected of manifesting autism or a related pervasive developmental disorder (Lord, Leventhal, & Cook, 2001; Lord et al., 1997; Lord, Rutter, & Le Couteur, 1994; Lord et al., 1993). The psychometric properties of the ADI-R have been studied (Lord et al., 2001). Reliability was assessed among preschool children with autism and mental retardation or language impairment, and validity was assessed among children with and without autism. The ADI-R was found to be reliable and valid for diagnosing autism in preschool children, demonstrating good interrater reliability and high internal consistency (Lord et al., 1994). The ADI-R distinguished autistic from nonautistic, mentally handicapped preschool children (matched on mental and chronological age) on all subdomains of *DSM-IV* and *ICD-10* algorithm criteria (except some aspects of stereotypic language). Fifty of 51 children with clinically diagnosed autism were correctly identified by the ADI-R, and only 2 of 30 nonautistic children 18 months of age and older were misdiagnosed (Lord et al., 1993).

In another study, the ADI-R was successful in differentiating children with autism from those with receptive language disorder (Mildenberger, Sitter, Noterdaeme, & Amorosa, 2001). All subjects had nonverbal IQs falling within the normal range. Only one child with autism and one with receptive language disorder were misclassified by the *ICD-10* algorithm criteria of the ADI-R. The reciprocal social interaction and language and communication domains were superior to the restricted and stereotyped behavioral domain in differentiating the subject groups (especially among school-age children; Mildenberger et al., 2001).

The degree of diagnostic agreement between the ADI-R and the CARS has been investigated among individuals suspected of manifesting autism (Pilowsky, Yirmiya, Shulman, & Dover, 1998). Concordance was reached in 85.7% of cases (highest among the oldest subjects). Participants who fulfilled ADI-R criteria for autism were older and received higher CARS scores than participants who did not. No sex differences were present between the two instruments.

The Autism Diagnostic Observation Schedule-Generic (ADOS-G) is a companion instrument to the ADI-R and is administered to the identified children and adults. The ADOS-G is a valid and reliable semistructured observation and interview protocol designed to provide clinical information relevant for diagnosing autism and related pervasive developmental disorders (Lord et al., 2000). The ADOS-G was developed in order to improve the accuracy and reliability of diagnoses within the autism spectrum. It consists of a series of "presses" for social and communicative interaction through the presentation of tasks, play activities, and conversational probes. Based on the age, communicative ability, and developmental level of the individual, one of four modules is selected for administration. The following items are included across the four modules: the quality of social greetings and request-helping initiatives; choice making; spontaneous, symbolic, and interactive play; social, functional, and symbolic imitation; joint attention and social referencing; responsiveness to name; responsive social smiling; the quality of help-requesting initiatives; anticipation of routines with objects and of social routines; nonverbal communication (through demonstration or mime); identification of social interactions and activities in pictures; appreciation of sequential plots and themes depicted in social stories; creative story telling; understanding of higher order social concepts (e.g., humor, intent, irony, and alternate points of view); general conversational ability; and insight regarding the nature of social topics (e.g., emotions and feelings, relationships—close friendship, family ties, romantic relationships, interpersonal conflict, loneliness, self-conception, future goals, and aspirations). Scoring of the ADOS is based on assessments of the quality of reciprocal social interaction, pragmatic communication, and play, as well as on the presence of restricted, stereotyped, and ritualistic behavior.

The psychometric properties of the ADOS-G have been assessed among 223 children and adults with autistic disorder, PDDNOS, and non-PDD disorders (Lord et al., 2000). Highly significant values for the following were found: interrater and test–retest reliability for individual items, interrater reliability within domains, and internal consistency. Autism and PDDNOS were accurately differentiated from non-PDD conditions; however, differentiation of autism from PDDNOS was less robust. Excellent sensitivity (87–100%) and specificity (90–94%) of the *DSM-IV* and *ICD-10* diagnostic algorithms were achieved for autism and PDDNOS relative to non-PDD disorders, with moderate differentiation of autism from PDDNOS (Lord et al., 2000).

Another investigator-based schedule for interviewing parents and caregivers is the Diagnostic Interview for Social and Communication Disorders (DISCO), currently in its ninth edition (Leekam, Libby, Wing, Gould, & Taylor, 2002). The DISCO was developed with the goal of gathering developmental and clinical information relevant to the broader autism spectrum and to aid in case formulation and clinical diagnosis. Unlike the ADI-R, the DISCO was not developed in concert with the major schemes of categorical diagnosis (i.e., *DSM* and *ICD*), and is more dimensional than categorical in its approach. Algorithms have been derived for *ICD-10* childhood autism and for the broader autistic spectrum. Measures of interrater reliability and diagnostic validity are good, particularly for the broader autistic spectrum (Leekam et al., 2002).

Summary: Definitions and Characteristics of the Spectrum

Autism and related PDDs are early-onset neurobiological conditions that share fundamental impairments in social reciprocity, pragmatic and semantic communication, reactions to environmental stimuli, and the nature of preferred interests and activities. Although there is a broad range of cognitive, linguistic, and adaptive functioning across the autism spectrum, impairments in social understanding, emotion perception, and pragmatic communication are universally present. Currently, there are several PDD (or ASD) subtypes recognized by the principal diagnostic systems, the *DSM-IV*, and the *ICD-10*: namely autistic disorder, disintegrative disorder, Rett's disorder, Asperger disorder, and PDDNOS.

Autism and related conditions are disorders of neurodevelopment connectivity, with suspected structural and functional abnormalities in brain regions that are primarily responsible for social, communicative, and executive functions (e.g., the orbitofrontal cortex and regions of the temporal lobe and related limbic system). There are many different proximal causes of autism, including genetic etiologies (i.e., autism-specific susceptibility genes, more global genetic disorders, such as some causes of tuberous sclerosis and fragile X syndrome). During the past decade, the reported prevalence of ASD has markedly increased because of earlier and more accurate diagnosis, recognition of a broader spectrum, and increased awareness among primary practitioners, educators, and parents. However, other factors may be operative as well.

Both clinical and basic science research regarding the etiology, pathogenesis, clinical pharmacology, and treatment of autism spectrum disorders has been expanding, particularly with regard to interdisciplinary investigations, international collaboration, and public–private funding. Given this impressive effort, it is likely that major advances in our understanding of these serious neurobiological conditions will be forthcoming during the next decade.

References

Adrien, J. L., Lenoir, P., Martineau, J., Perrot, A., Hameury, L., Larmande, C., et al. (1993). Blind ratings of early symptoms of autism based upon family home movies. *Journal of the American Academy of Child & Adolescent Psychiatry, 32*(3), 617–626.

Allen, D. A. (1988). Autistic spectrum disorders: Clinical presentation in preschool children. *Journal of Child Neurology, 3*(Suppl.), S48–S56.

American Psychiatric Association. (1980). *The diagnostic and statistical manual of mental disorders* (3rd ed.). Washington, DC: Author.

American Psychiatric Association. (1987). *The diagnostic and statistical manual of mental disorders* (3rd ed., rev.). Washington, DC: Author.

American Psychiatric Association. (1994). *The diagnostic and statistical manual of mental disorders* (4th ed.). Washington, DC: Author.

Amir, R. E., Van den Veyver, I. B., Wan, M., Tran, C. Q., Francke, U., & Zoghbi, H. Y. (1999). Rett syndrome is caused by mutations in X-linked MECP2, encoding methyl-CpG-binding protein 2 [comment]. *Nature Genetics, 23*(2), 185–188.

Asperger, H. (1944). Die "Autistischen Psychopathen" im Kindesalter [Autistic psychopathy of childhood]. *Archives fur Psychiatrie und Nervenkrankheiten, 117,* 76–136.

Auyeung, B., Baron-Cohen, S., Wheelwright, S., & Allison, C. (2008). The Autism Spectrum Quotient: Children's Version (AQ-Child). *Journal of Autism & Developmental Disorders, 38*(7), 1230–1240.

Auyeung, B., Wheelwright, S., Allison, C., Atkinson, M., Samarawickrema, N., & Baron-Cohen, S. (2009). The children's empathy quotient and systemizing quotient: Sex differences in typical development and in autism spectrum conditions. *Journal of Autism and Developmental Disorders, 39,* 1509–1521.

Bailey, A., Palferman, S., Heavey, L., & Le Couteur, A. (1998). Autism: The phenotype in relatives. *Journal of Autism & Developmental Disorders, 28*(5), 369–392.

Baird, G., Charman, T., Baron-Cohen, S., Cox, A., Swettenham, J., Wheelwright, S., et al. (2000). A screening instrument for autism at 18 months of age: A 6-year follow-up study. *Journal of the American Academy of Child & Adolescent Psychiatry, 39*(6), 694–702.

Baranek, G. T. (1999). Autism during infancy: A retrospective video analysis of sensory-motor and social behaviors at 9–12 months of age. *Journal of Autism & Developmental Disorders, 29*(3), 213–224.

Baron-Cohen, S., Cox, A., Baird, G., Sweettenham, J., & Nightingale, N. (1996). Psychological markers in the detection of autism in infancy in a large population. *British Journal of Psychiatry, 168*(2), 158–163.

Baron-Cohen, S., Hoekstra, R. A., Knickmeyer, R., & Wheelwright, S. (2006). The Autism-Spectrum Quotient (AQ)–Adolescent Version. *Journal of Autism and Developmental Disorders, 36*(3), 343–350.

Baron-Cohen, S., Jolliffe, T., Mortimore, C., & Robertson, M. (1997). Another advanced test of theory of mind: Evidence from very high functioning adults with autism or Asperger Syndrome. *Journal of Child Psychology and Psychiatry, 38*(7), 813–822.

Baron-Cohen, S., O'Riordan, M., Stone, V., Jones, R., & Plaisted, K. (1999). Recognition of faux pas by normally developing children and children with Asperger syndrome or high-functioning autism. *Journal of Autism & Developmental Disorders, 29*(5), 407–418.

Baron-Cohen, S., Scott, F. J., Allison, C., Williams, J., Bolton, P., Matthews, F. E., et al. (2009). Prevalence of autism-spectrum conditions: UK school-based population study. *British Journal of Psychiatry, 194*(6), 500–509.

Baron-Cohen, S., Wheelwright, S., Cox, A., Baird, G., Charman, T., Swettenham, J., et al. (2000). Early identification of autism by the Checklist for Autism in Toddlers (CHAT). *Journal of the Royal Society of Medicine, 93*(10), 521–525.

Baron-Cohen, S., Wheelwright, S., Skinner, R., Martin, J., & Clubley, E. (2001). The autism spectrum quotient (AQ): Evidence from Asperger syndrome/high-functioning autistic males and females, scientists and mathematicians. *Journal of Autism & Developmental Disorders, 31*(1), 5–17.

Bellini, S. (2006). The development of social anxiety in adolescents with autism spectrum disorders. *Focus on Autism and Other Developmental Disabilities, 21*(3), 138–145. doi: http://dx.doi.org/10.1177/10883576060210030201

Bernabei, P., Camaioni, L., & Levi, G. (1998). An evaluation of early development in children with autism and pervasive developmental disorders from home movies: Preliminary findings. *Autism, 2*(3), 243–258.

Berument, S. K., Rutter, M., Lord, C., Pickles, A., & Bailey, A. (1999). Autism screening questionnaire: Diagnostic validity. *British Journal of Psychiatry, 175,* 444–451.

Bishop, D. V. (1998). Development of the Children's Communication Checklist (CCC): A method for assessing qualitative aspects of communicative impairment in children. *Journal of Child Psychology & Psychiatry & Allied Disciplines, 39*(6), 879–891.

Bishop, D. V. (2000). Pragmatic language impairment: A correlate of SLI, a distinct subgroup, or part of the autistic continuum? In D. V. M. Bishop & L. B. Leonard (Eds.), *Speech and language impairments in children: Causes, characteristics, intervention and outcome* (pp. 99–113). Hove, UK: Psychology Press

Bishop, D. V., & Adams, C. (1989). Conversational characteristics of children with semantic pragmatic disorder. II: What features lead to a judgement of inappropriacy? *British Journal of Disorders of Communication, 24*(3), 241–263.

Bishop, D. V., & Norbury, C. F. (2002). Exploring the borderlands of autistic disorder and specific language impairment: A study using standardised diagnostic instruments. *Journal of Child Psychology & Psychiatry & Allied Disciplines, 43*(7), 917–929.

Bishop, D. V. M., & Rosenbloom, L. (1987). Classification of childhood language disorders. In W. Y. M. Rutter (Ed.), *Language development and disorders* (Vol. 22, pp. 61–81). London: Mac Keith Press.

Boris, N. W., Zeanah, C. H., Larrieu, J. A., Scheeringa, M. S., & Heller, S. S. (1998). Attachment disorders in infancy and early childhood: A preliminary investigation of diagnostic criteria. *American Journal of Psychiatry, 155*(2), 295–297.

Brereton, A. V., Tonge, B. J., Mackinnon, A. J., & Einfeld, S. L. (2002). Screening young people for autism with the Development Behavior Checklist. *Journal of the American Academy of Child & Adolescent Psychiatry, 41*(11), 1369–1375.

Bryson, S. E., Clark, B. S., & Smith, I. M. (1988). First report of a Canadian epidemiological study of autistic syndromes. *Journal of Child Psychology & Psychiatry & Allied Disciplines, 29*(4), 433–445.

Buitelaar, J. K., Van der Gaag, R., Klin, A., & Volkmar, F. (1999). Exploring the boundaries of pervasive developmental disorder not otherwise specified: Analyses of data from the DSM-IV Autistic Disorder Field Trial. *Journal of Autism & Developmental Disorders, 29*(1), 33–43.

Burgoine, E., & Wing, L. (1983). Identical triplets with Asperger's syndrome. *British Journal of Psychiatry, 143,* 261–265.

Carter, A. S., Black, D. O., Tewani, S., Connolly, C. E., Kadlec, M. B., & Tager-Flusberg, H. (2007). Sex differences in toddlers with autism spectrum disorders. *Journal of Autism and Developmental Disorders, 37,* 86–97.

Centers for Disease Control and Prevention. (2007). Prevalence of autism spectrum disorders—autism and developmental disabilities monitoring network, 14 sites, United States, 2002, Autism, Developmental Disabilities Monitoring Network Surveillance Year, Principal Investigators, Centers for Disease Control and Prevention. *Morbidity & Mortality Weekly Report Surveillance Summaries, 56*(1), 12–28.

Charman, T., & Baird, G. (2002). Practitioner review: Diagnosis of autism spectrum disorder in 2- and 3-year-old children. *Journal of Child Psychology & Psychiatry & Allied Disciplines, 43*(3), 289–305.

Charman, T., Baron-Cohen, I., Baird, G., Cox, A., Wheelwright, S., Swettenham, J., et al. (2001a). Commentary: The Modified Checklist for Autism in Toddlers. *Journal of Autism & Developmental Disorders, 31*(2), 145–148.

Charman, T., Baron-Cohen, I., Baird, G., Cox, A., Wheelwright, S., Swettenham, J., et al. (2001b). Commentary: The Modified Checklist for Autism in Toddlers. *Journal of Autism & Developmental Disorders, 31*(2), discussion, 149–151.

Chick, J., Waterhouse, L., & Wolff, S. (1979). Psychological construing in schizoid children grown up. *British Journal of Psychiatry, 135,* 425–437.

Cohen, D. J., Paul, R., & Volkmar, F. R. (1986). Issues in the classification of pervasive and other developmental disorders: Toward DSM-IV. *Journal of the American Academy of Child Psychiatry, 25*(2), 213–220.

Cohen, D. J., Towbin, K. E., Mayes, L., & Volkmar, F. (1994). Developmental psychopathology of multiplex developmental disorder. In S. L. Friedman & H. C. Haywoods (Eds.), *Developmental follow-up: Concepts, domains, and methods* (pp. 155–179). San Diego, CA: Academic Press.

Dawson, G., Webb, S., Schellenberg, G. D., Dager, S., Friedman, S., Aylward, E., et al. (2002). Defining the broader phenotype of autism: Genetic, brain, and behavioral perspectives. *Development & Psychopathology, 14*(3), 581–611.

Deckner, C. W., Soraci, S. A., Jr., Deckner, P. O., & Blanton, R. L. (1982). The Rimland E-2 assessment of autism: Its relationship with other measures. *Exceptional Children, 49*(2), 180–182.

DeLong, G. R., & Dwyer, J. T. (1988). Correlation of family history with specific autistic subgroups: Asperger's syndrome and bipolar affective disease. *Journal of Autism & Developmental Disorders, 18*(4), 593–600.

Demb, H. B., & Noskin, O. (2001). The use of the term Multiple Complex Developmental Disorder in a diagnostic clinic serving young children with developmental disabilities: A report of 15 cases. *Mental Health Aspects of Developmental Disabilities, 4*(2), 49–60.

DiLalla, D. L., & Rogers, S. J. (1994). Domains of the Childhood Autism Rating Scale: Relevance for diagnosis and treatment. *Journal of Autism & Developmental Disorders, 24*(2), 115–128.

DiMartino, A., & Tuchman, R. F. (2001, September). Antiepileptic drugs: Effective use in autism spectrum disorders. *Pediatric Neurology, 25*(3), 199–207.

Ehlers, S., Gillberg, C., & Wing, L. (1999). A screening questionnaire for Asperger syndrome and other high-functioning autism spectrum disorders in school age children. *Journal of Autism & Developmental Disorders, 29*(2), 129–141.

Einfeld, S. L., & Tonge, B. J. (1991). Psychometric and clinical assessment of psychopathology in developmentally disabled children. *Australia & New Zealand Journal of Developmental Disabilities, 17*(2), 147–154.

Einfeld, S. L., & Tonge, B. J. (1995). The Developmental Behavior Checklist: The development and validation of an instrument to assess behavioral and emotional disturbance in children and adolescents with mental retardation. *Journal of Autism & Developmental Disorders, 25*(2), 81–104.

Ellaway, C., & Christdoulou, J. (1999a). Rett syndrome: Genetic breakthrough. *Journal of Paediatrics & Child Health, 35*(6), 593.

Ellaway, C., & Christodoulou, J. (1999b). Rett syndrome: Clinical update and review of recent genetic advances. *Journal of Paediatrics & Child Health, 35*(5), 419–426.

Esbensen, A. J., Seltzer, M. M., Lam, K. S. L., & Bodfish, J. W. (2009). Age-related differences in restricted repetitive behaviors in autism spectrum disorders. *Journal of Autism and Developmental Disorders, 39,* 57–66.

Farrugia, S., & Hudson, J. (2006). Anxiety in adolescents with Asperger syndrome: Negative thoughts, behavioral problems, and life interference. *Focus on Autism and Other Developmental Disabilities, 21,* 25–35.

Filipek, P. A., Accardo, P. J., Ashwal, S., Baranek, G. T., Cook, E. H., Dawson, G., et al. (2000). Practice parameter: Screening and diagnosis of autism—Report of the Quality Standards Subcommittee of the American Academy of Neurology and the Child Neurology Society. *Neurology, 55*(4), 468–479.

Filipek, P. A., Accardo, P. J., Baranek, G. T., Cook, E. H., Jr., Dawson, G., Gordon, B., et al. (1999a). The screening and diagnosis of autistic spectrum disorders. *Journal of Autism & Developmental Disorders, 29*(6), 439–484.

Filipek, P. A., Accardo, P. J., Baranek, G. T., Cook, E. H., Jr., Dawson, G., Gordon, B., et al. (1999b). The screening and diagnosis of autistic spectrum disorders. *Journal of Autism & Developmental Disorders, 29*(6), 439–484. [Erratum appears in *Journal of Autism & Developmental Disorders.* (2000, February), *30*(1), 81].

Folstein, S. E., Santangelo, S. L., Gilman, S. E., Piven, J., Landa, R., Lainhart, J., et al. (1999). Predictors of cognitive test patterns in autism families. *Journal of Child Psychology & Psychiatry & Allied Disciplines, 40*(7), 1117–1128.

Fombonne, E. (2003). Epidemiological surveys of autism and other pervasive developmental disorders: An update. *Journal of Autism & Developmental Disorders, 33*(4), 365–382.

Fombonne, E., Du Mazaubrun, C., Cans, C., & Grandjean, H. (1997). Autism and associated medical disorders in a French epidemiological survey. *Journal of the American Academy of Child & Adolescent Psychiatry, 36*(11), 1561–1569.

Fombonne, E., Simmons, H., Ford, T., Meltzer, H., & Goodman, R. (2001). Prevalence of pervasive developmental disorders in the British Nationwide Survey of Child Mental Health. *Journal of the American Academy of Child & Adolescent Psychiatry, 40*(7), 820–827.

Ghaziuddin, M. (2002). Asperger syndrome: Associated psychiatric and medical conditions. *Focus on Autism and Other Developmental Disabilities, 17,* 138–144.

Gunter, H. L., Ghaziuddin, M., & Ellis, H. D. (2002). Asperger syndrome: Tests of right hemisphere functioning and interhemispheric communication. *Journal of Autism & Developmental Disorders, 32*(4), 263–281.

Gura, T. (1999). Gene defect linked to Rett syndrome. *Science, 286*(5437), 27.

Hagberg, B. (2002). Clinical manifestations and stages of Rett syndrome. *Mental Retardation & Developmental Disabilities Research Reviews, 8*(2), 61–65.

Hagberg, B., Hanefeld, F., Percy, A., & Skjeldal, O. (2002). An update on clinically applicable diagnostic criteria in Rett syndrome (Comments to Rett Syndrome Clinical Criteria Consensus Panel Satellite to European Paediatric Neurology Society Meeting, Baden Baden, Germany, September 11, 2001). *European Journal of Paediatric Neurology, 6*(5), 293–297.

Hakak, Y., Walker, J. R., Li, C., Wong, W. H., Davis, K. L., Buxbaum, J. D., et al. (2001). Genome-wide expression analysis reveals dysregulation of myelination-related genes in chronic schizophrenia. *Proceedings of the National Academy of Sciences of the United States of America, 98*(8), 4746–4751.

Harris, S. L., & Delmolino, L. (2002). Applied behavior analysis: Its application in the treatment of autism and related disorders in young children. *Infants & Young Children, 14*(3), 11–17.

Hartley, S. L., & Sikora, D. M. (2009). Sex differences in autism spectrum disorder: An examination of developmental functioning, autistic symptoms, and coexisting behavior problems in toddlers. *Journal of Autism and Developmental Disorders, 39,* 1715–1722.

Hellings, J. A. (1999). Psychopharmacology of mood disorders in persons with mental retardation and autism. *Mental Retardation & Developmental Disabilities Research Reviews, 5*(4), 270–278.

Hollander, E., Dolgoff-Kaspar, R., Cartwright, C., Rawitt, R., & Novotny, S. (2001). An open trial of divalproex sodium in autism spectrum disorders. *Journal of Clinical Psychiatry, 62*(7), 530–534.

Holtmann, M., Bolte, S., & Poustka, F. (2007). Autism spectrum disorders: Sex differences in autistic behavior domains and coexisting psychopathology. *Developmental Medicine & Child Neurology, 49,* 361–366.

Iacoboni, M., & Dapretto, M. (2006). The mirror neuron system and the consequences of its dysfunction. *Nature Reviews in Neuroscience, 7,* 942–951.

Ingersoll, B., Schreibman, L., & Stahmer, A. (2001). Brief report: Differential treatment outcomes for children with autistic spectrum disorder based on level of peer social avoidance. *Journal of Autism & Developmental Disorders, 31*(3), 343–349.

Joseph, R. M., Tager-Flusberg, H., & Lord, C. (2002). Cognitive profiles and social-communicative functioning in children with autism spectrum disorder. *Journal of Child Psychology & Psychiatry & Allied Disciplines, 43*(6), 807–821.

Kanner, L. (1943). Autistic disturbances of affective contact. *Nervous Child, 2,* 217–253.

Kim, J. A., Szatmari, P., Bryson, S. E., Streiner, D. L., & Wilson, F. J. (2000). The prevalence of anxiety and mood problems among children with autism and Asperger syndrome. *Autism, 4*(2), 117–132.

King, B. H. (2000). Pharmacological treatment of mood disturbances, aggression, and self injury in persons with pervasive developmental disorders. *Journal of Autism & Developmental Disorders, 30*(5), 439–445.

Klin, A., Lang, J., Cicchetti, D. V., & Volkmar, F. R. (2000). Brief report: Interrater reliability of clinical diagnosis and DSM-IV criteria for autistic disorder: Results of the DSM-IV Autism Field Trial. *Journal of Autism & Developmental Disorders, 30*(2), 163–167.

Klin, A., Mayes, L. C., Volkmar, F. R., & Cohen, D. J. (1995). Multiplex developmental disorder. *Journal of Developmental & Behavioral Pediatrics, 16*(Suppl.3), S7–S11.

Klin, A., Schultz, R. T., Rubin, E., Bronen, R., & Volkmar, F. R. (2001). Asperger's disorder: Reply. *American Journal of Psychiatry, 158*(3), 502–503.

Klin, A., & Volkmar, F. R. (2003). Asperger syndrome: Diagnosis and external validity. *Child & Adolescent Psychiatric Clinics of North America, 12*(1), 1–13.

Klin, A., Volkmar, F. R., Sparrow, S. S., Cicchetti, D. V., & Rourke, B. P. (1995). Validity and neuropsychological characterization of Asperger syndrome: Convergence with nonverbal learning disabilities syndrome. *Journal of Child Psychology & Psychiatry & Allied Disciplines, 36*(7), 1127–1140.

Knickmeyer, R. C., Wheelwright, S., Baron-Cohen, S. B. (2008). Sex-typical play: Masculinization/defeminization in girls with an autism spectrum condition. *Journal of Autism and Developmental Disorders, 38,* 1028–1035.

Kogan, M. D., Blumberg, S. J., Schieve, L. A., Boyle, C. A., Perrin, J. M., Ghandour, R. M., et al. (2009). Prevalence of parent-reported diagnosis of autism spectrum disorder among children in the US, 2007. *Pediatrics, 124*(5), 1395–1403.

Kolevzon, A., Gross, R., Reichenberg, A., Kolevzon, A., Gross, R., & Reichenberg, A. (2007). Prenatal and perinatal risk factors for autism: A review and integration of findings [Review]. *Archives of Pediatrics & Adolescent Medicine, 161*(4), 326–333.

Kopp, S., & Gillberg, C. (1992). Girls with social deficits and learning problems: Autism, atypical Asperger syndrome of a variant of these conditions. *European Child & Adolescent Psychiatry, 1*(2), 89–99. doi: http://dx.doi.org/10.1007/BF02091791

Krug, D. A., Arick, J., & Almond, P. (1980). Behavior checklist for identifying severely handicapped individuals with high levels of autistic behavior. *Journal of Child Psychology & Psychiatry & Allied Disciplines, 21*(3), 221–229.

Kuusikko, S., Pollock-Wurman, R., Jussila, K., Carter, A. S., Mattila, M., Ebeling, H., et al. (2008). Social anxiety in high-functioning children and adolescents with autism and Asperger syndrome. *Journal of Autism and Developmental Disorders, 38,* 1697–1709.

Lam, K. S., & Aman, M. G. (2007). The Repetitive Behavior Scale-Revised: Independent validation in individuals with autism spectrum disorders. *Journal of Autism and Developmental Disorders, 37*(5), 855–866. doi: http://dx.doi.org/10.1007/s10803-006-0213-z

Lawson, J., Baron-Cohen, S., & Wheelwright, S. (2004, June). Empathising and systemising in adults with and without Asperger Syndrome. *Journal of Autism and Developmental Disorders,* 301–310.

LeCouteur, A., Bailey, A., Goode, S., Pickles, A., Robertson, S., Gottesman, I., et al. (1996). A broader phenotype of autism: The clinical spectrum in twins. *Journal of Child Psychology & Psychiatry & Allied Disciplines, 37*(7), 785–801.

Leekam, S. R., Libby, S. J., Wing, L., Gould, J., & Taylor, C. (2002). The diagnostic interview for social and communication disorders: Algorithms for ICD-10 childhood autism and Wing and Gould autistic spectrum disorder. *Journal of Child Psychology & Psychiatry & Allied Disciplines, 43*(3), 327–342.

Lincoln, A. J., Allen, M. H., & Kilman, A. (1995). The assessment and interpretation of intellectual abilities in people with autism *Learning and cognition in autism* (pp. 89–117). New York, NY: Plenum.

Lincoln, A. J., Courchesne, E., Kilman, B. A., Elmasian, R., & Allen, M. (1988). A study of intellectual abilities in high-functioning people with autism. *Journal of Autism & Developmental Disorders, 18*(4), 505–524.

Liss, M., Fein, D., Allen, D., Dunn, M., Feinstein, C., Morris, R., et al. (2001). Executive functioning in high-functioning children with autism. *Journal of Child Psychology & Psychiatry & Allied Disciplines, 42*(2), 261–270.

Liss, M., Harel, B., Fein, D., Allen, D., Dunn, M., Feinstein, C., et al. (2001). Predictors and correlates of adaptive functioning in children with developmental disorders. *Journal of Autism & Developmental Disorders, 31*(2), 219–230.

Lord, C. (1995). Follow-up of two-year-olds referred for possible autism. *Journal of Child Psychology & Psychiatry & Allied Disciplines, 36*(8), 1365–1382.

Lord, C., Schopler, E., & Revicki, D. (1982). Sex differences in autism. *Journal of Autism and Developmental Disorders, 12*(4), 317–330. doi: http://dx.doi.org/10.1007/BF01538320

Lord, C., Leventhal, B. L., & Cook, E. H., Jr. (2001). Quantifying the phenotype in autism spectrum disorders. *American Journal of Medical Genetics, 105*(1), 36–38.

Lord, C., Pickles, A., McLennan, J., Rutter, M., Bregman, J., Folstein, S., et al. (1997). Diagnosing autism: Analyses of data from the Autism Diagnostic Interview. *Journal of Autism & Developmental Disorders, 27*(5), 501–517.

Lord, C., Risi, S., Lambrecht, L., Cook, E. H., Jr., Leventhal, B. L., DiLavore, P. C., et al. (2000). The Autism Diagnostic Observation Schedule-Generic: A standard measure of social and communication deficits associated with the spectrum of autism. *Journal of Autism & Developmental Disorders, 30*(3), 205–223.

Lord, C., Rutter, M., & Le Couteur, A. (1994). Autism Diagnostic Interview-Revised: A revised version of a diagnostic interview for caregivers of individuals with possible pervasive developmental disorders. *Journal of Autism & Developmental Disorders, 24*(5), 659–685.

Lord, C., Storoschuk, S., Rutter, M., & Pickles, A. (1993). Using the ADI–R to diagnose autism in preschool children. *Infant Mental Health Journal, 14*(3), 234–252.

Mahoney, W. J., Szatmari, P., MacLean, J. E., Bryson, S. E., Bartolucci, G., Walter, S. D., et al. (1998). Reliability and accuracy of differentiating pervasive developmental disorder subtypes. *Journal of the American Academy of Child & Adolescent Psychiatry, 37*(3), 278–285.

McLennan, J. D., Lord, C., & Schopler, E. (1993). Sex differences in higher functioning people with autism. *Journal of Autism and Developmental Disorders, 23*(2), 217–227. doi: http://dx.doi.org/10.1007/BF01046216

Mildenberger, K., Sitter, S., Noterdaeme, M., & Amorosa, H. (2001). The use of the ADI–R as a diagnostic tool in the differential diagnosis of children with infantile autism and children with receptive language disorder. *European Child & Adolescent Psychiatry, 10*(4), 248–255.

Miller, J. N., & Ozonoff, S. (2000). The external validity of Asperger disorder: Lack of evidence from the domain of neuropsychology. *Journal of Abnormal Psychology, 109*(2), 227–238.

Miranda-Linne, F. M., & Melin, L. (2002). A factor analytic study of the Autism Behavior Checklist. *Journal of Autism & Developmental Disorders, 32*(3), 181–188.

Militerni, R., Bravaccio, C., Falco, C., Fico, C., & Palermo, M. T. (2002). Repetitive behaviors in autistic disorder. *European Child & Adolescent Psychiatry, 11*(5), 210–218.

Moog, U., Smeets, E. E., van Roozendaal, K. E., Schoenmakers, S., Herbergs, J., Schoonbrood-Lenssen, A. M., et al. (2003). Neurodevelopmental disorders in males related to the gene causing Rett syndrome in females (MECP2). *European Journal of Paediatric Neurology, 7*(1), 5–12.

Ollendick, T. H., King, N. J., & Muris, P. (2004). Phobias in children and adolescents. In M. Maj., H. S. Akiskal, J. J. Lopez-Ibor, & A. Okasha (Eds.), *Phobias* (pp. 245–279). London: Wiley.

Osterling, J. A., Dawson, G., & Munson, J. A. (2002) . Early recognition of 1-year-old infants with autism spectrum disorder versus mental retardation. *Development & Psychopathology, 14*(2), 239–251.

Ozonoff, S. (1995). Executive functions in autism. In E. Schopler & G. B. Mesibov (Eds.), *Learning and cognition in autism: Current issues in autism* (pp. 199–219). New York: Kluwer.

Ozonoff, S. (1997). Components of executive function in autism and other disorders. In J. Russell (Ed.), *Autism as an executive disorder* (pp. 179–211). New York: Kluwer.

Ozonoff, S., & Griffith, E. M. (2000). Neuropsychological function and the external validity of Asperger syndrome. In A. Klin & F. R. Volkmar (Eds.), *Asperger syndrome* (pp. 72–96). New York: Guilford Press.

Paul, R., Cohen, D., Klin, A., & Volkmar, F. (1999). Multiplex developmental disorders: The role of communication in the construction of a self. *Child & Adolescent Psychiatric Clinics of North America, 8*(1), 189–202.

Pelios, L. V., & Lund, S. K. (2001). A selective overview of issues on classification, causation, and early intensive behavioral intervention for autism. *Behavior Modification, 25*(5), 678–697.

Pennington, B. F., Rogers, S. J., Bennetto, L., Griffith, E. M., Reed, D., & Shyu, V. (1997). Validity tests of the executive dysfunction hypothesis of autism. In J. Russell (Ed.), *Autism as an executive disorder* (pp. 143–178). Oxford, UK: Oxford University Press.

Pilowsky, T., Yirmiya, N., Shulman, C., & Dover, R. (1998). The Autism Diagnostic Interview–Revised and the Childhood Autism Rating Scale: Differences between diagnostic systems and comparison between genders. *Journal of Autism & Developmental Disorders, 28*(2), 143–151.

Rett Syndrome Diagnostic Criteria Work Group. (1988). Diagnostic criteria for Rett syndrome. *Annals of Neurology, 23*, 425–428.

Richters, M. M., & Volkmar, F. R. (1994). Reactive attachment disorder of infancy or early childhood. *Journal of the American Academy of Child & Adolescent Psychiatry, 33*(3), 328–332.

Robins, D. L., Fein, D., Barton, M. L., & Green, J. A. (2001). The Modified Checklist for Autism in Toddlers: An initial study investigating the early detection of autism and pervasive developmental disorders. *Journal of Autism & DevelopmentalDisorders, 31*(2), 131–144.

Rogers, S. J. (1998). Empirically supported comprehensive treatments for young children with autism. *Journal of Clinical Child Psychology, 27*(2), 168–179.

Rourke, B. P. (Ed.). (1995). *Syndrome of nonverbal learning disabilities: Neurodevelopmental manifestations.* New York: Guilford Press.

Rourke, B. P., & Tsatsanis, K. D. (2000). Nonverbal learning disabilities and Asperger syndrome. In A. Klin & F. R. Volkmar (Eds.), *Asperger syndrome* (pp. 231–253). New York: Guilford Press.

Ruttenberg, B. A., Dratman, M. L., Fraknoi, J., & Wenar, C. (1966). An instrument for evaluating autistic children. *Journal of the American Academy of Child Psychiatry, 5*(3), 453–478.

Ruttenberg, B. A., Wolf-Schein, E. G., & Wenar, C. (1991). *BRIAAC: Behavior rating instrument for autistic and other atypical children* (2nd ed.). Chicago: Stoelting.

Rutter, M. (1974). The development of infantile autism. *Psychological Medicine, 4*(2), 147–163.

Rutter, M. (1978). Diagnosis and definition of childhood autism. *Journal of Autism & Childhood Schizophrenia, 8*(2), 139–161.

Rutter, M. (1979). Language, cognition, and autism. *Research Publications—Association for Research in Nervous & Mental Disease, 57,* 247–264.

Scambler, D., Rogers, S. J., & Wehner, E. A. (2001). Can the checklist for autism in toddlers differentiate young children with autism from those with developmental delays? *Journal of the American Academy of Child & Adolescent Psychiatry, 40*(12), 1457–1463.

Scheeringa, M. S. (2001). The differential diagnosis of impaired reciprocal social interaction in children: A review of disorders. *Child Psychiatry & Human Development, 32*(1), 71–89.

Schopler, E., Reichler, R. J., DeVellis, R. F., & Daly, K. (1980). Toward objective classification of childhood autism: Childhood Autism Rating Scale (CARS). *Journal of Autism & Developmental Disorders, 10*(1), 91–103.

Schreibman, L. (2000). Intensive behavioral/psychoeducational treatments for autism: Research needs and future directions. *Journal of Autism & Developmental Disorders, 30*(5), 373–378.

Serra, M., Minderaa, R., van Geert, P., & Jackson, A. (1999). Social–cognitive abilities in children with lesser variants of autism: Skill deficits or failure to apply skills? *European Child & Adolescent Psychiatry, 8*(4), 301–311.

Shamay-Tsoory, S., Tomer, R., Yaniv, S., & Aharon-Peretz, J. (2002). Empathy deficits in Asperger syndrome: A cognitive profile. *Neurocase, 8*(3), 245–252.

Shattuck, P. T., Seltzer, M. M., Greenberg, J. S., Orsmond, G. I., Bolt, D., Kring, S., et al. (2007). Change in autism symptoms and maladaptive behaviors in adolescents and adults with an autism spectrum disorder. *Journal of Autism and Developmental Disorders, 37,* 1735–1747.

Shields, J. R. (1991). Semantic–pragmatic disorder: A right hemisphere syndrome? *British Journal of Disorders of Communication, 26*(3), 383–392.

Shields, J., Varley, R., Broks, P., & Simpson, A. (1996a). Hemispheric function in developmental language disorders and high-level autism. *Developmental Medicine & Child Neurology, 38*(6), 473–486.

Shields, J., Varley, R., Broks, P., & Simpson, A. (1996b). Social cognition in developmental language disorders and high-level autism. *Developmental Medicine & Child Neurology, 38*(6), 487–495.

Sicotte, C., & Stemberger, R. M. (1999). Do children with PDDNOS have a theory of mind? *Journal of Autism & Developmental Disorders, 29*(3), 225–233.

Sionoff, E., Pickles, A., Charman, T., Chandler, S., Loucas, T., & Baird, G. (2008). Psychiatric disorders in children with autism spectrum disorders: Prevalence, comorbidity and associated factors in a population-derived sample. *Journal of the American Academy of Child and Adolescent Psychiatry, 47,* 921–929.

Stella, J., Mundy, P., & Tuchman, R. (1999). Social and nonsocial factors in the Childhood Autism Rating Scale. *Journal of Autism & Developmental Disorders, 29*(4), 307–317.

Stone, W. L., Coonrod, E. E., & Ousley, O. Y. (2000). Brief report: Screening tool for autism in two-year-olds (STAT): Development and preliminary data. *Journal of Autism & Developmental Disorders, 30*(6), 607–612.

Sturm, H., Fernell, E., & Gillberg, C. (2004). Autism spectrum disorders in children with normal intellectual levels: Associated impairments and subgroups. *Developmental Medicine & Child Neurology, 46,* 444–447.

Sukhodolsky, D. G., Scahill, L., Gadow, K. D., Arnold, L. E., Aman, M. G., McDougle, C. J., et al. (2008). Parent-rated anxiety symptoms in children with pervasive developmental disorders: Frequency and association with core autism symptoms and cognitive functioning. *Journal of Abnormal Child Psychology, 36,* 117–128.

Szatmari, P., Archer, L., Fisman, S., Streiner, D. L., & Wilson, F. (1995). Asperger's syndrome and autism: Differences in behavior, cognition, and adaptive functioning. *Journal of the American Academy of Child & Adolescent Psychiatry, 34*(12), 1662–1671.

Tonge, B. J., Brereton, A. V., Gray, K. M., & Einfeld, S. L. (1999). Behavioural and emotional disturbance in high-functioning autism and Asperger syndrome. *Autism, 3*(2), 117–130.

Tonge, B. J., Einfeld, S. L., Krupinski, J., Mackenzie, A., McLaughlin, M., Florio, T., et al. (1996). The use of factor analysis for ascertaining patterns of psychopathology in children with intellectual disability. *Journal of Intellectual Disability Research, 40*(3), 198–207.

Towbin, K. E. (1997). Pervasive developmental disorder—not otherwise specified. In F. R. Volkmar (Ed.), *Handbook of autism and pervasive developmental disorders* (2nd ed., pp. 165–200). New York: Wiley.

Towbin, K. E., Dykens, E. M., Pearson, G. S., & Cohen, D. J. (1993). Conceptualizing "borderline syndrome of childhood" and "childhood schizophrenia" as a developmental disorder. *Journal of the American Academy of Child & Adolescent Psychiatry, 32*(4), 775–782.

Tsai, L., Stewart, M. A., & August, G. (1981). Implication of sex differences in the familial transmission of infantile autism. *Journal of Autism and Developmental Disorders, 11*(2), 165–173. doi: http://dx.doi.org/10.1007/BF01531682

Tuchman, R. (2000). Treatment of seizure disorders and EEG abnormalities in children with autism spectrum disorders. *Journal of Autism & Developmental Disorders, 30*(5), 485–489.

Van den Veyver, I. B., & Zoghbi, H. Y. (2002). Genetic basis of Rett syndrome. *Mental Retardation & Developmental Disabilities Research Reviews, 8*(2), 82–86.

Volkmar, F. R. (1992). Childhood disintegrative disorder: Issues for DSM-IV. *Journal of Autism & Developmental Disorders, 22*(4), 625–642.

Volkmar, F. R. (1996). The disintegrative disorders: Childhood disintegrative disorder and Rett's disorder. In F. R. Volkmar (Ed.), *Psychoses and pervasive developmental disorders in childhood and adolescence* (pp. 223–248). Washington, DC: American Psychiatric Association.

Volkmar, F. R. (2000). Medical problems, treatments, and professionals. In M. D. Powers (Ed.), *Children with autism: A parents' guide* (2nd ed., pp. 67–90). Bethesda, MD: Woodbine House.

Volkmar, F. R., Cicchetti, D. V., Dykens, E., Sparrow, S. S., Leckman, J. F., & Cohen, D. J. (1988). An evaluation of the Autism Behavior Checklist. *Journal of Autism & Developmental Disorders, 18*(1), 81–97.

Volkmar, F. R., & Cohen, D. J. (1991). Comorbid association of autism and schizophrenia. *American Journal of Psychiatry, 148*(12), 1705–1707.

Volkmar, F. R., Cook, E. H., Jr., Pomeroy, J., Realmuto, G., & Tanguay, P. (1999). Practice parameters for the assessment and treatment of children, adolescents, and adults with autism and other pervasive developmental disorders (American Academy of Child and Adolescent Psychiatry Working Group on Quality Issues). *Journal of the American Academy of Child & Adolescent Psychiatry, 38*(Suppl.12), 32S–54S.

Volkmar, F. R., & Klin, A. (1998). Asperger syndrome and nonverbal learning disabilities. In E. Schopler, G. B. Mesibov, & L. J. Kunce (Eds.), *Asperger syndrome or high-functioning autism? Current issues in autism* (pp. 107–121). New York: Guilford Press.

Volkmar, F. R., & Klin, A. (Eds.). (1999). *Kaplan and Sadock's comprehensive textbook of psychiatry* (7th ed.). Baltimore, MD: Lippincott Williams & Wilkins.

Volkmar, F. R., Klin, A., Marans, W., & Cohen, D. (1997). Childhood disintegrative disorder. In R. Volkmar (Ed.), *Handbook of autism and pervasive developmental disorders* (2nd ed., pp. 123–147). New York: Wiley.

Volkmar, F. R., Klin, A., Siegel, B., Szatmari, P., Lord, C., Campbell, M., et al. (1994). Field trial for autistic disorder in DSM-IV. *American Journal of Psychiatry, 151*(9), 1361–1367.

Volkmar, F. R., & Rutter, M. (1995). Childhood disintegrative disorder: Results of the DSM-IV autism field trial. *Journal of the American Academy of Child & Adolescent Psychiatry, 34*(8), 1092–1095.

Volkmar, F. R., Shaffer, D., & First, M. (2000). PDDNOS in DSM-IV. *Journal of Autism & Developmental Disorders, 30*(1), 74–75.

Wadden, N. P., Bryson, S. E., & Rodger, R. S. (1991). A closer look at the Autism Behavior Checklist: Discriminant validity and factor structure. *Journal of Autism & Developmental Disorders, 21*(4), 529–541.

Wakabayashi, A., Baron-Cohen, S., Uchiyama, T., Yoshida, Y., Kuroda, M., & Wheelwright, S. (2007). Empathizing and systemizing in adults with and without autism spectrum conditions: Cross-cultural stability. *Journal of Autism and Developmental Disorders, 37*(10), 1823–1832. doi: http://dx.doi.org/10.1007/s10803-006-0316-6

Wakabayashi, A., Baron-Cohen, S., & Wheelwright, S. (2006). Individual and gender differences in Empathizing and Systemizing: Measurement of individual differences by the Empathy Quotient (EQ) and the Systemizing Quotient (SQ). *Japanese Journal of Psychology, 77*(3), 271–277.

Weisbrot, D. M., Gadow, K. D., DeVincent, C. J., & Pomeroy, J. (2005). The presentation of anxiety in children with pervasive developmental disorders. *Journal of Child and Adolescent Psychopharmacology, 15*, 477–496.

White, S. W., Oswald, D., Ollendick, T., & Scahill, L. (2009). Anxiety in children and adolescents with autism spectrum disorders. *Clinical Psychology Review, 29*, 216–229.

Williams, J. H. G. (2008). Self—other relations in social development and autism: multiple roles for mirror neurons and other brain bases. *Autism Research, 1*, 73–90.

Wing, L. (1981). Asperger's syndrome: A clinical account. *Psychological Medicine, 11*(1), 115–129.

Wing, L., & Gould, J. (1979). Severe impairments of social interaction and associated abnormalities in children: Epidemiology and classification. *Journal of Autism & Developmental Disorders, 9*(1), 11–29.

Wing, L., & Potter, D. (2002). The epidemiology of autistic spectrum disorders: Is prevalence rising? *Mental Retardation & Developmental Disabilities Research Reviews, 8*(3), 151–161.

Wolff, S. (2000). Schizoid personality in childhood and Asperger syndrome. In F. R. Volkmar (Ed.), *Asperger syndrome* (pp. 278–305). New York: Guilford Press.

Wolff, S., & Barlow, A. (1979). Schizoid personality in childhood: A comparative study of schizoid, autistic and normal children. *Journal of Child Psychology & Psychiatry & Allied Disciplines, 20*(1), 29–46.

Wolff, S., & Chick, J. (1980). Schizoid personality in childhood: A controlled follow-up study. *Psychological Medicine, 10*(1), 85–100.

Wolff, S., & McGuire, R. J. (1995). Schizoid personality in girls: A follow-up study: What are the links with Asperger's syndrome? *Journal of Child Psychology and Psychiatry, 36*(5), 793–817. doi: http://dx.doi.org/10.1111/j.1469-7610.1995.tb01330.

World Health Organization. (1992). *International statistical classification of diseases and health related problems: Tabular list* (10th ed.). Geneva, Switzerland: Author.

World Health Organization. (1993). *International statistical classification of diseases and health related problems: Instruction manual* (10th ed.). Geneva, Switzerland: Author.

Yeargin-Allsopp, M., Rice, C., Karapurkar, T., Doernberg, N., Boyle, C., & Murphy, C. (2003). Prevalence of autism in a U.S. metropolitan area [Comment]. *Journal of the American Medical Association, 289*(1), 49–55.

Zalsman, G., & Cohen, D. J. (1998). Multiplex developmental disorder. *Israel Journal of Psychiatry & Related Sciences, 35*(4), 300–306.

Zeev, B. B., Yaron, Y., Schanen, N. C., Wolf, H., Brandt, N., Ginot, N., ... Orr-Urtreger, A. (2002). Rett syndrome: Clinical manifestations in males with MECP2 mutations. *Journal of Child Neurology, 17*(1), 20–24.

3

IDENTIFICATION AND DIAGNOSIS OF AUTISM SPECTRUM DISORDERS

Constanza Colombi, So Hyun Kim, Alayna Schreier, and Catherine Lord

UNIVERSITY OF MICHIGAN, ANN ARBOR, MI,

Introduction

Autism spectrum disorders (ASD), also known as pervasive developmental disorders (PDD) are characterized by deficits in social interaction and communication and by repetitive behaviors and interests. As the definitions of ASD broaden and screening and diagnosis become more frequent and sophisticated, the prevalence of ASDs is increasing. The most recent figures reported have indicated prevalence rates of ASD of about 1 in 110 births (Rice, 2009). It is important to understand best practices for ASD screening and diagnoses so we can better serve this population.

Because there is not currently a genetic or biological marker for ASD, the diagnosis must be based upon both observable behavior and developmental history. Standardized diagnostic instruments based on criteria in the *Diagnostic and Statistical Manual on Mental Disorders* (*DSM-IV-TR*; American Psychiatric Association, 2000) and in the *International Statistical Classification of Diseases and Related Health Problems* (*ICD-10*; World Health Organization, 1990) have created relatively uniform standards, which have enabled researchers to compare samples across studies. Because ASD involves compound impairments it is important to examine multiple domains in the diagnostic process (Lord & Bishop, 2009). While language delay is often the first reason why parents of children with ASD seek help, additional communication, social and play behaviors, and related characteristics must also be considered in the context of overall development.

In this chapter, we outline the ASD identification and diagnostic processes. We discuss referral and screening as well as elements of a comprehensive diagnostic assessment and recommendations for future treatment. As a description and overview of the identification, screening, and diagnostic process we employ two case studies: John, a 24-month-old boy, and Kelly, a 13-year-old girl.

Diagnostic Classification: An Overview and Historical Background

Autism spectrum disorders (ASD) are clinically diagnosed based on criteria described in *DSM-IV-TR* (2000) and in *ICD-10* (1990). The *DSM* and *ICD* classification systems are similar; however, below we discuss the *DSM-IV* classification because of its wide-scale use in North America. Educators also routinely rely on *DSM* criteria for *ASD*, albeit educational diagnoses fall under the Individuals with Disabilities Education Act (1990).

Autistic Disorder

According to the current *DSM* (American Psychiatric Association, 2000) autistic disorder is characterized by the presence of symptoms in three domains: communication, social interaction, and restricted and repetitive patterns of behavior and interests. Moreover, onset of symptoms must occur before the age of 3. Manifestation of symptoms in this triad of impairments varies greatly depending on chronological and developmental age as well as myriad other factors such as the nature and severity of an individual's disability. Difficulties in the communication domain for a toddler may include late onset of single word use and phrase speech, diminished use of pointing, and limited attempts to direct another person's attention to objects or events of interest to the child. Examples of communication symptoms in an older individual with phrase speech are speech abnormalities such as irregularities in rhythm, odd intonation, inappropriate pitch, pronoun reversal (e.g., "you" to mean "I"), and difficulties in sustaining a reciprocal conversation. Impairments in social interaction in a young child may include delayed or no response to having his or her name called, and absence of behaviors such as giving and showing objects to another person. In an adolescent or adult, symptoms in the social area may include limited understanding of social relationships such as marriage or friendship and limited empathy for the emotions of other people.

Restricted, repetitive behaviors and interests (RRBs) may include a young child lining up cars rather than playing with them. Examples of such characteristics in an older individual may include obsessive and repetitive reciting of minutiae related to one specific subject, such as the Second World War.

Asperger Disorder

Asperger disorder (AS) is characterized by impairments in social interaction and the presence of restricted, repetitive behaviors, and interests. While onset of speech is not delayed in AS, atypicalities in communication such as difficulties in reciprocal conversations and flat intonation are often present. Diagnosis of autistic disorder must be excluded before a clinician may consider a diagnosis of AS.

Pervasive Developmental Disorders Not Otherwise Specified

Pervasive developmental disorders not otherwise specified (PDDNOS) are diagnosed when an individual's difficulties are related to symptoms of autistic disorder, but are not enough to fully meet standard criteria for ASD. A child with PDDNOS may fail to meet onset criteria for autistic disorder (before age 3) or may present symptoms in only two of the three domains or may present limited symptoms in each domain.

Rett Syndrome

Rett syndrome is caused in most cases by mutations to gene MECP2 (Monnerat, dos Santos Moreira, Alves, Bonvicino, & Vargas, 2010). Rett syndrome almost always affects girls and is characterized by a short period of apparently typical development followed by sudden onset of symptoms such as deceleration in head growth often resulting in microcephaly, and severe losses in fine and gross motor abilities, language, and social skills. Stereotypic hand movements such as mouthing or wringing are also present as well as significant intellectual disability.

Childhood Disintegrative Disorder

Childhood disintegrative disorder (CDD) is a rare condition (Fombonne, 2005) in which typical development is followed by severe regression in language, social interaction, motor skills, and adaptive behavior between 2 and 10 years of age. The regression occurring in CDD can be quite dramatic and fast. Children may speak fluently at 4 years of age and suddenly lose language within a couple of days to the extent that they become completely nonverbal (Palomo, Belinchón, & Ozonoff, 2006).

Description and Summary of the Identification and Diagnostic Process

In this section we describe and provide an overview of the identification and diagnostic process via the use of two case studies. The cases describe two children diagnosed with ASD, John, a 24-month-old boy, and Kelly, a teenage girl.

John W., Age 24 Months

Background: John was 24 months old when he was referred by his pediatrician to an autism clinic due to developmental concerns and a question of possible autism.

Family: John was the firstborn child of Sarah and Robert W. John had a younger brother, Timothy, who was 10 weeks old at the time of the assessment. Sarah was not working outside the home and Robert was employed as an engineer at a local manufacturing company. The parents reported the presence of learning disabilities, attention deficit disorder, anxiety disorder, and depression in the child's family members.

Medical History: John was the product of a normal 39-week pregnancy. Parents reported no concerns about him during the first year of life. John had seizures when he had a high fever at 15 months. No other medical conditions were reported.

Early Development: Early development appeared normal until about 15 months of age, although John reportedly vocalized less than other children his age and was on the lower end of the "normal range" for development of words. From history, John was a happy and social baby and toddler. He was interested in people, smiled, waved good-bye sometimes, had two words (*cat* and *outside*), and made eye contact. At about 15 months John gradually began to say words less often than he previously did. By 19 months John had stopped talking completely, would no longer wave, and displayed little interest in his parents and grandparents. His language began to develop again when he was just under 2 years old, when he learned new words but was still very different socially than he had been as an infant. At the time of the assessment he spoke approximately 20 words. He was very affectionate with his mother; however, he showed diminished interest in other people.

Behavioral Observation during the Clinic Visit.   John was described by clinical personnel as an adorable 2-year-old boy who adjusted quickly to being in an unfamiliar environment with new people. He was able to participate in several activities, especially when the examiner used toys to keep him engaged. John occasionally looked at the examiner. He vocalized often, but many of his utterances were not directed toward the examiner. He did not point to, request, or direct the adults' attention. John did not respond to his name over several repeated calls. By history, he would respond to his name about 50% of the time. His play involved manipulation of objects such as rolling cars, opening and closing a slinky, and pushing buttons of a cause-and-effect toy. He did not engage in pretend play. He smiled during physical games with his mother.

Overall, John was attentive to tasks and occasionally seemed to enjoy the activities with the examiner. However, his social and communicative skills, such as the use of gestures, directed vocalizations, and eye contact were diminished compared to other toddlers his age.

Parent Report of Early Development and Current Adaptive Behavior. Two screening questionnaires were administered, the Infant-Toddler Checklist (ITC; Wetherby & Prizant, 2002), a broad screener for early developmental problems, and the Modified Checklist for Autism in Toddlers (M-CHAT; Robins, Fein, Barton, & Green, 2001), a questionnaire that screens specifically for autism. By his mother's report, John's scores on both screeners were above the cutoffs indicative of the need for further developmental assessment. Specifically, John's mother reported that it was difficult to make eye contact with him, that he rarely showed objects to people, and that he did not always react when someone spoke to him. The Autism Diagnostic Interview-Revised (ADI-R), an interview protocol for caregivers referred for a possible diagnosis of autism spectrum disorder (ASD), was administered to John's mother and father. This interview revealed behaviors consistent with a diagnosis of ASD. John's parents also completed the Vineland Adaptive Behavior Scales, 2nd Edition (VABS-II; Sparrow, Cicchetti, & Balla, 2005), a standardized caregiver interview that measures adaptive skills in four areas: communication, daily living skills, socialization, and motor skills. John's profile on the VABS-II showed that his communication, socialization, and daily living skills were below average, while his motor skills were in the low average range.

Tests Results. The Mullen Scales of Early Learning (1995), a standardized instrument that measures development in four areas (fine motor, visual reception, and receptive and expressive language abilities), was administered to John by a psychologist. John's performance on the Mullen was uneven, with average visual reception skills, slightly delayed fine motor and expressive language skills, and very low receptive language skills.

The Autism Diagnostic Observation Schedule-Toddler Version (ADOS; Luyster, 2009) was also administered by the psychologist. John engaged with some of the test materials and it was not difficult to get his attention. His vocalizations consisted of jargon that was occasionally directed toward others. To make a request, John most frequently vocalized and reached without eye contact. John's eye contact was not used to support communication as expected for a toddler of his age. He typically did not look to other people or reference them. He occasionally glanced briefly at adults. He did not respond with a smile to the examiner's smile, but did smile back at his mother. John gave toys to adults for the purpose of getting help and when requested to clean up. John responded to the examiner's point by looking toward a toy in the distance. During activities of high interest, he focused his attention on toys or activities without shifting his attention between the object and the adults. He did not exhibit any pretend play or imitation. John's score on the ADOS-T was above the autism cutoff threshold.

Summary. John showed symptoms that are consistent with an autism spectrum disorder. His social communication skills were delayed. His eye contact was quite infrequent, and he did not use joint attention. Based on these findings and consistent with best-practice findings published by the National Research Council (2001) recommendations included the following:

1. Early intervention can promote progress in many skill areas. Research on early intervention suggests that for children ages 2 and up diagnosed with an autism spectrum disorder, 25 hours a week of behavioral or developmentally based intervention is necessary for the most effective changes in communication and social skills.

2. John would benefit from both individual and group speech therapy. He needs the individual time to establish reciprocal communication skills that, in turn, can be practiced in a group situation.

3. It is important for John to spend time with typically developing same-age peers. He would likely benefit from time spent in a regular day care center a few hours each week. Particular emphasis should be placed on helping him enjoy and be successful with this social interaction and play. Individual goals for John should include: increasing peer-directed social behavior, including learning appropriate social initiations and responses to peers, and developing appropriate parallel and interactive play skills.

4. Parent education is essential to provide guiding principles in the everyday life of raising a child with autism. John's parents should receive help from a therapist for behavior management and for strategies helpful to teaching John daily living skills.

Kelly, L., Age 13 Years

Background/Referral: Kelly was 13 years old when she was brought by her parents to an autism center at a local university. Kelly was originally referred to a pediatrician by her resource teacher at her middle school due to concern about her behavioral problems, including difficulty concentrating in class and verbal aggression toward others. The pediatrician administered several screening measures, including the Social Communication Questionnaire (SCQ; Rutter, Bailey, & Lord, 2003). Because the SCQ resulted in an elevated score, the pediatrician referred Kelly to the autism center for further assessment. After the referral was made a clinician at the autism center conducted a comprehensive diagnostic assessment battery, comprised of a parent interview, a clinical observation, and cognitive testing.

   Educational History: At the time of intake Kelly was a seventh grade middle school student enrolled in the general curriculum. She did, however, receive 10 hours per week of special education in a resource room. Kelly entered a general education preschool but her preschool teachers noticed difficulties in her speech and behavioral problems such as temper tantrums and aggressive behaviors. Soon after, she started a special education program and since then had been receiving special education services.

Clinician Observation and Cognitive Testing.
A clinician administered a semistructured observation to Kelly, the Autism Diagnostic Observation Scale (Lord, Rutter, DiLavore, & Risi, 1999). That measure revealed difficulties in the area of language and communication, reciprocal social interaction, and restricted and repetitive behaviors. For example, Kelly's language consisted of complex sentences but she made frequent grammatical errors. The clinician also noticed that even though Kelly was able to engage in conversation, her conversational range was more restricted than what would be expected for an adolescent her age. In the area of reciprocal social interactions, the clinician noted that Kelly's eye contact was inconsistent, and the ranges of her facial expressions were limited. In terms of restricted and repetitive behaviors, Kelly used some odd phrases such as "sun-belly" to describe a fish with a yellow underbody. Kelly met the ADOS cutoff scores for ASD. Additionally, the clinician administered a cognitive test, the Wechsler Intelligence Scale for Children (WISC; Wechsler, 1949). Kelly's cognitive scores were in the low average range.

Parent Report of Early Development and Current Adaptive Behavior.
Results of a parent interview, the Autism Diagnostic Interview-Revised (Le Couteur, Lord, & Rutter, 2003), revealed that Kelly had experienced difficulties in language and communication and reciprocal social interactions since her toddler years. During the interview, Kelly's parents reported that

she usually avoided social situations and had a tendency to engage in solitary activities, such as preferring to play hand-held games. She was also reported to show some restricted and repetitive behaviors, particularly, unusual interests in computer games and cartoons. Kelly met the cutoff scores for autism in all domains in the ADI-R. The parents also completed the Vineland Adaptive Behavior Scale (VABS; Sparrow, Balla, & Cicchetti, 1984), which also showed that Kelly was below average in the areas of communication, daily living skills, and socialization.

Summary/Recommendations. Based on the results from the screening and assessment, and consistent with effective practice methodology and data interpretation, the clinical team gave Kelly a diagnosis of ASD. Based on the evaluation the following best-practice-oriented recommendations were given to the parents:

1. Kelly's parents were advised to participate in a parent education class to learn strategies for managing behavior and teaching skills to children with ASD.
2. It was recommended that Kelly's eligibility for educational ASD certification and services under the Individuals with Disabilities Education Act (1990) be determined. It was also recommended that school personnel regularly assess Kelly's ASD-related needs over the course of her remaining school years.
3. Diagnostic staff recommended that staff trained and experienced in identifying and implementing interventions for youth with autism be used by school personnel. Diagnostic personnel also recommended staff training for school personnel (e.g., professional development training in applying the TEACCH methodology and behavioral methods) and regular consultation with a school district autism specialist in the areas of ASD curricula, intervention strategies, and behavior management.
4. It was recommended that Kelly's school IEP reflect specific social goals, such as increasing initiations with peers and increasing the duration of her sustained play interactions. The staff also recommended that school personnel, including her aide, be instructed in effective-practice procedures for supporting and prompting social interactions.
5. In response to a query from Kelly's teacher about the use of medications, the diagnostic team made the judgment that medications for Kelly were not warranted. This opinion was based on scientific evidence that medications for children and youth diagnosed with ASD are most effective when used to assist in controlling such behaviors as irritability, ADHD, extreme anxiety, OCD, and so forth. Because Kelly's difficulties did not primarily fall in the above areas, but rather were primarily related to the understanding of tasks, it was determined that she was not a good candidate for drug treatment.

Diagnostic Assessment of ASD: Effective Practices and an Interpretation of the Evidence Base

Diagnostic assessment of ASD can be performed by a variety of professionals including developmental pediatricians, psychiatrists, psychologists, and speech and language pathologists. Regardless of their specific areas of expertise, it is crucial that professionals who conduct ASD assessments use standardized measures, have appropriate clinical training, and are familiar with individuals with ASD. Diagnostic professionals also need to be able to interpret and apply data and other information from standardized instruments as well as apply their clinical experience relative to assessing and making appropriate scientifically based recommendations for individuals with ASD.

Beyond core deficits in communication, social interaction, and restricted behaviors and interests, individuals with ASD commonly have marked disruptions in several areas of development, including play, cognition, and adaptive behavior. Thus, assessment of individuals with ASD should include consideration of these areas of development, with special attention toward identifying strengths and weaknesses and their connection to functioning and treatment and educational recommendations.

Screening

General Characteristics of Screening.   Once a child or adolescent has been referred to a pediatrician or a mental health professional, and often prior to a diagnostic referral, if he or she is suspected of showing characteristics of ASD then screening can take place to detect signs or symptoms of the disorder. As the cases of John and Kelly illustrate, screening measures precede a more comprehensive diagnostic evaluation. Thus, screening can be defined as a brief assessment of a more comprehensive diagnostic evaluation for the risk of delay or disability (Meisels, 1985). Screening measures are different from diagnostic measures in that the purpose of screening in general is to indicate an individual's level of risk for a disability rather than to provide a definitive diagnosis. Thus screening measures tend to be less lengthy than diagnostic measures and require less training and experience for administrators.

There are two different levels for screening of ASD: Level 1 and Level 2. Level 1 screening measures are often used in pediatric practices and early intervention programs for all children, and they tend to cover a broad range of developmental disorders such as intellectual disability and language impairment. Level 2 screening measures are more focused and specific to ASD symptoms and are primarily used in mental health and other clinical settings. These measures are used to differentiate ASD from other developmental disorders in children. Different formats have been used for screening measures, including informant reports and clinician observations. Screening measures also vary by length of administration and interpretation time, level of administrator expertise and experience, and skill and knowledge in interpreting results. Level 1 measures are typically brief and easy to administer, and often come in the form of parent-report questionnaires. Level 2 measures require finer-grained analyses of developmental problems, and more time and training to administer, score, and interpret the results.

A screening measure can be selected based on consideration of the purpose and context for which it is intended. One of the important considerations is the sensitivity and specificity of each measure. Sensitivity is defined as the proportion of children with developmental problems who are correctly identified as being at risk by a screening measure. Specificity is the proportion of children without developmental problems who are identified as not being at risk for a particular condition (Aylward, 1997). A screening measure for ASD attempts to maintain the balance between its ability to identify as many children with symptoms of ASD as possible while successfully excluding children without ASD symptoms. Generally, a Level 1 screening measure has high sensitivity and is more inclusive because it is intended to include as many children with ASD symptoms as possible. However, for this reason, Level 1 screening measures may mislabel more children as being at risk for ASD than is actually the case. As a result, further diagnostic assessment is imperative. On the other hand, Level 2 screening measures are intended to have higher sensitivity than specificity levels, but the difference is less than in Level 1 screening measures.

Review of Evidence Based Screening Measures.   Various ASD-focused screening measures have been developed, and numerous studies have examined their predictive validity to help clinicians and researchers select evidence based screening measures. Level 1 screening measures can include nonspecific screening measures and ASD-specific screening measures

(Coonrod & Stone, 2005). Nonspecific screening measures are intended to identify children who have problems with a broad range of difficulties, such as impairments in cognitive skills, communication and language, motor skills, social skills, self-help skills, and behavior. Because children with ASD have impairments in these areas, these measures can be used to identify children with ASD symptoms. The Child Neurology Society and American Academy of Neurology practice parameters (Filipek et al., 1999) recommend the following measures for nonspecific screening: Ages and Stages Questionnaire (ASQ; Bricker & Squires, 1999), the Child Development Inventories (CDIs; Ireton & Glascoe, 1995), and Parent's Evaluation of Developmental Status (PEDS; Glascoe, 1998). Each of these measures has strong psychometric properties, is in the form of a parent questionnaire, and is designed for young children under 36 months. Another recommended measure is the Brigance Screens (Glascoe, 1996), a clinician observation method.

Screening measures for deficits in social and communication can also be used to identify children at risk for ASD, given that social and communication impairments are prevalent in children with ASD. For example, the case of John illustrates that John's parents were given one of the widely used screening measures, the Infant-Toddler Checklist from the Communication and Symbolic Behavior Scales of Developmental Profile (CSBS DP; Wetherby & Prizant, 2002), before John went through a comprehensive diagnostic evaluation. His mother's report indicated that John's score on the screener was above the cutoff threshold, thus indicating need for further developmental assessment. As illustrated earlier, the CSBS DP is based on parent report and can be used for children from 6 to 24 months of age. The checklist assesses three main areas: social (e.g., use of gestures), speech (e.g., use of sounds), and symbolic (e.g., use of objects).

Recommended ASD specific screening measures include the Checklist for Autism in Toddlers (CHAT; Baird et al., 2000), the Modified-Checklist for Autism in Toddlers (M-CHAT; Robins, Fein, Barton, & Green, 2001), and the Pervasive Developmental Disorders Screening Test-Stage 1 (PDDST-Stage 1; Siegel & Hayer, 1999). The M-CHAT is an extended parent report version of the CHAT, originally designed to screen 18-month-old infants during routine health care visits based on parent report. The M-CHAT comprises the original items from the CHAT and adds more items to assess additional ASD symptoms not assessed by the CHAT. The age range of screening for the M-CHAT is 24 months of age or older. Table 3.1 presents additional details about other Level 1 specific screening measures that are considered appropriate for use with children with ASD.

Effective and evidence-based Level 2 screening measures commonly used by clinicians and researchers include the Autism Behavioral Checklist (ABC; Krug, Arick, & Almond, 1980), the Childhood Autism Rating Scale (CARS; Schopler, Reichler, & Renner, 1988), the Gilliam Autism Rating Scale (GARS; Gilliam, 1995), and the Social Communication Questionnaire (SCQ; Berument et al., 1999). In the case illustration of Kelly, her parents were given a parent report questionnaire by the pediatrician before she was referred to an autism clinic. That referral for a more comprehensive diagnostic assessment was based on an elevated screening measure score (SCQ). The SCQ is designed to screen individuals age 4 and older; it measures reciprocal social interactions, language and communication, and repetitive and stereotyped behaviors. It can be completed within 10 minutes. The psychometric properties of the SCQ were examined in the original study, and it was found that the sensitivity and specificity for the SCQ ranged from 67 to 96%, depending on diagnostic comparisons (Corsello et al., 2007). Table 3.1 presents additional details about other recommended Level 2 screening measures.

Early detection of ASD is necessary for timely access to services and treatments, and these early intervention services are associated with better outcomes (Rogers, Young, Cook, Giolezetti, & Ozonoff, 2010). Increasingly both professionals and parents are aware of this fact, perhaps

TABLE 3.1 ASD Specific Screening Measures

Level 1 Screening Measures	Validity		Ages	Design	
	Sensitivity	Specificity		Format	Level of Expertise
Checklist for Autism in Toddlers (CHAT)	.18–.38. 65–.85	.98–1.0 1.0	T, C, A, Ad	Interview and interactive	Minimal
Modified Checklist for Autism in Toddlers (M-CHAT)	.95–.97a	.95–.99 a	T, C, A, Ad	Parent Questionnaire	None
Pervasive Developmental Disorders Screening Test-Stage 1 (PDDST-Stage 1)	.85	.71	I, T, C	Parent Questionnaire	None

Level 2 Screening Measures	Validity		Ages	Design	
	Sensitivity	Specificity		Format	Level of Expertise
Autism Behavior Checklist (ABC)	.35–.38	.76–.97	T, C, A, Ad	Behavioral Checklist	Minimal
Social Communication Questionnaire (SCQ)	.85–96	.67–.80	C, A, Ad	Parent Questionnaire	None
Childhood Autism Rating Scale (CARS)	.92–.98	.85	—	Behavioral Checklist	Minimal
Gilliam Autism Rating Scale (GARS)	.48	—	T, C, A	Behavioral Checklist	Minimal
Pervasive Developmental Disorders Screening Test-Stage 2 (PDDST-Stage 2)	.69–88	.25–.63	I, T, C	Parent Questionnaire	None
Screening for Autism in 2-Year-Olds (STAT)	.92	.85	T	Interactive	Requires training
Early Screening of Autistic Traits Questionnaire (ESAT)	Above .90	Above .80	I, T	Parent Questionnaire	None

Note: — = Not Reported; I = Infants; T = Toddlers; C = School-aged children; A = Adolescents; Ad = Adults
[a] These numbers represent estimates because follow-up with the no-risk group is not yet complete.
[b] Some data are available for children under 3 years old.

explaining why parents are seeking help for their children suspected of having ASD characteristics earlier than ever before. In recent studies, the average age of parental concern was between 15 and 18 months (Chawarska et al., 2007; DeGiacomo & Fombonne, 1998). Accordingly, based on the needs of families with young children with ASD and awareness of the positive impact of early intervention, researchers and clinicians have established the growing need for effective screening measures that are appropriate for toddlers and young preschoolers. Level 2 screening measures that are effective and have been specifically designed for young children include the PDDST-Stage 2 (Siegel & Hayer, 1999), the Early Screening of Autistic Traits Questionnaire (ESAT; Dietz, Swinkels, van Daalen, van Engeland, & Buitelaar, 2006), and the Screening Tool for ASD in Two-Year-Olds (STAT; Stone, Coonrod, & Ousley, 2000). The STAT is a widely used measure, and was designed to differentiate children between the ages of 24 and 36 months with ASD from nonspectrum disorder children. The STAT is interactive, comprised of items that are administered in a play-based context, and takes about 20 minutes to administer. Tests of the psychometric properties of the STAT showed that sensitivity levels ranged from 77 to 100% and specificities ranged from 86 to 91%. Stone et al. (2000) found similar STAT psychometric properties relative to children with ASD and those with nonspectrum disorders who were matched by mental ages. Another recent STAT study yielded a sensitivity of 0.95 and specificity of 0.73 for children under 24 months of age (Stone, McMahon, & Henderson, 2006).

Limitations of Screening Measures. Screening measures have a number of limitations. First, the psychometric properties of screening measures for toddlers and preschoolers in general need further study. By their very nature the behavioral patterns of young children and toddlers are idiosyncratic and a number of measures for this group have not been based on sound psychometric principles. Moreover, because symptom expression in young children is different from that of older children, and because some measures have been patterned after those of older children rather than specifically designed relative to young children, the predictive validity of a number of these measures with young children is unclear. In addition, many of the screening measures that are currently available have a tendency to underidentify more verbally able children or children with milder variants of ASD (Filipek et al., 1999). As a result of availability of less than completely accurate measures some children may miss opportunities for early intervention services (Howlin & Asgharian, 1999). For example, it was reported that the Autism Behavioral Checklist (ABC) did not identify the majority of more able children and adolescents with ASD even though it was effective in identifying children with more severe levels of ASD (Yirmiya, Sigman, & Freeman, 1994). Thus, revision of existing screening measures to identify high functioning children is a particular area of need.

Diagnostic Evaluation

The first step in a diagnostic evaluation, subsequent to collecting screening information, consists of gathering information regarding the physical health of the individual under study (for example, see the case study of John above). This information is necessary for two main reasons: medical issues may explain some autismlike behaviors; and medical issues may influence an individual's performance on standardized tests. For example, significant motor and visual impairments may impact performance on a cognitive test and hearing impairments may explain language difficulties and reduced responsivity (e.g., diminished response to name called) thus confusing an accurate diagnosis of ASD.

After collecting information regarding medical issues, a comprehensive developmental and cognitive evaluation needs to be undertaken, with the aim of identifying an individual's strengths and weaknesses. In this section we describe domains that require assessment. In Table 3.2 we provide a list of commonly used and effective-practice tests. We give particular importance to understanding the developmental level of an individual because this information is needed to formulate recommendations, including school and vocational placements and correctly interpreting symptoms of ASD. It is also particularly important to obtain an accurate estimate of both expressive and receptive language abilities because a child's language level impacts the interpretation of other test results and is an overall predictor of outcomes for individuals with ASD (Venter, Lord, & Schopler, 1992).

Because individuals with ASD often have impaired verbal abilities it may be necessary to use nonverbal tests to obtain an accurate comprehensive developmental level. For example, a full scale IQ of 80—in the low average range—may be obtained if an individual has a nonverbal IQ of 95 and a verbal IQ of 70. Thus, in this case, a simple inference about a child's needs based on a full scale IQ may be misleading, and a separate estimate of verbal and nonverbal skills would provide a more representative picture of an individual's strengths and weaknesses.

The next step in the evaluation consists of obtaining a measure of *adaptive functioning*—the abilities connected to personal and social independence and functioning in real life situations. Measures of adaptive functioning include assessment of motor, social, communication, and daily living skills. Assessment of adaptive functioning is necessary to make a diagnosis of intellectual disability, as well as to identify priorities for intervention.

After collecting information related to health issues, developmental level, and adaptive functioning, symptoms of ASD should be assessed via use of ASD diagnostic instruments, such as the ones described in the cases of John and Kelly. It is beyond the scope of this chapter to provide a comprehensive review of ASD diagnostic instruments; we recommend that readers review the measures evaluated by Lord and Corsello (2005). Here, we discuss two widely used clinical and research-practice instruments, the Autism Diagnostic Interview-Revised (ADI-R; Lord, Storoschuk, Rutter, & Pickles, 1994) and the Autism Diagnostic Observation Schedule (ADOS; Lord et al., 2000).

The ADI-R is a standardized, semistructured, investigator-based interview for caregivers of individuals referred for a possible diagnosis of ASD. It is based on *ICD-10* and *DSM-IV* criteria and needs to be administered by a trained clinician with expertise in interviewing skills and ASD. Information collected during the interview is supported by diagnostic algorithms, which provide classifications of "autism" or "nonspectrum." Recently, for purposes of research, an ASD cutoff was proposed as a means of identifying children who fall within the broad autism spectrum rather than only individuals with autism (Risi et al., 2006). In this connection, when interpreting results of the ADI-R, reference to developmental level is imperative, given that children with nonverbal mental ages below 18 months or individuals with profound to severe intellectual disabilities tend to fall within the cutoff threshold of ASD, regardless of their clinical diagnosis (Risi et al., 2006). Thus, while the ADI-R may be useful relative to collecting information regarding the behaviors of individuals with severe intellectual disabilities, the inferred diagnostic classifications should be interpreted with great caution.

The ADOS is a standardized semistructured observation for children and adults referred for a diagnosis of ASD. Like the ADI-R, the ADOS was developed based on *DSM-IV* diagnostic criteria. The ADOS protocol involves several activities that require 35 to 45 minutes to administer. These activities provide the clinician with the opportunity to observe social, communication, and restricted behaviors related to ASD. The ADOS comprises four different modules based on the child's level of language. Children with mental ages under 15 months often meet ADOS cut-off criteria for ASD, regardless of their true clinical diagnosis. To address this issue, a Toddler version of the ADOS (Luyster et al. 2009), appropriate for children between

TABLE 3.2 Evidenced-Based Assessment Measures

Area of Assessment	Design		
Cognitive/Developmental Level	*Ages*	*Format*	*Level of Expertise*
Mullen Scales of Early Learning (MSEL)	I, T, C	Interactive	Requires training
Bayley Scales of Infant & Toddler Development, 3rd Edition (Bayley-III)	I, T, C	Interactive and Parent Questionnaire	Minimal
Battelle Developmental Inventory, 2nd Edition (BDI-2)	I, T, C	Interview and Interactive	Minimal
Differential Ability Scales, 2nd Edition (DAS-II)	T, C, A	Interactive	Minimal
Stanford-Binet Intelligence Scales, 5th Edition (SB5)	T, C, A	Interactive	Requires training
Wechsler Intelligence Scale for Children, 4th Edition (WISC-IV)	C, A	Interactive	Requires training
Wechsler Adult Intelligence Scale, 4th Edition (WAIS-IV)	Ad	Interactive	Requires training
Wechsler Abbreviated Scale of Intelligence (WASI)	A, Ad	Interactive	Requires training
Adaptive Functioning			
Bayley III Social-Emotional and Adaptive Behavior Questionnaire	I, T, C	Parent Questionnaire	Minimal
Vineland Adaptive Behavior Scales, 2nd Edition (VABS-II)	I, T, C, A, Ad	Interview	Minimal
Autism-Related Behaviors			
Communication and Symbolic Behavior Scales: Developmental Profile (CSBS-DP)	I, T	Parent Questionnaire	None
Autism Observation Scale for Infants (AOSI)	I, T		
Autism Diagnostic Observation Schedule – Toddler (ADOS-T)	I, T	Interactive	Requires training
Autism Diagnostic Interview – Revised including subset of items relevant to toddlers (ADI-R)	I, T	Interview	Requires training
Autism Diagnostic Observation Schedule (ADOS)	T, C, A, Ad	Interactive	Requires training
Autism Diagnostic Interview – Revised (ADI-R)	T, C, A, Ad	Interview	Requires training
Diagnostic Interview for Social and Communication Disorders (DISCO)	T, C, A, Ad	Interview	Requires training

Note: I = Infants, T = Toddlers, C = School-aged children; A = Adolescents; Ad = Adults

12 and 30 months with no language or use of single words, has been developed for research use and will soon be available to clinicians.

At this point in the diagnostic process the clinician should have many of the pieces of the assessment puzzle in place and thus should be able to reach an accurate diagnostic conclusion. After the assessment, verbal and written diagnostic feedback should be provided to the family. The clinician should discuss the results of the assessments, provide information related to ASD, and provide appropriate and utilitarian recommendations, including those related to intervention strategies and educational or vocational plans (see, for example, the recommendations provided in the case study descriptions of John and Kelly). For individuals who are still in school, clinicians should talk with the teachers to identify and discuss recommendations that can be integrated into students' educational plans. If the clinician who carried out the assessment is not a medical professional it is recommended that the family be advised to consult a psychiatrist relative to providing medical supports. Similarly, recommendations need to include a comprehensive pediatric exam to rule out genetic disorders and manage health issues.

Future Directions

The field has been witness to significant progress and a rapid refinement of diagnostic instruments and assessment procedures for ASD over the past several years. The current organization of autism symptoms in three main domains—communication, social, and repetitive behaviors—may change. There is a movement in the field toward the reorganization of these domains to merge the social aspects of communication (e.g., nonverbal communication, as well as conversation) into a broader category of social deficits (Lecavalier et al., 2006). Moreover, researchers have proposed to divide the third domain, repetitive behaviors, into two subdomains (Cuccaro et al., 2003). One subdomain would include sensory interests and repetitive use of objects; the other domain would include compulsive behaviors, rituals, and insistence on routines. Repetitive sensory behaviors are common, affecting individuals with ASD across age and ability levels, while behaviors related to insistence on sameness are less common and tend to be more prevalent in older children (Bishop, Richler, & Lord, 2006).

Another proposed change in current diagnostic practice involves a shift from an ASD categorical approach to the use of a dimensional framework. Rather than using labels such as autism or PDDNOS, an individual's level of competence/impairment may be described using continuous measures of social and communication difficulties and repetitive behaviors. This would help in identifying areas of strength and weakness for the purpose of planning intervention programs and strategies. Using a dimensional framework may also lead to the development of more useful measures of severity. Currently, we are just beginning to develop ways to measure the severity of ASD, independent of intellectual disabilities and language delay (Gotham, Pickles, & Lord, 2009). Accordingly a dimensional framework may better describe an individual's severity level of ASD, developmental trajectories, and response to treatment.

Conclusions

In this chapter, we summarized current practices in the screening and diagnostic process of ASD. We emphasized the importance of having a clinician who conducts the evaluation be a professional who is experienced in developmental frameworks as well as clinical work with ASD. During the course of the evaluation, information should be obtained from multiple sources, including standardized observations of autism symptoms and markers, parent and teacher reports and developmental history, and standardized assessment of cognitive, language, and adaptive skills. The evaluation should lead to an accurate and functional diagnostic classification and identification of areas of strengths and weaknesses in cognitive/developmental level, adaptive functioning, social communication, and behavior. At the end of the diagnostic process, the clinician should verbally and in writing communicate the results of the evaluation to the parents. This information should provide an accurate diagnosis, identify follow-up and future assessment of both recommendations, and describe plans for intervention.

While the field has moved quickly in the last few years, challenges in the diagnostic process still remain. Researchers and clinicians are now working to identify more meaningful classifications of ASD (categorical versus dimensional) and developing more sensitive instruments for very young children and individuals with severe cognitive impairments. Future screening and diagnostic protocols must reflect these research-driven movements.

References

American Psychiatric Association. (1994). *Diagnostic and statistical manual of mental disorders* (4th ed.). Washington, DC: Author.

American Psychiatric Association. (2000). *The diagnostic and statistical manual of mental disorders* (4th ed., Text rev.). Washington, DC: Author.

Aylward, G. P. (1997). Conceptual issues in developmental screening and assessment. *Journal of Developmental and Behavioral Pediatrics, 18,* 340–349.

Baird, G., Charman, T., Baron-Cohen, S., Cox, A., Swettenham, J., Wheelwright, S., et al. (2000). A screening instrument for autism at 18 months of age: A 6-year follow-up study. *Journal of the American Academy of Child and Adolescent Psychiatry, 39,* 694–702.

Bishop, S. L., Richler, J., & Lord, C. (2006). Association Between Restricted and Repetitive Behaviors and Nonverbal IQ in Children with Autism Spectrum Disorders. *Child Neuropsychology, 12*(4-5), 247–267.

Bricker, D., & Squires, J. (1999). *Ages and stages questionnaires* (2nd ed.). Baltimore, MD: Brookes.

Chawarska, K., Paul, R., Klin, A., Hannigen, S., Dichtel, L., & Volkmar, F. (2007). Parental recognition of developmental problems in toddlers with autism spectrum disorders. *Journal of Autism and Developmental Disorders, 38*(1), 67–72.

Coonrod, E. E., & Stone, W. L. (2005). Screening for autism in young children. In D. J. Cohen & F. R. Volkmar (Eds.), *Handbook of autism and pervasive developmental disorders* (2nd ed., pp. 707–729). New York: Wiley.

Cuccaro, M. L., Shao, Y., Grubber, J., Slifer, M., Wolpert, C. M., Donnelly, S. L., & Pericak-Vance, M. A. (2003). Factor analysis of restricted and repetitive behaviors in autism using the Autism Diagnostic Interview-R. *Child Psychiatry and Human Development, 34*(1), 3–17.

Dietz, C., Swinkels, S., van Daalen, E., van Engeland, H., & Buitelaar, J. K. (2006). Screening for Autistic Spectrum Disorder in Children Aged 14-15 Months. II: Population Screening with the Early Screening of Autistic Traits Questionnaire (ESAT). Design and General Findings. *Journal of Autism and Developmental Disorders, 36*(6), 713–722.

DeGiacomo, A., & Fombonne, E. (1998). Parental recognition of developmental abnormalities in autism. *European Journal of Child and Adolescent Psychiatry, 7,* 131–136.

Filipek, P. A., Accardo, P. J., Baranek, G. T., Cook, E. H. Jr., Dawson, G., Gordon, B., et al. (1999). The screening and diagnosis of autistic spectrum disorders. *Journal of Autism and Developmental Disorders, 29,* 439–484.

Fombonne, E. (2005). The changing epidemiology of autism. *Journal of Applied Research in Intellectual Disabilities, 18*(4), 281–294.

Gilliam, J. E. (1995). *Gilliam autism rating scale.* Austin, TX: ProEd.

Glasgoe, F. P. (1996). *A variation study and the psychometric properties of the Brigance screens.* North Billerica, MA: Curriculum Associates.

Glasgoe, F. P. (1998). *Collaborating with parents: Using parents' evaluation of developmental status to detect and address developmental and behavioral problems.* Nashville, TN: Ellsworth & Vandermeer.

Gotham, K., Pickles, A., & Lord, C. (2009). Standardizing ADOS scores for a measure of severity in autism spectrum disorders. *Journal of Autism and Developmental Disorders, 39*(5), 693–705.

Howlin, P., & Asgharian, A. (1999). The diagnosis of autism and Asperger syndrome: Finding from a survey of 770 families. Developmental Medicine and Child Neurology, 41, 834–839.

Individuals with Disabilities Education Act of 1990, 20 U.S.C. § 1400 et seq. (1990).

Ireton, H., & Glasgoe, F. P. (1995). Assessing children's development using parents' reports: The Child Development Inventory. *Clinical Pediatrics, 34,* 248–255.

Krug, D. A., Arick, J., & Almond, P. (1980). Behavior checklist for identifying severely handicapped individuals with high levels of autistic behavior. *Journal of Child Psychology and Psychiatry, 21*(3), 221–229.

Lecavalier, L. (2005). An evaluation of the Gilliam autism rating scale. *Journal of Autism and Developmental Disorders,* online first. Retrieved from http://springerlink.com

Lecavalier, L., Aman, M. G., Scahill, L., McDougle, C. J., McCracken, J. T., Vitiello, B., et al. (2006). Validity of the autism diagnostic interview-revised. *American Journal of Mental Retardation, 111,* 199–215.

Le Couteur, A., Lord, C., & Rutter, M. (2003). *The Autism diagnostic interview – revised (ADI-R).* Los Angeles: Western Psychological Services.

Lord, C., & Bishop, S. L. (2009). The autism spectrum: Definitions, assessment and diagnoses. *British Journal of Hospital Medicine, 70*(3), 234–237.

Lord, C., & Corsello, C. (2005). Diagnostic instruments in autistic spectrum disorders. In F. R. Volkmar, R. Paul, A. Klin, & D. J. Cohen (Eds.), *Handbook of autism and pervasive developmental disorders, Vol. 2: Assessment, interventions, and policy* (3rd ed. pp. 730–771). Hoboken, NJ: Wiley.

Lord, C., Risi, S., Lambrecht, L., Cook, E. H., Leventhal, B. L., DiLavore, P., et al. (2000). The Autism Diagnostic Observation Schedule – Generic: A standard measure of social and communication deficits associated with the spectrum of autism. *Journal of Autism and Developmental Disorders, 30*(3), 205–223.

Lord, C., Rutter, M., DiLavore, P., & Risi, S. (1999). Autism diagnostic observation schedule (ADOS). Los Angeles: Western Psychological Services.

Lord, C., Storoschuk, S., Rutter, M., & Pickles, A. (1994). Using the ADI-R to diagnose autism in preschool children. *Infant Mental Health Journal, 14*(3), 234–252.

Luyster, R., Gotham, K., Guthrie, W., Coffing, M., Petrak, R., DiLavore, P., et al. (2009). The Autism Diagnostic Observation Schedule – Toddler Module: A new module of a standardized diagnostic measure for autism spectrum disorders. *Journal of Autism and Developmental Disorders, 39*9, 1305–1320.

Meisels, S. J. (1985). *Developmental screening in early childhood* (Rev. ed). Washington, DC: National Association for the Education of Young Children.

Monnerat, L., dos Santos Moreira, A., Alves, M., Bonvicino, C., & Vargas, F. (2010). Identification and characterization of novel sequence variations in MECP2 gene in Rett syndrome patients. *Brain & Development, 32*(10), 843–848.

National Research Council. (2001). *Educating children with autism* (Committee on Educational Interventions for Children with Autism, Division of Behavioral and Social Sciences and Education). Washington, DC: National Academy Press.

Palomo, R., Belinchón, M., & Ozonoff, S. (2006). Autism and Family Home Movies: A Comprehensive Review. *Journal of Developmental and Behavioral Pediatrics, 27*(Suppl. 2), 59–68.

Rice, C. (2009). Prevalence of autism spectrum disorders: Autism and developmental disabilities monitoring network, United States, 2006. CDC surveillance summaries. *Morbidity and Mortality Weekly Report, 58*(SS-10), 1–20.

Risi, S., Lord, C., Gotham, K., Corsello, C., Chrysler, C., Szatmari, P., et al. (2006). Combining information from multiple sources in the diagnosis of autism spectrum disorders. *Journal of the American Academy of Child and Adolescent Psychiatry, 45*(9), 1094–1103.

Robins, D. L., Fein, D., Barton, M. L., & Green, J. A. (2001). The Modified Checklist for Autism in Toddlers: An initial study investigating the early detection of autism and pervasive developmental disorders. *Journal of Autism and Developmental Disorders, 31*, 131–144.

Rogers, S. J., Young, G. S., Cook, I., Giolezetti, A., & Ozonoff, S. (2010). Imitating actions on objects in early-onset and regressive autism: Effects and implications of task characteristics on performance. *Development and Psychopathology, 22*(1), 71–85.

Rutter, M., Bailey, A., & Lord, C. (2003). *Social Communication Questionnaire*. Los Angeles, CA: Western Psychological Services.

Schopler, E., Reichler, R. J., & Renner, B. R. (1988). *The childhood autism rating scale (CARS)*. Los Angeles, CA: Western Psychological Services.

Siegel, B., & Hayer, C. (1999, April). *Detection of autism in the 2nd and 3rd year: The pervasive developmental disorders screening test (PDDST)*. Poster presented at the biennial meeting for the Society for Research in Child Development, Albuquerque, NM.

Sparrow, S., Balla, D., & Cicchetti, D. (1984). Vineland adaptive behavior scales. Circle Pines, MN: American Guidance Service.

Sparrow, S. S., Cicchetti, D. V., & Balla, D. A. (2005). *Vineland adaptive behavior scales* (2nd ed.). Circle Pines, MN: American Guidance Service.

Stone, W. L., Coonrod, E. E., & Ousley, O. Y. (2000). Screening tool for autism two-year-olds (STAT): Development and preliminary data. *Journal of Autism and Developmental Disorders, 30*, 607–612.

Stone, W. L., McMahon, C. R., & Henderson, L. M. (2008). Use of screening tool for autism in two-year-olds (STAT) for children under 24 months. *Autism, 12*(5), 557–573.

Venter, A., Lord, C., & Schopler, E. (1992). A follow-up study of high-functioning autistic children. *Journal of Child Psychology and Psychiatry, 33*(3), 489–507.

Wechsler, D.(1949). *Manual for the Wechsler intelligence scale for children*. New York: The Psychological Corporation.

Wetherby, A. M., & Prizant, B. M. (2002). *Communication and symbolic behavior scales developmental profile*. Baltimore, MD: Brookes.

World Health Organization. (1990). *International statistical classification of diseases and health related problems* (10th ed.). Geneva, Switzerland: Author.

Yirmiya, N., Sigman, M., & Freeman, B. J. (1994). Comparison between diagnostic instruments for identifying high-functioning children with autism. *Journal of Autism and Developmental Disorders, 24*, 281–291.

SECTION II

Approaches and Philosophies in Educating Students with Autism

4

APPLIED BEHAVIOR ANALYSIS AND LEARNERS WITH AUTISM SPECTRUM DISORDERS

Jack Scott and Kyle Bennett

FLORIDA ATLANTIC UNIVERSITY

Introduction

Autism spectrum disorder (ASD) is a complex disability, and many of the characteristics that children with ASD display are challenging to their caregivers and teachers and interfere with teaching new skills and behaviors (Iovannone, Dunlap, Huber, & Kincaid, 2003; Smith, 2001). Related to these challenges applied behavior analysis (ABA) has a long-standing history of being a scientifically based approach to educating and treating children and youth with ASD (Committee on Educational Interventions for Children with Autism, 2001; Simpson, 2005a). ABA is the science of human behavior whereby principles of behavior have been discovered, and tactics developed from these principles have been systematically applied to bring about socially important changes (Cooper, Heron, & Heward, 2007). ABA involves the study of human behavior in relation to environmental variables (Skinner, 1953); and it seeks to understand how behavior is learned, why it exists, and how it is controlled via the environment (Sulzer-Azaroff & Mayer, 1991). By understanding the basic principles of behavior analysis, researchers and practitioners have developed and validated many teaching strategies, as well as treatment options for problem behaviors, which have been successful in educating children with autism (Smith, 2001).

In this chapter, we offer an overview of interventions and approaches to educating students with ASD conceptualized under an ABA model. Such efforts rely on clearly defined goals and objectives, utilization of evidence-based tactics, precisely defined data collection and analysis methods, and data based decision making on the effectiveness of the programming. Although there is a history of using punishment and aversive procedures, modern behavior analysts rely on positive strategies to achieve worthy outcomes meaningful for the person of concern and society.

This chapter begins with an overview of the historical background of ABA and students with an ASD. The work of Lovaas (1987) plays an important role in this early history but many others made valuable contributions. Early ABA-focused work tended to concentrate on specific skills and the application of punishment to manage problem behaviors. While this may seem limited in scope or harsh to the modern reader, we must be reminded of the dreary state of affairs relative to our understanding of autism and autism interventions at the time. The legacy of Bettelheim (1967) and other "parent blamers" combined with fundamental misunderstandings about the atypical behavior of children with autism-related disabilities helped create a climate wherein expectations were low and progress was not always actively sought. This historical overview then moves forward to consider functional analysis of problem behavior and the emergence of the communication hypothesis for problem behaviors of children with an array of severe problem behaviors as well as autism. In this context the positive behavior support (PBS) approach (Horner et al., 1990) as a refinement of ABA is explored.

Next we offer a review of the basics of ABA. Here we look at the dimensions of the field and definitions and description of principles and techniques associated with ABA. The role of theory in ABA, or rather the relative lack of theory, is considered in light of the inductive nature of behavioral research. It is this scientific foundation for ABA that allows it, perhaps more than any other discipline focused on persons with disabilities, to be the quintessential evidence-based approach. In this section we also consider important trends and issues within ABA as it relates to interventions for children with ASD, with special attention to the provision of services in increasingly inclusive public school environments.

The heart of this chapter is a review of studies that provide the evidence base for ABA and students with ASD. While it is not possible to report on all these studies, this chapter highlights salient themes within the research and shows the evolving sophistication of behavioral intervention for students on the spectrum.

The chapter then moves to ABA-related future trends and issues in relation to ASD. Among these trends is the movement to use ever more positive interventions, procedural regulation of interventions, the professionalization of the field of behavior analysis, and the refinement of behavioral teaching strategies, especially early intervention methods and strategies that focus on teaching verbal behavior. We also discuss several important policy issues connected to ABA, including closer linkages with pediatricians; policy and procedural matters related to seclusion/ exclusion and timeout; safety, with a special focus on helping children remain free from unintentional injury; and vocational preparation and transition. This chapter concludes with a brief summary and a final statement on future trends.

Historical Background

It can now be difficult to envision just how crude treatment for children with autism was in the era prior to PL 94-142 (Education for All Handicapped Children, 1975, later codified as Individuals with Disabilities Education Act). Leo Kanner (1943) provided a clinical description of the disorder, and while on one hand recognizing the biological basis of the disorder, he used the other hand to point to the likelihood of parent contribution to the development of autism. Kanner was not the worst parent blamer, however, as this unfortunate distinction must surely go to Bruno Bettelheim. His books, including *The Empty Fortress: Infantile Autism and the Birth of Self* (1967), *A Home for the Heart* (1974), and *Dialogues with Mothers* (1962), as well as frequent magazine articles promoted the idea of parents rejecting their child and the child, in a desperate effort to survive, turning inward and becoming autistic. The Bettelheim recommendation was to institutionalize the child so as to remove the harmful influences of the parents and seek to get the parents into therapy in the hope of a successful reunification as both child and parent made progress. Bettelheim's thinking has been totally rejected (see Pollak, 1997); nonetheless Bettelheim had a profoundly negative impact on the culture of autism by blaming parents, specifically mothers, and minimized help and support for the children. School programs of the era often segregated children with autism and expectations for these learners were low.

Behavior analysts found autism an exciting population to which they could apply their often brash enthusiasm. Among the first behavioral studies of children with autism was by Wolf,

Risely, and Mees (1964). They used timeout and other behavioral procedures, and provided details on the parent and teacher training which accompanied their intervention efforts. Early behavioral research examined the use of reinforcement, but was, however, characterized by studies that emphasized punishment (Lovaas, Schaeffer, & Simmons, 1965; Lovaas & Simmons, 1969; Risley, 1968). A photographic feature article on Lovaas's work at the UCLA Neuropsychiatric Institute appeared in *Life Magazine* in 1965 and influenced the belief that punishment was an intrinsic part of effective treatment for children with autism. In their paper, with what to our modern sensibilities appears as a rather oxymoronic title, "Building Social Behavior in Autistic Children by the Use of Electric Shock," Lovaas, Schaeffer, and Simmons (1965) described using electric shock with two sets of identical twins with autism. Their results supported the conclusion that electric shock could work to encourage children with autism to approach adults to avoid shocks and could suppress tantrums and self-stimulation. Interestingly, Lovaas had earlier written about the benefits of treatments based on positive reinforcement (Lovaas, 1964).

Without trying to justify the use of aversive methods, it is possible to appreciate the treatment choice dilemma Lovaas and colleagues faced. Nonaversive methods would work with children with autism but they took tremendous time and effort. These elements, namely time and effort, would later come to characterize effective positive interventions for children with ASD. Shock and other forms of punishment were tried as shortcuts to overcome the severity of the impairments confronting early interventionists. Even Risley (and other early advocates for positive treatment of children), when confronted with a child with dangerous climbing behavior, was willing to use electric shock as a punisher (Risley, 1968). To be sure, the behavioral community was not shy about the use of punishers for persons with autism and those with other disabilities during this era. Empirical data gave strong evidence for the effectiveness of such practices, and in the absence of a viable collection of other intervention strategies, these methods were widely used. This early emphasis on punishment would leave a lingering resentment on the part of many and a distrust of any behavioral intervention for years to come.

In 1987, Lovaas published a landmark article; one that had a profound impact on the field of autism. Lovaas reported results on early and intensive behavioral intervention with a systematic program of sequenced training activities. Children with autism began treatment at an early age, and parents were enlisted as cotherapists. The results of the treatment were dramatic with nearly half of the study participants reported to achieve normal intellectual and educational functioning. Not surprisingly, controversy accompanied the publication of Lovaas's work and it continues today (Gresham & MacMillan, 1998). The work of Lovaas was assailed for both methodological weaknesses and attacked from a philosophical stance. Methodological weaknesses have been addressed in an enviable number of replications resulting in 22 peer-reviewed published reports (T. Smith, personal communication, October, 2010). These studies offer results in support of the original 1987 article. Those who raise philosophical objections may never be placated. Intensive delivery of any type of educational program presents significant challenges to schools (Scott & Baldwin, 2005), and in the absence of a definitive court ruling that mandates such services, many districts are reluctant to offer them. Others have criticized ABA interventions that take place in a child's home based on the notion that this setting does not represent many learning situations the child will encounter away from home (e.g., one-on-one instruction) and that it relies on developmentally inappropriate tactics. Critics of Lovaas and his methods have also voiced concern about the recommended 40 hours a week of intensive work. Supporters, on the other hand, have maintained that intensive therapies are routine for children with medically based conditions and that surgeries or other medical treatments may be much more intrusive; yet, these are delivered without objection. It is quite possible that no amount of empirical evidence will satisfy some critics or alter the prevailing nonintensive behavioral treatment orientation of some professionals. Nevertheless, the accumulating evidence for intensive behavioral intervention should cause even the most grudging critics to recognize the scientific evidence that supports ABA. It is becoming clearer that those children with higher IQs are more likely to make dramatic progress while those with lower IQs are more likely to achieve modest gains (Sallows & Graupner, 2005). The evidence section of this chapter provides additional treatment of this subject.

While Lovaas caused professional controversy, it was a parent of a child with autism who ignited worldwide interest in intensive behavioral intervention. Catherine Maurice provided an account of successful treatment of her daughter, and later her son, in *Let Me Hear Your Voice* (1993). This account began a movement of parents seeking *recovery* for their children. Maurice detailed the struggles she had in finding evidence-based treatments for her daughter and shared details of outmoded and sometimes ludicrous advice she received. Rejecting the playgroup for her daughter and the parent support group for herself, Maurice sought out Lovaas and set out to replicate his program for her daughter. Perhaps most importantly, Maurice was the first to articulate a goal of normal functioning for her child: "Anne-Marie would be whole and normal.... She would recover" (p. 67).

Verbal Behavior and ASD

The history of ABA was heavily influenced by the work of Skinner. In addition to his work with nonverbal behavior, Skinner was the first to conceptualize the development of language in behavior analytic terms (1957). His analysis was motivated by challenges from antibehavioral colleagues who believed it was not possible to describe the development of language from a behavioral perspective. Skinner's initial work on verbal behavior languished for many years until its utilitarian potential as a treatment for persons with autism and other developmental disabilities was recognized (Greer & Ross, 2007; Sundberg, 1991; Sundberg & Michael, 2001). In this connection, an important marker was the publication of the first issue of *The Analysis of Verbal Behavior* in 1982. Mark Sundberg and James Partington are widely credited with the development of assessments and interventions that focus on improving the verbal behavior of children with autism using behavior analytic tactics with Skinner's analysis of verbal behavior as their guide (Sundberg & Partington, 1998). This topic is addressed further in the next section of this chapter.

Functional Assessment and the Communication Hypothesis

Another of the most significant developments in understanding and treating problem behavior for children with ASD was the recognition that problem behaviors could serve important functions (Carr, 1977; Iwata, Dorsey, Slifer, Bauman, & Richman, 1982/1994). This idea is particularly significant in light of the early misunderstandings of autism as a form of psychosis. This concept was also critical in assessing the function or functions of problem behaviors relative to selecting and applying appropriate interventions (Carr & Durand, 1985).

The functional analysis approach to responding to problem behaviors had a profound impact on the field, most notably the "normalization" of even the most severe problem behaviors of children with autism. Based on this orientation behavior was not a mysterious expression of a bizarre or psychotic brain, but rather a form of communication. Broadly, in many instances problem behaviors are now seen as ways of communicating (albeit socially unacceptable in form), and thus are understandable and treatable. Furthermore, behavioral teaching and training offered the most effective methods of responding to these challenging behaviors. In accordance with this thinking, Carr and Durand (1985) emphasized the use of functional communication training as the main approach for dealing with problem behaviors. That is, once the purpose or function of a child's challenging behavior was understood it was possible to intervene using a functionally equivalent means of communication, one that was equally or more efficient and that could be taught to the child and reinforced by all persons who had contact with the child.

Edward "Ted" Carr was among the leaders in these developments and he had an immense impact on behavioral intervention (Carr et al., 1994). For Carr, decreasing problem behavior for a person with ASD was not the primary objective. Instead the goal was to create conditions or "environmental contexts" that supported prosocial and adaptive behavior in people with autism and other developmental disabilities. Carr's view was based on the notion that problems are context-dependent; that is, problem contexts produce problem behaviors (Moskowitz, Adamek, & Tenebaum, 2009). Hence, for Carr, changing nonproductive environments using "system change" methods and collaborative teaming, with a focus on skill development among students, was essential for treating problem behavior. Carr is credited with being a primary philosophical contributor to and cofounder of positive behavior support, highlighted later in this chapter.

Description and Overview

Applied behavior analysis (ABA) grew out of the laboratory tradition of the experimental analysis of behavior. ABA is now one of three branches of behavior analysis; the others are experimental analysis of behavior (with basic research as its emphasis) and behaviorism (the philosophy of the science of behavior). Since its inception, ABA has been most closely associated with helping persons with developmental disabilities, including those with ASD (Cooper et al., 2007; Green, 2010).

ABA is founded on the scientific model, with reliance on experimentation, precise measurement of observable behaviors, and conditions that may influence behaviors of interest (Skinner, 1953). Thus, behavior analysts seek to understand behaviors targeted for change primarily by being able to predict how an alteration of affecting conditions (independent variables) will impact behavior. With successful prediction comes a degree of experimental control. Being able to control the behavior enables the behavior analyst to successfully intervene and put in place new conditions that will reduce problem behaviors and strengthen desired behaviors. Replication of findings lends confidence to what is known. Questioning and scientific doubt is ongoing and reports by even the most respected authorities and experts will be doubted in the face of new evidence. This reliance on the scientific method, including sharing methods and results in peer-reviewed journals and other dissemination venues, has proven to be a relatively successful method. Over time, studies are replicated and extended, and proven strategies become accepted elements of the practice of behavior analysis. Currently, the Behavior Analyst Certification Board (n.d.) offers an international certification program (BCBA and BCABA Behavior Analyst Task List, 3rd ed.) based on these tenets.

The historical underpinnings of ABA were framed by Baer, Wolf, and Risley (1968) in the first issue of the *Journal of Applied Behavior Analysis*. These ABA pioneers provided a concise declaration of what the field of applied behavior analysis was all about, a statement that continues to define the field to this day. First, they clarified the meaning of "applied" by noting that "the behavior, stimuli, and/or organism under study are chosen because of their importance to man and society, rather than their importance to theory" (Baer et al., 1968, p. 92). This set ABA apart from earlier experimental analysis of behavior and other disciplines where researchers may be testing hypothetical theoretical constructs. Thus, the emphasis is on real world problems, studied in real world settings, and is focused on people facing real and immediate problems.

Second, they emphasized that ABA was by definition a *behavioral science*; that is, it is based on observable and measurable events, and thus is focused on what a person actually does rather than what they may think or wish to do.

ABA is also *analytic* in nature based on the requirement that there be "believable demonstrations of the events that can be responsible for the occurrence or non-occurrence of behavior" (Baer et al., 1968, pp. 93–94). Accordingly, control over behavior, in an experimental sense, occurs when researchers are able to demonstrate that independent (manipulated) variables are in fact responsible for observed changes in behavior. Identifying a *functional relationship* between a controlling variable and problem behavior (hence the term *functional behavioral analysis*) is paramount to this process. As ABA evolved from laboratory settings to real-world situations, the degree to which a subject's behavior could be overtly manipulated was of course minimized. Nevertheless, evidence for a functional relation between a treatment variable and corresponding behavior remains a critical goal of ABA. To achieve evidence for this functional relationship a broad array of behavioral or *single-subject* research designs has been developed. The best known of these is the reversal design, wherein baseline data are taken and then followed by an intervention. The intervention, or independent variable, is withdrawn or reversed while measurement continues, with the expectation that the behavior will revert to baseline rates. The intervention is then reinstated to again determine its impact on the behavior under study. The reversal design has obvious problems relative to treating some types of behaviors (e.g., it is unethical to cease treatment for some targets such as self-injurious behavior), thus other designs such as the multiple baseline design can achieve convincing demonstrations of control without abrupt withdrawal of an apparently effective intervention. Replication of effects, either within a study or between studies, further strengthens confidence in findings. Visual analysis of charted data, such as simple line charts, is the primary means of judging intervention effectiveness.

Baer et al. (1968) also argued that robust ABA studies are clear on descriptions of *technological* elements. In this connection the general rule of thumb is that the methods are clearly enough described to permit another trained interventionist "to produce the same results, given only a reading of the description" (p. 95).

Baer et al. (1968) also contributed to a basic understanding of the underlying principles of ABA by stressing the need for *conceptual systems*. They used this term to accentuate the importance of careful attention to terminology and using tactics derived from known principles of behavior. This included prohibitions against inventing new terms for techniques or principles already established in the literature, as well as similar rules that facilitate the sharing of information among behavior analytic researchers and practitioners working together as a cooperative discipline.

The basic foundations of ABA are also tied to demonstrations of effectiveness and utility. The definition of *effective* goes beyond gains on statistical tests or slight increments in progress. Instead, it calls for *social validity*, wherein the people closest to the person being helped provide testimony as to the effectiveness of an intervention. The last foundational element of ABA, *generality*, is among the most challenging. Intervention *generality* occurs when a behavioral change "proves durable over time, if it appears in a wide variety of possible environments, or if it spreads to a wide variety of related behaviors" (Baer et al., 1968, p. 96). In spite of challenges associated with achieving generalization this element of effective ABA remains vitally important.

Basic Principles of ABA

There are several basic principles that underlie all behavior analysis work. These principles are used throughout education and are known to be effective with all children, including those diagnosed with ASD (Horner, Carr, Strain, Todd, & Reed, 2002). These basic behavioral principles are based on empirically proven demonstrations of "functional relationships" between target behaviors and environmental variables. Several principles include reinforcement, punishment, extinction, and stimulus control (Cooper et al., 2007). *Reinforcement* is the most important of these behavioral principles. When a behavior is followed by a stimulus that increases the future probability of that behavior, reinforcement has occurred. In the case of *positive reinforcement* something is added to the behavioral equation. *Negative reinforcement* occurs when a stimulus is removed contingent upon a behavior, and that behavior increases. The term *negative* refers to the removal or termination of the stimulus and does not imply the presentation of a harsh or aversive stimulus. Thus, positive reinforcement teaches people to acquire (e.g., attention, food, drinks, and activities), and negative reinforcement teaches people to escape or avoid aversive situations (e.g., difficult work demands, social situations, and discomfort). Reinforcement is the most widely used principal of ABA and it is the basis for the vast majority of interventions, including those for learners with ASD.

Punishment, defined as following a behavior with a consequence that decreases "the future probability of the behavior" (Miltenberger, 1997, p. 566), is another basic principle of ABA. Timeout and verbal reprimands are two examples of commonly used classroom strategies that can function as punishers. Functionally, an intervention is only a punisher if it results in a decreased probability in the behavior. Accordingly, a teacher may consider sending a child with ASD to the office for bad behavior to be a punisher. However, in a behavioral sense it can only be described as a punisher if it decreases the probability of the behavior in the future.

Extinction calls for discontinuing reinforcement for behavior that had previously been reinforced. The impact will be a decrease in behavior (Cooper et al., 2007). Planned ignoring is an extinction-based tactic wherein the presumed reinforcement for a behavior is teacher attention. Preventing a child from escaping or avoiding math instruction is another extinction-based tactic wherein the likely reinforcer is delaying, terminating, or reducing the difficulty of the assignment.

Several other key concepts are essential to understanding the basic principles of behavior analysis. One of these elements is the three-term contingency, or (ABC) that is used to specify the relationship among antecedents, behaviors, and consequences (Cooper et al., 2007). **A**ntecedents are all discernible factors in place prior to the occurrence of a target behavior. Some antecedents set the occasion for behaviors to occur because reinforcement contingencies have followed in the past. Other antecedents abate the occurrence of behavior because extinction, or punishment contingencies have followed. Additionally, the term *setting events* is used to describe an expanded array of antecedents that can exert general control over behavior, including physiological states (e.g., food deprived because breakfast was missed, elevated or decreased sugar levels due to failure to take needed medication, etc.) and proximal or distal environmental events (e.g., fight with peers, extended morning bus ride to school, crowded/noisy environments, etc.). Antecedents do not cause a behavior; rather, they increase or decrease the likelihood of a behavior occurring resulting from past learning (i.e., consequences), or altering the saliency of a reinforcer (i.e., setting events).

Within the ABC conceptualization, the **B**ehavior is the observable and measurable action emitted by the person. A single instance of behavior is termed a *response*; the collection of all the behaviors of an individual is referred to as their *repertoire*. **C**onsequences constitute whatever follows the behavior of concern. As stated before, consequences can increase or decrease the probability of a behavior occurring. For instance, it may be planned reinforcement delivered by the teacher, or unplanned giggles offered by classmates. Loss of points or teacher frowns are two examples that may function as punishment consequences. Together this ABC sequence provides a way of describing and analyzing behavioral episodes. Functional assessment relies heavily on carefully observing and analyzing within this ABC format. When certain observed behaviors can reliably be suspected of producing a given function for a student a hypothesis as to the likely purpose of the behavior for that student can be developed and tested. In turn, the development of hypothesis driven interventions can be developed, and this is the cornerstone of functional assessment, ABA-based interventions, and treatment and instructional evaluation tactics.

Instructional Procedures for Students with ASD

Behavioral instructional strategies are crucial elements of educational programs for students with autism and are grounded in the three-term, or ABC, contingency discussed above. Among these strategies are discrimination training, prompting, time delay, shaping, imitation, chaining, task analysis, and reinforcement tactics, to name a few (Duker, Didden, & Sigafoos, 2004). Interestingly, these procedures are universally employed in behavioral instruction of persons with ASD; and widely used by teachers who might be reluctant to describe themselves as individuals who rely on behavioral methodology. In some cases, the unique learning characteristics of children with ASD have resulted in development of new strategies. Stimulus overselectivity, for example, first critically analyzed by Lovaas, Koegel, and Schreibman (1979), occurs when an individual has a strong preference for particular elements of an instructional stimulus or stimuli. Often this preference (e.g., a particular color or texture) is incompatible with making correct responses, and thus requires careful attention to the properties of the teaching materials as well as instructional modifications (Hundert, 2009; Schreibman, 1975).

Positive Behavior Support

Positive behavior support (PBS) stressed the importance of quality of life factors for persons with autism. Discussion of ABA strategies related to children with ASD must also include the contributions of the positive behavior support (PBS) movement, especially with its refinement and expansion of ABA such that it is more utilitarian, especially in schools and with families (Horner et al., 1990). PBS builds on the scientific foundation of ABA. It compliments ABA to include greater emphasis on features such as contextual fit of interventions, with particular attention to potentially supporting factors; person-centered planning, with an emphasis on long-term outcomes; use of support teams and collaborative efforts among practitioners and families; behavior assessment techniques refined for ease of use among teachers and families; interventions designed to prevent and replace problem behavior, and not merely decelerate challenging behaviors; and dramatic reduction of the use of aversive procedures. But Johnston, Foxx, Jacobson, Green, and Mulick (2006) among others, have criticized PBS suggesting that it offers little when contrasted to high quality ABA services. Ultimately, the goal of PBS is to integrate proven ABA tactics within a framework that increases accessibility among families and schools, with a particular interest in increasing the quality of life and happiness of persons with ASD and those involved in their care (Horner et al., 2002; Horner et al., 1990).

Theory and ABA

Baer et al. (1968) argued that theory was not a critical element of ABA, and this precept of behavior analysis persists today. Rather, addressing socially valid problems and preventing development of other challenges remains the most important objective of ABA. In spite of this guideline, however, there are clearly noteworthy theories about autism that have been advanced by behavior analysts. Ferster (1961), the first behavior analyst to offer a theory of autism, viewed the disability as manifestations of observable social interactions between parents and children. In this regard Ferster noted:

> In general, the autistic child's behavior will be analyzed by the functional consequences of the child's behavior rather than the specific forms. The major attempt will be to determine what specific effects the autistic child's performance has on that environment and how the specific effects maintain the performance. (p. 438)

By environment, Ferster was referring to the child's parents. Accordingly, in theory, it was his contention that having sufficient observations of parents and their responses, or failures to respond, to their children would make it possible to show the "actual contingencies applied by the parental environment to the child's behavior" (p. 443) that would lead to an understanding of the child's condition. Ferster failed to recognize autism as having a neurological etiology. Accordingly, his treatment recommendation was fully behavioral in nature: Directly observe how parents reinforce or fail to reinforce behaviors, and based on these data alter parental behaviors and thus offset the development of autism.

Twenty-eight years later a second major comprehensive behavioral theory of autism was advanced by Lovaas and Smith (1989). Their behavioral theory of autism had four tenets: (a) behaviors related to autism are consistent with basic laws of behavioral learning theory; (b) behavioral problems of learners with autism are best described as developmental delays; (c) when provided with the right learning settings, environments, and conditions, many children with autism are able to learn as much as others; and (d) the learning and behavioral difficulties of individuals with autism are not the result of a "disease," but rather a poor fit between an atypical nervous system and environments that lack accommodations and modifications. These tenets remain highly relevant to this day. To be sure, Lovaas and Smith recognized that children with ASD had learning strengths and that in optimal environments they could learn well. Perhaps most importantly, they recognized that a faulty neurological system was at the heart of autism, and not the result of parental inadequacy, action, or inaction. These authors stressed that behavioral treatment was the most effective treatment approach, and that building competent social repertoires at an early age was the most practical way of overcoming the delays associated with ASD.

The Evidence Base

Again, an exhaustive review of the literature is beyond the scope of this chapter. Representative historical studies and relevant current studies are presented to demonstrate the evidence base for using ABA strategies when working with children with ASD. We view the contributions of ABA along two broad categories: skill development and enhancement, and the understanding and resolution of problem behaviors. Henceforth, the behavior analytic studies highlighting the efficacy of ABA are presented within these categories.

The Evidence Base for Skill Development

There are a variety of educational and therapeutic strategies available for helping children with ASD; however, those based on ABA have been shown to be among the most promising and efficacious (Committee on Educational Interventions for Children with Autism, 2001; Howard, Sparkman, Cohen, Green, & Stanislaw, 2005; National Autism Center, 2009; Simpson 2005a). One specific ABA strategy that has shown particular utility and efficacy is discrete trial teaching (DTT). DTT is typically implemented in a distraction-free environment, and is comprised of the following components: (a) a cue in the form of a verbal or nonverbal stimulus presentation; (b) a prompt, if needed, used to evoke a correct response; (c) the child's response; (d) a consequence (e.g., reinforcement), contingent on a child's response; and (e) an intertrial interval, wherein there is a brief pause before the next trial begins. In his influential work on the behavioral treatment of children with autism, Lovaas (1987) demonstrated that children taught using DTT could make substantial improvements in multiple domains of functioning, including preacademic, academic, daily living, and communication skills, to name a few. Children in his study who participated in 40 hours per week of DTT for 2 to 3 years showed the most gains, while children participating in fewer hours of DTT, as well as those who did not participate in DTT at all, did not show comparable progress. In a follow-up study, McEachin, Smith, and Lovaas (1993) found the children from Lovaas's (1987) intensive behavioral treatment group maintained their treatment gains; confirming the resiliency and long-term nature of gains made using ABA methods.

Following the Lovaas (1987) study, a series of related studies on the effects of DTT with children with autism also reported favorable findings. Smith, Groen, and Wynn (2000) examined the effects of DTT with children in an intensive treatment group compared to those receiving DTT from their parents with clinical guidance. The children were randomly assigned to both groups. Those involved in the intensive treatment group participated in DTT implemented by trained staff for nearly 25 hours per week for 1 year. This was followed by a reduction in hours over the course of 1 to 2 years. The children in the parent-training group received DTT from their caregivers. Although the reported gains were less than those from the Lovaas (1987) and McEachin et al. (1993) studies, the results of this study showed that the children participating in the intensive treatment group significantly outperformed the children in the parent training group on many domains of functioning.

To extend previous findings on DTT, and to address concerns over intensity of treatment being a factor in the results of previous studies, Eikeseth, Smith, Jahr, and Eldevik (2002) examined the differences in children (ages 4–7 years) who participated in DTT compared to those who participated in an equally intense eclectic school program. Children assigned to the behavioral treatment group participated in DTT sessions similar to the Lovaas (1987) study. Children in the eclectic group participated in a combination of programming activities, based on elements from other (non-ABA) intervention approaches for children with autism. As with previous findings, children in the behavioral treatment group significantly outperformed those in the eclectic group. In accordance with these findings it was inferred that treatment intensity was not the single key factor that accounted for the gains. Rather, intensely and strategically delivered individualized programming based on ABA seemed to be the primary factors that led to the improvements. Additionally, this study demonstrated that children older than those who participated in previous studies using DTT received substantial benefit.

In a related study, Howard et al. (2005) evaluated the differences between children's gains when they participated in an intensive behavioral treatment program, an intensive eclectic-oriented intervention program in a special education class, and a nonintensive early intervention program. Results were similar to those reported by Eikeseth et al. (2002). That is, children in the intensive behavioral group scored significantly higher on all domains, except gross motor skills, compared to the other groups. Additionally, rates of learning increased substantially for many of the children in the intensive behavioral treatment group, a learning pattern that was different from that of the majority of children assigned to the other groups. These results provide further evidence that the type of intervention (DTT), not simply the intensity with which a particular intervention is applied, is a key factor accounting for instructional progress among children with ASD.

The studies reviewed above, in conjunction with other studies advance the position that intensive behavioral treatment produces significant improvements in children with autism (Green, Brennan, & Fein, 2002; Sheinkopf & Siegel, 1998; Smith, Eikeseth, Klevstrand, & Lovaas, 1997). Notwithstanding these positive results, DTT has been the target of criticism, especially the work of Lovaas (1987). Several authors, including Gresham and MacMillan (1998), and more recently, Tews (2007) have alleged methodological concerns related to DTT research. These purported research design and procedural flaws include questions about sample representativeness, random assignment of participants to experimental and control groups, and treatment and outcome claims. Others note that there is inadequate evidence to reliably document the number of treatment hours required to achieve desired outcomes (Simpson, 2005b). Additionally, some have noted that DTT produces limited behavioral spontaneity, especially with language skills, and a lack of stimulus and response generalization (Committee on Educational Interventions for Children with Autism, 2001).

Natural teaching approaches, especially incidental teaching, have been used in response to claims of inflexible and stilted initiations and poor skill generalization among students with whom traditional ABA methods such as DTT instructional methods have been used (Committee on Educational Interventions for Children with Autism, 2001; Simpson 2005b). In this regard incidental teaching has been successfully used to effectively and efficiently develop a variety of skills, including receptive language skills of youth with autism (McGee, Krantz, Mason, & McClannahan, 1983), increased meaningful vocalizations and increased social proximity of young children with autism (McGee, Morrier, & Daly, 1999), and increased initiation and generalization of adjective use among children with autism (Miranda-Linne & Melin, 1992). In addition to natural teaching strategies, such as incidental teaching, other ABA methods have also contributed to the enhanced effectiveness of ABA methodology, including tactics such as errorless learning, prompting and fading strategies, natural reinforcers, and instruction that capitalizes on the students' motivation (Leblanc, Esch, Sidener, & Firth, 2006).

Researchers and practitioners have also increasingly recognized the importance of incorporating Skinner's (1957) analysis of verbal behavior findings and recommendations into behavior analytic language training programs (LeBlanc et al., 2006; Sundberg & Michael, 2001; Sundberg & Partington, 1998). Traditional approaches to the habilitation of children with language disabilities have focused on teaching them to receptively and expressively identify items, pictures, actions, and so forth (Leblanc et al., 2006). It was reasoned that if children were taught these identification skills they would automatically use these assets, without additional training, to request, comment, or have conversations. Such skill transfer often occurs quickly among children without language deficits; generalization of this type among children with language disorders, such as those with autism, is rare (Sundberg & Partington, 1998). Other formal properties of speech and language efficiently taught via ABA are also relevant targets for children with ASD, including grammar, prosody, and articulation (Sundberg & Partington, 1998).

In contrast to relying on traditional approaches to teaching language, Skinner (1957) emphasized a functional analysis of verbal behavior. This approach highlighted the independent development of independent verbal operants and the interconnections of reciprocal verbal interactions. Skinner (1957) described several basic functions of a person's verbal behavior. *Verbal operants* are controlled by either motivational factors or direct environmental events: these include echoics (e.g., vocal imitations), mands (e.g., requesting, demanding, or protesting), tacts (e.g., labeling items or actions that come into contact with one of the five senses), intraverbals (e.g., conversation), and a variety of listener behaviors (e.g., receptive language skills). Skinner

(1957) indicated that each of these verbal operants develops functionally independent of each other and each is controlled by different environmental variables. For instance, a child who has learned to request a cookie when she is hungry may not necessarily be able to label the cookie when asked to do so; or be able to talk about cookies that were eaten earlier in the day. Although each of these skills is related to the topic of cookies, each skill develops independently of others; and application of language skills within a variety of contexts requires different methods (Sundberg & Partington, 1998). This Skinner-based concept of independent functional use of verbal behavior is fundamental to current ABA language instruction and analysis. Two studies support the assertion of the independent development of different verbal operants. Hall and Sundberg (1987) demonstrated that two individuals who were deaf failed to learn to request when taught to label items; however, they successfully learned to request when given direct mand training. Similarly, based on research with an individual with a severe intellectual disability, Stafford, Sundberg, and Braam (1988) reported that the consequences that control mands were different from those that control tacts.

The implications of Skinner's analysis of verbal behavior and corresponding recommendations for teaching verbal skills to children with ASD are significant. In fact these notions were the foundation for changes in how language intervention programs for children with autism were designed to incorporate maximally effective practice elements (Carbone, Morgenstern, Zecchin-Tirri, & Kolberg, 2010; Sundberg & Michael, 2001; Sundberg & Partington, 1999). In this regard an elemental and effective-practice verbal operant that is taught to children is the mand (i.e., requesting, demanding, protesting, and so forth) because this skill has direct benefit and sets the stage for children to learn speaker/listener roles and relationships (Sundberg & Partington, 1999). Mand instruction, based on use of errorless learning, prompting, fading, and reinforcement, has successfully been used to teach young children with autism to make independent requests (Sweeney-Kerwin, Carbone, O'Brien, Zecchin, & Janecky, 2007). In a related study, Yi, Christian, Vittimberga, and Lowenkron (2006) applied the verbal behavior model to teach elementary-aged children with autism to protest; that is, to use mands that were maintained by negative reinforcement. Similarly, other ABA-oriented researchers have successfully taught children with ASD a variety of functional language skills, including vocal play, echoic responses, tacts, and intraverbal skills, using the verbal behavior model strategies (Goldsmith, Leblanc & Sautter, 2007; Ingvarsson & Hollobaugh, 2010; Kelly, Shillingburg, Castro, Addison, & LaRue, 2007; Kodak & Clements, 2009; Partington, Sundberg, Newhouse, & Spengler, 1994; Ward, Osnes, & Partington, 2007). The extant literature provides a body of empirical evidence that strongly supports the verbal behavior model as a scientifically valid and practical way to teach language skills to children with autism.

In addition to verbal skills, behavior analytic procedures such as DTT and incidental teaching have been successfully used to teach a variety of functional skills to learners diagnosed with autism. These skills include dressing, grooming, hygiene, eating and drinking, and play and leisure skills (Howard et al., 2005; Smith, 2001).

The Evidence Base for Understanding and Resolving Problem Behaviors

Children and youth with ASD commonly manifest problem behaviors, including aggression, self-injury, property destruction, and disruption of routines and activities. These problem behaviors are typically most prominent among individuals with skill deficits (Carr et al., 1994). ABA significantly contributes to the education and treatment of children and youth with ASD by providing an evidence-based problem solving process as well as a multitude of effective strategies to ameliorate these problem behaviors.

Carr (1977), a pioneer in the area of ABA-focused problem solving, identified potential purposes (functions) of self-injurious behavior, including positive social reinforcement (e.g., attention and access), negative social reinforcement (e.g., escape and avoidance), automatic positive reinforcement (e.g., sensory stimulation), and automatic negative reinforcement (e.g., pain attenuation). Carr argued that understanding these functions of behavior could lead to more effective interventions and an efficacious means of reducing problem behavior. Iwata et al. (1982/1994) studied and developed assessment methods designed to determine the functions of problem behavior. These efforts to identify functions of behavior have evolved over the last several decades to become what is currently known as functional behavior assessment (FBA). That is, the FBA process is designed to identify the contingencies that maintain problem behaviors via understanding the relationship between problem behavior(s), antecedent events (e.g., setting events and discriminative stimuli), and consequent events (e.g., positive and negative reinforcement) (Horner et al., 1990; O'Neill et al., 1997). A typical FBA consists of reviewing relevant records, interviewing caregivers and teachers, conducting direct observations, and developing and testing hypotheses related to functional explanations for problem behaviors (Iwata et al., 1982/1994; Neef & Peterson, 2007; Northup et al., 1991; O'Neill et al., 1997). FBA findings are subsequently used to design and implement evidence-based interventions, particularly ones that prevent, replace, or otherwise improve behavior. A number of studies have reported on the utility of conducting an FBA to aide in developing effective behavior intervention plans (BIP) and related interventions for individuals with autism (Machalicek, O'Reilly, Beretvas, Sigafoos, & Lancioni, 2007; Mancil, 2006). For instance, Ingvarsson, Kahng, and Hausmand (2008) determined that a girl with autism emitted aggressive, disruptive, and self-injurious behavior to escape demands and gain access to food. An intervention designed to address these specific functions consisted of applying noncontingent reinforcement (NCR) on different schedules and differential reinforcement of alternative behaviors (DRA) (in this case, a preferred item was presented contingent on compliance with demands). The results showed that low density NCR and high density NCR resulted in a reduction in the child's problem behaviors. The NCR and DRA conditions produced similar results, suggesting that strategic environmental arrangements could be used to reduce problem behavior and increase appropriate behaviors.

Other investigators sought to build functionally equivalent behavior; that is, to develop appropriate behavior that would replace problem behaviors. In one such functional analysis study Hagopian, Contrucci-Huhn, Long, and Rush (2005) determined that three children with ASD engaged in aggression, self-injury, and destruction because these problems behaviors served a communicative function. A multiple component BIP was implemented, consisting of functional communication training (FCT) to develop new communicative behaviors and extinction to abate the problematic behaviors. Results of the study demonstrated the intervention was successful in replacing the problem behaviors; supporting the notion that problem behaviors can be reduced by teaching alternative and more socially appropriate ways of communication (Carr & Durand, 1985; Durand & Carr, 1991).

In a similar study, Kahng, Hendrickson, and Vu (2000) determined that a boy with autism emitted aggressive, self-injurious, and destructive behaviors to gain access to desired items. A FCT intervention consisting of teaching the child several communicative responses reduced the problem behaviors. The researchers also reported that teaching multiple replacement responses was more effective than teaching one response. This finding supports the importance and utility of teaching multiple functional and meaningful behaviors to children with autism.

ABA is an applied science whose goal is to facilitate socially significant societal changes and improvement. In this regard ABA has contributed substantially to improvements in scientifically based teaching strategies and problem solving methods that have benefitted countless learners with autism. As clearly illustrated in this section ABA is strongly grounded in empirical evidence and thus carries credentials of effective practice. Over the last several decades the science of applied behavior analysis has grown and evolved. This growth and evolution will continue, and with it improvements that will continue to benefit and support individuals with autism.

Future Directions

What is the future for behavioral services for children with ASD? Behavior analytic interventions for students with ASD will continue to become more widely available and more specialized. Many more trained and certified behavior analysts will be available. Interestingly, and not surprisingly, within the Association for Behavior Analysis International (the primary behavior analytic professional organization) the largest program area for the 2010 annual convention was ASD. Future directions likely will be influenced by teachers and other practitioners who have had early behavioral intervention training and experiences with learners with ASD, not just in traditional public school settings but also in home, special charter, and other nontraditional school settings. While it is never possible to know what will happen in the future, here are 10 trends we think are important to pursue.

1. *The evidence base for ABA for students with ASD.* The research base for behavior analytic interventions for children with autism is impressive. Efforts and movements to recognize ABA as an evidence-based practice for public school use are growing and becoming ever more prominent. The National Standards Report (2009) by the Nation Autism Center represents a significant effort to identify effective and less or ineffective interventions. Behavior analytic interventions generally receive high marks; in contrast "Facilitated Communication" and "Sensory Integrative Package," for example, have an "evidence level" of "unestablished" (National Standards Report, 2009). It remains unclear what impact this and similar reports will have on practices that affect learners with ASD. We are hopeful that the outcome will be a willingness for the field to recognize and use evidence-based methods such as ABA; and to eliminate or significantly reduce use of methods that lack proven efficacy.
2. *Prevention of serious problem behavior in children with ASD.* The ABA community currently has in place a strong technology and recommended practices that can prevent or mitigate the development of serious problem behaviors among most children with ASD. The general pattern by which children with ASD use problem behaviors to communicate their needs and protest is increasingly well understood. Our hope is that these tools will become increasingly a part of the educational and treatment scene landscape, including timely, direct parent support and contextualized training.
3. *Crisis management.* Crisis management must be considered as part of a comprehensive behavior support agenda (Carr et al., 1994) for students diagnosed with ASD. Because the majority of crisis management programs used by schools claim to be behaviorally based, the ABA community has at least some responsibility to see that crisis management is done correctly. In particular ABA protocol and thinking can play a leadership role in dealing with issues related to restraint and seclusion timeout. In fact, the Association for Behavior Analysis International has issued a position statement on the use of restraint and seclusion (August 5, 2010). The position includes a strongly worded statement that opposes "inappropriate and/or unnecessary use of seclusion, restraint, or other intrusive interventions" (p. 1).
4. *Linkage with pediatricians and other medical personnel.* Pediatricians and other medical personnel are typically a primary source of support for young children with ASD and their families. Thus, it is essential that professionals with behavior analytic skills work and collaborate

with these professionals, including sharing information about prevention and treatment of problem behaviors (Friman, 2010).

5. *Research in support of verbal behavior.* Verbal behavior clearly has both potential and signs of being an evidence-based method (Sweeney-Kerwin et al., 2007; Ward et al., 2007). The next step in advancing these methods should involve comprehensive and large-scale demonstrations of effectiveness, especially in school settings.

6. *Safety.* Safety from unintentional injury for children with ASD is an important target for behavioral intervention. The risk of serious injury and death among children with ASD is estimated to be two to three times greater than that of typically developing children (Shavelle, Strauss, & Pickett, 2001). Because there is a paucity of literature on this topic and related to the obvious positive role that ABA can play on this front it will be important for ASD stakeholders, including the ABA community, to more aggressively consider behavioral safety interventions for individuals with ASD.

7. *Access to consumer-friendly ABA training materials for teachers and parents.* Clearly there is a need for teacher- and family-friendly behavioral support materials. There is no question that ABA methodology bodes well for individuals with ASD. The future challenge will be to develop and disseminate ABA-focused literature that will permit teachers, parents and others to use ABA techniques with integrity and fidelity. Some materials are currently available (e.g., Harris & Weiss, 2007; Partington, 2008); and additional development of these documents will hopefully fill an ever growing need for evidence-based ABA information.

8. *Address the social-behavior needs of students with ASD.* By definition individuals with ASD have social deficits and experience lifelong social challenges. To be sure there is no question that instruction and support of appropriate social behavior is a significant need in the field and one to which ABA can make a significant contribution. Yet current K–12 school programming often includes minimal support of students' social needs. Thus, future initiatives must include greater emphasis on applications of behavior analytic teaching and support efforts to improve core social competency deficits among students with ASD.

9. *Career and vocational preparation for students with ASD.* Assisting adolescents and young adults with ASD prepare for life beyond high school is critical. In this regard behavior analysts in the future must be able to refine and adapt current ABA methods approaches to make them more utilitarian for assisting older students and adults as they prepare for and enter the world of work and deal with other life challenges.

10. *Continue the transition from reduction to instruction.* Behavior analysts have lingered far too long under the guise of playing the role of "reduction professional." That is, members of the discipline have not been sufficiently assertive in pressing for instructional opportunities and alternatives to punishment for unacceptable behavior. In this role we see future ABA professionals being far more actively involved as evidence-based advocates for specialized behavioral instructional methods and other strategies that advance quality of life for persons with ASD and their families. We see these future roles playing out in a variety of settings, including homes, communities, and schools.

Conclusion and Summary

Applied behavior analysis is a scientific method for understanding and changing behavior that has long been used to help persons with autism. ABA relies on scientific methods: experimentation; precise measurement; careful analysis aided by visual display of data; replication to establish principles of learning; and a broad array of evidence-based behavior change procedures. The ABA community has struggled at times, as have other disciplines that have faced the challenge of addressing the needs of persons with ASD. Early ABA applications, unfortunately, tended to rely on punishment; to not adequately consider setting and context factors; and to not fully consider the unique characteristics of children with ASD. In spite of this history ABA has made enormous advances in the understanding, treatment, and support of persons with ASD; and the discipline offers a strong beacon of hope for individuals with autism-related disabilities and their families. Early on behavioral pioneers saw the success of behavior analysis with children with autism, and these early-stage successes have continually been refined. As a result ABA methods are being used in a progressively more contextualized and positive fashion.

Behavior analysts are largely responsible for developing and refining a broad array of specialized teaching tactics that form the foundation for home and school evidence-based programming for learners with ASD. The field of ABA will continue to develop, and will carry on its long-standing tradition of identifying and validating empirically valid and scientifically based methods that will improve the lives of individuals with ASD, their families, and their communities.

References

Association for Behavior Analysis International. (2010). *Statement on restraint and seclusion*. Retrieved from http://www.abainternational.org/ABA/statements/RestraintSeclusion.asp

Baer, D. M., Wolf, M. M., & Risley, T. R. (1968). Some current dimensions of applied behavior analysis. *Journal of Applied Behavior Analysis, 1,* 91–97.

Behavior Analysis Certification Board. (n.d.). *BCBA and BCABA behavior analyst task list* (3rd ed.). Retrieved from http://www.bacb.com/cues/frame_about.html

Bettelheim, B. (1962). *Dialogues with mothers*. Glencoe, IL: Free Press.

Bettelheim, B. (1967). *The empty fortress: Infantile autism and the birth of the self*. New York: Free Press.

Bettelheim, B. (1974). *A home for the heart*. New York: Knopf.

Carbone, V. J., Morgenstern, B., Zecchin-Tirri, G., & Kolberg, L. (2010). The role of the reflexive-conditioned motivating operation (CMO-R) during discrete trial instruction of children with autism. *Focus on Autism and Other Developmental Disabilities, 25*(2), 110–124.

Carr, E. G., (1977). The motivation of self-injurious behavior: A review of some hypotheses. *Psychology Bulletin, 84,* 800–816.

Carr, E. G., & Durand, V. M. (1985). Reducing behavior problems through functional communication training. *Journal of Applied Behavior Analysis, 18,* 111–126.

Carr, E. G., Levin, L., McConnachie, G., Carlson, J. I., Kemp, D. C., & Smith, C. E. (1994). *Communication-based interventions for problem behavior: A user's guide for producing positive change*. Baltimore, MD: Brookes.

Committee on Educational Interventions for Children with Autism: Division of Behavioral and Social Sciences and Education: National Research Council. (2001). *Educating children with autism*. Washington, DC: National Academy Press.

Cooper, J. O., Heron, T. E., & Heward, W. L. (2007). *Applied behavior analysis* (2nd ed.). Upper Saddle River, NJ: Pearson Educational.

Duker, P. C., Didden, R., & Sigafoos, J. (2004). *One-to-one training: Instructional procedures for learners with developmental disabilities*. Austin, TX: Pro-Ed.

Durand, V. M., & Carr, E. G. (1991). Functional communication training to reduce challenging behavior: Maintenance and application in new settings. *Journal of Applied Behavior Analysis, 24,* 251–256.

Eikeseth, S., Smith, T., Jahr, E., & Eldevik, S. (2002). Intensive behavioral treatment at school for 4- to 7-year-old children with autism. *Behavior Modification, 26*(1), 49–68.

Ferster, C. B. (1961). Positive reinforcement and the behavioral deficits of autistic children. *Child Development, 32,* 437–456.

Friman, P. C. (2010). Come on in, the water is fine: Achieving mainstream relevance through integration with primary medical care. *The Behavior Analyst, 33,* 19–36.

Goldsmith, T. R., LeBlanc, L. A., & Sautter, R. A. (2007). Teaching intraverbal behavior to children with autism. *Research in Autism Spectrum Disorders, 1,* 1–13.

Green, G. (2010). *Applied behavior analysis for autism*. Cambridge Center for Behavioral Studies. Retrieved from http://www.behavior.org/resource.php?id=300

Green, G., Brennan, L. C., & Fein, D. (2002). Intensive behavioral treatment for a toddler at high risk for autism. *Behavior Modification, 26*(1), 69–102.

Greer, R. D., & Ross, D. E. (2007). *Verbal behavior analysis: Inducing and expanding new verbal capabilities in children with language delays.* Boston, MA: Allyn & Bacon.

Gresham, F. M., & MacMillan, D. L. (1998). Early intervention project: Can its claims be substantiated and its effects replicated? *Journal of Autism and Developmental Disorders, 28,* 5–13.

Hagopian, L. P., Contrucci-Kuhn, S. A., Long, E. S., & Rush, K. S. (2005). Schedule thinning following communication training: Using competing stimuli to enhance tolerance to decrements in reinforcer density. *Journal of Applied Behavior Analysis, 38,* 177–193.

Hall, G. A., & Sundberg, M. L. (1987). Teaching mands by manipulating conditioned establishing operations. *The Analysis of Verbal Behavior, 5,* 41–53.

Harris, S. L., & Weiss, M. J. (2007). *Right from the start: Behavioral intervention for young children with autism.* Bethesda, MD: Woodbine House.

Horner, R. H., Carr, E. G., Strain, P. S., Todd, A. W., & Reed, H. K. (2002). Problem behavior interventions for young children with autism: A research synthesis. *Journal of Autism and Developmental Disorders, 32,* 423–446.

Horner, R. H., Dunlap, G., Koegel, R. L., Carr, E. G., Sailor, W., Anderson, J. ... O'Neill, R. E. (1990). Toward a technology of "nonaversive" behavioral support. *The Journal of the Association for Persons with Severe Handicaps, 15,* 125–132.

Howard, J. S., Sparkman, C. R., Cohen, H. G., Green, G., & Stanislaw, H. (2005). A comparison of intensive behavior analytic and eclectic treatments for young children with autism. *Research in Developmental Disabilities, 26,* 359–383.

Hundert, J. (2009). *Inclusion of students with autism: Using ABA-based supports in general education.* Austin, TX: Pro-ed.

Ingvarsson, E. T., & Hollobaugh, T. (2010). Acquisition of intraverbal behavior: Teaching children with autism to mand for answers to questions. *Journal of Applied Behavior Analysis, 43,* 1–17.

Ingvarsson, E. T., Kahng, S., & Hausman, N. L. (2008). Some effects of noncontingent positive reinforcement on multiply controlled problem behaviors and compliance in a demand context. *Journal of Applied Behavior Analysis, 41,* 435–440.

Iovannone, R., Dunlap, G., Huber, H., & Kincaid, D. (2003). Effective educational practices for students with autism spectrum disorder. *Focus on Autism and Other Developmental Disabilities, 18*(3), 150–165.

Iwata, B. A., Dorsey, M. F., Slifer, K. J., Bauman, K. E., & Richman, G. S. (1994). Toward a functional analysis of self-injury. *Journal of Applied Behavior Analysis, 27,* 197–209. (Reprinted from *Analysis and Intervention in Developmental Disabilities, 2,* 3–20, 1982)

Johnston, J. M., Foxx, R. M., Jacobson, J. W., Green, G., & Mulick, G. A. (2006). Positive behavior support and applied behavior analysis. *The Behavior Analyst, 29,* 51–74.

Kahng, S., Hendrickson, D. J., & Vu, C. P. (2000). Comparison of single and multiple functional communication training responses for the treatment of problem behavior. *Journal of Applied Behavior Analysis, 33,* 321–324.

Kanner, L. (1943). Autistic disturbances of affective contact. *Nervous Child, 2,* 217–250.

Kelly, M. E., Shillingburg, M. A., Castro, M. J., Addison, L. R., & LaRue, R. H. (2007). Further evaluation of emerging speech in children with developmental disabilities: Training verbal behavior. *Journal of Applied Behavior Analysis, 40,* 431–445.

Kodak, T., & Clements, A. (2009). Acquisition of mands and tacts with concurrent echoic training. *Journal of Applied Behavior Analysis, 42,* 839–843.

LeBlanc, L. A., Esch, J., Sidener, T. M., & Firth, A. M. (2006). Behavioral language interventions for children with autism: Comparing applied verbal behavior and naturalistic teaching approaches. *The Analysis of Verbal Behavior, 22,* 49–60.

Lovaas, O. I. (1964). Control of food intake in children by reinforcement of relevant verbal behavior. *Journal of Abnormal and Social Psychology, 68,* 672–678.

Lovaas, O. I. (1987). Behavioral treatment and normal educational and intellectual functioning in young autistic children. *Journal of Consulting and Clinical Psychology, 55,* 3–9.

Lovaas, O. I., Koegel, R. L., & Schreibman, L. (1979). Stimulus overselectivity in autism: A review of the literature. *Psychological Bulletin, 86,* 1236–1254.

Lovaas, O. I., Schaeffer, B., & Simmons, J. Q. (1965). Building social behavior in autistic children by use of electric shock. *Journal of Experimental Studies in Personality, 1,* 99–109.

Lovaas, O. I., & Simmons, J. Q. (1969). Manipulation of self-destruction in three retarded children. *Journal of Applied Behavior Analysis, 2,* 143–157.

Lovaas, O. I., & Smith, T. (1989). A comprehensive behavior theory of autistic children: Paradigm for research and treatment. *Journal of Behavior Therapy and Experimental Psychiatry, 20,* 17–29.

Machalicek, W., O'Reilly, M. F., Beretvas, N., Sigafoos, J., & Lancioni, G. E. (2007). A review of interventions in school settings for students with autism spectrum disorder. *Research in Autism Spectrum Disorders, 1,* 229–246.

Mancil, G. R. (2006). Functional communication training: A review of the literature related to children with autism. *Education and Training in Developmental Disabilities, 41,* 213–224.

Maurice, C. (1993). *Let me hear your voice: A family's triumph over autism.* New York: Knopf.

McEachin, J. J., Smith, T., & Lovaas, O. I. (1993). Long-term outcome for children with autism who received early intensive behavioral treatment. *American Journal on Mental Retardation, 97,* 359–372.

McGee, G. G., Krantz, P. J., Mason, D., & McClannahan, L. E. (1983). A modified incidental teaching procedure for autistic youth: Acquisition and generalization of receptive object labels. *Journal of Applied Behavior Analysis, 16,* 329–338.

McGee, G. G., Morrier, M. J., & Daly, T. (1999). An incidental teaching approach to early intervention for toddlers with autism. *The Journal of the Association for Persons with Severe Handicaps, 24,* 133–146.

Miltenberger, R. G. (1997). *Behavior modification: Principles and procedures.* Pacific Grove, CA: Brooks/Cole.

Miranda-Linne, F., & Melin, L. (1992). Acquisition, generalization, and spontaneous use of color adjectives: A comparison of incidental teaching and traditional discrete trial procedures for children with autism. *Research in Developmental Disabilities, 13,* 191–210.

Moskowitz, L. J., Adamek, L., & Tenebaum, S. P. (2009). Edward G. Carr 1947–2009: An obituary. *Journal of Autism and Developmental Disorders, 39.* 1762–1764. doi 10.1007/s10803-009-0876-3

National Autism Center. (2009). *Evidence-based practices and autism in the schools: A guide to providing appropriate interventions to students with autism spectrum disorders.* Randolph, MA: National Autism Center.

Neef, N. A., & Peterson, S. M. (2007). Functional behavior assessment. In J. O. Cooper, T. E. Heron, & W. L. Heward (Eds.), *Applied behavior analysis* (2nd ed., pp. 500–524). Upper Saddle River, NJ: Pearson Educational.

Northup, J., Wacker, D., Sasso, G., Steege, M., Cigrand, K., Cook, J., & DeRaad, A. (1991). A brief functional analysis of aggressive and alternative behavior in an outclinic setting. *Journal of Applied Behavior Analysis, 24,* 509–522.

O'Neill, R. E., Horner, R. H., Albin, R. W., Sprague, J. R., Storey, K., & Newton, J. S. (1997). *Functional assessment and program development for problem behavior: A practical handbook* (2nd ed.). Pacific Grove, CA: Brooks/Cole.

Partington, J. W. (2008). *Capturing the motivation of children with autism or other developmental delays.* Pleasant Hill, CA: Behavior Analysts.

Partington, J. W., Sundberg, M. L., Newhouse, L., & Spengler, S. M. (1994). Overcoming an autistic child's failure to acquire a tact repertoire. *Journal of Applied Behavior Analysis, 27,* 733–734.

Pollak, R. (1997). *The creation of Dr. B: A biography of Bruno Bettelheim.* New York: Simon & Schuster.

Risley, T. R. (1968). The effects and side effects of punishing the autistic behaviors of a deviant child. *Journal of Applied Behavior Analysis, 1,* 21–34.

Sallows, G. O., & Graupner, T. D. (2005). Intensive behavioral treatment for children with autism: Four-year outcome and predictors. *American Journal on Mental Retardation, 110,* 417–438.

Schreibman, L. (1975). Effects of within-stimulus and extra-stimulus prompting on discrimination learning in autistic children. *Journal of Applied Behavior Analysis, 8,* 91–112.

Scott, J., & Baldwin, W. L. (2005). The challenge of early intensive intervention. In D. Zager (Ed.), *Autism spectrum disorders: Identification, education, and treatment* (3rd ed., pp. 173–228). Mahwah, NJ: Erlbaum.

Shavelle, R. M., Strauss, D. J., & Pickett, J. (2001). Causes of death in autism. *Journal of Autism and Developmental Disorders, 31,* 569–576.

Sheinkopf, S. J., & Siegel, B. (1998). Home-based behavioral treatment of young children with autism. *Journal of Autism and Developmental Disorders, 28*(1), 15–23.

Simpson, R. L. (2005a). Evidence-based practices and students with autism spectrum disorders. *Focus on Autism and Other Developmental Disabilities, 20*(3), 140–149.

Simpson, R. L. (2005b). *Autism spectrum disorders: Interventions and treatments for children and youth.* Thousand Oaks, CA: Corwin.

Skinner, B. F. (1953). *Science and human behavior.* New York: Macmillan.

Skinner, B. F. (1957). *Verbal behavior.* Acton, MA: Copley.

Smith, T. (2001). Discrete trial training in the treatment of autism. *Focus on Autism and Other Developmental Disabilities, 16*(2), 86–92.

Smith, T., Eikeseth, S., Klevstrand, M., & Lovaas, O. I. (1997). Intensive behavioral treatment for preschoolers with severe mental retardation and pervasive developmental disorder. *American Journal on Mental Retardation, 102,* 238–249.

Smith, T., Groen, A. D., & Wynn, J. W. (2000). Randomized trial of intensive early intervention for children with pervasive developmental disorder. *American Journal on Mental Retardation, 105,* 269–285.

Stafford, M. W., Sundberg, M. L., & Braam, S. (1988). A preliminary investigation of the consequences that define the mand and the tact. *The Analysis of Verbal Behavior, 6,* 61–71.

Sulzer-Azaroff, B., & Mayer, G. R. (1991). *Behavior analysis for lasting change.* Orlando, FL: Harcourt Brace Jovanovich.

Sundberg, M. L. (1991). 301 research topics from Skinner's book *Verbal behavior. The Analysis of Verbal Behavior, 9,* 81–96.

Sundberg, M. L., & Michael, J. (2001). The benefits of Skinner's analysis of verbal behavior for children with autism. *Behavior Modification, 25*(5), 698–724.

Sundberg, M. L., & Partington, J. W. (1998). *Teaching language to children with autism or other developmental disabilities.* Pleasant Hill, CA: Behavior Analysts.

Sundberg, M. L., & Partington, J. W. (1999). The need for both discrete trial and natural environment language training for children with autism. In P. M. Ghezzi, W. L. Williams, & J. E. Carr (Eds.), *Autism: Behavior analytic perspectives* (pp. 139–156). Reno, NV: Context Press.

Sweeney-Kerwin, E. J., Carbone, V. J., O'Brien, L., Zecchin, G., & Janecky, M. N. (2007). Transferring control of the mand to the motivating operation in children with autism. *The Analysis of Verbal Behavior, 23,* 89–102.

Tews, L. (2007). Early intervention for children with autism: Methodologies critique. *Developmental Disabilities Bulletin, 35,* 148–168.

Ward, S. J., Osnes, P. J., & Partington, J. W. (2007). The effects of a delay of noncontingent reinforcement during a pairing procedure in the development of stimulus control of automatically reinforced vocalizations. *The Analysis of Verbal Behavior, 23,* 103–111.

Wolf, M. M., Risley, T. R., & Mees, H. L. (1964). Application of operant conditioning procedures to the behavior problems of an autistic child. *Behavior Research and Therapy, 1,* 305–312.

Yi, J. I., Christian, L., Vittimberga, G., & Lowenkron, B. (2006). Generalized negatively reinforced manding in children with autism. *The Analysis of Verbal Behavior, 22,* 21–33.

5

DIR—THE DEVELOPMENTAL, INDIVIDUAL DIFFERENCE, RELATIONSHIP-BASED MODEL

A Dynamic Model for the 21st Century[1]

Serena Wieder

INTERDISCIPLINARY COUNCIL OF DEVELOPMENTAL AND LEARNING DISORDERS, DIR INSTITUTE

Introduction

The daunting challenge of educating children with autism involves the uniqueness of each child and how to promote the fundamental capacities necessary for development. The developmental, individual difference, relationship-based (DIR) model addresses the core deficits by emphasizing developmentally appropriate experiences needed to build higher levels of emotional and intellectual capacities through affect-based interactions based on each child's individual profile. It goes beyond focusing on specific behaviors, symptoms, or rote learning by examining how infants and children use everyday functioning to carry out emotionally meaningful goals based on their developmental levels. Each child has a unique profile characterized by types and degrees of limitations in fundamental developmental areas of functioning, such as joint attention and regulation, engagement across a wide range of emotions, two-way communication, complex problem solving, and symbolic and abstract thinking. In addition, each child has a unique profile with respect to individual differences in sensory reactivity, visual–spatial and auditory/language processing, and purposeful movement, the neurological pathways through which experience is understood. And each child must also be understood in the context of his or her family, community, and culture. By taking all three areas into account the foundation for learning can be established (Greenspan & Wieder, 1997a, 1998, 2006, 2007; Wieder & Greenspan, 1993, 2001). Parents are at the center of developmental, relationship-based approaches because of the importance of their emotional relationships with the child and the ongoing opportunities to support development. Teachers, therapists, and other caregivers play a vital role through their interactions in helping the child develop (Wieder & Greenspan, 2006).

The DIR model provides a developmental framework for assessment and intervention (Greenspan & Wieder, 2000; Wieder & Greenspan, 2001). Central to these interventions are the ways in which the child's natural emotions and emotional interactions affect intelligence and related cognitive and language abilities, as well as social and self-regulation skills. While DIR emphasizes early identification and intervention with preschool and school aged children, as a developmental model it provides a life span perspective which guides intervention for those with continuing uneven developmental capacities and emotional, behavioral, and cognitive challenges.

DIR theory hypothesizes that deficits occur in autism stem from compromise in the infant's ability to connect emotions or intent to motor planning and sequencing to sensations and, later, to early forms of symbolic expression (Greenspan, 2001; Greenspan, DeGangi, & Wieder, 2001; Greenspan & Wieder, 1998, 2003a; Greenspan & Shanker, 2004). Creating states of heightened pleasurable and other affects tailored to the child's unique motor and sensory-processing profile helps to develop and strengthen the connection between sensation, affect, and motor action. This leads to more purposeful affective behavior, with increased reciprocal signaling as the child is engaged and interacting more continuously, becoming increasingly aware of who she is and how she affects others, creating the opportunities for greater symbolic functioning through language, play, and higher-level thinking skills. DIR stresses the importance of emotional and sensory processing areas and focuses on affect-based interactions to strengthen the connections between these areas to promote development (Greenspan & Wieder, 1999: Wieder, 1994). Currently neuroscience highlights the poor connectivity between brain regions which derail the intake, comprehension, and integration of information essential for learning and functioning (Garber, 2007; Minshew, Goldstein, & Siegel, 1997; Mostofsky et al., 2006; Williams & Minshew, 2007). Emerging neuroscience research is also beginning to reflect the impact of interventions related to connectivity (Dziuk et al., 2007).

Historical Background

Developmental approaches are based on an understanding of development which recognizes the importance of relationships, interactions with parents and caregivers as well as peers, in various environments. Developmental approaches take into account the individual differences in the way infants and children process and comprehend sensations and plan actions and provide the interactive experiences which allow it to develop. This became very evident in a 6-year long NIMH research study, the Clinical Infant Development Program, directed by Greenspan and Wieder in the late 1970s and early 1980s with high risk infants in multiproblem families (Greenspan et al., 1987). It utilized the Developmental-Structuralist framework, later known as the Functional Emotional Developmental Levels (Greenspan, 1979, 1989, 1992b, 1997; Greenspan, DeGangi, & Wieder, 2001) and integrated the emerging understanding of individual differences and infant mental health approaches concerned with emotional development and parent–infant interactions. The study considered both theoretical models of emotional and cognitive development and the rich clinical intervention and research of such pioneers as Brazelton (Brazelton & Kramer, 1990), Mahler, Pine, and Bergman (1975), Fraiberg (1980), Lourie (1971), Provence (1983), and others concerned with foundations for healthy development and its challenges. This group rejected the psychogenic theory of autism which blamed parents for their children's autism as implied by Kanner, Asperger, and Bettelheim in prior decades (Asperger, 1944; Bettelheim, 1967; Kanner, 1943). At the time, few thought of genetically based sources, or parent accommodation to their child's hypersensitivities, or parents' despair over unresponsive children.

During the NIMH study it became apparent that developmental and relationship-based approaches were not yet part of the developmental disability world. Autism was first being defined in the *Diagnostic and Statistical Manual of Mental Disorders* (*DSM-III;* American Psychiatric Association, 1980) and Ivor Lovaas was developing the behavioral models to treat autism based on principles of reinforcement and conditioning (Lovaas, 1987). It was also at this time when laws were passed to ensure special education for children with special needs and structured teaching models were already underway (Marcus, Semrau, & Schopler, 1977)

Greenspan and Wieder shifted their attention to the diagnosis and treatment of children with multisystem developmental disorders and autism, recognizing the critical impact of sensory and motor processing challenges and integrating these with the emotional and relationship based approaches from infant mental health and work with parents. They recognized the need for a multidimensional approach to diagnosis and treatment of autism and developmental disabilities within the broader framework of diagnostic classification of infants and young children. Greenspan and Wieder cochaired Zero to Three's Diagnostic Classification Task Force which published *Diagnostic Classification: 0–3: Diagnostic Classification of Mental Health and Developmental Disorders of Infancy and Early Childhood* (Wieder, 1994b), a relationship-based guide to understanding emotional and developmental disorders of infancy and early childhood, introducing regulatory disorders and the functional emotional developmental levels in a diagnostic framework. Later, an interdisciplinary clinical diagnostic guide for infant mental health, as well as neurodevelopmental, language, visual–spatial, and learning differences for children through age 5 was published (The Interdisciplinary Council on Developmental and Learning Disorders, 2005). The intervening years were devoted to developing the principles and methods of the DIR model for children on the autism spectrum. These were described in various articles (Greenspan, 1992b; Greenspan & Wieder, 1997, 1999, 2001, 2003; Wieder, 1996b; Wieder & Greenspan, 2001) and in *The Child with Special Needs* (Greenspan & Wieder, 1998) and *Engaging Autism* (Greenspan & Wieder, 2006). Attention was also given to the role of DIR in assessment and intervention in education (Wieder, 1996b; Wieder & Greenspan, 1993; Wieder & Kalmanson, 2000).

The field at large also started to embrace developmental approaches in terms of their focus on affective engagement necessary for a child to learn and relationship-based approaches became part of a broader category of working with children with autism and other special needs (Gutstein, 2002; Rogers & Dawson, 2010; Wetherby, Prizant, & Hutchinson, 1998). In spite of support for and greater interest in the role of emotions in human development, emotions took a back seat to cognition, language, and memory. Until recently, most research outcomes were reported in terms of IQ scores, class placement, and language measures rather than measures of the developmental levels and pathways through which such distinctly human capacities as symbol formation, language, and reflective thinking emerge in the life of each new infant and child. Explorations of the types of thinking that are part of skillful social interactions (i.e., emotional intelligence), and concepts of multiple intelligences also supported and increased interest in the role of emotions (Gardner, 1983; Goleman, 1995). In a clinical outcome study reported below, Greenspan and Wieder showed that by working on emotional interactions, a subgroup of children diagnosed with autistic spectrum disorders can learn to engage with others, enjoy peers, think creatively, logically, and reflectively, and do well academically in regular classes (Greenspan & Wieder, 2005a).

The DIR Pathways to Core Psychological Deficits in Autism

Various deficits have been suggested in autism including empathy and seeing the world from another person's perspective (Baron-Cohen, Leslie, & Frith, 1985); higher-level abstract thinking, including making inferences (Minshew et al., 1997); shared attention, including social referencing and problem solving (Mundy, Sigman, & Kasari, 1990); emotional reciprocity (Baranek, 1999; Dawson & Galpert, 1990); and functional (pragmatic) language (Wetherby & Prizant, 1993). Clinical work and research suggest that the deficits in the abilities listed above stem from a compromised earlier capacity to connect emotions or intent to motor planning and sequencing and to sensations, and later to early forms of symbolic expression of their intent or emotions. It is hypothesized that the biological differences associated with ASD may express themselves through the derailing of this connection, leading to both the primary and secondary features of ASD (Greenspan & Shanker, 2004; Greenspan & Wieder, 2003a,b, 2007).

In healthy development, an infant connects the sensory system to the motor system through affect; for example, seeing and turning to look at a caregiver's smiling face or wooing voice and beginning to recognize patterns as they share attention, take pleasure in interactions, read each others' cues, and respond to each other over and over again through gaze, vocalizations, and gestures. By the end of the first year the infant recognizes variations in his caregiver's affect as well as his own feelings related to such emotions as love, anger, feeling proud, or caregiver's disapproval. By the second year of life, these patterns lead to a sense of self as a purposeful agent and a differentiated sense of others, and ultimately enable a child to form and give meaning to symbols conveyed through affect leading to higher levels of thinking. Understanding this complex process in typical development has enabled the earlier identification of very young children with challenges and guides the interventions tailored to the child's biological profile and vulnerabilities. Such early intervention increases the likelihood of developing abilities for joint attention, theory of mind, and higher levels of language and symbolic thinking (Greenspan & Shanker, 2004; Wieder & Greenspan, 2003).

The D, the I, and the R

The DIR model identifies the child's **D**evelopmental level of emotional and intellectual functioning; determines his or her **I**ndividual way of reacting to and comprehending movement, sounds, sights, and other sensations; and formulates learning **R**elationships and affect based interactions at home, in school, and in different therapies (speech, occupational/physical, visual–spatial therapy) geared to the child's profile. The individualized learning relationships utilize the child's natural interests and emotions and create interactions that help him or her master the capacities for relating, communicating, and thinking.

The "D"—Developmental Levels of Emotional and Intellectual Functioning, or Functional Emotional Developmental Levels (FEDL)

1. *Regulation and Joint Attention (between infant and caretaker).* From birth to 3 months of age, an infant's capacity grows for calm, focused interest in the sights and sounds of the outer world while she begins to share her interests with the caregiver. This first level or capacity expands in duration, range, and stability as the child develops.
2. *Forming Attachments and Engaging in Relationships.* During the first 4 to 5 months, the infant and his parents become more and more intimate as they interact with each other with warmth, trust, and familiarity. They use their senses to enjoy each other through looks, hugs, songs, and dancing together. Over time the infant will need to remain related and engaged across the full range of emotions, even when disappointed, scared, or angry or feeling other stresses.
3. *Intentional Two-Way Affective Communication.* Between 4 and 10 months, the purposeful, continuous flow of interactions with gestures and reciprocating emotions gets underway. The infant begins to act purposefully, now that she has matured and is more aware of her body and the functions it can perform. As the infant gains motor control over her body and intent, she is better able to communicate her desires. With the emerging abilities to reach, sit and turn, crawl and creep, and give and take or drop objects, the infant's awareness of the interpersonal world is growing, as is her awareness of her body in space and in relation to others who may also be moving.
4. *Complex Social Problem Solving.* Between 9 and 18 months, an infant—now an emerging toddler—develops the capacity to problem-solve using social interactions without interrupting the flow. He has learned the back and forth rhythm of interactive emotional signaling and

begins to use this ability to think about and solve his problems; that is, to help get or do what he wants and finds emotionally meaningful such as taking Daddy by the hand and pulling him to the door to go outside and play. All of the child's senses work with his motor system as he interacts with others to solve problems. Difficulties arise when he becomes aware that things are not as they should be based on prior experiences as recorded in his mind; and he encounters new difficulties to solve as his experience expands.

5. *Emotional Ideas*. Between 18 and 36 months, the toddler begins to represent or symbolize her intentions, feelings, and ideas in imaginative play or language, using gestures, words, and symbols. The toddler now picks up the toy phone to call, sets up a picnic or tea party, takes the sick baby to the doctor, or repairs his car in the garage before driving somewhere. These first ideas come from experiences in real life that can now be enacted in pretend dramas as the child experiments with different roles and feelings.

6. *Emotional Thinking, Logic, and Sense of Reality*. At about 3 years, the young child begins to combine ideas together to tell a story as she develops more logical thinking and better understanding of herself and others, and of what is real or not real. Her stories may still use imaginative characters and animal figures who talk and even are magical as she discovers she needs more power to encounter the conflicts in life, but her reasoning skills click in to understand sequential bridges, and the stories become increasingly logical and realistic. Over the next few years, the child's emotional and mental abilities move toward abstract thinking and she develops the ability to distinguish reality from fantasy, self from nonself, and one feeling from another; and to make distinctions concerning time and space.

7. *Multicausal and Comparative Thinking*. At this level the child "deepens the plot" as he can explore multiple motives, get opinions, and compare and contrast ideas. The child can express how he would feel "in your shoes" and predicts what you will do based on your "affect cues" such as deception, fairness, and justice.

8. *Relativistic or Gray-Area Thinking*. Here, the child differentiates more of her thoughts, rather than thinking only in "black and white" terms. The lion may pay a price for killing the zebra, or the bear devouring all the honey will disappoint her friend. The child now considers different possibilities and contingencies, and is aware of different outcomes and of how she would feel under different circumstances.

9. *Self-Reflection or Thinking Using an Internal Standard*. Now the child has a sense of himself; he can look at and reflect on his performance and feelings. He can question why he is feeling a certain way and contrast this with how he usually feels, or he can compare his current efforts with earlier ones. This kind of thinking allows him to make inferences about himself and others, and creates new choices and ideas.

At all levels variations may exist in robustness, stability, and completeness of the child's efforts. Stress related to health or learning difficulties, family change, moves, and other events can throw a child off course. It is critical to meet each child at the level she is in at the moment; both over- and underestimating a child has risks. A developmental perspective calls for lifelong learning; the time this takes each child may vary, but ascension to each level should be pursued (Greenspan & Wieder, 2003a, 2007).

The "I"—Individual Differences in Sensory Modulation, Sensory Processing, Sensory Affective Processing, and Motor Planning and Sequencing

These biologically based individual differences are the result of genetic, prenatal, perinatal, and maturational variations or deficits, and can be characterized in at least four ways:

1. Sensory modulation, including hypo- and hyperreactivity in each sensory modality, including touch, sound, smell, vision, and movement in space.

2. Sensory processing in each sensory modality, including auditory processing and language and visual–spatial processing. Processing includes the capacity to register, decode, and comprehend sequences and abstract patterns. Without comprehension development cannot move forward.
3. Sensory–affective processing in each modality (e.g., the ability to process and react to affect, including the capacity to connect "intent" or affect to motor planning and sequencing, language, and symbols). This processing capacity may be especially relevant for ASD.
4. Motor planning and sequencing, including the capacity to sequence actions, behaviors, and symbols, including symbols in the form of thoughts, words, visual images, and spatial concepts.

The "R"—Relationships and Interactions

Relationship and affective interaction patterns include developmentally appropriate, or inappropriate, interactive relationships with parent, caregiver, and family patterns. Interaction patterns between the child and caregivers and family members bring the child's biology into the larger developmental progression and can contribute to the negotiation of the child's functional developmental capacities. Developmentally appropriate interactions mobilize the child's intentions and affects and enable the child to broaden his or her range of experience at each level of development and to move from one functional developmental level to the next. In contrast, interactions that do not deal with the child's functional developmental level or individual differences can undermine progress. For example, a caregiver who is aloof may not be able to engage an infant who is underreactive and self-absorbed; or there can be constrictions of affect, anxiety, rigidities and obsessions, or acting out behavior in a child who does not have the interactive support of a parent to explore negative emotions symbolically.

Theory into Practice: DIR Assessment and Intervention Model Assessment

A comprehensive assessment of all the relevant functional areas requires the following components, which can take a number of sessions with the child and family to complete (Greenspan & Wieder, 2000). These include (a) two or more clinical observations of 45 minutes each, of child–caregiver or clinician–child interactions; (b) developmental history and review of current functioning; (c) review of family and caregiver functioning; (d) review of standard diagnostic assessments, current programs, and patterns of interaction; (e) consultation with speech pathologists, occupational and physical therapists, educators, and mental health colleagues, including the use of structured tests as needed; and (f) neurological/biomedical evaluation (see Interdisciplinary Council on Developmental and Learning Disorders, n.d.).

The assessment leads to an individualized functional profile that captures each child's unique developmental features outlined above in the description of DIR and creates individually tailored intervention programs (i.e., tailoring the program to the child rather than fitting the child to a general program). The profile describes each of the child's functional developmental capacities (D), contributing biological processing differences (I), and environmental interactive patterns, including the different interaction patterns available to the child at home, at school, with peers, and in other settings (R).

Understanding children's developmental variations has enabled the dynamic formulation of subtypes for neurodevelopmental disorders of relating and communicating (NDRC), which can guide treatment and research as well as training. While almost all the children with an NDRC or ASD diagnosis evidence language and visual–spatial thinking sequencing challenges, they may show very different biologically based patterns of sensory and emotional reactivity, processing, and motor planning (Greenspan & Wieder, 1999). For example, the child may tend to be overresponsive to sensations, such as sound or touch (e.g., covers ears or gets dysregulated with lots of light touch), or crave sensory experience (e.g., actively seeks touch, sound, and different movement patterns), or be underresponsive to sensations (e.g., requires highly energized vocal or proprioceptive support to be alert and attend), or some combination of the above. Similarly, the child may show relative strength in motor planning and sequencing and be very purposeful and able to execute intent (e.g., carries out many-step action patterns, such as negotiating obstacle courses or building complex block designs, etc.), or show relative weakness in motor planning and sequencing (e.g., can barely carry out simple movements and may tend to simply bang blocks or do other one- to two-step action patterns). Some may have relative strength in auditory memory (remembers or repeats long statements or materials from books, TV, records, etc.) or have difficulty remembering even simple sounds or words. Others have strong visual memory and tend to remember what is seen (such as book covers, pictures, eventually words, etc.) or have difficulty comprehending even simple pictures or objects. Many have difficulty making sense of what they see and have poor awareness of their bodies in space, and difficulty with movement, thinking, and logic, bound to repeat what they remember. These variations will require different emphases in the intervention program (Greenspan & Wieder, 2000).

The DIR Intervention Program

The theory summarized earlier has enabled the formation of a comprehensive intervention program at all ages for ASD and other developmental challenges that involves reestablishing the developmental sequence that went awry (with a special focus on helping the child become affectively connected and intentional). The program determines which of the functional emotional levels described earlier have been mastered fully, partially, or not at all. It also uses an understanding of children's individual differences in sensory modulation, processing, and motor planning to establish a relationship that creates interactive, affective opportunities to negotiate the partially mastered or yet mastered functional emotional developmental process. Rather than focus only on isolated behaviors or skills, the DIR approach focuses on these more essential functional emotional developmental processes and differences that underlie particular symptoms or behaviors (Greenspan & Wieder, 1998, 2000, 2006).

For example, rather than trying to teach a child who is perseveratively opening and closing the door to play with something else or to open and close the door for some purpose, it would use the child's interest and, warmly smiling, open the door for him to close, or start a peekaboo game, or send a stuffed animal through each time he opened the door to get reciprocal, affective interaction going and make him available for the joint experiences he needs to discover and expand the use of his body actions and mind to play more purposefully. The goal is to pinpoint what is compromised, what is getting in the way of the "next step," and construct the developmental foundations for shared attention, engagement, and reciprocity, the early building blocks for healthy emotional, social, and intellectual functioning. The DIR model, however, is not an assessment tool or a discrete intervention. It helps to systematize many of the traditionally helpful assessments and interventions and to emphasize elements of a comprehensive approach that are often ignored or left unrelated to each other.

All the elements in the DIR model have a long tradition, including speech and language therapy, occupational therapy, visual spatial cognitive therapy, special and early childhood education, and Floortime type interactions with parents consistent with the developmentally appropriate practice guidelines of the National Association for the Education of Young Children (NAEYC; Bredekamp & Copple, 1997). The DIR model, however, further defines the child's developmental level, individual processing differences, and the need for certain types of affective interactions where all the needed elements can work together toward common goals selected and balanced to fit the profile of the child and the family (Greenspan & Wieder, 2000). These elements include:

- Floortime, unstructured "play" sessions where the child initiates the ideas, and the adult both follows and challenges the child to support spontaneous, purposeful and flowing reciprocal interactions at both presymbolic and symbolic levels. Floortime, and later reflective Talktime, remain constant.
- Family consultation and counseling to help parents design and implement their comprehensive programs, support family functioning, and provide advocacy where needed.
- Semistructured activities support imitative and ritualized learning such as social games, drama, or sports, as well as problem solving activities to learn sequencing and independence. As the child progresses, various activities will become part of a child's social activities such as clubs, sports, music, and drama.
- Educational programs with parent collaboration. For children who can interact and imitate gestures or words and engage in preverbal problem solving, either an integrated inclusion program or a regular preschool program with an aide. For children not yet able to engage in preverbal problem solving or imitation, a special education program where the major focus is on engagement, purposeful gestural interaction, preverbal problem solving (a continuous flow of back-and-forth communication), and especially movement. As children prepare for academic learning, some may require individualized instruction or tutoring in reading, mathematics, visual thinking, as well as specific learning techniques. Other considerations involve smaller class size and facilitative environments which do not overwhelm the child (Greenspan & Wieder, 2000; Wieder & Kalmanson, 2000).
- Augmentative technologies and consideration of nutrition and diet, biomedical interventions, and when indicated, medications which address regulation and anxiety, possible seizures, and enhance motor planning and sequencing, concentration, and learning.

Most children on the autism spectrum need the majority if not all of these components at the start to address each major area that requires further development; each component provides the countless opportunities for successful spontaneous and semistructured interactions which have been derailed. It is a dynamic program and the frequency or changes in the program depend on the child's progress.

In this model, the therapeutic program must begin as early as possible and recent improvements in early identification now make it possible to screen and identify challenges in children under a year of age. However, the DIR model can be started at any age because it is a developmental framework which is not necessarily linked to the age of the child, and can be used with older children, adolescents, and even adults, development being a lifelong process.

The DIR intervention is different in fundamental ways from behavioral, skill building, play therapy, or psychotherapy. The primary goal of this intervention is to enable children to form a sense of themselves as intentional, interactive individuals, to develop cognitive, language, and social capacities from this basic sense of intentionality, and to progress through the functional emotional developmental capacities. Most typical children develop the first six levels by school age. Children with sensory-motor processing challenges in language comprehension and visual–spatial knowledge can develop further when affect is brought into the treatment. Affect based interactions connect these processing areas to improve comprehension and carry out intent. Affect cuing helps transform labels into meanings and support comprehension of symbolic imagery as well as communication of thoughts and feelings. These affective transformations lead to and promote abstract reasoning, gray and multicausal thinking, as well as reflective capacities of self and others (Greenspan & Shanker, 2004; Greenspan & Wieder, 1998).

Evidence-Based Practice and Research

For a disorder as complex and as heterogeneous as autism many methods of gathering evidence from various disciplines need to be considered. These include studies in developmental psychology, early intervention, infant mental health, deficits in autism spectrum disorders, and the rapidly emerging studies in neuroscience examining the role of affect and connectivity in the brain. DIR theory has informed and been informed by these various fields of practice and research. This discussion of evidenced-based practice and research will first describe the clinical reports and research supported evidence stemming from the DIR model as well as various streams and methods of related developmental and intervention research.

Built on years of research that underscores the importance of early relationships and family functioning noted earlier, the DIR model has also integrated research contributions from various disciplines, such as speech and language pathology (Gerber & Prizant, 2000; Wetherby & Prizant, 1993; Wetherby, et al., 1998), occupational therapy (Ayres, 1979; Case-Smith & Miller, 1999; Williamson & Anzalone, 1997), and social work (Shahmoon-Shanok, 2000), all of which support different elements of its complex model. These are important to consider because autism and related disorders are very diverse and various disciplines contribute to the understanding of the individual differences in children with autism as well as the variations in parent–child interactions which support development.

The first study to show evidence for the DIR/Floortime model was published in 1997 when Greenspan and Wieder reviewed charts of 200 children who were part of a cohort of children seen by the authors for a minimum of 2 years of treatment during a period of 8 years (Greenspan & Wieder, 1997b). The goal of the review was to reveal patterns in presenting symptoms, underlying processing difficulties, early development, and response to intervention in order to generate hypotheses for future studies. All the children met the criteria of autism or pervasive developmental disorder (PDDNOS) as described in *DSM-III-R* and *DSM-IV* (American Psychiatric Association, 1987, 1994) and scored in the autism range on the Childhood Autism Rating Scale (Schopler, Reichler, DeVellis, & Daly, 1980). The children ranged in age from 22 months to 4 years, with the majority between 2.5 and 3.5 at the initial evaluation. The study identified sensory processing and modulation difficulties in all the children and the authors hypothesized that difficulties connecting affect and sequencing capacities could be a possible common denominator derailing complex purposeful gestural communication (see Table 5.1).

Outcomes showed that after 2 years of intervention, 58% of treated children showed improvements and no longer met the criteria for ASD. These children became capable of joyful relationships, empathy, affective reciprocity, creative thinking, and healthy peer relationships. They all mastered basic capacities such as reality testing, impulse control, organization of thoughts and emotions, differentiated sense of self, and ability to experience a range of emotions. They no longer showed symptoms such as self-absorption, avoidance, self-stimulation, or perseveration. On the Childhood Autism Rating Scale (CARS), they shifted into the nonautistic range, although some still evidenced auditory or visual–spatial difficulties (which were improving) and most had some degree of fine or gross motor planning challenges. Furthermore, children who made progress tended to improve in a certain sequence. First, within several months they began showing more emotion and pleasure in relating to others. Contrary to the stereotypes of autism, they seemed eager for emotional contact; but had trouble figuring out how to achieve it. They seemed grateful when their parents helped them express their desire for interaction. After parents learned to draw them out and engage them by various Floortime approaches, even children who had been very avoidant and self-absorbed began seeking out their parents for relatedness. The results of the 200 case series, a landmark description of the full range of challenges faced by children on the autism spectrum, led to the publication of the full description of the DIR/Floortime Model in the *Clinical Practice Guidelines* (The Interdisciplinary Council for Developmental and Learning Disorders, 2005) (see Table 5.1).

In 2005, they reported a 10- to 15-year follow-up study (since the start of treatment) of a subset of 16 children diagnosed with ASD that were part of the first 200 case series and were part of the 58% of children who showed great improvements (Greenspan & Wieder, 2005a). The children were all boys, ranged in age between 12 and 17, with a mean of 13.9 years and had at least 2 years (maximum 5) of DIR intervention, between 2.0 and 8.5 years of age. Ten to 15 years following the end of intervention, this group presented as empathetic, creative, and reflective adolescents, with healthy peer relationships and solid academic skills. Based on these findings, the authors suggested that some children with ASD can master the core deficits and reach levels of development formerly thought unattainable.

TABLE 5.1 200 Cases of Children with Autistic Spectrum Disorders: Presenting Profiles

	Patients with Mild to Severe Impairment	*Description of Functional Emotional Developmental Component (FEDL)*
Presenting Functional, Emotional, Developmental Levels	24%	Partially engaged and purposeful with limited use of symbols (ideas)
	40%	Partially engaged with limited complex problem-solving interactive sequences (half of this group evidenced only simple purposeful behavior)
	31%	Partially engaged with only fleeting purposeful behavior
	5%	No affective engagement
Sensory Modulation	19%	Over-reactive to sensation
	39%	Under-reactive to sensation (with 11% craving sensation)
	36%	Mixed reactivity to sensation
	6%	Not classified
Motor Planning Dysfunction	52%	Mild to moderate motor planning dysfunction
	48%	Severe motor planning dysfunction
Low Muscle Tone	17%	Motor planning dysfunction with significant degree of low muscle tone
Visual-spatial Processing Dysfunction	22%	Relative strength (e.g., can find toys, good sense of direction)
	36%	Moderate impairment
	42%	Moderate to severe impairment
Auditory Processing and Language	45%	Mild to moderate impairment with intermittent abilities to imitate sounds and words or use selected words
	55%	Moderate to severe impairment with no ability to imitate or use words

The DIR model also served as the theoretical framework to develop the Greenspan Social-Emotional Growth Chart (SEGC; Greenspan, 2004). This norm-referenced surveillance of key social–emotional milestones in 1,500 infants and children from birth to 42 months of age was able to identify infants at risk for ASD with a sensitivity of 87% and specificity of 90%. It is now part of the revised Bayley Scales of Infant and Early Childhood Development (Bayley, 2005).

In 2007, Dr. Solomon and colleagues published a pilot study of The P.L.A.Y. Project Home Consultation, a widely disseminated program that trains parents of children with autism spectrum disorders in the DIR/Floortime model. Sixty-eight children 2 to 6 years old (average 3.7 years) completed an 8- to 12-month program where parents were encouraged to deliver 15 hours per week of 1:1 interaction (Solomon, Necheles, Ferch, & Bruckman, 2007). Pre–post ratings of videotapes by blind raters using the Functional Emotional Assessment Scale (FEAS) showed significant increases (p ≤ 0.0001) in child subscale scores. That is, 45.5% of children made good to very good functional developmental progress. Parent satisfaction was 90% overall and average cost of intervention was $2,500/year. Despite some limitations, the pilot study suggested that the model has potential to both enhance developmental progress of young children with autism and to be a cost-effective intervention. The P.L.A.Y. model evolved from a small, university-based clinical program into a low-cost train-the-trainer model that has the capacity to be disseminated nationally. Based on the strength of this study, in 2009 NIMH awarded Dr. Solomon the funds for a large scale randomized, controlled, community-based clinical trial of the P.L.A.Y. Project (Phase II SBIR grant), with children 3 to 5 years old with ASD.

Another randomized controlled trial DIR study is underway by Shanker, Casenheiser, and Stieben of York University, Canada assessing the efficacy of a 12-month intensive DIR/Floortime treatment for children ages 30 to 51 months old examining language and interaction outcomes. It is also the first study to use neurophysiologic changes to measure the efficacy of intervention using ERP measures in response to different facial expressions and compares typical children to the group that received DIR intervention and an untreated group.

Other neuroimaging research also provides evidence of how experience affects developing brains. For example, Siegel has shown how attuned relationships in infancy change brain structure in ways that later affect social and emotional development (Siegel, 2001). Minshew and colleagues (Minshew et al., 1997; Williams & Minshew, 2007), as well as Mostofsky and colleagues (Mostofsky et al., 2006) report evidence for the poor neural connectivity between different brain regions that might account for the poor information processing and connectivity seen in autism, which underlie individual differences.

There have also been years of developmentally based research confirming the value of intervention programs focused on supporting parent–child relationships, particularly in examining joint attention and emotional attunement. As far back as 1990, Mundi, Sigman, and Kasari reported on the benefits of focusing on joint attention and language development in autistic children (Mundi et al., 1990). Later, short term studies using randomized, controlled trials looked at joint attention and symbolic play in 58 children with autism and found that expressive language gains were greater for treatment groups which used developmental approaches compared with the control group that was based only on behavioral interventions (Kasari, Freeman, & Paparella, 2006; Kasari, Freeman, Paparella, & Jahromi, 2008).

Other behavioral–developmental researchers include Sally Rogers who developed the Early Start Denver model (Rogers, Hall, Osaki, Reaven, & Herbison, 2000), and in 2010, Dawson, Rogers, and colleagues reported positive results of a randomized controlled trial of a comprehensive developmental behavioral intervention for improving outcomes of toddlers (18–30 months) with ASD in a 2-year program (Dawson et al., 2010). They reported significant improvement in language, adaptive behavior, and change in the autism diagnosis. Their cohort maintained growth in adaptive behavior compared with a normative sample, reflecting the benefits of early intervention.

While randomized controlled trial studies are considered to be the gold standard in research, various researchers have pointed out that it has not yet been possible to do a comparison of different methods because of the numerous challenges in identifying uniform treatment groups in the heterogeneous population of autism, isolating treatments, ensuring fidelity of treatment approaches, and the lack of validated measurement tools (Committee on Educational Interventions for Children with Autism, 2001; Costa & Witten, 2009; Spreckley & Boyd, 2009).

Drew and colleagues (Drew et al., 2002), and Mahoney and Perales (2003) have suggested that other methodology be considered in lieu of randomized controlled trials, such as norm referenced scores and logic models. Mahoney and Perales showed positive results using developmental relationship based approaches (Mahoney & Perales, 2004, 2005). Gernsbacher showed intervention can change the way parents interact to increase reciprocity and that these changes are correlated with changes in social engagement and in language (Gernsbacher, 2006).

Clinically observed evidence for the DIR model continues to grow and find support evidenced by recognition as an accepted therapy by the American Academy of Pediatrics, Easter Seal Home Programs, the Centers for Disease Control, and Autism Speaks. DIR is consistent with the recommendation of the National Academy of Sciences to use comprehensive approaches that work with child and family in terms of each child's unique profile of strengths and weaknesses, and called for more appropriate outcome measures such as improvement in initiation of spontaneous communication in functional activities, and generalization of language across activities, people, and settings (Committee on Educational Interventions for Children with Autism, 2001). In 2009, Zwaigenbaum and colleagues highlighted the challenges related to early detection, diagnosis, and treatment of ASD in very young children (Zwaigenbaum et al., 2009). The authors outline the principles of effective intervention for infants and toddlers with suspected or confirmed diagnosis of ASD, including responsive and sensitive caretaking, enriched language environments using responsive rather than directive interaction styles, environments that provide opportunities for toddlers to take initiative in their learning, and interventions that are individualized and targeted to specific skills. These elements are consistent with the DIR model.

The field is advancing as evidence-based practice and evidence-based research strive to improve outcomes for children on the autism spectrum but are still bound by inherent challenges and limitations. DIR provides a dynamic and humanistic developmental model to guide this pursuit.

Training in the DIR Model

The value of a model resides in its effective implementation by well trained providers. The Interdisciplinary Council on Learning and Developmental Disorders (ICDL), founded by Stanley Greenspan and Serena Wieder, offers a range of educational opportunities through conferences, the DIR Institute, the ICDL Graduate School, online courses, books and videos, and the development of research tools (see www.icdl.com). Parents participate in many of these activities, as do professionals from the fields of education, psychology, developmental pediatrics and optometry, child psychiatry and neurology, speech, language, occupational, physical, sensory motor, and creative arts therapists. The DIR Institute uses an integrated competency-based approach to training licensed professionals of all disciplines at the DIR Institute in comprehensive assessment and intervention (Wieder, 2005). This is a case based approach that requires long term experience and work with a range of children with developmental and learning disorders to educate candidates in the competencies necessary to tailor intervention to individual differences in various settings, including schools, clinics, home programs, and individual therapy offices. Following introductory courses, candidates complete a curriculum that includes model cases, presentation of their cases, small-group process discussions, interdisciplinary seminars on assessment, intervention, and outcome evaluations. Ongoing reflective tutoring is required throughout the course of study and leads to the DIR Certificate. The DIR Institute also offers a "Training the Trainers" program and a program to support educators and consultants working with the DIR Model in Schools. The ICDL Graduate School offers the first PhD in infant mental health and developmental disorders. As the field moves toward a national credentialing system, ICDL will also develop a Floortime credential.

Conclusion

This chapter presents an overview of the DIR/Floortime model and discusses its implications for assessment, intervention, and research based on the developmental pathways related to autistic spectrum and other developmental disorders. It also presents clinical reports and research based studies supportive of the DIR/Floortime model and identifies an emerging consensus on the importance of developmental models as we move into the 21st century. DIR offers a dynamic functional developmental, relationship-based approach that can change not only the way we think about developmental disorders, how we work with children and families based on profiles of individual differences, how affect transformations lead to successively higher developmental levels, but what needs to be included in the research base to improve outcomes. The field is finally going beyond reporting IQ scores and educational placement and research needs to pursue the critical developmental deficits derailing development represented by the DIR model. Neuroscience is both revealing the pathogenesis and poor connectivity as well as the plasticity of the brain and how it can also change in response to early and intensive intervention. Assessment, intervention, and research are best defined by the relevant areas of developmental functioning as described here and focus on the primary goals for each child and family. Future research will need to pursue the complexity of developmental disorders with long term intervention outcome studies that focus on the critical junctures of development for different subtypes along the autism spectrum. Educational models are needed which utilize affect based curriculums to make learning experiences meaningful and comprehended to build the developmental foundations for higher levels of emotional and cognitive functioning. As children grow into adolescence and adulthood, the DIR model will provide the continuity of a relationship based model to guide personal, social, and community goals.

Note

1. Dedicated to the memory of Stanley Greenspan whose brilliance, caring, and dedication to children and families enhanced so many lives as he taught us to understand development and the vital force of relationships and affect to change the world.

References

American Psychiatric Association. (1980). *Diagnostic and statistical manual of mental disorders* (3rd ed.). Washington, DC: Author.

American Psychiatric Association. (1987). *Diagnostic and statistical manual of mental disorders* (3rd ed., rev.). Washington, DC: Author.

American Psychiatric Association. (1994). *Diagnostic and statistical manual of mental disorders* (4th ed.) Washington, DC: Author.

Asperger, H. (1991). Autistic psychopathology in childhood. In U. Frith (Ed.), *Autism and Asperger syndrome* (pp. 37–92). New York: Cambridge University Press. (Original work published 1944)

Ayres, J. (1979). *Sensory integration and the child.* Los Angeles, CA: Western Psychological Services.

Baranek, G. T. (1999). Autism during infancy: A retrospective video analysis of sensory-motor and social behaviors at 9–12 months of age. *Journal of Autism Developmental Disorders, 29,* 213–224.

Baron-Cohen, S., Leslie, A. M., & Frith, U. (1985). Does the autistic child have a "theory of mind"? *Cognition, 21,* 37–46.

Bayley, N. (2005). *Bayley scales of infant and toddler development* (3rd ed.; *Bayley-III*). Bulverde, TX: Psychological Corp.

Bettelheim, B. (1967). *The empty fortress: Infantile autism and the birth of the self.* New York: Free Press.

Brazelton, T., & Kramer, B. (1990). *The earliest relationship: Parents, infants, and the drama of early attachment.* Reading, MA: Addison-Wesley.

Bredekamp, S., & Copple, C. (1997). *Developmentally appropriate practices in early childhood programs.* Washington, DC: National Association for the Education of Young Children.

Case-Smith, J., & Miller, H. (1999). Occupational therapy with children with pervasive developmental disorders. *American Journal of Occupational Therapy, 53,* 506–513.

Committee on Educational Interventions for Children with Autism, National Research Council (2001). *Educating children with autism* (C. Lord & J. McGee, Eds.). Washington, DC: National Academy Press.

Costa, G. & Witter M. R. (2009). Pervasive developmental disorders. In B. A. Mowder, F. Rubenstein, & A. E. Yasik (Eds.), *Evidence based practice in infant and early childhood psychology* (pp. 467–499). New York: Wiley.

Dawson, G., & Galpert, I. (1990). Mother's use of imitative play for facilitating social responsiveness and toy play in young autistic children. *Developmental Psychopathology, 2,* 151–162.

Dawson, G., Rogers, S., Munson, J., Smith, M., Winter, J., Greenson, J., et al. (2010). Randomized, controlled trial of an intervention for toddlers with autism: The Early Start Denver Model. *Pediatrics, 125,* 17–23.

Diagnostic Classification Task Force. (1994). *Diagnostic classification: 0-3: Diagnostic classification of mental health and developmental disorders of infancy and early childhood.* S. I. Greenspan (Chair). Arlington, VA: Zero to Three/National Center for Clinical Infant Programs.

Drew, A., Baird, G., Baron-Cohen, S., Cox, A., Slonim, V., Wheelwright, S., et al. (2002). A pilot randomized control trial of parent training intervention for pre-school children with autism. *European Child & Adolescent Psychiatry, 11,* 266–272.

Dziuk, M., Gidley Larson, J., Apostu, A., Mahone, E., Denckla, M., & Mostofsky, S. (2007). Dyspraxia in autism: Association with motor, social, and communicative deficits. *Developmental Medicine & Child Neurology, 49,* 734–739.

Fraiberg, S. *Clinical studies in infant mental health: The first year of life.* New York: Basic Books.

Garber, K. (2007). Neuroscience: Autism's cause may reside in abnormalities at the synapse. *Science, 17,* 190–191.

Gardner, H. (1983) *Frames of mind: The theory of multiple intelligences.* New York: Basic Books.

Gerber, S., & Prizant, B. (2000). Speech, language and communication assessment and intervention for children. In S. G. Greenspan (Ed.), *ICDL clinical practice guidelines: Redefining the standards of care for infants, children, and families with special needs* (pp. 85–122). Bethesda, MD: The Interdisciplinary Council on Developmental and Learning Disorders.

Gernsbacher, M. (2006). Toward a behavior of reciprocity. *Journal of Developmental Processes, 1,* 139–152.

Goleman, D. (1995). *Emotional intelligence: Why it can matter more than IQ for character, health and lifelong achievement.* New York: Bantam Books.

Greenspan, S. (1979). *Intelligence and adaptation: An integration of psychoanalytic and Piagetian developmental psychology* (Psychological Issues, Monograph No. 47–48). New York: International Universities Press.

Greenspan, S. (1989). *The development of the ego: Implications for personality theory, psychopathology, and the psychotherapeutic process.* Madison, CT: International Universities Press.

Greenspan, S. (1992a). *Infancy and early childhood: The practice of clinical assessment and intervention with emotional and developmental challenges.* Madison, CT: International Universities Press.

Greenspan, S. (1992b). Reconsidering the diagnosis and treatment of very young children with autistic spectrum or pervasive developmental disorder. *Zero to Three, 13,* 1–9.

Greenspan, S. (1997). *The growth of the mind and the endangered origins of intelligence.* Reading, MA: Addison Wesley Longman.

Greenspan, S. (1999). *Building healthy minds: The six experiences that create intelligence and emotional growth in babies and young children.* Cambridge, MA: Perseus Books.

Greenspan, S. (2001). The affect diathesis hypothesis: The role of emotions in the core deficit in autism and the development of intelligence and social skills. *Journal of Developmental Learning Disorders, 5,* 1–45.

Greenspan, S. (2004a). *Greenspan social–emotional growth chart.* Bulverde, TX: Psychological Corp.

Greenspan, S. (2004b). *The Greenspan social–emotional growth chart: A screening questionnaire for infants and young children.* Bulverde, TX: Psychological Corp.

Greenspan, S., DeGangi, G., & Wieder, S. (2001). *The functional emotional assessment scale (FEAS) for infancy and early childhood: Clinical and research applications.* Bethesda, MD: Interdisciplinary Council on Developmental and Learning Disorders.

Greenspan, S., & Shanker, S. (2004). *The first idea: How symbols, language and intelligence evolved from our primate ancestors to modern humans.* Reading, MA: Perseus Books.

Greenspan, S., & Wieder, S. (1993). Regulatory disorders. In C. H. Zeanah (Ed.), *Handbook of infant mental health* (pp. 280–290). New York: Guilford Press.

Greenspan, S., & Wieder, S. (1997a). An integrated developmental approach to interventions for young children with severe difficulties in relating and communicating. *Zero to Three, 17,* 5–18.

Greenspan, S., & Wieder, S. (1997b). Developmental patterns and outcomes in infants and children with disorders in relating and communicating: A chart review of 200 cases of children with autistic spectrum diagnoses. *Journal of Developmental Learning Disorders, 1,* 87–141.

Greenspan, S., & Wieder, S. (1998). *The child with special needs: Encouraging intellectual and emotional growth.* Reading, MA: Perseus Books.

Greenspan, S., & Wieder, S. (1999). A functional developmental approach to autism spectrum disorders. *JASH, 24,* 147–161.

Greenspan, S., & Wieder, S. (2000). Principles of clinical practice for assessment and intervention: Developmentally appropriate interactions and practices: Developmentally based approach to the evaluation process. In *Interdisciplinary Council on Developmental and Learning Disorders: Clinical practice guidelines* (pp. 261–282). Bethesda, MD: Interdisciplinary Council on Developmental and Learning Disorders.

Greenspan, S., & Wieder, S. (2001). *Floortime techniques and the DIR model for children and families with special needs: A guide to the training videotape series.* Bethesda, MD: Interdisciplinary Council on Developmental and Learning Disorders.

Greenspan, S., & Wieder, S. (2003a). Assessment and early identification of autism spectrum and other disorders of relating and communicating: A functional developmental approach to autism spectrum disorders. In E. Hollander (Ed.), *Medical psychiatry: Vol. 24. Autism spectrum disorders* (pp. 57–86). New York: Dekker.

Greenspan, S., & Wieder, S. (2003b). Diagnostic classification in infancy and early childhood. In A. Tasman, J. Kay, & J. Lieberman (Eds.), *Psychiatry* (2nd ed., pp. 677–686). Hove, UK: Wiley.

Greenspan, S., & Wieder, S. (2005a). Can children with autism master the core deficits and become empathetic, creative and reflective? A ten to fifteen year follow-up of a subgroup of children with autism spectrum disorders (ASD) who received a comprehensive developmental, individual-difference, relationship-based (DIR) approach. *Journal of Developmental Learning Disorders, 9,* 39–61.

Greenspan, S., & Wieder, S. (2005b). *Diagnostic manual for infancy and early childhood.* Bethesda, MD: Interdisciplinary Council on Developmental and Learning Disorders.

Greenspan, S., & Wieder, S., (2005c). *Infant and early childhood mental health: A comprehensive developmental approach to assessment and intervention.* Arlington, VA: American Psychiatric Press.

Greenspan, S., & Wieder, S. (2006). *Engaging autism: The Floortime approach to helping children relate, communicate, and think.* Cambridge, MA: DaCapo Press/Perseus Books.

Greenspan, S., & Wieder, S. (2007). *The DIR/Floortime approach to autistic spectrum disorders.* In E. Hollander & E. Anagnostou (Eds.), *Clinical manual for the treatment of autism* (pp. 179–210). Arlington, VA: American Psychiatric Press.

Greenspan, S., Wieder, S., Lieberman, A., Nover, R., Lourie, R., & Robinson, M. (1987). *Infants in multirisk families: Case studies in preventive intervention* (Clinical Infant Reports, No. 3). New York: International Universities Press.

Gutstein, S. E., & Sheely, R. K. (2002). *Relationship development intervention with young children: Social and emotional developmental activities for Asperger syndrome, autism, PDD and NLD.* London: Jessica Kingsley.

Interdisciplinary Council on Developmental and Learning Disorders. (2005). *Diagnostic manual for infancy and early childhood (ICDL-DMIC).* Bethesda, MD: Interdisciplinary Council on Developmental and Learning Disorders.

Interdisciplinary Council on Developmental and Learning Disorders. (n.d.). *Clinical practice guidelines: Redefining the standards of care for infants, children, and families with special needs.* Retrieved from www.icdl.com.

Kanner, L. (1943). Autistic disturbances of affective contact. *Nervous Child, 2,* 217–250.

Kasari, C., Freeman, S., & Paparella, T. (2006). Joint attention and symbolic play in young children with autism: A randomized controlled intervention study. *Journal of Child Psychology and Psychiatry, 47,* 611–620.

Kasari, C., Freeman, S. F. N., Paparella, T &. Jahromi, L. B. (2008). Language outcome in autism: Randomized comparison of joint attention and play interventions. *Journal of Consulting and Clinical Psychology, 76,* 125–137.

Lord, C. & McGee, J. (Eds.). (2001). *Educating children with autism* (National Research Council). Washington, DC: National Academy Press.

Lourie, R. S. (1971). The first three years of life: An overview of a new frontier for psychiatry. *American Journal of Psychiatry, 127,* 1457–1463.

Lovaas, O. (1987). Behavioral treatment and normal educational and intellectual functioning in young autistic children. *Journal of Consulting and Clinical Psychology, 55,* 3–9.

Mahler, M. S., Pine, F., & Bergman, A. (1975). *The psychological birth of the human infant.* New York: Basic Books,

Mahoney, G., & Perales, F. (2003). Using relationship-focused intervention to enhance the social-emotional functioning of young children with autism spectrum disorders. *Topics in Early Childhood Special Education, 23,* 77–89.

Mahoney, G., & Perales, F. (2004). Relationship-focused early intervention with children with pervasive developmental disorders and other disabilities: A comparative study. *Journal of Developmental & Behavioral Pediatrics, 26,* 77–85.

Mahoney, G., & Perales, F. (2005). A comparison of the impact of relationship-focused intervention on young children with pervasive developmental disorders and other disabilities. *Journal of Developmental and Behavioral Pediatrics, 26,* 77–85.

Marcus, L., Semrau, L., & Schopler, E. (1977). *Division TEACCH: Toward a statewide network of public school services for the autistic child and his family* (pp. 34–44). Washington, DC: Coordinating Office for Regional Resource Centers.

Minshew, N., Goldstein, D., & Siegel, D. (1997). Neuropsychologic functioning in autism: Profile of a complex information processing disorder. *Journal of the International Neuropsychological Society, 3,* 303–316.

Mostofsky, S., Dubai, P., Jerath, V.,Jansiewicz, E., Goldberg, M., & Denckla, M. (2006). Developmental dyspraxia is not limited to imitation in children with autism spectrum disorders. *Journal of the International Neuropsychological Society, 12,* 314–326.

Mundy, P., Sigman, M., & Kasari, C. (1990). A longitudinal study of joint attention and language development in autistic children. *Journal of Autism and Developmental Disorders, 20,* 115–128.

Provence, S. (1983). *Infants and parents* (Clinical Case Reports, No. 2). New York: International Universities Press.

Rogers, S., Hall, T., Osaki, D., Reaven, J., & Herbison, J. (2000). The Denver model: A comprehensive, integrated educational approach to young children with autism and their families. In J. Handleman & S. Harris (Eds.), *Preschool education programs for children with autism* (2nd ed., pp. 95–133). Austin, TX: Pro-Ed.

Rogers, S. J., & Dawson, G. (2010). *Early start Denver model for young children with autism.* New York: Guilford.

Schopler, E., Reichler, R., DeVellis, R., & Daly, K. (1980). Toward objective classification of childhood autism: Childhood Autism Rating Scale (CARS). *Journal of Autism and Developmental Disorders, 10*(1), 91–103.

Shahmoon-Shanok, R. (2000). The action is in the interaction: Clinical practice guidelines for work with parents of children with developmental disorders. In S. G. Greenspan (Ed.), *ICDL clinical practice guidelines: Redefining the standards of care for infants, children, and families with special needs* (pp. 333–371). Bethesda, MD: The Interdisciplinary Council on developmental and Learning Disorders.

Siegel, D. (2001). Toward an interpersonal neurobiology of the developing mind: Attachment, "mindsight" and neural integration. *Infant Mental Health Journal, 22,* 67–94.

Solomon, R., Necheles, J., Ferch, D., & Bruckman, D. (2007). Pilot study of a parent training program for young children with autism: The P.L.A.Y. Project Home Consultation model. *Autism: The International Journal of Research and Practice, 11,* 205–224.

Spreckley, M., & Boyd, R. (2009). Efficacy of applied behavioral intervention in preschool children with autism for improving cognitive, language, and adaptive behavior: A systematic review and meta-analysis. *Journal of Pediatrics, 154,* 338–344.

Wetherby, A., & Prizant, B.(1993). Profiling communication and symbolic abilities in young children. *Journal of Childhood Communication Disorders, 15,* 23–32.

Wetherby, A. M., Prizant, B. M., & Hutchinson, T. (1998). Communicative, social-affective and symbolic profiles of young children with autism and pervasive developmental disorders. *American Journal of Speech-Language Pathology, 7,* 79–91.

Wieder, S. (1994a). Opening the door: Approaches to engage children with multisystem developmental disorders. *Zero to Three, 13,* 10–15.

Wieder, S. (Ed.). (1994b). *Diagnostic classification of mental health and developmental disorders of infancy and early childhood: DC 0–3.* Washington, DC: Zero to Three.

Wieder, S. (1994c). The separation-individuation process from a developmental-structuralist perspective: Its application to infants with constitutional differences. *Psychoanalytic Inquiry, 14,* 128–152.

Wieder, S. (1996a). Climbing the "symbolic ladder": Assessing young children's symbolic and representational capacities through observation of free play interaction. In S. Meisels & E. Fenichel (Eds.), *New visions for the developmental assessment of infants and young children* (pp. 267–287). Washington, DC: Zero to Three.

Wieder, S. (1996b). Integrated treatment approaches for young children with multisystem developmental disorder. *Infants & Young Children, 8,* 24–34.

Wieder, S. (1997). Multisystem developmental disorder. In A. Lieberman, S. Wieder, & E. Fenichel (Eds.), *DC: 0–3 Casebook* (pp. 295–333). Washington, DC: Zero to Three.

Wieder, S. (2005). The DIR certificate program: A case based competency training model. In K. M. Finello (Ed.), *The handbook of training and practice in infant and preschool mental health* (pp. 343–356). San Francisco, CA: Jossey-Bass.

Wieder, S., & Greenspan, S. (1993). The emotional basis of learning. In B. Spodek (Ed.), *Handbook of research on the education of young children* (pp. 77–87). New York: Macmillan.

Wieder, S., & Greenspan, S. (2001). The DIR (developmental, individual difference, relationship based) approach to assessment and intervention planning. *Zero to Three, 4*(21) 11–19.

Wieder, S., & Greenspan, S. (2003). Climbing the symbolic ladder in the DIR model through floortime/interactive play. *Autism, 7,* 425–436.

Wieder, S., & Greenspan, S. (2005). Developmental pathways to mental health: The DIR model for comprehensive approaches to assessment and intervention. In K. M. Finello (Ed.), *The handbook of training and practice in infant and preschool mental health* (pp. 377–401). San Francisco, CA: Jossey-Bass.

Wieder, S., & Greenspan, S. (2006). Infant and early childhood mental health: The DIR model. In G. Foley & J. Hochman (Eds.), *Mental health in early intervention: Achieving unity in principles and practice* (pp. 175–190). Baltimore, MD: Brookes.

Wieder, S., & Kalmanson, B. (2000). Educational guidelines for preschool children with difficulties in relating and communicating. In *Interdisciplinary Council on Developmental and Learning Disorders clinical practice guidelines* (pp. 261–282). Bethesda, MD: Interdisciplinary Council on Developmental and Learning Disorders.

Wieder, S., Kalmanson, B., & Fenichel, E. (1999). Diagnosing regulatory disorders using DC 0–3: A framework and a case illustration. *Infants & Young Children, 12,* 79–89.

Williams, D. L., & Minshew, N. J. (2007). Understanding autism and related disorders: What has imaging taught us? *Neuroimaging Clinics of North America, 17*(4), 495–509.

Williamson, G., & Anzalone, M. (1997). Sensory integration: A key component of the evaluation and treatment of young children with severe difficulties in relating and communicating. *Zero to Three, 17,* 29–36.

Zwaigenbaum, L., Bryson, S., Lord, C., Rogers, S., Carter, A., Carver, L., et al. (2009). Clinical assessment and management of toddlers with suspected autism spectrum disorder: Insights from studies of high-risk infants. *Pediatrics, 123,* 1383–1391.

6

STRUCTURED TEACHING AND THE TEACCH PROGRAM

Gary B. Mesibov and Victoria Shea

UNIVERSITY OF NORTH CAROLINA AT CHAPEL HILL

Stephanie McCaskill

NEW YORK CITY DEPARTMENT OF EDUCATION-DISTRICT 75

Introduction

Structured teaching is the name for the principles and strategies for educating and supporting individuals with autism that were developed within the TEACCH program. Treatment and Education of Autistic and Related Communication-Handicapped Children (TEACCH) is a program based at the University of North Carolina at Chapel Hill. Although TEACCH began as a program for children, it now works with individuals across the age span. (In this chapter, we will use the terms *students* and *individuals* interchangeably, and the term *autism* will refer to all autism spectrum disorders.)

We will begin with brief histories of the concept of evidence-based practices and of the TEACCH program. We will then describe the core principles and strategies of Structured Teaching along with suggestions for implementing them in classrooms. This is followed by an overview of the research literature related to these principles and strategies. We conclude with a perspective on what is known and what we do not yet know about interventions for autism, and suggestions for future directions in the area of evidence-based education for students with autism.

Historical Background

Evidence-Based Practice

The concept of basing clinical practice on systematic reviews of research began in the field of medicine in the early 1970s (Dunst, Trivette, & Cutspec, 2002). One version of the application of this concept, empirically validated treatment (EVT), was introduced into clinical psychology in the mid-1990s and was designed to be a list of specific, written treatment procedures that met certain research criteria. The original purpose of the EVT movement was to defend adult psychotherapy against competition from psychiatric medication and pressures from managed care insurance plans (Society of Clinical Psychology, 1995). EVT evolved over time, and in addition, other groups of psychologists developed somewhat different definitions and standards for the same general concept. Finally, after a "decade of both enthusiasm and controversy" (American Psychological Association, 2006, p. 272) the American Psychological Association decided upon the construct of "Evidence-Based Practice in Psychology," defined as the "integration of the best available research and clinical expertise within the context of patient characteristics, culture, values, and preferences" (2006, p. 273). This definition was thus significantly broader and more flexible than a list of treatment manuals.

In education, the term *scientifically-based research* (SBR) was introduced in the No Child Left Behind Act of 2001 (NCLB) as a required foundation for many school programs funded by the federal government; it was also used in the Education Sciences Reform Act of 2002 and incorporated by reference into the 2006 regulations for the Individuals with Disabilities Education Improvement Act of 2004. The focus of SBR was on issues in regular education (not special education), such as reading, math, and science curricula, and dropout prevention. The federal definition of SBR included both a preferred (not mandatory) research design (i.e., randomized controlled trials) and a requirement for specific forms of peer review, criteria that are significantly more prescriptive than the American Psychological Association definition of EBPP.

The Council for Exceptional Children (CEC) has established an evidence-based practice initiative for evaluating special educational practices (CEC, 2008). According to CEC, "the evidence-base must reflect the theoretical and research foundation; the inclusion of professional wisdom; and respect for family and community values" (p. 3).

In summary, use of the terms *evidence-*, *empirically*, or *scientifically-based* applied to treatment, practice, research, or intervention is a relatively recent construct and is defined differently by different professional groups. Both the American Psychological Association and CEC recognize the importance of integrating empirical studies with other elements in order to identify the evidence base for competent practice. The American Psychological Association describes these other elements as *clinical expertise* and *clients' characteristics*; CEC uses the terms *professional skill and wisdom* and *family and cultural values*.

In two recent papers (Mesibov & Shea, 2010, in press), we have discussed in detail the application of evidence-based principles and practices to interventions for individuals with autism. There are clear benefits to this approach, because the area of autism has generated some particularly questionable treatments, such as psychoanalysis (Schopler & Mesibov, 1984), facilitated communication (Smith, Haas, & Belcher, 1994), and chemical chelation of the blood (Offit, 2008). However, although there is general agreement that education based on a foundation of empirical studies is desirable, there are a number of difficulties associated with this goal. For example, students and families are complex and multifaceted. There are always other factors influencing their behavior and learning in addition to the intervention approach being studied. And there are practical and ethical issues involved in carrying out randomized group trials of interventions—families might not support the interventions to which their children have been assigned, and they might want to switch conditions or abandon the study. Another difficulty is that the additional elements of the evidence base, such as expertise, wisdom, and integration of values are particularly hard to define and measure. Further implementation of standardized interventions, while also individualizing treatment or education, has proven to be more complicated than it might seem. Also, those practitioners who attempt to use research reviews to identify empirically based practices have found that these reviews vary in many ways (e.g., studies reviewed, the authors' theoretical orientation and personal views, and even, in the case of very broad review articles, the author's familiarity with specifics and issues related to each topic) and so the results of such reviews vary too.

TEACCH

The precursor of the TEACCH program was a federal grant to its cofounder, psychologist Eric Schopler for research into a new service model for children with autism. At the time of that grant (1966), children with disabilities did not yet have a legal entitlement to public education, although many children were accepted into public schools, typically being served in classes for students with either emotional disorders or mental retardation (now called intellectual disability). The prevailing theory at the time was that autism was a result of parental psychopathology. In particular, an influential figure in both professional training and in the general public's view of autism was Bruno Bettelheim. Bettelheim was widely thought to be a psychiatrist, but he was not actually trained in medicine or mental health (Pollak, 1997). He compared parents to prison guards in Nazi concentration camps and recommended that children with autism be separated from their parents and placed in residential care. Less extreme theories at the time still suggested that the appropriate treatment model was psychotherapy for parents and unstructured play therapy for the children with autism.

Schopler was a student of Bettelheim's but came to see him as a "negative role model" (i.e., whatever Bettelheim did, Schopler tried the opposite). He developed a model of working with parents as cotherapists for their own children. Parents were taught how to teach their children new skills, and they were found to be quite effective in doing so (Marcus, Lansing, Andrews & Schopler, 1978; Short, 1984). Dr. Schopler also stressed the importance of structure in teaching children with autism. (Structure in Dr. Schopler's formulation meant that the adult planned the activity the student would do, the materials to be used, and the length of time each activity would last, and communicated this information clearly to the student.)

When the federal grant to Dr. Schopler ended, the TEACCH program was funded by the North Carolina General Assembly beginning in 1972. At that time, TEACCH consisted of three centers across the state that provided diagnostic and parent training services; TEACCH also supervised some classrooms in public schools. Eventually, all school systems in the United States were required by law to provide free appropriate public education (FAPE) for students with autism (and other disabilities). TEACCH no longer operates classrooms, but at the present time has nine clinical centers in North Carolina, plus model service programs in early intervention services, supported employment, and a residential/vocational program for adults.

Description and Overview of Structured Teaching

In the 1990s, professionals at TEACCH developed a theoretical conceptualization of autism, called the *culture of autism*, and an educational approach that flows from it, called *Structured Teaching* (Mesibov, Shea, & Schopler, 2005). Structured teaching is specifically designed for autism because autism is a unique disorder that is distinguishable from other developmental disabilities and from other causes of social difficulties and problematic behaviors (Volkmar & Klin, 2005). Although many individuals with autism also have an intellectual disability, the two disorders are not the same, and it is important to understand the unique characteristics of autism in order to develop effective intervention strategies.

The Culture of Autism

The concept of the culture of autism describes patterns of thinking and behavior that characterize individuals with autism. These are different from but compatible with formal diagnostic criteria (e.g., *DSM-IV-TR*; American Psychiatric Association, 2000). The culture of autism includes the following attributes:

1. Relative strength in and preference for processing *visual* information (compared to relative difficulties with auditory processing, particularly of language).
2. Heightened attention to *details* but difficulty with sequencing, integrating, connecting, or deriving meaning from them.
3. Variability in *attention* (individuals can be very distractible at times and at other times intensely focused, with difficulties shifting attention efficiently).
4. *Communication* problems that vary by developmental level, but always include impairments in the social use of language.
5. Difficulty with concepts of *time*, including moving through activities too quickly or too slowly and having problems with the *sequencing* of steps in an activity, including the concept of "finished."
6. A tendency to become *attached to routines* and the settings where they are established, so that skills may not generalize from the original learning situation, and disruptions in routines can be confusing or upsetting.
7. A strong *personal sense of order:* how things should look and how activities should be done (these preferences are unique to each individual and are not necessarily consistent with the organizational standards of the neurotypical world).
8. Intense *interests* and *impulses* to engage in favored activities and difficulties disengaging from them.
9. Marked *sensory* preferences and aversions.

We use the term *culture of autism* to highlight our view that autism is not just a collection of behavioral excesses and deficits, but a predictable pattern of information processing, thinking, and responding. By understanding this pattern, teachers, parents, and other professionals can function as "cross-cultural interpreters," seeing the world through the eyes of the student with autism and communicating information about and the expectations of our neurotypical world in forms that the student understands and finds meaningful.

Although the culture of autism describes patterns seen in all individuals with autism, there are also many sources of diversity within the population of students who share this diagnosis. It is sometimes said "if you have met one person with autism ... you have met one person with autism." Among the factors on which students with autism differ are age, IQ, language skills, social interests and skills, special interests and talents, sensory profile, and degree of rigidity in response to changes and surprises (see chapter 2).

Structured Teaching

Structured teaching uses students' visual strengths and personal sense of order to help them learn new concepts and skills, which in turn increases their comfort and motivation to participate in learning tasks. The goal is to help students with autism become confident learners who recognize that they can understand what they are being asked to do and can complete tasks successfully.

The fundamental principles of Structured Teaching are described as follows:

1. *Individualize all strategies and goals.* No two individuals with autism are alike, so it is not reasonable or even possible to write a standard curriculum or overall treatment manual. Plans that work for one student with autism are unlikely to be effective for another student without individualized modifications based on individualized assessment. Further, students develop and learn, so strategies and goals need ongoing assessment and updating as the student matures. Structured teaching therefore emphasizes the importance of applying general principles in unique, individualized ways for each student. Interventions using

Structured Teaching can be designed both for "concrete" learners who function, communicate, and learn best through the use of objects, pictures, and other tangible methods, and for "abstract" learners who find spoken and written language and other symbolic content meaningful.

2. *Provide external organization of space, time, and the design of tasks.* Because disorganization and difficulties with sequencing and time management are characteristic of students with autism, a basic principle of Structured Teaching is to provide external organizational supports. Typically we use a combination of physical structure of the environment and structuring of time using a visual schedule. We also use organizational strategies for tasks (e.g., stabilization of materials, tasks that move from left to right or top to bottom, tasks with a clear end point). We implement this principle in a variety of ways depending on the developmental level of the individual student (see specific examples in the following section).

3. *Use visual supports to supplement or at times substitute for verbal language.* Structured teaching relies strongly on the use of visual information for several reasons. First, individuals with autism are more easily engaged in productive activities that have a visual component. Second, visual supports tend to reduce the confusion and distress that can be caused when too much language processing is required. Third, visual supports can remain in place over time, while spoken instruction takes place in a discrete time period and then vanishes, and may not be adequately processed or remembered. There are many excellent commercial resources for materials and applications of visual supports (e.g., Arwood & Kaulitz, 2007; Hodgdon, 1995; Quill, 1997, Savner, n.d.; see also www.do2learn and www.UseVisual-Strategies.com). Note that for developmentally advanced students, visual supports would generally be in written form; for example, "to do" lists, directions, reminders, rules, explanations, or social stories (Gray, 1998; Mesibov, Shea, & Adams, 2001)

4. *Use special interests to engage attention and learning.* Most modern intervention approaches use students' special interests as rewards for successful completion of tasks, rather than using standard rewards such as candy or tickling. In addition, Structured Teaching incorporates individuals' special interests at other points in the educational process, such as using favorite cartoon characters in materials to teach academic skills (e.g., counting or writing about helicopters) or organizational strategies (e.g., Sponge Bob says, "Put your homework in the red basket"), to highlight a student's seat or cubby, or to draw a student's attention to his daily schedule.

Implementation in the Classroom

The core strategy of Structured Teaching can be summarized as follows: For each new learning activity and for each situation in which the student indicates, through words or behavior, that he is having difficulty staying focused on the activity, provide the student with *visual* answers to these five questions:

1. *Where* am I supposed to be? or *Where* am I going?
2. *What* work or activity will I do there?
3. *How long* will I do it or *how many* will I do?
4. How can I see that I am making *progress* and how will I know that I have *finished*?
5. What will I do *next*?

Naturally, given the tremendous variation of skills and understanding among students with an autism spectrum diagnosis, the ways in which these questions are answered differ markedly. The fundamental principle of providing this external organization for learning and for problematic situations does not change, however. Answering these questions typically involves a combination of the following approaches:

1. *Physical organization of space and materials.* Physical organization is one way of answering the questions "Where am I supposed to be?" and "What work or activity will I do there?" For young or developmentally delayed students, physical structure can take the form of arranging classroom spaces using fixed boundaries such as bookcases, filing cabinets, and screens that define areas for specific activities and help students remain in the assigned area and focus their attention on structured activities. For these students we would typically recommend the following areas: a place for 1:1 work with a teacher, an independent practice work area, a transition area where they check their schedules (see next section), a social or group work area, a snack area, and a leisure time area. For older and more capable students, physical organization might take the form of a diagram of the student's classrooms within the school building or college campus, or diagrams, containers, and folders for keeping lockers, desks, and notebooks organized.

In special education classrooms, along with designating specific areas for specific activities, it is necessary to plan how each area will be monitored and used by teachers and classroom personnel. Teachers can use a "man to man" approach and follow a student or small group from one area to another, or they can use a "zone" approach and stay in one area while students make transitions between areas. Whatever approach teachers select, it is important to communicate the plan to all classroom personnel, so that they know which student(s) or area they are responsible for.

2. *Schedules.* In Structured Teaching, the environment and learning activities are designed to help students with autism move beyond their perceptions of fragmented details and unexpected events, and begin to identify and understand meaningful connections in the world around them. We achieve this through the use of preplanned events whose sequence is communicated to students in ways they can understand. That is, rather than just taking a student from one activity to another, we use visual cues in advance of each activity to help each student understand where he or she is going and what he or she will do there. For young or developmentally delayed students, we might use an actual object that will be used in the upcoming activity (e.g., a cup for snack time, a ball for going outside, a block or marker for individual work with a teacher). For older and more advanced students, the schedule might take the form of photographs, picture symbols, written words, or even a typical class schedule. Schedules, among other effects, answer the question "What work or activity will I be doing?"

The most important features of schedules are that they are visible and meaningful to the student and that they can be easily changed and updated. Schedules do not need to be beautiful, computer-generated, or laminated. They should not be posted at adult eye level or laid on the teacher's desk. They especially do not have to be unchanging. We want the schedules to be realistic because you can't plan the whole week in advance, and even if you could, something would change (e.g., substitute teacher, fire drill, weather-related disruptions of plans). Further, we know that individuals with autism tend to be good at memorizing routines—what they have more difficulty with are changes from what they expect, and so we deliberately incorporate change into schedules so that students learn to look to the schedule for information. Schedules should provide accurate information of what is coming next, even if the information must be changed, removed, or added. For students who have significant difficulty with changes, we would use a "something is different" symbol on the schedule and begin teaching it with "good" changes and differences before starting to use the symbol in conjunction with less desired non-routine activities.

3. *Structured work systems.* Because students with autism are frequently disorganized, in Structured Teaching we preorganize learning activities to the degree needed for students to understand the task and complete it successfully. We count out materials, think through the sequence of steps in the task, or highlight a part of the task to make it the focus of attention. We

also want to encourage engagement with the task by showing students in advance how long the task will last or how many items they will do, so that students can see that they can be successful and that the task is not endless.

Methods for developmentally young students include keeping materials organized in containers, keeping tasks short and visually clear, designating a place to put the finished materials, and using an object or symbol to indicate the next activity. For a more developmentally advanced student, we might use step-by-step written directions checked off when completed, separate file folders or notebooks for different subject matter, or organizational supports for taking home a written list of homework assignments and corresponding materials. At home, a check-off system for the list of homework assignments would be a similar strategy. Task and activity organization answer the questions: "How long will I do it or how many will I do?" "How can I see that I am making progress and how will I know that I have finished?" and "What will I do next?"

For concrete learners, we almost always begin teaching each activity in 1:1 sessions with a teacher. Activities are taught using whatever techniques work with that particular student (e.g., demonstrations, gestures, hand-over-hand assistance [if the student accepts this], verbal explanations [if the student understands this], step-by-step visual directions, etc.). Tasks that have been mastered in this way are then practiced during independent work sessions at a different time in a different location. Tasks are then generalized to other materials and other kinds of variations (for example, after learning to sort blue and red blocks, the student could practice sorting blue, red, and yellow blocks, blue and red crayons, big vs. small blocks, sorting materials with another student, playing with sorting toys in the free play area or home, etc.). Classroom teachers thus create an environment where activities flow from task and concept acquisition to independence, generalization, and integration into the natural environment.

Evidence Base

Evidence for the Culture of Autism

We look first at evidence for our theoretical understanding of autism (i.e., the culture of autism) that is the basis of Structured Teaching. Various research reviews have described the evidence of patterns of neuropsychological functioning that are characteristic of autism. For example, Dawson (1996) summarized the extant research literature as indicating that most individuals with autism have "spared" (p. 180) skills in visual–spatial organization and some aspects of memory and learning, but impairments in organization, flexibility, and comprehension of complex verbal information. Tsatsanis's (2005) review of research into neuropsychological characteristics of autism described unusual responses to sensory stimulation, disorders of some aspects of attention (e.g., filtering distractions, shifting attentional focus), and difficulty with planning and organizing responses, all of which correspond to our experiences with the culture of autism. Similarly, Ozonoff, South, & Provencal (2005) reviewed evidence for difficulties with cognitive and attentional flexibility in individuals with autism. Research supporting the theoretical foundation for the TEACCH approach is discussed in more detail in Mesibov and Shea (2010).

Evidence for Elements of Structured Teaching

Structure. An early demonstration of the effectiveness of structure is found in the research of Rutter and Bartak (1973), who studied 50 children, aged 7 to 9 years at the beginning of the study, who were attending one of three different educational programs: (a) an autism-specific "regressive"/psychotherapeutic program, (b) a cross-categorical combined psychotherapeutic and special education program, or (c) an autism-specific structured special education program. After 3.5 to 4 years, the children in the structured program demonstrated significantly more on-task behavior and higher academic achievement than the children in the other settings. The general principle of using structure for students with autism (and other developmental disabilities) is now well accepted (Bodfish, 2004; National Research Council, 2001; Rogers, 1999).

Visual Strategies and Supports. Most researchers and clinicians have also accepted the importance of visual or written material for teaching and supporting individuals with autism (American Speech-Language-Hearing Association, 2006; Mesibov, Browder, & Kirkland, 2002; National Research Council, 2001; Quill, 1997; Stromer, Kimball, Kinney, & Taylor, 2006). Krantz, McClannahan, and MacDuff, in a series of studies using photographic or written material, taught youngsters to initiate social exchanges (Krantz & McClannahan, 1998) and to follow schedules of planned activities (Krantz, McDuff, & McClannahan, 1993; MacDuff, Krantz, & McClannahan, 1993). Pierce and Schreibman (1994) taught youngsters with autism to carry out daily living skills independently using picture cues. Bryan and Gast (2000) reported that students spent significantly more time on tasks and completed more tasks correctly when they used visual activity schedules. Massey and Wheeler (2000) reported similar results in terms of increased task engagement as well as reduction of challenging behaviors. Several studies have also demonstrated that picture cues were effective in reducing disruptive or aggressive behavior during transitions between activities (Dettmer, Simpson, Myles, & Ganz, 2000; Dooley, Wilczenski, & Toren, 2001; Schmit, Alper, Raschke, & Ryndak, 2000), and that written or picture cues served to increase social interaction skills (Sarokoff, Taylor, & Poulson, 2001; Thiemann & Goldstein, 2001) and play skills (Morrison, Sainato, Benchaaban, & Endo, 2002).

Structured Work Systems. Hume and Odom (2007) demonstrated the effectiveness of structured work systems for three individuals with autism (ages 6, 7, and 20 years). Using an ABAB single subject design, they found marked increases of on-task behavior and marked reduction of teacher prompting when individualized structured work systems were implemented. Similarly, Hume (2009) documented increased on-task behavior and accuracy, decreased adult prompting and task completion duration, and generalization to other conditions when structured work systems were experimentally studied with three 7-year-old children. Structured work systems are considered to have a confirmed evidence base by the National Professional Development Center on Autism Spectrum Disorders (n.d.). Similarly, the National Standards Report of the National Autism Center (n.d.) considers antecedent packages and schedules to be established treatments, and Structured Teaching to have an emerging research base.

Evidence for Applications of Structured Teaching

Principles and strategies of Structured Teaching can be used successfully in a wide variety of settings, including homes, regular and special education classrooms, recreation programs, medical, dental, and therapy appointments, employment settings, and others. Although didactic preparation, supervised training, and experience are valuable, we have seen Structured Teaching carried out effectively, if imperfectly, by a variety of practitioners.

Ozonoff and Cathcart (1998) conducted a study in which parents of 11 preschool-age children were taught to implement a Structured Teaching home program. All children also attended school or other day treatment programs. The group whose parents provided Structured Teaching improved significantly more than the control group overall on the Psychoeducational Profile-Revised (PEP-R; Schopler, Lansing, Reichler, & Marcus, 2005) and on the imitation, fine motor, gross motor, and cognitive-performance subscales; they also showed marked progress on the perception and cognitive-verbal subscales.

Panerai, Ferrante, and Zingale (2002) studied the effects of Structured Teaching interventions on the developmental skills of a group of eight children and adolescents with autism and severe mental retardation in an Italian residential program, compared with a matched group of children who lived at home and attended regular Italian public school classrooms with a support teacher, which is the standard Italian special education model. After one year, the group in the Structured Teaching program had made significantly more progress on the PEP-R (Schopler et al., 2005) than the control group had made. In a later study, Panerai et al. (2009) compared PEP-R and adaptive behavior scores of three groups of school-aged youngsters with autism and severe mental retardation. As in the earlier study, one group received Structured Teaching interventions in the residential program and one group received the standard Italian special education; in addition, a third group attended regular public school but their support teachers and parents were trained in Structured Teaching. Results indicated significantly better developmental progress and fewer maladaptive behaviors in both groups in which Structured Teaching techniques were used.

Van Bourgondien, Reichle, and Schopler (2003) looked at the skills, negative behaviors, and satisfaction of the families of six adults with autism 18 months after the clients entered a residential program based on Structured Teaching principles, compared to those factors for 26 similar adults who had also applied for the program but were not selected. Those not admitted continued to live either in family homes, group homes, or institutions. Eighteen months after admission, serious negative behaviors were significantly lower for the Structured Teaching program group than the others, and the families of those in the program were significantly more satisfied than those with children in group homes.

Welterlin's (2009) dissertation research looked at the effectiveness of a 12-session intervention that taught Structured Teaching strategies to parents of 10 2- and 3-year old children with autism. Compared to children in the waiting list control condition, the treatment group had significant increases in fine motor skills, decreased maladaptive behavior, increased independence, measurable increases in visual receptive skills, improved parental teaching skills, and marked decreases in parental distress.

Evidence of Professional Wisdom/Clinical Expertise

Although both the American Psychological Association and CEC include professional wisdom or clinical expertise as core elements of the concept of evidence-based practice, those constructs are rarely, if ever, assessed in evaluations of the evidence base of specific interventions. Rather, such evaluations have focused almost exclusively on elements of experimental research design (such as the number of subjects or studies, random assignment to experimental or control condition, fidelity of the intervention to a written manual, validity of test measures, etc.). Elements such as these are obviously easier to quantify and measure than "wisdom" or "expertise." However, what is difficult to measure might be at least as important as what can be easily counted or rated. Also, what is *difficult* to measure is not *impossible* to measure; and with creative effort, operationalization of abstract concepts might be achievable.

In psychology and education, a marker of wisdom or expertise might be professional recognition within one's field. This might be operationalized by some of the following ways:

- Number of publications in peer-reviewed journals
- Number of publications in prestigious journals
- Years of service on editorial boards of such journals
- Number of invited chapters
- Number of books written or edited
- Number of citations by others in their articles and chapters
- Book sales
- Professional awards
- Demand for clinical services, consultations, and training

Looking at the professional reputation of individuals who have been affiliated with the TEACCH program in terms of these criteria yields strong evidence for professional wisdom and clinical expertise. For example, chapters from TEACCH have been invited for many prominent publications, including all three editions of *The Handbook of Autism and Pervasive Developmental Disorders* (Cohen, Donnellan, & Paul, 1987; Cohen & Volkmar, 1997; Volkmar, Paul, Klin, & Cohen, 2005a, 2005b), and Schopler and Mesibov were editors of the most highly ranked autism journal in the world (the *Journal of Autism and Developmental Disorders*). Mesibov received the 1997 American Psychological Association Award for Distinguished Professional Contributions in Public Service, and Eric Schopler (posthumously) was the 2006 recipient of the American Psychological Foundation Gold Medal Award for Life Achievement in the Application of Psychology. Training in Structured Teaching has been provided to thousands of professionals through invited presentations at universities and autism programs in the United States. The widespread international use of Structured Teaching is also noteworthy, with training or consultation relationships in more than 20 countries. (The implementation of Structured Teaching in other countries was described in detail in a special issue of the *International Journal of Mental Health*; Schopler, 2000.)

Evidence of Integration of Client, Family, and Cultural/Community Values

This is another element of the evidence base of interventions that is frequently overlooked when specific interventions are evaluated. Within TEACCH, the emphasis on individualization is a clear reflection of the importance of respecting the uniqueness of each student and family. Schopler and colleagues developed assessment tools for measuring developmental skills and needs (*Psychoeducational Profile*, now in its 3rd edition; and *TTAP: TEACCH Transition Assessment Profile*, now in its 2nd edition; Mesibov, Thomas, Chapman, & Schopler, 2007). Family involvement is a core principle of our approach, and has been since Schopler's early rejection of the notion that parents caused their child's autism. The principle is put into action by communicating openly with parents, requesting their information, perspectives, and preferences about what and how to teach their children, and including them as full partners in decision making about the child.

Conclusion and Future Directions

The concept of evidence-based special education for autism has been easy to support and somewhat difficult to implement, for several reasons. First, autism interventions have a limited research base compared to medicine or mental health where the concept of evidence-based practice originated. Second, the population of students with autism is very heterogeneous, spanning the range of intelligence, age, language skills, academic levels, and behavior patterns. There really is no other developmental disability with such a diverse presentation and range of skills and needs (Mash & Barkley, 2003). Third, research related to autism interventions is published in many different journals, most of which are not accessible to typical teachers (e.g., *Journal of Autism and Developmental Disabilities, Research in Autism Spectrum Disorders, Journal of Child Psychology and Psychiatry, Journal of Applied Behavior Analysis, Journal of Applied Research in Intellectual Disabilities*). Finally, most teachers (and clinical and school psychologists) are not expert in critically assessing the details of research design and statistical analysis, even if they had the time and access needed for reviewing and keeping up with research.

In terms of autism, here is some of what we think the fields of special education and psychology know:

1. Autism is a specific disorder, distinguishable from intellectual disability, other psychiatric disorders, and generic behavior problems.
2. Individuals with autism have a characteristic pattern of intact or relatively well-preserved visual skills and relative difficulty with language processing and executive functions.
3. Educational methods, including Structured Teaching, that use visual and written supports are meaningful and effective.
4. Providing external organization (e.g., the physical structure and structured work systems of Structured Teaching) is also helpful and effective.

Specifically in terms of Structured Teaching, here are some questions we need to know more about:

1. Does answering the five Structured Teaching questions help students at all ages and developmental levels?
2. Are any of the five Structured Teaching questions more important than others?
3. Are there students for whom Structured Teaching is ineffective?

We suggest that in coming years professionals concerned with the education of students with autism move in the following directions:

- Look at additional dependent variables beyond academic achievement (e.g., independent daily functioning, adult outcome, and "soft" variables like life satisfaction).
- Temper the enthusiasm for manualized interventions and randomized controlled trials, because strategies and variables that are easy to measure are not necessarily those that are most meaningful.
- Develop additional ways to measure professional skill and wisdom.
- Reduce the emphasis on the horse race (Lampropoulos, 2000) among "name-brand" programs, devoting more resources to identifying effective techniques for specific age levels, skill levels, and tasks.
- Maintain respect for individual differences in responses to interventions—group studies don't necessarily predict individual results.

References

American Psychiatric Association. (2000). *Diagnostic and statistical manual of mental disorders* (4th ed., Text rev.). Washington, DC: Author.

American Psychological Association. (2006). Evidence-based practice in psychology. *American Psychologist, 61,* 271–285.

American Speech-Language-Hearing Association. (2006). *Guidelines for speech-language pathologists in diagnosis, assessment, and treatment of autism spectrum disorders across the life span.* Retrieved from http://www.asha.org/docs/html/GL2006-00049.html

Arwood, E. L., & Kaulitz, C. (2007). *Learning with a visual brain in an auditory world: Visual language strategies for individuals with autism spectrum disorders.* Shawnee Mission, KS: Autism Asperger.

Bodfish, J. W. (2004). Treating the core features of autism: Are we there yet? *Mental Retardation and Developmental Disabilities Research Reviews, 10,* 318–326.

Bryan, L. C., & Gast, D. L. (2000). Teaching on-task and on-schedule behaviors to high-functioning children with autism via picture activity schedules. *Journal of Autism and Developmental Disorders, 30,* 553–567.

Council for Exceptional Children. (2008). CEC evidence-based practice initiative. Retrieved from www.cec.sped.org/Content/NavigationMenu/ProfessionalDevelopment/ProfessionalStandards/CEC_EBP_Initiative_ppt.pdf

Cohen, D. J., Donnellan, A. M., & Paul, R. (Eds.). (1987). *Handbook of autism and pervasive developmental disorders.* New York: Holt, Rinehart and Winston.

Cohen, D. J., & Volkmar, F. R. (Eds.). (1997). *Handbook of autism and pervasive developmental disorders* (2nd ed.). New York: Wiley.

Dawson, G. (1996). Brief report: Neuropsychology of autism: A report on the state of the science. *Journal of Autism and Developmental Disorders, 26,* 179–184.

Dettmer, S., Simpson, R. L., Myles, B. S., & Ganz, J. B. (2000). The use of visual supports to facilitate transitions of students with autism. *Focus on Autism and Other Developmental Disabilities, 15,* 163–169.

Dooley, P., Wilczenski, F. L., & Torem, C. (2001). Using an activity schedule to smooth school transitions. *Journal of Positive Behavior Interventions, 3,* 57–61.

Dunst, C. J., Trivette, C. M., & Cutspec, P. A. (2002). Toward an operational definition of evidence-based practices. *Centerscope, 1,* 1–10. (Asheville, NC: Winterberry Press) Retrieved from http://www.wbpress.com/index.php?main_page=product_book_info&products_id=369&zenid=752af676bd3df8a9961580e7a5d8bb9e

Gray, C. A. (1998). Social stories and comic strip conversations with students with Asperger syndrome and high-functioning autism. In E. Schopler, G. B. Mesibov, & L. J. Kunce (Eds.), *Asperger syndrome or high functioning autism?* (pp. 167–198). New York: Plenum Press.

Hodgdon, L. (1995). *Visual communication: Practical supports for school and home.* Troy, MI: QuirkRoberts.

Hume, K. (2009). *Effects of an individual work system on independence, task acquisition and duration, and generalization in students with autism.* Manuscript submitted for publication.

Hume, K., & Odom, S. (2007). Effects of an individual work system on the independent functioning of students with autism. *Journal of Autism and Developmental Disorders, 37*(6), 1166–1180.

Krantz, P. J., MacDuff, M. T., & McClannahan, L. E. (1993). Programming participation in family activities for children with autism: Parents' use of photographic activity schedules. *Journal of Applied Behavior Analysis, 26,* 137–138.

Krantz, P. J., & McClannahan, L. E. (1998). Social interaction skills for children with autism: A script-fading procedure for beginning readers. *Journal of Applied Behavior Analysis, 31,* 191–202.

Lampropoulos, G. K. (2000). A reexamination of the empirically supported treatments critiques. *Psychotherapy Research, 10,* 474–487.

MacDuff, G. S., Krantz, P. J., & McClannahan, L. E. (1993). Teaching children with autism to use photographic activity schedules: Maintenance and generalizations of complex response chains. *Journal of Applied Behavior Analysis, 26,* 89–97.

Marcus, L. M., Lansing, M., Andrews, C. E., & Schopler, E. (1978). Improvement of teaching effectiveness in parents of autistic children. *Journal of the American Academy of Child Psychiatry, 17,* 625–639.

Mash, E. J., & Barkley, R. A. (2003). *Child psychopathology* (2nd ed.). New York: Guilford.

Massey, N. G., & Wheeler, J. J. (2000). Acquisition and generalization of activity schedules and their effects on task engagement in a young child with autism in an inclusive pre-school classroom. *Education and Training in Mental Retardation and Developmental Disabilities, 35,* 326–335.

Mesibov, G. B., Browder, D. M., & Kirkland, C. (2002). Using individualized schedules as a component of positive behavioral support for students with developmental disabilities. *Journal of Positive Behavioral Interventions, 4,* 73–79.

Mesibov, G. B., & Shea, V. (2010). The TEACCH program in the era of evidence-based practice. *Journal of Autism and Developmental Disorders, 40*(5), 570–579.

Mesibov, G. B., & Shea, V. (in press). Evidence-based practices and autism. *Autism: The International Journal of Research and Practice.*

Mesibov, G. B., Shea, V., & Adams, L. W. (2001). *Understanding Asperger syndrome and high-functioning autism.* New York: Springer.

Mesibov, G. B., Shea, V., & Schopler, E. (with Adams, L., Burgess, S., Chapman, S. M., et al.). (2005). *The TEACCH approach to autism spectrum disorders.* New York: Springer.

Mesibov, G. B., Thomas, J. B., Chapman, S. M., & Schopler, E. (2007). *TTAP: TEACCH transition assessment profile* (2nd ed.). Austin, TX: Pro-ed.

Morrison, R. S., Sainato, D. M., Benchaaban, D., & Endo, S. (2005). Increasing play skills of children with autism using activity schedules and correspondence training. *Journal of Early Intervention, 25,* 58–72.

National Autism Center. (n.d.). *National standards report.* Retrieved from http://www.nationalautismcenter.org/affiliates/

National Professional Development Center on Autism Spectrum Disorders. (n.d.). Retrieved from http://autismpdc.fpg.unc.edu/

National Research Council, Committee on Educational Interventions for Children with Autism: Division of Behavioral and Social Sciences and Education. (2001). *Educating children with autism.* Washington, DC: National Academy Press.

Offit, P. A. (2008). *Autism's false prophets: Bad science, risky medicine, and the search for a cure.* New York: Columbia University Press.

Ozonoff, S., & Cathcart, K. (1998). Effectiveness of a home program intervention for young children with autism. *Journal of Autism and Developmental Disorders, 28,* 25–32.

Ozonoff, S., South, M., & Provencal, S. (2005). Executive functions. In F. R. Volkmar, R. Paul, A. Klin, & D. Cohen (Eds.). *Handbook of autism and pervasive developmental disorders, Vol. 1: Diagnosis, development, neurobiology, and behavior* (3rd ed., pp. 606–627). Hoboken, NJ: Wiley.

Panerai, S., Ferrante, L., & Zingale, M. (2002). Benefits of the treatment and education of autistic and communication handicapped children (TEACCH) programme as compared with a non-specific approach. *Journal of Intellectual Disability Research, 46,* 318–327.

Panerai, S., Zingale, M., Trubia, G., Finocchiaro, M., Zuccarello, R., Ferri, R., et al. (2009). Special education versus inclusive education: The role of the TEACCH program. *Journal of Autism and Developmental Disorders, 39*(6), 874–882.

Pierce, K. L., & Schreibman, L. (1994). Teaching daily living skills to children with autism in unsupervised settings through pictorial self-management. *Journal of Applied Behavior Analysis, 27,* 471–481.

Pollak, R. (1997). *The creation of Dr. B: A biography of Bruno Bettelheim.* New York: Simon & Schuster.

Quill, K. A. (1997). Instructional considerations for young children with autism: The rationale for visually cued instruction. *Journal of Autism and Developmental Disorders, 27,* 697–714.

Rogers, S. J. (1999). Intervention for young children with autism: From research to practice. *Infants and Young Children, 12,* 1–16.

Rutter, M., & Bartak, L. (1973). Special educational treatment of autistic children: A comparative study—II. Follow-up findings and implications for services. *Journal of Child Psychology and Psychiatry, 14,* 241–270.

Sarokoff, R. A., Taylor, B. A., & Poulson, C. L. (2001). Teaching children with autism to engage in conversational exchanges: Script fading with embedded textual stimuli. *Journal of Applied Behavior Analysis, 34,* 81–84.

Savner, J. (n.d.). *Visual supports in the classroom* [Video]. Shawnee Mission, KS: Autism Asperger.

Schmit, J., Alper, S., Raschke, D., & Ryndak, D. (2000). Effects of using a photographic cueing package during routine school transitions with a child who has autism. *Mental Retardation, 38,* 131–137.

Schopler, E. (Ed.). (2000). International priorities for developing autism services via the TEACCH model [Special issue]. *International Journal of Mental Health, 29.*

Schopler, E., Lansing, M. D., Reichler, R. J., & Marcus, L .M. (2005). *PEP-3: TEACCH individualized psychoeducational assessment* (3rd ed.). Austin, TX: Pro-ed.

Schopler, E., & Mesibov, G. B. (1984). *The effects of autism on the family.* New York: Plenum.

Short, A. B. (1984). Short-term treatment outcome using parents as co-therapists for their own autistic children. *Journal of Child Psychology and Psychiatry, 25,* 443–458.

Smith, M.D., Haas, P.J., & Belcher, R.G. (1994). Facilitated communication: The effects of facilitator knowledge and level of assistance on output. *Journal of Autism and Developmental Disorders, 24*(3), 357–367.

Society of Clinical Psychology. (1995). Task force on promotion and dissemination of psychological procedures. *The Clinical Psychologist, 48,* 1–17.

Stromer, R., Kimball, J. W., Kinney, E. M., & Taylor, B. A. (2006). Activity schedules, computer technology, and teaching children with autism spectrum disorders. *Focus on Autism and Other Developmental Disabilities, 21,* 14–24.

Thiemann, K. S., & Goldstein, H. (2001). Social stories, written text cues, and video feedback: Effects on social communication of children with autism. *Journal of Applied Behavior Analysis, 34,* 425–446.

Tsatsanis, K. D. (2005). Neuropsychological characteristics in autism and related conditions. In F. R. Volkmar, R. Paul, A. Klin, & D. Cohen (Eds.), *Handbook of autism and pervasive developmental disorders: Vol. 1. Diagnosis, development, neurobiology, and behavior* (3rd ed., pp. 365–381). Hoboken, NJ: Wiley.

Van Bourgondien, M. E., Reichle, N. C., & Schopler, E. (2003). Effects of a model treatment approach on adults with autism. *Journal of Autism and Developmental Disorders, 33,* 131–140.

Volkmar, F. R., & Klin, A. (2005). Issues in the classification of autism and related conditions. In F. R. Volkmar, R. Paul, A. Klin, & D. Cohen (Eds.), *Handbook of autism and pervasive developmental disorders: Vol. 1. Diagnosis, development, neurobiology, and behavior* (3rd ed., pp. 5–41). Hoboken, NJ: Wiley.

Volkmar, F. R., Paul, R., Klin, A., & Cohen, D. (Eds.). (2005a). *Handbook of autism and pervasive developmental disorders: Vol. 1. Diagnosis, development, neurobiology, and behavior* (3rd ed.). Hoboken, NJ: Wiley.

Volkmar, F. R., Paul, R., Klin, A. & Cohen, D. (Eds.). (2005b). *Handbook of autism and pervasive developmental disorders:Vol. 2.Assessment, interventions, and policy* (3rd ed.). Hoboken, NJ: Wiley.

Welterlin, A. (2009). The Home TEACCHing Program: A study of the efficacy of a parent training early intervention model (Unpublished doctoral dissertation). Rutgers University, New Brunswick, NJ.

7

ACADEMIC DEVELOPMENT THROUGH INTEGRATED BEHAVIORAL EXPERIENTIAL TEACHING

Dianne Zager and Francine Dreyfus

PACE UNIVERSITY

Individuals on the autism spectrum require specialized instructional programs that take into account their complex learning characteristics. These characteristics may include severe language impairment, uneven skill development, extreme behaviors, and challenges in learning and in relating to other people (Zager & Shamow, 2005), all of which significantly impact academic performance. Teachers of children who are on the spectrum are often confronted with the conundrum of choosing instructional methods from a variety of conflicting programs and curricula. The intent of this chapter is to contribute to the existing body of knowledge in the field of autism in order to provide guidance for designing instruction that can meet the diverse and unique learning needs associated with autism. The chapter presents a description of the integrated behavioral experiential teaching (IBET) model (Zager, 2009). IBET (as in *I bet you can!*) is grounded in the tenet that all students can learn realistic, relevant skills when instruction is presented through strategies that are well-matched to individual learner characteristics and when instructional activities and materials hold intrinsic motivation specific to the learner.

In providing an overview of the IBET model, the chapter presents an educational construct that incorporates principles and practices related to *integrated* curriculum, *behavioral* strategies, *and experiential teaching* into a newly configured instructional model. A reflective historical review of the literature in the area of educational intervention for students with autism and related disabilities is provided to build an understanding of the underpinnings of IBET, as well as an appreciation of the relatedness of the theories upon which the approach was founded. An examination of the evidence-base that supports the underlying framework of the IBET approach is presented throughout the chapter, and practices are considered in the light of the historical context in which they were developed and employed.

Introduction: What is IBET?

IBET is an instructional model for teaching basic skills to children with autism spectrum disorders (Zager & Feinman, 2006). Through an integrated approach that incorporates behavioral principles into teaching programs that are based on real-life situations and presented in multisensory contexts, IBET helps children with autism learn basic academic skills. This multisensory, language-based approach uses visual, auditory, kinesthetic, and tactile (VAKT) instructional materials along with photographs of actual experiences, through which children with receptive and expressive language processing challenges are able to comprehend their environment and respond to demands that are placed upon them. IBET is derived from the study of evidence-based multisensory approaches (e.g., Birsh, 2005; Frostig, 1963; Strauss & Lehtinen, 1947); every component of this new intervention reflects practices that have been documented in the special education literature as effective.

Interestingly, one question that has arisen of late pertains to the actual value of the existing literature with regard to evaluating the effectiveness of educational methods. This chapter examines the research base related to practices included in the IBET model to aid educators in making informed decisions about whether or how to use the approach. Theories, principles, and practices are examined through the lens of quantitative and qualitative studies. Strategies on which IBET is founded are considered in light of their historical relevance and the strength of their evidence base. The chapter provides information related to both theory and practice. It is not a how-to chapter, but rather focuses on providing an overview of scientific evidence through which to consider the practice of integrated behavioral experiential teaching. As is demonstrated in the chapter through the historical overview and the examination of relevant studies, the underpinnings of the IBET model are embedded in the history of instructional interventions for students with autism.

Historical Background: Theories and Practices Preceding IBET

The IBET approach is built upon theories related to multisensory instruction, applied behavior principles, and cognitive processing as they pertain to the remediation of reading, math, and information processing disabilities (Frostig, 1963). These theories and strategies provide the framework for teaching basic academic skills and for achieving successful learning outcomes for individuals on the autism spectrum.

Applied Behavioral Principles

The research base for the IBET model begins with Jean Itard's study in the 18th century. Itard applied behavioral principles in his teaching of Victor, the so-called wild boy of Aveyron, a 12-year-old boy with significant delays (Groff, 1932). In his famous study, Itard attempted to teach Victor cognitive, behavioral, and functional living skills, and socialization skills (Martens, 1936). Itard proposed principles of learning or "moral treatment" (Groff, p. 251) to guide instruction for Victor. He identified goals to increase Victor's cognitive development, teach him verbal speech through imitation, and implement an individualized, systematic, and child centered curriculum for instruction. By pairing procedures of modeling/imitation with tangible reinforcements, Itard was able to progressively shape Victor's positive responses. As a result of the behavioral principles employed by Itard, Victor learned to verbally identify letters, write the word *milk*, and use objects in his environment to play games and construct visual patterns.

More than a century later, B. F. Skinner reaffirmed Itard's theories, proposing that learning was a function of change in an individual's observable behaviors. Skinner's cognitive behavior theory was predicated on the assumption that by changing the interaction of the antecedent (stimuli) and consequence of the behavior (i.e., rewarding the correct response), desired behaviors would be developed (Skinner, 1963). Accordingly, with the continued use of rewards that were delivered using varied reinforcement delivery schedules, maintenance of learned behaviors could be facilitated. Further, by utilizing naturally occurring reinforcement in a variety of settings, acquired behaviors could be generalized and sustained. Applications of Skinner's theories of stimulus-response patterns form the foundation of direct instruction programs for teaching academic skills. These theories are the basis of the IBET program.

Skinner's principles and procedures became known as applied behavior analysis (ABA), a research validated methodology that has been shown to be an effective approach for teaching behavioral, social, and cognitive skills to individuals on the autism spectrum (Cohen, Heller, Alberto, & Frederick, 2008; Dunlap, Kern & Worcester, 2001; Flores & Ganz, 2007; Hayward, Svein, Gale, & Morgan, 2009; Heflin & Alberto, 2001; Howard, Sparkman, Cohen, Green, & Stanislaw, 2005; Iovannone, Dunlap, Huber, & Kincaid, 2003; Simpson, 2001; Tincani, 2007). According to Simpson (2001), ABA is an effective practice that can promote change in individuals' behavior and skills. Further, Iovannone et al. (2003) concluded, in their meta-analysis of studies related to effective education practices, that the use of ABA strategies with individuals with autism actually increased the rate of acquisition and generalization of new skills.

Howard et al. (2005) compared the effects of three treatment approaches (intensive behavior therapy, a combination of strategies, and nonintensive behavior strategies) with preschool age children. They concluded that the group that received intensive behavior intervention (i.e., 1:1 adult/child ratio, 25–40 hours per week), had higher mean standard scores in language, cognitive, and adaptive skills as compared to the other two groups. In a more recent study, Hayward et al. (2009) showed the effectiveness of behavioral intervention by examining the progress of two groups of children with autism who received individualized behavioral intervention for 36 hours per week over one year. One group of 23 children that received ABA services in a clinic and another group of 21 children that received ABA services from parents with professional supervision were included. Both groups of children improved significantly, as measured by their growth in cognitive, language, social, motor, and adaptive behavior skills.

IBET Incorporates ABA Principles.   Based on principles of systematic and sequential instruction, structured learning environments, and shaping and rewarding desired responses as detailed in Itard's work and Skinner's cognitive behavior theory, IBET can promote academic skill acquisition for children who have been resistant to instruction. IBET's structured tasks facilitate fluency, generalization, and maintenance through the repetition of skills and use intrinsic rewards throughout the program. By combining mathematical problem solving and decoding within stories and employing a structured ABA approach, IBET programming helps children acquire and generalize literacy and mathematics skills. Skill acquisition is enhanced through materials that contain motivating visual prompts and cues. Throughout the program, students are sequentially prompted and rewarded for correct responses, therein increasing the rate of learning and the fluency of skills.

Multisensory Learning

IBET's instructional strategies are anchored in the research findings of Grace Fernald, Samuel Orton, and Samuel Kirk on language and reading disabilities. Grace Fernald's strategies for teaching reading focused on teaching sight words (whole words) while students simultaneously used all four modalities, visual, auditory, kinesthetic, and tactile (VAKT), to cognitively process words (Fernald, 1943). Fernald's method included four phases: (a) the teacher (auditory model) pronounced the word; (b) the student looked at the word (visual); (c) the student traced the letters of the word (kinesthetic and tactile); and (d) the student rhythmically pronounced all the syllables of the word. Included in Fernald's strategy were the behavioral strategies of repetition (the student repeated the word until ready to write it), self-regulation (checking to see if the written word was correct), and errorless learning (providing visual cues to check the student's writing, and repeating the process until the student mastered writing the word correctly) (Oakland, Black, Stanford, Nussbaum, & Balise, 1998). By implementing applied behavioral principles and systematic direct instruction, Fernald's method taught students to read, write, and spell words using multisensory strategies.

Samuel Orton hypothesized that approximately 10% of all students had reading disabilities (Ritchey & Goeke, 2006). According to Orton, reading disabilities were caused by a lack of dominance in the brain where language was processed, resulting in mirror images (i.e., reversals) and word blindness, which Orton referred to as *strephosymbolia* (Hallahan & Mercer, 2001; Ritchey & Goeke, 2006). The instructional reading program that Orton developed with Anna Gillingham was a sequential, multisensory approach to teach reading, spelling, and writing designed to remediate word processing problems associated with dyslexia (Rose & Zirkel, 2007). Incorporating Fernald's VAKT strategy, Orton's program emphasized a multisensory approach to learning. A basic strategy of the program focused on using visual, kinesthetic, and tactile modalities to facilitate the representation and structure of written language (Oakland et al., 1998). In contrast to Fernald's whole word strategy for learning to read and spell words, the basis of Orton's approach was phonological awareness and phonics (Oakland et al., 1998). In Orton's program, instruction began with recognizing phonemes and progressed to vocabulary and reading comprehension. A significant component of the program was continual drill and practice to ensure retention due to deficits in short-term visual memory (Oakland et. al., 1998). The approach used direct, explicit instruction in written language through a systematic and cumulative process (Ritchey & Goeke, 2006). By progressing through this sequence of instruction, students were able to learn new skills, while practicing already learned skills to ensure mastery.

In his early research with children with reading disabilities, Samuel Kirk concluded it was essential that reading readiness skills be explicitly taught in order to remediate information processing deficits in the areas of visual and auditory discrimination, as well as visual short-term memory (Bos & Vaughn, 1998; Deshler, 1998). The single most important requirement for learning to read, according to Kirk, was the development of the ability to process information. He believed that information processing ability could be improved through the use of systematic explicit instruction, frequent drill and repetition, and experiential learning (Bos & Vaughn, 1998). He suggested that children begin learning sounds with activities such as nursery rhymes to promote the development of auditory discrimination and memory (Bos & Vaughn, 1998). The stages of reading formulated by Kirk included Fernald's VAKT strategy with multisensory learning to compensate for deficits in sensory processing. Kirk formulated three stages of reading development: (a) reading sentences that are experiential and developed with the child, (b) learning phonics to associate the sound with the alphabetic symbol words and then the structure of words, and (c) the last stage in which the child decodes with automaticity (Bos & Vaughn, 1998). Kirk emphasized the need to use instructional strategies based on sound principles of behavior, progressive systematic instruction with frequent repetition, and a reward system to facilitate skill development and maintenance.

There have been studies that have examined the use of direct instruction and multisensory strategies for teaching reading comprehension and decoding skills to school-age children and adolescents on the autism spectrum (Broun, 2004; Chiang & Lin, 2007; Flores & Ganz, 2007). Flores and Ganz (2007) conducted a research investigation using direct instruction with four elementary school students with a scripted teacher manual and visual cues in the areas of statement inference, factual information, and analogies. Similar, to Orton and Kirk's interventions, in the Flores and Ganz study, the teacher used direct instruction combined with principles of applied behavior (immediate correction procedures, positive reinforcement for correct responses, and modeling). All students achieved to criterion in each of the three areas.

Several recent studies have further confirmed the effectiveness of multisensory teaching. Based on their meta-analysis of 11 studies focusing on instruction in reading comprehension for students with autism spectrum disorders, Chiang and Lin (2007) suggested a multisensory approach to sight word comprehension that included multimedia instruction, picture cues, and flash cards combined with discrete trial training and direct instruction. Broun's (2004) implementation of a visual, auditory, kinesthetic, and tactile approach to teach whole sight words is similar to Fernald's methodology. Broun also suggested that students put words together to create sentences and then design books using these sentences based on their own interests, a strategy suggested by Kirk for teaching initial reading instruction that was based on the student's own experiential writing.

IBET Is Multisensory. Through IBET, children learn mathematics and literacy skills through an integrated multisensory process using Fernald's VAKT methodology, as well as through systematic direct instruction proposed by Orton and Kirk, and confirmed by numerous other studies (e.g., Broun, 2004; Chiang & Lin, 2007; Flores & Ganz, 2007). The multisensory manipulative items used in IBET have textures, shapes, and colors to increase tactile and kinesthetic input. Individuals with autism have difficulty processing auditory information; and by using a multisensory approach, students' strengths in perceptual and other sensory skills can be used to foster learning (Helfin & Alberto, 2001). The use of concrete visual, tactile, and kinesthetic cues enables students with autism to attend to relevant stimuli in tasks, organize information for comprehension, and generalize skills across environments (Heflin & Alaimo, 2007). IBET integrates students' personal experiences to teach literacy and math skills as suggested by Kirk's teaching and learning principles in the development of reading. Furthermore, in keeping with the findings of Orton (Oakland et al., 1998) and Kirk (Bos & Vaughn, 1998), the IBET Program includes a phonics based approach for decoding skills and sequentially teaches literal, inferential, and problem solving comprehension skills.

Cognition Related to Visual Perception

The theories and interventions advocated by Frostig, Cruickshank, and Deshler address deficits in cognitive skills related to the neurological functions of perception, language, and memory. The work of these researchers focuses on implementing visual and perceptual motor strategies to facilitate learning. The results of Cruickshank's work with children with cerebral palsy indicated that the children were severely impaired on tasks focusing on visual and tactual motor skills. Given black-and-white line drawings of objects with the background covered with lines, shapes, and other abstract forms, the children focused on the background information, indicating that they had deficits in figure–ground discrimination (Dolphin & Cruickshank, 1951). Cruickshank concluded that perceptual motor problems affected learning; and therefore, the environment needed to be structured to emphasize relevant stimuli and assist students to manage their distractibility (Hallahan & Mercer, 2001).

Frostig suggested that areas of the brain were interdependent in psychological functions and affected language, motor, and perceptual skills (Frostig & Maslow, 1979). The theoretical construct of her work focused on the value of perceptual and motor training to facilitate remediation in these areas. According to Frostig, children with learning disabilities who demonstrated difficulty in integrative functions had difficulty in integrating the two hemispheres of the brain (Frostig & Maslow, 1979). She concluded from her research that brain functioning could be changed through educational interventions and that intelligence was a "conglomerate of interrelated abilities" (Frostig & Maslow, p. 44). Frostig suggested specific interventions for children with left hemisphere deficits which included the use of visual, tactile, or kinesthetic materials to facilitate reading and writing skills.

Similarly, for children with deficits in the right hemisphere whose strengths were verbal and auditory skills, training was implemented through the use of visual patterns. Frostig also suggested that using a multimodality approach with tactile cues would facilitate visual memory for students with right hemisphere disabilities (e.g., the student might write the letter on the back of his or her hand; Frostig & Maslow, 1979).

From his work with secondary-age students with learning disabilities, Deshler devised strategies for improving reading comprehension and overall classroom achievement (Deshler, 1998). Deshler's intervention focuses on teaching students with disabilities how to connect new knowledge to information they previously have been taught (Deshler, Schumaker, Bulgren, & Lenz, 2001). The purpose of the strategic instruction model (SIM) created by Deshler is to assist students with disabilities to actively participate in the learning process by: (a) paraphrasing details and main ideas in their own words, (b) utilizing self-questioning techniques to monitor comprehension, (c) using visual imagery to create a visual representation of the passage/ information, and (d) decoding unfamiliar words by context clues and word analysis (Clapper, Bremer, & Kachgal, 2002; Clark, Deshler, Schumaker, Alley, & Warner, 1984). Components of SIM, the Content Enhancement Routines, and the Anchoring Table (a visual organizer), were developed to ensure that students were actively involved in their own learning, These strategies visually present abstract concepts concretely and distinguish important information from extraneous information. The Anchoring Table explicitly teaches students how to learn content information (Clark et al., 1984).

Studies focused on teaching reading skills indicate that using graphic organizers, visual mapping, and reference to background knowledge to new skills and information are critical learning strategies for students on the autism spectrum (Gately, 2008; Kim, Vaughn, Wanzek, & Wei, 2004; O'Connor & Klein, 2004). In a study of 20 students with autism spectrum disorders, the effect of three strategies (answering prereading question, completing cloze sentences from information in the test, and anaphoric cueing a target referent) were examined by O'Connor and Klein (2004). The results of the study indicated anaphoric cueing was the most successful intervention for students to promote improvement in their comprehension skills. In their meta-analysis of 21 studies conducted between 1963 and 2001, Kim et al. (2006) concluded that graphic organizers were effective instructional tools for teaching comprehension in specific reading passages for students with learning disabilities. Gately (2008) described visual mapping and think-alouds as strategies to facilitate higher order comprehension skills. Think-alouds were used to assist students with the skills of "predicting, questioning, clarifying, and summarizing," (Gately, 2008, p. 42), similar to the strategies devised by Deshler in his strategic instruction model (Deshler et al., 2001).

IBET Emphasizes Visual Cues. The research of Cruickshank, Frostig, and Deshler is threaded throughout IBET instruction. Cruickshank (1977) advocated structuring educational environments to eliminate extraneous stimuli so that students could attend to salient information. Through visual and tactile stimuli that are embedded in instructional stimuli, the IBET multisensory materials promote attention to salient aspects of tasks. Students learn to "read" the materials in order to solve problems. For instance, in IBET math, the block that represents the number 10 is consistently color coded as red, with 10 bumps and 10 distinct segments; and it is 10 inches in length. Such cues provided in learning tasks increase the likelihood that children will respond correctly to questions and learn new skills.

Frostig's (1963) ideas about educational interventions promoted multimodality instruction, such as IBET, for teaching reading and writing skills to students who have atypical sensory processing abilities. Photographs are used in the IBET program to maximize the visual skills that are often the strongest learning modality for individuals on the autism spectrum. Similar to Deshler's (1998) interventions that often teach through visual perceptual skills, the IBET approach encourages students to use visual imagery to create a visual representation of mathematical concepts and operations. The IBET program reflects Deshler's suggestions to use students' own experiences as a basis for learning. Individuals with autism have difficulty understanding the meaning of inferential or abstract concepts and perform better using literal information and comprehension. Through the incorporation of real-life experiential learning in IBET instruction, abstract mathematical and literacy concepts become associated with meaningful experiences.

Evidence-Based Principles Underlying IBET Practices

While most existing programs for children with autism focus primarily on visual methods of instruction (Hodgon, 2000), the IBET approach utilizes a VAKT (visual, auditory, kinesthetic, tactile) system of instruction: *auditory* refers to input perceived through the sense of hearing; *kinesthetic* refers to input through muscular movement; and *tactile* input is perceived through the sense of touch. In IBET, multisensory instruction interconnects several subject areas and learning modalities simultaneously.

Integration of Methods and Content

As its name implies, IBET blends several educational practices, bringing together methods that since the early 1980s have been successful with children with learning and behavior differences. By combining varied practices, an empirically eclectic system has been developed in which data analysis helps to identify specific practices that are most helpful for particular students. By integrating approaches, students are able to simultaneously benefit from a variety of approaches that often have been considered to be in opposition to each other. Effective teachers use reflective planning to select and design instructional strategies (Gartin & Murdick, 2008), interweaving and blending practices. When decision making in education is based on scientific evidence rather than on philosophical bias instructional practices enhance learning (Shelden & Hutchins, 2008). Because IBET is grounded in evidence-based methodology and because of its student-centered focus, it is congruent with other research-based programs.

In the title, *IBET, integrated* refers to combining practices and integrating strategies from different approaches so that teachers are able to design instruction to match the unique characteristics and needs of individual learners. Subject matter is not considered from isolated perspectives, but is mixed and combined in such a manner that reinforces learning. Specifically, *integrated* in the IBET program means that learning can best be accomplished if information is presented to students in a systematic fashion that utilizes and integrates the four major learning perceptual channels to maximally utilize student strengths. *Integrated* also refers to integrating subject matter, so that reading and other literacy skills are integrated into math, science, social studies, social skills, and other lessons. Material learned in one lesson is reinforced in other lessons throughout the program. Subject matter is not considered from isolated perspectives, but is mixed and combined in such a manner that reinforces learning. Finally, *integrated* implies that instruction that is provided by an integrated transdisciplinary team of professionals and family members fosters generalized learning, especially for children with cognitive challenges.

Behavioral Principles

The IBET model incorporates behavioral principles to motivate, engage, and reinforce learners while progress is systematically monitored and analyzed in order to refine instruction as needed. The term *behavioral* in IBET attests to the fact that principles of applied behavioral analysis have been demonstrated to be effective in teaching students who have autism spectrum disorders (Bregman, Zager, & Gerdtz, 2005; Schreibman & Ingersoll, 2005).

In IBET instruction, students are prompted using a logical sequence of prompts that increases the rate of learning and skill acquisition through minimizing chance error, rewarding correct responses, and increasing the likelihood of desired responses by prearranging the learning environment and learning tasks. IBET strategies foster skill fluency, generalization and maintenance through the incorporation of prompts embedded within stimuli, frequent repetitions, scheduled reinforcement and naturally occurring reinforcement. Skills that are taught through this model are considered to be learned or mastered after the student is (a) able to demonstrate the skill in a natural setting in which the skill typically would be needed, (b) initiate and carry out the skill at in the absence of artificial prompts, and (c) perform the skill at an acceptable rate of fluency.

Experiential Learning

The presence of language deficits and cognitive processing difficulties in individuals with autism dictates that, in order to be effective, instruction for students with this disorder whenever possible should be directly related to personal experiences through which concepts can be understood and skills can be mastered. Real experiences add meaning to language and concepts that otherwise would be abstract in nature. Experiences are necessary for the development of language. Students' own experiences form the basis of IBET learning. Because children with autism tend to have difficulty grasping underlying meaning and do better with literal comprehension rather than inferential or critical comprehension skills, working with directly stated literal facts about personally experienced events makes learning easier. Words and numbers themselves have no meaning, but when repeatedly associated with real-life experiences children are able to attach meaning to specific symbols. In the IBET model, students' own experiences, as related by them, are used to introduce and teach literacy and math skills. In order to maximize visual abilities, which are often the strongest perceptual modality for individuals on the spectrum, and to teach students to attend to relevant aspects of events, photographs play a vital role in the IBET model.

Literacy and Mathematics Instruction in IBET

This section addresses the research base and underlying principles for IBET instructional strategies in the areas of mathematics and literacy. Both the IBET literacy and math models utilize a VAKT approach combined with personal experiences and inquiry-based methods that lend meaning and purpose to the acquisition of concepts and skills. Mathematics and literacy are not separated in IBET instruction. In fact, when mathematics instruction is integrated with literacy instruction and provided in a meaningful context, growth occurs in both core academic areas (van Garderen, 2008). Math skills taught through IBET include basic counting, addition, subtraction, multiplication, and division; fractions; time-telling; money skills; calendar skills; problem solving; and matching/sorting/patterns. Literacy skills addressed in IBET instruction include basic phonic decoding skills with letter matrices/rimes; sight word development based on language experience and Fernald methods; and literal, inferential, critical, and problem solving comprehension skills.

IBET Math

Mathematics disabilities, one of the most prominent features of learning disabilities, are shared by approximately 25% of students with high functioning autism and Asperger syndrome (Williams, Goldstein, Kojkowski, & Minshew, 2008). A study by Mayes and Calhoun (2005) found that 67% of students with autism also exhibited learning disabilities. Students with disabilities that affect math achievement, demonstrate difficulty learning basic facts, generalizing math skills to the community, determining salient factors from irrelevant information, and performing multistep calculations (Maccini & Gagnon, 2006). Some explicit instruction techniques that have proven effective for students with special needs have included task analysis, mnemonics, flash cards, and direct instruction (Vaughn, Gersten, & Chard, 2000). In spite of the research base for these techniques, in recent years educators have shifted toward more inquiry-based strategies and away from direct instruction (Cole & Wasburn-Moses, 2010). Inquiry-based teaching engages children in solving problems collaboratively. Problems in inquiry-based learning require use of math skills in natural settings and in real-life contexts. Math educators often differentiate between higher and lower level math skills, associating higher level math with inquiry-based learning, and lower level skills with direct instruction.

Interestingly, the National Mathematics Advisory Panel (2008) reviewed the extant research on these two supposedly diverse approaches and recommended a balanced approach that combines inquiry-based instruction and direct instruction. IBET practices are based, in large measure, on these findings that teaching and learning core academic skills is a complementary process that should combine both direct instruction and collaborative-based activities (Donaldson & Zager, 2010). It is clear that both approaches should be combined in order to meet the needs of diverse learners in varied situations (Bottge, Rueda, LaRoque, Serlin, & Kwon, 2007).

One strategy that has been used in math instruction for students with autism is *self-regulation*. Similar to cognitive behavior modification, self-regulation instruction involves students learning to utilize assistive tools, such as checklists as they perform calculation, with reminders or prompts built in for each step. Dunlap and Dunlap (1989) found that, with self-regulation, student solution accuracy increased and attitude toward tasks became more positive (Dunlap & Dunlap, 1989). Verbal feedback strategies, in which students were required to repeat salient directions to reinforce skills, helped to create structure, and ensure development of comprehension for each step (Spreen, Risser, & Edgell, 1995).

Direct instruction is a scientifically supported strategy that is used frequently in special education (Zager & Shamow, 2005). Direct instruction involves the use of systematic teaching to help students learn how to perform specific tasks, using prompts to guide the learner to reinforce correct responses. Accurate responses are rewarded; inaccurate responses are redirected, with an emphasis on students learning strategies for computation or problem solving. Utilizing a direct instruction intervention for computation, Van Houten and Rolider (1990) taught students to match a numeral to a specific color to teach number names, with two-thirds of the subjects tested demonstrating 100% accuracy 4 months following (Van Houten & Rolider, 1990). In another direct instruction intervention for problem solving, Wilson and Sindelar (1991) successfully taught addition and subtraction word problems to students with special needs.

A well-known strategy, *concrete-representational-abstract* (CRA), has been used to teach academic skills to students with information processing deficits. In CRA, students are first shown concrete examples (e.g., two halves of a cookie), then they might be shown a representation (a picture of two halves of a square), followed by the abstract depiction of the concept (the fraction ½). Miller and Mercer (1993) determined that students who learned word problems, having no exposure to word problems previously, when taught using a concrete-representational-abstract sequence, performed at a mean level of 87%. Because of their difficulty processing abstract concepts, a concrete-to-representational-to-abstract sequence of instruction has been shown to be especially helpful for teaching math to students with autism spectrum disorders (Rourke & Strang, 1978).

The IBET approach has been used to teach children with autism spectrum disorders fundamental academic skills (Zager, 2007). IBET utilizes elements of direct instruction in its use of behavioral principles; and CRA in its emphasis on concrete presentation of stimuli first (through photographs of actual experiences followed by abstract symbols) to teach skills and concepts through vivid concrete representations. Students' direct personal experiences are utilized to make learning meaningful, through photographs and experiential learning in combination with errorless learning and systematic reinforcement. To enhance the power of educational materials, prompts and cues are embedded directly within the instructional stimuli (Zager & Feinman, 2006).

IBET Literacy Instruction

Literacy skills addressed in IBET instruction include basic phonic decoding with letter matrices/rimes; sight word development based on language experience; VAKT methods for literacy (Fernald, 1943); and literal, inferential, critical, and problem solving comprehension skills. The IBET literacy approach focuses on instruction of decoding and comprehension through interactive lessons based on children's own stories. Because IBET utilizes the student's own experiences as the basis for reading instruction and the raw material is created by the student, lessons are inherently motivating and meaningful. Students proceed at their own rate as they learn through reading, writing, and problem solving. An integrated approach across subjects that includes direct and indirect instruction through interactive lessons that utilize experiential learning is advantageous for learning (Marchant & Womack, 2010).

Similar to the IBET math approach, in literacy instruction the technique of self-regulation instruction involves students learning to utilize self-editing and corrective strategies (Dunlap & Dunlap, 1989; Spreen, Risser, & Edgell, 1995), with cues within the reading prompts built in for each step. Teacher feedback maintains structure by directly teaching and reinforcing skills, to ensure development of comprehension. Inquiry-based learning complements the explicit instruction and increases the level of student engagement.

Concrete-representational-abstract (CRA) has been used successfully to improve acquisition of comprehension skills and to facilitate progression to higher levels of cognition. Through use of photographs and problem solving stories, students are able to learn decoding and comprehension concomitantly. The concrete-to-representational-to-abstract sequence of instruction has been shown to be effective for presenting new information to students with autism spectrum disorders because of their difficulty processing abstract concepts (Rourke & Strang, 1978).

Summary

To understand and appreciate new methods in autism intervention, especially those that integrate varied research-based components in an innovative manner, it is helpful to understand the historical trends and earlier research underlying these new approaches. The IBET model is derived from a combination of tried and true methods, each with a long history of researched effectiveness.

There are five key components of the IBET model: (a) content across subject areas is combined in an integrated model so that students are concomitantly learning more than one skill; (b) instruction is systematic and structured following behavioral principles for teaching and learning; (c) prompts and cues are embedded within instructional to stimuli to ensure learner success; (d) multisensory instruction is provided to facilitate information processing; and (e) learning of new information is related to personal experiences to infuse meaning through real-life situations. By combining and integrating these parts, the whole configuration is greater than the sum of the parts.

Acknowledgment

This chapter was supported in part by the Michael C. Koffler endowment to Pace University and by MetSchools, New York.

References

Birsh, J. (2005). *Multisensory teaching of basic language skills* (2nd ed.). Baltimore, MD: Brookes.

Bos, C.S., & Vaughn, S. (1998). Samuel Kirk's legacy to teaching reading: The past speaks to the present. *Learning Disabilities Research & Practice, 13,* 22–28.

Bottge, B. A., Rueda, E., LaRoque, P. T., Serlin, R. B., & Kwon, J. (2007). Integrating reform-orientated math instruction in special education settings. *Learning Disabilities Research and Practice, 22*(2), 96–109.

Bregman, J. D., Zager, D., & Gerdtz, J. (2005). Behavioral interventions. In F. R. Volkmar, R. Paul, A. Klin, & D. Cohen (Eds.), *Handbook on autism and pervasive developmental disabilities* (3rd ed., Vol. 2, pp. 897–924). Hoboken, NJ: Wiley.

Broun, L. T., (2004). Teaching students with autistic spectrum disorders to read. *Teaching Exceptional Children, 36,* 36–40.

Chiang, H. M., & Lin, Y. H. (2007). Reading comprehension instruction for students with autism spectrum disorders: A review of the literature. *Focus on Autism and Other Developmental Disabilities, 22,* 259–267.

Clapper, A. T., Bremer, C. D., & Kachgal, M. M. (2002). Never too late: Approaches to reading instruction for secondary students with disabilities. *National Center on Secondary Education and Transition Research to Practice Brief, 1,* 1–5.

Clark, F. L., Deshler, D. D., Schumaker, J. B., Alley, G., & Warner, M. M. (1984). Visual imagery and self-questioning: Strategies to improve comprehension of written material. *Journal of Learning Disabilities, 17,* 145–149. Retrieved from http://www.sagepublications.com

Cohen, E. T., Heller, K. W., Alberto, P., & Fredrick, L. D. (2008). Using a three-step decoding strategy with constant time delay to teach word reading to students with mild and moderate mental retardation. *Focus on Autism and Other Developmental Disabilities, 23,* 67–78.

Cole, J. E., & Wasburn-Moses, L. H. (2010). A special educator's guide to understanding and assisting with inquiry-based teaching in mathematics. *Teaching Exceptional Children, 42*(4), 14–20.

Cruickshank, W. (1977). Myths and realities in learning disabilities. *Journal of Learning Disabilities, 10*(1), 51–58.

Deshler, D. D. (1998). Grounding interventions for students with learning disabilities in "powerful ideas." *Learning Disabilities Research & Practice, 13,* 22–28.

Deshler, D., Schumaker, J., Bulgren, J., & Lenz, K. (2001). Making learning easier: Connecting new knowledge to things students already know. *Teaching Exceptional Children 33,* 82–86.

Dolphin, J. E., & Cruickshank, W. (1951). The figure–ground relationship in children with cerebral palsy. *Journal of Clinical Psychology, 7,* 228–231. Retrieved from http://www3.interscience.wiley.com/journal

Donaldson, J., & Zager, D. (2010). Mathematics interventions for students with high functioning autism/Asperger's syndrome. *Teaching Exceptional Children, 42*(6), 40–46.

Dunlap, L. K., & Dunlap, G. (1989). A self-monitoring package for teaching subtraction with regrouping to students with learning disabilities. *Journal of Applied Behavior Analysis, 22,* 309–314.

Dunlap, G., Kern, L., & Worcester, J. (2001). ABA and academic instruction. *Focus on Autism and Other Developmental Disorders, 16,* 129–136.

Fernald, G. M. (1943). *Remedial techniques in basic school subjects.* New York: McGraw-Hill.

Flores, M. M., & Ganz, J. B., (2007). Effectiveness of direct instruction for teaching statement inference, use of facts, and analogies to students with developmental disabilities and reading delays. *Focus on Autism and Other Developmental Disorders, 4,* 244–251.

Frostig, M. (1963). *Visual perception in the brain-injured child.* New York: Wiley.

Frostig, M., & Maslow, P. (1979). Neuropsychological contributions to education. *Journal of Learning Disabilities, 12,* 40–53. Retrieved from http://www.sagepublications.com

Gartin, B. C., & Murdick, N. L. (2008). Meeting the needs of all students through instructional design. In H. P. Parette & G. Peterson-Karlan (Eds.), *Research-based practices in developmental disabilities* (2nd ed., pp. 171–182). Austin, TX: Pro-Ed.

Gately, S. E., (2008). Facilitating reading comprehension for students on the autism spectrum. *Teaching Exceptional Children, 40,* 40–45.

Groff, M. L. (1932). Jean Marc Gaspard Itard (1775–1838). *The Psychological Clinic,* 246–256.

Hallahan, D. P., & Mercer, C. D. (2001). Learning disabilities: Historical perspectives. In R. Bradley, L. Danielson, & D. P. Hallahan (Eds.), *Identification of learning disabilities: Research to practice* (pp.1–67). Mahwah, NJ: Erlbaum.

Hayward, D., Svein, E., Gale, C., & Morgan, S. (2009). Assessing progress during treatment for young children with autism receiving intensive behavioural interventions, *Autism: The International Journal of Research and Practice, 13,* 613–633.

Heflin L. J., & Alaimo, D.F. (2007). *Students with autism disorders: Effective instructional practices.* Upper Saddle River, NJ: Pearson.

Heflin, L. J., & Alberto, P. (2001). Establishing a behavioral context for learning for students with autism. *Focus on Autism and Other Developmental Disabilities, 16,* 93–101.

Hodgon, L. (2000). *Visual strategies for improving communication: Practical supports for school and home.* Troy, MI: Quirks Roberts.

Howard, J. S., Sparkman, C., Cohen, H., Green, G., & Stanislaw, H. (2005). A comparison of intensive behavior analytic and eclectic treatments for young children with autism. *Research on Developmental Disabilities, 26,* 359–383.

Iovannone, R., Dunlap, G., Huber, H., & Kincaid, D. (2003). Effective educational practices for students with autism spectrum disorders. *Focus on Autism and Other Developmental Disabilities, 18,* 150–165.

Kim, A. H., Vaughn, S., Wanzek, J., & Wei, S. (2004). Graphic organizers and their effects on the reading comprehension of students with LD: A synthesis of research. *Journal of Learning Disabilities, 37,* 105–118.

Maccini, P., & Gagnon, J. C. (2006). Perceptions and applications of NCTM standards by special and general education teachers. *Exceptional Children, 68,* 325–344.

Marchant, M., & Womack, S. (2010). Book in a bag: Blending social skills and academics. *Teaching Exceptional Children, 42*(4), 6–12.

Martens, E. H. (1936). A conference for curriculum for mentally retarded children. *Journal of Exceptional Children, 2,* 92–97.

Mayes, S. D., & Calhoun, S. L. (2005). Frequency of reading, math, and writing disabilities in children with clinical disorders. *Learning and individual differences, 16*(2), 145–157.

Miller, S. P., & Mercer, C. D. (1993). Using data to learn about concrete, semi-concrete, and abstract instruction for students with math disabilities. *Learning Disabilities Research and Practice, 8,* 89–96.

National Mathematics Advisory Panel. (2008). *Foundations for success: The final report of the National Mathematics Advisory Panel.* Washington, DC: U.S. Department of Education.

Oakland, T., Black, J. L., Stanford, G., Nussbaum, N. L., & Balise, R. R. (1998). An evaluation of the dyslexia training program: A multisensory method for promoting reading in students with reading disabilities. *Journal of Learning Disabilities, 31,* 140–147.

O'Connor, I. M., & Klein, P. D. (2004). Exploration of strategies for facilitating the reading comprehension of high-functioning students with autism spectrum disorders. *Journal of Autism and Developmental Disabilities, 34,* 115–127.

Ritchey, K. D., & Goeke, J. L. (2006). Orton-Gillingham and Orton-Gillingham-based reading instruction: A review of the literature. *The Journal of Special Education, 40,* 171–183.

Rose, T. E., & Zirkel, P. (2007). Orton-Gillingham methodology for students with reading disabilities: 30 years of law. *The Journal of Special Education, 41,* 171–185.

Rourke, B. P., & Strang, J. D. (1978). Neuropsychological significance of variations in patterns of academic performance: Motor, psychomotor, and tactile-perceptual abilities. *Journal Pediatric Psychology, 3*(2), 62–66.

Schreibman, L., & Ingersoll, B. (2005). Behavioral interventions to promote learning in individuals with autism. In F. R. Volkmar, R. Paul, A. Klin, & D. Cohen (Eds.), *Handbook on autism and pervasive developmental disabilities* (3rd ed., Vol. 2, pp. 882–897). Hoboken, NJ: Wiley.

Shelden, D. L., & Hutchins, M. P. (2008). Personalized curriculum development. In H. P. Parette & G. Peterson-Karlan (Eds.), *Research-based practices in developmental disabilities* (2nd ed., pp. 235–268). Austin, TX: Pro-Ed.

Simpson, R. L. (2001). ABA and students with autism spectrum disorders: Issues and considerations for effective practice. *Focus on Autism and Other Developmental Disorders, 16,* 68–71. Retrieved from http://www.sagepublications.com

Skinner, B. F. (1963). Operant behavior. *American Psychologist, 18,* 503–515.

Spreen, O., Risser, A. T., & Edgell, D. (1995). *Developmental neuropsychology.* New York: Oxford Press.

Strauss, A. A., & Lehtinen, L. E. (1947). *Psychopathology and education of the brain injured child.* New York: Grune & Stratton.

Tincani, M. (2007). Moving forward: Positive behavior support and applied behavior analysis. *The Behavior Analyst Today, 8,* 492–499.

Van Garderen, D. (2008). Middle school special education teachers' instructional practices for solving mathematical word problems: An exploratory study. *Teacher Education and Special Education, 31*, 132–144.

Van Houten, R., & Rolider, A. (1990). The use of color mediation techniques to teach number identification and single digit multiplication problems to children with learning problems. *Education and Treatment of Children, 13*, 216–224.

Vaughn, S., Gerwsten, R., & Chard, D. J. (2000). The underlying message in LD intervention research: Findings from research synthesis. *Exceptional Children, 67*, 99–114.

Williams, D. L., Goldstein, G., Kojkowski, N., & Minshew, N. J. (2008). Do individuals with high functioning autism have the IQ profile associated with nonverbal learning disability? *Research in Autism Spectrum Disorders, 2*(2), 353–361.

Wilson, C. L., & Sindelar, P. T. (1991). Direct instruction in math word problems: Students with learning disabilities. *Exceptional Children, 57*, 512–519.

Zager, D. (2007). *Current trends in educating students with autism: Selecting evidence-based methods.* Presentation at pre-conference workshop, Arkansas CEC Annual Conference, Hot Springs, AR.

Zager, D. (2009, May). *IBET: Integrated behavioral experiential teaching.* Presentation to PCI staff and consultants. San Antonio, TX.

Zager, D., & Feinman, S. (2006, April). *Integrated behavioral experiential teaching: Teaching math skills to students with autism.* Paper presented at the International Council for Exceptional Children, Salt Lake City, UT.

Zager, D., & Shamow, N. (2005). Teaching students with autism spectrum disorders. In D. Zager (Ed.), *Autism spectrum disorders: Identification, education, and treatment* (3rd ed., pp. 295–326). Mahwah, NJ: Erlbaum.

8

EVIDENCE-BASED PRACTICES

The Ziggurat Model and a Comprehensive Autism Planning System

Brenda Smith Myles

AUTISM SOCIETY

Sheila M. Smith

OHIO CENTER FOR AUTISM AND LOW INCIDENCE

Ruth Aspy and Barry G. Grossman

THE ZIGGURAT GROUP

Shawn Henry

OHIO CENTER FOR AUTISM AND LOW INCIDENCE

In 2009, two reports were published on the prevalence of autism spectrum disorders (ASD). One identified the prevalence of ASD as 1 in 110 (Centers for Disease Control and Prevention, 2009) and the other reported a prevalence rate of 1 in 91 (Kogan et al., 2009). At approximately the same time, three reports were published that attempted to identify evidence-based practices (EBP) for children and youth on the spectrum. These documents were authored or contracted by the following organizations: (a) National Professional Development Center on Autism Spectrum Disorders (NPDC; n.d.), (b) National Autism Center (NAC; 2009), and (c) Centers for Medicare and Medicaid (CMS; 2010). In order to determine whether studies on interventions were scientifically rigorous, the NPDC (n.d.) used the following criteria for articles on interventions used with individuals with ASD (excluding intervention packages): (a) at least two experimental or quasi-experimental group design studies carried out by independent investigators, (b) at least five single case design studies from at least three independent investigators, or (c) a combination of at least one experimental/quasi-experimental study and three single case design studies from independent investigators. The authors of the second report (NAC, 2009) developed a Scientific Merit Rating Scale (SMRS) that analyzed (a) research design, (b) measurement of the dependent variable, (c) measurement of the independent variable or procedural fidelity, (d) participant ascertainment, and (e) generalization (p. 16). Each of these elements within an article was rated on a 5-point Likert scale with scores of 3, 4, or 5 indicating scientific rigor. The third report, commissioned by CMS (2010) sought to identify scientific evidence regarding the efficacy, effectiveness, safety, and availability of ASD–related psychosocial services and supports for children, transitioning youth, and adults with ASD. Articles on interventions were classified as evidence-based using the criteria adopted by the NPDC on ASD and the categories identified by the NAC. Table 8.1 overviews the interventions identified as effective or established in each of the aforementioned reports. Because one of the three documents used different intervention terminology and descriptions, the authors attempted to categorize the three lists using language from each report so that the reader could determine the level of overlap between the reports.

TABLE 8.1 Evidence-based Practices (EBP) (identified as Established EBP by CMS and NAC)

Intervention	Centers for Medicare and Medicaid Services (CMS)	National Autism Center (NAC)[1]	National Professional Development Center on ASD (NPDC)
Antecedent Package	(0–16) (17–21) Modifications of events that typically precede the occurrence of a target behavior. These alterations are made to increase the likelihood of success or reduce the likelihood of problems occurring.	(3–18) Behavior chain interruption; behavioral momentum; choice; cueing/ prompting; environmental enrichment/modification; errorless learning; incorporating echolalia, special interests, thematic activities, or ritualistic/ obsessional activities; maintenance interspersal; noncontingent access/ reinforcement; priming; stimulus variation; time delay.	*Antecedent-based Interventions* (EC-MH) Include 1) using highly preferred activities/items to increase interest level, 2) changing schedule/ routine, 3) implementing preactivity interventions, 4) offering choices, 5) altering manner in which instruction is provided, and 6) enriching the environment for access to sensory stimuli that serve the same function as the interfering behavior.
Behavioral Package	(0–16) Interventions designed to reduce problem behavior and teach functional alternative behaviors or skills through the application of basic principles of behavior change.	(0–21) Chaining; contingency contracting; contingency mapping; delayed contingencies; DR; DTT; FCT; generalization training; mand training; noncontingent escape; reinforcement; shaping; stimulus-stimulus pairing; successive approximation; task analysis; token economy.	
Differential Reinforcement (DR)			(EC-H) Reinforcement is provided for desired behaviors, while inappropriate behaviors are ignored.
Extinction			(EC-MH) Extinction involves withdrawing or terminating the positive reinforcer that maintains an inappropriate interfering behavior.

(continued)

TABLE 8.1 Continued

Intervention	Centers for Medicare and Medicaid Services (CMS)	National Autism Center (NAC)[1]	National Professional Development Center on ASD (NPDC)
Prompting			(EC-MH) Any help given to learners that assist them in using a specific skill.
Reinforcement			(EC-MH) A relationship between learner behavior and a consequence that follows the behavior. This relationship is only considered reinforcement if the consequence increases the probability that a behavior will occur in the future, or at least be maintained.
Time Delay			(E) Fading the use of prompts during instructional activities. With this procedure, a brief delay is provided between the initial instruction and any additional instructions or prompts.
Cognitive Behavioral Intervention Package	(0–16) Interventions designed to change negative or unrealistic thought patterns/behaviors to positively influencing emotions/life functioning.		
Comprehensive Behavioral Treatment for Children	(0–16) Interventions involving a combination of instructional and behavior change strategies and a curriculum that addresses core and ancillary symptoms and behaviors of ASD.	(0–8) Using ABA strategies (e.g., DTT, incidental teaching, errorless learning, shaping). Criteria: {a} defined ASD symptoms, {b} treatment manuals, {c} intensive treatment, and {d} measuring program effectiveness.	

Intervention	Centers for Medicare and Medicaid Services (CMS)	National Autism Center (NAC)[1]	National Professional Development Center on ASD (NPDC)
Discrete Trial Training (DTT)			(EC, E) DTT is a one-to-one instructional approach. Used when a learner needs to learn a skill best taught in small repeated steps. Each trial or teaching opportunity has a definite beginning and end. The use of antecedents and consequences is carefully planned and implemented.
Functional Behavior Assessment			(EC-MH) Systematic strategies that determine underlying behavior function, so that an effective intervention plan can be developed.
Joint Attention Intervention	(0–16) Interventions involving teaching a child to respond to the nonverbal social bids of others or to initiate joint attention interactions.	(0–5) Often taught using DTT, examples include pointing, showing items/activities to another person, and following eye gaze.	
Modeling	(0–16) Interventions relying on an adult or peer providing a demonstration of the target behavior that should result in an imitation by the person with ASD.	(3–18) Examples include live modeling and video modeling.	*See Video Modeling*
Multicomponent Package	(0–16) These interventions involve a combination of multiple treatment procedures that are derived from different fields of interest or different theoretical orientations. They do not better fit one of the other treatment "packages" in this list nor are they associated with specific programs.		

(continued)

TABLE 8.1 Continued

Intervention	Centers for Medicare and Medicaid Services (CMS)	National Autism Center (NAC)[1]	National Professional Development Center on ASD (NPDC)
Naturalistic Teaching Strategies	(0–16) Primarily child-directed interactions to teach functional skills in natural environment. Providing a stimulating environment, modeling how to play, encouraging conversation, providing choices and direct/natural reinforcers, and rewarding reasonable attempts.	(0–9) Different names include *focused stimulation, incidental teaching, milieu teaching, embedded teaching, responsive education,* and *prelinguistic milieu teaching.*	(EC-MH) Includes environmental arrangement, interaction techniques, behavioral strategies designed to encourage specific target behaviors. Builds more elaborate learner behaviors that are naturally reinforcing and appropriate to the interaction.
Parent Implemented Interventions			(EC-E) Parent-implemented Intervention entails parents directly using individualized intervention practices with their child to increase positive learning opportunities and acquisition of important skills.
Peer Training Package	(0–16) These interventions involve teaching children without disabilities strategies to facilitate play and social interactions with children on the autism spectrum. Peers often include classmates or siblings.	(3–14) There are many different peer training programs, including Project LEAP, peer networks, circle of friends, buddy skills package, Integrated Play Groups, peer initiation training, and peer-mediated social interaction training.	(EC-MH) *Peer-Mediated Instruction/ Intervention* Peers are systematically taught ways of engaging learners with ASD in social interactions in both teacher-directed and learner-initiated activities
Picture Exchange Communication System (PECS)	(0–16) Involves the application of a specific AAC system based on behavioral principles that are designed to teach functional communication to children with limited verbal and/or communication skills.		(EC-E) Learners are taught to give a picture of a desired item to a communicative partner in exchange for the item.
Pivotal Response Treatment	(0–16) Focuses on targeting "pivotal" behavioral areas —such as motivation to engage in social communication, self-initiation, self-management, and responsiveness to multiple cues.	(3–9) This treatment is an expansion of Natural Language Paradigm.	(EC-MH) *Pivotal Response Training* Creates a more efficient and effective intervention by enhancing four pivotal variables: motivation, responding to multiple cues, self-management, and self-initiations.

Intervention	Centers for Medicare and Medicaid Services (CMS)	National Autism Center (NAC)[1]	National Professional Development Center on ASD (NPDC)
Response Interruption and Redirection			(EC-MH) RIR contains two main components: During the response interruption component, practitioners stop the learner from engaging in the interfering behavior. Redirection focuses on prompting the learner to engage in a more appropriate, alternative behavior.
Self-management	(0–16) These interventions teach individuals with ASD to regulate their behavior by recording the occurrence/nonoccurrence of the target behavior, and securing reinforcement for doing so.	(3–18) These interventions promote independence by teaching individuals with ASD to regulate their behavior by recording the target behavior, and securing reinforcement for doing so.	(EC-MH) Learners with ASD are taught to discriminate between appropriate and inappropriate behaviors, monitor and record their own behaviors, and reward themselves.
Social Communication Intervention	(0–16) These psychosocial interventions involve targeting some combination impairments such as pragmatic communication skills, and the inability to successfully read social situations.		
Social Skills Groups			(EC-MH) Social skills groups typically involve small groups of two to eight individuals with disabilities and a teacher or adult facilitator. Most social skill group meetings include instruction, role-playing or practice, and feedback.

(continued)

TABLE 8.1 Continued

Intervention	Centers for Medicare and Medicaid Services (CMS)	National Autism Center (NAC)[1]	National Professional Development Center on ASD (NPDC)
Social Skills Package	(0–16) These interventions seek to build social interaction skills by targeting basic responses (e.g., eye contact, name response) to complex social skills (e.g., how to initiate or maintain a conversation). They seek to build social interaction skills in children with ASD by targeting basic responses (e.g., eye contact, name response) to complex social skills (e.g., how to initiate or maintain a conversation).		
Story-based Intervention Package	(0–16) These treatments involve a written description of the situations under which specific behaviors are expected to occur. Stories may be supplemented with additional components.	(6–14) Social Stories™ are the best known story-based interventions and they seek to answer the "who," "what," "when," "where," and "why" in order to improve perspective-taking.	
Social Narratives			(EC-MH) Social narratives describe social situations in detail by highlighting relevant cues and offering examples of appropriate responses.
Speech Generating Devices (SGD)			(EC-MH) SGD are electronic devices that are portable in nature and can produce synthetic or digital speech for the user. SGD may be used with graphic symbols, as well as with alphabet keys.
Structured Teaching	(0–16) This intervention involves a combination of procedures that rely on the physical organization of a setting, predictable schedules, and individualized use of teaching methods.		(EC-MH) *Structured Work Systems* The individual work system is a visually organized space where learners independently practice skills that have been mastered under direct supervision.
Task Analysis			(EC-MH) Breaking a skill into smaller, more manageable steps to teach the skill.

Intervention	Centers for Medicare and Medicaid Services (CMS)	National Autism Center (NAC)[1]	National Professional Development Center on ASD (NPDC)
Technology-based Treatment	(0–16) The presentation of instructional materials using the medium of computers or related technologies.		
Computer-aided Instruction			(E-MH) Using computers to teach academic skills and to promote communication skills. It includes computer modeling and computer tutors.
Video Modeling			(E-MH) A mode of teaching that uses video recording and display equipment to provide a visual model.
Visual Supports			(EC-MH) Any tool presented visually that supports an individual as he or she moves through the day. Might include, but is not limited to, pictures, written words, objects, arrangement of the environment or visual boundaries, schedules, maps, labels, organization systems, timelines, and scripts.
Schedules	(0–16) Interventions involving the presentation of a task that communicates a series of activities or steps required to complete a specific activity.	(3–14) These interventions involve the presentation of a task list that communicates a series of activities or steps required to complete a specific activity.	

Note.   EC = early childhood, E = elementary, MH = middle/high school.
    1 Reported exact age—not age or grade range.

While we now have an understanding of EBP in isolation, it is essential that we determine whether a particular intervention or, more likely, sets of interventions, match a learner's strengths and needs. Thus, it is important to begin with a thorough understanding of the student's needs, especially those related to the underlying characteristics of ASD. Fixsen, Blasé, Horner, and Sugai (2009) stated that "evidence-based practices must be carefully selected to meet student needs AND they must be implemented well in order to achieve educational benefit" (p. 5). Next occurs the process of identifying long-term and short-term goals for the learner. Establishment of these goals will help in selecting the most appropriate instructional strategies (cf. Kraemer, Cook, Browning-White, Mayer, & Wallace, 2008). The next critical step is to integrate these strategies systematically and comprehensively throughout the individual's day by developing a comprehensive daily schedule for the student. This schedule should embed the supports needed for success. In addition, it should provide continual development of student skills and measurement of those skills with a vision of how this will affect the student now and in the future (National Research Council, 2001). This is the comprehensive planning process.

This implementation usually requires changes in the daily activities of staff, related service providers, administrators, and even parents. It takes cohesive team planning, clearly defined objectives, and professional development of all personnel to ensure that the chosen EBPs are implemented with fidelity and across all settings (National Implementation Research Network, 2008).

The purpose of this article is to introduce two linked comprehensive planning models that meet the rigor required by No Child Left Behind (NCLB), Response to Intervention (RTI), and School Wide Positive Behavior Supports (SWPBS): the Ziggurat Model (Aspy & Grossman, 2007) and the comprehensive autism planning system (CAPS; Henry & Myles, 2007).

Figure 8.1 depicts the process of comprehensive planning using the Ziggurat Model and CAPS.

What Is the Ziggurat Model?

The Ziggurat Model is a comprehensive planning model for individuals with ASD (Aspy & Grossman, 2007; Okada, Ohtake, & Yanagihara, 2010). Its premise is that in order for a program to be successful for an individual with ASD, his unique needs and strengths must be identified and then directly linked to interventions (Aspy & Grossman, 2007). Therefore, the Ziggurat Model is designed to utilize students' strengths to address true needs or underlying deficits that result in social, emotional, and behavioral concerns. The ziggurat approach centers on a hierarchical system, consisting of five levels that must be addressed for an intervention plan to be comprehensive: (a) sensory/biological, (b) reinforcement, (c) structure and visual/tactile supports, (d) task demands, and skills to teach.

When designing a comprehensive program, it is essential to consider the *context of the underlying autism spectrum disorder*. This is overlooked all too often (Mesibov & Shea, 2010). Targeting the individual's specific needs defined by ASD characteristics leads to interventions that are more proactive and effective (Koenig, De Los, Reyes, Cicchetti, Scahill, & Klin, 2009; Mesibov & Shea, 2011). In comparison, interventions that address only surface or observable behavior without consideration of underlying ASD characteristics are potentially less effective and less likely to result in sustained behavior change.

As such, the process of intervention design should begin with an assessment of the presenting characteristics of ASD (see Figure 8.1). A thorough assessment of underlying characteristics helps parents and professionals to plan a program that takes into account the individual's strengths and needs (Thomas, Bartholomew, & Scott, 2009). Further, assessment of underlying characteristics provides insight into which skills should be taught and how to design instruction in order to facilitate learning and bring about meaningful and long-lasting change. The Underlying Characteristics Checklist (UCC) offers a comprehensive perspective as a basis for program planning (Aspy & Grossman, 2007; Fogerty, 2010).

The Underlying Characteristics Checklist

The Underlying Characteristics Checklist (UCC) is an informal assessment designed to identify ASD characteristics for the purpose of intervention. Three versions of the UCC have been

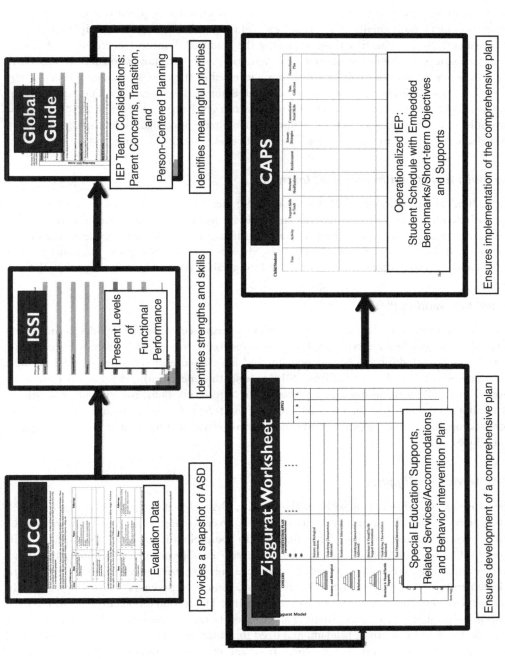

FIGURE 8.1 Process of comprehensive planning using the Ziggurat and CAPS.

developed: one intended for use with individuals who are high functioning (UCC-HF), including those with Asperger syndrome (AS); one for use with those with a more classic presentation (UCC-CL) in cognition and speech-language skills; and one for young children at the early invention stage, the UCC-EI. Designed to be completed by parents, teachers, or other service providers, individually or as a team, each of the UCCs is comprised of eight areas (Aspy & Grossman, 2007). The first three represent the traditional autism spectrum triad: social, restricted patterns of behavior interests and activities, and communication (cf. Wing, 1981). Characteristics often associated with ASD are addressed in the next four areas: sensory differences, cognitive differences, motor differences, and emotional vulnerability. The eighth underlying area is known medical and other biological factors (cf. Zecavati & Spence, 2009). Based on the results of completing the UCC, a comprehensive intervention plan is developed that targets ASD characteristics by incorporating each of the five levels of the ziggurat.

The Individual Strengths and Skills Inventory

The Individual Strengths and Skills Inventory (ISSI), designed to accompany the UCC, ensures that an individual's underlying strengths and skills are incorporated in the intervention design process. For example, one student may have a strength in imitation whereas another has an intense interest in, and knowledge of animals (Winter-Messiers, 2007). These assets can easily become key to addressing underlying skill deficits. The ISSI parallels the first seven areas of the UCC.

Global Intervention Plan

The global intervention plan helps users complete a person-centered plan by identifying short- and long-term goals and targeting the UCC areas and items that would have the greatest impact on the individual's ability to be independent and have a sense of well-being across multiple environments (McConkey & Collins, 2010). Using this mechanism, ASD-related areas are selected that will be meaningful in the short- and long-term. Thus, the student's educational plan will be tied directly to the individual leading a self-determined life as an adult replete with increased opportunities, happiness, and other aspects related to a high quality of life (Wigham et al., 2008).

The Intervention Ziggurat

The centerpiece and the framework of the Ziggurat Model is the intervention ziggurat (IZ). It was designed to help parents and educators avoid overlooking critical areas that impact the effectiveness of any intervention plan as they build a comprehensive program (Sansosti, Powell-Smith, & Cowan, 2010). The IZ is comprised of five critical levels structured into a hierarchy: sensory differences and biological needs, reinforcement, structure and visual/tactile supports, task demands, and skills to teach. The first level, sensory differences and biological needs, addresses basic internal factors that impact functioning. The second level addresses motivational needs prerequisite to skill development. The third level draws on individuals' strength of visual processing and addresses their fundamental need for order and routine. The final two levels of the IZ emphasize the importance of expectations and skill development relative to the characteristics of individuals with ASD. Each of the levels is essential and contributes to the effectiveness of the others. Thus, if needs on all levels are not addressed, the intervention will not be as effective and skills will not develop (Aspy & Grossman, 2007; Okada et al., 2010). The following is a brief discussion of the five levels of the Intervention Ziggurat.

Sensory Differences and Biological Needs. The first level of the IZ represents what can be considered the foundation of behavior, biology (Ganzel, Morris, & Wethington, 2010). Consideration of biological factors is important due to the strong genetic and neurological underpinnings of this disorder. Sensory differences and biological needs often present some of the greatest challenges for individuals on the spectrum. The existence of one of these areas, sensory, is being formalized by its proposed inclusion in the fifth edition of the American Psychiatric Association's *Diagnostic and Statistical Manual of Mental Disorders* (*DSM-V*, 2010). Research exists on sensory interventions for individuals with ASD. In fact over 50 studies have been conducted on sensory interventions (cf. Baranek, 2002; Case-Smith & Arbesman, 2008). Much of the research on biological interventions has centered on the use of medications, both conventional (Angley, Young, Ellis, Chan, & McKinnon, 2007) and complementary and alternative (Angley, Semple, Hewton, Paterson, & McKinnon, 2007).

Reinforcement. All intervention plans ultimately target the development or increase in effectiveness of a behavior or skill (Skinner, 1938). This goal can only be accomplished by incorporating the EBP reinforcement (CMS, 2010; NAC, 2009; NPDC, n.d.) into a comprehensive plan because the purpose of reinforcement is to increase the likelihood that a behavior will occur again. Without reinforcement, there is no intervention (Frost & Bondy, 2002) and, as such, reinforcement is included as the second level of the intervention ziggurat. It is often challenging to identify appropriate reinforcers for those on the spectrum. It is often helpful to consider the student's preoccupations or special interests (Winter-Messiers, 2007). Indeed, research has found that activities or objects related to obsessions are often more effective reinforcers than food for individuals on the autism spectrum (cf. Charlop-Christy, Kurtz, & Casey, 1990).

Structure and Visual/Tactile Supports. Individuals with ASD function best when predictability is established across the school day, including schedules, routines, environments, behavioral and academic expectations, and interpersonal interactions (cf. Machalicek et al., 2009: Wheeler, Baggett, Fox, & Blevins, 2006). Because verbal communication deficits are evident in ASD, supports that are visual are critical (Mesibov & Shea, 2010). For students with ASD and a vision impairment, tactile supports should be considered. Visual supports, such as pictures, written schedules, and task strips have been shown to be effective for decreasing behavior problems, increasing on task behavior, and enhancing independence (cf. Wheeler et al., 2006). The three reports on EBP have used various terms to identify this set of interventions: structured teaching (CMS, 2010), structured work systems (NPDC, n.d.), and schedules (NAC, 2009).

Task Demands. The term task demand can be thought of as obstacle removal (E. Blackwell, personal communication, 2007). In designing quality interventions, obstacles that could prevent an individual from succeeding either independently or with assistance should be removed (Reichle, Johnson, Monn, & Harris, 2010; Vygotsky, 1978). For example, a team may recognize that because a child lacks the skills to negotiate peer conflict, he will be provided with a trained peer "buddy" during group activities until he is able to master strategies for compromise. The obstacle: lacking the skills to negotiate peer conflict; how it is removed: a trained peer buddy who can help the child in situations that require negotiation. Task demands with the IZ include academic demands but go beyond, to include social, communication, organizational, sensory, and other areas of functioning. Numerous interventions reduce demands. For example, peer-mediated interventions, including peer networks, circle of friends, and peer buddies have been found to be beneficial in promoting social skills (CMS, 2010; NAC, 2009; NPDC, n.d.).

Skills to Teach.   The first four levels of the ziggurat set the stage for skill acquisition. It is possible to resolve many behavior concerns using strategies on the first four levels without ever teaching skills. Indeed, many improvements may be seen as a direct result of attending to an individual's biological needs, providing meaningful reinforcers, addressing the need for structure and predictability, and carefully matching demands to ability. Comfortable with behavior gain, intervention teams may overlook this crucial last level. However, such a "partial" approach to intervention will have negative long-term outcomes because it does not allow for independence or promote generalization or growth. It is for this reason that the authors view skills to teach as the ultimate goal of any intervention plan (Aspy & Grossman, 2007). Several approaches to teaching skills to individuals with ASD have been supported in the literature, including instruction during social skills groups and pivotal response training (PRT; cf. CMS, 2010; NAC, 2009; NPDC, n.d.). The Ziggurat Model does not promote one teaching methodology over another. The multidisciplinary team, including parents, identifies the specific instructional method(s) that match the student's learning style.

Ziggurat Worksheet

With a new understanding of the student's needs based on (a) completion of the UCC, (b) information on strengths and current skill level provided through completion of the ISSI, and (c) development of long- and short-term goals and prioritized UCC areas and items, using the *global intervention plan*, the team is prepared to design an intervention plan that is targeted to the individual student (Aspy & Grossman, 2007; Fogerty, 2010). Using the aforementioned information, the team uses the ziggurat worksheet to guide them through the development of a comprehensive intervention plan. All interventions incorporated into the plan must address underlying needs from the UCC. This provides a safeguard from developing a plan that addresses only surface concerns or from recycling interventions that have been used with other students with ASD without careful consideration of the specific student. Further, the ziggurat worksheet promotes collaboration by helping parents and professionals to understand their part in the larger intervention picture (Aspy & Grossman, 2007; Keenan, Dillenburger, Doherty, Byrne, & Gallagher, 2010). After completion of the ziggurat worksheet, the team is ready to discuss how these interventions will be embedded throughout the school day. While the ziggurat worksheet allows a team to know that the intervention plan is thorough and targeted, the CAPS provides a structure for implementation.

What Is the Comprehensive Autism Planning System (CAPS)?

CAPS provides an overview of a student's daily schedule by time and activity and specifies supports that he or she needs during each period. Thus, the CAPS enables professionals and parents to answer the fundamental question: What supports does the student need for each activity?

   Once a multidisciplinary team, including the parents, has identified the student's needs through completion of the UCC (CL, HF, or EI) and ISSI, established goals for the student and prioritized UCC items that lead to these goals, and has developed interventions across the six areas of the ziggurat that match the student's UCC- and ISSI-identified strengths and concerns, the team is ready to complete the CAPS. That is, based on information developed using the Ziggurat Model, the CAPS provides a framework to list a student's tasks and activities, the times they occur, along with a delineation of the supports needed for success (Henry & Myles, 2007; Myles, Grossman, Aspy, Henry, & Coffin, 2007). In addition, the CAPS includes a place for recording the results of ongoing data collection and consideration of how skills are to be generalized to other settings.

Components of CAPS

The CAPS contains the following components:

1. *Time.* This section indicates the clock time of each activity that the student engages in throughout the day.
2. *Activity.* Activities include *all* tasks and activities throughout the day in which the student requires support. Academic periods (e.g., reading), nonacademic times (e.g., recess, lunch), as well as transitions between classes are all be considered activities.
3. *Targeted Skills to Teach.* This may include individualized education program (IEP) goals, state standards, or skills that lead to school success for a given student.
4. *Structure/Modifications.* Structures/modifications can consist of a wide variety of supports, including placement in the classroom, visual supports, peer networks, and instructional strategies (e.g., priming, self-monitoring).
5. *Reinforcement.* Student access to specific types of reinforcement as well as reinforcement schedules are listed here.
6. *Sensory Strategies.* Sensory supports and strategies identified by an occupational therapist or others are listed in this CAPS area.
7. *Communication/Social Skills.* Specific communication goals or activities as well as supports are delineated in this section. Goals or activities may include (a) requesting for help, (b) taking turns in conversation, or (c) protesting appropriately. Supports may encompass language boards or augmentative communication systems.
8. *Data Collection.* This space is for recording the type of data as well as the behavior to be documented during a specific activity. Typically, this section relates directly to IEP goals and objectives.
9. *Generalization Plan.* Because individuals with ASD often have problems generalizing information across settings, this section of the CAPS was developed to ensure that generalization of skills is built into the child's program.

The CAPS, as well as the Ziggurat Model, are applicable from early intervention to adulthood across home, school, employment, university or postsecondary training, and community. However, some slight modifications in the CAPS are needed as the individual enters high school and beyond. For example, the daily structure of school changes when students transition to middle and high school. Students may have as many as nine teachers in nine different classrooms. Despite their movement from classroom to classroom, the activities in which the students participate in each academic class are similar. That is, in each class students are likely to be required to participate in (a) independent work, (b) group work, (c) tests, (d) lectures, and (e) homework. From this standpoint, the activities in English class and geometry are the same. The fundamental differences between the structure of elementary school and middle/high school require that the CAPS must be modified accordingly. The modified comprehensive autism planning system (M-CAPS; Henry & Myles, 2007) is an effective means of communicating to educators who teach academic subjects the types of supports that students need during each activity (Sue Klingshirn, personal communication, April, 2006). The multidisciplinary team that plans the program for a high school student with ASD who spends extensive time in general education classrooms develops the student's program using the M-CAPS. As a result, each of the student's academic teachers shares the same document. The M-CAPS used in biology is the same as the M-CAPS used in sociology. Likewise, the supports for a given student are the same. Additional examples of CAPS and M-CAPS across the lifespan can be found at www. texasautism.com.

Case Study for Mickey: From Ziggurat to CAPS

Mickey, a fifth-grade child who has moved to a new school district, was recently diagnosed with Asperger syndrome by a medical professional and identified as having autism by his school district multidisciplinary team. His mother reported that from infancy Mickey was a "challenging child." He never established a sleeping or eating routine, was irritable, had constant ear infections, and once upset did not calm easily. He became toilet trained at age 5. Mickey was kicked out of two neighborhood preschools because of his failure to follow teacher directions, lack of cooperative play skills, and his near-constant temper tantrums despite his above average intelligence. Mickey's mother sought assistance from Mickey's pediatrician who reported that 3-year-old Mickey was bright but socially immature. She sought assistance from three other physicians, including a psychiatrist, who indicated that Mickey's behaviors were due to (a) immaturity or (b) inconsistent parenting. Through her diligence, Mickey was finally identified as having AS at age 9. Currently, Mickey's vocabulary is more advanced than that of his peers. He can follow one-step directions with prompts and visual cues. He is extremely literal, has a special interest in washers and dryers, and does not know how to play cooperatively with peers. Mickey does not appear to know how to regulate himself. He often tantrums when minor changes occur in the environment or when the sequence of events does not match his expectations. Once he becomes upset, it is difficult for him to become calm and focused. Parents and teachers believe that if Mickey could develop social skills and learn to self-regulate, he would make more progress at home and in school.

Interventions tried in his prior school included positive reinforcement, timeout, and wait time. Parents reported that these interventions have brought about no change in Mickey's behaviors and skill acquisition. Currently, Mickey receives outpatient speech therapy and outpatient occupational therapy sessions three times per week.

Mickey's multidisciplinary team, including his parents, met to develop his program. They completed an ISSI (see Figure 8.2), an UCC-HF, and Global Planning Guide (see Figure 8.3 for the guide that also includes UCC-HF items). Using information from these activities, Mickey's team completed the ziggurat worksheet (see partial copy in Figure 8.4). Finally, they created a CAPS for his school program (see partial copy in Figure 8.5). This process helped the team match Mickey's needs and strengths to interventions that could be implemented throughout his day.

Summary

The Ziggurat Model and CAPS provide a unique way to develop and implement a meaningful and comprehensive program for students on the spectrum. The structure fosters consistent use of supports to ensure student success as well as data collection to measure that success. Compatible with current trends in education of children with ASD, the Ziggurat Model and CAPS are easily implemented for individuals across the spectrum and age ranges as well as across environments and tasks.

Individual Strengths and Skills Inventory

Ruth Aspy, Ph.D., and Barry G. Grossman, Ph.D.

In designing effective intervention plans, it is important to be aware of individual strengths. Please describe strengths in the following areas:

Social
Enjoys sharing his interests with others
Able to work among peers

Behavior, Interests, and Activities
Has strong interests
Diligent in pursuit of interests – writes, builds
Copes with unfamiliar individuals and unfamiliar circumstances (film crew)
Orients to the listener

Sensory
Tolerates heat
Tolerates range of textures of clothing

Cognitive
Able to work on academic tasks in large group with assistance of aide

Motor
Able to complete some handwriting tasks
Able to make detailed replicas of washing machines and dryers

Emotional
Copes with unfamiliar individuals and unfamiliar circumstances (film crew)
Finds pleasure in pursuing interests

Biological
Sleeps well
Passed hearing and vision screening

FIGURE 8.2 Individual Strengths and Skills Inventory: Mickey. From Aspy, R., & Grossman, B. G. (2008). *The Ziggurat model.* Shawnee Mission, KS: Autism Asperger Publishing Company. Reproduced with permission.

Global Intervention Plan: Guide to Establishing Priorities

Ruth Aspy, Ph.D., and Barry G. Grossman, Ph.D.

Directions: Following completion of the UCC and ISSI, the next step is to identify UCC **areas** and **items** that will result in a *meaningful* Global Intervention Plan. Consideration of priorities and strengths for an individual facilitates selection of UCC areas and items. The following questions are provided as a guide.

Selecting UCC Areas

VISION   "Begin with the end in mind" – Stephen R. Covey

- What is the long and short-term vision of/for the individual?
Note that "short-term" and "long-term" may be defined differently in order to be meaningful.

- Long Term:
  - Develop friendships
  - Increased independence
  - Improved coping skills
- Short Term:
  - Ask for help
  - Increase positive peer interactions (reduce verbal outbursts)
  - Increase participation in group activities
  - Accurately identify feelings of self and others
  - Identify alternatives to yelling and arguing

◉ Which UCC **areas** would have the greatest impact on achieving this vision?

- Social, Communication, and Emotional Vulnerability

SETTINGS

- In what settings does the individual participate?

  - School (e.g., classroom, PE, lunchroom, hallways)
  - Home
  - Community (e.g., grocery store, mall)

◉ Which UCC **areas** have the greatest impact on the individual's ability to function in multiple settings?

- Social, Communication, and Emotional Vulnerability

QUALITY OF LIFE

- What is most important to the individual? What provides a sense of well-being?
Consider independence, relationships, play/leisure activities, safety, health, etc.

Talking about interests and making friends

◉ Which UCC **areas** have the greatest impact on the individual's quality of life?

- Social, Communication, and

Based on your answers to the questions above, place a check √ next to the key UCC **areas**
*Transfer to the **Areas of Concern** section of the Ziggurat Worksheet.*

☒ Social   ☐ Cognitive Differences
☐ Restricted Patterns of Behavior Interests, and   ☐ Motor Differences
   Activities   ☒ Emotional Vulnerability
☒ Communication   ☐ Known Medical or Other Biological Factors
☐ Sensory Differences

KEY UCC ITEMS

Select key UCC **items** for *each* of the UCC **areas** listed above. Choose items that are essential (necessary for progress) and developmentally appropriate. Emphasize items that are more pivotal (building blocks for additional skills). Avoid selecting redundant items.

Write key item numbers and descriptions below. These items will be used to develop interventions keeping strengths and skills (identified on the ISSI) in mind.

*Transfer items to the **Selected UCC Item** section of the Ziggurat Worksheet. Develop interventions.*

Selecting UCC Items

1 Mindblindness

5 Has difficulty making or
     keeping friends

#7 Is naïve, easily taken
    advantage of, or bullied

#28 Has difficulty starting,
     joining, and/or ending
     conversation

#29 Has difficulty asking for help

#39 Has difficulty talking about
     others' interests

#76 Is easily stressed — worries
     obsessively

#87 Has difficulty identifying,
     quantifying, expressing,
     and/or controlling emotions

FIGURE 8.3 Ziggurat Model. Shawnee Mission, KS: Autism Aspergers Publishing Company, www. asperger.net; used with permission.

Mickey—Global Intervention Plan

ZIGGURAT WORKSHEET

Ruth Aspy, Ph.D., and Barry G. Grossman, Ph.D.

BEHAVIOR/AREAS OF CONCERN	FOR SPECIFIC INTERVENTION PLAN Operationalized Behaviors	PRIORITIZED UCC ITEMS	CHECK ALL THAT APPLY		
			A	B	C
Social ● Communication ● Emotional Vulnerability ●		[1] Mindblindness [5] Has difficulty making or keeping friends [7] Is naïve, easily taken advantage of, or bullied [28] Has difficulty starting, joining, and/or ending a conversation	[29] Has difficulty asking for help [39] Has difficulty talking about others' interests [76] Is easily stressed—worries obsessively [87] Has difficulty identifying, quantifying, expressing, and/or controlling emotions	√		√
Sensory/Biological Needs	Sensory/Biological Intervention:	• Provide physical education activities in smaller setting • Provide individual sport activities for PE • Intersperse calming activities (high interest) with challenging tasks. Provide area in classroom to keep catalogs, models, etc. for access at these times • Provide sensory assessment by occupational therapist to follow up with consult to staff and parents regarding sensory interventions			√
	Underlying Characteristics Addressed:	[76] Is easily stressed—worries obsessively [87] Has difficulty identifying, quantifying, expressing, and/or controlling emotions			
Reinforcement	Reinforcement Intervention:	• Reinforce Mickey for practicing social and communication skills. Provide additional reinforcement for demonstrating skills during actual interactions. • Intersperse calming activities (high interest) with challenging tasks • Provide a visual menu of reinforcers. • Provide a written list of alternatives to yelling or arguing when frustrated. Reinforce for using one of the identified alternatives. • Reinforce prompted and modeled behaviors (recognize that number of reinforcers earned will likely be higher on challenging days)	√	√	√
	Underlying Characteristics Addressed:	[1] Mindblindness [5] Has difficulty making or keeping friends [28] Has difficulty starting, joining, and/or ending a conversation [29] Has difficulty asking for help [76] Is easily stressed—worries obsessively			
Structure & Visual/Tactile Supports	Structure/Visual/Tactile Support Intervention:	• Use visual checklists of steps to an assignment. Put visual reminder of reinforcer to be earned as the last step. • Involve Mickey in a carefully selected extracurricular club or activity. Train peers. • Teach Mickey skills for conversational turn-taking on preferred and less preferred topics – use modeling, role play, narration, and video • Provide a visual menu of reinforcers. • Provide a written list of alternatives to yelling or arguing when frustrated. Reinforce for using one of the identified alternatives. • Video tape Mickey in actual learning activities and social interactions. Review the video while Mickey is calm and narrate the behaviors observed. • Identify stressful situations and help Mickey to quantify the level of stress using a dryer heat scale – develop strategies for each situation	√	√	√
	Underlying Characteristics Addressed:	[1] Mindblindness [5] Has difficulty making or keeping friends [29] Has difficulty asking for help [76] Is easily stressed—worries obsessively [87] Has difficulty identifying, quantifying, expressing, and/or controlling emotions			

Mickey—Global Intervention Plan

Task Demands	Task Demand Intervention:	• Provide physical education activities in smaller setting • Identify stressful situations and help Mickey to quantify the level of stress using a dryer heat scale – develop strategies for each situation • Intersperse calming activities (high interest) with challenging tasks. Provide area in classroom to keep catalogs, models, etc. for access at these times • Teach Mickey skills for conversational turn-taking on preferred and less preferred topics – use modeling, role play, narration, and video • Provide individual sport activities for PE • Train circle of friends to support Mickey in less structured activities (PE, recess, lunch) – teach Mickey to "follow their lead" when uncertain • Provide school wide training for "bully prevention" and reinforce prosocial behaviors in school wide program • Provide visual supports (see visual support level) • Adjust proportion of calming activities on high demand days	√	
	Underlying Characteristics Addressed:	[1] Mindblindness [5] Has difficulty making or keeping friends [7] Is naïve, easily taken advantage of, or bullied [29] Has difficulty asking for help [76] Is easily stressed—worries obsessively [87] Has difficulty identifying, quantifying, expressing, and/or controlling emotions		√
Skills to Teach	Skill Intervention:	• Teach Mickey how to recognize his emotional state – use modeling, role play, narration, and video • Teach Mickey how to recognize emotions of others – use modeling, role play, narration, and video • Teach Mickey skills for conversational turn-taking on preferred and less preferred topics – use modeling, role play, narration, and video • Provide individual and group speech therapy services to support communication goals – include another student with similar needs in instruction and practice activities – (lunch bunch) • Teach Mickey to recognize when he needs help • Identify stressful situations and help Mickey to quantify the level of stress using a dryer heat scale – develop strategies for each situation		√
	Underlying Characteristics Addressed:	[1] Mindblindness [5] Has difficulty making or keeping friends [28] Has difficulty starting, joining, and/or ending a conversation [29] Has difficulty asking for help [39] Has difficulty talking about others' interests [76] Is easily stressed—worries obsessively [87] Has difficulty identifying, quantifying, expressing, and/or controlling emotions		

FIGURE 8.4 Intervention of individuals with high-functioning autism and Asperger syndrome: The Ziggurat Model. From Aspy, R., & Grossman, B. G. (2008). Shawnne Mission, KS: Autism Asperger Publishing Company, www.aapctextbooks.net, used with permission.

Comprehensive Autism Planning System (CAPS)

Child/Student: Mickey

Time	Activity	Targeted Skills to Teach	Structure/ Modifications	Reinforcement	Sensory Strate- gies	Communication Social Skills	Data Collection	Generalization Plan
8:00	Priming	Turn-taking Asking for help Emotion recognition in self Self-regulation	Visual schedule Resource room (ECLIPSE curriculum, Integrated Self-Advocacy curriculum) Train peers	Review special interest catalogs after priming Verbally reinforce targeted skills	Koosh ball Disco seat to sit on	List of alternatives for screaming and yelling Dryer heating scale (5-point scale)	Turn taking (yes/no, M, 15m) Asking for help (# T 15m) Identification of emotion in self (correct/ incorrect D) Rumbling and rage (# D)	Dryer hearing scale Alternatives to yelling and screaming (inside notebook and at home)
8:15 9:00 1:00 1:45	Reading Math Language Arts Social Studies/ Science	State standards Asking for help	Visual checklist of assignment steps Keyboard or dictate assignments Quiet area for tests and assignments Home base card Fewer problems	Reinforcer menu at end of class (for asking for help) Catalogs in classroom	Disco seat to sit on Calming activity after assignment; run an errand, put away materials Break between reading and math/LA and SS/SC	List of alternatives for screaming and yelling Dryer heating scale Conversation starters card	Mastery of state standards Asking for help (I/P, #, W, 15m) Rumbling and rage (# D) # of times to home base (D)	Dryer hearing scale Alternatives to yelling and screaming (inside notebook and at home)
9:45	Bathroom	Appropriate urinal use	Early release (Urinal Test Pro [UTP])	None	None	None	Y/N self-report Score on UTP	None

Note. D = Daily; I = Independent; P = Prompt

FIGURE 8.5 Comprehensive Autism Planning System (CAPS): Mickey (partial).

References

American Psychiatric Association. (2010). *DSM-5 development.* Retrieved from http://www.dsm5.org

Angley, M., Semple, S., Hewton, C., Paterson, F., & McKinnon, R. (2007). Children and autism: Part 2—Management with complementary medicines and dietary interventions. *Australian Family Physician, 36*(10), 827–830.

Angley, M., Young, R., Ellis, D., Chan, W., & McKinnon, R. (2007). Children and autism: Part 1—Recognition and pharmacological management. *Australian Family Physician, 36*(9), 741–744.

Aspy, R., & Grossman, B. G. (2007). *The Ziggurat Model: A framework for designing comprehensive interventions for individuals with high-functioning autism and Asperger syndrome.* Shawnee Mission, KS: Autism Asperger.

Baranek, G. T. (2002). Efficacy of sensory and motor interventions for children with autism. *Journal of Autism and Developmental Disorders, 32*(5), 397–422.

Case-Smith, J., & Arbesman, M. (2008). Evidence based review on interventions for autism used in occupational therapy. *The American Journal of Occupational Therapy, 62*(4), 416–429.

Centers for Disease Control and Prevention. (2009). *Prevalence of autism spectrum disorders—Autism and Developmental Disabilities Monitoring Network, United States, 2006, 58*(SS-10), 1–10.

Centers for Medicare and Medicaid Services. (2010). *Autism spectrum disorders: Final report on environmental scan.* Washington, DC: Author.

Charlop-Christy, M. H., Kurtz, P. F., & Casey, F. (1990). Using aberrant behaviors as reinforcers for autistic children. *Journal of Applied Behavior Analysis, 23*, 163–181.

Fixsen, D., Blasé, K., Horner, R., & Sugai, C. (2009). *Concept paper: Develop the capacity for scaling up the effective use of evidence-based programs in state departments of education.* Unpublished document, University of North Carolina, Chapel Hill.

Fogerty, R. E. (2010). *Learning to negotiate the social world through occupation* (Unpublished master's thesis). University of St. Augustine for Health Sciences, St. Augustine, Florida.

Frost, L., & Bondy, A. (2002). *PECS: The Picture Exchange Communication System training manual.* Newark, DE: Pyramid Educational Products.

Ganzel, B. L., Morris, P. A., & Wethington, E. (2010). Allostasis and the human brain: Integrating models of stress from the social and life. *Psychological Review, 117*(1), 134–174.

Henry, S. A., & Myles, B. S. (2007). *The comprehensive autism planning systems (CAPS) for individuals with Asperger syndrome, autism and related disabilities: Integrating best practices throughout the student's day.* Shawnee Mission, KS: Autism Asperger.

Keenan, M., Dillenburger, K., Doherty, A., Byrne, T., & Gallagher, S. (2010). The experiences of parents during diagnosis and forward planning for children with autism spectrum disorder. *Journal of Applied Research in Intellectual Disabilities, 23*(4), 390–397.

Koenig, K., De Los Reyes, A., Cicchetti, D., Scahill, L., & Klin, A. (2009). Group intervention to promote social skills in school-age children with pervasive developmental disorders: Reconsidering efficacy. *Journal of Autism and Developmental Disorders, 29*(8), 1163–1172.

Kogan, M. D., Blumberg, S. J., Schieve, L. A., Boyle, C. A., Perrin, J. M., Ghandour, R. M., … van Dyck, P. (2009). Prevalence of parent-reported diagnosis of autism spectrum disorder among children in the US, 2007. *Pediatrics, 124*(5), 1395–1403.

Kraemer, B. R., Cook, C. R., Browning-Wright, D., Mayer, G. R., & Wallace, M. D. (2008). Effects of training on the use of the behavior support plan quality evaluation guide with autism educators. *Journal of Positive Behavior Interventions, 10*, 179–189.

Machalicek, W., Shogren, K., Lang, R., Rispoli, M., O'Reilly, M. F., Franco, J. H., & Sigafoos, J. (2009). Increasing play and decreasing the challenging behavior of children with autism during recess with activity schedules and task correspondence training. *Research in Autism Spectrum Disorders, 3,* 547–555.

McConkey, R., & Collins, S. (2010). Using personal goal setting to promote the social inclusion of people with intellectual disability living in support accommodation. *Journal of Intellectual Disability Research, 54*(2), 135–143.

Mesibov, G., & Shea, V. (2010). The TEACCH program in the era of evidence-based practice. *Journal of Autism and Developmental Disorders, 40,* 570–579.

Mesibov, G. B., & Shea, V. (2011). Evidence-based practices and autism. *Autism, 15,* 114–133.

Myles, B. S., Grossman, B. G., Aspy, R., Henry, S. A., & Coffin, A. B. (2007). Planning a comprehensive program for students with autism spectrum disorders using evidence-based practices. *Education and Training in Developmental Disabilities, 42*(4), 398–409.

National Autism Center. (2009). *National standards report: Addressing the need for evidence-based practice guidelines for autism spectrum disorders.* Randolph, MA: Author.

National Implementation Resource Network. (2008). What is NIRN? Retrieved from http://www.fpg.unc.edu/~nirn/default.cfm

National Professional Development Center on Autism Spectrum Disorders. (n.d.). *Evidence based practice briefs.* Retrieved from http://autismpdc.fpg.unc.edu/content/briefs.

National Research Council. (2001). *Educating children with autism*. Washington, DC: National Academy Press.

Okada, S., Ohtake, Y., & Yanagihara, M. (2010). Improving the manners of a student with autism: The effects of manipulating perspective holders in Social Stories™: A pilot study. *International Journal of Disability, Development and Education, 57*(2), 207–219

Reichle, J., Johnson, L., Monn, E., & Harris, M. (2010). Task engagement and escape maintained challenging behavior: Differential effects of general and explicit cues when implementing a signaled delay in the delivery of reinforcement. *Journal of Autism and Developmental Disorders, 40*, 709–720.

Sansosti, F. J., Powell-Smith, K. A., & Cowan, R. (2010). *High-functioning autism/Asperger syndrome in schools: Assessment and intervention*. New York: Guilford.

Skinner, B. F. (1938). *The behavior of organisms: An experimental analysis*. New York: Appleton-Century-Crofts.

Thomas, C. A., Bartholomew, C. C., & Scott, L. A. (2009). *Universal design for transition: A roadmap for planning and instruction*. Baltimore, MD: Brookes.

U.S. Department of Education. (2002). *No Child Left Behind: A desktop reference*. Washington, DC: Education Publications Center.

Vygotsky, L. (1978). *Mind in society: The development of higher psychological processes*. Cambridge, MA: Harvard University Press.

Wheeler, J. J., Baggett, B. A., Fox, J., & Blevins, L. (2006). Treatment integrity: A review of intervention studies conducted with autism. *Focus on Autism and Other Developmental Disabilities, 21*, 45–55.

Wigham, S., Robertson, J., Emerson, E., Hatton, C., Elliott, J., Mcintosh, B., ... Joyce, T. (2008). Reported goal setting and benefits of person centered planning for people with intellectual disabilities. *Journal of Intellectual Disabilities, 12*, 143–152.

Wing, L. (1981). Asperger's syndrome: A clinical account. *Psychological Medicine, 11*, 115–129.

Winter-Messiers, M. A. (2007). From tarantulas to toilet brushes: Understanding the special interest areas of children and youth with Asperger syndrome. *Remedial and Special Education, 28*, 140–152.

Zecavati, N., & Spence, S. J. (2009). Neurometabolic disorders and dysfunction in autism spectrum disorders. *Neurology and Neuroscience Reports, 9*, 129–136.

SECTION III

Education through the Developmental Stages

9

CULTURAL AND LINGUISTIC DIVERSITY AND LEARNERS WITH AUTISM SPECTRUM DISORDERS

Elizabeth West

UNIVERSITY OF WASHINGTON

Pei-Yu Chen

NATIONAL TAIPEI UNIVERSITY OF EDUCATION

Our future student growth is predictable. In 35 years, White students will be a minority in every category of public education as we know it (Garcia & Cuellar, 2006). The term *cultural linguistic diversity* refers to "behavioral, value, linguistic, and other differences ascribed to people's cultural backgrounds. Cultural diversity almost invariably includes some level of diversity in how language is understood and used … [the terms] cultural diversity and cultural linguistic diversity [are often used] synonymously" (Barrera, Corso, & Macpherson, 2003, p. 6). The U.S. Department of Education estimates that students from culturally and linguistically diverse backgrounds constitute approximately 32% of the general school population, and a large number of these students are identified as having disabilities and receiving services in special education programs (National Research Council, 2002; Sileo & Prater, 1998).

According to the National Research Council (2001), the effects of high quality early intervention have been verified to improve long-term development of students with autistic spectrum disorders (ASD) in social, communication, and behavioral areas. Access to care for autism-related services, however, has been identified to be limited for racial and ethnic minority families with low parent education, living in nonmetropolitan areas (Thomas, Ellis, McLaurin, Daniels, & Morrissey, 2007). Furthermore, cultural language diversity (CLD) families' language barriers and beliefs about disabilities may also influence the type and amount of services that children with ASD receive. Having educated parents appears to be a protective factor that may assist in access to early and accurate diagnosis. This diagnosis assists families as it leads to services that are critical to improving long-term development. For example, 10 areas in California have been considered to be "autism clusters" and are associated with areas of higher parental education and close proximity to major autism treatment centers (Van Meter et al., 2010). Schwartz and Sandall (2010) state, "we worry, however, that establishing an early and accurate diagnosis may be related more to where a family lives, whether the parents went to college, and what medical insurance they have than to the young children's behavioral profiles" (p. 106). In addition to underrepresentation in ASD services, children of minority race and ethnicity with ASD have been reported to receive a different mix of services when compared to White children and appear to receive these services at a later age (Levy, Mandell, Merher, Ittenback, & Pinto-Martin, 2003; Mandell, Listerud, Levy, & Pinto-Martin, 2002).

Although a substantial amount of research has paid attention to important issues in the early experiences of families that have children with developmental disabilities (e.g., diagnosis, services, coping, adaptation), these studies have been conducted with predominantly European American families (Zhang & Bennett, 2003; Zionts, Zionts, Harrison, & Bellinger, 2003). The majority of research in the field of ASD has largely ignored or minimized diversities in race and culture (Connors & Donnellan, 1998). For CLD families that have recently arrived in the United States and who have a child diagnosed with ASD, the challenges can be heightened given the additional psychological, social, and economic costs of immigration (Welterlin & LaRue, 2007). In addition, it may be difficult to access appropriate services and health care (Welterlin & LaRue, 2007). The National Research Council (2001) has acknowledged that there is limited literature which focuses on the experiences of recent immigrant families of learners with ASD in the United States. Further, little is known about how these families access and benefit from services (Welterlin & LaRue, 2007). Despite the limited research that relates to recent immigrant families and CLD families who have resided in the United States for longer periods of time, it is clear that these families exist and are in need of appropriate services.

Wilder, Dyches, Obiakor, and Algozzine (2004) identify a host of culture-specific strategies for meeting the needs of students with ASD. These universal strategies are applicable to children from culturally and linguistically diverse backgrounds (of which immigrant families are a part) that have disabilities, including ASD. This chapter uses these strategies as a benchmark to expand upon evidence-based principles and practices for learners with ASD who are also culturally and linguistically diverse. Specifically, this chapter highlights cultural understanding, teacher expectations, language issues, cultural pluralism in curriculum, and implications for teacher preparation programs.

Historical Background

Studies are beginning to document the underdiagnosis and referral bias of ASD in ethnic communities (Begeer, Bouk, Boussaid, Terwogt, & Koot, 2009). Mandell et al. (2002) have suggested that professionals screen for ASD less often in children from minority than majority groups. Rosenberg, Daniels, Law, Law, and Kaufmann (2009) reported on the trends in ASD diagnoses between 1994 and 2007. Data collected by these researchers suggest that many factors influence initial diagnosis, including ethnicity, race, evaluator types, region, and urbanicity. These findings are congruent with Mandell and Palmer (2005) and Mandell et al. (2008) that indicate disparities in overall diagnosis and treatment patterns in autism by race and ethnicity. These disparities in diagnosis may be the result of professionals' lack of cultural understanding about behavior expectations and presentations of a specific culture as well as families' language barriers and various beliefs about the etiology of disabilities. For instance, studies exist to document differences in race and socioeconomic status for African American and Hispanic and Latino/a children; however, little is known about Asian Americans. Parette, Chuang, and Huer (2004) identify Asian individuals as viewing disability very differently from European Americans. Further, these authors "assert that individual family cultural backgrounds have strong effects on a family's values and beliefs" (p. 115). Chan (1997) reported that Asian parents tend to attribute the cause of a child's disability to supernatural influences or sins committed by the child's ancestors. There have been studies of Chinese and Chinese American families that identify parents' reactions to their children with developmental and physical disabilities. Ryan and Smith (1989) found that almost half of the parents they studied did not understand their children's problem, due in part to complicated explanations by physicians and limited English fluency. Thus, a child's race and socioeconomic status may influence the age at which a diagnosis is made.

Brown and Rogers (2003) identify the research base for the effects of cultural factors in ASD as being miniscule. Clearly, a greater focus on multicultural perspectives and ASD is needed. Wilder et al. (2004) and Dyches, Wilder, Sudweeks, Obiaker, and Algozzine (2004) provide a call to action based on the belief that understanding diversity is critical to the development of effective programs for students with autism. Culture does mediate learning.

The field of special education faces the challenge of providing culturally responsive services to adequately meet the needs of children and families from diverse linguistic, cultural, and religious backgrounds. Professionals who serve these families and their children are predominantly from middle class European American cultures and their practices and beliefs may differ dramatically from those of the families they work with (Harry, 1992). Eighty-six percent of special educators are European American while 32% of students in special education are culturally and linguistically diverse (Rosenberg & Sindelar, 2003). The makeup of elementary and secondary teachers in general education is not appreciably different (Gay & Howard, 2000).

Description and Overview

Using scientific-based research to support practices for students with disabilities, including ASD, has been emphasized by the Individuals with Disabilities Education Act (IDEIA; 2004). It is necessary to identify and understand the treatments and methods that produce positive outcomes as proven by research. This research assists by clarifying "what works," which enables evidence-based treatment decisions. Evidence-based practices for families and children from culturally and linguistically diverse backgrounds must be respectful and responsive. These practices are critical to assessment and intervention because they promote equity and access to programs which are culturally congruent. All interventions for children and families must respect families' wishes and priorities as a component of family-based service provision (Sandall, McLean, & Smith, 2000).

Several organizations have responded to the call to establish the evidence base for autism. The Council for Exceptional Children (CEC) provides a set of criteria to assist educators and other professionals in determining effective interventions for students with disabilities (CEC, 2008). In addition, a Report of the Children's Services Evidence-Based Practice Committee identifies a host of best practices for students with ASD (Maine Department of Health and Human Services [MDHHS] & the Maine Department of Education [MDE, 2009]). Results from the MDHHS and MDE Report (2009) identified three interventions to have established evidence: (a) applied behavior analysis (ABA) for challenging behavior, communication, and early intervention behavioral intervention (IBI), (b) picture exchange communication system (PECS), and (c) pharmacological treatments including Haldol, Ritalin, and Risperidol. While various interventions are supported by scientific research, the extent to which the interventions address the needs of CLD children with ASD is unclear.

An emphasis on the development and evaluation of intervention programs for CLD students to improve their reading achievement or English language development has emerged. The What Works Clearinghouse (What Works) publishes intervention reports that evaluate research on curricula and instructional strategies for English language learners. These curricula and instructional strategies focus on students in grades K-6 and are intended to increase skills in reading achievement, mathematics achievement, and English language development. Thirty-one interventions have been reviewed which relate to English language learners and nine interventions are identified as being "potentially positive."

While the What Works report acknowledges that some programs demonstrate promising effects in improving CLD students' reading and English learning development, the extent to which these programs meet the needs of students with ASD is not addressed. In addition, the incorporation of multicultural representations into interventions, a critical CLD intervention component (Wilder et al., 2004), was not directly examined. Further, the What Works report focuses primarily on a single type of research methodology—randomized experimental group designs (also called randomized clinical trials [RCTs]; What Works, 2003). The complexities of this situation have several implications for research. Researchers must specify clearly for whom the practice is effective and in what context (Guralnick, 1997). Learners who are CLD and have ASD are a very heterogeneous population and do pose a significant challenge to designs such as RCTs. This heterogeneity can be a challenge because it is difficult to establish equivalent groups. In addition, RCTs require a relatively large number of participants to build the power of the analysis. This power is difficult to achieve with low prevalence rates within diverse populations as compared to learners who are White.

This evidence base leaves practitioners with some supporting scientific evidence of programs for either CLD students or for children with ASD; however, to date no evidence base exists which has examined the combination of CLD and ASD. Effective programs are essential to enhance learning outcomes of CLD students and students with ASD. To address the needs of CLD students with ASD, we build on existing evidence-based practice by reviewing key components of services for CLD students and for students with ASD. The following review provides an overview of considerations in the key service dimension areas of diagnosis and assessment, family involvement, and personnel preparation issues for CLD students with ASD. Next, a list of evaluation criteria is generated to (a) help define critical components of culturally responsive interventions for children with ASD and (b) enhance our understanding about the extent to which existing evidence-based intervention programs for students with ASD addresses the needs of CLD students. Specifically, we compare the critical components of services for children with ASD identified by the National Research Council (2001), the intervention strategies for CLD students with ASD (Wilder et al., 2004), and the educational guidelines for CLD students discussed by Vaughn, Bos, and Schumm (2011).

Considerations for Diagnosis and Assessment, Family Involvement, and Personnel Preparation

As discussed earlier, underrepresentation of CLD students amongst students with ASD has been documented across studies. Further, when diagnosed as having an ASD, learners who are CLD have reportedly received a mix of services and such services may be delayed. This problematic phenomenon calls for a close examination and review of relevant issues regarding diagnosis and assessment procedures. The National Research Council (2001), Wilder et al. (2004), and Vaughn et al. (2011) describe guidelines of practice to address assessment, family involvement, and personnel preparation issues (see Table 9.1) to guide high-quality services for CLD students and students with ASD.

As shown in Table 9.1, the practice in diagnosis and assessment, family involvement, and personnel preparation for students with ASD and for CLD students emphasizes an "ecocultural approach." This approach proposes assessment and intervention procedures based upon contextual fit (Brookman-Frazee, 2004; Moes & Frea, 2002) and considers the sociocultural environment of the child and family and how it impacts family dynamics. Successful application of the

TABLE 9.1

Dimensions of Service	Students with ASD (NRC, 2001)	CLD students with ASD (Wilder et al., 2004)	CLD students (Vaughn et al., 2011)
Diagnosis and Assessment	1. Multidisciplinary evaluation 2. Systematic gathering of information from parents	1. Involving bilingual diagnostic professional 2. Language and ecological assessment of communication needs	1.Implementing culturally responsive assessment
Family Involvement	1. Providing parent training (e.g., skill instruction and behavior reduction)	1. Identifying important language and skills as educational goals and objectives	1. Exploring best ways to communicate with parents (i.e., letters in parents' native language)
	2. IEP team member		2. Including a translator to support parent conferences
	3. Providing mental health support services for stressed families		3. Incorporating parents as resources at home or at school
Personnel Preparation	1. Practicum within multidisciplinary teams	1. Being culturally sensitive when identifying and interpreting behavioral patterns	1. Staff sharing, learning about, and respecting their own diversity
	2. Including personnel with ASD expertise in support system	2. Being responsive to cultural learning styles and incorporating cultural contexts in instructions and curricula	2. Conceptualizing multicultural education as much more than a curriculum or a subject to teach
	3. Research-based curriculum	3. Understanding and interacting with families	3. Understanding programs for second language acquisition

ecocultural approach results in accommodating the needs, values, goals, and systems that make up the ecocultural niche of a family. A limited understanding of cultural differences may alienate diverse families during the diagnosis and assessment process and may cause low treatment adherence if interventions are inconsistent with a family's cultural beliefs. Welterlin and La Rue (2007) suggest that "by incorporating the components of a family's social and cultural environment is to create a 'best fit' intervention" (p. 756).

Working in collaboration with families is important to facilitate successful outcomes for individuals with disabilities. Learners with ASD are members of families across ethnicities and cultures. A key factor in ensuring student success is teachers' understanding and appreciation of how culture shapes academic and social development. This is particularly crucial when students are from cultures different from the teachers' own. As discussed by the National Research Council (2001), Wilder et al. (2004), and Vaughn et al. (2011), during diagnosis and assessment, contextual fit could be addressed by involving families of CLD students with ASD to help understand the culture of the family, provide information regarding their child's strengths and communication needs, and identify target areas that the child with ASD needs to work on. When collaborating with educators, however, families of CLD students with ASD should be involved and empowered as equal partners (Harry, Kalyanpur, & Day, 1999). To achieve this goal, language supports, parental training, and other relevant supports should be available for families of CLD students with ASD (NRC, 2001; Vaughn et al., 2011).

Family involvement is a key component of service provision for students with ASD and for CLD students. Unfortunately, cultural awareness and collaborating with CLD families have historically been lacking in personnel preparation programs which focus on students with ASD (National Research Council, 2001). Without preparatory courses that focus on cultural knowledge and the importance of a pluralistic perspective in education, the possibility of negative outcomes for CLD students due to clashes between the culture of special education and family cultures is omnipresent (Harry et al., 1999). A key factor in ensuring student success is teachers' understanding and appreciation of how culture shapes academic and social development. This is particularly crucial when students come from cultures different from the teachers' own.

Educators who use culturally responsive teaching practices will achieve optimal outcomes for culturally and linguistically diverse learners (Gay, 2000), which also holds true for those learners who have disabilities. To improve outcomes for learners who are CLD with ASD, both general education and special education teachers should incorporate learners' language and culture into the curriculum, demonstrate that they value the learners' culture and language, have high expectations of their students' ability to learn, and make accommodations so that they can learn successfully. To prepare personnel who implement culturally responsive teaching (CRT) for CLD students with ASD, teacher training programs should help teachers to "recognize the differences between their students and themselves and strive to become nonjudgmental" (Cartledge, Gardner, & Ford, 2009, p.18).

Professionals must be knowledgeable about the considerations highlighted in Table 9.1. In addition, they must be aware of a variety of critical components related to aspects of an intervention. These components relate to the structure, content, and outcome of an intervention.

Evaluation Criteria of Intervention Programs

A list of critical intervention components for CLD students with ASD is generated to help identify evidence-based interventions for this group. These components have emerged from the literature reviewed (specifically, National Research Council, 2001; Vaughn et al., 2011; Wilder et al. 2004). Table 9.2 describes the scope and definition of each intervention component.

As shown in Table 9.2, the intervention programs for CLD students with ASD should have sufficient intensity and appropriate objectives to address the needs of CLD students with ASD, including social, communication, behavioral, and English language learning. In addition, the intervention programs should use continuous assessments to monitor students' learning outcome and to guide intervention implementation.

In a subsequent section, we use the intervention components presented in Table 9.2 to review three intervention programs, including ABA, PECS, and sheltered instruction observation protocol (SIOP). Specifically, ABA and PECS are identified as evidenced-based practices for students with ASD (MDHHS & MDE, 2009). There is, however, insufficient evidence to support using SIOP with CLD students (What Works, 2009) even though SIOP is widely used for English language learners in the United States. Rationale for intervention program selection is detailed below and the components of these three programs are compared to the key components of intervention for CLD students with ASD.

The Evidence Base

The purpose of this chapter is to identify evidence-based practices for CLD students with ASD. There is a wide range of intervention programs with different focuses developed for CLD students and for students with ASD (MDHHS & MDE, 2009). However, the programs discussed

TABLE 9.2 Intervention Components for CLD Students with ASD

Intervention Aspects	Critical components	Definition of the Components
Structure of Intervention	1. Intensive instruction and planned teaching opportunities to meet individual goals 2. Low student/teacher ratios 3. Having high expectations	-Number of hours of services provided for students -Guidelines for planning are prevalent -Providing high level adult attention -Using curriculum and teaching strategies that promote coherence, relevance, progression, and continuity -Teaching higher order thinking
Content of Intervention	4. Functional communication, social, play, cognitive, and academic skills 5. Functional approach to address problem behaviors 6. Infusing multicultural representation in schools and curriculum 7. English Language Learning	-Individualized based on students' needs -Adapting teaching to meet students' learning styles -Based on assessment results -Integrating students' native language and dialect, culture, and community into classroom or instruction session -Providing ESL services if necessary and interventions that improve communication
Outcome of Intervention	8. Ongoing assessment	-Providing explicit instruction to monitor students' progress and providing immediate feedback

in this chapter focus on interventions that increase students' communication ability. This focus is used because of the significant importance of functional communication skills among CLD students with ASD. Based on the results of the intervention review reported by MDHHS and MDE (2009) and What Works (2009), we include two established-evidence interventions, ABA for communication and PECS, and one popular program for English language learners, SIOP. Although there are not sufficient scientific studies examining the effects of SIOP, we include it in subsequent discussion given that it is widely used by teachers and practitioners in the United States.

Methods used to assist in establishing the evidence base include a review of the CEC standard of evaluating intervention programs (CEC, 2008) to ensure that the intervention programs have *positive effects* from evidence-based practices. Next, we use the key intervention components reviewed in Table 9.3 along with another component, "family involvement," to examine the extent to which the three intervention programs (ABA, PECS, and SIOP) meet the needs of CLD students with ASD.

CEC Standards for Evidence-Based Practice

In 2008, CEC proposed a procedure to help identify evidence-based practices in special education. Similar to the MDHHS and MDE Report (2009), CEC (2008) included three levels of evidence with a different label and criteria for each level of evidence, including positive effects, insufficient effects, and negative effects. The major difference between criteria proposed by CEC and MDHHS and MDE (2009) lies in the number of studies that help determine each level of evidence. Compared to MDHHS and MDE (2009), CEC includes three types of study designs, group experiment and quasi experimental, single subject, and correlation design studies. For each design, both CEC and MDHHS and MDE (2009) identify a list of quality indicators with which to examine the studies. Given the similar quality indicators proposed by CEC (2008) and MDHHS and MDE (2009), we include the studies of ABA for communication (n = 6) and PECS (n = 7) reviewed by MDHHS and MDE (2009) in the current review. Although ABA for development of communication skills and PECS are identified as established evidence by MDHHS and MDE (2009), we also use the CEC standard (2008) to examine the level of evidence of ABA for communication and PECS. In addition, we include SIOP studies examined by What Works and use CEC standards to help determine the level of evidence for this language intervention program for CLD students.

Among the six ABA for communication studies reviewed by MDHHS and MDE (2009), five studies are considered to be strong research reports (Charlop & Carpenter, 2000; Charlop & Trasowech, 1991; Charlop-Christy & Kelso, 2003; Ingersoll, Lewis, & Kroman, 2007; Jones, Feeley, & Takacs, 2007), and the other report (Lee, McComas, & Jawor, 2002) is identified as being moderately strong. In addition, these studies were conducted by four research teams. According to the CEC standards (2008), if an intervention program has at least five strong single subject design studies that are well implemented with positive effects from at least three research teams and shows no negative effects, that intervention program can be considered as "positive effects evidence-based." Therefore, the ABA for communication studies reviewed by MDHHS and MDE (2009) meet the CEC standard and can be considered as positive effects evidence-based.

Similarly, the seven PECS studies (Charlop-Christy, Carpenter, Le, LeBlanc, & Kellet, 2002; Frea, Arnold, & Vittimberga, 2001; Ganz & Simpson, 2004; Ganz, Simpson, Corbin-Newsome, 2008; Kravits, Kamps, Kemmerer, & Potucek, 2002; Tincani, 2004; Yoder, & Stone, 2006) reviewed by MDHHS and MDE (2009) meet the same level of evidence. Specifically, PECS demonstrates positive effects in increasing the communication ability of students with ASD across three well implemented single subject design studies conducted by three independent research teams, and demonstrated moderate positive effects in two other well-implemented studies conducted by different research teams. Hence, both ABA for communication and PECS meet the highest level of evidence criteria defined by CEC standards (2008) and are considered as positive effects evidence-based practices.

In contrast, among the seven SIOP studies reviewed by What Works, only one peer-reviewed study directly examined the effects of SIOP on English language learners' writing achievement (Echevarria, Short, & Powers, 2006). The other study, which investigated the effects of SIOP on that population's vocabulary and comprehension, also revealed positive effects (Dennis, 2004). The study by Dennis (2004) is a master's thesis and has not been published in a peer-reviewed journal. The rest of the studies reviewed by What Works either examined the use of SIOP observation protocols or provided an overview of SIOP that does not directly examine the effects of SIOP on students' communication performance. Therefore, to determine whether SIOP has a positive effect on students' communication skills, we focus on the studies conducted by Echevarria et al. (2006) and Dennis (2004). The results of these two studies demonstrate that SIOP increased English language learners' writing ability and vocabulary; however, the methodology of both studies does not show adequate quality in their designs. Specifically, the two studies lack comparison groups, show no control of students' abilities across groups prior to experiment, or have low implementation fidelity. Therefore, SIOP cannot be identified as having any level of evidence using the CEC standards (2008). This finding indicates that more well-controlled studies need to be conducted to document the effects or lack of effects of using SIOP to increase these students' learning outcomes. This need is particularly evident given the frequency of SIOP's use in the classroom.

Critical Intervention Components for CLD Students with ASD

According to the CEC standards (2008), ABA for communication and PECS are considered as positive effects, evidence-based practice for students with ASD; however, the extent to which these programs address the needs of CLD students with ASD is not addressed in the CEC standards. That is, an intervention program may show positive results for students with ASD but the components of the program may not work as well for CLD students with ASD without further examining the participants in the studies and the components of the intervention. Below, we discuss the components of ABA for communication, PECS, and SIOP and compare them to the critical components discussed in Table 9.2. Specifically, we include the studies that demonstrated strong research quality based on MDHHS and MDE (2009) and the intervention studies reviewed by What Works in the current review. Since these studies all show positive effects on students' learning, the following review focuses on the participants and procedures described in these studies (Tables 9.3 to 9.5).

ABA for Communication.   As shown in Table 9.3, the studies implementing ABA for purposes of developing communication skills demonstrate strong supports for students with ASD but do not address the components that CLD students with ASD may need. Specifically, three out of five studies conducting ABA for communication involved families before or during intervention to help identify target behaviors and assess students with ASD (Charlop & Trasowech, 1991; Charlop-Christy & Kelso, 2003; Ingersoll et al., 2007). In addition, most of these studies provide intensive interventions with a low student–teacher ratio during intervention. About 50% of the studies (n = 2) set up high expectations for students with ASD by connecting the intervention objectives to the behaviors of same-age typically developing children. This consideration also makes the content of interventions more functional for students with ASD because these students have more opportunities to observe and perform the behaviors during their daily life. In addition, because of the nature of single subject design, students' progress is closely monitored through ongoing assessment to guide intervention.

The components regarding challenging behaviors, English language learning, and cultural needs of CLD students with ASD, however, are not addressed across these studies. Although the authors mention that students' undesired responses did not receive predetermined reinforcement during intervention, the function of students' undesired responses is not discussed. Furthermore, the connection between the use of a specific reinforcer and the function of the behaviors of students with ASD is not addressed.

All studies lacked information about the cultural and ethnic background of the participants. The omission of this information makes it difficult to determine whether the intervention procedure considers the language and cultural needs of the family and students with ASD. In sum, the components of ABA for communication demonstrate adequate supports for students with ASD in general but need to incorporate cultural and English language learning into intervention procedures to better address the needs of CLD students with ASD.

PECS.   The studies implementing PECS demonstrate strong support for students with ASD by involving families, providing one-on-one instructions, focusing on functional communication abilities across studies, and providing ongoing assessments. Families and parents of students with ASD are involved to help identify reinforcers for their child or evaluate the overall effects and feasibility of the interventions rather than implementing PECS in home settings. This type of family involvement may be required because of the specific training needed to implement PECS. The PECS studies, however, do not appear to set up particularly high expectations for CLD students with ASD (Table 9.4). This may be due in part to the difficulty the trainers

TABLE 9.3 Critical Components of ABA for Communication

Critical Components	Charlop & Trasowech (1991)	Charlop & Carpenter (2000)	Charlop-Christy & Kelso (2003)	Jones, Feeley & Takacs (2007)	Ingersoll, Lewis, & Kroman (2007)
1. Family Involvement	Settings, routine, and target behavior		Generalization probes	N/A	Inform consent, and determine language age
2. Intensive instruction and planned teaching opportunities to meet individual goals	Daily for 1 year, including follow up		Twice a week	1–6 sessions/ day for about 3 days	1 hour/day 2 days/week 10 weeks of intervention
3. Low student/teacher ratios	1:1		1:1	1:1	1:1
4. Having high expectations	Use typically developing students' phrases as standard		Use student interests and typically developing peers' conversation topics	N/A	N/A
5. Functional communication, social, play, cognitive, and academic skills	Verbalization		Conversation	Spontaneous Communi- cation	Gesture Imitation
6. Functional approach to address problem behaviors	N/A		N/A	N/A	N/A
7. Infusing multicultural representation in schools and curriculum	N/A		N/A	N/A	N/A
8. English Language Learning	N/A		N/A	N/A	N/A
9. Ongoing assessment	Daily recording		Continuous probes	Continuous probes	Continuous probe, Pre- and post-motor assessment

have in reaching the higher order instruction which generally occurs at levels 5 and 6 of the PECS protocol. Initial objectives of most PECS interventions focus on teaching students with moderate to severe ASD to request objects or initiate interaction with others. CLD students may not be provided with sufficient training to move beyond the initial levels to reach the higher order instruction.

Similar to ABA for communication, most of these PECS studies do not address problem behaviors. Charlop-Christy et al. (2002) do describe the antecedents of students' challenging behaviors; however, the functions of these problem behaviors are not clearly addressed. Therefore, the connection between the behavior management strategies used in this study and the function of the student's behavior is not clear. Furthermore, the cultural needs of the CLD students across these studies are not addressed. Specifically, while the ethnicity backgrounds of the student participants are described in most studies, the extent to which the intervention is adapted to make the intervention more culturally responsive for these students is not discussed.

TABLE 9.4 Critical Components of PECS

Critical Components	Charlop-Christy, Carpenter, Le, LeBlanc, & Kellet (2002)	Kravits, Kamps, Kemmerer, & Potucek (2002)	Tincani (2004)	Yorder, & Stone (2006)
1. Family Involvement	Generalization, Preference assessment	Home as one of intervention settings	Social validity	Social validity, Parent information session
2. Intensive instruction and planned teaching opportunities to meet individual goals	15 minutes session, twice a week	5–35 minutes (15–71 trials) over five training periods	21 sessions of intervention	1 hour/ week for 6 months
3. Low student/teacher ratios	1:1	1:1	1:1	1:1 & 2:1
4. Having high expectations	N/A	N/A	N/A	N/A
5. Functional communication, social, play, cognitive, and academic skills	Verbal Speech	Spontaneous initiation and interaction	Motor imitation, mand, and word vocalization	Spoken communication
6. Functional approach to address problem behaviors	Planned Ignoring, A contingent "no," DRO	N/A	N/A	N/A
7. Infusing multicultural representation in schools and curriculum	N/A	N/A	N/A	N/A
8. English Language Learning	Ethiopian, Chinese, and Korean American	N/A	African and Asian American	Excluding ELL students
9. Ongoing assessment	Observation data/session	Language Sample and Observation data/session	Observation data/session	Time 1, Time 2, and Time 3

The students with ASD in these studies may not have needs in learning English but their diverse ethnic backgrounds may influence their communication style and the priority of words that they need to learn to communicate with their family. Therefore, to provide a culturally responsive PECS intervention, families may need to be involved beyond assessing social validity of the intervention to help infuse multicultural representation in PECS intervention.

SIOP.   The two SIOP studies reviewed examined the effects of SIOP on English language learners' writing, vocabulary, and comprehension skills (Dennis, 2004; Echevarria et al., 2006). As shown in Table 9.5, the studies implementing SIOP demonstrate adequate supports for typically developing CLD students but may not address the components that CLD students with ASD may need. Specifically, both studies have a strong focus on setting up high expectations and provide language supports for CLD students throughout the lesson. These studies, however, do not involve family before or during intervention to help identify target behaviors and show high student–teacher ratio and low intervention intensity. In addition, considerations regarding multicultural representation and challenging behavior during intervention are not addressed.

TABLE 9.5 Critical Components of SIOP

Critical Components	Echevarria et al. (2006)	Dennis (2004)
1. Family Involvement	N/A	N/A
2. Intensive instruction and planned teaching opportunities to meet individual goals	N/A	1 lesson
3. Low student/teacher ratios	12:1	31:1
4. Having high expectations	Focus on language production, focus, support or elaboration, organization, and mechanics	Access content of History lesson
5. Functional communication, social, play, cognitive, and academic skills	Academic—writing	Academic—vocabulary and comprehension
6. Functional approach to address problem behaviors	N/A	N/A
7. Infusing multicultural representation in schools and curriculum	N/A	N/A
8. English language learning	Have specific language objective	Have specific language objective and scaffold academic language
9. Ongoing assessment	Pre- and postwriting assessment	Pre- and postvocabulary and comprehension tests

The SIOP does demonstrate a strong focus on language learning and positive results in increasing English language learners' performance; however, the SIOP components may require further modification to better address the needs of CLD students with ASD. For instance, parents and teachers can incorporate SIOP features when implementing ABA for communication, PECS, or other evidence-based intervention for students with ASD to meet the language needs of CLD students with ASD.

The three programs reviewed do not demonstrate multicultural considerations and do not address problem behaviors of CLD students with ASD. Future studies need to incorporate the above mentioned components into interventions to address the language, behavior, social, and cultural needs of CLD students with ASD.

Future Directions

We must use science to improve education for *all* children, not just for some children. There are many sociocultural and language implications of autism, especially given the core characteristics of autism which include difficulties with social interactions and problems in language development and understanding. These implications, coupled with a cultural and linguistic profile which differs from the mainstream, may marginalize those learners who are CLD and have an ASD diagnosis. Sociocultural factors are important in learning and teaching methods must be used that meet the needs of CLD students with autism. We must generate research which seeks to answer the questions around what interventions are evidence based for learners who are CLD and have been diagnosed with an ASD. These interventions can then be used in culturally responsive ways to improve outcomes. As we have outlined in this chapter there are a host of factors that require attention.

Different methodologies are important for addressing different questions. The exclusive use of RCTs will not serve students who are CLD and have ASD as well. Other methodologies are experimental and may fit this population better (i.e., single-subject designs). Researchers might find benefit in using Levin, O'Donnell, and Kratochwill's stages of programs of research (2003) to inform future intervention design efforts and research. These stages illustrate science on a continuum rather than a fixed point where Stage 1 involves preliminary ideas, hypothesis, observations, and pilot works; Stage 2 reflects controlled laboratory experiments or classroom-based demonstrations and design experiments; Stage 3 research incorporates knowledge from prior stages into RCTs or single-subject design studies in classroom or naturalistic settings; and Stage 4 is where classroom practice is informed. Many methodologies and disciplines could be used to generate useful information. Clearly, research on ASD and CLD is at Stage 1 where pilot work is emerging. We must progress to the next step and begin to focus on the development of experiments to prove effectiveness of an intervention in naturalistic settings. As we focus on finding evidence for "what works" it is critical to find out what works with whom (Cunningham & Fitzgerald, 1996).

It is not only important to know what works, it is critical to train professionals to implement the intervention in culturally responsive ways. To meet the needs of an increasingly heterogeneous society, it is imperative that professionals be prepared to respond effectively to families and children from varying cultural and linguistic backgrounds. If service providers and related professionals fail to understand the role that culture plays in the construction of disability and social development, the risk of impeding the success of children from cultural orientations different from our own remains. Partnering with families can increase understanding of individual and cultural perspectives, provide the opportunity to bridge this gap of incompatibility, and create an opportunity for all children to reach their potential. There is a critical need to understand the experiences of families to provide sufficient levels of support and culturally responsive services. Current school practices and the normative curriculum are responsive to the dominant culture in society, yet they are generally not responsive to communities whose cultural practices differ from those of the mainstream (Ladson-Billings, 1995). Cultural issues require us to adopt the "posture of cultural reciprocity" as suggested by Kalyanpur and Harry (1997). Using this posture suggests that both parties involved in the interactions respect, listen, and learn about each other's cultural identity and model. The result can be successful outcomes that are valued by all and mirror family values in culturally responsive ways.

This chapter provides a framework for extrapolating evidence-based practices from research done with CLD students and from research performed with students who have ASD. Underlying this framework is a host of critical components that should be in place for the learner who is CLD and has an ASD. Future researchers could use this framework as a starting point to design research that attends to the critical components and includes diverse participants where demographics are fully described.

Conclusion and Summary

Professionals who work with CLD children with autism should be very concerned about the paucity of research around evidence-based practices. CLD children with autism and their families are challenged on many levels and must receive equitable services and culturally responsive resources at every stage, from identification to assessment and intervention.

A first step toward evidence-based practice is creating awareness of the content of the best available research. It is no longer enough to use what we believe works, we must consider what we know works in order to close the gap between science and practice, utilize limited resources wisely, and best serve CLD children who have ASD. Clearly, research for this population is still at the "what we believe works" stage. We must progress into generating sound proof of effective interventions using multiple methodologies. Resources must be allocated to enable researchers to conduct this large-scale work.

The goal of multicultural education is to change the structure of schools so that students, including those diagnosed with ASD from different cultural groups have an equal chance to achieve in school. It is imperative that we generate a solid evidence base of interventions to positively influence outcomes for these individuals.

References

Barrera, I., Corso, R. M., & Macpherson. D. (2003). *Skilled dialogue: Strategies for responding to cultural diversity.* Baltimore, MD: Brookes.

Begeer, S., El Bouk, S., Boussaid, W., Meerum Terwogt, M., & Koot, H. M. (2009). Underdiagnosis and referral bias of autism in ethnic minorities. *Journal of Autism and Developmental Disorders, 39,* 142–148.

Brookman-Frazee, L. (2004). Parent–professional partnerships in parent education interventions for children with autism. *Journal of Positive Behavior Interventions, 6,* 195–213.

Brown, J. R., & Rogers, S. J. (2003). Cultural issues in autism. In S. Ozonoff, S. J. Rogers, & R. L. Hendren (Eds.), *Autism spectrum disorders: A research review for practitioners* (pp. 209–226). Arlington, VA: American Psychiatric Publishing.

California Department of Developmental Services. (2003, April). *Autistic spectrum disorders. Changes in the California caseload: An update: 1999 through 2002.* Retrieved from http://www.dds.ca.gov

Cartledge, G., Gardner, R. III., & Ford, D. Y. (2009). *Diverse learners with exceptionalities: Culturally responsive teaching in the inclusive classroom.* Upper Saddle River, NJ: Merrill/Pearson Education.

Chan, S. (1997). Families with Asian roots. In E. W. Lynch & M. J. Hanson (Eds.), *Developing cross-cultural competence: A guide for working with children and their families* (2nd ed.). Baltimore, MD: Brookes.

Charlop, M. H., & Carpenter, M. H. (2000). Modified incidental teaching sessions: A procedure for parents to increase spontaneous speech in their children with autism. *Journal of Positive Behavioral Interventions, 2*(2), 98–112.

Charlop, M. H., & Trasowech, J. E. (1991). Increasing autistic children's daily spontaneous speech. *Journal of Applied Behavior Analysis, 24*(4), 747–761.

Charlop-Christy, M. H., Carpenter, H. M., Le, L., LeBlanc, L. A., & Kellet, K. (2002). Using the picture exchange communication system (PECS) with children with autism: Assessment of PECS acquisition, speech, social-communicative behavior, and problem behavior. *Journal of Applied Behavior Analysis, 35,* 213–231.

Charlop-Christy, M. H., & Kelso, S. E. (2003). Teaching children with autism conversational speech using a cue card/written script program. *Education and Treatment of Children, 26*(2), 108–127.

Connors, J. L., & Donnellan, A. M. (1998). Walk in beauty: Western perspectives on disability and Navajo family/cultural resilience. In H. I. McCubbin, E. A. Thompson, A. I. Thompson, & J. E. Fromer (Eds.), *Resiliency in Native American and immigrant families* (pp. 159–182). New York: Sage.

Council for Exceptional Children. (2008). *Classifying the state of evidence for special education professional practices: CEC practice study manual.* Retrieved from http://www.cec.sped.org/Content/NavigationMenu/ProfessionalDevelopment/ProfessionalStandards/.

Cunningham, J. W., & Fitzgerald, J. (1996). Epistemology and reading. *Reading Research Quarterly, 31,* 36–60.

Dennis, R. L. (2004). The effects of the sheltered instruction observation protocol model on the vocabulary development of English language learners in the content area. *Masters Abstracts International, 43*(04), 101–1073.

Dyches, T. T., Wilder, L. K., Sudweeks, R. R, Obiakor, F. E., & Algozzine, B. (2004). Multicultural issues in autism. *Journal of Autism and Developmental Disorders, 34*(2), 211–222.

Echevarria, J., Short, D., & Powers, K. (2006). School reform and standards-based education: A model for English-language learners. *Journal of Educational Research, 99*(4), 195–210.

Frea, W. D., Arnold, C. L., & Vittimberga, G. I. (2001). A demonstration of the effects of augmentative communication on the extreme aggressive behavior of a child with autism within an integrated preschool setting. *Journal of Positive Behavior Interventions, 3*(4), 194–198.

Ganz J. B., & Simpson, R. L. (2004). Effects of communicative requesting and speech development of the picture exchange communication system in children with characteristics of autism. *Journal of Autism and Developmental Disorders, 34*(4), 395–409.

Ganz, J. B., Simpson, R. L., & Corbin-Newsome, J. (2008). The impact of the picture exchange communication system on requesting and speech development in preschoolers with autism spectrum disorders and similar characteristics. *Research in Autism Spectrum Disorders, 2,* 157–169.

Garcia, E., & Cuellar, D. (2006). Who are these linguistically and culturally diverse students? *Teachers College Record, 108*(11), 2220–2246.

Gay, G. (2000). *Culturally responsive teaching: Theory, research, and practice.* New York: Teachers College Press.

Gay, G., & Howard, T. C. (2000). Multicultural teacher education for the 21st century. *The Teacher Educator, 36*, 1–16.

Gee, J. P. (2001). A sociocultural perspective on early literacy development. In S. B. Neuman & D. K. Dickinson (Eds.), *Handbook of early literacy research* (pp. 30–42). New York: Guilford Press.

Guralnick, M. J. (1997). Second generation research in the field of early intervention. In M. J. Guralnick (Ed.), *The effectiveness of early intervention* (pp. 3–22). Baltimore, MD: Brookes.

Harry, B. (1992). Cultural diversity, families, and the special education system. New York: Teachers College Press.

Harry, B., Kalyanpur, M., & Day, M. (1999). *Building cultural reciprocity with families: Case studies in special education.* Baltimore, MD: Brookes..

Individuals With Disabilities Education Improvement Act of 2004 (IDEIA), Pub. L. No. 108-446, 20 U.S.C. §§ 1400.

Ingersoll, B., Lewis, E., & Kroman, E. (2007). Teaching the imitation and spontaneous use of descriptive gestures in young children with autism using a naturalistic behavioral intervention. *Journal of Autism and Other Developmental Disorders, 37,* 1446–1456.

Jones, E. A., Feeley, K. M., & Takacs, J. (2007). Teaching spontaneous responses to young children with autism. *Journal of Applied Behavior Analysis, 40*(3), 565–570.

Kalyanpur, M., & Harry, B. (1997). A posture of reciprocity: A practical approach to collaboration between professionals and parents of culturally diverse backgrounds. *Journal of Child and Family Studies, 6*(4), 487–509.

Kravits, T. R., Kamps, D. M., Kemmerer, K., & Potucek, J. (2002). Brief report: Increasing communication skills for an elementary-aged student with autism using the picture exchange communication system. *Journal of Autism and Developmental Disorders, 32*(3), 225–230.

Ladson-Billings, G. J. (1995). Toward a theory of culturally relevant pedagogy. *American Education Research Journal, 35,* 465–491.

Lee, R., McComas, J. J., & Jawor, J. (2002). The effects of differential and lag reinforcement schedules on varied verbal responding by individuals with autism. *Journal of Applied Behavior Analysis, 35*(4), 391–402.

Levin, J. R., O'Donnell, A. M., & Kratochwill, T. R. (2003). Educational/psychological intervention research. In W. Reynolds & G. Miller (Eds.), *Handbook of psychology: Vol. 7. Educational psychology* (pp. 557–581). Hoboken, NJ: Wiley.

Levy, S., Mandell, D., Merher, S., Ittenback, R., & Pinto-Martin, J. (2003). Use of complementary and alternative medicine among children recently diagnosed with autism spectrum disorder. *Journal of Developmental and Behavioral Pediatrics, 24,* 418–423.

Maine Department of Health and Human Services & the Maine Department of Education. (2009, October). *Interventions for autism spectrum disorders: State of the evidence* (Report of the Children's Services Evidence-Based Practice Advisory Committee). Augusta, ME: Author.

Mandell, D. S., Listerud, J., Levy, S. E., & Pinto-Martin, J. A. (2002). Race differences in the age at diagnosis among Medicaid-eligible children with autism. *Journal of the American Academy of Child and Adolescent Psychiatry, 41,* 1447–1453.

Mandell, D. S., Morales, K. H., Marcus, S. C., Stahmer, A. C., Doshi, J., & Polsky, D. E. (2008). Psychotropic medication use among Medicaid-enrolled children with autism spectrum disorders. *Pediatrics, 121*(3), e441-e448. doi:10.1542/peds.2007-0984.

Mandell, D. S., & Novak, M. (2005). The role of culture in families' treatment decisions for children with autism spectrum disorders. *Mental Retardation and Developmental Disabilities, 11,* 110–115.

Mandell, D. S., & Palmer, R. (2005). Differences among states in the identification of autistic spectrum disorders. *Archives of Pediatrics and Adolescent Medicine, 159*(3), 266–269. doi:10.1001/archpedi.159.3.266

Moes, D., & Frea, W. (2002). Contextualized behavioral support in early intervention for children with autism and their families. *Journal of Autism & Developmental Disorders, 32*(6), 519.

National Research Council. (2001). *Educating children with autism* (C. Lord & J. P. McGee, Eds.). (Committee on Educational Interventions for Children with Autism, Division of Behavioral and Social Sciences and Education). Washington, DC: National Academy Press.

National Research Council. (2002). *Minority students in special and gifted education* (M. S. Donovan & C. T. Cross, Eds.). (Committee on Minority Representation in Special Education). Washington, DC: National Academy Press.

Parette, P., Chuang, S. L., & Huer, M. B. (2004). First-generation Chinese American families' attitudes regarding disabilities and educational interventions. *Focus on Autism and Other Developmental Disabilities, 97,* 114–123.

Rosenberg, M. S., & Sindelar, P. T. (2003). *The proliferation of alternative routes to certification in special education: A critical review of the literature* (COPSSE Document Number RS-10E). Gainesville: University of Florida, Center on Personnel Studies in Special Education.

Rosenberg, R. E., Daniels, A. M., Law, J. K., Law, P. A., & Kaufmann, W. E. (2009). Trends in autism spectrum disorder diagnoses: 1994–2007. *Journal of Autism and Developmental Disorders, 39,* 1099–1111.

Ryan, A., & Smith, M. (1989). Parental reactions to developmental disabilities in Chinese American families. *Child and Adolescent Social Work, 6,* 283–299.

Sandall, S., McLean, M. E., & Smith, B. J. (Eds.). (2000). *DEC recommended practices in early intervention/early childhood special education.* Longmont, CO: Sopris West.

Schwartz, I. S., & Sandall, S. R. (2010). Is autism the disability that breaks part c? [A commentary on "Infants and toddlers with autism spectrum disorder: Early identification and early intervention," by B. A. Boyd, S. C. Odom, B. P. Humphreys, & A. H. Sam]. *Journal of Early Intervention, 32*(2), 105–109.

Sileo, T. W., & Prater, M. A. (1998). Preparing professionals for partnerships with parent of students with disabilities: Textbook considerations regarding cultural diversity. *Exceptional Children, 64*(4), 513–529.

Thomas, K. C., Ellis, A. R., McLaurin, C., Daniels, J., & Morrissey, J. P. (2007). Access to care for autism-related services. *Journal of Autism and Developmental Disorders, 37,* 1902–1912.

Tincani, M. (2004). Comparing the picture exchange communication system and sign language training for children with autism. *Focus on Autism and Other Developmental Disabilities, 19*(3), 152–163.

Vaughn, S. R., Bos, C. S., & Schumm, J. S. (2011). *Teaching students who are exceptional, diverse, and at risk in the general education classroom.* Upper Saddle River, NJ: Merrill.

Van Meter, K. C., Christiansen, L. E., Delwiche, L. D., Azari, R., Carpenter, T. E., & Herz-Picciotto, I. (2010). Geographic distribution of autism in California: A retrospective birth cohort analysis. *Autism Research, 3*(1), 19–29.

Welterlin, A., & LaRue, R. (2007). Serving the needs of immigrant families of children with autism. *Disability and Society, 22*(7), 747–760.

What Works Clearinghouse. (2003). Standards. Washington, DC: Author. Retrieved from http://www.w-w-c.org/standards.html

What Works Clearinghouse. (2009). English Language Learners. Retrieved April 2, 2010, from http://ies.ed.gov/ncee/wwc/reports/topic.aspx?tid=10

Wilder, L. K., Dyches, T. T., Obiakor, F. E., & Algozzine, B. (2004). Multicultural perspectives on teaching students with autism. *Focus on Autism and Other Developmental Disabilities, 19,* 105–113.

Yorder, P., & Stone, W. L. (2006). A randomized comparison of the effect of two prelinguistic communication interventions on the acquisition of spoken communication in preschoolers with ASD. *Journal of Speech, Language, and Hearing Research, 49,* 698–711.

Zhang, C., & Bennett, T. (2003). Facilitating the meaningful participation of culturally and linguistically diverse families in the IFSP and IEP process. *Focus on Autism and Other Developmental Disabilities, 18*(1), 51–59.

Zionts, L. T., Zionts, P., Harrison, S., & Bellinger, O. (2003). Urban African American families' perceptions of cultural sensitivity within the special education system. *Focus on Autism and Other Developmental Disabilities, 18*(1), 41–50.

10

EARLY INTERVENTION AND EARLY CHILDHOOD YEARS

E. Amanda Boutot

TEXAS STATE UNIVERSITY

Jennifer Loncola Walberg

DEPAUL UNIVERSITY

Introduction

Since the early 1990s, improvements in screening and diagnostic capabilities have increased the numbers of young children under age 3 who are diagnosed with autism (Boyd, Odom, Humphreys, & Sam, 2010), and in many cases children are being identified by age 2 (Zwaigenbaum et al., 2009). With this increase comes the opportunity and need for early intervention and early childhood special education services for youngsters with autism. Strong evidence suggests that the earlier children begin receiving appropriate, individualized interventions, the better their future prognosis (National Research Council, 2001). The purpose of this chapter is to provide information on the state of understanding within the autism community on infants, toddlers, and preschoolers with autism. Specifically, we will briefly cover the historical context for early intervention and early childhood special education for children with autism. We will present evidence suggesting that our understanding, as a field, of autism in infants, toddlers, and preschoolers is itself in its infancy, with much to be learned through continued research. We will also present an overview of legal mandates specific to this age group. Next we will discuss the literature on early identification and how research has led to earlier screening and diagnostic instruments for children under age 3 in particular. Given that early intervention services cannot begin until a child has been targeted as needing such services, early identification and diagnosis are crucial at this developmental level. We will also provide an overview of those interventions that are found to be scientifically based for use with infants, toddlers, and preschoolers with autism. In addition, the authors will provide suggestions for future directions and research.

Historical Foundations

A review of the literature reveals that until the early 1980s little specific attention was paid to very young children with autism, and that was nearly 40 years after Kanner (1943, as cited in Gonzalez, Cassel, & Boutot, 2011) first described the syndrome. Until that time, research on autism focused primarily on school-aged children. As diagnostic advances were made, and public awareness of the disorder grew, the age at which children received the diagnosis dropped

(Boyd et al., 2010). Today infants are being screened for autism by their first birthday in most states (Johnson & Myers, 2007), leading to an increase in infants and toddlers identified with autism. Since the early eighties, more research on early identification and early treatment for autism has been steadily on the rise as well (Boyd et al., 2010). Perhaps what has contributed to the increase in numbers of infants and toddlers identified as having autism and who receive services for the disorder, are the legal mandates requiring both identification and provision of services for all children with disabilities. The next section provides an overview of the legal requirements specific to infants, toddlers, and preschoolers with disabilities, including those with autism.

Legal Mandates

The Individuals with Disabilities Education Act (IDEA; 2004) is the law that specifies the educational rights of children with disabilities. Originally enacted in 1975, IDEA has undergone many revisions since its inception. Most relevant to this chapter was the 1986 revision of the Education for All Handicapped Children Act, which extended services to 3- to 5-year-olds. A brief history follows below. As will be discussed later in the chapter, early intervention is crucial to remediating some of the deficits involved with autism. In fact, a cost–benefit analysis of early intensive behavioral therapy demonstrates that even for young children who make modest gains with the therapy the net savings can be in the millions (Jacobson, Mulick, & Green, 1998). Therefore, provision of early intervention services is critical.

When first enacted in 1975, IDEA, then known as Education for All Handicapped Children Act, provided for a free and appropriate public education for children with disabilities aged 6 to 21. Over the years, additional amendments to the original act have changed its name and extended the rights provided to students with disabilities. Most significant to our discussion here is the Education of All Handicapped Children Act Amendments of 1986 (20 U.S.C. §§ 1471 et seq and 1419 et seq). These amendments extend services to 3- to 5-year-olds, requiring that services be gradually implemented and formally mandated by 1990. They also provided incentives to states to deliver early intervention services for infants and toddlers from birth to 36 months. In 1990, the name of the act was officially changed from the Education of All Handicapped Children Act to the Individuals with Disabilities Education Act. IDEA was reauthorized in 1997 and 2004 and is currently divided into four parts: Part A—General Provisions; Part B—Assistance for Education of All Children with Disabilities; Part C—Infants and Toddlers with Disabilities; Part D—National Activities to Improve Education of Children with Disabilities. Part C, concerning infants and toddlers with disabilities is the component of the law that has shaped the way we provide services for very young children.

Section 631 of IDEA Part C states: "It is the policy of the United States to provide financial assistance to States...to develop and implement a statewide, comprehensive, coordinated, multidisciplinary, interagency system that provides early intervention services for infants and toddlers with disabilities and their families." Early intervention services include a multidisciplinary family-centered assessment of the child, assessment of the resources and supports needed by the family in order to best serve the child, and the creation of an individualized family service plan (IFSP), which includes what services are needed for transition to an early childhood special education program (Part B).

According to Part C regulations, the IFSP must contain the following information: (1) Statements related to: (A) The infant or toddler's present level of functioning across physical and developmental areas. (B) Family resources or concerns around development. (C) Expected outcomes of early intervention services related to the achievement of the infant or toddler in areas such as preliteracy, and language (written as goals). (D) Specific early intervention service, based on peer-reviewed research, needed to meet the goals stated above, including frequency, method, and intensity of services. (E) The environment where the services will take place (i.e. home or center-based). (2) Projected start date for services and anticipated duration and frequency. (3) The identification of a service coordinator who can oversee the plan and coordinate services across disciplines. (4) Steps that will be taken to support toddlers with disabilities and their families in the transition to preschool. (IDEA 20 U.S.C. §§ 1400 et seq). The individualized family service plan (IFSP) is similar to an individualized education plan (IEP) that is written for children aged 3 to 21. The main difference between the two is that in an IEP the focus is on the child, while in an IFSP, the focus is on the entire family.

Once children reach the age of 3, they begin the process of transitioning to Part B services. Among other things, Part B of the Individuals with Disabilities Education Act spells out the different disability categories, defines the process for referral to special education, gives guidance on evaluation of the student and development of the IEP, and discusses the importance of educating students in the least restrictive environment. Part B also gives eligibility criteria and specific information regarding state preschool grants that enable funding of special education services for children aged 3 to 5. The legal mandates of Part C and B of the Individuals with Disabilities Education Act set the stage for how school district personnel and other early intervention personnel refer, assess, and implement interventions for infants, toddlers, and young children with autism.

Description and Overview

In a meeting of the Autism Coordinating Board of the National Institutes of Health in 1998, early identification and diagnosis of autism was ranked as the second most important priority for research, behind etiology (Goin & Myers, 2004). Since then, many research articles have been published exploring the characteristics of autism in infants and toddlers, to provide clues to the features that can lead to pinpointing those youngsters who will and will not be diagnosed with autism in the future, as well as with methods for identifying autism at earlier ages. This research into early characteristics has taken two forms: retrospective and prospective. Retrospective studies have taken the form of a parent interview, retrospective videotape analysis, while prospective studies actually track infants in real time, observing and recording behaviors, and comparing these behaviors across those who get an autism diagnosis in the future and those who do not. Retrospective studies are not without limitations, though they provided much of the earliest research leading to the more recent prospective studies. Specifically, disadvantages of retrospective studies involving parent interview are that often the parents were interviewed many years, or even decades, after their child was in the infant–toddler stage (Goin & Myers, 2004). Memory issues are cited as possible flaws with interviews, as is the fact that by the time the parent is interviewed, their child has an autism diagnosis. It is possible that the parents' perception of their child's developmental history is influenced by this knowledge in present time. Retrospective video analysis was employed to address the concern over memory and parent perspective, yet it also has methodological limitations: specifically, the quality of the home movies and settings and contexts of the videos (Boyd et al., 2010).

Retrospective Methods

Parent Interview

One of the earliest methods for attempting to uncover the characteristics of autism in very young children was through the use of the parent interview. Researchers would ask parents to review their child's developmental history and discuss specific characteristics that might be associated with autism or that were well outside the norm for typical development (e.g., communication and social delays). Results of some of these studies revealed that beginning around ages 12 to 18 months, families reported noticing differences in language and social development. Most parents reported their concerns to their pediatricians (Siegel, 2001), though most children did not receive a diagnosis of autism for at least one year following these initial reports of concern. Parents reported a number of other concerns including failure to echo adult sounds, lack of pointing behavior, failure to imitate others, failure to engage in social games (e.g., peekaboo), not seeking to cuddle, lack of searching for parents, lack of interest in animals or same-aged peers, failure to seek comfort, not waving hello or goodbye, perseverative play with an object, not raising arms to be picked up, lack of eye contact, no verbal turn-taking, and failure to respond to name (Coonrod, Turner, Pozdol, & Stone, 2001; Robins, Fein, Barton, & Green, 2001; Vostanis et al., 1998; Wimpory, Hobson, Williams, & Nash, 2000).

Another area of interest in parent interview research involved those children who developed symptoms of autism after a period of apparent typical development (Goin & Myers, 2004). Researchers sought to determine at what age and in what developmental areas this regression occurs. Williams and Ozonoff (2001) found that regression was first noted by parents in the areas of communication and socialization at a mean age of 16.6 months. Werner and Munson (2001) noted that motor development was observed as regressing in children, even when social and language delays were not noted.

Among those families whose children did not display regressive onset of autistic symptoms, compared to typically developing children, they reported a perception that their child behaved differently from birth, though concerns were not reported to physicians until specific delays became obvious (e.g., communication). Examples of behaviors noted as different from birth included uncontrollable crying, appearing deaf, resistance to being held, and constant tantrums (Goin & Myers, 2004). Of interest is the consistent report by parents that upon expressing these concerns to their pediatricians, they were most often advised to take a "wait and see" approach, due to differences and variations in typical child development.

Retrospective Videotape Analysis

Another approach to the study of autism in infancy is retrospective video analysis. In this method, researchers study home videos of infants/toddlers who are later diagnosed with autism, identifying developmental characteristics that differentiate these children from matched controls involving typically developing peers or peers with other developmental disabilities or delays. A benefit to the use of videos is that they do not rely on parent memory (Goin & Myers, 2004). Saint-Georges et al. (2010) reviewed the literature on use of family home movies in identification of characteristics of autism in young children finding 41 such research studies, both in the United States and abroad (18 of which were of sufficiently high quality to warrant review in their article). Ages of infants ranged from zero to 48 months, with most studies (11 of 18) analyzing videotapes longitudinally. Sample sizes ranged from 1 to 56 for subjects and zero to 25 for controls. In addition, some studies (9 of the 18) examined differences between children later diagnosed with autism and not only neurotypical controls, but also to those with other disabilities, such as mental retardation or developmental delay. Most studies used blind review of videotapes by at least two trained coders, most often using some evaluation scale to rate behaviors (Goin & Myers, 2004). According to the review by Saint-Georges et al. (2010), most studies sought statistical significance of differences between the autism and control groups, though some studies were more descriptive and did not rely on statistical analyses (p. 359). In addition to seeking to identify specific behavioral differences between youngsters with autism and those who are typically developing, other retrospective video analyses have also been conducted to determine at what ages these differences were first observable. Adrien et al. (1993) and Zakian, Malvy, Desombre, Roux, and Lenour (2000) found differences, such as distractibility, lack of social smile, no social interaction, inappropriate facial expression, and more docile behavior in the first year, and noted these differences tended to worsen as the children approached age 2. In a classic study, Osterling and Dawson (1994) reviewed first birthday party videotapes of children later diagnosed with autism and neurotypical children. Findings included a failure to bring a favorite object or toy to show an adult, failure to respond to their name when called, lack of pointing behavior, and lack of eye contact. Similar results were found when observing home videos of infants aged 8 to 10 months (Werner, Dawson, Osterling, & Dinno, 2000). Carmagnat-Dubois et al. (1997) found in reviewing home videos that differences in behavior became noticeable as early as 6 months of age, and worsened by the first year, including failure to respond to others, lack of vocalization, and no social smile. Atypical motor development has also been observed through analysis of family home videos (Teitelbaum, Teitelbaum, Nye, Fryman, & Maurer, 1998), including delays in rolling over, sitting up, crawling, walking, and poor coordination. Sensory-motor differences have also been noted using a retrospective video analysis method. Baranek (1999) examined differences in typically developing infants, those with developmental delays, and those with autism aged 9 to 12 months. Both the autism group and the developmental delay group displayed unusual postures, while the developmental delay group exhibited more stereotypical play behaviors and fewer references to the camera person than either the typical group or the autism group. However, the autism group consistently exhibited less response to name, failure to reference visual stimuli, more mouthing of objects, and aversion to touch than the other two groups, all behaviors noted by Baranek as predictive of autism.

In addition to identifying characteristic symptoms of infants later diagnosed with autism, two single-case studies reviewed by Saint-Georges et al. (2010) specifically targeted infants who displayed delayed onset of autistic symptoms, or regression. "The first child waved good-bye, played peek-a-boo, babbled often, played normally and used protodeclarative pointing before the occurrence of an acute regression around 12 months" (p. 360). In the second study, the child displayed typical developmental characteristics until age 22 months, when he began to exhibit "repetitive and stereotyped behavior, isolation, language stagnation, and decline of mental age" (p. 360).

Prospective Studies

Most early research into the early signs and symptoms of autism relied heavily on parental interview or retrospective video analysis of children known to have been later diagnosed with the disorder. Information from these early studies led to the identification of warning signs that were later used to predict infants considered at risk for autism. Identifying infants at risk for autism has allowed researchers to observe and study these children prospectively, meaning that they do not have to rely on retrospection or interview but can make observations in real time. In addition, prospective studies have also examined infant siblings of children with autism given that autism is known to occur more frequently in siblings than in the general population (Boyd et al., 2010). Some of the symptoms found through prospective studies include lack of social engagement, impaired communication, limited or lack of response to name, limited receptive language, fewer gestures, irritability, stereotyped behaviors, distress, and affective impairments (Saint-Georges et al., 2010). Results from prospective studies tend to confirm those from retrospective video analysis (Saint-Georges et al., 2010).

Early studies into the characteristics of autism in infants and toddlers were aimed at differentiating ages of onset of symptoms as well as different disabilities or delays so that earlier and better screening and diagnostic instruments could be developed for this population of youngsters. Today it is understood that a wait and see approach is detrimental to children who display these early symptoms, with parent and professional education on the early signs of autism a priority. First Signs (www.firstsigns.org) is a national nonprofit organization dedicated to educating parents and professionals on the red flags of autism in infants and toddlers. Further, the American Academy of Pediatrics now recommends developmental screenings for autism no later than 18 to 24 months old, with a strong recommendation to screen for early warning signs at 9 months (Boyd et al., 2001).

Early Screening and Diagnosis

With a better understanding of what autism looks like in very young children, improvements have been made in screening for the disorder and in early diagnosis (Boyd et al., 2010). In their review of the literature, Boyd and colleagues discuss a number of early screeners and diagnostic tools for use specifically with very young children under age 3. While, with the early warning signs research has come increased work to create and validate such measures, Boyd et al. comment that many of the tools are still in the validation process. However, some tools have been in use for some time. The Checklist for Autism in Toddlers (CHAT; Baron-Cohen, Allen, & Gillberg, 1992) is a widely used instrument for use with infants and toddlers, and according to Boyd et al. is widely used by medical professionals with families to screen for possible autism. Two newer versions of the CHAT are also available: the Modified Checklist for Autism in Toddlers (MCHAT) is available for free download from the Internet (www.firstsigns.org/downloads/m-chat.PDF) and extends the age range to 30 months; the Quantitative Checklist for Autism in Toddlers (QCHAT) is for ages 18 to 24 months specifically (Boyd et al., 2010). Two other measures in use for screening for autism in young children include the Screening Tool for Autism in Two-Year-Olds (Stone, Coonrod, & Ousley, 2000), a clinician-administered instrument (Boyd et al., 2010), and the First Year Inventory (Reznick, Baranek, Reavis, Watson, & Crais, 2007), which is a parent questionnaire (Boyd et al., 2010).

Assessment instruments for older children, until recently, "were simply adjusted for use with infants and toddlers, which could be problematic because those diagnostic indicators were based on more chronologically or developmentally advanced expressions for autism" (Boyd et al., 2010, p. 83). Early diagnostic instruments are less readily available, though Boyd and colleagues report that studies of validity on some instruments is underway. For example, a toddler version of the "gold standard" in diagnostic instruments (Boyd et al., 2010) the Autism Diagnostic Observation Schedule (ADOS; Lord, Rutter, DiLavore, & Risi, 1999) is being validated currently and Bryson, Zwaigenbaum, McDermott, Rombough, and Brian (2008) have developed the Autism Observation Scale for Infants.

Family Issues

When a child is first diagnosed, it is common for parents and other family members to feel upset or even grieve over the "loss" of the child they were expecting. Though parents may eventually accept the diagnosis and come to terms with the impact it has on their lives, professionals must be aware that depression, anger, and denial can reappear at any time, especially in the first few years after diagnosis. Additional children may also be born around this time, creating sibling issues such as resentment and rivalry. Parents may experience feelings of concern over the well-being of their typically developing children, and there may be guilt associated with the extra time and attention they must bestow on their child with autism. This situation can be made more complex when families are engaged in intensive early intervention that may eat up limited familial resources that might otherwise be shared among all their children. Again, this can contribute to feelings of guilt and resentment on the part of both parents and siblings of children with autism.

In these early years, families are learning to navigate the educational system, researching treatments, and perhaps trying a variety of options to determine what works best. As the child gets older, many parents mention a feeling of urgency, and this urgency may create a feeling of panic that time is "running out" to find the best treatment approach. Further, with some parents and even professionals suggesting that autism can be cured with a particular treatment, or that children may "outgrow" their autism, the early years may be a time of both hope and disappointment as the parents begin to face the reality that autism is a lifelong disorder. The move from early intervention (EI) to early childhood special education is the first of many *transitions* for a child with autism. IDEA 2004, allows for an EI professional to accompany a parent to an IEP meeting to help ease transition issues and to help the parent feel more comfortable with the process.

The Evidence Base

In discussions so far in this chapter, we have focused on the background and what is known about the manifestation of autism in infants, toddlers, and preschoolers. We have further addressed specific issues for this age group, including Part C and Part B early childhood special education services, diagnostic and screening instruments, and issues related to families and caregivers. With new and improved understanding of the symptoms of autism in young children, better abilities to screen for and predict those with and at risk for autism, and upcoming diagnostic tools specific to this age group, the one question that remains unanswered is, "What are evidence-based practices for infants, toddlers, and preschoolers with autism?" In this section, we will explore the challenges related to studying this age group, review the literature on evidence-based practices as they are currently understood, and discuss issues related to personnel preparation and professional development in evidence-based practices.

As has been discussed in previous chapters, evidence-based practices are not only required by law, they are recommended for all children with autism (National Research Council, 2001). Therefore, we will not enter into a discussion here of what constitutes evidence-based practice. However, important to understanding the evidence base as it relates to very young children with autism is the recognition, again, that research with this age group is relatively scant and recent (Boyd et al., 2010). Much of what is understood about evidence-based practices for students with autism comes from research using subjects who are older than age 3, in some cases older than age 6. Far fewer studies have looked at those interventions that specifically target infants and toddlers with autism, perhaps because of the relatively recent screening and diagnostic improvements discussed previously. Accordingly, practitioners serving this age child have had to rely on the strategies known to be effective for older children and to adapt down to the age of the young children they served (Corsello, 2005). While more studies have included 3- to 5-year-olds, discussion of issues relating to infants and toddlers under age 3 remain uncommon in the literature today. In this section we will review the literature on evidence-based practices as well as promising practices for both zero to 3 and 3- to 5-year-old children.

A review of the literature on treatment for autism for young children reveals several common factors, which are supported by recommendations by the National Research Council (2001), as well as the *National Standards Report* (National Autism Center, 2009). Among these recommendations are that children with autism receive a minimum of 25 hours per week of intensive (often described as one-to-one) intervention and that such intervention must start as early as possible. In working with younger children, literature consistently points to parent training and family-implemented programs as factors associated with child gains (Boyd et al., 2010). Within the literature on treatment for young children with autism, there are two classifications: (a) intervention practices and (b) comprehensive treatment models (CTMs) (Boyd et al., 2010). Focused intervention practices are specific teaching procedures or strategies known to improve learning or decrease challenging behaviors (Boyd et al., 2010). In contrast, CTMs are intervention packages that draw from multiple theoretical or philosophical frameworks and provide a comprehensive model for remediation of specific skills. These models tend to involve instruction "across developmental domains, across longer periods, across the employment of a variety of focused practices" (p. 84).

Focused Intervention Practices

A number of specific instructional practices or teaching strategies have been identified in the literature, such as discrete trial training, incidental teaching, use of visual supports, and story based social interventions (National Autism Center, 2009). Much of the literature in support of specific strategies comes from the field of applied behavior analysis (ABA), which is discussed in chapter 4 of this text. Much of ABA practice involves what is known as the three-term contingency (Olive, Boutot, & Tarbox, 2011). The three-term contingency involves an antecedent (A), behavior or response (B), and a consequence (C). Interventions designed to teach a specific behavior or response (B) through application of specific antecedent cues and consequences designed to increase these behaviors can be thought of as behavioral interventions. Other interventions, which are designed to manipulate antecedents and to teach skills in order to prevent or remediate challenging behaviors can be thought of as positive behavior supports (Boyd et al., 2010). It should be noted that many behavioral intervention strategies serve to prevent inappropriate behavior while many of those considered as positive behavior supports also teach specific target skills.

Among specific strategies for young children with autism, perhaps the most often studied has been the use of discrete trial training. In the original study by Lovaas (1987), subjects were a mean age of 32 to 35 months at the start of the intensive behavioral treatment. Over a 3-year period, the study compared 19 children who received 40 hours per week of intervention, 19 children receiving 10 hours per week, and 21 control subjects who received no treatment. Results indicated that based on IQ scores pre- and postintervention, the high intensity (40 hours/week) group made significantly larger gains than either of the other two groups (Lovaas, 1987). Other researchers studying DTT for youngsters have included those younger than age 2 (Smith, Groen, & Wynn, 2000). In their study, Smith and colleagues compared gains in IQ, language, behavior, and adaptive behavior in children ages 18 to 42 months who received either 30 hours per week of DTT, 5 hours per week of DTT provided by their parents, and a control group of children in special classes. Results were somewhat less promising that those found in the original Lovaas study or the McEachin, Smith, and Lovaas (1993) follow-up study. The children who received higher intensity treatment performed better than the low intensity/parent trained group in IQ and language, but no differences were noted between the two groups on either behavior (problems) or adaptive behavior skills. A common concern with regard to the delivery of DTT and other ABA-based intervention programs is the number of hours per week required for effectiveness. Some researchers have found positive outcomes for young children with autism with fewer than the original 40 hours per week in the Lovaas study or that recommended by Green (1996) of 30 hours per week at a minimum. For example, Anderson, Avery, DiPietro, Edwards, & Christian (1987) demonstrated improvements for 14 children with autism on measures of mental age and social age in programs averaging 15 to 25 hours per week (mean age of participants: 43 months). Similarly, Luiselli and colleagues (2000) found that while intensity of service did reveal differences, those children (mean age 2.6 or 3.9 years) who were receiving services for longer duration achieved greater gains (Luiselli, Cannon, Ellis, & Sisson, 2000). Additionally, these researchers compared results for those children younger than age 3 (mean age 2.6) and those older than 3 (mean age 3.9) finding that there were no significant differences between the two groups, though the children in the under 3 group did have larger gain scores compared to the older children, suggesting that they had "fewer abilities at the onset of treatment" (p. 435).

Several other studies have been published focusing on other aspects of the behavioral intervention strategies, including parent-implement interventions, pivotal response training, PECS, and naturalistic teaching. Parents have been successfully taught to implement home-based treatment programs for their toddlers (Schertz & Odom, 2007) and preschoolers (Moes & Frea, 2002) with autism, with improvements in children's communication and joint attention, and decreases in challenging behaviors. Preschoolers (Stahmer, 1998) and toddlers (Jones, Carr, & Freely 2006) have been taught symbolic play and joint attention skills through use of PRT. Yoder and Stone (2006a, 2006b) found that PECS was an appropriate strategy for 2-year-olds with autism.

Comprehensive Treatment Models

Five CTMs were reviewed by Boyd and colleagues (2010), and are similar to those reviewed in previous literature (Corsello, 2005). These include: Children's Toddler School (CTS), Project Data for Children (PDT), Early Start Denver Model (ESDM), Early Social Interaction Project (ESIP), and the Walden Toddler Program (WTP). These specific models were selected because of their focus on young children and early autism intervention (Boyd et al., 2010). Each of these models incorporates similar strategies for toddlers with autism. For example, three of the five models (CTS, PDT, and WTP) educate the children with autism along with typically developing peers; all five program models include some element of parent training and support, with two of them including parent-implemented home-based intervention as a key component (ESDM and ESIP). In addition two of the models include extra hours per week specifically for the children with autism, over and above what their neurotypical peers receive (CTS and PDT). Research regarding the effectiveness of these models themselves is ongoing.

Though there is limited research in support of specific strategies or models of intervention for infants and toddlers with autism, practices found effective for preschoolers with autism may hold promise for this younger group. As the literature suggests, early intervention is key, and thus research is ongoing as to what specific strategies are most effective, and to what intensity level.

Issues for Practitioners

One issue brought up in recent publications on early intervention for children with autism (Boyd et al., 2010; Schwartz & Sandall, 2010) is whether or not it is feasible to provide the recommended services to children younger than age 3, who are being served by Part C (National Research Council, 2001). Boyd and colleagues recommended broad changes to state policy and funding mechanisms to allow for more intensive and comprehensive treatment of young children with autism served through early intervention. However, Schwartz and Sandall question whether such changes to the system would make the costs of providing such services too great, thus making the services unachievable. This debate may continue until such time as states are able to create policies or provide funding for every child served in Part C with autism. However, Boyd and colleagues recommended that other mechanisms of support, such as Medicare and private insurance be explored as a means of getting services to all children.

Another issue involves personnel training and professional development. The extent to which early intervention service providers (Part C) or early childhood special education teachers (Part B) are trained in autism-specific strategies is not readily understood, particularly those with an evidence base to support their use with young children. Specialized training is needed to successfully work with individuals with autism (Scheuermann, Webber, Boutot, & Goodwin, 2003) and failure to provide such specialized training, not only in specific strategies but also in the disorder itself, can lead to detrimental effects for the children. Perhaps the greatest obstacle related to this issue is, as Boyd et al., pointed out, that there is scant literature on what constitutes evidence-based practices for the younger children, particularly for those in early intervention. Training is necessary, yet exact understanding of what that training should be is limited.

Future Directions

The literature base pertaining to treatment for young children with autism is limited, though growing (Boyd et al., 2010). The field has made strides in the identification of symptoms of autism in infants and toddlers, as well as in the development of screening measures based on these findings. It is imperative now that diagnostic measures be developed and validated with this population. Future research should seek to examine factors associated with early treatment of autism. Among them, the extent to which age at onset of services impacts treatment outcomes; intensity of services at various ages and across the different interventions; parent-implemented versus teacher/therapist-implemented approaches; the extent to which parent training in specific strategies impacts treatment outcomes; location of services; impact of access to typically developing peers; and duration of services to name a few. Extrapolating from the literature base for older children (Boyd et al., 2010) is not sufficient to determine what works for infants, toddlers, and preschoolers with autism. Furthermore, increases in the numbers of young children identified with or at risk of autism as a result of improvements in screening and diagnostics will lead to increases in the numbers of youngsters needing services. Such increases necessitate that future research begin to focus on evaluations of specific interventions so that families and professionals can make appropriate programming decisions.

References

Adrien, J. L., Lenour, P., Martineau, J., Perot, A., Hameury, L., Larmande, C., et al. (1993). Blind ratings of early symptoms of autism based upon family home movies. *Journal of the American Academy of Child and Adolescent Psychiatry, 32*, 617–627.

Anderson, A. S., Avery, D. L., DiPietro, E., Edwards, G. L., & Christian, W. P. (1987). Intensive home-based early intervention with autistic children. *Education and treatment of children, 10*, 352–366.

Baranek, G. T. (1999). Autism during infancy: A retrospective video analysis of sensory-motor and social behaviors at 9–12 months of age. *Journal of Autism and Developmental Disorders, 29*, 213–224.

Baron-Cohen, S., Allen, J., & Gillberg, C. (1992). Can autism be detected at 18 months? The needle, the haystack, and the CHAT. *British Journal of Psychiatry, 161*, 839–843.

Boyd, B. A., Odom, S. L., Humphreys, B. P., & Sam, A. H. (2010). Infants and toddlers with autism spectrum disorder: Early identification and early intervention. *Journal of Early Intervention, 32*, 75–98.

Bryson, S. E., Zwaigenbaum, L., Brian, J., Roberts, W., Szatmari, P., Rombough, V., et al. (2007). A prospective case series of high-risk infants who developed autism. *Journal of Autism and Developmental Disorders, 37*, 12–24.

Carmagnat-Dubois, F., Desombre, H., Perrot, A., Roux, S., LeNoir, P., Sauvage, D., et al. (1997). Autism and Rett syndrome: A comparison study during infancy using family home videos. *L'Encephale, 23*, 273–279.

Coonrod, E., Turner, L., Pozdol, S., & Stone, W. (2001, April). *The parent interview for autism (PIA) for children under the age of three.* Paper presented at the biannual meeting of the Society for Research in Child Development, Minneapolis, MN.

Corsello, C. M. (2005). Early intervention in autism. *Infants and Young Children, 18*, 74–85.

Education for All Handicapped Children Act. Amendments of 1986, 20 U.S.C. §§ 1471 et seq. and 1419 et seq.

Goin, R. P., & Myers, B. J. (2004). Characteristics of infantile autism: Moving toward earlier detection. *Focus on Autism and Other Developmental Disabilities, 19*, 5–12.

Gonzalez, K., Cassel, T., & Boutot, E.A. (2011). Overview of autism spectrum disorders. In E. A. Boutot & B. S. Myles (Eds.), *Autism spectrum disorders: Foundations, characteristics, and effective strategies* (pp. 1–33). Upper Saddle River, NJ: Pearson.

Green, G. (1996). Early behavioral intervention for autism: What does research tell us? In C. Maurice, G. Green, & S. Luce (Eds.), *Behavioral intervention for young children with autism* (pp. 29–44). Austin, TX: Pro-Ed.

Individuals with Disabilities Education Act 20 of 2004 U.S.C. §§ 1400 et seq.

Jacobson, J. W., Mulick, J. A., & Green, G. (1998). Cost benefit estimates for early-intensive behavioral intervention for young children with autism—General model and single case state. *Behavioral Interventions, 13*, 201–226.

Johnson, C. P., & Myers, S. M. (2007). Identification and evaluation of children with autism spectrum disorders. *Pediatrics, 120*, 1183–1215.

Jones, E. A., Carr, E. G., & Feeley, K. M. (2006). Multiple effects of joint attention intervention for children with autism. *Behavior Modification, 30*, 782–834.

Lord, C., Rutter, M., DiLavore, P., & Risi, S. (1999). *The autism diagnostic observation schedule (ADOS).* Los Angeles, CA: Western Psychological Corporation.

Lovaas, I. O. (1987). Behavioral intervention and normal educational and intellectual functioning in young autistic children. *Journal of Consulting and Clinical Psychology, 55*, 3–9.

Luiselli, J. K., Cannon, B. O., Ellis, J. T., & Sisson, R. W. (2000). Home-based behavioral intervention for young children with autism/pervasive developmental disorder: A preliminary evaluation of outcome in relation to child age and intensity of service delivery. *Autism, 4*, 426–438.

McEachin, J. J., Smith T., & Lovaas, I. O. (1993). Long-term outcome for children with autism who received early intensive behavioral intervention. *American Journal on Mental Retardation, 55*, 359–372.

Moes, D. R., & Frae, W. D. (2002). Contextuallized behavioral support in early intervention for children with autism and their families. *Journal of Autism and Developmental Disorders, 32*, 519–534.

National Autism Center. (2009). *The national standards report.* Retrieved from http://www.nationalautismcenter.org/affiliates/model.php

National Research Council. (2001). *Educating children with autism.* Washington, DC: National Academy Press.

Olive, M., Boutot, E. A., & Tarbox, J. (2011). Teaching students with autism using the principles of applied behavior analysis. In E. A. Boutot & B. S. Myles (Eds.), *Autism spectrum disorders: Foundations, characteristics, and effective strategies* (pp. 141–162). Upper Saddle River, NJ: Pearson.

Osterling, J., & Dawson, G. (1994). Early recognition of children with autism: A study of first birthday home videotapes. *Journal of Autism and Developmental Disabilities, 24*, 247–257.

Reznick, J. S., Baranek, G. T., Reavis, S., Watson, L. R., & Crais, E. R. (2007). A parent-report instrument for identifying one-year olds at risk for an eventual diagnosis of autism: The First Year Inventory. *Journal of Autism and Developmental Disorders, 37*, 1691–1710.

Robins, D. L., Fein, D., Barton, M. L., & Green, J. A. (2001). The modified checklist for autism in toddlers: An initial study investigating the early detection of autism and pervasive developmental disorders. *Journal of Autism and Developmental Disabilities, 31*, 131–144.

Saint-Georges, C., Cassel, R. S., Cohen, D., Chetounai, M., Laznik, M., Maestro, S., et al. (2010). What studies of family home movies can teach us about autistic infants: A literature review. *Research in Autism Spectrum Disorders, 4*, 355–366.

Schertz, H. H., & Odom, S. L. (2007). Promoting joint attention in toddlers with autism: A parent-mediated developmental model. *Journal of Autism and Developmental Disorders, 37*, 1562–1575.

Scheuermann, B., Webber, J., Boutot, E. A., & Goodwin, M. (2003). Issues in personnel preparation in autism. *Focus on Autism and Other Developmental Disorders, 18*(3), 197–206.

Schwartz, I. S., & Sandall, S. R. (2010). Is autism the disability that breaks Part C? [A commentary on "Infants and toddlers with autism spectrum disorder: Early identification and early intervention" by B. A. Boyd, S. C. Odom, B. P. Humphreys, and A. H. Sam]. *Journal of Early Intervention, 32*, 105–109.

Siegel, B. (2001). *Pervasive developmental disorders screening test II.* Retrieved from www.firstsigns.org/downloads/I_PDDST_II_5_01_01.PDF

Smith, T., Groen, A. D., & Wynn, J. W. (2000). Randomized trial of intensive early intervention for children with pervasive developmental disorder. *American Journal on Mental Retardation, 105,* 269–285.

Stahmer, A. C. (1998). Teaching symbolic play skills to children with autism using pivotal response training. *Journal of Autism and Developmental Disorders, 25,* 123–141.

Stone, W. L., Coonrod, E. E., & Ousley, O. Y. (2000). Brief report: Screening tool for autism in two-year-olds (STAT): Development and preliminary data. *Journal of Autism and Developmental Disorders, 30,* 607–612.

Teitelbaum, P., Teitelbaum, O., Nye, J., Fryman, J., & Maurer, R. G. (1998). Movement analysis in infancy may be useful for early diagnosis of autism. *Proceedings of the National Academy of Sciences, 95,* 13982–13987.

Vostanis, P., Smith, B., Corbett, J., Sungum-Paliwal, R., Edwards, A., Gingell, K., et al. (1998). Parental concerns of early development in children with autism and related disorders. *Autism, 2,* 229–242.

Werner, E., Dawson, G., Osterling, J., & Dinno, N. (2000). Brief report: Recognition of autism spectrum disorder before one year of age: A retrospective study based on home videotapes. *Journal of Autism and Developmental Disorders, 30*(2), 157–162.

Werner, E. B. & Munson, J. A. (2001, April). *Regression in autism: A description and validation of the phenomenon using parent report and home video tapes.* Paper presented at the biannual meeting of the Society for Research in Child Development, Minneapolis, MN.

Williams, B. J., & Ozonoff, S. (2001). *Parental report of the early development of autistic children who experience a regression.* Paper presented at the Biannual Meeting of the Society for Research in Child Development, Minneapolis, MN.

Wimpory, D. C., Hobson, R. P., Williams, J. M. G., & Nash, S. (2000). Are infants with autism socially engaged? A study of recent retrospective parental reports. *Journal of Autism and Developmental Disabilities, 30,* 525–536.

Yoder, P., & Stone, W. (2006a). A randomized comparison of the effect of two prelinguistic communication interventions on the acquisition of spoken communication in preschoolers with ASD. *Journal of Speech, Language, and Hearing Sciences, 49,* 698–711.

Yoder, P., & Stone, W. (2006b). Randomized comparison of two communication interventions for preschoolers with autism spectrum disorders. *Journal of Consulting and Clinical Psychology, 74,* 426–435.

Zakian, A., Malvy, J., Desombre, H., Roux, S., & Lenour, P. (2000). Early signs of autism: A new study of family home movies. *L'Encephale, 26,* 38–44.

Zwaigenbaum, L., Bryson, S., Lord, C., Rogers, S., Carter, A., Carver, L., et al. (2009). Clinical assessment and management of toddlers with suspected autism spectrum disorder: Insights from studies of high-risk infants. *Pediatrics, 123,* 1383–1391.

11

EDUCATION THROUGH THE DEVELOPMENTAL STAGES

School-Age Children and Adolescents

L. Juane Heflin and Jackie S. Isbell

GEORGIA STATE UNIVERSITY

Although early intervention greatly improves prognosis, children with autism spectrum disorders (ASD) do not outgrow the disorder (Farley et al., 2009; Volkmar, Lord, Bailey, Schultz, & Klin, 2004). Differences in nonverbal communication, including unusual eye gaze, are common among individuals across ages and functioning levels (Gotham, Risi, Pickles, & Lord, 2007) and into adulthood (Rumsey, Rapoport, & Sceery, 1985). Unlike typically developing children, young children with ASD tend to be more engrossed in objects than people (Dawson, Meltzoff, Osterling, Rinaldi, & Brown, 1998; Klin, Jones, Schultz, Volkmar, & Cohen, 2002), and do not seek to make eye contact with others (Jones, Carr, & Klin, 2008). This preference for the inanimate rather than the social world, even as the children get older, results in a

> preponderance of learning about the physical environment (e.g., physical over social contingencies), rote speech over contextualized communication, hyperlexia over conceptual reading, and memorization of facts and information over episodic and personal information—all of which are features well noted in the later-life clinical expression of autism. (Jones & Klin, 2009, p. 473)

All of these features are readily apparent in children and adolescents who have acquired spoken language, as they attempt to share everything they know about their favorite topics such as trains, presidential history, cryptozoology, and so forth. Children and adolescents who have not acquired spoken language will demonstrate their fascination with the physical world by collecting things, manipulating objects, arranging items, and so forth.

Although the social impairments persist (Tsatsanis, 2003), other characteristics of ASD abate as the children grow into adolescence and then adulthood (Richler, Huerta, Bishop, & Lord, 2010). Adolescents with ASD demonstrate fewer repetitive behaviors than children with ASD (Bishop, Richler, & Lord, 2006). Conversational abilities of youth with Asperger syndrome (AS) in 1:1 interactions improve, although attention difficulties become more pronounced (Gilchrist et al., 2001). After an increase in problem behavior in adolescence, parents of children with AS report reduced severity of symptomatology as the youth became adults (Cederlund, Hagberg, & Gillberg, 2010). These same authors found that adults with AS reported more problems with executive functioning that severely inhibit their daily functioning than individuals with traumatic brain injury or schizophrenia.

To discuss the educational implications of teaching youth whose learning is not based in the social world and who will continue to experience challenges with planning and executing actions, we must make a rather arbitrary distinction. Although some have suggested that the terms *high functioning* and *low functioning* are discriminatory (Bashe & Kirby, 2005), youth with ASD must receive an education that is tailored to their individual needs and strengths, which are often dictated by cognitive characteristics as they influence academic achievement (White, Scahill, Klin, Koenig, & Volkmar, 2007). With the ultimate goal of independent functioning, empirical data are used to support particular educational interventions as beneficial for youth who have near-typical to gifted intelligence; these are differentiated from interventions found to be effective for students with intellectual disability (Lord & Bishop, 2010). For this reason, this chapter will be divided into two strands. In the first strand, research relevant to the needs of youth with ASD who have intellectual disability ("low functioning ASD" [LFASD]) will be discussed. These are the children and youth most likely to have clinical diagnoses of autistic disorder.

The second strand will contain research germane to the education of youth with ASD with near-typical to gifted intelligence ("high functioning ASD" [HFASD]). HFASD is a broad category that encompasses individuals who have been diagnosed with AS, pervasive developmental disorders not otherwise specified (PDDNOS), and autistic disorder and who are high functioning (Volker et al., 2010). The designations *HFASD* and *LFA* have been used by others (Bauminger, Solomon, & Rogers, 2010; Begeer, Terwogt, Lunenburg, & Stegge, 2009; Mayes et al., 2009), but the LFASD counterpart to HFASD will be used in this chapter. These distinctions are not meant to be offensive; we are not calling youth "high" or "low" in a derogatory manner. Instead, we are providing a nomenclature in recognition of the fact that empirically based interventions differ according to the cognitive functioning of these unique children and adolescents.

Educational Placement

Before discussing educational research targeting older children and adolescents with ASD, the topic of educational placement must be mentioned briefly because instructional practices are correlated with educational setting. As noted, instructional goals for youth across the autism spectrum emphasize independent functioning; however, instructional targets will vary by cognitive ability. Students with LFASD are more likely to be working on acquisition of functional skills with the aim of performance across settings. Students with HFASD are more likely to be working on performance of acquired skills across settings with the objective of acquiring higher level academic skills. For these reasons, students with LFASD are more likely to be educated in specialized settings (White et al., 2007) in order to acquire skills that will allow them to benefit from inclusive environments (Mulick & Butter, 2002). Indeed, students with LFASD make meaningful progress in useful skills when they are educated in specialized settings using structured teaching (Panerai et al., 2009). Spanish parents surveyed believe that teachers in self-contained classrooms are more qualified to educate their children and have access to more resources and supports than teachers in general education classrooms (Moreno, Aguilera, & Saldana, 2008). Although it may be easier to emphasize functional skills in segregated settings, students with LFASD have access to a full continuum of placements, and decisions about the percentage of time spent in any of the settings will be made by the student's educational decision making team.

Students with HFASD are more likely to receive their education in general classroom settings (Whitby & Mancil, 2009), although the impact of their disability may dictate placement in more specialized settings for at least part of the school day. The increase in the number of individuals with ASD has been partially attributed to the inclusion of HFASD in prevalence estimates; in 2009, almost 50% of over 78,000 parents reported that at least one of their children had a mild form of ASD (Kogan et al., 2009). When compared to their same-age peers, youth with HFASD become more noticeably challenged as they get older (Klin et al., 2007), which explains why most of these children will not receive diagnoses until they are about 11 years of age (Howlin & Asgharian, 1999). As competent as they appear academically, older children and adolescents must receive support services to participate in general education classrooms (Lord & Bishop, 2010).

Students with ASD in general education settings frequently receive support from an individually assigned paraprofessional (Suter & Giangreco, 2009). This practice can be problematic unless these paraprofessionals are trained to a high level of competence. Even with adequate training, paraprofessionals may not use the skills they've learned when working with students across settings (Hall, Grundon, Pope, & Romero, 2010), and caution is warranted because school districts which use paraprofessionals as the primary teacher for students with ASD have been required to provide compensatory education to those students (Etscheidt, 2005). Unfortunately, students with ASD tend to become dependent on a paraprofessional to remain engaged (Werts, Zigmond, & Leeper, 2001; White et al., 2007) and fail to attend to naturally occurring cues and directions (Giangreco, Yuan, McKenzie, Cameron, & Fialka, 2005). Researchers have found that the assignment of an individual paraprofessional for a student in the general education classroom discourages peers from interacting with the student with disabilities (Anderson, Moore, Godfrey, & Fletcher-Flinn, 2004; Carter, Sisco, Brown, Brickham, & Al-Khabbaz, 2008; Giangreco, Edelman, Luiselli, & MacFarland, 1997), possibly because of the stigmatization associated with the ever-present adult (Giangreco, 2010). General education teachers tend to relinquish instructional responsibility for students who are accompanied to class by paraprofessionals (Giangreco & Broer, 2005). Educational decision-making teams which create the student's individualized educational program (IEP) may want to consider a variety of options to support students with ASD in general education settings (e.g., assigning paraprofessionals to support a group of students, developing peer supports, hiring additional special educators, enhancing general educators' abilities to teach students with disabilities) before deciding to rely on individual paraprofessional assignment (Giangreco & Broer, 2005; Giangreco, Halvorsen, Doyle, & Broer, 2004; Giangreco, Suter, & Doyle, 2010). Since researchers have investigated instructional strategies and supports, including use of paraprofessionals, based on functioning levels of individuals with disabilities, empirically based educational implications for older children and adolescents with LFASD will be discussed next, followed by a discussion of what is known about educating older children and adolescents with HFASD.

Students with ASD and Intellectual Disability (LFASD)

Odom, Boyd, Hall, and Hume (2010) identified 30 comprehensive treatment models (CTMs) developed for children, youth, or adults with ASD. CTMs contain multiple components to address core deficits in ASD, and are provided for 25+ hours per week over a span of a year or more. The authors evaluated the models against criteria such as descriptions in peer-reviewed publications, and availability of manuals describing the content and procedures for implementation. Most of the 30 CTMs that met inclusion criteria are affiliated with a location (e.g., Alpine Learning Group Programs, Denver Model, Eden Institute, TEACCH). Almost half of the CTMs (n = 14) have been replicated at independent sites, but over half (n = 16) failed the criterion of producing peer-reviewed reports with empirical evidence to substantiate benefit.

Most of the CTMs have been available for many years, and 15 of the 30 are described as providing services for individuals with ASD over the age of 14 years; however, research validation for the programs tends to be based on young children; and studies in which the outcomes for adolescents and young adults are demonstrated are nonexistent. Research is needed to provide evidence of effectiveness for middle and high school populations as well as analyze similarities and differences among the programs (Ingersoll, 2010; Lord & Bishop, 2010; Rogers & Vismara, 2008).

Unless professionals are trained and supported in the use of a comprehensive treatment model, most will continue to develop programs for their students from among focused-intervention practices (which individually become components of the CTMs). Focused interventions are implemented for weeks or months instead of years and target specific behaviors rather than the core deficits of ASD (Lord & Bishop, 2010). Hundreds of effectiveness studies support the utility of focused-intervention practices across populations of individuals with disabilities, including ASD (S. Anderson, & Romanczyk, 1999). The strength of the empirical validation for these interventions varies according to methodological rigor and experimental control. The National Autism Center (2009) conducted a systematic evaluation of over 700 focused interventions used specifically for individuals with ASD. Interventions were categorized as *Established, Emerging, Unestablished,* and *Ineffective/Harmful,* but the categorizations have already been challenged (Simpson, Mundschenk, & Heflin, in press) and the utility of the resultant groupings (e.g., 22 generic strategies combined to form "antecedent interventions") is doubtful due to the lack of precision.

Given the sparse research with older children and adolescents in the CTMs and the debatable benefit of the attempt to evaluate focused-intervention practices for this population, the question naturally arises: What are the most effective interventions for children and adolescents with LFASD? To address this question, we must look to empirical literature to identify patterns and analyze researchers' conclusions. Toward that end, the instruction of students with LFASD will be discussed based on the two most common approaches researched for the population, discrete trial training and naturalistic applications of applied behavior analysis, and the associated implications for classroom settings, including useful accommodations. Two widely used interventions to support communication and behavior, functional communication training and the picture exchange communication system, will be reviewed, followed by considerations related to the mental health of older children and adolescents with LFASD.

Instruction

Discrete Trial Training.   Applied behavior analysis (ABA) is the only instructional approach widely recognized as effective for children with ASD (Granpeesheh, Tarbox, & Dixon, 2009; National Research Council, 2001; Volker & Lopata, 2008). ABA provides the theoretical underpinnings of a broad array of interventions, but it is not uncommon for the lay public to use ABA as a synonym for discrete trial training (Heflin & Alaimo, 2007), or as Ghezzi (2007) convincingly argues, discrete trial teaching (DTT). Synonyms for DTT include discrete trial instruction (DTI), and early intensive behavioral intervention (EIBI). DTT is used in most programs provided by trainers in homes (Young, Ruble, & McGrew, 2009). Professionals and paraprofessionals in public (Bolton & Mayer, 2008) and private schools (Belfiore, Fritts, & Herman, 2008; Catania, Almeida, Liu-Constant, & Reed, 2009; Leblanc, Ricciardi, & Luiselli, 2005) are being trained to deliver a specified amount of skill instruction to students with LFASD via DTT.

Simply defined, DTT involves presenting a discriminative stimulus (S^D) to a student and then reinforcing or correcting the student's response. The trainer will then pause for the specified length of the intertrial interval (making each trial "discrete") before presenting the next S^D (Koegel, Russo, & Rincover, 1977). Decades of research on DTT, most conducted with young children, allow us to draw the following conclusions:

- More efficient learning occurs when materials used to teach identification include a distracter (Gutierrez et al., 2009). For example, when teaching a child to identify "ball," a field of at least two items is presented; one card with a picture of a ball and one card with a picture of something that is not a ball.
- More frequent reinforcement is needed for new or difficult skills (Hagopian, Toole, Long, Bowman, & Lieving, 2004).
- During DTT, it is important to use the S^D that the student will experience in natural environments (Woods, 1987).
- Providing the correct response immediately after an error is more effective for skill acquisition than providing the correct response after a delay (Bennett & Cavanaugh, 1998).
- The choice of error correction procedures (i.e., model correct, or say "no," or ignore and introduce next trail) can affect rates of learning (Smith, Mruzek, Wheat, & Hughes, 2006).
- Using error prevention (rather than error correction) procedures may result in more efficient learning (Carr & Felce, 2008).
- Students may be motivated to respond during DTT in the presence of atypical contingencies (e.g., toothpaste caps, swizzle sticks, globes; Charlop-Christy & Haymes, 1998).

DTT has been shown to increase single targeted responses, but is not useful for teaching responses that require chained actions including self-help skills and vocational skills (Steege, Mace, Perry, & Longenecker, 2007). Neef, Walters, and Egel (1984) discovered that even though students' responses during DTT remained at chance levels (50%), the students were able to demonstrate the skills with 80% accuracy in typical settings.

Paradoxically, the tendency to use DTT with students with LFASD appears contraindicated as IQ can reliably foreshadow children's responsiveness to the methodology (Ben-Itzchak & Zachor, 2009; Eikeseth, Smith, Jahr, & Eldevik, 2007; Granpeesheh, Tarbox, Dixon, Carr, & Herbert, 2009; Howlin, Magiati, & Charman, 2009). Children with IQs of less than 50 are less likely to benefit from intensive DTT (S. R. Anderson, Avery, DiPietro, Edwards, & Christian, 1987; Drew et al., 2002; Fenske, Zalenski, Krantz, & McClannahan, 1985; Harris and Handelman, 2000; Lovaas, 1987). Even after 4 years of intervention provided 30 to 40 hours per week (Sallows & Graupner, 2005), no participants in this category have been found to "recover" (Smith, Groen, & Wynn, 2000).

Age at the initiation of intervention also appears to correlate with effectiveness; the younger the child, the better the outcome (Granpeesheh, Dixon, Tarbox, Kaplan, & Wilke, 2009; Harris & Handleman, 2000; Stoelb et al., 2004). Unfortunately, there is a tendency to use DTT with students who have LFASD throughout their elementary school years (Rogers & Vismara, 2008) and into their middle school years, even though researchers have demonstrated conclusively that DTT is more effective for younger children (Lovaas, 1987), with 7 years of age being the oldest empirically shown to benefit (Eikeseth et al., 2007). Children who avoid social situations, such as many of those with LFASD, make less progress during intervention (Ingersoll, Schreibman, & Stahmer, 2001).

Family characteristics also predict children's response to DTT. Howard, Sparkman, Cohen, Green, and Stanislaw (2005) discovered that parents of children who made the most progress using DTT were better educated and more likely to be married. Similarly, children in families in which parents report having high levels of stress do not demonstrate the same gains as do children whose parents are less stressed (Osborne, McHugh, Saunders, & Reed, 2008). The tendency to implement DTT with children older than 7 years of age with below average IQs, in families with high levels of stress may explain why 50% (Rogers & Vismara, 2008) to 70% (Perry et al., 2011) of children with autism do not benefit from intensive DTT. Those who do acquire skills may have difficulty generalizing the application of those skills to people other than their trainers, or in settings other than the one in which they were trained (Cowan & Allen, 2007; McGee, Krantz, & McClannahan, 1985). Some children experience impairments in adaptive functioning (Rogers, 1999) as they wait to be told what to do (i.e., stimulus dependency). For these and other reasons, individually delivered DTT must not be the only intervention being used with students with LFASD (Smith, 2001); however, this approach will generate complex discrimination with strong stimulus control (Cowan & Allen, 2007). As a reminder, almost all of the research conducted to determine influential aspects and cautions related to DTT was done with young children; extrapolations are necessary for older children and adolescents.

Naturalistic ABA.   Concerns about the limitations of DTT have increased the visibility and use of ABA instructional strategies considered to be more naturalistic or "normalized" (Delprato, 2001, p. 315) when compared to the staged, nonfunctional, adult-directed format of DTT (Steege et al., 2007). Naturalistic ABA strategies have been referred to generically as "milieu" interventions (Warren & Gazdag, 1990, p. 62) and are used to teach skills that are relevant to the child, as shown by child initiation, within typical environments and normal routines, using logically related consequences (Delprato, 2001; Ingersoll, 2010). For example, during snack (a daily routine), a teacher may have slices of banana that are just out of reach of the student. When the student reaches for the banana (child initiation), the teacher models the request, and shapes the student's successive approximation of that request by giving the student some banana (logically related consequence). Table 11.1 contains a brief comparison of the differences between typical, structured DTT, and naturalistic ABA approaches (Cowan & Allen, 2007; Delprato, 2001; Ghezzi, 2007; Steege et al., 2007; Sundberg & Partington, 1998).

TABLE 11.1 Comparison of Structured DTT and Naturalistic ABA Approaches

Structured DTT	*Naturalistic ABA*
▪ Carefully controlled environment	▪ Typical environments with sabotaging
▪ Instruction occurs in same location each time	▪ Instruction occurs in a variety of locations
▪ Curriculum specified and easy to follow	▪ Curriculum loosely conceptualized
▪ Carefully constructed set of materials used repeatedly	▪ Materials change as environments change
▪ Correct response predetermined by adult	▪ Approximations accepted and shaped
▪ Adult gives SD and establishes pace	▪ Student initiates and establishes pace
▪ Specified sequence of prompts used to evoke student response	▪ Variety of prompts used as appropriate for context
▪ Contrived reinforcement unrelated to task	▪ Naturally occurring reinforcement related to task
▪ Student learns to respond to specific stimuli	▪ Student learns to respond to naturally occurring stimuli
▪ Skills taught in nonfunctional way can evoke escape-based behavior	▪ Student motivation enhanced by functional nature of instruction
▪ Quick acquisition but limited generalization	▪ Acquisition may take longer but good generalization

Naturalistic ABA interventions include pivotal response training (PRT); natural environment training (NET; Sundberg & Partington, 1998), which identifies behavior as tacts, mands, and so forth, and focuses on mands initially; and incidental teaching (IT; McGee, Krantz, Mason, & McClannahan, 1983), in which children are encouraged to elaborate on their initiated speech and are reinforced for the effort. Researchers have demonstrated that naturalistic ABA approaches are more effective for teaching language and were better accepted by parents than DTT (Delprato, 2001), in addition to facilitating better generalization when compared to DTT (Miranda-Linne & Melin, 1992).

Classroom Implications. Although teachers in public schools could be trained to implement any of the naturalistic ABA strategies, the fact that they are "branded" by being named as specialized approaches (Rogers & Vismara, 2008, p. 31) creates barriers to widespread use and disregards that components of the programs are being used already in many classrooms. Naturalistic ABA interventions are implemented in contexts in which the skills being taught are useful. Teachers apply this principle when they embed instruction within ongoing activities (Horn & Banerjee, 2009). Embedded instruction has been used to teach food categorization (Wolery & Anthony, 1997), vocabulary words (McDonnell et al., 2006), and initiating requests (Johnson, McDonnell, Holzwarth, & Hunter, 2004). The use of embedded instruction can increase correct responses as well as reduce maladaptive behavior and improve attitudes toward learning when compared to DTT (Sigafoos et al., 2006).

Accommodations for Learning. The most commonly used accommodation for students with LFASD is the provision of information in visual formats. Picture schedules are ubiquitous in classrooms where students with LFASD are being taught (Green et al., 2006) and can be used to promote smooth transitions between activities (Dettmer, Simpson, Myles, & Ganz, 2000; Ganz, 2007). In addition to visual schedules, Heflin and Alberto (2001) discussed the importance of using visual supports for helping children and youth with ASD comprehend expectations, including class rules. Reading instruction frequently begins with picture reading (Alberto, Fredrick, Hughes, McIntosh, & Cihak, 2007) and learning to read is more efficient for adolescents with LFASD when the text is associated with icons (Chen, Wu, Lin, Tasi, & Chen, 2009). The use of visually placed touch points on numerals has been shown to be more effective for teaching single-digit addition than using a number line (Cihak, & Foust, 2008). Although not explored specifically for students with LFASD, no difference was found for students with intellectual disability between visual prompts that were presented as pictures and those presented as videos, although students with attention deficits may perform slightly better using static pictures (Alberto, Cihak, & Gama, 2005).

Visual accommodations also may include scripts. Students can be given written scripts (that are systematically faded) to learn how to initiate and maintain conversations (Krantz & McClannahan, 1993). For emergent readers, scripts consist of one- or two-word phrases along with icons (Krantz & McClannahan, 1998). Even nonreaders can be taught scripted speech using recordings on cards pronounced by a Language Master machine (Stevenson, Krantz, & McClannahan, 2000). Interventions using visual or audio scripts result in collateral benefit as the use of unscripted initiations as well as the scripted initiations (Sarokoff, Taylor, & Poulson, 2001).

Communication and Behavior

Unlike children and adolescents with HFASD who rely on spoken language as their primary form of communication, youth with LFASD tend to rely on behavior rather than speech to communicate their needs and preferences (Sigafoos et al., 2006). Approximately 25% of children and adolescents with LFASD will not develop functional speech during their lifetimes (Volkmar et al., 2004). Fortunately speech is not requisite for communication; the challenge is to determine the messages being relayed via behavior. Two dominant interventions for facilitating reliable communication in individuals with LFASD are functional communication training (FCT) and the picture exchange communication system (PECS).

Functional Communication Training. FCT involves identifying the message being communicated through behavior (often maladaptive) and teaching youth a replacement behavior that conveys the same message or accomplishes the same function (Carr & Durand, 1985; Durand & Crimmins, 1987). FCT is considered an empirically supported intervention for addressing problem behavior (Durand & Merges, 2001). For example, if a student kicks others in order to be left alone, he or she could be taught to sign "break" to accomplish the same outcome in a less aggressive manner. The replacement behavior selected must be one that the student can perform and be just as efficient and effective at accomplishing the same function as the maladaptive behavior (Horner, Sprague, O'Brien, & Heathfield, 1990). Students who use spoken language can be taught to use phrases to get what they want and avoid what they don't want (e.g., "I want a snack" or "snack"; "I don't want to sit here"). Alternatively, students can be taught to use sign language or gestures (Wacker et al., 1990), point to pictures (Harding et al., 2009), or use speech-generating devices (Franco et al., 2009) to communicate in a more conventional manner. Indeed, Langdon, Carr, and Owen-DeSchryver (2008) documented that FCT could be used to target behaviors that were precursors to problem behaviors, resulting in a reduction of problem behavior. Researchers have specifically targeted students with ASD in studies on the effectiveness of FCT (Mancil, 2006). FCT can be implemented in general education classrooms (Casey & Merical, 2006) and community settings (Gerhardt, Weiss, & Delmolino, 2003). When combined with a naturalistic approach (i.e., milieu therapy), FCT effectively reduced maladaptive behavior (i.e., pinching, hitting, tantrums) while reducing participants' dependence on adult prompts (Mancil, Conroy, & Haydon, 2009)

Picture Exchange Communication System. PECS was developed to facilitate the development of spontaneous, intentional communication in individuals without spoken language (Bondy & Frost, 1994), and involves following a specific series of steps described in a manual to teach students to exchange a picture for a desired item or activity (Bondy, Tincani, & Frost, 2004). PECS is widely heralded as an intervention that is easy to implement and effective because it capitalizes on what children find motivating (Flippin, Reszka, & Watson, 2010). The results of independent analyses can be used to conclude that PECS provides a highly reliable method of communication, but may not always generate spoken language (Preston & Carter, 2009; Schlosser & Wendt, 2008). In criticizing the failure to generate spoken language, these researchers ignore the fact that PECS was not intended to produce speech; this outcome has been described as a collateral benefit (Sulzer-Azaroff, Hoffman, Horton, Bondy, & Frost, 2009). Although not designed to facilitate speech, PECS will not inhibit speech production (Tincani, Crozier, & Alazetta, 2006). PECS may be differentially effective for children who are interested in objects, do not imitate well, and have poor joint attention (Flippin et al., 2010). In addition to providing a reliable means of communication, PECS also has been used to evoke descriptive and improvised communication (Marckel, Neef, & Ferreri, 2006), and explored as a mean of facilitating literacy (Rehfeldt & Root, 2005).

Mental Health

Unlike those with HFASD, children and adolescents with LFASD do not become depressed or suicidal; however, they may experience commensurate levels of anxiety. Leo Kanner, in his 1943 article defining autism, stated "the child's behavior is governed by an anxiously obsessive-desire for the maintenance of sameness" (p. 245). Researchers suggest that individuals with ASD engage in stereotypical behaviors as a way to deal with their anxiety (Berkson, 2002; Militerni, Bravaccio, Falco, Fico, & Palermo, 2002). Although this idea has been challenged (Kennedy, Meyer, Knowles, & Shukla, 2000), there appears to be a strong correlation between increasing anxiety and increased stereotypical behaviors (e.g., twirling, hand flapping, echolalia; Howlin, 1998; Thomas et al., 1998). Interrupting the ritualistic behaviors of an individual with LFASD produces increased anxiety (Groden, Cautela, Prince, & Berryman, 1994; Rutter, 1985). Self-injurious behaviors (SIB) are associated with anxiety (Morgan, 2006), and can be reduced by behavioral interventions that alleviate anxiety (O'Reilly, Sigafoos, Lancioni, Edrisinha, & Andrews, 2005).

Medications for students with LFASD are prescribed primarily to address high activity levels, inattention, ritualistic behavior, self-injurious behavior, and aggression (Rosenberg et al., 2010). Only 50 to 60% of individuals with ASD respond to stimulant medications commonly prescribed for hyperactivity (Aman & Langworthy, 2000), and stimulant medications are noted for increasing irritability and stereotypies (des Portes, Hagerman, & Hendren, 2003). Selective serotonin reuptake inhibitors (SSRIs), used to treat obsessive-compulsive behavior, tend to be tolerated better in adolescents with ASD than in younger children (Rogers & Vismara, 2008). There is a long history of using antipsychotics with individuals with LFASD, but concerns about negative side effects, including tardive dyskinesia (Campbell, Armenteros, Malone, & Adams, 1997), have led to increased reliance on atypical antipsychotics for treatment of repetitive and aggressive behavior (Findling, 2005). In 2007, the U.S. Federal Drug Administration for the first time designated a medication for autism, when it approved an atypical antipsychotic, risperidone, for the treatment of self-injury, aggression, and agitation.

Children and adolescents may take antiseizure medications because 33% of the population experiences seizures, which may manifest as they reach adolescence (Volkmar & Nelson, 1990). Canitano, Luchetti, and Zappella (2005) found that of the 35% of children in their study who had epilepsy, 22% had sudden electrical misfiring in their brains without seizures. Unusual changes in behavior as children with LFASD reach puberty, which are not responsive to behavioral interventions, could be symptomatic of an emerging seizure disorder.

Intervention can be provided as a comprehensive approach (i.e., via CTM), although there is little empirical data to substantiate the effectiveness of these treatments for older children and adolescents with LFASD. Typically, interventions for this population are selected from among many focused-intervention practices, a number of which have been researched specifically for youth with LFASD. As contradictory as it seems, based on research evidence suggesting that DTT is ineffective for youth over 7 years of age and with IQs <50, many students with LFASD receive at least some of their educational instruction via DTT. Naturalistic ABA practices hold more promise for engaging students with LFASD and promoting generalized use of meaningful skills. By sabotaging typically occurring events, professionals can use positive reinforcement to carefully shape adaptive responses. This is what usually occurs during embedded instruction. Visual supports, including scripts, are the most common accommodations provided to youth with LFASD. The most effective approaches for dealing with communication and behavior combine the two; there is strong empirical support for using FCT and PECS with youth with

LFASD. Finally, professionals must be aware that stereotypic and self-stimulatory behaviors may indicate high levels of stress and anxiety. Contexts must be examined to identify variables that can be modified to reduce anxiety. Although there are some behavioral similarities, youth with HFASD have needs that differ from those individuals with LFASD. Surprisingly little research has been conducted on educational interventions for students with HFASD, but we can examine their characteristic differences and identify topics of research which could be applied to this group of students.

Students with ASD without Intellectual Disability (HFASD)

The academic achievement of students with HFASD is a relatively new area of research and is still evolving. The No Child Left Behind Act of 2001 and the Individuals with Disabilities Education Act of 2004 created national education policies that place an enhanced emphasis on academic achievement for students with disabilities. With raised expectations for all students with disabilities, academic performance has become increasingly important in the education of students with HFASD. Educational goals for students with HFASD may include college or careers that require postsecondary training (Camarena & Sarigiani, 2009; VanBergeijk, Klin, &Volkmar, 2008). However, adult outcomes for this population have been disappointing. Even with improved educational opportunities, adults with HFASD have not achieved the same level of success in college, careers, personal relationships, and independent living as their typical peers (Barnhill, 2007; Eaves & Ho, 2008; Howlin, Goode, Hutton, & Rutter, 2004).

Although students with HFASD have average intelligence, they also have characteristics that may impede their educational progress. They often need individualized instruction and appropriate accommodations to be successful in school. Educators need an understanding of the academic functioning of this group to help students meet their long-term educational goals. A general academic profile associated with HFASD can serve as the foundation for developing effective instructional strategies matched to the academic strengths and weaknesses of the population. Given the heterogeneity of the population, educators must be able to tailor evidence-based strategies to meet the unique needs of individual students. Adaptive functioning is an equally important component in the education of students with HFASD. Students must develop social behavior that allows them to function independently in the complex social environment of school. A lack of independence may limit educational and social opportunities for students, so it is imperative that educators who support students with HFASD employ behavioral strategies that foster independence. Academic achievement and independence should be considered educational priorities for students with HFASD.

Academic Profile of Students with HFASD

A general academic profile of students with HFASD emerged from a synthesis of research conducted between 1981 and 2008 (Whitby & Mancil, 2009). Students with HFASD exhibited deficits in the areas of comprehension, written expression, handwriting skills, understanding of linguistically complex materials, complex processing across all domains, and problem solving. Reading, math, and writing were commensurate with IQ in most students with HFASD, and IQ appeared to increase up to the age of 8 years. Children younger than 8 years had weaker verbal skills, but the nonverbal and verbal intelligence gap closed between 9 and 10 years of age (Whitby & Mancil, 2009). Some individuals with HFASD may perform as well or better than typical peers until a certain grade level but then perform substantially below typical expectations in subsequent grades (Klin et al., 2007). Deficits in academic achievement may not become apparent until learning moves from concrete activities to more abstract concepts in upper elementary, middle, and high schools, at which point challenges in reading, writing, and math appear.

The academic profiles of some students with HFASD indicate a discrepancy between measured intelligence and achievement. Mayes and Calhoun (2003) estimate that 37% of students with HFASD met criteria for learning disabilities in reading, 60% for learning disabilities in writing, and 23% for learning disabilities in mathematics. Students with HFASD may have highly developed knowledge and skills in a specific area of interest and experience learning difficulties in other content areas (Attwood, 2007; Myles & Simpson, 2003). Global scores in ability or achievement do not identify deficits adequately that affect academic functioning. Analysis of subtest domains may be needed to determine the strengths and weaknesses of individual students with HFASD (Mayes & Calhoun, 2006; Whitby & Mancil, 2009). Current research in reading, writing, and math is summarized below.

Reading Characteristics

Students with HFASD exhibit comprehension deficits. In contrast, basic reading and decoding skills appear to be intact for this population (Asberg, Kopp, Berg-Kelly, & Gillberg, 2010; Huemer & Mann, 2010; Whitby & Mancil, 2009). Hyperlexia, associated with autism spectrum disorders, indicates a discrepancy between word-reading skills and reading comprehension (Grigorenko et al., 2002; Grigorenko, Volkmar, & Klin, 2003). Advanced word recognition skills of students with HFASD have been investigated to determine the importance of phonological decoding versus visual memory in single-word recognition skills. Most recently, T. M. Newman et al. (2007) found that students with HFASD who demonstrated hyperlexia relied on phonological decoding like typical readers and hyperlexic readers without ASD. When students with HFASD and hyperlexia were required to glean content in text, their fluency was significantly slower than the fluency of typical readers but similar to students with HFASD without hyperlexia.

During early school years, students may demonstrate reading skills at or about the same level as their neurotypical peers. However, as the focus of reading instruction shifts to comprehension and becomes less explicit, students begin to falter in reading (Huemer & Mann, 2010; Whitby & Mancil, 2009). By upper elementary grades, the structure of written text becomes more complex and may include figurative language. Reading instruction begins to include abstract concepts such as main idea, cause and effect, theme, and inferences. Higher order thinking such as critical thinking and verbal reasoning are required to attribute meaning to implicit text. The tendency to focus on details out of context (Happé & Frith, 2006), the inability to take the perspective of another (Baron-Cohen, 2006), and the inability to organize and process information to predict outcomes (Ozonoff, Strayer, McMahon, & Filloux, 1994) are contributing factors to the reading comprehension difficulties of students with HFASD. Sentence-level language in working memory (Berninger et al., 2010) and weaknesses in the suppression of irrelevant information in the verbal domain of working memory (Pimperton & Nation, 2010) are predictive of deficits in reading comprehension in readers who are skilled at decoding but struggle with comprehension. Executive dysfunction has been identified in students with HFASD (Robinson, Goddard, Dritschel, Wisley, & Howlin, 2009) and appears to be responsible for reading comprehension deficits. *Executive function* is the umbrella term for cognitive processes used to process and store information, as well as plan, regulate, and monitor behavior (See Table 11.2). Understanding the underlying causes of reading comprehension deficits is important for educators who support students with HFASD because reading skills affect achievement across academic content areas.

TABLE 11.2 Cognitive Processes in Executive Function

Cognitive Process	Description
Planning	A complex cognitive skill that requires constant monitoring, evaluating, and updating of a sequence of planned actions; requires disengaging from the current situation and looking ahead to identify alternatives, make choices, and then implement the plan and revise it as needed.
Mental Flexibility	The ability to shift to a different thought or action in response to changes in a situation; disengaging from one unfinished task to engage in another task.
Response Inhibition	The ability to suppress irrelevant or interfering information or impulses; discerning relevant from irrelevant input in the environment; ability to suppress natural responses to follow arbitrary rules that have no rationale.
Generativity	The ability to generate and regulate novel ideas and behaviors spontaneously; engaging in pretense; adapting behaviors to novel situations.
Self-monitoring	The ability to monitor one's own thoughts, actions, or words; the ability to self-correct thoughts, words, and actions according to situation.

Reading Instruction. Few researchers have investigated the effects of evidence-based reading instruction on the reading achievement of students with HFASD. To review reading comprehension instruction for students with ASD, Chiang and Lin (2007) screened 754 articles to identify studies that included at least one participant with ASD, data related to reading comprehension, and an experimental design. The researchers found 11 studies that met the inclusion criteria. Of these 11 studies, only three included students with HFASD. Classwide peer tutoring (Kamps, Barbetta, Leonard, & Delquadri, 1994) and cooperative learning (Kamps, Leonard, Potucck, & Harrell, 1995) were effective in increasing reading comprehension of students with HFASD in the inclusive classroom. O'Connor and Klein (2004) conducted the first study to investigate the use of strategy instruction with students with HFASD. The researchers used procedural facilitation to compare the effects of answering prereading questions (as a form of priming), the use of a cloze task, and anaphoric cueing (assigning a reference word to a target pronoun) on reading comprehension. All three interventions produced positive results, but cueing students to assign a reference word to a target pronoun produced the largest gains in reading comprehension.

Whalon and Hanline (2008) extended reading comprehension research by combining peer tutoring with strategy instruction in an intervention package that included visual supports and an interactive storyboard. The approach increased reading comprehension by teaching students with HFASD to generate and answer "wh-" questions during reading. Flores and Ganz (2007) expanded the efficacy of direct instruction to adolescents with HFASD who exhibited hyperlexia. The intervention targeted statement inference, use of facts, and analogies to increase reading comprehension.

The National Institute of Child Health and Human Development (2000) identified reading comprehension instruction as an evidence-based practice for increasing reading skills. Peer-mediated interventions, cognitive strategy instruction, and explicit instruction have been used effectively to increase reading comprehension of students with HFASD. Based on the results of reading intervention studies, Whalon, Al Otaiba, and Delano (2009) concluded that students with HFASD can benefit from reading instruction consistent with reading research.

Writing Achievement

Students with HFASD exhibit deficits in handwriting and written expression (Whitby & Mancil, 2009). Myles, Huggins, Rome-Lake, Hagiwara, Barnhill, and Griswold (2003) found that students with HFASD had less legible handwriting than their neurotypical peers. The students with HFASD produced as many sentences as typical writers, but the writing had qualitative differences. The sentences produced by students with HFASD were brief, less complex in structure, and contained fewer details than the writing of neurotypical peers.

No empirical studies have investigated the cause of handwriting deficits in students with HFASD. Deficits may be caused by motor coordination difficulties. In the general population orthographic-motor integration, the process of retrieving letter forms from memory and then producing them in written form (Cahill, 2009; Christensen, 2004), visual motor integration, and fine motor control have been associated with handwriting difficulties (Daly, Kelley, & Krauss, 2003; Volman, van Schendel, & Jongmans, 2006).

Deficits in executive function, particularly in the area of planning (Robinson et al., 2009), may have a negative impact on the ability of students with HFASD to organize their thoughts and transfer them to paper. Difficulties with generating original ideas (Low, Goddard, & Melser, 2009) and taking the perspective of another person may also have a negative effect on writing product (Jolliffe & Baron-Cohen, 1999). In order to create imaginative stories with fully developed characters students are required to take the perspective of another to determine inner emotional state, motivation, and course of action. Deficits in writing achievement most likely are the result of weak motor coordination in combination with processing deficits (Whitby & Mancil, 2009).

Writing Instruction   Handwriting interventions that address deficits specific to students with HFASD have not been investigated. Berninger et al. (2006) evaluated the effects of interventions on handwriting skills of struggling students and found that combining orthographic training with motor training was most effective in increasing handwriting skills. Formation of legible letters typically leads to automatic handwriting. Legible letter writing and automaticity are not enough to ensure the development of text-writing skills. However, automaticity allows students to concentrate on retrieving and organizing words stored in memory to create a composition. Assistive technology can remove the barrier that handwriting deficits present in the development of writing skills. Voice recognition software allows students with deficits that interfere with handwriting and keyboarding to dictate and compose on a computer (Alper & Raharinirini, 2006).

The efficacy of cognitive strategy instruction to improve the written expression of students with HFASD is emerging in the literature. Self-regulated strategy development (SRSD; Graham, Harris, MacArthur, & Schwartz, 1991) provides planning and self-monitoring strategies for all stages of writing. A scaffolded approach teaches students to select and implement strategies independently. SRSD has been used alone and with video modeling with positive results (Asaro & Saddler, 2009). Students with HFASD experienced powerful gains in quality and quantity of writing output, producing stories with more complex structure and more detail. SRSD is a promising writing intervention for students with HFASD that warrants further study.

Mathematics

Most students with HFASD have average mathematical abilities and may perform as well as their neurotypical peers in the early years of school (Whitby & Mancil, 2009). Computational abilities appear to be intact. However, students with HFASD have difficulty with complex problem solving required in the application of mathematics. Achievement in mathematics may be affected by deficits in cognitive processes such as planning, organization, and attention. Reading comprehension also may have a negative impact on mathematical achievement. Chiang and Lin (2007) reported that the mathematical achievement scores of some students with

HFASD were significantly lower than full scale IQ scores, indicating mathematical weakness. In the same review, the scores of some students with HFASD indicated mathematical giftedness. Identified deficits in other areas may help explain the discrepancy between intelligence and mathematical achievement exhibited by some students with HFASD.

Mathematics Instruction.   There are no empirical studies concerning effective mathematic instruction specifically for students with HFASD. Given that students with deficits in mathematical achievement may share characteristics with students identified with learning disabilities in math, effective strategies from the learning disabilities literature should be explored, such as schema-based instruction, cognitive strategies, peer-mediated instruction, concrete-representational-abstract (CRA) sequence, and mnemonics (e.g. Fuchs et al., 2010; Kunsch, Jitendra, & Sood, 2007; Maccini, Mulcahy, & Wilson, 2007; Test & Ellis, 2005; Witzel, 2005). Cognitive strategy instruction for students with HFASD has produced positive results in reading and writing. The effects of strategy instruction on math achievement should be considered an area of interest for future research.

Accommodations for Academic Success

Students with HFASD may require instructional accommodations to access and benefit from the general education curriculum. Curricular accommodations alter how teachers present grade-level content and how students demonstrate mastery of grade-level knowledge and skills without changing curriculum standards. Environmental accommodations adapt the learning environment to individual learning needs to support academic achievement. The presence and implementation of accommodations in the general education setting are critical to the success of students with disabilities (Ketterlin-Geller, Alonzo, Braun-Monegan, & Tindal, 2007; Lee, Wehmeyer, Soukup, & Palmer, 2010; Webb, Patterson, Syverund, & Seabrooks-Blackmore, 2008).

Instructional strategies specified as accommodations in IEPs of students with HFASD benefit students with and without disabilities in classrooms where teachers use principles of universal design for learning (UDL) to deliver differentiated instruction that meets needs of diverse learners (Hitchcock & Stahl, 2004; McGuire, Scott, & Shaw, 2006). UDL is an approach to developing curricula that promotes access, participation, and progress in the general education curriculum for all learners by proactively embedding accommodations into instruction to meet learning needs of all students, instead of adding accommodations retroactively to address needs of students with disabilities (Center for Applied Special Technology [CAST], 2008). An illustration of how accommodations can be incorporated into UDL is provided in Table 11.3.

Visual support strategies often are recommended to enhance the performance of students with HFASD in the classroom (Attwood, 2007; Myles & Simpson, 2003). Visual cues may help make abstract concepts more concrete, allow for longer processing time than auditory information, and promote recognition of stored information, activating prior knowledge stored in short- or long-term memory. Visual supports can be used as part of an intervention package to enhance academic achievement across content areas and educational settings (Myles & Adreon, 2001). Some of the visual strategies that can be incorporated into the inclusive classroom are advance organizers (Laushey, Heflin, Shippen, Alberto, Fredrick, 2009), graphic organizers, task cards or Power Cards (Boutot, 2009), study guides, and outlines (Myles & Simpson, 2003).

TABLE 11.3 Essential Qualities of Universal Design for Learning (UDL)

Essential Qualities of UDL	Embedded Accommodations
Multiple Means of Representation	• Visual schedules
	• Key points written on whiteboard or in printed advance organizer
	• Visually uncluttered handouts, worksheets, and assessments
	• Models of finished products
	• Printed study guides
	• Computer-assisted instruction
	• Visual representation of abstract concepts
Multiple Means of Expression	• Dictation of answers to peers, teachers, digital recorder, or computer
	• Structured interview with teacher
	• Multimedia production
	• Musical composition
	• Artistic/graphic design
	• Physical demonstration of concept or skill
	• Grades for effort and participation
Multiple Means of Engagement	• Completion of assignments in pairs or groups
	• Use of hands-on activities
	• Integration of motor activities
	• Incorporation of special interests
	• Task cards for multi-step procedures
	• Use of calculators and manipulatives in math
	• Simplified text for independent reading
	• Text read aloud or use of audio books
	• Text-to-voice and voice-to-text software
	• Computer games and activities

Note: UDL embeds instructional strategies into curriculum to accommodate diverse learning needs of all students. UDL Guidelines available at www.udlcenter.org/aboutudl/udlguidelines.

Social Behavior

Students with HFASD have difficulty developing independence (Hume, Loftin, & Lantz, 2009; VanBergeijk et al., 2008). Even students with superior intelligence may be overly dependent on others to help them function in the school environment. It is important for educators to use explicit instruction to teach age-appropriate social behavior and personal management skills such as, coping skills, social communication, social interaction skills, and classroom study skills. Challenging classroom behaviors such as interrupting, noncompliance, and disruption may be related to deficits in social skills or a lack of understanding of behavioral expectations (Volker et al., 2010). More subtle behaviors that interfere with learning, such as insistence on sameness, inattention, disorganization, and lack of problem solving may be related to cognitive processing deficits associated with HFASD (Hill, 2004). After behavioral expectations and task-specific skills have been taught and students have demonstrated acquisition of the skills, educators should incorporate strategies into daily routines that support independent performance of age-appropriate social behavior by students with HFASD.

Priming and Home Base

Priming refers to the introduction of information, assignments, instructional material, or activities before they are used during typical instruction in the classroom (Wilde, Koegel, & Koegel, 1992). Priming is well-suited to students with HFASD because they rely on routine and react to unexpected events with stress and anxiety. Myles and Adreon (2001) describe the benefits of priming as familiarizing students with instructional material, introducing predictability, and increasing the likelihood of success. For students who may spend most of their days in general education settings, priming may take place in Home Base. Home Base is a designated place outside the general education classroom where students can check in to organize themselves for the day, visit during the day to remove themselves from stressful situations or work in a quiet environment, and check out at the end of the day to prepare to go home (Myles & Southwick, 1999). Both priming and Home Base address characteristics of HFASD and can be individualized to meet the needs of students who receive academic instruction in the general education classroom.

Self-Management

Self-management interventions foster independence in the school environment by transferring the responsibility of managing behavior from a teacher or parent to the student. This transfer of control makes teaching self-management a viable strategy for promoting independence (Ganz, 2007; Hume et al., 2009). Self-management empowers individuals to control their behavior and reduces their dependence on others. Interventions that use self-management techniques can vary widely, but an extensive body of literature supports the efficacy of self-management for promoting independence across age, disabilities, behaviors, and settings (Briesch & Chafouleas, 2009; Lee, Simpson, & Shogren, 2007). Combining components of self-management provides the opportunity to create intervention packages designed to meet individual student needs. The elements used most commonly are personal goal setting, self-monitoring, self-evaluation and recording, self-reinforcement, and self-charting.

Until recently, special education teachers used self-management interventions almost exclusively in special education settings (Lee et al., 2007). A body of research is accumulating that indicates self-management interventions also produce positive results for students with HFASD in inclusive classrooms. Self-management interventions increased independence by helping students manage transitions (Newman & Buffington, 1995), increase social interaction with peers (Apple, Billingsley, & Schwartz, 2005; Boutot, 2009; Morrison, Kamps, Garcia, & Parker, 2001; Palmen, Didden, & Arts, 2008), increase completion of academic tasks (Mruzek, Cohen, & Smith, 2007; Wilkinson, 2005), and decrease self-injurious behavior (Tiger, Fisher, & Bouxsein, 2009). A self-management plan is a portable, inexpensive, low-tech intervention that fosters independence and generalization of skills and has a history of efficacy. Educators can develop self-management interventions tailored to the diverse needs of students with HFASD across academic content areas and educational settings.

Mental Health

Anxiety is among the most common mental health concern for school-age children and adolescents with HFASD (Ghaziuddin, 2002). Prevalence data on diagnosed anxiety disorders are variable, but youth with HFASD experience more problems with anxiety than many other clinical and nonclinical populations (White, Oswald, Ollendick, & Scahill, 2009). Possible causes of co-occurrence of anxiety with HFASD include genetic predisposition, neurological differences, and neurochemical disturbances. The presentation of anxiety in students with HFASD appears be influenced by age, level of cognitive functioning, and degree of social impairment, which may complicate diagnoses (White et al., 2009).

The relationship between anxiety and social skills remains unclear. For example, physiological hyperarousal and social deficits were predictive of social anxiety (Bellini, 2006). However, investigations into the relationship between anxiety, loneliness, and social impairment were inconclusive. Bauminger, Shulman, and Agam (2003) found that students with HFASD who reported elevated anxiety also reported more feelings of social and emotional loneliness compared to neurotypical peers. In a later study, students with HFASD who reported elevated anxiety also reported experiencing social loneliness but not emotional loneliness (White & Roberson-Nay, 2009). The authors offered possible explanations for the inconsistent results. Participants may have had difficulties recognizing their inner emotional state, or they may have desired social peers but did not seek emotional bonding outside existing family relationships. Both explanations are plausible and offer future directions for research.

Cognitive–Behavioral Therapy. Cognitive–behavioral therapy (CBT) is a promising intervention for the treatment of anxiety in students with HFASD. Treatment programs for child anxiety disorders were modified to meet the needs of students with HFASD by simplifying cognitive activities, using visual supports to clarify abstract concepts, and adding components associated with applied behavioral analysis (ABA), such as systematic prompting and differential reinforcement (Lang, Regester, Lauderdale, Ashbaugh, & Haring, 2010). CBT training helps youth recognize affective arousal in themselves, restructure faulty cognition, and practice altered ways of thinking in practice situations before applying the newly learned skills to real life. In vivo exposure involved facing feared situations repeatedly while using learned coping skills and remaining in the situation until habituation occurs. Parents receive training on supporting in vivo exposures, using positive reinforcement, using communication skills to encourage children's independence, and preventing relapse (Chalfant, Rapee, & Carroll, 2007; Reaven et al., 2009; Sofronoff, Attwood, & Hinton, 2005; White, Ollendick, Scahill, Oswald, & Albano, 2009; Wood et al., 2009). Although there are differences in the number of sessions and specific skills targeted in various CBT programs, they shared similar treatment designs. The efficacy of CBT was demonstrated by the reduction of anxiety in children and adolescents with HFASD who received treatment. All CBT studies took place in clinical settings. Future research should explore the feasibility of special education teachers providing CBT in the school environment to give students with HFASD broader access to effective treatment for anxiety.

Bullying. A growing area of concern regarding the effect of school experiences on the mental health of students with HFASD is an increasing recognition of the extent of bullying and associated detrimental outcomes. Between 65% (Carter, 2009) to 94% (Little, 2002) of students with HFASD are estimated to be the targets of bullies in general education classrooms. Of those youth with HFASD who report being bullied, 87% indicate they are bullied at least once a week, and 40% report daily occurrences of bullying (Wainscot, Naylor, Sutcliffe, Tantam, & Williams, 2008). The devastating effect on mental health is a worsening of depression and an emergence of suicidal ideation (Anonymous, 2007; Collom, 2005). Some youth with HFASD are succumbing to "bullycide" (LaSalle, 2009, para 1) as they choose to end their lives because of the abuse. Ironically, when students with HFASD receive educational services in specialized settings outside of general education classrooms, the occurrence of bullying declines dramatically (van Roekel, Scholte, & Didden, 2010), possibly as a result of normalization of social deficits associated with ASD and teacher–pupil ratios that permit better supervision.

The trend, however, is for students with HFASD to receive their educational services in general education classrooms. Davidson (2010) analyzed autobiographies of individuals with HFASD to glean suggestions for creating physical and social classroom environments that support successful participation and achievement. A key implication that emerged is that concerted effort needs to be exerted to implement interventions that protect students with HFASD from bullying. Some of this effort should be directed at creating a school climate that does not tolerate bullying directed at any student. Effort also must be directed toward systematically teaching youth with HFASD how to avoid becoming the targets for bullies. For example, there are simple solutions such as teaching these students to always be in proximity to a group of other students (Attwood, 2004). Students with HFASD need to be taught how to advocate for themselves, which is a skill addressed in social skills training. Unfortunately, social skills training may not be included as a support service. White et al. (2007) found that the parents of 101 students in 25 states reported that their children with ASD did not receive social skills training in the seventh and eighth grades.

The complex needs of students with HFASD present challenges to school systems and personnel responsible for providing their education. Increased emphasis on academic achievement requires students to access and benefit from rigorous general education curriculum. Researchers and practitioners must take into consideration the academic profiles of students with HFASD and the characteristics associated with the disorder to develop and deliver effective interventions that promote academic achievement and social development. Adult outcomes have not been good for this group of students with disabilities. There is an urgent need for research and development of effective instructional practices that lead to improved educational outcomes and increased independence to ensure the future success of students with HFASD in postsecondary education, careers, and personal relationships.

Conclusion

An understanding of the most effective educational interventions for older children and adolescents with ASD remains elusive because most intervention research has been conducted with young children (Lord & Bishop, 2010) in clinical settings, with few focused–intervention strategies being conducted in natural settings (Mancil et al., 2009). Practitioners must extrapolate the conclusions drawn by researchers studying younger children in order to attempt to make informed decisions regarding educational programming for older children and adolescents. The challenge is to ensure that the extrapolation takes into account the changes that occur related to the new patterns of deficits that emerge as the presence of ASD affects how individuals interact with the environment, which in turn affects the expression of the disability (Mundy, Sullivan, & Mastergeorge, 2009).

More research has been conducted with youth with LFASD when compared to a paucity of empirical scrutiny of interventions for those with HFASD. For youth with LFASD, DTT and naturalistic ABA should be used together to promote the best outcomes (Cowan & Allen, 2007;

Delprato, 2001), bearing in mind the limitations of each. Education should emphasize capturing motivation by facilitating the development of meaningful skills. This task is made more challenging by federal requirements that IEP goals be aligned with general education standards of chronologically matched typically developing peers. The education of students with HFASD is guided by common practices, such as using Home Base and incorporating components of UDL, but few of the practices have been adequately researched with this population.

There is strong consensus that no one educational intervention will be effective for all children and adolescents with ASD (National Research Council, 2001; Steege et al., 2007). Regardless of whether or not the intervention is empirically based or extrapolated, ongoing progress monitoring is necessary to document students' gains during intervention (Ferraioli, Hughes, & Smith, 2005). Children and adolescents who do not show progress with one intervention, are highly likely to benefit from a different intervention (Sherer & Schreibman, 2005). Similarly, there is an urgent need to identify child and family demographics that affect intervention outcomes (Baker-Ericzén, Stahmer, & Burns, 2007). More research, particularly studies involving randomized controlled trials (RCTs), are necessary before we can answer the critical question: "Which teaching approaches appear most effective for teaching specific skills given certain profiles of child and contextual characteristics?" (Rogers & Vismara, 2008, p. 30) as it applies to older children and adolescents with ASD.

References

Alberto, P., Cihak, D., & Gama, R. (2005). Use of static picture prompts versus video modeling during simulation instruction. *Research in Developmental Disabilities, 26*, 327–339.

Alberto, P., Fredrick, L., Hughes, M., McIntosh, L., & Cihak, D. (2007). Components of visual literacy: Teaching logos. *Focus on Autism and Other Developmental Disabilities, 22*, 234–243.

Alper, S., & Raharinirini, S. (2006). Assistive technology for individuals with disabilities: A review and synthesis of the literature. *Journal of Special Education Technology, 21*, 47–64.

Aman, M., & Langworthy, K. (2000). Pharmacotherapy for hyperactivity in children with autism and other pervasive developmental disorders. *Journal of Autism & Developmental Disorders, 30*, 451.

Anderson, A., Moore, D. W., Godfrey, R., & Fletcher-Flin, C. M. (2004). Social skills assessment of children with autism in free-play situations. *Autism, 8*, 369–385.

Anderson, S. R., Avery, D. L., DiPietro, E. K., Edwards, G. L., & Christian, W. P. (1987). Intensive home-based early intervention with autistic children. *Education & Treatment of Children, 10*, 352–366.

Anderson, S., & Romanczyk, R. (1999). Early intervention for young children with autism: Continuum-based behavioral models. *Journal of the Association for Persons with Severe Handicaps, 24*, 162–173.

Anonymous. (2007). Giving up on school: One family's story. *Education Canada, 47*(3), 38–42.

Apple, A. L., Billingsley, F., & Schwartz, I. S. (2005). Effects of video modeling alone and with self-management on compliment-giving behaviors of children with high-functioning ASD. *Journal of Positive Behavior Interventions, 7*, 33–46.

Asaro, K., & Saddler, B. (2009). Effects of planning instruction on a young writer with Asperger Syndrome. *Intervention in School and Clinic, 44*, 268–275.

Asberg, J., Kopp S., Berg-Kelly, K., & Gillberg, C. (2010). Reading comprehension, word decoding, and spelling in girls with autism spectrum disorders (ASD) or attention-deficit/hyperactivity disorder (AD/HD): Performance and predictors. *International Journal of Language and Communication Disorders, 45*, 61–71.

Attwood, T. (2004). Strategies to reduce the bullying of young children with Asperger syndrome. *Australian Journal of Early Childhood, 29*, 15–23.

Baker-Ericzén, M., Stahmer, A., & Burns, A. (2007). Child demographics associated with outcomes in a community-based pivotal response training program. *Journal of Positive Behavior Interventions, 9*, 52–60.

Barnhill, G. P. (2007). Outcomes in adults with Asperger syndrome. *Focus on Autism and Other Developmental Disabilities, 22*, 116–126.

Baron-Cohen, S. (2006). The autistic child's theory of mind: A case of specific developmental delay. *Journal of Child Psychology and Psychiatry, 30*, 285–297.

Bashe, P. R., & Kirby, B. L. (2005). *The OASIS guide to Asperger syndrome* (Rev. ed.). New York: Crown.

Bauminger, N., Shulman, C., & Agam, G. (2003). Peer interaction and loneliness in high-functioning children with autism. *Journal of Autism and Developmental Disorders, 33*, 489–507.

Bauminger, N., Solomon, M., & Rogers, S. (2010). Predicting friendship quality in autism spectrum disorders and typical development. *Journal of Autism and Developmental Disorders, 40*, 751–761.

Begeer, S., Terwogt, M., Lunenburg, P., & Stegge, H. (2009). Brief report: Additive and subtractive counterfactual reasoning of children with high-functioning autism spectrum disorders. *Journal of Autism and Developmental Disorders, 39*, 1593–1597.

Belfiore, P., Fritts, K., & Herman, B. (2008). The role of procedural integrity: Using self-monitoring to enhance discrete trial instruction (DTI). *Focus on Autism and Other Developmental Disabilities, 23*, 95–102.

Bellini, S. (2006). The development of social anxiety in adolescents with autism spectrum disorders. *Focus on Autism & Other Developmental Disabilities, 21*, 138–145.

Ben Itzchak, E., & Zachor, D. (2009). Change in autism classification with early intervention: Predictors and outcomes. *Research in Autism Spectrum Disorders, 3*, 967–976.

Bennett, K., & Cavanaugh, R. (1998). Effects of immediate self-correction, delayed self-correction, and no correction on the acquisition and maintenance of multiplication facts by a fourth-grade student with learning disabilities. *Journal of Applied Behavior Analysis, 31*, 303–306.

Berkson, G. (2002). Feedback and control in the development of abnormal stereotyped behaviors. In R. L. Sprague & K. M. Newell (Eds.), *Stereotyped movements: Brain and behavior relationships* (pp. 3–15). Washington, DC: American Psychological Association.

Berninger, V. W., Abbott, R. D., Swanson, H. L., Lovitt, D., Trivedi, P., Lin, S., … Amtmann, D. (2010). Relationship of word- and sentence-level working memory to reading and writing in second, fourth, and sixth grade. *Language, Speech, and Hearing Services in Schools, 41*, 179–193.

Berninger, V., Rutberg, J., Abbott, R., Garcia, N., Anderson-Youngstown, M., Brooks, A., & Fulton, C. (2006). Tier 1 and Tier 2 early intervention for handwriting and composing. *Journal of School Psychology, 44*, 3–30.

Bishop, S., Richler, J., & Lord, C. (2006). Association between restricted and repetitive behaviors and nonverbal IQ in children with autism spectrum disorders. *Child Neuropsychology, 12*, 247–267.

Bolton, J., & Mayer, M. (2008). Promoting the generalization of paraprofessional discrete trial teaching skills. *Focus on Autism & Other Developmental Disabilities, 23*, 103–111.

Bondy, A. S., & Frost, L. A. (1994). The picture exchange communication system. *Focus on Autistic Behavior, 9*(3), 1–20.

Bondy, A., Tincani, M., & Frost, L. (2004). Multiply controlled verbal operants: An analysis and extension to the picture exchange communication system. *Behavior Analyst, 27*, 247–261.

Boutot, E. A. (2009). Using "I Will" cards and social coaches to improve social behaviors of students with Asperger syndrome. *Intervention in School and Clinic, 44*, 276–281.

Briesch, A. M. & Chafouleas, S. M. (2009). Review and analysis of literature on self-management interventions to promote appropriate classroom behaviors (1988–2008). *School Psychology, 24*, 106–118.

Cahill, S. (2009). Where does handwriting fit in? Strategies to support academic achievement. *Intervention in School & Clinic, 44*, 223–228.

Camarena, P. M., & Sarigiani, P. A. (2009). Postsecondary educational aspirations of high-functioning adolescents with autism spectrum disorders and their parents. *Focus on Autism and Other Developmental Disabilities, 24*, 115–128.

Campbell, M., Armenteros, J., Malone, R., & Adams, P. (1997). Neuroleptic-related dyskinesias in autistic children: A prospective, longitudinal study. *Journal of the American Academy of Child & Adolescent Psychiatry, 36*, 835–843.

Canitano, R., Luchetti, A., & Zappella, M. (2005). Epilepsy, electroencephalographic abnormalities, and regression in children with autism. *Journal of Child Neurology, 20*, 27–31.

Carr, E. G., & Durand, V. M. (1985). Reducing behavior problems through functional communication training. *Journal of Applied Behavior Analysis, 18*, 111–126.

Carr, D., & Felce, J. (2008). Teaching picture-to-object relations in picture-based requesting by children with autism: A comparison between error prevention and error correction teaching procedures. *Journal of Intellectual Disability Research, 52*, 309–317.

Carter, E. W., Sisco, L. G., Brown, L., Brickham, D., & Al-Khabbaz, Z. A. (2008). Peer interactions and academic engagement of youth with developmental disabilities in inclusive middle and high school classrooms. *American Journal on Mental Retardation, 113*, 479–494.

Carter, S. (2009). Bullying of students with Asperger syndrome. *Issues in Comprehensive Pediatric Nursing, 32*, 145–154.

Casey, S., & Merical, C. (2006). The use of functional communication training without additional treatment procedures in an inclusive school setting. *Behavioral Disorders, 32*, 46–54.

Catania, C., Almeida, D., Liu-Constant, B., & Digennaro Reed, F. (2009). Video modeling to train staff to implement discrete-trial instruction. *Journal of Applied Behavior Analysis, 42*, 387–392.

Cederlund, M., Hagberg, B., & Gillberg, C. (2010). Asperger syndrome in adolescent and young adult males: Interview, self- and parent assessment of social, emotional, and cognitive problems. *Research in Developmental Disabilities, 31*, 287–298.

Center for Applied Special Technology. (2008). *Universal design for learning guidelines version 1.0.* Wakefield, MA: Author.

Chalfant, A. M., Rapee, R., & Carroll, L. (2007). Treating anxiety disorders in children with high functioning autism spectrum disorders: A controlled trial. *Journal of Autism and Developmental Disorders, 37*, 1842–1857.

Charlop-Christy, M., & Haymes, L. (1998). Using objects of obsession as token reinforcers for children with autism. *Journal of Autism & Developmental Disorders, 28*, 189–198.

Chen, M., Wu, T., Lin, Y., Tasi, Y., & Chen, H. (2009). The effect of different representations on reading digital text for students with cognitive disabilities. *British Journal of Educational Technology, 40*, 764–770.

Chiang, H., & Lin, Y. (2007). Reading comprehension instruction for students with autism spectrum disorders: A review of the literature. *Focus on Autism and Other Developmental Disabilities, 22*, 259–267.

Christensen, C. (2004). Relationship between orthographic-motor integration and computer use for the production of creative and well-structured written text. *British Journal of Educational Psychology, 74*, 551–564.

Cihak, D., & Foust, J. (2008). Comparing number lines and touch points to teach addition facts to students with autism. *Focus on Autism and Other Developmental Disabilities, 23*, 131–137.

Collom, E. (2005). The ins and outs of homeschooling: The determinants of parental motivations and student achievement. *Education and Urban Society, 37*, 307–335.

Cowan, R., & Allen, K. (2007). Using naturalistic procedures to enhance learning in individuals with autism: A focus on generalized teaching within the school setting. *Psychology in the Schools, 44*, 701–715.

Daly, C., Kelley, G., & Krauss, A. (2003). Relationship between visual-motor integration and handwriting skills of children in kindergarten: A modified replication study. *American Journal of Occupational Therapy, 57*, 459–462.

Davidson, J. (2010). "It cuts both ways": A relational approach to access and accommodation for autism. *Social Science and Medicine, 70*, 305–312.

Dawson, G., Meltzoff, A. N., Osterling, J., Rinaldi, J., & Brown, E. (1998). Children with autism fail to orient to naturally occurring social stimuli. *Journal of Autism and Developmental Disorders, 28*, 479.

Delprato, D. (2001). Comparisons of discrete-trial and normalized behavioral language intervention for young children with autism. *Journal of Autism and Developmental Disorders, 31*, 315–325.

des Portes, V., Hagerman, R. J., & Hendren, R. L. (2003). Pharmacotherapy. In S. Ozonoff, S. J. Rogers, & R. L. Hendren (Eds.), *Autism spectrum disorders: A research review for practitioners* (pp. 161–186). Washington, DC: American Psychiatric Association.

Dettmer, S., Simpson, R., Myles, B., & Ganz, J. (2000). The use of visual supports to facilitate transitions of students with autism. *Focus on Autism and Other Developmental Disabilities, 15*, 163–169.

Drew, A., Baird, G., Baron-Cohen, S., Cox, A., Slonims, V., Wheelwright, S., …Charman, T. (2002). A pilot randomized control trial of a parent training intervention for preschool children with autism. *European Child & Adolescent Psychology, 11*, 266–272.

Durand, V. M., & Crimmins, D. B. (1987). Assessment and treatment of psychotic speech in an autistic child. *Journal of Autism and Developmental Disorders, 17*, 17–28.

Durand, V. M., & Merges, E. (2001). Functional communication training: A contemporary behavior analytic intervention for problem behaviors. *Focus on Autism & Other Developmental Disorders, 16*, 110–119.

Eaves, L. C., & Ho, H. H. (2008). Young adult outcome of autism spectrum disorders. *Journal of Autism and Developmental Disorders, 38*, 739–747.

Eikeseth, S., Smith, T., Jahr, E., & Eldevik, S. (2007). Outcome for children with autism who began intensive behavioral treatment between ages 4 and 7: A comparison controlled study. *Behavior Modification, 31*, 264–278.

Etscheidt, S. (2005). Paraprofessional services for students with disabilities: A legal analysis of issues. *Research and Practice for Persons with Severe Disabilities, 30*, 60–80.

Farley, M., McMahon, W., Fombonne, E., Jenson, W., Miller, J., Gardner, M., … Coon, H. (2009). Twenty-year outcome for individuals with autism and average or near-average cognitive abilities. *Autism Research, 2*, 109–118.

Fenske, E. C., Zalenski, S., Krantz, P. J., & McClannahan, L. E. (1985). Age at intervention and treatment outcome for autistic children in a comprehensive intervention program. *Analysis and Intervention for Developmental Disabilities, 5*, 49–58.

Ferraioli, S., Hughes, C., & Smith, T. (2005). A model for problem solving in discrete trial training for children with autism. *Journal of Early and Intensive Behavior Intervention, 2*, 224–246.

Findling, R. (2005). Pharmacologic treatment of behavioral symptoms in autism and pervasive developmental disorders. *The Journal of Clinical Psychiatry, 66*, 1026–1031.

Flippin, M., Reszka, S., & Watson, L. (2010). Effectiveness of the picture exchange communication system (PECS) on communication and speech for children with autism spectrum disorders: A meta-analysis. *American Journal of Speech-Language Pathology, 19*, 178–195.

Flores, M. M., & Ganz, J. B. (2007). Effectiveness of direct instruction for teaching statement inference, use of facts, and analogies to students with developmental disabilities and reading delays. *Focus on Autism and Other Developmental Disabilities, 22*, 244–251.

Franco, J., Lang, R., O'Reilly, M., Chan, J., Sigafoos, J., & Rispoli, M. (2009). Functional analysis and treatment of inappropriate vocalizations using a speech-generating device for a child with autism. *Focus on Autism and Other Developmental Disabilities, 24,* 146–155.

Fuchs, L. S., Powell, S. R., Seethaler, P. M., Cirino, P. T., Fletcher, J. M., Fuchs, D., & Hamlett, C. L. (2010). The effects of strategic counting instruction, with and without deliberate practice, on number combination skill among students with mathematics difficulties. *Learning and Individual Differences, 20,* 89–100.

Ganz, J. (2007). Classroom structuring methods and strategies for children and youth with autism spectrum disorders. *Exceptionality, 15,* 249–260.

Gerhardt, P., Weiss, M., & Delmolino, L. (2003). Treatment of severe aggression in an adolescent with autism. *Behavior Analyst Today, 4,* 386–394.

Ghaziuddin, M. (2002). Asperger syndrome: Associated psychiatric and medical conditions. *Focus on Autism and Other Developmental Disabilities, 17,* 138–144.

Ghezzi, P. (2007). Discrete trials teaching. *Psychology in the Schools, 44,* 667–679.

Giangreco, M. (2010). One-to-one paraprofessionals for students with disabilities in inclusive classrooms: Is conventional wisdom wrong? *Intellectual and Developmental Disabilities, 48,* 1–13.

Giangreco, M. F. & Broer, S. M. (2005) Questionable utilization of paraprofessionals in inclusive schools: Are we addressing symptoms or root causes? *Focus on Autism and other Developmental Disabilities, 20,* 10–26.

Giangreco, M. F., Edelman, S. W., Luiselli, T. E., & MacFarland, S. Z. (1997). Helping or hovering? Effects of instructional assistant proximity on students with disabilities. *Exceptional Children, 64,* 7–18.

Giangreco, M., Halvorsen, A., Doyle, M., & Broer, S. (2004). Alternatives to overreliance on paraprofessionals in inclusive schools. *Journal of Special Education Leadership, 17,* 82–90.

Giangreco, M., Suter, J., & Doyle, M. (2010). Paraprofessionals in inclusive schools: A review of recent research. *Journal of Educational & Psychological Consultation, 20,* 41–57.

Giangreco, M., Yuan, S., McKenzie, B., Cameron, P., & Fialka, J. (2005). "Be careful what you wish for...": Five reasons to be concerned about the assignment of individual paraprofessionals. *Teaching Exceptional Children, 37*(5), 28–34.

Gilchrist, A., Green, J., Cox, A., Burton, D., Rutter, M., & Le Couteur, A. (2001). Development and current functioning in adolescents with Asperger syndrome: A comparative study. *Journal of Child Psychology and Psychiatry, 42,* 227–240.

Gotham, K., Risi, S., Pickles, A., & Lord, C. (2007). The Autism Diagnostic Observation Schedule: Revised algorithms for improved diagnostic validity. *Journal of Autism & Developmental Disorders, 37,* 613–627.

Graham, S., Harris, K., MacArthur, C., & Schwartz, S. (1991). Writing and writing instruction for students with learning disabilities: Review of a research program. *Learning Disability Quarterly, 14,* 89–114.

Granpeesheh, D., Dixon, D., Tarbox, J., Kaplan, A., & Wilke, A. (2009). The effects of age and treatment intensity on behavioral intervention outcomes for children with autism spectrum disorders. *Research in Autism Spectrum Disorders, 3,* 1014–1022.

Granpeesheh, D., Tarbox, J., & Dixon, D. (2009). Applied behavior analytic interventions for children with autism: A description and review of treatment research. *Annals of Clinical Psychiatry, 21,* 162–173.

Granpeesheh, D., Tarbox, J., Dixon, D., Carr, E., & Herbert, M. (2009). Retrospective analysis of clinical records in 38 cases of recovery from autism. *Annals of Clinical Psychiatry, 21,* 195–204.

Green, V., Pituch, K., Itchon, J., Choi, A., O'Reilly, M., & Sigafoos, J. (2006). Internet survey of treatments used by parents of children with autism. *Research in Developmental Disabilities, 27,* 70–84.

Grigorenko, E. L., Klin, A., Pauls, D. L., Senft, R., Hooper, C., & Volkmar, F. (2002). A descriptive study of hyperlexia in a clinically referred sample of children with developmental delays. *Journal of Autism and Developmental Disorders, 32,* 3–12.

Grigorenko, E. L., Volkmar, F., & Klin, A. (2003). Hyperlexia: Disability or superability? *Journal of Child Psychology and Psychiatry, 44,* 1079–1091.

Groden, J., Cautela, J. R., Prince, S., & Berryman, J. (1994). The impact of stress and anxiety on individuals with autism and developmental disabilities. In E. Schopler & G. Mesibov (Eds.), *Behavioral issues in autism* (pp. 177–193). New York: Plenum Press.

Gutierrez, A., Hale, M., O'Brien, H., Fischer, A., Durocher, J., & Alessandri, M. (2009). Evaluating the effectiveness of two commonly used discrete trial procedures for teaching receptive discrimination to young children with autism spectrum disorders. *Research in Autism Spectrum Disorders, 3,* 630–638.

Hagopian, L., Toole, L., Long, E., Bowman, L., & Lieving, G. (2004). A comparison of dense-to-lean and fixed lean schedules of alternative reinforcement and extinction. *Journal of Applied Behavior Analysis, 37,* 323.

Hall, L. J., Grundon, G. S., Pope, C., & Romero, A. B. (2010). Training paraprofessionals to use behavioral strategies when educating learners with autism spectrum disorders across environments. *Behavioral Interventions, 25,* 37–51.

Happé, F., & Frith, U. (2006). The weak coherence account: Detail-focused cognitive style in ASD. *Journal of Autism and Developmental Disorders, 36,* 5–25.

Harding, J., Wacker, D., Berg, W., Winborn-Kemmerer, L., Lee, J., & Ibrahimovic, M. (2009). Analysis of multiple manding topographies during functional communication training. *Education & Treatment of Children, 32,* 21–36.

Harris, S. L., & Handleman, J. S. (2000). Age and IQ at intake as predictors of placement for young children with autism: A four- to six-year follow-up. *Journal of Autism and Developmental Disorders, 30,* 137–142.

Heflin, L. J. & Alaimo, D. F. (2007). *Students with autism spectrum disorders: Effective instructional practices.* Upper Saddle River, NJ: Pearson/Merrill/Prentice Hall.

Heflin, L., & Alberto, P. (2001). Establishing a behavioral context for learning for students with autism. *Focus on Autism & Other Developmental Disabilities, 16,* 93–101.

Hill, E. L. (2004). Evaluating the theory of executive dysfunction in autism. *Developmental Review, 24,* 189–233.

Hitchcock, C., & Stahl, S. (2004). Assistive technology, universal design, Universal Design for Learning: Improved learning outcomes. *Journal of Special Education Technology, 18,* 45–52.

Horn, E., & Banerjee, R. (2009). Understanding curriculum modifications and embedded learning opportunities in the context of supporting all children's success. *Language, Speech, & Hearing Services in Schools, 40,* 406–415.

Horner, R. H., Sprague, J. R., O'Brien, M., & Heathfield, L. T. (1990). The role of response efficiency in the reduction of problem behaviors through functional equivalence training: A case study. *Journal of the Association for Persons with Severe Handicaps, 15,* 91–97.

Howard, J., Sparkman, C., Cohen, H., Green, G., & Stanislaw, H. (2005). A comparison of intensive behavior analytic and eclectic treatments for young children with autism. *Research in Developmental Disabilities, 26,* 359–383.

Howlin, P. (1998). *Children with autism and Asperger syndrome: A guide for practitioners and carers.* Chichester, England: Wiley.

Howlin, P., & Asgharian, A. (1999). The diagnosis of autism and Asperger syndrome: Findings from a survey of 770 families. *Developmental Medicine & Child Neurology, 41,* 834–839.

Howlin, P., Goode, S., Hutton, J., & Rutter, M. (2004). Adult outcomes for children with autism. *Journal of Child Psychology and Psychiatry, 45,* 212–229.

Howlin, P., Magiati, I., & Charman, T. (2009). Systematic review of early intensive behavioral interventions for children with autism. *American Journal on Intellectual and Developmental Disabilities, 114,* 23–41.

Huemer, S. V., & Mann, V. (2010). A comprehensive profile of decoding and comprehension in autism spectrum disorders. *Journal of Autism and Developmental Disorders, 40,* 485–493.

Hume, K., Loftin, R., & Lantz, J. (2009). Increasing independence in autism spectrum disorders: A review of three focused interventions. *Journal of Autism and Developmental Disorders, 39,* 1329–1338.

Individuals with Disabilities Education Improvement Act of 2004, 20 U.S.C. § 1400 *et seq.* (2004) (reauthorization of the Individuals with Disabilities Education Act of 1990).

Ingersoll, B. (2010). Teaching social communication: A comparison of naturalistic behavioral and development, social pragmatic approaches for children with autism spectrum disorders. *Journal of Positive Behavior Interventions, 12,* 33–43.

Ingersoll, B., Schreibman, L., & Stahmer, A. (2001). Brief report: Differential treatment outcomes for children with autistic spectrum disorder based on level of peer social avoidance. *Journal of Autism & Developmental Disorders, 31,* 343–349.

Johnson, J., McDonnell, J., Holzwarth, V., & Hunter, K. (2004). The efficacy of embedded instruction for students with developmental disabilities enrolled in general education classes. *Journal of Positive Behavior Interventions, 6,* 214–227.

Jolliffe, T., & Baron-Cohen, S. (1999). The Strange Stories Test: A replication with high-functioning adults with autism or Asperger syndrome. *Journal of Autism and Developmental Disorders, 29,* 395–406.

Jones, W., Carr, K., & Klin, A. (2008). Absence of preferential looking to the eyes of approaching adults predicts level of social disability in 2-year-old toddlers with autism spectrum disorder. *Archives of General Psychiatry, 65,* 946–954.

Jones, W., & Klin, A. (2009). Heterogeneity and homogeneity across the autism spectrum: The role of development. *Journal of the American Academy of Child & Adolescent Psychiatry, 48,* 471–473.

Kamps, D. M., Barbetta, P. M., Leonard, B. R., & Delquadri, J. (1994). Classwide peer tutoring: An integration strategy to improve reading skills and promote peer interactions among students with autism and general education peers. *Journal of Applied Behavior Analysis, 27,* 49–61.

Kamps, D. M., Leonard, B., Potucek, J., & Harrell, G. (1995). Cooperative learning groups in reading: An integration strategy for students with autism and general education peers. *Behavioral Disorders, 21,* 89–109.

Kanner, L. (1943). Autistic disturbances of affective contact. *The Nervous Child, 2,* 217–250.

Kennedy, C. H., Meyer, K. A., Knowles, T., & Shukla, S. (2000). Analyzing the multiple functions of stereotypical behaviors for students with autism: Implications for assessment and treatment. *Journal of Applied Behavior Analysis, 33,* 559–571.

Ketterlin-Geller, L. R., Alonzo, J., Braun-Monegan, J., & Tindal, G. (2007). Recommendations for accommodations: Implications of (in)consistency. *Remedial and Special Education, 28,* 194–206.

Klin, A., Jones, W., Schultz, R., Volkmar, F., & Cohen, D. (2002). Defining and quantifying the social phenotype in autism. *The American Journal of Psychiatry, 159,* 895–908.

Klin, A., Saulnier, C., Sparrow, S., Cicchetti, D., Volkmar, F., & Lord, C. (2007). Social and communication abilities and disabilities in higher functioning individuals with autism spectrum disorders: The Vineland and the ADOS. *Journal of Autism and Developmental Disorders, 37*, 748–759.

Koegel, R., Russo, D., & Rincover, A. (1977). Assessing and training teachers in the generalized use of behavior modification with autistic children. *Journal of Applied Behavior Analysis, 10*, 197–205.

Kogan, M., Blumberg, S., Schieve, L., Boyle, C., Perrin, J., Ghandour, R., … van Dyck, P. C. (2009). Prevalence of parent-reported diagnosis of autism spectrum disorder among children in the US, 2007. *Pediatrics, 124*, 1395–1403.

Krantz, P., & McClannahan, L. (1993). Teaching children with autism to initiate to peers: Effects of a script-fading procedure. *Journal of Applied Behavior Analysis, 26*, 121–133.

Krantz, P., & McClannahan, L. (1998). Social interaction skills for children with autism: A script-fading procedure for beginning. *Journal of Applied Behavior Analysis, 31*, 191–202.

Kunsch, C. A., Jitendra, A. K., & Sood, S. (2007). The effects of peer-mediated instruction in mathematics for students with learning problems: A research synthesis. *Learning Disabilities Research and Practice, 22*, 1–12.

Lang, R., Regester, A., Lauderdale, S., Ashbaugh, K., & Haring, A. (2010). Treatment of anxiety in autism spectrum disorders using cognitive behavior therapy: A systematic review. *Developmental Neurorehabilitation, 13*, 53–63.

Langdon, N., Carr, E., & Owen-DeSchryver, J. (2008). Functional analysis of precursors for serious problem behavior and related intervention. *Behavior Modification, 32*, 804–827.

LaSalle, R. (Reporter). (2009, November 12). North Georgia parents seek harsher punishment for bullies after son's suicide. *WDEF News 12*. Retrieved from http://wdef.com/news/north_georgia_parents_seek_harsher_punishment_for_bullies_after_sons_suicide/11/09

Laushey, K. M., Heflin, L. J., Shippen, M., Alberto, P. A., & Fredrick, L. (2009). Concept mastery routines to teach social skills to elementary children with high functioning autism. *Journal of Autism and Developmental Disorders, 39*, 1435–1448.

Leblanc, M., Ricciardi, J. N., & Luiselli, J. K. (2005). Improving discrete trial instruction by paraprofessional staff through an abbreviated performance feedback intervention. *Education and Treatment of Children, 28*, 76–82.

Lee, S., Simpson, R. L., & Shogren, K. A. (2007). Effects and implications of self-management for students with autism: A meta-analysis. *Focus on Autism and Other Developmental Disabilities, 22*, 2–13.

Lee, S., Wehmeyer, M. L., Soukup, J. H., & Palmer, S. B. (2010). Impact of curriculum modifications on access to the general education curriculum for students with disabilities. *Exceptional Children, 76*, 213–233.

Little, L. (2002). Middle-class mothers' perceptions of peer and sibling victimization among children with Asperger's syndrome and nonverbal learning disorders. *Issues in Comprehensive Pediatric Nursing, 24*, 43–57.

Lord, C., & Bishop, S. L. (2010). Autism spectrum disorders: Diagnosis, prevalence, and services for children and families. *Social Policy Report, 24*(2), 1–21.

Lovaas, O. I. (1987). Behavioral treatment and normal education and intellectual functioning in young autistic children. *Journal of Consulting and Clinical Psychology, 55*, 3–9.

Low, J., Goddard, E., & Melser, J. (2009). Generativity and imagination in autism spectrum disorder: Evidence from individual differences in children's impossible entity drawings. *British Journal of Psychology, 27*, 425–444.

Maccini, P., Mulcahy, C. A., & Wilson, M. G. (2007). A follow-up of interventions for secondary students with learning disabilities. *Learning Disabilities Research and Practice, 22*, 58–74.

Mancil, G. (2006). Functional communication training: A review of the literature related to children with autism. *Education and Training in Developmental Disabilities, 41*, 213–224.

Mancil, G., Conroy, M., & Haydon, T. (2009). Effects of a modified milieu therapy intervention on the social communicative behaviors of young children with autism spectrum disorders. *Journal of Autism & Developmental Disorders, 39*, 149–163.

Marckel, J., Neef, N., & Ferreri, S. (2006). A preliminary analysis of teaching improvisation with the picture exchange communication system to children with autism. *Journal of Applied Behavior Analysis, 39*, 109–115.

Mayes, S. D., & Calhoun, S. L. (2003). Ability profiles in children with autism: Influence of age and IQ. *Autism, 6*, 65–80.

Mayes, S., Calhoun, S., Murray, M., Morrow, J., Yurich, K., Mahr, F., … Petersen, C. (2009). Comparison of scores on the checklist for autism spectrum disorder, Childhood Autism Rating Scale, and Gilliam Asperger's Disorder Scale for children with low functioning autism, high functioning autism, Asperger's disorder, ADHD, and typical development. *Journal of Autism and Developmental Disorders, 39*, 1682–1693.

McDonnell, J., Johnson, J., Polychronis, S., Riesen, T., Jameson, M., & Kercher, K. (2006). Comparison of one-to-one embedded instruction in general education classes with small group instruction in special education classes. *Education and Training in Developmental Disabilities, 41*, 125–138.

McGee, G., Krantz, P., Mason, D., & McClannahan, L. (1983). A modified incidental-teaching procedure for autistic youth: Acquisition and generalization of receptive object labels. *Journal of Applied Behavior Analysis, 16*, 329–338.

McGee, G., Krantz, P. J., & McClannahan, L. E (1985). The facilitative effects of incidental teaching on preposition use by autistic children. *Journal of Applied Behavior Analysis, 18*, 17–31.

McGuire, J., Scott, S. S., & Shaw, S. F. (2006). Universal design and its applications in educational environments. *Remedial and Special Education, 27,* 166–175.

Militerni, R., Bravaccio, C., Falco, C., Fico, C., & Palermo, M. T. (2002). Repetitive behaviors in autistic disorder. *European Child and Adolescent Psychiatry, 11,* 210–218.

Miranda-Linne, F., & Melin, L. (1992). Acquisition, generalization, and spontaneous use of color adjectives: A comparison of incidental teaching and traditional discrete-trial procedures for children with autism. *Research in Developmental Disabilities, 13,* 191–210.

Moreno, J., Aguilera, A., & Saldana, D. (2008). Do Spanish parents prefer special schools for their children with autism? *Education and Training in Developmental Disabilities, 43,* 162–173.

Morgan, K. (2006). Is autism a stress disorder? What studies of nonautistic populations can tell us. In M. G. Baron, J. Groden, G. Groden, & L. P. Lipsitt (Ed), *Stress and coping in autism* (pp. 129–182). New York: Oxford University Press.

Morrison, L., Kamps, D., Garcia, J., & Parker, D. (2001). Peer mediation and monitoring strategies to improve initiation and social skills for students with autism. *Journal of Positive Behavior Interventions, 3,* 237–250.

Mruzek, D. W., Cohen, C., & Smith, T. (2007). Contingency contracting with students with ASD in a public school setting. *Journal of Developmental and Physical Disabilities, 19,* 103–114.

Mulick, J., & Butter, E. (2002). Educational advocacy for children with autism. *Behavioral Interventions, 17,* 57–74.

Mundy, P., Sullivan, L., & Mastergeorge, A. (2009). A parallel and distributed-processing model of joint attention, social cognition and autism. *Autism Research, 2,* 2–21.

Myles, B. S., & Adreon, D. (2001). Asperger Syndrome and adolescence: Practical solutions for school success. Shawnee Mission, KS: Autism Asperger Publishing.

Myles, B. S., Huggins, A., Rome-Lake, M., Hagiwara, T., Barnhill, G. P., & Griswold, D. E. (2003). Written language profile of children and youth with Asperger syndrome: From research to practice. *Education and Training in Developmental Disabilities, 38,* 362–369.

Myles, B. S., & Simpson, R. L. (2003). *Asperger syndrome: A guide for educators and parents* (2nd ed.). Austin, TX: Pro-Ed.

Myles, B. S., & Southwick, J. (1999). *Asperger Syndrome and difficult moments: Practical solutions for tantrums, rage, and meltdowns.* Shawnee Mission, KS: Autism Asperger Publishing.

National Autism Center. (2009). *National standards project: Addressing the need for evidence-based practice guidelines for autism spectrum disorders.* Retrieved from http://www.nationalautismcenter.org/about/national.php

National Institute of Child Health and Human Development. (2000). *Report of the National Reading Panel. Teaching children to read: An evidence-based assessment of the scientific research literature on reading and its implications for reading instruction* (NIH Publication No. 00-4769). Washington, DC: U.S. Government Printing Office.

National Research Council. (2001). *Educating children with autism* (Committee on Educational Interventions for Children with Autism. Division of Behavioral and Social Sciences and Education). Washington, DC: National Academy Press.

Neef, N. A., Walters, J., & Egel, A. L. (1984). Establishing generative yes/no responses in developmentally disabled children. *Journal of Applied Behavior Analysis, 17,* 453–460.

Newman, B., & Buffington, D. M. (1995). Self-management of schedule following in three teenagers with autism. *Behavioral Disorders, 20,* 190–196.

Newman, T. M., Macomber, D., Naples A. J., Babitz, T., Volkmar, F., & Grigorenko, E. L. (2007). Hyperlexia in children with autism spectrum disorders. *Journal of Autism and Developmental Disorders, 37,* 760–774.

No Child Left Behind Act of 2001, 20 U.S.C. 70 § 6301 *et seq.* (2002).

O'Connor, I., & Klein, P. (2004). Exploration of strategies for facilitating the reading comprehension of high-functioning students with autism spectrum disorders. *Journal of Autism & Developmental Disorders, 34,* 115–127.

Odom, S., Boyd, B., Hall, L., & Hume, K. (2010). Evaluation of comprehensive treatment models for individuals with autism spectrum disorders. *Journal of Autism and Developmental Disorders, 40,* 425–436.

O'Reilly, M., Sigafoos, J., Lancioni, G., Edrisinha, C., & Andrews, A. (2005). An examination of the effects of a classroom activity schedule on levels of self-injury and engagement for a child with severe autism. *Journal of Autism & Developmental Disorders, 35,* 305–311.

Osborne, L., McHugh, L., Saunders, J., & Reed, P. (2008). Parenting stress reduces the effectiveness of early teaching interventions for autistic spectrum disorders. *Journal of Autism and Developmental Disorders, 38,* 1092–1103.

Ozonoff, S., Strayer, D., McMahon, W., & Filloux, F. (1994). Executive function abilities in autism and Tourette syndrome: An information processing approach. *Journal of Child Psychology & Psychiatry & Allied Disciplines, 35,* 1015–1032.

Palmen, A., Didden, R., & Arts, M. (2008). Improving question asking in high functioning adolescents with autism spectrum disorders. *Autism: The International Journal of Research & Practice, 12,* 83–98.

Panerai, S., Zingale, M., Trubia, G., Finocchiaro, M., Zuccarello, R., Ferri, R., & Maurizio, E. (2009). Special education versus inclusive education: The role of the TEACCH program. *Journal of Autism & Developmental Disorders, 39,* 874–882.

Perry, A., Cummings, A., Geier, J., Freeman, N. L., Hughes, S., Managhan, T., & ... Williams, J. (2011). Predictors of outcome for children receiving intensive behavioral intervention in a large, community-based program. *Research in Autism Spectrum Disorders, 5,* 592–603.

Pimperton, H., & Nation, K. (2010). Suppressing irrelevant information from working memory: Evidence for domain-specific deficits in poor comprehenders. *Journal of Memory and Language, 62,* 380–391.

Preston, D., & Carter, M. (2009). A review of the efficacy of the picture exchange communication system intervention. *Journal of Autism and Developmental Disorders, 39,* 1471–1486.

Reaven, J. A., Blakely-Smith, A., Nichols, S., Dasari, M., Flanigan, E., & Hepburn, S. (2009). Cognitive-behavioral group treatment for anxiety symptoms in children with high-functioning autism spectrum disorders: A pilot study. *Focus on Autism and Other Developmental Disabilities, 24,* 27–37.

Rehfeldt, R., & Root, S. (2005). Establishing derived requesting skills in adults with severe developmental disabilities. *Journal of Applied Behavior Analysis, 38,* 101–105.

Richler, J., Huerta, M., Bishop, S., & Lord, C. (2010). Developmental trajectories of restricted and repetitive behaviors and interests in children with autism spectrum disorders. *Development & Psychopathology, 22,* 55–69.

Robinson, S., Goddard, L., Dritschel, B., Wisley, M., & Howlin, P. (2009). Executive functions in children with autism spectrum disorders. *Brain and Cognition, 71,* 362–368.

Rogers, S. J. (1999). Intervention for young children with autism: From research to practice. *Infants and Young Children, 12,* 1–16.

Rogers, S., & Vismara, L. (2008). Evidence-based comprehensive treatments for early autism. *Journal of Clinical Child & Adolescent Psychology, 37,* 8–38.

Rosenberg, R., Mandell, D., Farmer, J., Law, J., Marvin, A., & Law, P. (2010). Psychotropic medication use among children with autism spectrum disorders enrolled in a national registry, 2007–2008. *Journal of Autism and Developmental Disorders, 40,* 342–351.

Rumsey, J., Rapoport, J., & Sceery, W. (1985). Autistic children as adults: Psychiatric, social, and behavioral outcomes. *Journal of the American Academy of Child Psychiatry, 24,* 465–473.

Rutter, M. (1985). The treatment of autistic children. *Journal of Psychology and Psychiatry, 26,* 193–214.

Sallows, G., & Graupner, T. (2005). Intensive behavioral treatment for children with autism: Four-year outcome and predictors. *American Journal on Mental Retardation, 110,* 417–438.

Sarokoff, R., Taylor, B., & Poulson, C. (2001). Teaching children with autism to engage in conversational exchanges: Script fading with embedded textual stimuli. *Journal of Applied Behavior Analysis, 34*(1), 81–84.

Schlosser, R., & Wendt, O. (2008). Effects of augmentative and alternative communication intervention on speech production in children with autism: A systematic review. *American Journal of Speech-Language Pathology, 17,* 212–230.

Sherer, M. R., & Schreibman, L. (2005). Individual behavioral profiles and predictors of treatment effectiveness for children with autism. *Journal of Consulting and Clinical Psychology, 73,* 525–538.

Sigafoos, J., O'Reilly, M., Ma, C., Edrisinha, C., Cannella, H., & Lancioni, G. (2006). Effects of embedded instruction versus discrete-trial training on self-injury, correct responding, and mood in a child with autism. *Journal of Intellectual & Developmental Disability, 31,* 196–203.

Simpson, R. L., Mundscenk, N., & Heflin, L. J. (in press). Issues, policies, and recommendations for improving the education of learners with autism. *Journal of Disability Policies Study.*

Smith, T. (2001). Discrete trial training in the treatment of autism. *Focus on Autism and Other Developmental Disabilities, 16,* 86–92.

Smith, T., Groen, A., & Wynn, J. (2000). Randomized trial of intensive early intervention for children with pervasive developmental disorder. *American Journal on Mental Retardation, 105,* 269–285.

Smith, T., Mruzek, D., Wheat, L., & Hughes, C. (2006). Error correction in discrimination training for children with autism. *Behavioral Interventions, 21,* 245–263.

Sofronoff, K., Attwood, T., & Hinton, S. (2005). A randomized controlled trial of a CBT intervention for anxiety in children with Asperger syndrome. *Journal of Child Psychology and Psychiatry, 46,* 1152–1162.

Steege, M., Mace, F., Perry, L., & Longenecker, H. (2007). Applied behavior analysis: Beyond discrete trial teaching. *Psychology in the Schools, 44,* 91–99.

Stevenson, C., Krantz, P., & McClannahan, L. (2000). Social interaction skills for children with autism: A script-fading procedure for nonreaders. *Behavioral Interventions, 15,* 1–20.

Stoelb, M., Yarnal, R., Miles, J., Takahashi, T., Farmer, J., & McCathren, R. (2004). Predicting responsiveness to treatment of children with autism: A retrospective study of the importance of physical dysmorphology. *Focus on Autism & Other Developmental Disabilities, 19,* 66–77.

Sulzer-Azaroff, B., Hoffman, A., Horton, C., Bondy, A., & Frost, L. (2009). The picture exchange communication system (PECS): What do the data say? *Focus on Autism and Other Developmental Disabilities, 24,* 89–103.

Sundberg, M. L., & Partington, J. W. (1998). *Teaching language to children with autism or other developmental disabilities.* Pleasant Hill, CA: Behavior Analysts.

Suter, J. C., & Giangreco, M. F. (2009). Numbers that count: Exploring special education and paraprofessional service delivery in inclusion-oriented schools. *Journal of Special Education, 43*, 81–93.

Test, D. W., & Ellis, M. F. (2005). The effects of LAP fractions on addition and subtraction of fractions with students with mild disabilities. *Education and Treatment of Children, 28*, 11–24.

Thomas, G., Barratt, P., Clewley, H., Joy, H., Potter, M., & Whitaker, P. (1998). *Asperger syndrome*. Cambridge, England: Cambridge University Press.

Tiger, J. H., Fisher, W. W., Bouxsein, K. J. (2009). Therapist and self-monitored DRO contingencies as a treatment for the self-injurious skin picking of a young man with Asperger syndrome. *Journal of Applied Behavior Analysis, 42*, 315–319.

Tincani, M., Crozier, S., & Alazetta, L. (2006). The picture exchange communication system: Effects on manding and speech development for school-aged children with autism. *Education and Training in Developmental Disabilities, 41*, 177–184.

Tsatsanis, K. (2003). Outcome research in Asperger syndrome and autism. *Child and Adolescent Psychiatric Clinics of North America, 12*, 47–63.

VanBergeijk, E., Klin, A., & Volkmar, F. (2008). Supporting more able students on the autism spectrum: College and beyond. *Journal of Autism and Developmental Disorders, 38*, 1359–1370.

van Roekel, E., Scholte, R. H. J., & Didden, R. (2010). Bullying among adolescents with autism spectrum disorders: Prevalence and perceptions. *Journal of Autism and Developmental Disorders, 40*, 63–73.

Volker, M., & Lopata, C. (2008). Autism: A review of biological bases, assessment, and intervention. *School Psychology Quarterly, 23*, 258–270.

Volker, M. A., Lopata, C., Smerbeck, A. M., Knoll, V. A., Thomeer, M. L., Toomey, J. A., & Rodgers, J. D. (2010). BASC-2 PRS profiles for students with high-functioning autism spectrum disorders. *Journal of Autism and Developmental Disorders, 40*, 188–199.

Volkmar, F., Lord, C., Bailey, A., Schultz, R., & Klin, A. (2004). Autism and pervasive developmental disorders. *Journal of Child Psychology and Psychiatry, 45*, 135–170.

Volkmar, F., & Nelson, D. (1990). Seizure disorders in autism. *Journal of the American Academy of Child and Adolescent Psychiatry, 29*, 127–129.

Volman, M., van Schendel, B., & Jongmans, M. (2006). Handwriting difficulties in primary school children: A search for underlying mechanisms. *American Journal of Occupational Therapy, 60*, 451–460.

Wacker, D., Steege, M., Northup, J., & Sasso, G., Berg, W., Reimers, T., … Donn, L. (1990). A component analysis of functional communication training across three topographies of severe behavior problems. *Journal of Applied Behavior Analysis, 23*, 417–429.

Wainscot, J. J., Naylor, P., Sutcliffe, P., Tantam, D., & Williams, J. V. (2008). Relationships with peers and use of the school environment of mainstream secondary school pupils with Asperger syndrome (high-functioning autism): A case-controlled study. *International Journal of Psychology and Psychological Therapy, 8*, 25–38.

Warren, S., & Gazdag, G. (1990). Facilitating early language development with milieu intervention procedures. *Journal of Early Intervention, 14*, 62–86.

Webb, K. W., Patterson, K. B., Syverud, S. M., & Seabrooks-Blackmore, J. J. (2008). Evidence based practices that promote transition to postsecondary education: Listening to a decade of expert voices. *Exceptionality, 16*, 192–206.

Werts, M. G., Zigmond, N., & Leeper, D. C. (2001). Paraprofessional proximity and academic engagements: Students with disabilities in primary age classrooms. *Education and Training in Mental Retardation and Developmental Disabilities, 36*, 424–440.

Whalon, K., Al Otaiba, S., & Delano, M. (2009). Evidence-based reading instruction for individuals with autism spectrum disorders. *Focus on Autism and Other Developmental Disabilities, 24*, 3–16.

Whalon, K., & Hanline, M. (2008). Effects of a reciprocal questioning intervention on the question generation and responding of children with autism spectrum disorder. *Education and Training in Developmental Disabilities, 43*, 367–387.

Wilde, L., Koegel, L., & Koegel, R. (1992). *Increasing success in school through priming: A training manual*. Santa Barbara: University of California.

Whitby, P. J. S., & Mancil, G. R. (2009). Academic achievement profiles of children with high functioning autism and Asperger syndrome: A review of the literature. *Education and Training in Developmental Disabilities, 44*, 551–560.

White, S. W., Ollendick, T., Scahill, L., Oswald, D., & Albano, A. M. (2009). Preliminary efficacy of a cognitive-behavioral treatment program for anxious youth with autism spectrum disorders. *Journal of Autism and Developmental Disorders, 39*, 652–1662.

White S. W., Oswald D., Ollendick, T., & Scahill, L. (2009). Anxiety in children and adolescents with autism spectrum disorders. *Clinical Psychology Review, 29*, 216–229.

White, S. W. & Roberson-Nay, R. (2009). Anxiety, social deficits, and loneliness in youth with autism spectrum disorders. *Journal of Autism and Developmental Disorders, 39*, 1006–1013.

White, S. W., Scahill, L., Klin, A., Koenig, K., & Volkmar, F. R. (2007). Educational placements and service use patterns of individuals with autism spectrum disorders. *Journal of Autism and Developmental Disorders, 37*, 1403–1412.

Wilkinson, L. A. (2005). Supporting the inclusion of a student with Asperger syndrome: A case study using conjoint behavioural consultation and self-management. *Educational Psychology in Practice, 21,* 307–326.

Witzel, B. S. (2005). Using CSR to teach algebra to students with math difficulties in inclusive settings. *Learning Disabilities, 3,* 49–60.

Wolery, M., & Anthony, L. (1997). Training elementary teachers to embed instruction during classroom activities. *Education & Treatment of Children, 20,* 40–58.

Wood, J. J., Drahota, A., Sze, K., Har, K., Chiu, A., & Langer, D. A. (2009). Cognitive behavioral therapy for anxiety in children with autism spectrum disorders: A randomized, controlled trial. *Journal of Child Psychology and Psychiatry, 50,* 224–234.

Woods, T. (1987). Programming common antecedents: A practical strategy for enhancing the generality of learning. *Behavioural Psychotherapy, 15,* 158–180.

Young, A., Ruble, L., & McGrew, J. (2009). Public vs. private insurance: Cost, use, accessibility, and outcomes of services for children with autism spectrum disorders. *Research in Autism Spectrum Disorders, 3,* 1023–1033.

12

SOCIAL SKILLS INTERVENTIONS AND PROGRAMMING FOR LEARNERS WITH AUTISM SPECTRUM DISORDERS

Richard L. Simpson

UNIVERSITY OF KANSAS

Jennifer B. Ganz and Rose Mason

TEXAS A&M UNIVERSITY

Introduction

From the original writings on autism spectrum disorder (ASD) by pioneers such as Kanner (1943) and Asperger (1944), and extending to judgments and perspectives of current organizations (e.g., Autism Society of America, 2009), researchers (Legoff & Sherman, 2006; Reichow & Volkmar, 2009), and practitioners (Garcia Winner, 2008; Thiemann & Kamps, 2008), there is consensus that social skills and interaction impairments are defining characteristics of ASD (American Psychiatric Association, 2000). For that reason there is strong agreement that development and practice of age-appropriate social skills and opportunities for high quality and positive social interaction opportunities are essential for people, particularly students, with ASD. Researchers and practitioners have demonstrated the benefits and social validity of improved social skills capacity among people diagnosed with autism-related disabilities (Lee, Odom, & Loftin, 2007; Stichter, Randolph, Gage, & Schmidt, 2007) as well as the negative effects and outcomes associated with failure to develop and support appropriate social skills (Thiemann & Kamps, 2008). To be sure, social skills and competent social interaction capacity positively impact academic and school-related outcomes, employment success, leisure opportunities, independent living capability, quality of life, and myriad other facets connected to successful human experiences throughout the life cycle (Cotugno, 2009).

The obvious need for social skills instruction and support for students with ASD is challenged by the undeniable reality that improving social behavior is difficult and that many commonly used social skills interventions and supports are untested and lack scientific validity (Gresham, 1998; Simpson, 2008). Social skills instruction and social engineering methods for people with ASD are also less studied and understood, compared to interventions for communication, behavior, and other salient features of autism (Reichow & Volkmar, 2009). Thus, there are relatively few evidence-based social enhancement and support programs appropriate for students with ASD from which practitioners may choose. Finally, a variety of factors commonly reduce attention and time available for school-based social skills instruction and social activities for students with ASD and other disabilities, such as increased emphasis on preparing pupils for high stakes academic assessments (Simpson, 2008).

Stakeholders involved in educating, supporting, and parenting children and youth with ASD can recognize myriad social excesses and problems worthy of intervention. They also recognize that identifying and implementing scientifically based social skills development strategies can mitigate these problems; and that social skills improvement bodes well for enhanced school, home, and community success (Thieman & Kamps, 2008). Yet, lack of well-designed and practitioner-friendly evidence-based social skills instruction and interaction support methods limit efficient and effectual support of learners' social skills needs (Gresham, 1998). In this connection, this chapter discusses social skills intervention and social interaction support strategies. Particular attention is given to the effective-practice credentials of these intervention strategies, underlying theoretical and scientific support for the methods, and their scientific and practical capacity to bring about desired outcomes. Methods are reviewed by three basic groupings: (a) explicit social skills instruction strategies; (b) social understanding, social problem solving, and interpretation methods; and (c) peer-mediated programs.

Historical Background and Overview of Social Skills Considerations

Across the spectrum, people diagnosed with ASD have difficulty understanding and following rules that govern human conduct as well as comprehending and complying with accepted protocol for interacting with others (Cotugno, 2009; Thieman & Kamps, 2008). To be fair, the conventions, customs, and standards connected to social expectations and rules are complex and variable, making them especially difficult to teach and practice with learners with ASD. Social rules and expectations also vary across settings, situations, people, ages, cultures, and countless other variables; and social principles that govern conduct tend to be situation- and circumstance-specific, rather than rigid and universally applicable. Social skills and social interaction instruction and programming must thus emphasize quality and situation suitability rather than merely increasing the quantity of social initiations or responses (Baker, 2004).

Varied explanations for social skills and social interaction problems among people with ASD, based on a variety of theoretical models, have been advanced. Explanations include problems of executive function, emotional regulation difficulties, and deficits in theory of mind (Baron-Cohen & Swettenham, 1997; Thieman & Kamps, 2008).

Executive Functioning

Individuals with ASD are commonly believed to have impairments in cognitive and self-regulatory processes known as *executive functioning*. Executive function encompasses the ability to complete complex tasks by employing self-regulatory skills and focus on attainment of goals (Calhoun, 2006). Executive functioning specifically involves (a) inhibition (i.e., preventing behaviors or responses that are counter to goal-attainment); (b) cognitive flexibility or set-shifting (i.e., interpreting ideas in multiple ways, having novel thoughts, and adjusting thought processes to work toward reaching goals); (c) working memory (i.e., holding information in short-term memory for the purpose of the task at hand); and (d) planning (i.e., thinking through strategies and completing multiple steps toward a goal; Pennington, 1997). Albeit cognitive in nature, executive functioning skills are fundamental elements of successful social functioning.

People with ASD typically display impairments in executive functioning that manifest as sociocommunicative problems (Calhoun, 2006). In this connection, they often struggle with executive performance and execution, which negatively impacts their social functioning (Pennington & Ozonoff, 1996). Such impairments include difficulty inhibiting socially unacceptable responses (Ozonoff, 1997). An inability to produce multiple solutions and options for problems and scenarios, compared to same-aged peers, impacts social problem solving and the ability for younger children with ASD to do such things as engage with peers in novel pretend play activities (Hill, 2004). Restricted interests and repetitive behaviors, which may be a manifestation of cognitive inflexibility, frequently are associated with social rejection (Turner, 1999). Mental inflexibility also impacts social situations by making it difficult to engage in new, more effective social strategies, in favor of more comfortable, practiced, but less effective or ineffective social strategies. Planning skills and problem solving related to social matters are difficult for individuals with ASD as well, including complex planning, following through, and reevaluating plans related to unexpected changes (Calhoun, 2006; Joseph, 1999; Solomon, Goodlin-James, & Anders, 2004).

Emotional Regulation

Emotional dysregulation is another area that has been used to account for social-emotional functioning problems of people with ASD. Emotional regulation is a type of self-monitoring and self-regulation skills. Self-regulation is a complex skills set that is believed to be underdeveloped in persons with autism-related disabilities, likely as a result of executive functioning impairments (Hill, 2004; Joseph, McGrath, & Tager-Flusberg, 2005). Self-monitoring, an element of self-regulation, involves being aware of one's own behaviors and internal thoughts, as well as the ability to modify one's own thoughts and behaviors. Impairments in the ability to self-monitor are associated with problems in planning and execution of socially appropriate initiations and responses, cognitive flexibility, and inhibition. Further, people with ASD, even if they have relatively strong language skills, may fail to use self-governing language, such as internal self-talk, for self-regulation purposes (Joseph et al., 2005).

Emotional regulation includes the ability to (a) endure varied sensory and social stimuli (e.g., tolerate loud noise in the cafeteria or sudden social interactions); (b) monitor one's own responses relative to novel situations; (c) communicate one's own emotional state in a socially acceptable manner; and (d) request assistance or preferences in a socially appropriate manner (Laurent & Rubin, 2004). These skills impact an individual's ability to build and maintain friendships, engage in interactions, manage novel situations, and participate successfully in activities with groups (Laurent & Rubin, 2004; National Research Council, 2000; Prizant, Wetherby, Rubin, & Laurent, 2003).

Children and adults with ASD have numerous difficulties with emotional regulation. They have difficulties appropriately communicating their own intentions and comprehending the intentions of others; distinguishing affective and preferential expressions of others and using appropriate affective expressions themselves; using conventional means to communicate emotions; and understanding the social-contextual meaning of expressions of others and responding to them appropriately (Bauminger, 2007; Blacher, 2007; Winner, 2008). Some people with high functioning ASD have demonstrated the ability to recognize basic emotions such as happiness, sadness, anger, and fear (Capps, 1992; LaCava, Golan, Baron-Cohen, & Myles, 2007), yet they often have difficulty recognizing more complex emotions, such as guilt or pride; and difficulty explaining the contexts underlying complex emotional states.

It is believed that many people with ASD engage in nonconventional behaviors—such as self-stimulatory behaviors, tantrums, inappropriate affective expressions, and fleeing stressful and nonpreferred social and sensory situations—as a result of these emotional regulation challenges (Laurent & Rubin, 2004). For example, although typical 10-year-olds can express unhappiness verbally, a 10-year-old with autism may resort to a tantrum if told by the teacher that recess is over. Such behaviors often result in decreased access to social and academic opportunities and may contribute to negative perceptions of students with ASD, such as assumptions that students with autism-related disabilities are generally unmotivated, egocentric, manipulative, aggressive, or noncompliant (Prizant et al., 2003).

Theory of Mind

Theory of mind impairments is another theoretical model used to account for social under-standing and social interaction shortcomings and difficulties among people diagnosed with ASD (Baron-Cohen, 1995). Theory of mind impairments may also be related to and the result of executive functioning problems and skills deficits (Ozonoff, 1997; Perner & Lang, 2000). The-ory of mind involves the skills of comprehending and assessing others' behavior based on mak-ing correct interpretations and judgments about their internal or mental states, including their beliefs, perceptions, knowledge and perspectives, emotions, and goals (Tager-Flusberg, 2007).

A classic assessment of theory of mind, the Sally-Anne false-belief test (Frith, 1989), involves presenting a story in which two dolls, Sally and Anne, are together. Sally puts a marble in a basket and leaves. Then, Anne moves the marble to a box and Sally then returns. Respondents participating in the Salle-Anne test are asked where Sally will look for her marble. Children with autism tend to incorrectly say that Sally will look in the box, demonstrating difficulties considering situations from another's point of view. This incorrect judgment is believed to reflect a theory of mind deficit. Recently, more complex tests of theory of mind skills have been developed. The Strange Stories test (Happé, 1994) involves presentation of a series of stories in which characters say things that they do not mean literally, while providing contextual information that infers the characters' mental states and motivation. Adolescents and adults with ASD have performed relatively poorly on such tests when compared to typically developing peers.

Successful social interactions are thought to rely heavily on intact theory of mind skills (Simpson, Myles, & LaCava, 2008). Researchers have documented difficulties people with ASD have with the ability to infer others' thinking (Lawson, Baron-Cohen, & Wheelwright, 2004) and make predictions of others' behavior based on social understanding (Morton, Frith, & Leslie, 1991). Theory of mind impairments among children with ASD are evident as early as 4 years, evidenced by lack of orientation toward people, difficulty judging social expectations connected to setting and environmental factors, and difficulties with joint attention (Tager-Flusberg, 2007). Consistent with theory of mind theoretical models, such impairments are inferred to relate to sociocommunicative difficulties involving understanding others' emotional states based on behavioral and contextual cues (Joseph, 1999). Theory of mind impairments seem to be linked to social skills, expressive language, and abstract language understanding deficits, which are common in children with ASD, even those with relatively normal language and cognitive abilities (Tager-Flusberg, 2007). It is interesting to consider that some people with ASD, particularly those with normal language and intellectual functioning (e.g., Asperger syndrome and higher-functioning autism) are able to perform simple theory of mind tasks. They typically, however, do not perform as well as peers on more complex theory of mind tasks (Kaland, Callesen, Moller-Nielsen, Mortensen, & Smith, 2008).

Theory of mind impairments are evident across the lifespan for people with ASD, although those skills in people with ASD range from individuals who are generally unaware that others have different thoughts than themselves, to those who understand that people may have different thoughts and feelings but have difficulty in seeing and understanding these differences (Cashin &

Baker, 2009). For example, in young children with ASD, pretend play may be difficult because it requires that the child is able to manipulate objects that are substitutes for real objects and to project thoughts to dolls (Leslie, 1987). Older people with ASD commonly have difficulties inferring the intended messages or feelings of their peers during social interactions, which may be related to theory of mind impairments (Levy, 2007).

Based on the aforementioned theoretical models and related explanations for social skills problems among people with ASD, a variety of interventions and improvement programs have been developed and used with learners with social difficulty. These strategies and methods vary; however, there are several important points of agreement among designers, promoters, and users of social skills improvement interventions and programs. One such element of agreement is that social skills that are particularly important for children and youth with ASD are those that are foundational and suitable for a variety of situations (Thiemann & Kamps, 2008). Skills such as knowing how close to stand to another person when conversing and requesting and giving information appropriately can be used in school, home, and community settings; with a variety of individuals and groups in multiple situations; and in a flexible fashion relative to other circumstances. Thus, problems associated with teaching discrete social skills that are applicable only in limited situations versus more utilitarian foundational skills are commonly recognized (de Boer, 2009).

Another point of general agreement is that social skills targets should address different areas that correspond to differing social requirements and situations (Quill, 2000; Reichow & Volkmar, 2009). To function successfully in social settings, students need basic social interaction, relationship, and cooperation skills; self-management and personal responsibility skills; and school and academically related social skills (Simpson et al., 2008).

Social Interaction, Relationship, and Cooperation Skills. Social interaction, relationship, and cooperation skills include such behaviors as playing cooperatively with others, initiating and responding to social bids, sharing, engaging in age-appropriate conversations, participating in group problem solving activities, showing age-appropriate affection, recognizing and appropriately responding to authority and rules, and giving and accepting age-appropriate consequences and feedback.

Self-Management and Personal Responsibility Skills. Self-management and personal responsibility skills include self-awareness and communication of social interaction preferences (e.g., group size, activity, age, and gender of preferred peers), appropriate avoidance strategies (e.g., how to exit or avoid uncomfortable social situations), appropriate attention-seeking strategies, and recognizing and appropriately responding to authority and rules.

School and Academic Social Skills. School and academic social skills specifically recognize the importance of social aptitude in school and classroom settings, such as following classroom rules, direction compliance, and appropriate social behavior and participation skills within small group and cooperative group activities.

Overview of Categories of Social Skills Interventions

Based on different theoretical models and explanations for social deficits, multiple strategies for teaching social skills and engineering social interaction opportunities have been recommended (e.g., Garcia Winner, 2008; McGinnis & Goldstein, 1997; Quill, 2000; Sigafoos, O'Reilly, & de la Cruz, 2007). Many of these methods, however, lack confirmed effective practice credentials and firm scientific support (National Autism Center, 2009; Simpson et al., 2005). Thus prospective users of these programs often have limited objective means by which to vet their potential utility. All too often, practitioners are wholly dependent on informal and unreliable evaluations such as blogs, commercial brochures and Web sites, and word of mouth. To be sure there is much room for improvement in the way purported social skills training options are classified relative to their effective practice capacity.

This chapter focuses on three major forms of social skills instruction and support: (a) explicit instruction methods; (b) social understanding, interpretation, and problem solving strategies; and (c) peer-mediated programs.

Explicit Instruction of Identified Social Targets. Explicit instruction of identified social targets refers to teaching specific behaviors using structured instructional methods. Commonly employed explicit instructional methods include coaching students to correctly perform particular social behaviors; offering models of desired social behavior; providing opportunities for students to role play, practice, and rehearse identified skills; providing feedback and reinforcement to students relative to demonstrating specific skills; and providing opportunities for using and practicing skills in natural settings. Specific ways of implementing explicit instructional methods include adult social prompting and coaching, commercial and teacher-made social skills curricula and programs, and social scripts and video modeling.

Social Understanding and Social Problem Solving Interventions. Social understanding and social problem solving interventions are based on the premise that social difficulties and weaknesses of people diagnosed with ASD are primarily a result of deficient social-cognitive awareness and inadequate social problem solving skills. In accordance with this assumption, this approach to improving social communication and relationships involves teaching functional social cognition skills to students with ASD, especially students with Asperger disorder and higher-functioning autism. Strategies such as social stories (Gray & Garand, 1993) and social problem solving curricula (Baker, 2004) are used and thus assist students to understand social situations and the corresponding appropriate social behaviors; identify and interpret emotions (their own and those of others); understand the perspectives of others; expand and improve their theory of mind abilities; become more aware of verbal and nonverbal emotional cues that accompany social situations; improve their social executive capabilities and resources; and use social problem solving strategies.

Peer-Mediated Strategies. Peer-mediated strategies involve teaching socially competent peers of students with ASD to initiate, respond, and support social interactions with children and youth with ASD. Following training, peers are placed in social situations where they participate in social activities with learners with ASD. Subsequent to orientation and training, students with ASD and their peers participate in social activities generally independent of direct adult involvement. These natural peer interactions are used to develop social skills, facilitate peer interactions, and support development of peer relationships. Peer-mediated strategies often overlap with the previously described categories, particularly explicit instructional methods, in that they involve the implementation of such methods with the involvement of peer models or peers in the place of adult instructors.

The Evidence Base

In an effort to provide a synthesis of the evidence and to add to the existing body of literature reviews (Chan et al, 2009; Disalvo & Oswald, 2002; Matson, Matson, & Rivet, 2007; Reichow

& Volkmar, 2009) and meta-analyses (Bellini et al., 2007) of social skills interventions with people with ASD, 31 studies from peer-reviewed journals were reviewed. We included five literature reviews and meta-analyses. Although not exhaustive, our review of the evidence (see Table 12.1) provides a succinct understanding of the existing social skills research literature.

Consistent with the results of other literature reviews (Bellini et al., 2007; Reichow & Volkmar, 2009), the majority of the studies were conducted with participants 10 years of age and younger and the majority of these participants were male. With the exception of two social scripts studies (Loveland & Tunali, 1991; Stevenson, Krantz, & McClannahan, 2000), social interpretation and problem solving interventions were the only ones to include adolescents and adults, particularly for those interventions that focused on recognizing and understanding emotions. This is consistent with the analyses of others that limited research is available to support social skills interventions with secondary and postsecondary participants (Reichow & Volkmar, 2009; Stichter, Randolph, Gage, & Schmidt, 2007).

A crucial factor in producing meaningful target behavior changes, in addition to choosing evidenced-based practices, involves selecting practices that best correspond to the target behavior being addressed (Bellini, Peters, Benner, & Hopf, 2007). Results of this review indicate that both explicit strategies and peer-mediated strategies appear to have evidence of increasing specific conversation and communication skills such as initiation, play, and compliment-giving. Social interpretation and problem solving strategies do not have evidence for increasing these skills. The literature suggests that social interpretation strategies are best for increasing emotional recognition, recognizing and understanding what others might be thinking or feeling, and responding appropriately to social cues.

Results of our review generally revealed that the strongest evidence was for interventions based on explicit instructional methods and peer-mediated strategies (Bellini et al., 2007; Reichow & Volkmar, 2009; White, Keonig, & Scahill, 2007). Specific interventions with relatively strong effective-practice credentials include video modeling, script- and story-based strategies, peer training, and environmental supports (e.g., preferred social activities within predictable and structured settings; Marans, Rubin, & Laurent, 2005; Stichter, Randolph, Gage, & Schmidt, 2007).

Explicit Social Skills Instruction Research Base

The majority of research on improving social skills of people with ASD to date has fallen within the direct, explicit social skills instruction category. Such intervention approaches often have a strong basis in applied behavior analysis (Thiemann & Kamps, 2008). There are a variety of models of implementing explicit instruction, including social skills curricula and social skills groups (Rogers, 2000). Interventions that were found to have significant research support included modeling and script-based interventions (Reichow & Volkmar, 2009). Additional interventions (e.g., natural language paradigm, naturalistic teaching strategies) have been demonstrated to be a relatively promising means of improving communication and related social skills as well (National Autism Center, 2009; Ogletree, Oren, & Fischer, 2007).

We are particularly impressed with the effective practice qualifications of video modeling, including video self-modeling and video modeling with adults or peer models, and interventions involving instructing learners to use scripts. In this regard we are in agreement with conclusions of other researchers (e.g., Bellini & Akullian, 2007; Ganz et al., 2008; Matson, Matson, & Rivet, 2007; National Autism Center, 2009; Wang & Spillane, 2009) that these methods appear to have the potential to bring about desired social outcomes with a wide range of age groups, multiple levels of severity, and various socially valid target behaviors.

TABLE 12.1 Social Skills Intervention Research Summaries

Author/Year Publication	Subject Description (age range, sex, diagnostic category)	Procedures/Methods	Research Design	Targeted Social Behaviors	Summary of Outcomes/Findings
Social Skills Intervention Literature Reviews and Meta-analyses					
Bellini et al. (2007)	157 children with ASD	Meta-analysis of 55 single-subject design social skills intervention studies in school settings; social skills interventions included peer mediated methods and three other types	Effectiveness was calculated via effect size (i.e., PND)	Collateral (play skills, conversation and communication skills, joint attention, eye contact, prosocial skills) social skills; social interaction skills (initiations, responses, social participation)	Authors concluded that "social skills interventions are minimally effective" (p. 159); not statistically significant, but interventions were most effective with secondary-age youth; results not presented by type of intervention
Chan et al. (2009)	172 individuals with ASD	Review of 42 studies that involved peer-mediated interventions	Systematic review of literature	Sociocommunicative interactions (responses to initiations, joint attention, sharing, affection, behavior, academic behaviors)	Results suggested that peer-mediated interventions with individuals diagnosed with autism spectrum disorders are robust and potentially effective
Matson et al. (2007)	Approximately 240 participants with ASD	Review of 79 studies of social skills interventions with children with ASD; review was not exhaustive; studies each employed a recognized group or single subject research design	Systematic review of literature	"Social skills" were defined as "interpersonal responses with specific operational definitions that allow the child to adapt to the environment through verbal and nonverbal communication" (p. 683)	Increasing popularity of peer mediated, script-based, and modeling and reinforcement social skill training methods was documented

Author/Year Publication	Subject Description (age range, sex, diagnostic category)	Procedures/Methods	Research Design	Targeted Social Behaviors	Summary of Outcomes/Findings
Reichow & Volkmar (2009)	513 individuals with ASD	Review of 65 studies on social skill interventions; studies appeared in peer-reviewed journals between 2001 and 2008	Systematic review of literature	Social interactions, attention and engagement, joint attention, social initiations and play, language and communication, social imitations, greetings	Review results show that multiple utilitarian social skill interventions may be effective, including peer-mediated (recommended practice); social skill groups and video modeling were judged to be established and evidence based and promising evidence base practices, respectively

Explicit Instructional Methods (Modeling and Video Modeling)

Author/Year Publication	Subject Description (age range, sex, diagnostic category)	Procedures/Methods	Research Design	Targeted Social Behaviors	Summary of Outcomes/Findings
Apple et al. (2005)	Study 1: 5 years old; 2 boys; Asperger syndrome and autism Study 2: 4 to 5 years old; 2 boys and 1 girl; Asperger syndrome and autism	Study 1: Videos of peers as models, including three phases: video alone, video plus reinforcement, and reinforcement alone Study 2: Two phases: video modeling with peer models, self-management	Single-case multiple baseline across participants	Compliment-giving initiations and responses	Study 1: Compliment giving increased and maintained Study 2: Compliment giving responses increased with video modeling and maintained during self-management phase; initiations increased during self-management
Charlop & Milstein (1989)	6 to 7 years old; 3 boys; autism	Adult models of short conversations	Single-case multiple baseline across participants	Conversation skills	Conversation skills were quickly learned and generalized and maintained
Charlop-Christy et al. (2000)	7 to 11 years old; 4 boys and 1 girl; autism	Compared in vivo (live) modeling to video modeling	Single-case multiple baseline design across participants	Labeling emotions, play skills, conversation skills (additional non-social skills were also addressed)	Video modeling led to quicker acquisition of skills than in vivo modeling for most participants. Skills generalized
Gena et al. (2005)	3 to 5 years old; 2 boys and 1 girl; autism	Compared in-vivo to video modeling; both were combined with token and praise reinforcement	Single-case multiple baseline across participants	Verbal affective responses within corresponding contexts	Both interventions increased affective responses; results maintained and generalized to novel scenarios, people

(continued)

TABLE 12.1 Continued

Author/Year Publication	Subject Description (age range, sex, diagnostic category)	Procedures/Methods	Research Design	Targeted Social Behaviors	Summary of Outcomes/Findings
Kroeger et al. (2007)	4 to 6 years old; two groups (direct teach group had 9 boys and 4 girls, video modeling group had 11 boys and 1 girl); autism	One group participated in a direct instruction social skills group; one group participated in a video modeling instruction social skills group; both conditions divided into two groups of 4 to 6 children	Controlled group study; children matched by functioning level then randomly assigned	Responses, interactions, initiations, and pro-social behaviors	Both groups made gains; direct teach group more gains than video modeling group
Nikopoulos & Keenan (2004)	7 to 9 years old; 3 boys; autism	Video modeling with peer and adult model	Single-case multiple baseline design across participants	Initiations and interactive play	Social initiations, interactive play skills improved and maintained
Nikopoulos & Keenan (2007)	6 to 7 years old; 3 boys; autism (repeated with additional 7-year-old girl with autism)	Video modeling with peer and adult models	Single-case multiple baseline across participants (repetition consisted of A-B design)	Social initiations, interactive play, imitations, object play	Behaviors increased and generalized with novel peer, maintained at least 2 months (repetition with additional participant successful)
Sansoti & Powel-Smith (2008)	6 to 10 years old; 3 boys; autism and Asperger syndrome	Computerized Social Stories™ and video modeling	Single-case multiple baseline design across participants	Social communication	Social communication increased; results maintained for 2 weeks; one participant generalized skills
Schrandt et al. (2009)	4 to 8 years old; 3 boys and 1 girl; autism	Training package that included modeling, role playing, prompts, and reinforcement	Single-case multiple baseline across participants; multiple baseline across emotional categories	Empathetic statements and motor behavior	Statements, behaviors increased with intervention; results generalized to novel stimuli
Sherer et al. (2001)	4 to 11 years old; 5 boys; autism	Compared video self modeling versus peer video modeling	Single-case multiple baseline design with embedded alternating treatment design	Answering conversation questions	Participants who acquired skills (4 of the 5 participants) did so equally in both conditions

Author/Year Publication	Subject Description (age range, sex, diagnostic category)	Procedures/Methods	Research Design	Targeted Social Behaviors	Summary of Outcomes/Findings
Explicit Instructional Methods (Visual and Written Scripts)					
Ganz, Kaylor, et al. (2008)	7 to 12 years old; 2 boys and 1 girl; autism and PDDNOS (all verbal)	Written scripts and visual cues; school-based program; participants paired with classmates with developmental delays other than ASDs	Single-case multiple baseline design across activities with an embedded withdrawal design	Scripted statements (statements listed on cue cards), unscripted statements (different from what was listed on cue cards), and preservative speech	Increased appropriate and communicative speech; decreased preservative speech
Krantz & McClannahan (1998)	4 to 5 years old; 3 boys with autism	Scripts imbedded into children's visual schedules during play activities; scripts instructed to say, "look," or, "watch me"	Single-case multiple baseline design across participants	Verbalizations to request help: untrained verbalizations	Increased scripted and unscripted phrases; results maintained and generalized to novel communicative partners, activities
Lovel & Tunali (1991)	5 to 27 years old; 13 children with autism, 13 children with Down syndrome	During a tea party, the examiner feigned being robbed. Verbal social scripts of appropriate affect were modeled	Controlled group design; participants matched by mental age	Appropriate verbal affective responses	Students with Down syndrome used more affective verbalizations; students with autism required more modeling; fewer children with autism used appropriate verbalizations
Stevenson et al. (2000)	10 to 15 years old; 4 boys with autism (nonreaders)	Scripts were audio recorded and participants were taught to self-prompt with the audio device	Single-case multiple probe design across participants	Scripted and unscripted verbalizations	Scripted and unscripted phrases increased with an adult; results maintained when scripts were faded
Peer-Mediated Interventions					
Ganz & Flores (2008)	4 to 5 years old; 3 boys; autism; 4 typically developing preschool children (1 boy, 3 girls)	Visual scripts with line drawings and written words implemented during pretend play activities with typically developing peers; peers received visual supports to teach peer-mediation skills	Single-case changing criterion design	Scripted phrases, context-relevant comments, use of any speech, unscripted phrases, verbal responses	Scripted phrases, context-relevant comments, use of any speech increased in all participants; unscripted phrases, verbal responses variable; scripts were not entirely faded; results repeated with 2 additional activities, scripts

(continued)

TABLE 12.1 Continued

Author/Year Publication	Subject Description (age range, sex, diagnostic category)	Procedures/Methods	Research Design	Targeted Social Behaviors	Summary of Outcomes/Findings
Owen-DeSchryver et al. (2008)	7 to 10 years old; 3 boys; autism and Asperger syndrome; 7 typically developing peers	Typical peers trained in peer mediation; observations were during lunch and recess	Single-case multiple baseline design across participants	Social initiations and responses of typical students towards students with ASD	Peers increased social initiations with students with ASD; peers increased responses to social initiations by students with ASD; untrained peers increased interactions toward students with ASD
Sawyer et al. (2005)	4 years old; boy; autism (limited speech and receptive language)	Took place in integrated preschool; priming, prompting, and praise were implemented during play with typically developing peers	Single-case alternating treatment design	Verbal and physical sharing with typically developing peer	Improved verbal, physical sharing with nondisabled peer
Thiemann & Goldstein (2004)	6 to 9 years old; 5 boys with autism or Asperger syndrome and 101 typically developing peers	Children with autism paired with peers; peers were trained in peer-mediation; children with ASD and their teachers generated scripts	Single-case multiple baseline design across participants	Verbal requests, comments, compliments, asking for information, responses	Peer training increased initiations, responses in 2 children with ASD; direct instruction of scripts increased dependent variables for all participants; social validity positive
Social Problem-Solving Interventions					
Golan & Baron-Cohen (2006) – Experiment 1	Study 1: home group: 19 adults; Asperger syndrome, autism; Control Group: 22 adults; Asperger syndrome, autism; Typical Control Group: 24 adults Study 2: 13 adults in each group (software/tutor, social skills course, control); Asperger syndrome, autism, typically developing	Study 1: 10 weeks of *Mindreading* intervention Study 2: 10 weeks of *Mindreading* intervention plus tutoring or social skills group intervention	RCT	Emotional recognition	Study 1: Intervention group improved significantly ($p < .001$ or $p < .005$) on emotional recognition tasks Study 2: Software group improved significantly ($p < .01$, $p < .001$) on tasks assessed; social skills group did not

Author/Year Publication	Subject Description (age range, sex, diagnostic category)	Procedures/Methods	Research Design	Targeted Social Behaviors	Summary of Outcomes/Findings
Lacava et al. (2007)	8 to 11 years old; 6 boys, 2 girls; Asperger syndrome	10 weeks of *Mindreading* software instruction	Nonequivalent pre- and posttest experimental group design	Theory of Mind: understanding emotions	Significant difference ($p < .05$) between pre- and posttest for all 3 areas assessed
Silver & Oakes (2001)	10 to 18 years old; 11; autism, Asperger syndrome	"Normal" instruction or the *Emotion Trainer* 10 times over 10 days	RCT	Emotional understanding; emotional recognition and prediction	Statistically significant ($p < .05$) improvement in experimental group versus control in all areas assessed
McKay & Dunlop (2007)	6 to 16 years old; 38 boys, 10 girls; autism, Asperger syndrome, unspecified ASD	Social skills groups including direct instruction and unstructured activity	Pre- and posttest assessment (effect size measures) of self and parent reports	Perspective taking, friendship skills, conversation skills	Statistically significant gains in all areas assessed; limited information regarding instruction that occurred during groups, no fidelity checks of groups
Solomon et al. (2004)	8 to 12 years old; 18 boys (9 in an experimental group and 9 in a control group); autism, Asperger syndrome, PDDNOS (IQ of 75 or above)	Pre- and postassessment following implementation of *The Social Adjustment Enhancement Curriculum* and parent training	RCT	Emotional recognition, theory of mind, problem solving	Facial expression intervention participants made statistically significant increase ($p = .003$); theory of mind: not a statistically significant increase for Strange Stories Test; statistically significant improvement on Faux Pas Stories task increase ($p > .001$)
Chan & O'Reilly (2008)	5 to 6 years old; 2 boys; autism	10 to 20 minute sessions of reading Social Story™, discussing questions, and role play	Single-case multiple baseline design across behaviors	Social interactions, hand-raising, initiations, vocalizations	Improvement in all behaviors; results maintained
Delano & Snell (2006)	6 and 9 years old; 3 boys; autism	Reading Social Story™, comprehension check, and play session	Single-case multiple probe design across participants	Social engagement	Increase in social engagement for all participants; maintenance and generalization

(continued)

TABLE 12.1 Continued

Author/Year Publication	Subject Description (age range, sex, diagnostic category)	Procedures/Methods	Research Design	Targeted Social Behaviors	Summary of Outcomes/Findings
Dodd et al. (2008)	9 and 12 years old; 2 boys; PDDNOS	Parents read picture and text Social Story™ to participant prior to engagement in play session with siblings 3 times weekly for 4 weeks	Single-case multiple baseline design across participants; multiple baseline design across behaviors	Compliments, Directions from adults	Direction giving increased, compliments decreased for one participant; compliments initially increased for second participant, followed by decreasing trend
Reichow & Sabornie (2009)	11 years old; 1 boy; autism	Participant independently read illustrated social story prior to school; visual cue card implemented	Single-case reversal design	Verbal greeting	Initiations increased with story, decreased when withdrawn; cue cards maintained frequency of initiations
Sansoti & Powell-Smith (2008)	6 to 10 years old; 3 boys, autism, Asperger syndrome	Participants watched computerized Social Story™ followed by a video model	Single-case multiple baseline design across participants	Joining in and maintaining conversations	Intervention alone increased target behavior for one participant; other participants required a verbal reminder to use skill, resulting in increased target behavior
Hutchins & Prelock (2006)	6 and 12 years old; 1 boy and 1 girl; unspecified ASD	Implementation of Social Stories™ and comic strip conversations	Single case A-B design for each	Cooperation, perspective taking, theory of mind	Improvement; however, but significant limitations due to design and assessment method
Wellman et al. (2002)	5 to 18 years old; 16 boys and 1 girl; autism	Utilized Sally Anne figures and thought bubbles to teach question answering regarding others' thoughts	Pre- and posttest (t-test)	False beliefs, theory of mind	Statistically significant improvement in answering questions except for Smarties task; no generalization assessed

Note: ASD = autism spectrum disorders; PND = percentage of non-overlapping data; RCT = randomized controlled trial

Social Understanding and Problem Solving Research Base

Social understanding, interpretation, and problem solving skills and strategies aimed at increasing theory of mind and perspective taking are increasingly being considered pivotal elements in teaching effective social exchanges (Feng, Lo, Tsai, & Cartledge, 2008; Garcia Winner, 2008; Lawson, Baron-Cohen, & Wheelwright, 2004). Undeniably, difficulties experienced by people with ASD in evaluating social interactions and responding accordingly, whether in group or one-to-one situations, result in problems in making initial contacts and forming and maintaining long-term relationships (Lacava, Golan, Baron-Cohen, & Myles, 2007; MacKay, Knott, & Dunlop, 2007). Several interventions have been developed in an effort to increase social awareness and social understanding skills among people with ASD. That these interventions are based on the recognition that it is impossible to teach every distinctive, specific skills appropriate for unique circumstances needed for social success makes them attractive. Moreover, addressing underlying social understanding and related problems such as abstract skills deficits suggests that these methods will be better able to promote independent social functioning and skills generalization. Yet, in spite of these strengths and the obvious importance of this type of training, the research on enhancing social understanding and social problem solving skills is limited (Mackay et al., 2007; Reichow & Sabornie, 2009).

There appears to be some evidence to support story-based interventions, such as social narratives and Comic Strip Conversations™. For instance Simpson et al. (2005) identified social stories as a promising practice and cartooning as a method with limited supporting information. Others, such as the *National Standards Report* (National Autism Center, 2009), noted that the evidence in support of theory of mind training was emerging. Yet others, such as Brunner and Seung (2009), reported that there is an absence of sound social skills intervention literature to support the effectiveness of Social Stories™. In accordance with existing literature, we are of the opinion that the current evidence base does not sustain social interpretation, understanding, and problem solving as well-established, evidence-supported strategies.

Peer-Mediated Social Skills Interventions Research Base

For decades, practitioners and researchers have used peers to model and prompt appropriate social initiations, responses, and other age and situation appropriate behaviors of children and youth with ASD (Chan et al., 2009; Owen-DeSchryver, Carr, Cale, & Blakeley-Smith, 2008). These peer-mediated strategies are based on the assumption that peers are uniquely and naturally equipped to effectively instruct children and youth with ASD in acceptable social behaviors within natural settings, and that this form of social skills instruction will facilitate skills maintenance and generalization (Sawyer, Luiselli, Ricciardi, & Gower, 2005). That a salient underpinning of these methods is that peer-mediated activities used to develop social skills, facilitate peer interactions, and support development of peer relationships frequently operate independently of direct adult supervision and direction, subsequent to completion of initial peer training, is testament to the strength of the aforementioned assumptions.

Especially in comparison to some other types of social instruction, there is relatively strong support for peer mediated strategies (Chan et al., 2009; Matson et al., 2007). Use of these strategies has resulted in an increase in a variety of positive, appropriate behaviors by students with ASD, increased peer acceptance, and development of supportive peer relationships (Thieman & Kamps, 2008). We are in general agreement with the *National Standards Report* (National Autism Center, 2009) that "peer training" is an "established treatment." Thus we are comfortable in recommending peer-mediated social skills methods. In our opinion, it falls short of clearly crossing the threshold as a scientifically valid practice. Nevertheless, it has relatively strong credentials and clearly has demonstrated capacity to produce positive outcomes.

Future Directions

The literature on social skills interventions for individuals with ASD points to several needed areas of research development. Future research should investigate remediation of basic impairments and foundational structures that are likely causes of social difficulties, including theory of mind, executive functioning, and emotional regulation, as well as social problem solving/ understanding and comprehensive social skills interventions that address numerous deficit areas concurrently (Chan & O'Reilly, 2008; Matson et al., 2007). Further research, including single-case studies demonstrating experimental control and randomized controlled trials, is required to determine the efficacy of widely used methods that have not been well studied. These methods include developmental relationship-based interventions, imitation and initiation instruction, certain forms of peer-mediated instruction, social skills packages and curricula, and theory of mind training. Little research has been conducted to compare the effectiveness of various social skills interventions with each other; thus, such studies would provide practitioners with valuable information regarding efficient and effective use of instructional time (Matson et al., 2007). Finally, most social skills intervention research has been conducted in clinical settings and with researchers as implementers. Research on interventions implemented by teachers and family members in applied settings, rather than controlled or clinical settings, is needed to assess their real-world potential (Matson et al., 2007).

Conclusion and Summary

By any measure the research that underpins social skills and social interactions interventions for learners with ASD is not especially strong. Yet there are encouraging signs. First there is an overall increase in the amount of social skills research that is being conducted and published, including interventions that are most geared to produce socially valid outcomes (Reichow & Volkmar, 2009). This pattern bodes well for work that will lead to a better understanding of social skills characteristics of persons with ASD as well as identification and development of empirically supported intervention strategies. There are also increasingly signs of consensus among stakeholders that children and youth with ASD have significant social excesses and problems that require attention, and that failing to address these needs portends poorly for students' futures and that social deficits can have devastating long-term effects. We are also encouraged that practitioners have available for current use several methods that appear to have relatively strong effective-practice qualifications. These methods, including valid explicit instructional methods and peer-mediated strategies, can serve relatively well the social instruction needs of many children and youth with ASD. While obviously not the total solution to the current challenge of efficiently and effectively teaching social skills and engineering high quality social learning opportunities, they offer practitioners basic options that have a proven capacity to produce desired social outcomes.

References

American Psychiatric Association. (2000). *Diagnostic and statistical manual of mental disorders* (4th ed., Text rev.). Washington, DC: Author.

Apple, A. L., Billingsley, F., & Schwartz, I. S. (2005). Effects of video modeling alone and with self-management on complement-giving behavior of children with high-functioning ASD. *Journal of Positive Behavior Interventions, 7,* 33–46.

Asperger, H. (1944). Die "Autistischen Psychopathen" im Kindesalter. ["Autistic psychopathy" in childhood]. *Archiv fur Psychiatrie und Nervenkrankheiten, 117,* 76–136.

Autism Society of America. (2009). What are autism spectrum disorders? Retrieved from http://www.autism-society.org

Baker, J. (2004). *Social skills training for children and adolescents with Asperger syndrome and social communication problems.* Shawnee Mission, KS: Autism Asperger.

Baron-Cohen, S. (1995). *Mindblindness: An essay on autism and theory of mind.* Cambridge, MA: MIT Press.

Baron-Cohen, S., & Swettenham, J. (1997). Theory of mind in autism: Its relationship to executive function and central coherence. In D. J. Cohen & F. R. Volkmar (Eds.), *Handbook of autism and pervasive developmental disorders* (pp. 880–893). New York: Wiley.

Bauminger, N. (2007). Brief report: Group social-multimodal intervention for HFASD. *Journal of Autism and Developmental Disorders, 37,* 1605–1615.

Bellini, S., & Akullian, J. (2007). A meta-analysis of video modeling and video self-modeling interventions for children and adolescents with autism spectrum disorders. *Exceptional Children, 73,* 264–287.

Bellini, S., Peters, J. K., Benner, L., & Hopf, A. (2007). A meta-analysis of school-based social skills interventions for children with autism spectrum disorders. *Remedial and Special Education, 28,* 153–162.

Blacher, J. (2007). Unlocking the mystery of social deficits in autism: Theory of mind as key. *Exceptional Parent, 37,* 96–97.

Brunner D. L., & Seung H. (2009). Evaluation of the efficacy of communication-based treatments for autism spectrum disorders: A literature review. *Communication Disorders Quarterly, 31*(1), 15–41.

Capps, L. (1992). Understanding of simple and complex emotions in non-retarded children with autism. *Journal of Child Psychology and Psychiatry and Allied Disciplines, 33,* 1169–1182.

Calhoun, J. A. (2006). Executive functions: A discussion of the issues facing children with autism spectrum disorders and related disorders. *Seminars in Speech and Language, 27,* 60–71.

Cashin, A., & Barker, P. (2009). The triad of impairment in autism revisited. *Journal of Child and Adolescent Psychiatric Nursing, 22,* 189–193.

Chan, J., Lang, R., Rispoli, M., O'Reilly, M., Sigafoos, J., & Cole, H. (2009). Use of peer-mediated interventions in the treatment of autism spectrum disorders: A systematic review. *Research in Autism Spectrum Disorders, 3,* 876–889.

Chan, J., & O'Reilly, M. O. (2008). A social story intervention package for students with autism in inclusive classroom settings. *Journal of Applied Behavior Analysis, 41,* 405–409.

Charlop, M. H., & Milstein, J. P. (1989). Teaching autistic children conversational speech using video modeling. *Journal of Applied Behavior Analysis, 22,* 275–285.

Charlop-Christy, M. H., Le, L., & Freeman, K. A. (2000). A comparison of video modeling with in vivo modeling for teaching children with autism. *Journal of Autism and Developmental Disorders, 30,* 537–552.

Cotugno, A. (2009). Social competence and social skills training and intervention for children with autism spectrum disorders. *Journal of Autism and Developmental Disorders, 39,* 1268–1277.

deBoer, S. (2009). *Successful inclusion for students with autism.* San Francisco, CA: Jossey-Bass.

Delano, M., & Snell, M. (2006). The effects of social stories on the social engagement of children with autism. *Journal of Positive Behavior Interventions, 8,* 29–42.

DiSalvo, C. A., & Oswald, D. P. (2002). Peer-mediated interventions to increase the social interaction of children with autism: Consideration of peer expectancies. *Focus on Autism and Other Developmental Disabilities, 17,* 198–207.

Dodd, S., Hupp, S. D. A., Jewell, J. D., & Krohn, E. (2008). Using parents and siblings during a social story intervention for two children diagnosed with PDD-NOS. *Journal of Developmental and Physical Disabilities, 20,* 217–229.

Feng, H., Lo, Y., Tsai, S., & Cartledge, G. (2008). The effects of theory-of-mind and social skill training on the social competence of a sixth-grade student with autism. *Journal of Positive Behavior Interventions, 10,* 228–242.

Frith, U. (1989). *Autism: Explaining the enigma.* Oxford, England: Blackwell.

Ganz, J. B., & Flores, M. M. (2008). Effects of the use of visual strategies in play groups for children with autism spectrum disorders and their peers. *Journal of Autism and Developmental Disorders, 38,* 926–940. doi: 10.1007/s10803-007-0463-4

Ganz, J., Kaylor, M., Bourgeois, B., & Hadden, K. (2008). The impact of social scripts and visual cues on verbal communication in three children with autism spectrum disorders. *Focus on Autism and Other Developmental Disabilities, 23,* 79–94.

Garcia Winner, M. (2008). *Think social: A social thinking curriculum for school-age students.* San Jose, CA: Think Social.

Gena, A., Couloura, S., & Kymissis, E. (2005). Modifying the affective behavior of preschoolers with autism using in-vivo or video modeling and reinforcing contingencies. *Journal of Autism and Developmental Disorders, 35,* 545–556.

Golan, O., & Baron-Cohen, S. (2006). Systemizing empathy: Teaching adults with Asperger syndrome or high-functioning autism to recognize complex emotions using interactive multimedia. *Development and Psychopathology, 18*, 591–617.

Gray, C., & Garand, J. (1993). Social stories: Improving responses of students with autism with accurate social information. *Focus on Autistic Behavior, 8*, 1–10.

Gresham, F. M. (1998). Social skills training: Should we raze, remodel or rebuild? *Behavioral Disorders, 24*, 19–25.

Happé, F. (1994). An advanced test of theory of mind: Understanding of story characters' thoughts and feelings by able autistic, mentally handicapped and normal children and adults. *Journal of Autism and Developmental Disorders, 30*, 225–236.

Hill, E. L. (2004). Evaluating the theory of executive dysfunction in autism. *Developmental Review, 24*, 189–233.

Hutchins, T. L., & Prelock, P. A. (2006). Using social stories and comic strip conversations to promote socially valid outcomes for children with autism. *Seminars in Speech and Language, 27*, 47–59.

Joseph, R. M. (1999). Neuropsychological frameworks for understanding autism. *International Review of Psychiatry, 11*, 309–325.

Joseph, R. M., McGrath, L. M., & Tager-Flusberg, H. (2005). Executive dysfunction and its relation to language ability in verbal school-aged children with autism. *Developmental Neuropsychology, 27*, 361–378.

Kaland, M., Callesen, K., Moller-Nielsen, A., Mortensen, E. L., & Smith, L. (2008). Performance of children and adolescents with Asperger syndrome or high-functioning autism on advanced theory of mind tasks. *Journal of Autism and Developmental Disorders, 38*, 1112–1123.

Kanner, L. (1943). Autistic disturbances of affective content. *The Nervous Child, 2*, 217–250.

Krantz, P. J., & McClannahan, L. E. (1998). Social interaction skills for children with autism: A script-fading procedure for beginning readers. *Journal of Applied Behavior Analysis, 31*, 191–202.

Kroeger, K. A., Schultz, J. R., & Newsom, C. (2007). A comparison of two group-delivered social skills programs for young children with autism. *Journal of Autism and Developmental Disorders, 37*, 808–817.

LaCava, P., Golan, O, Baron-Cohen, S., & Myles, B. (2007). Using assistive technology to teach emotion recognition to students with Asperger syndrome. *Remedial and Special Education, 28*, 174–181.

Laurent, A. C., & Rubin, E. (2004). Challenges in emotional regulation in Asperger syndrome and high-functioning autism. *Topics in Language Disorders, 24*, 286–297.

Lawson, W., Baron-Cohen, S., & Wheelwright, S. (2004). Empathizing and systemizing in adults with and without Asperger syndrome. *Journal of Autism and Developmental Disorders, 34*, 301–310.

Lee, S., Odom, S., & Loftin, R. (2007). Social engagement with peers and stereotypic behavior of children with autism. *Journal of Positive Behavior Interventions, 9*, 67–79.

Legoff, D. B., & Sherman, M. (2006). Long-term outcome of social skills intervention based on interactive LEGO© play. *Autism, 10*, 317–329.

Leslie, A. M. (1987). Pretense and representation: The origins of theory of mind. *Psychology Review, 4*, 412–426.

Levy, F. (2007). Theories of autism. *Australian and New Zealand Journal of Psychiatry, 41*, 859–868.

Loveland, K. A., & Tunali, B. (1991). Social scripts for conversational interactions in autism and Down syndrome. *Journal of Autism and Developmental Disorders, 21*, 177–186.

MacKay, T., Knott, F., & Dunlop, A.W. (2007). Developing social interaction and understanding in individuals with autism spectrum disorder: A groupwork intervention. *Journal of Intellectual and Developmental Disabilities, 32*, 279–290.

Marans, W., Rubin, E., & Laurent, A. (2005). Addressing social communication skills in individuals with high-functioning autism and Asperger syndrome: Critical priorities in educational programming. In F. Volkmar, R. Paul, A. Klin, & D. Cohen (Eds.), *Handbook of autism and pervasive developmental disorders: Vol. 2. Assessment, interventions and policy* (pp. 977–1002). Hoboken, NJ: Wiley.

Matson, J. L., Matson, M. L., & Rivet, T. T. (2007). Social-skillss treatments for children with autism spectrum disorders. *Behavior Modification, 31*, 682–707.

McGinnis, E., & Goldstein, A.P. (1997). *Skill streaming the elementary school child: New strategies and perspectives for teaching prosocial skills.* Champaign, IL: Research Press.

Morton, J., Frith, U., & Leslie, A. (1991). The cognitive basis of a biological disorder: Autism. *Trends in Neurosciences, 14*, 434–438.

National Autism Center. (2009). *National standards report.* Randolph, MA: Author.

National Research Council. (2000). *From neurons to neighborhoods* (Committee on Integrating the Science of Early Childhood Development, Institute of Medicine). Washington, DC: National Academy Press.

Nikopoulos, C. K., & Keenan, M. (2004). Effects of video modeling on social initiations by children with autism. *Journal of Applied Behavior Analysis, 37*, 93–96.

Nikopoulos, C. K., & Keenan, M. (2007). Using video modeling to teach complex social sequences to children with autism. *Journal of Autism and Developmental Disorders, 37*, 678–693. doi: 10.1007/s10803-006-0195-x

Ogletree, B., Oren, T., & Fischer, M. (2007). Examining effective intervention practices for communication impairment in autism spectrum disorder. *Exceptionality, 15*, 233–247.

Owen-DeSchryver, J. S., Carr, E. G., Cale, S. I., & Blakeley-Smith, A. (2008). Promoting social interactions between students with autism spectrum disorders and their peers in inclusive school settings. *Focus on Autism and Other Developmental Disabilities, 23*, 15–28.

Ozonoff, S. (1997). Components of executive function in autism and other disorders. In J. Russell (Ed.), *Autism as an executive disorder* (pp. 179–211). Oxford, England: Oxford University Press.

Pennington, B. F. (1997). Dimensions of executive functions in normal and abnormal development. In N. Krasnegor, G. R. Lyon, & P. S. Goldman-Rakic (Eds.), *Development of the prefrontal cortex: Evolution, neurobiology, and behavior* (pp. 721–733). Baltimore, MD: Brookes.

Pennington, B. F., & Ozonoff, S. (1996). Executive functions and developmental psychopathology. *Journal of Child Psychology and Psychiatry, 37*, 51–87.

Perner, J., & Lang, B. (2000). Theory of mind and executive function: Is there a developmental relationship. In S. Baron-Cohen, T. Tager-Flusberg, & D. Cohen (Eds.), *Understanding other minds: Perspectives from developmental cognitive neuroscience* (pp. 150–181). Oxford, England: Oxford University Press.

Prizant, B. M., Wetherby, A. M., Rubin, E., & Laurent, A. C. (2003). The SCERTS Model: A family-centered, transactional approach to enhancing communication and socioemotional abilities of young children with ASD. *Infants and Young Children, 16*, 296–316.

Quill, K. (2000). *Do-watch-say-listen: Social and communication intervention for children with autism.* Baltimore, MD: Brookes.

Reichow, B., & Sabornie, E. J. (2009). Brief report: Increasing verbal greeting initiations for a student with autism via a social story intervention. *Journal of Autism and Developmental Disorders, 39*, 1740–1743.

Reichow, B., & Volkmar, F. R. (2009). Social skill interventions for individuals with autism: Evaluation for evidence-based practices within a best evidence synthesis framework. *Journal of Autism and Developmental Disorders, 40*, 149–166.

Rogers, S. (2000). Interventions that facilitate socialization in children with autism. *Journal of Autism and Developmental Disorders, 30*, 399–409.

Sansosti, F. J., & Powell-Smith, K. A., (2008). Using computer-presented social stories and video models to increase the social communication skills of children with high functioning autism spectrum disorders. *Journal of Positive Behavior Interventions, 10*, 162–178. doi: 10.1177/1098300708316259

Sawyer, L., Luiselli, J., Ricciardi, J., & Gower, J. (2005). Teaching a child with autism to share among peers in an integrated preschool classroom: Acquisition, maintenance, and social validation. *Education and Treatment of Children, 28*, 1–10.

Schrandt, J. A., Townsend, D. B., & Poulson, C. L. (2009). Teaching empathy skills to children with autism. *Journal of Applied Behavior Analysis, 42*(1), 17–32.

Sherer, M., Pierce, K. L., Pareded, S., Kisacky, K. L., Ingersoll, B., & Schreibman, L. (2001). Enhancing conversation skills in children with autism via video technology: Which is better, "self" or "other" as a model? *Behavior Modification, 25*, 140–158.

Sigafoos, J., O'Reilly, M., & de la Cruz, B. (2007). *How to use video modeling and video prompting.* Austin, TX: Pro-Ed.

Silver, M., & Oakes, P. (2001). Evaluation of a new computer intervention to teach people with autism or Asperger syndrome to recognize and predict emotions in others. *Autism, 5*, 299–316.

Simpson, R., deBoer-Ott, S. R., Griswold, D. E., Myles, B. S., Byrd, S. E., Ganz, J. B., … Adams, L. G. (2005). *Autism spectrum disorders: Interventions and treatments for children and youth.* Thousand Oaks, CA: Corwin Press.

Simpson, R., Myles, B., & LaCava, P. (2008). Understanding and responding to the needs of children and youth with autism spectrum disorders. In R. Simpson & B. Myles (Eds.), *Educating children and youth with autism* (pp. 1–59). Austin, TX: Pro-Ed.

Simpson, R. L. (2008). Children and youth with autism spectrum disorders: The search for effective methods. *Focus on Exceptional Children, 40*, 1–14.

Solomon, M., Goodlin-James, B. L., & Anders, T. F. (2004). A social adjustment enhancement intervention for high functioning autism, Asperger's syndrome, and pervasive developmental disorder, NOS. *Journal of Autism and Developmental Disorders, 34*, 649–668.

Stevenson, C. L., Krantz, P. J., & McClannahan, L. E. (2000). Social interaction skills for children with autism: A script-fading procedure for nonreaders. *Behavioral Interventions, 15*, 1–20.

Stichter, J., Randolph, J., Gage, N., & Schmidt, C. (2007). A review of recommended social competency programs for students with autism spectrum disorders. *Exceptionality, 15*, 219–232.

Tager-Flusberg, H. (2007). Evaluating the theory-of-mind hypothesis of autism. *Current Directions in Psychological Science, 16*, 311–315.

Thiemann, K. S., & Goldstein, H. (2004). Effects of peer training and written text cueing on social communication of school-age children with pervasive developmental disorder. *Journal of Speech, Language, and Hearing Research, 47*, 126–144.

Thiemann, K., & Kamps, D. (2008). Promoting social communicative competence of children with autism in integrated environments. In R. Simpson & B. Myles (Eds.), *Educating children and youth with autism* (pp. 267–298). Austin, TX: Pro-Ed.

Turner, M. (1999). Repetitive behavior in autism: A review of psychological research. *Journal of Child Psychology and Psychiatry, 40,* 839–849.

Wang, P., & Spillane, A. (2009). Evidence-based social skills interventions for children with autism: A meta-analysis. *Education and Training in Developmental Disabilities, 44,* 318–342.

Wellman, H. M., Baron-Cohen, S., Caswell, R., Gomez, J. C., Swettenham, J., Toye, E., & K. Lagattuta. (2002). Thought bubbles help children with autism acquire an alternative to a theory of mind. *Autism, 6,* 343–363.

White, S., Keonig, K., & Scahill, L. (2007). Social skills development in children with autism spectrum disorders: A review of the intervention research. *Journal of Autism and Developmental Disorders, 37,* 1858–1868.

13

PROMOTING SELF-DETERMINATION AND SOCIAL INCLUSION

A Review of Research-Based Practices

Michael L. Wehmeyer

UNIVERSITY OF KANSAS

Tom E. C. Smith

UNIVERSITY OF ARKANSAS

This chapter provides an overview of research-based practices that have been shown to be effective with students with autism spectrum disorders (ASD) or with other students with disabilities. Importantly, we propose that given the issues that affect students with ASD regarding social interactions and communication, efforts to encourage self-determination are best approached and most appropriate in the overarching context of promoting social skills, social competence, and social inclusion.

Self-Determination and Social Interactions

Efforts to promote the self-determination of adolescents with disabilities are a component of high quality special education services in secondary education and transition services (Wehmeyer, Abery, Mithaug, & Stancliffe, 2003; Wehmeyer, Agran, et al., 2007) and, increasingly, there is an acknowledgment that efforts to do so must begin in early childhood and elementary school (Cho, Wehmeyer, & Kingston, in press; Cho, Wehmeyer, Kingston, & Palmer, in press). Self-determination status has been linked to the attainment of more positive academic (Fowler, Konrad, Walker, Test, & Wood, 2007; Konrad, Fowler, Walker, Test, & Wood, 2007; Lee, Wehmeyer, Soukup, & Palmer, 2010) and transition outcomes, including more positive employment and independent living (Martorell, Gutierrez-Rechacha, Pereda, & Ayuso-Mateos, 2008; Wehmeyer & Palmer, 2003; Wehmeyer & Schwartz, 1997); recreation and leisure outcomes (McGuire & McDonnell, 2008); and a more positive quality of life and life satisfaction (Lachapelle et al., 2005; Nota, Ferrari, Soresi, & Wehmeyer, 2007; Shogren, Lopez, Wehmeyer, Little, & Pressgrove, 2006; Wehmeyer & Schwartz, 1998).

Importantly, teachers believe that teaching students to become more self-determined is important (Carter, Lane, Pierson, & Stang, 2008; Thoma, Pannozzo, Fritton, & Bartholomew, 2008; Wehmeyer, Agran, & Hughes, 2000) and there are numerous curricular and instructional models identified to enable them to provide this instructional focus (Test, Karvonen, Wood, Browder, & Algozzine, 2000; Wehmeyer & Field, 2007). In a meta-analysis of single subject and group subject design studies, Algozzine, Browder, Karvonen, Test, and Wood (2001) found evidence for the efficacy of instruction to promote component elements of self-determined behavior, including interventions to promote self-advocacy, goal setting and attainment, self-awareness, problem-solving skills, and decision-making skills. Cobb, Lehmann, Newman-Gonchar, and Morgen (2009) conducted a narrative metasynthesis—a narrative synthesis of multiple meta-analytic studies—which covered seven existing meta-analyses that examined self-determination and concluded that there is sufficient evidence to support the promotion of self-determination as effective.

Self-Determination

This chapter approaches self-determination as a general psychological construct within the organizing structure of theories of human agency. Human agency is "the sense of personal empowerment, which involves both knowing and having what it takes to achieve one's goals" (Little, Hawley, Henrich, & Marsland, 2002, p. 390). An agentic person is the

> origin of his or her actions, has high aspirations, perseveres in the face of obstacles, sees more and varied options for action, learns from failures, and overall, has a greater sense of well being. In contrast, a non-agentic individual can be a pawn to unknown extra-personal influences, has low aspirations, is hindered with problem-solving blinders, often feels helpless and, overall, has a greater sense of ill-being. (Little et al. 2002, p. 390)

Human agentic theories "share the meta-theoretical view that organismic aspirations drive human behaviors" (Little, Snyder, & Wehmeyer, 2006, p. 61). An organismic perspective views people as active contributors to, or "authors" of, their behavior, where behavior is described as self-regulated and goal-directed *action*. Unlike stimulus-response accounts of behavior, actions are defined as purposive and self-initiated activities (Brandtstädter, 1998; Chapman, 1984; Harter, 1999). Further, an organismic approach to self-determination requires an explicit focus on the interface between the self and context (Little et al., 2002). In this chapter we argue that for students with ASD the critical context is the social context. Organisms influence and are influenced by the contexts in which they live and develop. Through this person–context interaction people become agents of their own action.

The meaning of the term has its roots in the philosophical doctrine of determinism (Wehmeyer et al., 2003), which posits that all events, including human behavior and thought, are caused by events that occurred before the event. There are now numerous theoretical frameworks that serve as a basis for instructional design to promote self-determination for students with ASD and other disabilities (Wehmeyer et al., 2003), as well as specially designed instructional methods, materials, strategies, and assessments to promote and measure self-determination (Wehmeyer, Agran, Hughes, Martin, et al., 2007; Wehmeyer & Field, 2007).

Wehmeyer, Kelchner, and Richards (1996) proposed a functional theory of self-determination—actions are viewed as self-determined based upon the function they serve for the individual—in which self-determination is viewed as a dispositional characteristic (enduring tendencies used to characterize and describe differences between people). Self-determined behavior refers to "volitional actions that enable one to act as the primary causal agent in one's life and to maintain or improve one's quality of life" (Wehmeyer, 2005, p. 117). The term *causal agency* implies that it is the person who makes or causes things to happen in his or her life; that the individual acts with an eye toward *causing* an effect to accomplish a specific end or to cause or create change. Self-determined actions are identified by four essential characteristics: (a) the person acts autonomously; (b) the behavior is self-regulated; (c) the person initiates and responds to the event(s) in a psychologically empowered manner; and (d) the person acts in a self-realizing manner. The functional model sees self-determination as an integral part of the process of individuation and adolescent development. This model has been empirically validated (Shogren et al., 2008; Wehmeyer, Kelchner, & Richards, 1996); operationalized by the development of an assessment linked to the theory (Wehmeyer, 1996); served as the foundation for intervention development, particularly with regard to the development of the self-determined learning model of instruction and related efforts (Wehmeyer, Palmer, Agran, Mithaug, & Martin, 2000); and provided impetus for a variety of research activities (see Wehmeyer et al., 2007). Finally, the functional model conceptualizes self-determination within a person–environment interaction framework, so it is relevant to the social–ecological approach to intervention we propose.

Abery and colleagues (e.g., Abery & Stancliffe, 1996) proposed an ecological model of self-determination that defines the self-determination construct as "a complex process, the ultimate goal of which is to achieve the level of personal control over one's life that an individual desires within those areas the individual perceives as important" (p. 27). The ecological model views self-determination as driven by the intrinsic motivation of all people to be the primary determiner of their thoughts, feelings, and behavior. It may involve, but is not synonymous with, independence and autonomy. Rather, it entails the person determining in what contexts and to what extent each of these behaviors/attitudes will be manifested. Self-determination, accordingly, is the product of both the person and the environment—of the person using the skills, knowledge, and beliefs at his or her disposal to act on the environment with the goal of obtaining valued and desired outcomes. The ecological model was derived from Bronfenbrenner's ecological perspective (1979, 1989), within which the way that people develop and lead their lives is viewed as consisting of four levels: the microsystem, mesosystem, exosystem, and macrosystem (see Wehmeyer et al., 2003 for more detail). The ecological model has been empirically evaluated (Abery, McGrew, & Smith, 1994; Abery, Simunds, & Cady, 2006; Stancliffe, Abery, & Smith, 2000), operationalized in the development of assessments (Abery, Simunds, & Cady, 2002; Abery, Stancliffe, Smith, McGrew, & Eggebeen, 1995a, 1995b), and has also provided a foundation for intervention (Abery, Arndt et al., 1994; Abery & Eggebeen, 1995) and research (Abery, Simunds, & Cady, 2006).

Mithaug (Wehmeyer et al., 2003) hypothesized that self-determination is an unusually effective form of self-regulation markedly free of external influence in which people who are self-determined regulate their choices and actions more successfully than others. Mithaug suggested that individuals are often in flux between existing states and goals or desired states. When a discrepancy exists between what one has and wants, an incentive for self-regulation and action becomes operative. With the realization that a discrepancy exists, the person may set out to achieve the goal or desired state. The ability to set appropriate expectations is based on the person's success in matching his or her capacity with the present opportunity. Capacity is the person's assessment of existing resources (e.g., skills, interests, motivation), and opportunity refers to aspects of the situation that allow the individual to achieve the desired gain. Mithaug referred to optimal prospects as "just-right" matches in which people are able to correctly match their capacity (i.e., skills, interests) with existing opportunities (e.g., potential jobs). The experience generated during self-regulation is a function of repeated interactions between capacity and opportunity. Mithaug (1998) suggested that "self-determination always occurs in a social context" (p. 42) and that the social nature of the construct is worth reviewing because the distinction between "self-determination and other-determination is nearly always in play when assessing an individual's prospects for controlling their life in a particular situation" (p. 42).

A Social-Ecological Approach to Promoting Self-Determination

All of the above theoretical frameworks are developmental in approach; that is, they propose that self-determination emerges across the life span as children and adolescents learn skills and develop attitudes that enable them to be causal agents in their lives. These attitudes and abilities are the *component elements* of self-determined behavior (Wehmeyer et al., 2003). Although not intended as an exhaustive list, these component elements are particularly important to the emergence of self-determined behavior and form the basis for considering pedagogy to promote self-determination. These component elements include choice-making, decision-making, and problem-solving skills; goal-setting and attainment skills, self-management skills; and self-advocacy and leadership skills, as well as self-awareness and knowledge.

While characteristics of people with ASD may impact the development of these component elements, none preclude students with ASD from developing such skills and attitudes. In fact, as will be detailed subsequently, research shows that students with ASD can, with educational supports and accommodations, acquire such skills. The unique needs of students with ASD, because of their characteristic differences in communication and social interaction, must be considered when working to promote self-determination. In fact, these issues necessitate, we would suggest, taking a social-ecological approach to promoting self-determination.

Social-ecological models of intervention emphasize the complex interactions that occur between person- and environment-specific variables and that account for significant changes in human behavior and enhanced human functioning. Walker et al. (2010) suggested that this approach is one of the few intervention models that have the necessary breadth for conceptualizing the complex and reciprocal environmental and personal variables and dynamics required to effectively design and evaluate interventions to promote self-determination.

The emphasis in social-ecological models of interventions on enhancing both the capacity of the person and modifying the context or environment to enable success has particular relevance for students with ASD. As was noted by Mithaug (1998), self-determination always has a social context—by that we mean that self-determination refers to self- versus other-determined action. It stands to reason, then, that social variables play an important role in mediating the effect of interventions to promote self-determination. In fact, the "other" determinant in the self- vs. other-determination equation is almost always other people or circumstances in which the "will" of other people comes into play. Walker et al. (2010) proposed three forms of social behavior that serve as mediator variables to the promotion of self-determination: social effectiveness, social capital, and social inclusion.

Social Effectiveness. Social effectiveness is one's ability to use social skills, strategies, and behavioral competencies to achieve preferred quality of life outcomes and to access key opportunities (making friends, recruiting social support networks, joining groups, managing one's life and daily routines, negotiating, etc.). It is worth elaborating, at this point, on the relationship between social effectiveness and social skills, particularly in the context of promoting self-determination. Social skills are a set of skills needed to get along with others that are used by most people every day in the community, workplace, and in school. Acting the way people think you should, getting along with others, making and keeping friends, and knowing what to say and how to say it are all examples of social skills. Frequently, people are described as being social as a means to describe someone with effective social skills. Whenever two or more people are together, the presence or lack of social skills helps define the relationship (Smith, Gartin, & Murdick, in press).

First, social effectiveness (and, thus social skills) and self-determination share, most likely, a reciprocal relationship, in that enhanced self-determination will improve social effectiveness and enhanced social effectiveness (and social capital and social inclusion) will result in more opportunities to practice and learn skills leading to enhanced self-determination. It is difficult to be socially effective without being self-determined; being aware of one's self, knowing how to solve problems, make decisions, and self-advocate. Unfortunately, the opposite is also true; it is difficult to be self-determined without effective social skills.

Too often educators approach teaching social skills and the skills leading to greater self-determination separately because they fail to see the natural linkage between them. While the literature has noted that the best ways to teach social skills and self-determination is through natural activities in natural settings, the relationship between social effectiveness and self-determination has not been adequately acknowledged (Meadan & Monda-Amaya, 2008; Smith et al., in press). As we have emphasized, self-determination has, by definition, a social context and as a result social skills should be a strong consideration during instruction to promote self-determination. When approaching the instruction of these skills together, the natural relationship facilitates developing competence in both. Some strategies for teaching social skills and skills to promote self-determination together include:

- Encourage decision making with students working together in groups;
- Encourage mutual responsibility and goal setting in groups;
- Stress internal motivation;
- Infuse choice when possible in group settings;
- Provide opportunities in natural settings for students to work together in problem-solving activities;
- Provide opportunities for students to set goals together;
- Provide opportunities for group reflections after goal-setting and problem-solving activities.

Getting along with others and establishing friendships is a large part of being social. Friendship development—a "natural and essential part of human existence—involves a series of complicated social interactions" (Morris, 2002, p. 67). Friendships are important at all ages, beginning in early childhood and lasting throughout adulthood. The nature of friendships changes over time. Preschool children often develop friendships equally with children of both sexes. During elementary school same-sex friendships are more typical. Also, friends are usually from a similar age group. As children get older, friendship is expanded to a wider age range and to both sexes (Slavin, 2009).

Being social is important throughout a person's life; however, during the school years its importance can be critical, often mediating aspects of a student's school success (Smith & Gilles, 2003). At the secondary level, being social becomes even more important because friendships and other social activities may be more important than parental relationships and approval (Polloway, Miller, & Smith, in press). Social skills impact all areas during secondary school, including popularity. Boutot (2007) found that students' popularity among peers was related to their level of social skills. School clubs, athletic events, dances, parties, and daily interactions with other students are examples of the important social activities of students in secondary schools.

Unfortunately, while being social is important for success in school, community living, and work, students with ASD commonly have difficulty with social skills. Studies have found social skill difficulties in students across disability categories, but of course, social interaction difficulties are characteristic of students with ASD (Morris, 2002). Students with ASD experience difficulties in being social for a variety of reasons, which includes the lack of opportunities to develop social skills, inattention to environmental cues and models, and emotional problems that interfere with the development and use of appropriate social skills (Smith et al., in press). While limited social skills impact students across all disability categories, the impact on persons with ASD is even more significant. The *Diagnostic and Statistical Manual of Mental Disorders* (*DSM-IV-TR*) notes regarding the diagnosis of ASD: "the impairment in reciprocal social interaction is gross and sustained" (American Psychiatric Association, 2000, p. 70).

Social Capital. The second form of social behavior referenced in the model, social capital, refers to the networks of social ties, supports, relationships, trust, cooperation, affiliations, and social–behavioral reciprocity that enhance one's life quality, lead to improvements in life chances, and satisfy basic psychosocial needs.

Social Inclusion. Social inclusion refers primarily to the presence and societal acceptance of people with disabilities within school, work, and community settings.

A social–ecological approach to promote self-determination that emphasizes social effectiveness, social capital, and social inclusion as mediating variables provides a powerful frame within which to consider interventions to promote the self-determination of students with ASD. Figure 13.1 depicts the social ecological approach to promoting self-determination proposed by Walker et al. (2010). The first level of the model depicts person-specific and environment-specific variables that are derived from theory and research as related to self-determination. The second level identifies classes of person-specific and environment-specific intervention practices that are important as derived from the foundation of theory and research. The third and fourth levels of the model depict the mediating variables that impact the efficacy of the intervention practices identified in the second level, as well as the practices that are important to take advantage of the mediating effect of these variables in intervention. The final level depicts expected outcomes from interventions to promote self-determination using this approach.

Research-Based Practices to Promote the Self-Determination with ASD

It is worth noting at the onset of any discussion about practices to promote self-determination that although there is accumulating evidence of the efficacy of interventions to promote component elements of self-determined behavior and to promote self-determination itself, in most cases, this evidence falls short of the standards set for "evidence-based practices" (Odom et al., 2005), which typically require randomized trial studies to establish an evidence base. Certainly, though, research is emerging that is providing causal evidence of the impact of interventions to promote self-determination and which engage in RCT studies, and thus would establish an evidence base for interventions to promote self-determination, but for the most part, such evidence currently falls short of standards that establish true causality. A review of the evidence by the U.S. Department of Education supported National Secondary Transition Technical Assistance Center (Test, Fowler, Kohler, & Kortering, 2010) classified the level of evidence in the area of teaching self-determination as "moderate."

Given the above caveat, instruction in the component elements of self-determined behavior, such as those described previously, can be incorporated into existing interventions for students with ASD. A number of core strategies identified in the literature for supporting students with ASD can also be incorporated in interventions to promote these components. For example, students with ASD often interpret communications literally and have difficulty with abstract concepts; thus working to make abstract concepts concrete by providing clear definitions and examples of what does and does not constitute the behavior, along with visual depictions of the behavior (Krasny, Williams, Provencal, & Ozonoff, 2003) would better enable students with

A Social Ecological Approach to Promote Self-Determination

What Variables are Conceptually Related to Self-Determination?

Person-Specific Variables
1. Moderating variables
2. Motivational variables
3. Causal capacity variables
4. Agentic capacity variables
5. Adaptive behavior variables

Ecological-Specific Variables
1. Microsystem variables
2. Mesosystem variables
3. Exosystem variables
4. Macrosystem variables

What Intervention Practices are Important According to these Variables?

Person-Specific Intervention Practices
1. Promote goal setting, decision-making, problem solving, and related causal capacity skills.
2. Promote self-regulation, self-advocacy, coping, self-management, and other agentic capacity skills.
3. Promote independent living, self-sufficiency, personal-social responsibility, social competency, and other adaptive behavior skills.
4. Link interventions to preferences to enhance motivation.

Ecological-Specific Intervention Practices
1. Educate family members, professionals, support staff, and general public on practices to promote self-determination
2. Promote choice-making opportunities.
3. Maximize experiences leading to identification of preferences.
4. Maximize opportunities to utilize and practice person-specific skills.
5. Ensure access via universal design
6. Design funding and systems to promote greater choice making and consumer control.

What Mediating Variables Impact the Efficacy of These Intervention Practices?

Mediating Variables
1. Social effectiveness
2. Social capital
3. Social inclusion

What Intervention Practices are Important to Promote these Mediating Variables?

Intervention Practices
1. Promote social effectiveness skills
2. Facilitate friendship and social networking opportunities
3. Promote school, community, and work inclusion

What Outcomes Result from Implementation of Interventions to Promote Self-Determination?

Enhanced Self-Determination	Improved Quality of Life Outcomes	Enhanced Social Inclusion

1. Access to community resources and supports
2. Improved ability to manage one's daily life
3. Greater community participation/acceptance
4. Emotional/material/physical well-being
5. Breadth and variety of daily activities

FIGURE 13.1 A social-ecological approach to promote self-determination (Calkins, Wehmeyer, Bacon, Heller, & Walker, 2008).

ASD to understand concepts related to these component elements (Wehmeyer & Shogren, 2008).

Goal-Setting and Attainment

Having the skills to set and attain goals is central to self-determined behavior. Understanding the goal process is also important for social interactions, as understanding the goals and intentions behind the actions of others is critical to 'many such interactions (Hamilton, 2009). The process of promoting goal-setting skills involves working with students to enable them to identify and define a goal clearly and concretely, develop a series of objectives or tasks to achieve the goal, and specify the actions necessary to achieve the goal. Goal-setting activities can be easily incorporated into a variety of educational activities and instructional areas, as well as in educational planning. Held, Thoma, and Thomas (2004) developed a multicomponent intervention that incorporates multiple means to promote goal setting for an adolescent with autism, including using the self-determined learning model of instruction (Wehmeyer, 2000), described subsequently, assisting the student to set goals in his or her personal life (including social interactions), school work, and postschool outcomes.

Research suggests that students with ASD tend to be more sequential in their goal-directed behavior, have difficulty engaging in multiple goal-directed activities concurrently, and tend to jump from activity to activity in the process of goal attainment (Ruble & Scott, 2002). Several strategies could be utilized to address this issue: Complex goals could be broken down into smaller subgoals, with fewer steps, that the student could complete in a shorter amount of time. Students could make a list of goals they are working toward, so they have a concrete visual reminder of their goals to which they can easily refer. Further, strategies to promote self-regulated behavior (discussed below) could be utilized to enable students with ASD to self-monitor their progress toward their goals (Wehmeyer & Shogren, 2008).

Choice Making

Choice making involves, simply, the expression of a preference between two or more options. Opportunities to make choices should be infused throughout a student's day, as experiences with making choices teach students that they can exert some control over their environment. Relatedly, research has shown that when students with ASD are provided opportunities to make choices, reductions in problem behavior and increases in adaptive behaviors are observed (Cole & Levinson, 2002; Shogren, Faggella-Luby, Bae, & Wehmeyer, 2004). For example, Mechling, Gast, and Cronin (2006) provided choice opportunities as a component of an intervention that improved academic task completion time for students with ASD. Carter (2001) provided choice opportunities in game playing situations with children with autism, resulting in increased language and social interaction skills. Choice opportunities can be infused through the school day, and students can be provided opportunities to choose within or between instructional activities, with whom they engage in a task, where they engage in an activity, and so forth.

Problem Solving

A problem is an activity or task for which a solution is not known or readily apparent. The process of solving a problem involves: (a) identifying and defining the problem, (b) listing possible solutions, (c) identifying the impact of each solution, (d) making a judgment about a preferred solution, and (e) evaluating the efficacy of the judgment. Developing the skills associated with social problem solving may be particularly difficult for students with ASD, as research suggests they may have specific difficulties understanding social and emotional cues that, in turn, limit their ability to interact with others (Bacon, Fein, Morris, Waterhouse, & Allen, 1998; Sigman & Ruskin, 1999; Travis, Sigman, & Ruskin, 2001). If the social difficulties experienced by students with ASD are a result of difficulties in understanding social and emotional cues, interventions to promote social and emotional understanding via instruction in social skills and interpersonal problem solving have the potential to mediate the social difficulties often faced by students with ASD.

There have been several strategies developed to promote social problem solving in students with ASD. Bauminger (2002, 2007a, 2007b) devised a social–emotional intervention to promote social cognition and social interaction in students with ASD by teaching social and interpersonal problem solving skills. After receiving intervention, students generated more appropriate solutions to problems faced in social situations and initiated more social interactions with peers. Bernard-Opitz, Sriram, and Nakhoda-Sapuan (2001) developed a computer program to assist students with ASD to develop social problem-solving skills. The program presented pictures or videos of people experiencing social conflicts, and then guided students through an animated problem solving process, in which students were asked to generate alternative solutions. After identifying an alternate solution, a video clip of the actors resolving the problem was presented. As students had repeated experience with the program, they generated more alternative solutions. Bernad-Ripoli (2007) used video self-modeling as a strategy, combined with social stories, to assist a child with Asperger syndrome to understand emotions pertaining to social interactions and social problem solving. In addition, problem-solving instruction is a component of many self-regulation strategies, which are discussed subsequently.

Decision Making

Decision making, like problem solving, is a systematic process that involves coming to a judgment about which solution is best at a given time. Making effective decisions involves: (a) identifying alternative courses of action, (b) identifying the possible consequences of each action, (c) assessing the probability of each consequence occurring, (d) choosing the best alternative, and (e) implementing the decision (Beyth-Marom, Fischhoff, Quadrel, & Furby, 1991). Research shows that students with disabilities, including students with ASD, want to be involved in decisions related to their lives. Ruef and Turnbull (2002) studied the perspective of adults with cognitive disabilities or autism about their problem behavior, and found that participants repeatedly said they wanted to have "voice" in their lives. The participants wanted to be actively involved in decisions related to their supports, their living arrangements, and their employment.

To support students with ASD to learn decision-making skills, a number of strategies can be implemented throughout the student's educational career. Early on, students should be provided with a wide array of choice opportunities, and receive instruction on how to make effective choices, as discussed previously. As students age, they should be provided with overt training in the decision-making process. Students with ASD should also be encouraged to process the emotions associated with the decision-making process, given that this is often a process characterized by uncertainty (Beyth-Marom et al., 1991). By providing discrete instruction in uncertainty, the emotions associated with it, and how to evaluate alternatives even when there is no single correct answer, students with ASD may experience less anxiety in the decision-making process. The process of evaluating alternatives is also an area in which direct instruction can occur; students can be supported to develop lists of decision options, to evaluate the risk and benefit associated with each option, and to evaluate biases in their decision-making (Beyth-Marom et al., 1991). Students often evaluate risk somewhat differently from the way adults do, perhaps because they see the excitement of risk as positive rather than negative. By teaching students how to evaluate and conceptualize risk, however, both in terms of short-term and long-term consequences, these biases can be reduced (Wehmeyer, Abery et al., 2003).

Self-Regulation and Student-Directed Learning Skills

Self-regulation is the process of setting goals, developing action plans to achieve those goals, implementing and following the action plans, evaluating the outcomes of the action plan, and changing actions plans if the goal was not achieved (Mithaug, 1993). The skills associated with self-regulation enable us to examine our environments, evaluate our repertoire of possible responses, and implement and evaluate a response (Whitman, 1990). Self-regulation involves the use of self-management skills, such as self-observation or self-monitoring, self-evaluation, self-reinforcement, and self-instruction. Research has consistently shown that students with ASD can learn and practice these skills, with positive behavioral effects (L. K. Koegel, Harrower, & Koegel, 1999; R. L. Koegel, Frea, & Surratt, 1994; R. L. Koegel, Koegel, & Parks, 1995). A single-subject design meta-analysis of the effects of self-management strategies with students with autism (Lee, Simpson, & Shogren, 2007) found that across subjects, settings, and conditions, self-management strategies generally resulted in improvements in socially desired behaviors.

Research has shown that interventions promoting self-management skills in students with ASD have led to increases in problem-solving skills (R. L. Koegel et al., 1995), communicative behavior (Newman, Reinecke, & Meinberg, 2000), daily living skills (Sherer et al., 2001), and academic performance (Callahan & Rademacher, 1999), in addition to reductions in disruptive behavior (Mancina, Tankersley, Kamps, Kravits, & Parrett, 2000). Instruction in self-management can focus globally on all of the involved skills (self-observation/self-monitoring, self-evaluation, self-reinforcement, and self-instruction) or can focus specifically on one or more of the skills. Self-observation or self-monitoring involves teaching students to assess, observe, and record their own behavior. For example, Todd and Reid (2006) used self-monitoring to teach three adolescents with ASD two new physical activities (snowshoeing and walking/jogging). Self-evaluation involves teaching students to track their progress in achieving their goals, or evaluating the discrepancy between where they currently are in relation to a goal or task, and where they want to be in the future. Self-reinforcement involves students in identifying and providing their own reinforcement for performance of a given behavior or achievement of a goal. Self-instruction is the process of enabling students to take the primary role in solving academic or social problems. When they are engaged in self-instruction, students must be able to direct themselves through the process of addressing the problem or meeting their goal. For example, Lord (1996) taught a student with autism self-instruction strategies for reducing his obsessive behaviors and for coping with frustration. The student was able to "intervene" as soon as he began to experience obsessive or compulsive thoughts, and thus was more successful in slowing down the escalation of his problem behavior than if he had been waiting for a teacher or support person to notice and intervene.

Self-Advocacy

Students with ASD need to learn the skills to advocate on their own behalf. Perhaps the most frequently identified context in which to teach and practice such skills involves increasing student participation in educational planning meetings. A first step to enabling students to express their wants and needs during these meetings is educating students about their rights and responsibilities in these areas. When teaching students how to advocate for themselves, the focus should be on teaching students how to be assertive, how to effectively communicate their perspective (either verbally or in written or pictorial form), how to negotiate, how to compromise, and how to deal with systems and bureaucracies. Students need to be provided with real-world opportunities to practice these skills. This can be done by embedding opportunities for self-advocacy within the school day, by allowing students to set up a class schedule, work out their supports with a resource room teacher or other support provider, or, as noted, to participate in IEP and transition meetings (Wehmeyer & Shogren, 2008).

Self-Awareness and Self-Knowledge

For students to become more self-realizing, they must possess a reasonably accurate understanding of their strengths, abilities, unique learning and support needs, and limitations. Further, they must know how to utilize this understanding to maximize success and progress. However, self-awareness and knowledge is not something that can simply be taught through direct instruction. Instead, students acquire this knowledge by interacting with their environment. Unfortunately, students with ASD often learn to identify what they *cannot* do instead of what they can. This skews students' perceptions of themselves, and influences how they interact with people and systems they encounter.

Faherty (2000) developed an approach to guide children and youth with ASD through the process of developing an understanding of their strengths, their abilities, and the impact of autism on their lives. The process has a number of activities that encourage students to think about their strengths and abilities, and contains activities to support students to develop and reflect on how they learn, their sensory experiences, their artistic and technological abilities, their social and communication skills, their thoughts, and why they sometimes feel upset. It also helps students reflect on the people in their lives, including their school experiences. Finally, the approach provides students with facts about ASD. The focus is on promoting adaptive self-awareness and supporting the student in developing both understanding of autism and its limitations, but also their abilities and strengths as a person.

Self-Determined Learning Model of Instruction

The self-determined learning model of instruction (SDLMI; Wehmeyer, 2000) is an instructional model derived from theory in self-determination, the process of self-regulated problem solving, and research on student-directed learning (Agran, King-Sears, Wehmeyer, & Copeland, 2003). It is appropriate for students with and without disabilities across multiple content areas and enables teachers to engage students in their educational programs by increasing opportunities to self-direct learning. Implementation of the *SDLMI* consists of a three-phase instructional process, depicted in the Figures 13.2, 13.3, and 13.4. Each instructional phase presents a problem to be solved by the student. The student solves this problem by posing and answering a series of four Student Questions per phase that students learn, modify to make their own, and apply to reach self-selected goals. Each question is linked to a set of Teacher Objectives. Each phase includes a list of Educational Supports that teachers use to enable students to self-direct learning. In each phase, the student is the primary causal agent for choices, decisions, and actions, even when eventual actions are teacher-directed. The Student Questions in the model are constructed to direct the student through a problem-solving sequence in each instructional

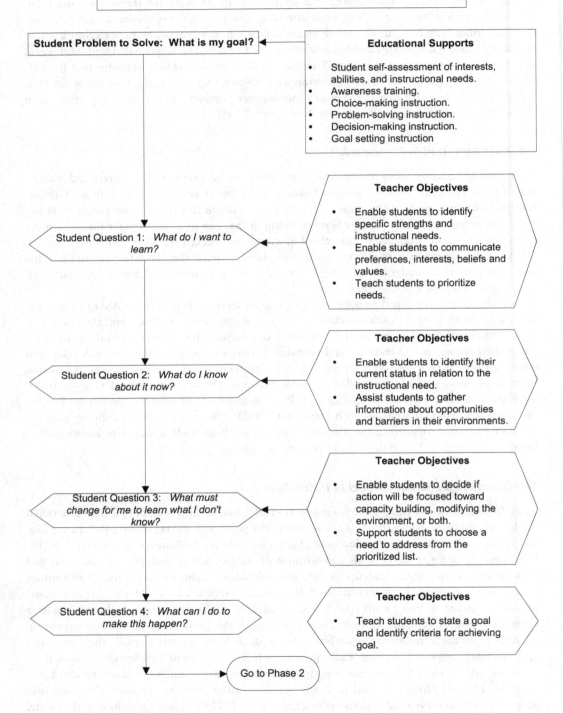

FIGURE 13.2 Phase 1 of the self-determined learning model of instruction (Wehmeyer, 1995).

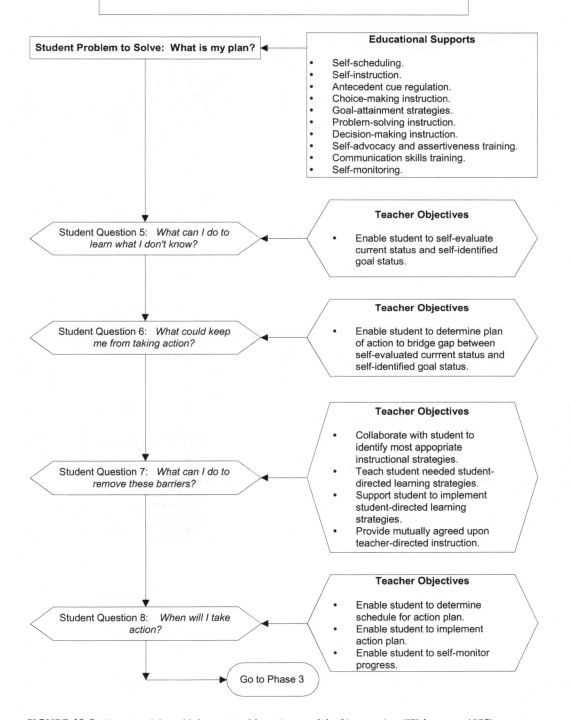

FIGURE 13.3 Phase 2 of the self-determined learning model of instruction (Wehmeyer, 1995).

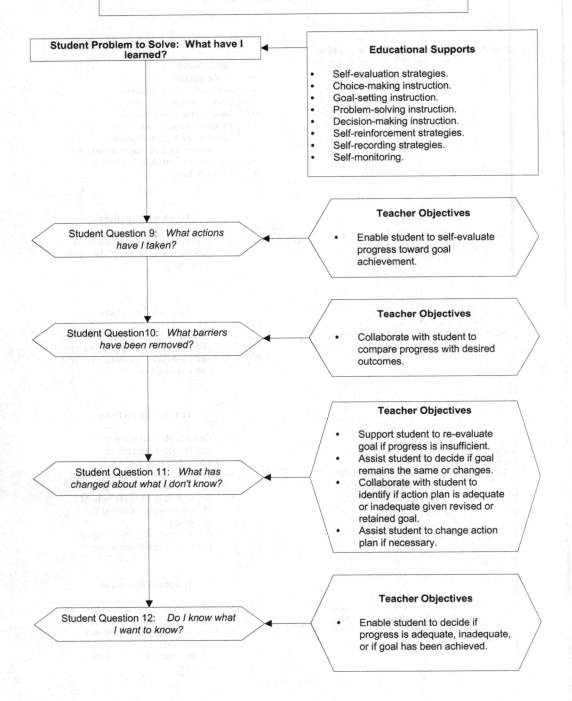

FIGURE 13.4 Phase 3 of the self-determined learning model of instruction (Wehmeyer, 1995).

phase. The solution to the problem in each phase leads to the problem-solving sequence in the next phase. Their construction was based on theory in the problem-solving and self-regulation literature that suggests there is a sequence of thoughts and actions, a means–ends problem solving sequence, which must be followed for any person's actions to produce results that satisfy their needs and interests. Teachers implementing the model teach students to solve a sequence of problems to construct a means–ends chain—a causal sequence—that moves them from where they are (an actual state of not having their needs and interests satisfied) to where they want to be (a goal state of having those needs and interests satisfied). We construct this means–ends sequence by having students answer the questions which connect their needs and interests to their actions and results via goals and plans.

To answer the questions, students must regulate their own problem solving by setting goals to meet needs, constructing plans to meet goals, and adjusting actions to complete plans. Thus, each instructional phase poses a problem the student must solve (What is my goal? What is my plan? What have I learned?) by solving a series of problems posed by the questions in each phase. The four questions differ by phase, but represent identical steps in the problem-solving sequence. That is, students answering the questions must (a) identify the problem, (b) identify potential solutions to the problem, (c) identify barriers to solving the problem, and (d) identify consequences of each solution. These steps are fundamental to any problem-solving process and form the means-end problem-solving sequence represented by the Student Questions in each phase. Because the model is designed for teachers to implement, the language used in the Student Questions is, intentionally, not written to be understandable by every student, nor does the model assume that students have life experiences that enable them to fully answer each question. The Student Questions are written in first-person voice in a relatively simple format with the intention that they are the starting point for discussion between the teacher and the student. Some students will learn and use all 12 questions as they are written. Other students will need to have the questions rephrased to be more understandable. Still other students, due to the intensity of their instructional needs, may need to have the teacher paraphrase the questions for them.

The Teacher Objectives within the model are the objectives a teacher will be trying to accomplish by implementing the model. In each phase, the objectives are linked directly to the Student Questions. These objectives can be met by utilizing strategies provided in the Educational Supports section of the model. The Teacher Objectives provide a road map for the teacher to enable students to solve the problem stated in the student question.

The Educational Supports are not actually a part of the model, but are what Joyce and Weil (1980) referred to as the model's syntax—how the model is implemented. However, because the implementation of the model requires teachers to teach students to self-direct learning, we believe it is important to identify some strategies and supports that could be used to successfully implement the model. The majority of these supports are derived from the self-management literature. A variety of strategies, like antecedent cue regulation, self-instruction, self-monitoring, self-evaluation, self-reinforcement, and goal setting, have been used to teach students, including students with cognitive disabilities, how to manage their own behavior across academic and functional content areas. The emphasis in the model on the use of instructional strategies and educational supports that are student-directed provides another means of teaching students to become causal agents in their lives. As important as it is to utilize the student-directed learning strategies, however, not every instructional strategy implemented will be student-directed. The purpose of any teaching model is to promote student learning. There are circumstances in which the most effective method or strategy to achieve a particular educational outcome will be a teacher-directed strategy. Within the *SDLMI* context, however, students are active in determining these educational plans, whether self- or teacher-directed.

There are a wide number of studies that have validated the efficacy of the SDLMI. Wehmeyer and colleagues (2000) conducted a field test of the model with students with intellectual and developmental disabilities. The efficacy of the model to enable students to achieve educationally valued goals was examined using the Goal Attainment Scaling (GAS) process, and found that the model was essentially effective in enabling students to attain educationally valued goals, with the majority of students achieving goals at an acceptable or above expected level. These findings have been confirmed and extended by other studies (Agran, Blanchard, & Wehmeyer, 2000; Agran, Cavin, Wehmeyer, & Palmer, 2006; Lee, Wehmeyer, Palmer, Soukup, & Little, 2008; McGlashing-Johnson, Agran, Sitlington, Cavin, & Wehmeyer, 2003; Palmer & Wehmeyer, 2003; Palmer, Wehmeyer, Gipson, & Agran, 2004).

Conclusions

There is clear evidence that students with ASD can learn the component skills that enable them to become more self-determined and that, for all students, enhanced self-determination is associated with more positive school and adult outcomes. For students with ASD, particularly, efforts to promote self-determination should be in the context of efforts to promote social effectiveness and social inclusion. Although there is an emerging evidence base pertaining to issues of promoting self-determination for students with ASD, there is a need to expand this evidence base and to identify those factors and interventions that will enable students with ASD to become more self-determined.

References

Abery, B. H., Arndt, K., Greger, P., Tetu, L., Eggebeen, A., Barosko, J., ... Rudrud, L. (1994). *Self-determination for youth with disabilities: A family education curriculum*. Minneapolis MN: University of Minnesota, Institute on Community Integration.

Abery, B. H., & Eggebeen, A. (1995). *Findings from a field-test of a self-determination capacity building curriculum* (Technical Report No. 3). Minneapolis MN: University of Minnesota, Institute on Community Integration.

Abery, B. H., McGrew, K., & Smith, J. (1994). *Validation of an ecological model of self-determination for children with disabilities* (Technical Report No. 2). Minneapolis, MN: University of Minnesota, Institute on Community Integration.

Abery, B. H., Simunds, E., & Cady, R. (2002). *The Minnesota health care self-determination scales*. Minneapolis, MN: University of Minnesota, Institute on Community Integration.

Abery, B. H., Simunds, E., & Cady, R. (2006). *The impact of health care coordination on the lives of adults with physical disabilities* (Technical Report #2). Minneapolis, MN: University of Minnesota, Institute on Community Integration.

Abery, B. H., & Stancliffe, R. J. (1996). The ecology of self-determination. In D. J. Sands & M. L. Wehmeyer (Eds.), *Self-determination across the life span: Independence and choice for people with disabilities* (pp. 111–145). Baltimore, MD: Brookes.

Abery, B. H., Stancliffe, R. J., Smith, J., McGrew, K., & Eggebeen, A. (1995a). *Minnesota opportunities and exercise of self-determination scale-adult edition*. Minneapolis, MN: University of Minnesota, Institute on Community Integration, Research and Training Center on Community Living.

Abery, B. H., Stancliffe, R. J., Smith, J., McGrew, K., & Eggebeen, A. (1995b). *Minnesota self-determination skills, attitudes, and knowledge evaluation scale-adult edition*. Minneapolis, MN: University of Minnesota, Institute on Community Integration, Research and Training Center on Community Living.

Agran, M., Blanchard, C., & Wehmeyer, M. L. (2000). Promoting transition goals and self-determination through student-directed learning: The self-determined learning model of instruction. *Education and Training in Mental Retardation and Developmental Disabilities, 35*, 351–364.

Agran, M., Cavin, M., Wehmeyer, M. L., & Palmer, S. (2006). Participation of students with severe disabilities in the general curriculum: The effects of the self-determined learning model of instruction. *Research and Practice for Persons with Severe Disabilities, 31*, 230–241

Agran, M., King-Sears, M, Wehmeyer, M. L., & Copeland, S. R. (2003). *Teachers' guides to inclusive practices: Student-directed learning strategies*. Baltimore, MD: Brookes.

Algozzine, B., Browder, D., Karvonen, M., Test, D. W., & Wood, W. M. (2001). Effects of interventions to promote self-determination for individuals with disabilities. *Review of Educational Research, 71*, 219–277.

American Psychiatric Association. (2000). *Diagnostic and statistical manual of mental disorders* (Vol. 4, Text rev.). Washington, DC: Author.

Bacon, A. L., Fein, D., Morris, R., Waterhouse, L., & Allen, D. (1998). The responses of autistic children to the distress of others. *Journal of Autism and Developmental Disorders, 28*(2), 129–142.

Bauminger, N. (2002). The facilitation of social-emotional understanding and social interaction in high-functioning children with autism: Intervention outcomes. *Journal of Autism and Developmental Disorders, 32*(4), 283–298.

Bauminger, N. (2007a).Brief report: Individual social-multi-modal intervention for HFASD. *Journal of Autism and Developmental Disorders, 37*, 1593– 1604.

Bauminger, N. (2007b). Brief report. Group social-multi-modal intervention for HFASD. *Journal of Autism and Developmental Disorders, 37*, 1605–1615.

Bernad-Ripoli, S. (2007). Using a self-as-model video combined with social stories to help a child with Asperger syndrome understand emotions. *Focus on Autism and Other Developmental Disabilities, 22*(2), 100–106.

Bernard-Opitz, V., Sriram, N., & Nakhoda-Sapuan, S. (2001). Enhancing social problem solving in children with autism and normal children through computer-assisted instruction. *Journal of Autism and Developmental Disorders, 31*(4), 377–398.

Beyth-Marom, R., Fischhoff, B., Quadrel, M. J., & Furby, L. (1991). Teaching decision making to adolescents: A critical review. In J. Baron & R. V. Brown (Eds.), *Teaching decision making to adolescents* (pp. 19–59). Hillsdale, NJ: Erlbaum.

Boutot, E.A. (2007). Fitting in: Tips for promoting acceptance and friendships for students with autism spectrum disorders in inclusive classrooms. *Intervention in School and Clinic, 42*, 156–161.

Brandtstädter, J. (1998). Action perspectives on human development. In R. M. Lerner (Ed.), *Theoretical models of human development: Vol. 1. Handbook of child psychology* (5th ed., pp. 807–863). New York: Wiley.

Bronfenbrenner, U. (1979). *The ecology of human development: Experiments by nature and design.* Cambridge MA: Harvard University Press.

Bronfenbrenner, U. (1989). Ecological systems theory. *Annals of Child Development, 6*, 187–249.

Callahan, K., & Rademacher, J. A. (1999). Using self-management strategies to increase the on-task behavior of a student with autism. *Journal of Positive Behavior Interventions, 1*(2), 117–122.

Carter, C. M. (2001). Using choice with game play to increase language skills and interactive behaviors in children with autism. *Journal of Positive Behavior Interventions, 3*, 131–152.

Carter, E. W., Lane, K. L., Pierson, M. R., & Stang, K. K. (2008). Promoting self-determinatoin for transition-age youth: Views of high school general and special educators. *Exceptional Children, 75*(1), 55–70.

Chapman, M. (1984). Intentional action as a paradigm for developmental psychology: A symposium. *Human Development, 27*(3–4), 113–144.

Cho, H. J., Wehmeyer, M. L., & Kingston, N. (in press). The impact of social and classroom ecological factors promoting self-determination in elementary school. *Preventing School Failure.*

Cho, H.J., Wehmeyer, M.L., Kingston, N., & Palmer, S. (in press). Self-determination and elementary education: Elementary school teachers' knowledge of and use of interventions to promote self-determination. *Journal of Special Education.*

Cobb, B., Lehmann, J., Newman-Gonchar, R., & Morgen, A. (2009). Self-determination for students with disabilities: A narrative metasynthesis. *Career Development for Exceptional Individuals, 32*(2), 108–114.

Cole, C. L., & Levinson, T. R. (2002). Effects of within-activity choices on the challenging behavior of children with severe developmental disabilities. *Journal of Positive Behavior Interventions, 4*, 29–39.

Faherty, C. (2000). *What does it mean to me? A workbook explaining self awareness and life lessons to the child or youth with high functioning autism or Aspergers.* Arlington, TX: Future Horizons.

Field, S., Sarver, M. D., & Shaw, S. F. (2003). Self-determination: A key to success in postsecondary education for students with learning disabilities. *Remedial and Special Education, 24*(6), 339–349.

Fowler, C. H., Konrad, M., Walker, A. R., Test, D. W., & Wood, W. M. (2007). Self-determination interventions' effects on the academic perfromance of students with developmental disabilities. *Education and Training in Developmental Disabilities, 42*(3), 270–285.

Hamilton, A. F. C. (2009). Research review: Goals, intentions and mental states: Challenges for theories of autism. *The Journal of Child Psychology and Psychiatry, 50*(8), 881–892.

Harter, S. (1999). *The construction of the self: A developmental perspective.* New York: Guilford Press.

Held, M. F., Thoma, C. A., & Thomas, K. (2004). "The John Jones Show": How one teacher facilitated self-determined transition planning for a young man with autism. *Focus on Autism and Other Developmental Disabilities, 19*(3), 177–188.

Joyce, B., & Weil, M. (1980). *Models of teaching* (2nd ed.). Englewood Cliffs, NJ: Prentice Hall.

Koegel, L. K., Harrower, J. K., & Koegel, R. L. (1999). Support for children with developmental disabilities in full inclusion classrooms through self-management. *Journal of Positive Behavior Interventions, 1*(1), 26–34.

Koegel, R. L., Frea, W. D., & Surratt, A. V. (1994). Self-management of problematic social behavior. In E. Schopler & G. B. Mesibov (Eds.), *Behavioral issues in autism: Current issues in autism* (pp. 81–97). New York: Plenum Press.

Koegel, R. L., Koegel, L. K., & McNerney, E. K. (2001). Pivotal areas in intervention for autism. *Journal of Clinical Child Psychology, 30*(1), 19–32.

Koegel, R. L., Koegel, L. K., & Parks, D. R. (1995). "Teach the individual" model of generalization: Autonomy through self-management. In R. L. Koegel & L. K. Koegel (Eds.), *Teaching children with autism: Strategies for initiating positive interactions and improving learning opportunities* (pp. 67–77). Baltimore, MD: Brookes.

Konrad, M., Fowler, C. H., Walker, A. R., Test, D. W., & Wood, W. M. (2007). Effects of self-determination interventions on the academic skills of students with learning disabilities. *Learning Disabilities Quarterly, 30*(2), 89–113.

Krasny, L., Williams, B. J., Provencal, S., & Ozonoff, S. (2003). Social skills interventions for the autism spectrum: Essential ingredients and a model curriculum. *Child and Adolescent Psychiatric Clinics of North America, 12*(1), 107–122.

Lachapelle, Y., Wehmeyer, M .L., Haelewyck, M. C., Courbois, Y., Keith, K. D., Schalock, R., … Walsh, P. N. (2005). The relationship between quality of life and self-determination: An international study. *Journal of Intellectual Disability Research, 49*, 740–744.

Lee, S. H., Simpson, R., & Shogren, K. (2007). Effects and implications of self-management for students with autism: A meta-analysis. *Focus on Autism and Other Developmental Disabilities, 22*(1), 2–13.

Lee, S. H., Wehmeyer, M. L., Palmer, S. B., Soukup, J. H., & Little, T. D. (2008). Self-determination and access to the general education curriculum. *The Journal of Special Education, 42*, 91–107.

Lee, S. H., Wehmeyer, M. L., Soukup, J. H., & Palmer, S. B. (2010). Impact of curriculum modifications on access to the general education curriculum for students with disabilities. *Exceptional Children, 76*(2), 213–233.

Little, T. D., Hawley, P. H., Henrich, C. C., & Marsland, K. (2002). Three views of the agentic self: A developmental synthesis. In E. L. Deci & R. M. Ryan (Eds.), *Handbook of self-determination research* (pp. 389–404). Rochester, NY: University of Rochester Press.

Little, T. D., Snyder, C. R., & Wehmeyer, M. (2006). The agentic self: On the nature and origins of personal agency across the lifespan. In D. K. Mroczek & T. D. Little (Eds.), *Handbook of personality development* (pp. 61–80). Mahwah, NJ: Erlbaum.

Lord, C. (1996). Treatment of a high-functioning adolescent with autism: A cognitive–behavioral approach. In M. A. Reinecke & F. M. Dattilio (Eds.), *Cognitive therapy with children and adolescents: A casebook for clinical practice* (pp. 394–404). New York: Guilford Press.

Mancina, C., Tankersley, M., Kamps, D., Kravits, T., & Parrett, J. (2000). Reduction of inappropriate vocalizations for a child with autism using a self-management treatment program. *Journal of Autism and Developmental Disorders, 30*(6), 599–606.

Martorell, A., Gutierrez-Recacha, P., Perda, A., & Ayuso-Mateos, J. L. (2008). Identification of personal factors that determine work outcome for adults with intellectual disability. *Journal of Intellectual Disability Research, 52*(12), 1091–1101.

McGuire, J., & McDonnell, J. (2008). Relationships between recreation and levels of self-determination for adolescents and young adults with disabilities. *Career Development for Exceptional Individuals, 31*(3), 154–163.

McGlashing-Johnson, J., Agran, M., Sitlington, P., Cavin, M., & Wehmeyer, M. L. (2003). Enhancing the job performance of youth with moderate to severe cognitive disabilities using the self-determined learning model of instruction. *Research and Practice for Persons with Severe Disabilities, 28*, 194–204.

Meadan, H., & Monda-Amaya, L. (2008). Collaboration to promote social competence for students with mild disabilities in the general classroom: A structure for providing support. *Intervention in School and Clinic, 43*, 158–167.

Mechling, L. C., Gast, D. L., & Cronin, B. A. (2006). The effects of presenting high-preference items, paired with choice, via computer-based video programming on task completion of students with autism. *Focus on Autism and Other Developmental Disabilities, 21*(1), 7–13.

Mithaug, D. E. (1993). *Self-regulation theory: How optimal adjustment maximizes gain.* Westport, CT: Praeger.

Mithaug, D. E. (1998). Your right, my obligation? *Journal of the Association for Persons with Severe Disabilities, 23*, 41–43.

Morris, S. (2002). Promoting social skills among students with nonverbal learning disabilities. *Teaching Exceptional Children, 34*, 66–70.

Newman, B., Reinecke, D. R., & Meinberg, D. L. (2000). Self-management of varied responding in three students with autism. *Behavioral Interventions, 15*(2), 145–151.

Nota, L., Ferrrari, L., Soresi, S., & Wehmeyer, M. L. (2007). Self-determination, social abilities, and the quality of life of people with intellectual disabilities. *Journal of Intellectual Disability Research, 51*, 850–865.

Odom, S. L., Brantlinger, E., Gersten, R., Horner, R. H., Thompson, B., & Harris, K. R. (2005). Research in special education: Scientific methods and evidence-based practices. *Exceptional Children, 71*, 137–148.

Palmer, S., & Wehmeyer, M. L. (2003). Promoting self-determination in early elementary school: Teaching self-regulated problem-solving and goal setting skills. *Remedial and Special Education, 24,* 115–126.

Palmer, S. B., Wehmeyer, M. L., Gipson, K., & Agran, M. (2004). Promoting access to the general curriculum by teaching self-determination skills. *Exceptional Children, 70,* 427–439.

Polloway, E. A., Miller, L., & Smith, T. E. C. (in press). *Language instruction for students with disabilities* (4th ed). Denver, CO: Love.

Ruble, L. A., & Scott, M. M. (2002). Executive functions and the natural habitat behaviors of children with autism. *Autism, 6*(4), 365–381.

Ruef, M. B., & Turnbull, A. P. (2002). The perspectives of individuals with cognitive disabilities and/or autism on their lives and their problem behavior. *Research and Practice for Persons with Severe Disabilities, 27*(2), 125–140.

Sherer, M., Pierce, K. L., Paredes, S., Kisacky, K. L., Ingersoll, B., & Schreibman, L. (2001). Enhancing conversation skills in children with autism via video technology: Which is better, "Self" or "Other" as a model? *Behavior Modification, 25*(1), 140–158.

Shogren, K., Faggella-Luby, M., Bae, S. J., & Wehmeyer, M. L. (2004). The effect of choice-making as an intervention for problem behavior: A meta-analysis. *Journal of Positive Behavior Interventions, 6,* 228–237.

Shogren, K. A., Lopez, S. J., Wehmeyer, M. L., Little, T. D., & Pressgrove, C. L. (2006). The role of positive psychology constructs in predicting life satisfaction in adolescents with and without cognitive disabilities: An exploratory study. *The Journal of Positive Psychology, 1,* 37–52.

Shogren, K. A., Wehmeyer, M. L., Palmer, S. B., Soukup, J. H., Little, T., Garner, N., ... Lawrence, M. (2008). Understanding the construct of self-determination: Examining the relationship between The Arc's Self-Determination Scale and the American Institute for Research Self-Determination Scale. *Assessment for Effective Instruction, 33,* 94–107.

Sigman, M., & Ruskin, E. (1999). Continuity and change in the social competence of children with autism, Down syndrome, and developmental delays. *Monographs of the Society for Research in Child Development, 64*(1), v–114.

Slavin, R. E. (2009). *Educational psychology: Theory and practice* (9th ed.). Columbus, OH: Merrill.

Smith, S. W., & Gilles, D.O. L. (2003). Using key instructional elements to systematically promote social skills generalization for students with challenging behavior. *Intervention in School and Clinic, 39,* 30–37.

Smith, T. E. C., Gartin, B., & Murdick, N. (in press). *Including adolescents with disabilities in general education classrooms.* Upper Saddle River, NJ: Pearson.

Stancliffe, R. J., Abery, B. H., & Smith, J. (2000). Personal control and the ecology of community living settings: Beyond living-unit size and type. *American Journal on Mental Retardation, 105,* 431–454.

Test, D. W., Fowler, C., Kohler, P., & Kortering, L. (2010). *Evidence-based practices and predictors in secondary transition: What we know and what we still need to know.* Charlotte, NC: National Secondary Transition Technical Assistance Center.

Test, D. W., Karvonen, M., Wood, W. M., Browder, D., & Algozzine, B. (2000). Choosing a self-determination curriculum: Plan for the future. *Teaching Exceptional Children, 33,* 48–54

Thoma, C. A., Pannozzo, G. M., Fritton, S. C., & Bartholomew, C. C. (2008). A qualitative study of preservice teachers' understanding of self-determination for students with significant disabiltiies. *Career Development for Exceptional Individuals, 31*(2), 94–105.

Todd, T., & Reid, G. (2006). Increasing physical activity in individuals with autism. *Focus on Autism and Other Developmental Disabilities, 21*(3), 167–176.

Travis, L., Sigman, M., & Ruskin, E. (2001). Links between social understanding and social behavior in verbally able children with autism. *Journal of Autism and Developmental Disorders, 31*(2), 119–130.

Walker, H. M., Calkins, C., Wehmeyer, M., Walker, L., Bacon, A., Palmer, S., ... Johnson, D. (2010). *A social-ecological approach to promote self-determination.* Manuscript submitted for publication.

Wehmeyer, M. L. (1996). A self-report measure of self-determination for adolescents with cognitive disabilities. *Education and Training in Mental Retardation and Developmental Disabilities, 31,* 282–293.

Wehmeyer, M. L. (2005). Self-determination and individuals with severe disabilities: Reexamining meanings and misinterpretations. *Research and Practice in Severe Disabilities, 30,* 113–120.

Wehmeyer, M. L., Abery, B., Mithaug, D. E., & Stancliffe, R. J. (2003). *Theory in self-determination: Foundations for educational practice.* Springfield, IL: Thomas.

Wehmeyer, M. L., Agran, M., & Hughes, C. (2000). A national survey of teachers' promotion of self-determination and student-directed learning. *Journal of Special Education, 34,* 58–68.

Wehmeyer, M. L., Agran, M., Hughes, C., Martin, J., Mithaug, D. E., & Palmer, S. (2007). *Promoting self-determination in students with intellectual and developmental disabilities.* New York: Guilford Press.

Wehmeyer, M. L., & Field, S. (2007). *Self-determination: Instructional and assessment strategies.* Thousand Oaks, CA: Corwin Press.

Wehmeyer, M. L., Kelchner, K., & Richards, S. (1996). Essential characteristics of self-determined behavior of individuals with mental retardation. *American Journal on Mental Retardation, 100,* 632–642.

Wehmeyer, M. L., & Palmer, S. B. (2003). Adult outcomes from students with cognitive disabilities three years after high school: The impact of self-determination. *Education and Training in Developmental Disabilities, 38*, 131–144.

Wehmeyer, M. L., Palmer, S., Agran, M., Mithaug, D., & Martin, J. (2000). Promoting causal agency: The self-determined learning model of instruction. *Exceptional Children, 66*, 439–453.

Wehmeyer, M. L., & Schwartz, M. (1997). Self-determination and positive adult outcomes: A follow-up study of youth with mental retardation or learning disabilities. *Exceptional Children, 63*, 245–255.

Wehmeyer, M. L., & Schwartz, M. (1998). The relationship between self-determination and quality of life for adults with mental retardation. *Education and Training in Mental Retardation and Developmental Disabilities, 33*, 3–12.

Wehmeyer, M.L., & Shogren, K. (2008). Self-determination and learners with autism spectrum disorders. In R. Simpson & B. Myles (Eds.), *Educating children and youth with autism: Strategies for effective practice* (2nd ed., pp. 433–476). Austin, TX: ProEd.

Whitman, T. L. (1990). Self-regulation and mental retardation. *American Journal on Mental Retardation, 94*(4), 347–362.

14

TRANSITION TO POSTSECONDARY EDUCATION, EMPLOYMENT, AND ADULT LIVING

Michael L. Wehmeyer

UNIVERSITY OF KANSAS

James R. D. Patton

UNIVERSITY OF TEXAS

For youth with autism spectrum disorders (ASD), receiving instruction using research- and evidence-based practices is, in part, a means to an end. That end is that the young person transitions from high school to some form of postsecondary education or gainful and fulfilling employment and assumes the roles and responsibilities of adulthood in his or her community. This chapter examines the research base for transition-related practices leading to these outcomes.

Overview of Transition and Transition Services

The concept of transition typically implies movement and change. Change, as it applies to students who are preparing to leave high school, is associated with those new situations in which they will find themselves. These new situations come with certain demands and challenges that require an array of knowledge and skill sets to function successfully. The nature of the transition planning process is aptly captured by the Japanese expression *shibumi*, which is loosely translated as "simple yet complex." The idea of planning for one's future seems straightforward and not too complicated until one engages the many facets of this process. The transition to the world after high school is complicated and needs systematic attention.

Vertical and Horizontal Transitions

We experience many transitions throughout our lives. Some of them are very predictable and others are unique to individual circumstances. As mentioned, important transitions occur along and across everyone's life span. Some of these are normative and predictable (vertical), whereas others are individual-specific and occur at some specific point in time (horizontal).

The life-span related (i.e., vertical) transitions are associated with predictable life events, such as beginning school, leaving elementary school, and growing older. Coordinated planning for these transitions can minimize the anxiety that may arise, and make such transitions smoother, but in reality, little comprehensive planning occurs in the lives of most individuals.

Horizontal transitions refer to movement from one situation or setting to another. One of the most important and frequently discussed horizontal transitions is the movement from separate settings to more inclusive ones. This is an example of a transition that is not age specific because opportunities for such movement are available throughout the life span for persons with disabilities.

Transition Defined

Transition from school to postschool settings has been defined in different ways since the early 1980s. The Division on Career Development and Transition (DCDT; Halpern, 1994) developed one of the most comprehensive definitions. This definition underscores the realities associated with change. It points out that, as students leave school, they will have to assume a variety of adult roles in the community. It also stresses the proactive aspects of transition education and the importance of actively involving students in this process whenever possible. The definition, written by Halpern (1994), reads as follows:

> Transition refers to a change in status from behaving primarily as a student to assuming emergent adult roles in the community. These roles include employment, participating in postsecondary education, maintaining a home, becoming appropriately involved in the community, and experiencing satisfactory personal and social relationships. The process of enhancing transition involves the participation and coordination of school programs, adult agency services, and natural supports within the community. The foundations for transition should be laid during the elementary and middle school years, guided by the broad concept of career development. Transition planning should begin no later than age 14, and students should be encouraged, to the full extent of their capabilities, to assume a maximum amount of responsibility for such planning. (p. 117)

Rationale and Mandate

To understand the importance of good transition planning and services, it is useful to consider the outcomes associated with successful functioning in adulthood, which is the ultimate goal of transition planning/services efforts. Teachers should be driven by the goal of assisting students to become participatory citizens across a number of inclusive adult settings. Moreover, a desire exists to ensure that students achieve some sense of personal fulfillment in their lives as adults. The transition process assists in achieving these goals by providing a mechanism that teaches the knowledge and skills required in adult settings and by linking students or their families to the services and supports that are needed as well.

It is important to recognize that the process whereby students are taught the knowledge and skills, as well as linked to the supports and services, that they will need later on is a shared responsibility. Whereas the school, which operates under the mandate of the Individuals with Disabilities Education Act (2004), which requires that transition planning be in place by age 16, is necessarily a primary agent in the transition process, the family, the student, and other service providers also play critical roles. Hence, this process should always be considered a shared process with the student as the key player. In other words, while many individuals need to be, and should be involved in this process, it is the student, whose life is being considered, who should drive and lead this process.

Key Elements of the Transition Planning/Services Process

The transition from school to life after high school is facilitated, if the following elements have been implemented: comprehensive assessment of strengths, needs, preferences, and interests; development of a set of transition activities/services that is included in the IEP; implementation of the elements included in the IEP; and need for coordination (i.e., cooperation, collaboration, communication) among key school and adult service agency personnel. Although other factors, such as motivation or disposition of the student making the transition, also should be recognized as important, the basic elements highlighted in this section are the sine qua non for successful transition.

Transition, Assessment, and Planning.   This first element primarily includes examining the student who will be going through a transition, in terms of what he or she wants to do when school is over. Specific strategies for assessment are discussed subsequently in the chapter, so our treatment here is at the big picture level. Such assessment involves a look at the student's strengths as well as those areas that require attention now (i.e., instruction or experience) and those that will arise in the future. This assessment process requires a systematic and comprehensive way to obtain this information.

This phase should also involve closely looking at the receiving setting(s) into which the student will be going when high school is completed. In other words, the more the student, his or her family, and school-based transition personnel know about the receiving environment (i.e., what is demanded to be successful) and the existing strengths and challenges of the person who must deal with this subsequent setting, the better the chances for creating an effective transition to this new setting.

The results of a comprehensive assessment process should be discussed at an IEP meeting that is dedicated to the topic of transition and then ultimately written into the IEP for the student. As discussed in more detail subsequently, whenever possible the student should be the one who leads the discussion of his or her transition preferences, interests, strengths, and needs.

Acting on the Plans.   Even high quality assessment and individualized planning become moot if the plan is not implemented effectively. Far too often, good plans are not put into effect. This important stage of the transition process suffers from two potential threats: (a) not being executed as planned and (b) some important aspects not being carried out because the assessment or the planning phase were performed inadequately.

School and Agency Coordination.   The element of a successful transition is the coordination that can and should occur among key parties involved in the transition itself. Such coordination requires ongoing cooperation, collaboration, and at very least communication. The movement of a student from school into any number of postschool settings such as a job or some type of further education setting is facilitated by coordination among various school and adult service providers.

Without comprehensive planning, effective implementation of the plan, and coordination of efforts, movement from one setting to another is likely to result only in physical relocation without the more meaningful outcomes associated with successful transition.

Guiding Principles

Certain principles are essential to guiding the transition process for students with autism. The guiding principles listed below represent a few of the many principles that should guide the transition process in schools and serve as a frame of reference for the implementation of transition planning and services.

- Transition efforts should start early.
- Planning must be comprehensive.
- The planning process must consider a student's preferences and interests.
- The transition planning process should be considered a capacity-building activity (i.e., consider a student's strengths).
- Student participation throughout the process is essential.
- Family involvement is desired, needed, and crucial.
- The transition planning process must be sensitive to diversity.
- Supports and services are useful and we all use them.
- Community-based activities can provide extremely beneficial experiences.
- Interagency commitment and coordination is essential.
- Timing is crucial if certain linkages are to be made and a seamless transition to life after high school is to be achieved.
- Ranking of transition needs must occur for students who have an extensive set of challenges.

Transition and Students with Autism Spectrum Disorders

There is a general acknowledgment that too few studies have focused on the educational attainment or outcomes of youth with ASD (Seltzer, Greenberg, Floyd, & Hong, 2004). It should come as no surprise, then, that there is a paucity of data with regard to transition-related outcomes for students with ASD. The most current and comprehensive understanding of secondary school experiences for transition-age youth with ASD comes from the U.S. Department of Education-funded *National Longitudinal Transition Study 2* (NLTS2; Newman, 2007). The NLTS2 is a 10-year study of transition-related outcomes of 12,000 youth who were aged 13 to 16 at the start of the study. Preliminary data pertaining to secondary school experiences for approximately 1,000 students with ASD were reported by Newman (2007).

From students with ASD in the NLTS2 sample, 77% had at least one vocational education course in secondary education, and, on average, vocational education coursework constitutes 20% of the average course load of these students. Of those vocational education courses, 76% of students received such course instruction in a special education setting. Of the 24% of students with ASD who received vocational education through a general education vocational education course, nearly three-quarters were identified as receiving the same curriculum and instructional materials as nondisabled peers, and nearly 70% were engaged in the same class activities as their nondisabled peers. Seventy-one percent of students with ASD took some life skills courses.

Hendricks and Wehman (2009) reviewed the literature pertaining to the transition from school to adulthood for students with ASD. The findings were not encouraging. These authors found that most young people with ASD continue to live at home with their parents following high school, that most young adults with ASD are unemployed (Standifer, 2009), and that many young adults with ASD are socially isolated and not included in their community's activities. Additionally, Hendricks and Wehman found that a minority of youth with ASD attended postsecondary education.

There is clearly a need for more research pertaining to transition-related outcomes for youth with ASD. It seems evident, however, from the research that exists, that transition-related outcomes for students with ASD are less positive than desired by educators, parents and family members, and people with ASD themselves. These findings also point to the need to focus on social competence and social skills acquisition in the transition process (see earlier chapters by

Simpson, Ganz, & Mason and Wehmeyer & Smith in the present work for more detailed analyses of the role of social skills and social competence in mediating outcomes for young people with ASD). Social skills and transition outcomes are inherently linked in the lives of people with ASD. Findings that young adults with ASD are socially isolated are self-evidently tied to issues of social competence and skills. Even outcomes such as employment, however, tie directly to these issues of social competence. Research shows that social skills limitations are a major reason that people with ASD have difficulty finding or retaining a job (Schall & Wehman, 2009). Other common issues that impinge on success in post high school settings include communication difficulties, and behavioral issues and concerns (Schall & Wehman) as well as, importantly, the lack of adequate supports within the system to mitigate the effects of these barriers (Targett & Wehman, 2009).

Transition Planning and IEP Development

Effective Practices in IEP Development for Transition

Effective transitions from high school to adulthood begin with effective transition planning for all students, including students with ASD. There are few studies that have examined the transition planning and IEP development process specifically for students with ASD, so most recommendations are generic in nature (e.g., pertaining to best practices for all students with disabilities). The NLTS2 did confirm that most students (85%) with ASD have a transition plan, though that says nothing about the quality of those plans. It is not feasible to go into detail about the federal requirements for educational planning, other than to note that the Individuals with Disabilities Education Act has, since 1992, required that the individualized education program of adolescent students (16 and older in the most recent reauthorization) include a discussion about needed transition goals and supports and include IEP goals and transition services leading to the attainment of such goals. It seems self-evident that such goals for students with ASD should address communication and social skills issues in the community (Schall, 2009; see Simpson, Ganz, & Mason, this volume); address key elements of instructional need in self-determination (e.g., problem solving, goal setting; see Wehmeyer & Smith, this volume); and focus on outcomes such as employment and community inclusion. That happens, currently, only to a limited extent. One report of the NLTS2 (Cameto, Levine, & Wagner, 2004) found that, among the IEPs of secondary-age students with ASD, 22% contained goals for competitive employment, 39% had goals for supported employment, and 39% contained goals for sheltered employment. That such a high percentage of goals target sheltered employment is discomforting. Goals pertaining to living skills were found on 58% of the IEPs, though only 28% focused on independent living. Only 23% of IEPs had goals pertaining to attending postsecondary education, while 57% had goals related to increasing friendships and social interactions. The latter are, of course, important, but the dearth of goals related to independent living, competitive employment, and postsecondary education suggests that there are limited expectations in schools now for such outcomes, an issue that needs to be remedied.

A common practice in quality transition planning involves the use of person-centered planning, which refers to approaches to planning for the delivery of educational and transition services and supports for students with disabilities that share common beliefs and attempt to put those beliefs into a planning framework. Such beliefs include:

- All individuals, regardless of the type or severity of their disability, benefit from services to support them in their communities and, through such supports, benefit the community itself (Schwartz, Jacobson, and Holburn, 2000);

- Direction for planning should come from the individual in shaping the planning process and formulating plans;
- The primacy of personal social relationships in supports to the individual and the consequent importance of the involvement of family and friends in the planning process;
- A focus on capacities and assets rather than limitations and deficiencies;
- An emphasis on settings, supports, and services available in the community as opposed to being disability-specific (O'Brien & Lovett, 1993).

Schwartz et al. (2000) used a consensus process to define "person-centeredness." This effort provides a useful picture of the values underlying person-centered planning as it exists today. Specifically, Schwartz and colleagues identified eight "hallmarks" of a person-centered planning process:

1. The person's activities, services, and supports are based upon his or her dreams, interests, preferences, strengths, and capacities.
2. The person and people important to him or her are included in lifestyle planning, and have the opportunity to exercise control and make informed decisions.
3. The person has meaningful choices, with decisions based on his or her experiences.
4. The person uses, when possible, natural and community supports.
5. Activities, supports, and services foster skills to achieve personal relationships, community inclusion, dignity, and respect.
6. The person's opportunities and experiences are maximized, and flexibility is enhanced within existing regulatory and funding constraints.
7. Planning is collaborative, recurring, and involves an ongoing commitment to the person.
8. The person is satisfied with his or her relationships, home, and daily routine (p. 238).

The characteristics of person-centered planning match, in many cases, the needs for the structure of planning for students with ASD; it is highly individualized, person-focused, collaborative, and emphasizes capacities and not deficits. Held, Thoma, and Thomas (2004) used a person-centered process in planning for the transition of a student with ASD, and concluded that the combination of strategies, beginning with the use of person-centered planning methods, and incorporating a focus on promoting self-determination and self-instruction, and the use of technology to give the student a "voice" in the process, was effective in creating high quality transition plans. Another important benefit of person-centered planning is that it creates a means to include parents and family members in meaningful ways in the planning process.

Student Involvement in Transition Planning

One means of ensuring that students with ASD have a "voice" in planning for their future is to ensure they are involved in such planning. The promotion of student involvement in educational planning and decision making has become best practice in the field of transition. Research documents the positive impact of efforts to promote student involvement in educational and transition planning on more positive transition outcomes (Martin et al., 2006; Mason, Field, & Sawilowsky, 2004; Test et al., 2004). Test and colleagues (2004), for example, reviewed articles reporting 16 studies designed to evaluate the effects of interventions to promote student involvement, and concluded that students across disability categories can become actively involved in the IEP process, and that instruction to promote such involvement results in enhanced student participation in the IEP process.

There are, now, a number of interventions designed to promote student involvement in educational and transition planning that have some evidence of their impact on one or more aspects of student involvement, including the *Self-Directed IEP* (Martin, Marshall, Maxson, & Jerman, 1993), the *Self-Advocacy Strategy* (2nd ed.) (Van Reusen, Bos, Schumaker, & Deshler, 2002), *Whose Future Is It Anyway?* (2nd ed.) (Wehmeyer et al., 2004), "Take Charge for the Future" (Powers et al., 2001), and the *Next S.T.E.P. Curriculum* (2nd ed.; Halpern, Herr, Doren, & Wolf, 2000), and there is an emerging database documenting the efficacy of these interventions. Martin et al. (2006), for example, conducted a randomized trial, control group study of the effectiveness of the Self-Directed IEP program involving 130 secondary students, with observations conducted in 130 IEP meetings. The results showed that involvement in the process significantly increased the percentage of time students talked and started or led their IEP meeting. Several studies have evaluated the efficacy of the *Whose Future Is It Anyway?* process (WFA; Wehmeyer et al., 2004). Wehmeyer and Lawrence (1995) implemented the WFA with 53 high school students with cognitive disabilities, and found that students involved with the process showed more positive perceptions about their capacity to self-direct planning and held more positive expectations for the success of such self-directed planning. Wehmeyer and Lawrence (2002) conducted a national replication of WFA with 290 students with intellectual disability across 21 states, measuring knowledge about transition planning and perceptions of transition planning efficacy pre- and postintervention. Students involved in the project gained knowledge about transition planning and had significantly more positive perceptions of self-efficacy about transition planning and more positive outcome expectations.

One of the frequently cited benefits of student involvement in educational planning and decision making has been that such efforts and experiences lead to the enhanced self-determination of adolescents with disabilities. Williams-Diehm, Wehmeyer, Palmer, Soukup, and Garner (2008) studied the differences in level of self-determination between 276 students with disabilities divided into groups that differed by level of student involvement in the IEP meeting. Multivariate analysis showed significant differences between self-determination scores using two different measures for students in a high involvement group versus students in a low involvement group, indicating that students who were more involved in their meetings were more self-determined. A second multivariate analysis found, though, that students who were more self-determined (two groups, high or low self-determination) were more likely to be involved in their IEP meeting. This replicated findings from Sands, Spencer, Gliner, and Swaim (1999), who showed that using structural equation modeling one measured component element of self-determined behavior predicted student involvement in transition-related activities, and both studies suggest a reciprocal relationship between self-determination and student involvement (e.g., greater self-determination leads to greater involvement, but greater involvement also leads to enhanced self-determination). Recently, Wehmeyer, Palmer, Lee, Williams-Diehm, and Shogren (in press) conducted a randomized trial evaluation of intervention with the WFA, finding a causal link between intervention with the WFA and greater self-determination and transition planning knowledge.

Cross, Cooke, Wood, and Test (1999) compared the effects of the MAPS person-centered planning process (Vandercook, York, & Forest, 1989) and the *Choosing Employment Goals* curriculum (Marshall, Martin, Maxson, & Jerman, 1997) on self-determination and found significant, positive differences in pre- and postintervention scores for groups receiving either intervention. Zhang (2001) examined the effects of the *Next S.T.E.P Curriculum* (Halpern et al., 1997) on the self-determination of high school students with learning disabilities, and found that intervention significantly improved the self-determination scores of a treatment group when compared with those of a control group.

As with transition planning in general, there is little research examining student involvement in educational planning specifically with students with ASD. In fact, among the 16 studies reviewed by Test and colleagues (2004), there were 309 students involved, and of those, only one was identified with autism. More recent studies, though, are including students with ASD. For example, the Wehmeyer et al. (in press) study of the effects of the *Whose Future* curriculum included 27 students with ASD. Again, however, there is a need for more research with regard to the effects of student involvement in transition planning on transition plans and outcomes for students with ASD.

Assessment in Transition

As is the case with instruction in any content area, assessment and instruction go hand-in-hand in efforts to promote an effective transition and, not surprisingly, little research has delved into the unique needs of students with ASD in this transition process. Determining instructional and curricular needs in transition will involve a combination of standardized and informal procedures incorporating input from multiple sources, including the student, his or her family, professionals, and others. Clark (1996) identified informal assessment from which transition-related decisions can be made as including: (a) situational or observational learning styles assessments; (b) curriculum-based assessment; (c) observational reports from teachers, employers, and family members; (d) situational assessments in home, community, and work settings; (e) environmental assessments; (f) personal-future planning activities; (g) structured interviews with students; (h) structured interviews with parents, guardians, advocates, or peers; (i) adaptive, behavioral, or functional skill inventories; (j) social histories; (k) employability, independent living, and personal-social skills rating scales; and (l) technology or vocational education skills assessments.

These types of assessment procedures enable planners to form a complete picture of student needs, interests, and abilities by gathering input from multiple sources, and are important for determining needed transition goals and services. Not only must data be gathered from multiple sources, however, such data collection must occur in multiple content areas, from career development and job skills to independent living and self-care. A comprehensive litany of such domains and assessment needs is beyond the scope of this chapter, but Schall (2009) identified several ways in which students with ASD might respond differentially to the assessment process than might other students, and those issues are worth pointing out.

First, some students with ASD may have difficulty generalizing skills to the environment in which that skill is to be used or other environments (Whalen, 2009). In such cases, as discussed briefly in the section on life skills and community-based instruction subsequently, such assessment should occur in the context in which it would be used and not just taught and assessed in one context with the presumption that it will be utilized in the appropriate setting. Second, Schall noted that some students with ASD can become prompt-dependent, meaning that they can perform a task or activity, but do not do so until they are prompted to do so. The issue here is one of prompt-fading in instruction, but the message for assessment is that assessors should recognize that a nonresponse by some students with ASD may reflect prompt-dependency, necessitating instruction to reduce such dependency, instead of skill deficits, instruction for which would be different. Third, and relatedly, some students with ASD exhibit stimulus overselectivity, often resulting in a focus on irrelevant or extraneous stimuli, and sometimes, resulting in difficulty in focusing on the target of the assessment. Finally, Schall noted that some students with ASD may have difficulty visioning themselves in different, future-oriented situations. Obviously, transition assessment and planning is future-oriented, so teachers must be wary of making presumptions from assessments that ask future-oriented questions unless it is clear that the student is comfortable and able to make such projections (Schall, 2009, p. 44).

As with any other instructional domains, issues of social skills and social competence are critically important in assessing for transition needs. For example, Schall, Doval, Targett, and Wehman (2006) discuss the unique needs of students with ASD in the traditional sequencing of job and career assessment and instruction. Typically, the development of specific job skills begins with assessment and instruction related to career awareness and career exploration, during which time students in middle/junior high and into high school learn about a broad range of career options, needed skills for particular types of careers, and then sample or explore some jobs across different careers of interest. That is followed, through high school, by a narrowing of the focus to specific career domains and jobs, job skills assessment and instruction, and, eventually, assessment specific to a particular job so as to inform instruction for skills within that job. Several issues may impact students with ASD in this sequence. Schall et al. (2006) noted that, for one thing, because of issues of social immaturity, many parents of students with ASD are hesitant to allow their children to hold jobs, even in career and job exploration phases. Further, as Schall et al. noted, some students with ASD don't connect what they learn from more exploratory activities to specific jobs.

There are only a few systems developed to assess transition needs, the most prominent one being, probably, the Transition Planning Inventory (TPI; Clark & Patton, 2006). The TPI is a testing system designed to identify and plan for the comprehensive transition needs of students, with data gathered from the student, parents, and school personnel, across all major transition domains. Recently, Rehfeldt, Clark, and Lee (in press) examined whether IEP teams that used the TPI generated significantly more transition-related IEP goals. They found that, among IEP teams for 56 students, including some students with ASD, those IEP teams who used the TPI developed significantly more transition-related goals.

One autism-specific planning system is the Comprehensive Autism Planning System-Transition (CAPS-TR; Henry & Myles, 2007; Myles & Steere, in press). The CAPS-TR is "a system that ties the type and intensities of supports that individuals require to their daily schedule of activities" (p. 14) and is organized around 10 elements, from the time of day and time of activity and associated tasks, to the training needed to be an effective employee, to social skills in transition areas, and to the types of supports needed for the student to succeed. For example, the CAPS-TR assists planning teams in the consideration of transition-related factors such as needed employee training; needed social skills and communication supports in daily living and transition-related domains; environmental supports, modifications, and accommodations needed to ensure greater independence; natural supports provided by coworkers, community members, neighbors, and others; and the types of data that can be collected to document progress in transition-related domains.

School-Based Transition-Related Instruction

Again, the literature pertaining to instruction to promote transition-related outcomes for students with ASD is not well differentiated from the literature pertaining to students with disabilities in general, except in the area of transition from high school to postsecondary education. The following sections address critical instructional areas with two notable exceptions; instruction to promote social skills and social inclusion and instruction to promote self-determination. These two are, of course, critical domains for students with ASD receiving transition instruction, and are not included in this chapter simply because other chapters in this text (Simpson et al. and Wehmeyer et al.) deal specifically with these issues, so readers are referred to those chapters.

Community-Based and Life Skills Instruction

The area of life skills instruction captures a broad array of skills needed to function in one's community and ranges from independent living skills to community inclusion skills and more. We begin this section, though, not with specific content domains, but with a brief discussion of the context in which such instruction should take place. As noted previously by Schall (2009), many students with ASD have difficulty generalizing a skill learned in one setting to a different setting. The solution to this issue is simple; instruction is provided in settings, typically called ecologically valid settings, in which the skill will be used.

Community-referenced planning and community-based instruction incorporate several basic characteristics. First, community-based instruction relies on community-referenced planning that is ecologically valid. Ryndak and Alper (1996) identified the steps of community-based instruction:

1. Select the instructional domain (e.g., vocation, recreation-leisure, independent living, etc.) based upon community-referenced assessment.
2. Identify current and future environments in this domain in which the student needs to learn skills and knowledge to better enable him or her to succeed.
3. Prioritize the need for instruction in specific subenvironments in each environment.
4. Identify activities within each subenvironment.
5. Task analyze the priority activities into their component skills.

So, for example, the instructional domain of a student with ASD might be vocational, and a student may have expressed a preference to work with animals. The ecological inventory might, then, identify a specific environment (pet store), and subenvironments within that environment (stock room, checkout counter, animal cages, etc.), prioritize the subenvironments in which the student will most likely function, identify tasks within prioritized subenvironments (cleaning cages, feeding animals, cleaning windows), and, finally, provide a task analysis for use in teaching each task. Obviously, community-based instruction is labor intensive, and many students with ASD will be able to learn in a school context and then generalize skills, but some students on the spectrum, and particularly students with a concomitant cognitive impairment, will benefit from this more intensive instructional approach.

The domains in which life skills and community-based instruction are needed vary, as is always the case, according to the student's unique strengths and areas of instructional need. Smith and Targett (2009) identified a number of major critical life skills domains in which students with ASD might require instruction: Mobility, recreation and leisure skills, health and safety, money management, and socialization. Two of these, mobility skills and recreation and leisure, have areas of instructional need that may be unique (or of particular priority) for students with ASD. Mobility skills involve those skills needed to successfully move around one's environment. The areas of instructional need for students with ASD identified by Smith and Targett involve the more generic issue of safety (e.g., obeying street signage when crossing streets), which is present in almost any instructional program pertaining to mobility skills, to the unique needs of some learners with ASD with regard to the expression of dangerous or disruptive behavior in vehicles or on public transportation. Instructional strategies in this area that might benefit students with ASD include targeted instruction in specific mobility skills (reading signs, learning addresses, etc.), social skills instruction pertaining to appropriate mobility and travel skills (e.g., social rules in public transportation), and behavior support plans for disruptive behavior.

The second domain identified by Smith and Targett involves the self-explanatory recreation and leisure skills area. This is an area that may be more salient to the transition needs of students with ASD than students with other disabilities, in fact, given that students with ASD often have restricted areas of interest (Vital, Ronald, Wallace & Happe, 2009) as well as difficulties in social skills in this area. Instruction to address these issues involves, quite simply, exposing students to a wide array of recreation and leisure activities and, as needed, providing skills training in those areas in which students show some interest, typically in community-based settings. For students whose areas of intense interest limit the range of recreational and leisure activities in which he or she engages, one strategy is to build on those interests so as to expand the types of other leisure activities in which the student might participate (Smith & Targett, 2009, p. 216).

Transition to Postsecondary Education

One of the few transition-related areas in which there is a growing literature base pertains to the transition from high school to postsecondary education settings, including 2-year and 4-year colleges. Briel and Getzel (2009) suggested that there were "several key areas" that are essential to the transition from secondary to postsecondary education for students with ASD, including a focus on self-determination and self-management skills (see Wehmeyer & Smith, this volume), using technology, and obtaining internships or other career-related activities. With regard to technology use, Mazzottie, Test, Wood, and Richter (2010) used multiple-baseline across behaviors design to demonstrate the positive effects of computer-assisted instruction of postschool options (employment, independent living, postsecondary education) with a young man with ASD.

Obviously, postsecondary education environments are different from secondary environments, with less contact with instructors, expectations of independent work, fewer tests covering more material, and increased social and independent living demands (Briel & Getzel, 2009, p. 191). These circumstances are difficult for many students to be successful in, and may pose particular challenges to students with ASD. Adreon and Durocher (2007) identified several key issues that must be addressed in the transition of students with ASD to postsecondary education, including the type and size of the college and living arrangements, level and sophistication of independent living skills, self-advocacy and self-awareness issues, and needed supports for both social and academic needs. These issues are, obviously, intertwined; students who have greater support needs—socially, academically, and with regard to independent living—will probably benefit from the increased opportunity for individualized supports and attentions often associated with community colleges rather than with larger universities. On the other hand, as Adreon and Durocher noted, there are drawbacks to community colleges that need to be considered, such as the fact that smaller schools may increase one's visibility or that if a student ultimately wants to obtain a bachelor's degree, he or she will have to make another transition from a community college to a university. VanBergeijk, Klin, and Volkmar (2008) refer to these as issues of "goodness of fit" and recommend that students consider both the environment and the supports that postsecondary education settings use to assist students on the spectrum.

There are a number of types of postsecondary education programs designed particularly for students with ASD and other developmental disabilities, ranging from substantially separate programs to inclusive supports. Hart, Grigal, Sax, Martinez, and Will (2006) described the latter as consisting of students receiving individualized supports, such as tutors, technology supports, and so forth, while enrolled in college classes, certificate programs, or degree programs.

Alpern and Zager (2007) emphasized, particularly with regard to inclusive settings, the importance of addressing the communication needs of students in postsecondary settings. These authors recommend that transition teams consider goals addressing joint attention, social reciprocity, language skills, and behavioral and emotional self-regulation when preparing students for life in college.

An important issue in postsecondary education related to self-advocacy is that of "disclosure" (see Wehmeyer and Smith, this volume for a treatment of self-advocacy skills for students with ASD): whether or not to disclose to school officials and others that one has an ASD, and thus is eligible for supports available to students with disabilities. Again there are benefits and disadvantages to disclosure (Shore, 2001), but students and transition planning teams need to consider whether such disclosure is necessary to obtain the types of supports—particularly academic supports such as preferential seating, note taking, or modifications to examinations—that might contribute to the student's success.

As is the case in most areas, social issues come to the forefront in considering postsecondary education for students with ASD. Myles and Adreon (2001) suggested the use of a liaison that the person can go to in times of anxiety, isolation, or stress. This person, who might be another student (mentor) or a staff/faculty person, would not only be available for the student, but would check in periodically to ensure that the student is functioning and to assist in problem solving (Briel & Getzel, 2009).

Transition to Employment

Of course, a primary purpose of postsecondary education is to prepare young adults for the world of work. As noted previously, a disproportionate number of people with ASD are unemployed or underemployed (e.g., working in sheltered workshops). There is a consensus that the preferred and attainable goal for youth with ASD should be eventual employment in integrated settings (Targett & Wehman, 2009), whether that is upon graduation from postsecondary education or directly upon graduation from high school. As Targett and Wehman emphasized, research is clear that with appropriate and adequate supports, people with ASD can work in a variety of jobs in their communities. For example, Hillier and colleagues (2007) demonstrated the efficacy of a vocational support program over 2 years in finding and maintaining competitive employment for employees with ASD.

Once again, there is a dearth of research specifically pertaining to supporting people with ASD in integrated, competitive work settings, and most of the strategies suggested are drawn from the broader fields of supported employment and natural supports, which are beyond the scope of this chapter (see Wehman, Smith, & Schall, 2009) for a comprehensive treatment of such strategies). These authors do recommend several "guiding principles" for on-the-job skills training for people with ASD, suggesting that they be:

- Based on proven state-of-the-art practices;
- Developed from functional assessment outcomes (such as those discussed previously);
- Provide a variety of individualized supports;
- Evaluated by outcome-based measures. (Targett & Wehman, 2009, p. 169)

Targett and Wehman (2009) identified a number of instructional strategies that provide the individualized supports needed by people with ASD to obtain and maintain competitive employment, including applied behavior analysis, using visual schedules, restructuring work routines, using visual instructions and cues, and manipulation or alteration of antecedent cues that signal work behaviors. Many of these strategies are familiar from other instructional domains, and still others focus on modifying the environment, job tasks, work settings, or antecedents or consequences of behavior, all of which are the hallmark of strategies such as supported and customized employment. Strategies that have been shown to be effective in educating students with ASD include limiting or modifying sensory experiences, providing concrete instructions on tasks, providing visual prompts, and managing the environment to minimize disruption related to transitions from one task or time to another. These strategies should all be equally effective in supporting people with ASD in work settings. With regard to sensory experiences, social and work interactions may be affected due to a student's sensory perception issues; the student may be overly sensitive to light, sound, noise, or specific smells, which in turn may limit success in transition-related environments and tasks. Schall and McFarland-Whisman (2009) suggested three general strategies to address these issues in the classroom that would be equally relevant to other settings: (a) determine if the source of the sensory input can be eliminated or avoided; (b) determine if the source of the sensory input can be modified to minimize disruption; and (c) determine if the student can be taught to self-regulate his or her behavior as it pertains to the sensory input (e.g., identifying the sensory input as a problem and reporting it or in some way changing behavior to minimize the disruption).

Perhaps in no other domain of transition are the importance of effective communication and social skills so readily apparent. Research has demonstrated that people with disabilities are as likely to lose a job because of poor communication or social skills as because of deficient job skills (Wehman, 2006). Using the above-mentioned strategies to support people within the work environment to communicate more effectively and to handle social interactions with employers and coworkers should be critical components of transition to employment planning, especially for persons on the spectrum.

Conclusions

The transition years are difficult for most adolescents, as they struggle with the establishment of an identity, the biological changes happening to their bodies, the social pressures of secondary education, and the identification of postgraduation goals. That this already complex process is further complicated by the presence of an autism spectrum disorder is hardly surprising. Research shows that transition outcomes, almost across the board (Cameto et al., 2004) are less favorable for youth with ASD than for their nondisabled peers. But, as we know from research with many other students with disabilities, disability is not destiny when it comes to achieving positive social, independent living, postsecondary education, and employment outcomes. There is a desperate need for more research with regard to the transition of youth with ASD, but the extant research and the knowledge from transition-related research with other students with disabilities suggests, at the very least, that we have the methods and strategies to solve this complex problem for virtually all students with ASD.

References

Adreon, D., & Durocher, J. S. (2007). Evaluating the college transition needs of individuals with high-functioning autism spectrum disorders. *Intervention in School and Clinic, 42*(5), 271–279.

Alpern, C., & Zager, D. (2007). Addressing communication needs of young adults with autism in a college-based inclusion program. *Education and Training in Developmental Disabilities, 42*(4), 428–436.

Briel, L. W., & Getzel, E. E. (2009). Postsecondary education for students with autism. In P. Wehman, M. D. Smith, & C. Schall (Eds.), *Autism and the transition to adulthood: Success beyond the classroom* (pp. 189–207). Baltimore, MD: Brookes.

Cameto, R., Levine, P., & Wagner, M. (2004). *Transition planning for students with disabilities: A special topic report from the National Longitudinal Transition Study–2* (NLTS-2). Menlo Park, CA: SRI International.

Clark, G., & Patton, J. (2006). *Transition planning inventory—updated version.* Austin, TX: ProEd.

Clark, G. M. (1996). Transition planning assessment for secondary-level students with learning disabilities. In J. R. Patton & G. Blalock (Eds.), *Transition and students with learning disabilities: Facilitating the movement from school to adult life* (pp. 131– 156). Austin, TX: ProEd.

Cross, T., Cooke, N. L., Wood, W. W., & Test, D. W. (1999). Comparison of the effects of MAPS and ChoiceMaker on student self-determination skills. *Education and Training in Mental Retardation and Developmental Disabilities, 34,* 499–510.

Halpern, A. S. (1994). The transition of youth with disabilities to adult life: A position statement of the Division on Career Development and Transition. *Career Development for Exceptional Individuals, 17*(2), 115–124.

Halpern, A. S., Herr, C. M., Doren, B., & Wolf, N. K. (2000) *Next S.T.E.P.: Student transition and educational planning* (2nd ed.). Austin, TX.: ProEd.

Halpern, A. S., Herr, C. M., Wolf, N. K., Doren, B., Johnson, M. D., & Lawson, J. D. (1997). *Next S.T.E.P.: Student transition and educational planning.* Austin, TX: Pro-Ed.

Hart, D., Grigal, M., Sax, C., Martinez, D., & Will, M. (2006). Postsecondary education options for students with intellectual disabilities. *Research to Practice, 45,* 1–4.

Held, M. F., Thoma, C. A., & Thomas, K. (2004). "The John Jones Show": How one teacher facilitated self-determined transition planning for a young man with autism. *Focus on Autism and Other Developmental Disabilities, 19,* 177–188.

Hendricks, D. R., & Wehman, P. (2009). Transition from school to adulthood for youth with autism spectrum disorders: Review and recommendations. *Focus on Autism and Other Developmental Disabilities, 24,* 77–88.

Henry, S. A., & Myles, B. S. (2007) *The comprehensive autism planning systems (CAPS) for individuals with Asperger syndrome, autism, and related disabilities: Integrating best practices throughout the student's day.* Shawnee Mission, KS: Autism Asperger.

Individuals with Disabilities Education Improvement Act of 2004, 20 U.S.C.A. § 1400 *et seq.*

Hillier, A., Campbell, H., Mastriani, K., Izzo, M. V., Kool-Tucker, A. K., Cherry, L., … Beversdorf, D. Q. (2007). Two-year evaluation of a vocational support program for adults on the autism spectrum. *Career Development for Exceptional Individuals, 30*(1), 35–47.

Marshall, L. H., Martin, J. E., Maxson, L. L., & Jerman, P. A. (1997). *Choosing employment goals.* Longmont, CO: Sopris West.

Martin, J. E., Marshall, L., Maxson, L. L., & Jerman, P. (1993). *Self-directed IEP.* Longmont, CO: Sopris West.

Martin, J. E., Van Dycke, J., Christense, W. R., Greene, B. A., Gardner, J. E., & Lovett, D. L. (2006). Increasing student participation in IEP meetings: Establishing the self-directed IEP as an evidenced-based practice. *Exceptional Children, 72,* 299–316.

Mason, C., Field, S., & Sawilowsky, S. (2004). Implementation of self-determination activities and student participation in IEPs. *Exceptional Children, 70,* 441–451.

Mazzotti, V. L., Test, D. W., Wood, C. L., & Richter, S. (2010). *Career Development for Exceptional Individuals, 33*(1), 25–40.

Myles, B. S., & Adreon, D. (2001). *Asperger syndrome and adolescence: Practical solutions for school success.* Shawnee Mission, KS: Autism Asperger.

Myles, B. S., & Steere, D. E. (in press). Transition for students with autism spectrum disorders. In M. L. Wehmeyer & K. Webb (Eds.), *Handbook of transition for youth with disabilities.* New York: Routledge.

Newman, L. (2007, April). *Facts from NLTS2: Secondary school experiences of students with autism.* Menlo Park, CA: SRI International. Retrieved from www.nlts2.org/fact_sheets/nlts2_fact_sheet_2007_04.pdf.

O'Brien, J., & Lovett, H. (1993). *Finding a way toward everyday lives: The contribution of person-centered planning.* Harrisburg: Pennsylvania Office of Mental Retardation.

Powers, L. E., Turner, A., Westwood, D., Matuszewski, J., Wilson, R., & Phillips, A. (2001). Take charge for the future: A controlled field-test of a model to promote student involvement in transition planning. *Career Development for Exceptional Individuals, 24*(1), 89–103.

Rehfeldt, J. D., Clark, G. M., & Lee, S. W. (in press). The effects of using the transition planning inventory and a structured IEP process as a transition planning intervention on IEP meeting outcomes. *Remedial and Special Education.*

Ryndak, D., & Alper, S. (1996). *Curriculum content for students with moderate and severe disabilities in inclusive settings.* Boston, MA: Allyn & Bacon.

Sands, D., Spencer, K., Gliner, J., & Swaim, R. (1999). Structural equation modeling of student involvement in transition-related actions: The path of least resistance. *Focus on Autism and Other Developmental Disabilities, 14,* 17–27.

Schall, C. (2009). Educational and transition planning. In P. Wehman, M. D. Smith, & C. Schall (Eds.), *Autism and the transition to adulthood: Success beyond the classroom* (pp. 39–94). Baltimore, MD: Brookes.

Schall, C., Doval, E. C., Targett, P. S., & Wehman, P. (2006). Applications for youth with ASD spectrum disorders. In P. Wehman (Ed.), *Life beyond the classroom: Transition strategies for young people with disabilities* (4th ed., pp. 535–575). Baltimore, MD: Brookes.

Schall, C., & McFarland-Whisman, J. (2009). Meeting transition goals through inclusion. In P. Wehman, M. D. Smith, & C. Schall (Eds.), *Autism and the transition to adulthood: Success beyond the classroom* (pp. 95–110). Baltimore, MD: Brookes.

Schall, C., & Wehman, P. (2009). Understanding the transition from school to adulthood for students with autism. In P. Wehman, M. D. Smith, & C. Schall (Eds.), *Autism and the transition to adulthood: Success beyond the classroom* (pp. 1–14). Baltimore, MD: Brookes.

Schwartz, A. A., Jacobson, J. W., & Holburn, S. (2000). Defining person-centeredness: Results of two consensus methods. *Education and Training in Mental Retardation and Developmental Disabilities, 35,* 235–258.

Seltzer, M. M., Greenberg, J. S., Floyd, F. J., & Hong, J. (2004). The trajectory of development in adolescents and adults with autism. *Mental Retardation and Developmental Disabilities Research Reviews, 10,* 234–247.

Shore, S. (2001). *Beyond the wall: Personal experiences with autism and Asperger syndrome.* Shawnee Mission, KS: Autism Asperger.

Smith, M. D. & Targett, P. S. (2009). Critical life skills. In P. Wehman, M. D. Smith, & C. Schall (Eds.), *Autism and the transition to adulthood: Success beyond the classroom* (pp. 209–231). Baltimore, MD: Brookes.

Standifer, S. (2009). *Adult autism and employment: A guide for vocational rehabilitation professionals.* Columbia: University of Missouri.

Targett, P. S., & Wehman, P. (2009). Integrated employment. In P. Wehman, M. D. Smith, & C. Schall (Eds.), *Autism and the transition to adulthood: Success beyond the classroom* (pp. 163–188). Baltimore, MD: Brookes.

Test, D. W., Mason, C., Hughes, C., Konrad, M., Neale, M., & Wood, W. M. (2004). Student involvement in individualized education program meetings. *Exceptional Children, 70,* 391–412.

VanBergeijk, E., Klin, A., & Volkmar, F. (2008). Supporting more able students on the autism spectrum: College and beyond. *Journal of Autism and Developmental Disorders, 38,* 1359–1370.

Vandercook, T., York, J., & Forest, M. (1989). The McGill action planning system (MAPS): A strategy for building the vision. *The Journal of the Association for Persons with Severe Handicaps, 14,* 205–215.

Van Reusen, A. K., Bos, C. S., Schumaker, J. B., & Deshler, D. D. (2002). *The self-advocacy strategy for enhancing student motivation and self-determination.* Lawrence, KS: Edge Enterprises.

Vital, P. M., Ronald, A., Wallace, G. L., & Happe, F. (2009). Relationship between special abilities and autistic-like traits in a large population-based sample of 8-year olds. *Journal of Child Psychology and Psychiatry, 50*(9), 1093–1101.

Wehman, P. (2006). Life beyond the classroom: *Transition strategies for young people with disabilities* (4th ed.). Baltimore, MD: Brookes.

Wehman, P., Smith, M. D., & Schall, C. (Eds.). (2009). *Autism and the transition to adulthood: Success beyond the classroom.* Baltimore, MD: Brookes.

Wehmeyer, M. L., & Lawrence, M. (2002). *A national replication of a student-directed transition planning process: Impact on student knowledge of and perceptions and transition planning.* Lawrence, KS: Beach Center on Disability.

Wehmeyer, M., Lawrence, M., Kelchner, K., Palmer, S., Garner, N., & Soukup, J. (2004). *Whose future is it anyway? A student-directed transition planning process* (2nd ed.). Lawrence, KS: Beach Center on Disability.

Wehmeyer, M. L., Palmer, S. B., Lee, Y., Williams-Diehm, K., & Shogren, K. A. (in press). A randomized-trial evaluation of the effect of *Whose future is it anyway?* on self-determination. *Career Development for Exceptional Individuals.*

Whalen, C. (2009). *Real life, real progress for children with autism spectrum disorders: Strategies for successful generalization in natural environments.* Baltimore, MD: Brookes.

Williams-Diehm, K., Wehmeyer, M. L., Palmer, S., Soukup, J. H., & Garner, N. (2008). Self-determination and student involvement in transition planning: A multivariate analysis. *Journal on Developmental Disabilities, 14,* 25–36.

Zhang, D. (2001). The effect of Next S.T.E.P Instruction on the self-determination skills of high school studetns with learning disabilities. *Career Development for Exceptional Individuals, 24*(2), 121–132.

15

FAMILY SUPPORT AND INVOLVEMENT THROUGHOUT THE SCHOOL YEARS

Teresa Taber-Doughty and Emily Bouck

PURDUE UNIVERSITY

Historical Background

The issue of family is integrally tied to autism and difficult to isolate from other issues in educating students with autism spectrum disorders (ASD). It was professionals who first articulated the connection between family and autism (Kanner, 1943), and it was mothers who were originally blamed for their children's behavior. Bettleheim (1967) claimed the syndrome resulted from maternal emotional frigidity and coined the term *refrigerator mothers*. Today the theory of parents being responsible for ASD has long been disproven, but the important role of parents and other family members in relation to a relative with ASD remains, especially regarding education of students with ASD (Autism Society of America, 2000; Dyches, Wilder, Sudweeks, Obiakor, & Algozzine, 2004; Rimland, 1964).

Science has made it clear that no one is "to blame" for a diagnosis of ASD (Rimland, 1964), but nonetheless, pressure on parents and other family members, albeit of a different kind, has not lessened. For example, research shows that stress may be greater for parents of a child with ASD than it is for parents of children with other disabilities or children who are developmentally typical (Boyd, 2002; Rao & Beidel, 2009; Sanders & Morgan, 1997). Further, emerging evidence exists that parental stress may limit the effectiveness of particular educational interventions in children with ASD (e.g., Osborne, McHugh, Saunders, & Reed, 2008; Robbins, Dunlap, & Plienis, 1991). The Association for Children's Mental Health (2004), although it was not specifically talking about children with ASD, stated, "one of the most important components of any treatment including an evidence-based practice is family involvement" (p. 7). Consequently, it is important to explore and understand family support for and family involvement with children who have ASD throughout the school years.

Family, and specifically parental involvement, is important in the education of *all* students, but especially for students with disabilities. In fact, parental participation in the education of students with disabilities is mandated in the Individuals with Disabilities Education Act (IDEA; 1997), and the Individuals with Disabilities Education Improvement Act (2004; R. Turnbull, Huerta, & Stowe, 2006). Parental participation is one of the six principles of IDEA and it is intended to involve families (i.e., parents and students) in partnership with educational agencies (R. Turnbull et al., 2006). In fact, the reauthorization of IDEA in 2004 placed greater ownership of and responsibility for the educational process with parents. With IDEA 2004, in fact, parental consent must be obtained for the initial evaluation and services (Yell & Dragow, 2007), and they now have the power to refuse evaluation of their child for services as well as reject services after the evaluation. Parents, as such, should be active partners in determining the education of their child with ASD (McCabe, 2007; R. Turnbull et al., 2006).

Although parental participation is emphasized in IDEA (2004), parents and educators do not always act as true partners in the education of students with ASD, and at times the relationship can be adversarial (Cohen, 2006; Ivey, 2004; Stoner & Angell, 2006; Stoner et al., 2005). For example, Stoner and colleagues reported that parents often express distrust toward educational professionals and feel as though they have to fight for services. Further, parents voiced concerns about problems communicating with school personnel. The potentially adversarial relationship between parents and educators over services surrounds parental wishes for the *best* services and a school's legal obligation to provide appropriate services from which students might reasonably benefit (*Board of Education of Hendrick Hudson Central School District v. Rowley,* 1982; Hersh & Johansen, 2007). Thus, families and educational systems can be on separate sides when working to make decisions about the education of a child with ASD.

Beyond these legal issues, parents of students with ASD often assume visible roles in advocating for their children (National Research Council, 2001; Stoner & Angell, 2006). Several grassroots organizations and other informal support groups have formed to provide support and advocacy for families and their children's educational process; however, little evaluation of these groups exists (Perry, Factor, & Freeman, 1992). For example, the Autism Society is a grassroots organization that "exists to improve the lives of all affected by autism" by

> advocating for appropriate services for individuals across the lifespan, and providing the latest information regarding treatment, education, research and advocacy. (Autism Society, n.d.)

Family support groups—including both parent and sibling support groups—assist families in learning how to advocate for their child, offer support, and can reduce family stress (Lessenberry & Rehfeldt, 2004; Yau & Li-Tsang, 1999). Yau and Li-Tsang found that participation in support groups assisted family members to cope with parenting a child with a developmental disability. Law, King, Steward, and King (2001) reported that parents gained a "sense of belonging" and parenting skills in addition to receiving support (p. 30). Research regarding family support groups, however, is limited.

Chapter Overview

Given the limited literature, this chapter explores issues related to family and education in a larger context. Specifically, the chapter pulls from the general literature relative to families, the literature on families with a child with a disability, and the literature on families who have children with ASD. The chapter presents information regarding family systems theory (A. Turnbull, Turnbull, Erwin, & Soondak, 2006) as well as family-centered practice with a research base. We discuss the impact of family dynamics that arise from having a child with ASD as well as the specific challenges families face when collaborating with schools. The chapter concludes with recommendations regarding family involvement and family support that are drawn from the general literature as well as the literature specific to students with ASD.

Description and Overview

Despite the historical and current importance of family support and family involvement in the education of students with ASD, an overall lack of research exists, particularly experimental or quasi-experimental research (Gersten, Irvin, & Keating, 2002; Kraus, 1997; Singer, 2002). It is difficult to address family support and family involvement in terms of evidence-based practices given the limited literature base and the conventional and collective wisdom that family involvement results in better outcomes for students with ASD and family support improves family functioning and the well-being of students with ASD. Given the lack of sufficient literature on this topic to align with the standard interpretation in the field as to what constitutes an evidence-base (see the special issue of *Exceptional Children* regarding evidence-based practices; Odom et al., 2005), we applied the U.S. Department of Education (2002) definition of evidence-based education: "the integration of professional wisdom with the best available empirical evidence in making decisions about how to deliver instruction." Empirical evidence includes scientifically based practices or practices with empirical data as to their effectiveness, and professional wisdom that consists of information ascertained through personal experiences or consensus (U.S. Department of Education, 2002).

Socially valid practices are those considered socially acceptable by recipients of such services, those who administer them, and people within the community (Alberto & Troutman, 2006; Kazdin, 1977; Wolf, 1978). It is critical to identify evidence-based practices, but Callahan, Henson, and Cowan (2008) argued that parents and school personnel must also consider if practices are socially valid. Failure of school personnel and parents to consider evidence-based *and* socially validated practices may result in the implementation of ineffective and inappropriate practices for children with ASD (Callahan et al., 2008). In addition, implementation of practices that are not socially valid may interfere with successful collaboration between school personnel and families due to the lack of agreement regarding appropriate strategies (Arick, Krug, Fullerton, Loos, & Falco, 2005; Yell, Katsiyannis, Drasgow, & Herbst, 2003).

As increasing prevalence rates of ASD are reported (Centers for Disease Control, 2010), it receives attention typically not given to other disabilities. While increased attention can be beneficial (i.e., increased focus on positive educational experience, increased awareness of early interventions), one negative aspect is the implementation of practices that are neither evidence-based nor socially valid. Parents, and some professionals, can become desperate to find a cure or a treatment that is effective for their individual child. When they encounter an intervention that shows promise for their son or daughter, they may enthusiastically present their results to the public as an effective treatment without a research base or social validation to support its use. Lack of a research base can lead to dangerous practices, misinformation, and potential harm. For example, incorrect information about the linkage between the MMR vaccine and ASD led many parents to withhold vaccinating their children from these diseases. Practices without validation can result in harm; in this case, harm both to the children who were not vaccinated as well as others whom they put at risk (Marcus, Kunce, & Schopler, 2005). While the issue of vaccination is just one example, many practices are implemented that lack social validation. For example, in a review of 37 studies from 1990 to 2002 examining evidence-based practices for young children with ASD, social validity was assessed in less than 11% (Odom et al., 2003). Researchers need to not only report the effects of practices but also their social validity, especially because parents of children with ASD

> contend with the reckless promoters of faddish therapies and the pressure to find a cure, both of which reinforce the natural tendency to doubt or deny the chronicity of the disorder, [so] professionals must remain sensitive to the vulnerable situation parents are placed

in and their need for support and for sound, empirically-based interventions. (Marcus et al., 2005, p. 1079)

Regardless of the research-base, or lack thereof, the issues surrounding family involvement and family support in the education of students with ASD are of utmost importance. Family or parental involvement is a hallmark of special education services for all students with disabilities (IDEA, 2004; A. Turnbull et al., 2006). Family involvement has been cited as critical for the success of students with disabilities in a variety of contexts, such as transition (Morningstar, Turnbull, & Turnbull, 1995), self-determination (Wehmeyer, 1996), and general student outcomes (Dettmer, Thurston, & Dyck, 2005). In education in general, parental involvement is valued due to the association between parents being engaged in their child's school and their child's learning (Hoover-Dempsey & Sandler, 1999). When parents are involved with school personnel, researchers reported positive academic outcomes, lower dropout rates, decreases in retention and placements in special education, completion of homework, positive behavioral outcomes, learning and success, and greater enrollment in postsecondary education (Anderson & Minke, 2007; Gutman & Midgley, 2000; Izzo, Weissberg, Kasprow, & Fendrich, 1999; McWayne, Hampton, Fantuzzo, Cohen, & Sekino, 2004; Miedel & Reynolds, 1999; Senechal & LeFevre, 2002).

Despite the presumption of the positive benefits accrued as a result of parental involvement in the education of students with disabilities, previous research suggests low rates of involvement may actually exist in terms of formal participation (e.g., attending an IEP meeting; Vacc et al., 2005). However, parental involvement is not necessarily related to parental satisfaction with special education services. In other words, regardless of parents' level of involvement, they can still express satisfaction for the educational programming of their child. For example, Westling (1996) reported that 80 to 85% of parents were satisfied with the educational services for their child with a disability. More recently, Bitterman, Daley, Misra, Carlson, and Markowitz (2008) reported that the majority of parents perceived the services for their child to be good or excellent, although the satisfaction of parents of students with ASD tended to be slightly lower than parents of children with other disabilities. Bitterman and colleagues also found high rates of parental satisfaction for their child's teacher and his or her specific program.

Family support can serve an important role in the lives of parents, siblings, other family members, and especially in regard to children with ASD (Singer & Irvin, 1989). All families experience stressors, but Benson (2006) suggested that families of students with ASD are at risk for heightened levels of stress, including siblings (e.g., Giallo & Gavidia-Payne, 2006; Nixon & Cummings, 1999). Although research regarding the impact on developmentally typical siblings of a sibling with ASD has increased in recent years, Benson and Karlof (2008) cautioned that support for siblings still needs to be further considered, especially in terms of attention by school personnel and other support organizations or individuals.

A Common Meaning

Although few researchers provide a formal definition of family involvement when considering the education of students with disabilities, we constructed an understanding from multiple sources. The term *parental involvement* is often used by schools and in federal and state education legislation, yet, no consensus exists on its definition. For example, many schools defined parental involvement as "the support and participation of parents at home, in the community, and at the school site that directly and positively affect the educational performance of all children" (San Diego County Office of Education, n.d.). This definition differs from the ways that

Christenson (2003) proposed family involvement in education could be conceptualized: (a) behavioral, intellectual, and personal resources provided by parents to their child (Grolnick, Benjet, Kurowski, & Apostleris, 1997); (b) as a partnership with schools that involve mutual participation, collaboration, and support (Moles & D'Angelo, 1993); and (c) as a nurtured, proactive relationship acting as a partnership focused on student success and joint responsibility (Christenson & Sheridan, 2001). An underlying trend is active, constructive involvement resulting in positive success for children.

The education of students with ASD typically means more than just parental involvement, but includes the involvement of siblings, other family members, and even friends (National Research Council, 2001; Xu & Filler, 2008). Siblings' lives are affected by having a child with ASD in the family; yet, the effect can be both positive and negative (Konidaris, 1997). Siblings can assist parents in understanding situations at school, particularly if they attend the same school, as well as help school personnel understand the child with ASD (National Research Council). The African proverb "it takes a village to raise a child" (Clinton, 2006) resonates with parents of students with ASD (Firestone, 2008).

While many different conceptualizations of family support may exist, throughout this chapter we will apply Singer's (2002) definition of family support: "formal and informal efforts to strengthen families' capabilities to facilitate autonomy, inclusion, care, and a satisfying quality of life for members with disabilities while maintaining family well-being" (p. 148). In considering family support, we are not solely focusing on providing support for parents but also siblings. Siblings can play critical roles in the lives of children with ASD and often roles that cannot be played by parents. For example, Blacher and Begum (2009) indicated that siblings can play a teaching role in terms of helping the child with ASD to develop social competence as well as acting as playmates.

Research has documented mixed results concerning the impact on a sibling when a child with ASD is part of the family (e.g., higher self-concept; Macks & Reeve, 2007), with both more behavior problems being reported for siblings (Hastings, 2003) as well as no effects on the siblings being reported (Smith & Perry, 2005). Finally, the literature is consistent in promoting the need for sibling support (Glasberg, Martins, & Harris, 2006). The family's ability to cope with the resulting stress, or, in other words, family quality of life, is clearly at the forefront of current themes and trends involving family support and family involvement in the education of students with ASD (A. P. Turnbull, Turnbull, Summers, & Poston, 2008).

Family Involvement and Support and Professionals: The Other Dimension

In addition to considering the research base on family involvement and family support for students with ASD, it is critical to evaluate how professionals are trained to address these issues as well as how to manage them in practice. Despite the documented relationship between parental involvement and positive student outcomes (Arvizu, 1996; Hoover-Dempsey & Sandler, 1999), research suggests teachers are not well-prepared for this aspect of their job (de Acosta, 1996; Epstein & Dauber, 1991). Yet, exposure to issues related to parental involvement during the preservice years can increase confidence and create more positive attitudes in teacher candidates in this respect (Morris & Taylor, 1998).

The Evidence Base

When examining the literature focused on family involvement in the education of students with disabilities through the school years, empirically based information is severely lacking

(Ivey, 2004). For example, when exploring how school personnel communicate information to families, the literature suggests that this often occurs through electronic or print materials as well as by bringing families together for a meeting with school personnel (Ballen & Moles, 1994. Although these strategies are reportedly widely used, Perry and Condillac (2003) found little evidence as to the effectiveness of any of these approaches for assisting families in obtaining greater knowledge or information about their child with ASD. A second example of the lack of empirically based information linked to working with families is in relation to collaboration. A cornerstone of IDEA is the collaborative partnerships called for between parents and schools (H. R. Turnbull & Turnbull, 2000), although the partnerships are often unsuccessful (Salembier & Furney, 1998). Blue-Banning, Summers, Frankland, Nelson, and Beegle (2004) noted that the value of collaborative partnerships with parents often leads to resolving differences of opinion before more costly legal interventions become necessary. They, along with others (Harry, Rueda, & Kalyanpur, 1999; Turnbull & Turnbull, 2001), suggested that the failure to create working relationships between school personnel and family members may lead to a general collapse in communication and mutual trust, leading to a worsening of effective skills in relation to the child by both parents and teachers, and loss of mutual respect. Because families are the focus for collaborative school partnerships and support, it is important to begin with an understanding of family characteristics, dynamics, and culture and the impact these play as school personnel prepare to work with the parents of children with ASD.

A Family Systems Theory Approach

Family systems theory is a whole-family approach that centers on the entire family and studies the effect the child with a disability has on that family (Turnbull et al., 2006). This theory asserts family relationships are interdependent and each member influences the other (Minuchin, 1974). Additionally, it provides a framework for determining how family characteristics (i.e., characteristics of the whole family and individual members) and functions within the family interact and how problems in one area (e.g., affection, self-esteem, economics) can have an impact on other areas (e.g., socialization, recreation, education; Turnbull, Summers, & Brotherson, 1984; Turnbull, Turnbull, Erwin, & Soondak, 2006). Child-specific characteristics that impact family functioning include the severity of the child's disability as well as any accompanying behavioral challenges (Hastings, 2002; Wang et al., 2004). Family-specific characteristics that influence family functioning may include family income (Park, Turnbull, & Turnbull, 2002; Yau & Li-Tsang, 1999) and fathers' participation in childcare (Park, Turnbull, & Turnbull, 2002; Willoughby & Glidden, 1995). Davis and Gavidia-Payne (2009) found a high correlation between income levels and quality of life satisfaction for families with children with disabilities. When families had increased income levels, they had greater access to resources and the ability to cope with the demands of their child's disability. They also indicated that professional support was one of the strongest predictors of family quality of life. Overall, researchers noted the importance of focusing on the whole family and maintaining a family-focused approach when providing quality support and effective interventions to families of young children with disabilities (Dunst, Trivette, & Hamby, 2007; Trivette, Dunst, Boyd, & Hamby, 1995; Trivette, Dunst, & Hamby, 1996).

Stress.   In families that have a child with ASD, child caring demands can lead to high rates of parental stress (Davis & Gavidia-Payne, 2009; Keen, Couzens, Muspratt, & Rodger, 2010). It is important to identify the needs of each family member and especially the needs of parents. If parents' needs are not met and stress is experienced, it may negatively impact their capacity to seek out resources for their child and participate in and support their child's education (Head & Abbeduto, 2007). Parental stress is linked to decreased service usage, delayed child development, poorer early intervention outcomes for children, and increased levels of child antisocial behavior (Keen et al., 2010; O'Connor, 2002).

For parents of children with ASD, Sharpley, Bitsika, and Efremidis (1997) identified the three primary sources of stress for parents: (a) apprehension over how permanent their child's disability would be over time, (b) the acceptability of their child's behaviors by others, and (c) the marginal amount of social support they received. Throughout the literature, mothers are frequently cited as bearing the greatest burden when caring for children with ASD (Phetra-suwan & Miles, 2008; Rao & Beidel, 2009) and both parents report limited time for leisure activities, job-related stress and employment restrictions, giving up family vacations and family outings, and stress within the marital relationship (Herring et al., 2006; Montes & Halterman, 2008; Sanders & Morgan, 1997). While few studies focus on how to support parents while con-currently reducing their stress levels, Keen et al. (2010) found even a brief parent-focused inter-vention could be successful in lessening child-related stress in parents of children with ASD. Reducing parent stress may improve their family conditions as well as their ability to focus on enhanced behavior and social outcomes for their child with ASD (Hoffman, Sweeney, Hodge, Lopez-Wagner, & Looney, 2009). Other issues that influence a family member's capacity to be actively involved in school-related activities include taking extra work in order to cover the cost of expensive therapies, transporting the child with ASD to various appointments, and the inability to locate childcare (Dunst, 1999; Perry & Condillac, 2003).

Family Centered Practices

Educational practices that involve parents, siblings, and extended family members are now recognized as essential elements of an effective working model for serving children and their families (American Academy of Pediatrics, 1992; Dunst et al., 2007; Xu & Filler, 2008). These practices grew from the early intervention field and include a focus on child learning opportuni-ties, parenting supports, family/community supports, and growth/development opportunities for young children (Dunst, 1999). For children with ASD, these early services may play a criti-cal role in increasing social, language, and behavioral skills (Corsello, 2005). In fact, evidence shows that children who begin intervention programs at earlier ages make greater gains than children who do so when they are older (Harris & Handleman, 2000). These family-centered services provide parents and other family members with an opportunity to be actively involved in educational decisions and choices for meeting individualized developmental goals and out-comes (Dunst, 2002).

While intensive early intervention programs for children with ASD tend to focus on pre-school age children (i.e., 4 to 5 years old), and while evidence exists to support the effectiveness of these programs (e.g., TEACCH program, ABA-based programming, the Denver model), Corsello (2005) noted many interventionists are currently seeking to introduce programming for children who are even younger. The author also noted, however, that while children who begin intervention sooner typically achieve greater gains than those who do so at a later age, there is currently no empirical evidence to support the effectiveness of the current evidence-based interventions with children under the age of 4.

As children transition to elementary and secondary school levels, evidence related to fam-ily centered practices similar to those seen in early intervention models is rarely found (Dunst, 2002). At the elementary level, the focus often shifts to family–school collaboration and col-laborative partnerships, where school-initiated practices are set in motion to connect school personnel and families so as to meet the educational and social needs of all students (Wolfendale, 1983). These practices promote positive parent participation, but those that center on the family continue to demonstrate evidence of their success (Dunst, 1999; Epstein & Lee, 1995). Efforts with demonstrated success emphasize parents' role as home-teachers and closely involve them in the development and acquisition of their child's learning goals (Epstein, Polloway, Foley, & Patton, 1993). Conflicting findings, however, were recently reported. In a review of 24 studies that examined the impact of parent involvement on improving children's academic achievement and behavior (K-7) and including parent involvement of children with disabilities, Fishel and Ramirez (2005) found no conclusive evidence to support broad parent involvement. They noted their findings replicated those of previous investigators (Mattingly, Prislin, McKenzie, Rodriguez, & Kayzar, 2002) but components of parent involvement (e.g., parent home tutoring and parent encouragement) bore promising evidence for improving children's academic performance. Specifically for parents of children with disabilities, their involvement resulted in greater maintenance of interventions for their children, increased parent satisfaction, and more successful identification of approaches for addressing student behaviors (Koegel, Koegel, & Schreibman, 1991; Newmann & Wehlage, 1995). The benefits of family–school collaboration clearly exist for children with disabilities, but more work needs to be done to empirically validate the broad approach of involving families whose child or children have ASD.

Difficulties with Family–School Collaboration

Despite the benefits of family support and family involvement, effective family–school collaboration does not always occur (Minke & Anderson, 2005). Numerous difficulties are cited as being experienced by both parents and school personnel alike and often serve as barriers to parents getting involved when they attempt to participate in their child's education. For example, several studies report parents have little to no involvement in special education services such as in developing IEP objectives, instructional or behavioral interventions, or evaluation, and that their overall satisfaction with such services is often minimal (Goldstein, Strickland, Turnbull, & Curry, 1980; Lynch & Stein, 1982; Spann, Kohler, & Soenksen, 2003). Many conclude this lack of involvement may be attributed to parents not being given choices in the services for their children (McWilliam et al., 1995), a general lack of notification when services or programming for their children change (Covert, 1995; Kohler, 1999), and poor communication between teachers and parents with teachers unwilling to consider parents' ideas or perspectives for instruction (Turnbull & Ruef, 1997). Spann et al. (2003) noted that when communication did occur between school and families it tended to revolve around the child's needs and performance such as addressing problem behavior at school rather than planning. In addition, parents reported they initiated the majority of interactions with school personnel and they carried the burden of maintaining that communication. In general, parents reported school personnel were not addressing their children's most significant needs.

Concomitant to reports of parent dismay regarding family–school collaboration, school personnel concerns are also cited in the literature (Anderson & Minke, 2007; Gilliam & Coleman, 1981; Lawson, 2003; McAfee & Vergason, 1979; Powell, Hecimovic, & Christensen, 1993; Rosin, 1996; Salisbury & Dunst, 1997; Spann et al., 2003). Interestingly, initial issues with family involvement may simply stem from how it is interpreted by schools and families. According to Anderson and Minke (2007), school personnel may interpret family involvement as parents being present at school, whereas families may perceive it as keeping their children safe and ensuring that their children arrive at school. These differences in definition may lead teachers to blame parents for challenges experienced by students and lead parents to not feel appreciated for their efforts with their children (Lawson, 2003). Some educators also possess negative perceptions about families (Spann et al., 2003), with many holding the belief that parents are not reliable resources for providing realistic information about their children's skills and abilities (Gilliam & Coleman, 1981; McAfee & Vergason, 1979). Others suggest school personnel may view families as potentially dysfunctional and oppositional (Powell et al., 1993; Rosin, 1996; Salisbury & Dunst, 1997). At a time when families are being inundated with information about ASD from the media and presented with uncertain and unsubstantiated practices targeted toward the autism community (Marcus et al., 2005), it is imperative that school personnel work closely with families to provide a measure of support. School personnel must look beyond the mere physical presence of parents at a meeting or in the school building and seek strategies to bridge the collaboration gap between home and school. Parents need the support and information available from trained school personnel in order to make informed decisions for their children. Concurrently, school personnel need parent and family support in order to develop more effective instructional and behavioral programs for the students they serve.

Recommended Strategies from the General Education Literature

A search of the literature revealed that the desire for greater involvement and information is not limited to parents of children with disabilities. Christenson and Hurley (1997) found that parents generally want more involvement in their children's education. These authors found that parents identified four areas of greater involvement: receiving information on school policies (e.g., school schedules, homework, attendance); how to teach specific skills to a student; structuring learning at home (e.g., how to help with homework); and on social, emotional, and academic child development. Parents indicated they were least interested in a school-based parent center or home visits, both of which are considered effective for students at risk (Liontos, 1992).

Blue-Banning et al. (2004) used a qualitative methodology to identify six themes of collaborative family partnerships: communication, commitment, equality, skills, trust, and respect. Communication was defined as expressing understanding and respect among members as well as being viewed as a key component within the partnership. Indicators of quality communication included sharing resources, listening, being honest, and communicating frequently. Commitment was viewed as each member's loyalty to the child and family as well as dedication to the targeted goals. Signs of commitment included being flexible, and on the part of school personnel, regarding work as "more than a job" (p. 174), being consistent, and being accessible. Equality was viewed as the true partnership of each member working together to achieve outcomes. Indicators included validating each member, avoiding turfism, exploring options, and empowering partners. Skills were perceived as those that each member brought to the team and partnership. All members were recognized for their competence. Positive demonstrations of collaborative family–professional skills include having expectations for a child's progress, individualized attention for each child on the part of school personnel, being willing to learn, and being active participants in the child's care. Trust was identified as sharing a sense of confidence about the fidelity and honesty of each member within the partnership. Displays of trust could be demonstrated through discretion, reliability, and ensuring the safety and security of the child. Finally, respect was considered as demonstrating "esteem through actions and communication" (p. 174) for each member within the family–school partnership. This was evidenced through being nonjudgmental, courteous to each member, valuing the child, and being nondiscriminatory. While each of these themes may not generalize to every family–school partnership team, they may be useful as a foundation for improving strategies when working with families (Blue-Banning et al., 2004).

Recommended Strategies from the Autism Literature

Numerous studies have recognized that challenges exist for supporting and involving families who have children on the autism spectrum, and a variety of practices are recommended, not only for serving these children but also for ensuring that parents and other family members were the focus of support. Iovannone, Dunlap, Huber, and Kincaid (2003) identified effective practices with empirical support for assisting young children on the autism spectrum and their families. Practices specifically associated with increasing family–school collaboration and partnerships that included elements of family involvement were frequently cited (Lorimer, Simpson, Myles, & Ganz, 2002). Aspects included considering family and child preferences and interests (Hurth, Shaw, Izeman, Whaley, & Rogers, 1999) and tailoring supports and services to match each family's unique characteristics (Dunlap, 1999). Corsello (2005) echoed these strategies and noted that when making recommendations to parents about early programs, professionals should ensure the provision of common elements such as parental involvement, intensity of intervention, a predictable environment, incorporating the child's interests, actively engaging the child, and focusing on individualized developmental goals.

One important recommendation for involving parents was the importance of their training and that of other family members to implement interventions. Odom et al. (2003) identified three studies in which evidence-based practices engaged family members in the development and implementation of interventions. They reported that when trained to implement specific intervention strategies in the home, parents could have a positive influence on their child's behavior (Dunlap & Fox, 1999). Parents could also be taught to embed their child's communication instruction within home-based routines, resulting in successful increases in their child's communication levels (Stiebel, 1999). Third, siblings could play a critical role in increasing the social skills of their younger siblings with ASD through social play activities (Baker, 2000). Thus, when parents and other family members were engaged in home–school collaboration, it resulted in children with ASD making developmental gains and increasing control over their environment (Dunlap & Fox, 1999). In addition, these studies demonstrated that with minimal training, parents and other family members can easily be involved in interventions that become part of the regular family routines and lead to increased social, behavioral, and communication skills for their children with ASD.

It is important to recognize, though, that the evidence serving as a foundation for family support and involvement remains limited (Ivey, 2004). In an attempt to provide additional support for evidence-based practices in the area of autism, Callahan et al. (2008) focused on the element of social validity as a means of providing additional support for programming components. They surveyed parents, teachers, and administrators and found consistent support fell in five major areas: "(a) individualized programming, (b) data collection, (c) the use of empirically-based strategies, (d) active collaboration, and (e) a focus on long-term outcomes" (p. 678). When reviewing how evidence-based practices were ranked, the authors found the 10 practices receiving the highest overall mean score were: (a) ensuring that teachers and service providers were knowledgeable, experienced, and qualified in the area of autism; (b) implementing an individualized program that resulted in educational benefits for students; (c) providing relevant and ongoing staff training; (d) conducting regular measurement, providing documentation and reports of student progress to parents; (e) implementing assessment of all relevant domains using a variety of methods in order to develop goals and objectives; (f) carrying out ongoing monitoring of intervention effectiveness; (g) providing a classroom environment that is "safe, interesting, and pleasurable" (p. 680); (h) revising methods and practices based on lack of student progress; (i) ensuring that sufficient administrative support and resources are available to school personnel and families; and (k) using specialized methods in the instruction of social skills.

These 10 practices represented not only those considered evidence-based but those also considered socially valid by school personnel and families alike for serving children with ASD. Of these top 10 practices, only one was directly related to collaborating with parents and focused on reporting student progress to parents. Of the 84 survey items Callahan et al. (2008) reported, only five additional items directly targeted parents and received overall mean scores in the top half of survey items. These included: directly engaging family members in the school program; providing extensive training to parents for direct intervention service provision; presenting greater collaborative planning to parents for better family support; actively and meaningfully including parents in every step of the IEP process; and making available individualized parent training in specific autism-related topics. These survey results are important because they demonstrate a measure of social validity for evidence-based practices in the ASD area. Failure to attend to socially validated practices may result in lack of agreement in programming between parents and school personnel (Arick et al., 2005; Yell et al., 2003) and make ongoing collaboration difficult (Callahan et al., 2008). These results may serve as a basis for the provision of effective family support and involvement practices in the ASD field.

Conclusion

While information exists regarding family involvement (e.g., current references), limited evidence is available concerning family supports. Formal or informal support groups (e.g., Autism Society) or other sources of support (e.g., Internet) are increasingly available and they are used; yet, without an empirical foundation, understanding their role or effect is difficult. Researchers and practitioners need to understand how family supports, including support groups, connect with and impact on the education of children with ASD. Support groups and the Internet often serve as sources where families acquire information as well as receive support beyond what they receive from school personnel. Thus, understanding the dynamic of family supports should be an area for future investigations. In addition, further research and replication studies are needed to confirm the impact of sibling support on the learning and behavior development of individuals with ASD. Early investigations demonstrate the positive impact siblings have on social play activities (Baker, 2000) and social competence (Blacher & Begum, 2009). Future investigations might examine the impact of the sibling role on increases in the ability to learn and the acquisition of more effective behavior skills for the sibling with ASD.

A primary focus for researchers and practitioners should be identification and use of empirically and socially validated practices. Callahan et al. (2008) identified several evidence-based and socially valid practices for involving and supporting families. Although minimally validated practices exist, the authors provided a starting point at which researchers might begin replicating their results and practitioners might begin implementing identified socially validated practices with families. The result may be greater home–school collaboration, family involvement in school activities and in implementing practices in the home, and more effective delivery of appropriate family supports.

References

Alberto, P. A., & Troutman, A. C. (2006). *Applied behavior analysis for teachers* (7th ed.). Columbus, OH: Pearson/ Merrill Prentice Hall.

American Academy of Pediatrics, Ad Hoc Task Force on Definition of the Medical Home. (1992). The medical home. *Pediatrics, 90,* 774.

Anderson, K. J., & Minke, K. M. (2007). Parent involvement in education: Toward an understanding of parents' decision making. *The Journal of Educational Research, 100*, 311–323.

Arick, J. R., Krug, D. A., Fullerton, A., Loos, L., & Falco, R. (2005). School-based programs. In F. R. Volkmar, R. Paul, A. Klin, & D. Cohen (Eds.), *Handbook of autism and pervasive developmental disorders* (pp. 1003–1028). Hoboken, NJ: Wiley.

Arvizu, S. F. (1996). Family, community, and school collaboration. In J. Sikula (Ed.), *Handbook of research on teacher education* (pp. 814–819). New York: Simon & Schuster.

Association of Children's Mental Health. (2004). *For families: Evidence-based practices: Beliefs, definitions, suggestions.* Retrieved from http:// www.acmh-mi.org/41447_ACMH_Booklet.pdf

The Autism Society. (n.d.) About us? *Autism Society: Improving the lives of all affected by autism.* Retrieved from http:// www.autism-society.org/site/PageServer?pagename=asa_home.

Autism Society of America. (2000). What is autism? *The Advocate: The Newsletter of the Autism Society of America, 33*(3), 13.

Baker, M. J. (2000). Incorporating the thematic ritualistic behaviors of children with autism into games: Increasing social play interactions with siblings. *Journal of Positive Behavior Interventions, 2*, 66–84.

Ballen, J., & Moles, O. (1994). *Strong families, strong schools: Building community partnerships for learning. A research base for family involvement in learning.* Washington, DC: U.S. Department of Education. (Eric Document Reproduction Service No. ED371909)

Benson, P. R. (2006). The impact of symptom severity on depressed mood among parents of children with ASD. *Journal of Autism and Developmental Disorders, 36*, 685–695.

Benson, P. R., & Karlof, K. L. (2008). Child, parent, and family predictors of latter adjustment in siblings of children with autism. *Research in Autism Spectrum Disorder, 2*, 583–600.

Bettelheim, B. (1967). *The empty fortress: Infantile autism and the birth of the self.* New York: Free Press.

Bitterman, A., Daley, T. C., Misra, S., Carlson, E., & Markowitz, J. (2008). A national sample of preschoolers with autism spectrum disorders: Special education services and parent satisfaction. *Journal of Autism and Developmental Disabilities, 38*, 1509–1517.

Blacher, J., & Begum, G. (2009). The social and the socializing sibling: Positive impact on children with autism. *The Exceptional Parent, 39*(5), 56–57.

Blue-Banning, M., Summers, J. A., Frankland, H. C., Nelson, L. L., & Beegle, G. (2004). Dimensions of family and professional partnerships: Constructive guidelines for collaboration. *Exceptional Children, 70*(2), 167–184.

Board of Education of Hendrick Hudson Central School District, Westchester County v. Rowley, 458 U.S. 176, 203, 102 S. Ct. 3034, 3049, 73 L.Ed.2d 690 (1982). Retrieved from http://www.faculty.piercelaw.edu/redfield/library/WordDocs/case-board.rowley.doc

Boyd, B. A. (2002). Examining the relationship between stress and lack of social support in mothers of children with autism. *Focus on Autism and Other Developmental Disabilities, 17*, 208–215.

Callahan, K., Henson, R. K., & Cowan, A. K. (2008). Social validation of evidence-based practices in autism by parents, teachers, and administrators. *Journal of Autism and Developmental Disorders, 38*, 678–692.

Centers for Disease Control and Prevention. (2010). *How many children have autism?* Retrieved from http://www.cdc.gov/ncbddd/features/counting-autism.html

Christenson, S. L. (2003). The family–school partnership: An opportunity to promote the learning competence of all students. *School Psychology Quarterly, 18*, 454–482.

Christenson, S. L., & Hurley, C. M. (1997). Parents' and school psychologists' perspectives on parent involvement activities. *School Psychology Review, 26*(1) 111–131.

Christenson, S. L., & Sheridan, S. M. (2001). *Schools and families: Creating essential connections for learning.* New York: Guilford Press.

Clinton, H. R. (2006). *It takes a village to raise a child and other lessons children teach us.* New York: Simon & Schuster.

Cohen, J. (2006). *Guns a'blazing: How parents of children on the autism spectrum and schools can work together—without a shot being fired.* Shawnee Mission, KS: Autism Asperger.

Corsello, C. M. (2005). Early intervention in autism. *Infants & Young Children, 18*(2), 74–85.

Covert, S. B. (1995). Supporting families. In J. Nisbet (Eds.), *Natural supports in school, at work, and in the community for people with severe disabilities* (pp. 121–163). Baltimore, MD: Brookes.

Davis, K., & Gavidia-Payne, S. (2009). The impact of child, family, and professional support characteristics on the quality of life in families of young children with disabilities. *Journal of Intellectual & Developmental Disability, 34*, 153–162.

de Acosta, M. (1996). A foundational approach to preparing teachers for family and community involvement in children's education. *Journal of Teacher Education, 47*(1), 9–15.

Dettmer, P., Thurston, L. P., & Dyck, N. J. (2005). *Consultation, collaboration, and teamwork for students with special needs* (5th ed.). Boston, MA: Allyn & Bacon/Longman.

Dunlap, G. (1999). Consensus, engagement, and family involvement for young children with autism. *The Journal of the Association for Persons with Severe Handicaps, 24*, 222–225.

Dunlap, G., & Fox, L. (1999). A demonstration of behavioral support for young children with autism. *Journal of Positive Behavior Interventions, 1*, 77–87.

Dunst, C. J., (1999). Responses to Mahoney et al.: Placing parent education in conceptual and empirical context. *Topics in Early Childhood Special Education, 19*(3), 141–147.

Dunst, C. J. (2002). Family-centered practices: Birth through high school. *The Journal of Special Education, 36*(3), 139–147.

Dunst, C. J., Trivette, C. M., & Hamby, D. W. (2007). Meta-analysis of family-centered help giving practices research. *Mental Retardation and Developmental Disabilities Research Reviews, 13*, 370–378.

Dyches, T. T., Wilder, L. K., Sudweeks, R. R., Obiakor, F. E., & Algozzine, B. (2004). Multicultural issues in autism. *Journal of Autism and Developmental Disabilities, 34*, 211–222.

Epstein, J., & Dauber, S. (1991). School programs and teacher practices of parent involvement in inner-city elementary and middle schools. *The Elementary School Journal, 91*, 279–289.

Epstein, J., & Lee, S. (1995). National patterns of school and family connections. In B. Ryan, G. Adams, T. Gullota, R. Weissberg, & R. Hampton (Eds.), *The family–school connection: Theory, research and practice* (pp. 108–154). Thousand Oaks, CA: Sage.

Epstein, M. H., Polloway, E. A., Foley, R. M., & Patton, J. R. (1993). Homework: A comparison of teachers' and parents' perceptions of the problems experienced by students identified as having behavioral disorders, learning disabilities, or no disabilities. *Remedial and Special Education, 14*, 40–50.

Firestone, B. (2008). *Autism heroes: Portraits of families meeting the challenge.* London: Kingsley.

Fishel, M., & Ramirez, L. (2005). Evidence-based parent involvement interventions with school-aged children. *School Psychology Quarterly, 20*, 371–402.

Foster Middle School. (2009). *Parent involvement policy.* Retrieved from http://www.tulsaschools.org

Giallo, R., & Gavidia-Payne, S. (2006). Child, parent, and family factors as predictors of adjustment for siblings of children with a disability. *Journal of Intellectual Disability Research, 50*, 937–948.

Gersten, R., Irvin, L., & Keating, T. (2002). Critical issues in research on families: Introduction to the special issue [Special issue]. *The Journal of Special Education, 36*, 122–124.

Gilliam, J. E., & Coleman, M. C. (1981). Who influences IEP committee decisions? *Exceptional Children, 47*, 642–644.

Glasberg, B. A., Martins, M., & Harris, S. L. (2006). Stress and coping among family members of individuals with autism. In M. G. Baron, J. Groden, G. Groden, & L. P. Lipsitt (Eds.), *Stress and coping in autism* (pp. 277–301). New York: Oxford University Press.

Goldstein, S., Strickland, B., Turnbull, A. P., & Curry, L. (1980). An observational analysis of the IEP conference. *Exceptional Children, 46*, 278–286.

Grolnick, W. S., Benjet, C., Kurowski, C. O., & Apostleris, N. H. (1997). Predictors of parent involvement in schooling. *Journal of Educational Psychology, 89*, 538–548.

Gutman, L. M., & Midgley, C. (2000). The role of protective factors in supporting the academic achievement of poor African American students during the middle school transition. *Journal of Youth and Adolescence, 29*, 233–248.

Harris, S. L., & Handleman, J. S. (2000). Age and IQ at intake as predictors of placement for young children with autism: A four- to six-year follow-up. *Journal of Autism and Developmental Disorders, 30*(2), 137–142.

Harry, B., Rueda, R., & Kalyanpur, M. (1999). Cultural reciprocity in sociocultural perspective: Adapting the normalization principal for family collaboration. *Exceptional Children, 66*, 123–136.

Hastings, R. P. (2002). Parental stress and behaviour problems of children with developmental disability. *Journal of Intellectual & Developmental Disability, 27*, 149–160.

Hastings, R. P. (2003). Brief report: Behavior adjustment of siblings of children with autism. *Journal of Autism and Developmental Disorders, 33*, 99–104.

Head, L. S., & Abbeduto, L. (2007). Recognizing the role of parents in developmental outcomes: A systems approach to evaluating the child with developmental disabilities. *Mental Retardation and Developmental Disabilities Research Reviews, 13*, 293–301.

Herring, S., Gray, K., Taffe, J., Tonge, B., Sweeney, D., & Einfeld, S. (2006). Behaviour and emotional problems in toddlers with pervasive developmental disorders and developmental delay: Associations with parental mental health and family functioning. *Journal of Intellectual Disability Research, 50*, 874–882.

Hersh, C. L., & Johansen, I. M. (2007). Free appropriate public education in the fourth circuit. *School Law Bulletin, 38*(1), 1–15. Retrieved from http://www.sog.unc.edu/pubs/electronicversions/slb/slbwin07/article1.pdf

Hoffman, C. D., Sweeney, D. P., Hodge, D., Lopez-Wagner, M. C., & Looney, L. (2009). Parenting stress and closeness: Mothers of typically developing children and mothers of children with autism. *Focus on Autism and Other Developmental Disabilities, 24*, 178–187.

Hoover-Dempsey, K. V., & Sandler, H. M. (1997). Why do parents become involved in their children's education? *Review of Educational Research, 67*(1), 3–42.

Hurth, J., Shaw, E., Izeman, S. G., Whaley, K., & Rogers, S. J. (1999). Areas of agreement about effective practices among programs serving young children with autism spectrum disorders. *Infants and Young Children, 12*(2), 17–26.

Individuals with Disabilities Education Act Amendments of 1997. Retrieved from http://www.ed.gov/office/OSERS/Policy/IDEA/the_law.html

Individuals with Disabilities Education Improvement Act of 2004, Pub. L. No. 108-446 (2004). Retrieved from http://www.ed.gov/office/OSERS/Policy/IDEA/the_law.html

Iovannone, R., Dunlap, G., Huber, H., & Kincaid, D. (2003). Effective educational practices for students with autism spectrum disorders. *Focus on Autism and Other Developmental Disabilities, 18*, 150–165.

Ivey, J. K. (2004). What do parents expect? A study of the likelihood and importance issues for children with autism spectrum disorders. *Focus on Autism and Other Developmental Disabilities, 19*, 27–33.

Izzo, C. V., Weissberg, R. P., Kasprow, W. J., & Fendrich, M. (1999). A longitudinal assessment of teacher perceptions of parent involvement in children's education and school performance. *American Journal of Community Psychology, 27*, 817–839.

Kanner, L. (1943). Autistic disturbances of affective contact. *Nervous Child, 2*, 217–250.

Kazdin, A. E. (1977). Assessing the clinical or applied significance of behavior change through social validation. *Behavior Modification, 1*, 427–452.

Keen, D., Couzens, D., Muspratt, S., & Rodger, S. (2010). The effects of a parent-focused intervention for children with a recent diagnosis of autism spectrum disorder on parenting stress and competence. *Research in Autism Spectrum Disorders, 4*, 229–241.

Koegel, R. L., Koegel, L. K., & Schreibman, L. (1991). Assessing and training parents in teaching pivotal behaviors. In R. Prinz (Ed.), *Advances in behavioral assessment of children and families* (pp. 36–52). London: Kingsley.

Kohler, F. K. (1999). Examining the services received by young children with autism and their families: A survey of parent responses. *Focus on Autism and Other Developmental Disabilities, 14*, 150–158.

Konidaris, J. A. (1997). A sibling's perspective on autism. In D. Cohen & F. Volkmar (Eds.), *Handbook of autism and pervasive developmental disorders* (2nd ed., pp. 1021–1031). New York: Plenum Press.

Kraus, M. W. (1997). Two generations of family research in early intervention. In M. J. Guralnik (Ed.), *The effectiveness of early intervention* (pp. 611–624). Baltimore, MD: Brookes.

Law, M., King, S., Stewart, D., & King, G. (2001). The perceived effects of parent-led support groups for parents of children with disabilities. *Physical & Occupational Therapy in Pediatrics, 21*(2/3), 29–48.

Lawson, M. A. (2003). School–family relations in context: Parent and teachers perceptions of involvement. *Urban Education, 38*, 77–133.

Lessenberry, R. M., & Rehfeldt, R. A. (2004). Evaluating stress levels of parents of children with disabilities. *Exceptional Children, 70*, 231–244.

Liontos, L. G. (1992). *At-risk families & schools: Becoming partners* (ERIC Clearinghouse on Educational Management: ED342055). Eugene, OR: University of Oregon.

Lorimer, P. A., Simpson, R. L., Myles, R. L., & Ganz, J. B. (2002). The use of social stories as a preventative behavioral intervention in a home setting with a child with autism. *Journal of Positive Behavior Interventions, 4*, 53–60.

Lynch, E. W., & Stein, R. (1982). Perspectives on parent participation in special education. *Exceptional Education Quarterly, 3*(2), 56–63.

Macks, R. J., & Reeves, R. E. (2007). The adjustment of non-disabled siblings of children with autism. *Journal of Autism and Developmental Disorders, 37*, 1060–1067.

Marcus, L. M., Kunce, L. J., & Schopler, E. (2005). Working with families. In D. J. Cohen & F. R. Volkmar (Eds.), *Handbook of autism and pervasive developmental disorders* (3rd ed., pp. 1055–1085). New York: Wiley.

Mattingly, D. J., Prislin, R., McKenzie, T. L., Rodriguez, J. L., & Kayzar, B. (2002). Evaluating evaluations: The case of parent involvement programs. *Review of Educational Research, 72*, 549–576.

McAfee, J. K., & Vergason, G. A. (1979). Parent involvement in the process of special education: Establishing the new partnership. *Focus on Exceptional Children, 11*(5), 1–15.

McCabe, H. (2007). Parent advocacy in the face of adversity: Autism and families in the People's Republic of China. *Focus on Autism and Other Developmental Disabilities, 22*(1), 39–50.

McWayne, C., Hampton, V., Fantuzzo, J., Cohen, H. L., & Sekino, Y. (2004). A multivariate examination of parent involvement and the school and academic competencies of urban kindergarten children. *Psychology in the Schools, 41*, 363–377.

McWilliam, R. A., Lang, L., Vandivere, P., Angell, R., Collins, L., & Underdown, G. (1995). Satisfaction and struggles: Family perceptions of early intervention services. *Journal of Early Intervention, 19*, 43–60.

Miedel, W. T., & Reynolds, A. J. (1999). Parent involvement in early intervention for disadvantaged children: Does it matter? *Journal of School Psychology, 37*, 379–402.

Minke, K. M., & Anderson, K. J. (2005). Family–school collaboration and positive behavior support. *Journal of Positive Behavior Interventions, 7*(3), 181–185.

Minuchin, S. (1974). *Families and family therapy.* Cambridge, MA: Harvard University Press.

Moles, O. C., & D'Angelo, D. (Eds.). (1993). *Building school-family partnership: Workshops for urban educators.* Washington, DC: U.S. Department of Education, Office of Educational Research and Improvement (OERI).

Montes, G., & Halterman, J. S. (2008). Psychological functioning and copying among mothers of children with autism: A population-based study. *Pediatrics, 199,* e1040–e1046.

Morningstar, M. E., Turnbull, A. P, & Turnbull, H. R. (1995). What do students with disabilities tell us about the importance of family involvement in the transition from school to adult life. *Exceptional Children, 62,* 249–260.

Morris, V. G., & Taylor, S. I. (1998). Alleviating barriers to family involvement in education: The role of teacher education. *Teaching and Teacher Education, 14,* 219–231.

National Research Council. (2001). *Educating children with autism.* Washington, DC: National Academy Press.

Newman, F. M., & Wehlage, G. C. (1995). *Successful school restructuring.* Madison: University of Wisconsin, Center on Organization and Restructuring of Schools, School of Education.

Nixon, C. L., & Cummings, M. E. (1999). Sibling disability and children's reactivity to conflicts involving family members. *Journal of Family Psychology, 13,* 274–285.

O'Connor, T. G. (2002). The "effects" of parenting reconsidered: Findings, challenges and applications. *Journal of Child Psychology and Psychiatry, 43,* 555–572.

Odom, S. L., Brown, W. H., Frey, T., Karasu, N., Smith-Canter, L. L., & Strain, P. S. (2003). Evidence-based practices for young children with autism: Contributions for single-subject design research. *Focus on Autism and Other Developmental Disabilities, 18,* 166–175.

Odom, S. L., Brantlinger, E., Gersten, R., Horner, R. H., Thompson, B., & Harris, K. R. (2005). Research in special education: Scientific methods and evidence-based practices. *Exceptional Children, 71,* 137–148.

Osborne, L. A., McHugh, L., Saunders, J., & Reed, P. (2008). Parenting stress reduces the effectiveness of early teaching interventions for autistic spectrum disorders. *Journal of Autism and Developmental Disabilities, 38,* 1092–1103.

Park, J., Turnbull, A. P., & Turnbull, H. R., III. (2002). Impacts of poverty on quality of life in families of children with disabilities. *Exceptional Children, 68,* 151–170.

Perry, A., & Condillac, R. (2003). *Evidence-based practices for children and adolescents with autism spectrum disorders: Review of the literature and practice guide.* Toronto, Canada: Children's Mental Health Ontario.

Perry, A., Factor, D. C., & Freeman, N. L. (1992). The effect of parent groups on stress in families of children with autism. *Children's Mental Health, 5*(2), 18–23.

Phetrasuwan, S., & Miles, M. S. (2008). Parenting stress in mothers of children with autism spectrum disorders. *Journal for Specialists in Pediatric Nursing, 14*(3), 157–165.

Powell, T. H., Hecimovic, A., & Christensen, L. (1993). Meeting the unique needs of families. In L. E. Berkell (Ed.), *Autism: Identification, education, and treatment* (pp. 187–224). Hillsdale, NJ: Erlbaum.

Rao, P. A., & Beidel, D. C. (2009). The impact of children with high-functioning autism on parental stress, sibling adjustment, and family functioning. *Behavior Modification, 33,* 437–451.

Rimland, R. P. (1964). *Infantile autism.* New York: Appleton-Century-Crofts.

Robbins, F. R., Dunlap, G., & Plienis, A. J. (1991). Family characteristics, family training, and the progress of young children with autism. *Journal of Early Intervention, 15,* 173–184.

Rosin, P. (1996). *Parent and service provider partnerships in early intervention.* In P. Rosin, A. D. Whitehead, L. I. Tuchman, G. S. Jesien, A. L. Begun, & L. Irwin (Eds.), *Partnerships in family-centered care* (pp. 65–80). Baltimore, MD: Brookes.

Salembier, G., & Furney, K. (1998). Speaking up for your child's future. *Exceptional Parent, 28*(7), 62–64.

Salisbury, C. L., & Dunst, C. J. (1997). Home, school, and community partnerships: Building inclusive teams. In B. Rainforth & J. York-Barr (Eds.), *Collaborative teams for students with disabilities* (pp. 57–88). Baltimore, MD: Brookes.

Sanders, J. L., & Morgan, S. B. (1997). Family stress and management as perceived by parents of children with autism or Down syndrome: Implications for intervention. *Child and Family Behavior Therapy, 19,* 15–32.

San Diego County Office of Education. (n.d.). *Six types of parent involvement.* Retrieved from http://www.sdcoe.net/lret2/family/pdf/6-p.pp

Senechal, M., & LeFevre, J. (2002). Parental involvement in the development of children's reading skill: A five-year longitudinal study. *Child Development, 73,* 445–460.

Sharpley, C. F., Bitsika, V., & Efremidis, B. (1997). Influence of gender, parental health, and perceived expertise of assistance upon stress, anxiety, and depression among parents of children with autism. *Journal of Intellectual and Developmental Disability, 22,* 19–28.

Singer, G. H. S. (2002). Suggestions for a pragmatic program of research on families and disability. *Journal of Special Education, 36,* 148–154.

Singer, G. H. S., & Irvin, L. K. (1989). *Support for care giving families: Enabling positive adaptation to disability.* Baltimore, MD: Brookes.

Smith, T., & Perry, A. (2005). A sibling support group for brothers and sisters of children with autism. *Journal of Developmental Disabilities, 11,* 77–88.

Spann, S. J., Kohler, F. W., & Soenksen, D. (2003). Examining parents' involvement in and perceptions of special education services: An interview with families in a parent support group. *Focus on Autism and Other Developmental Disabilities, 18*, 228–237.

Stiebel, D. (1999). Promoting augmentative communication during daily routines. *Journal of Positive Behavior Interventions, 1*, 159–169.

Stoner, J. B., & Angell, M. E. (2006). Parent perspectives on role engagement: An investigation of parents of children with ASD and their self-reported roles with education professionals. *Focus on Autism and Other Developmental Disabilities, 21*, 177–189.

Stoner, J. B., Bock, S. J., Thompson, J. R., Angell, M. E., Heyl, B. S., & Crowley, E. P. (2005). Welcome to our world: Parent perceptions of interactions between parents of young children with ASD and education professionals. *Focus on Autism and Other Developmental Disabilities, 20*, 39–51.

Trivette, C. M., Dunst, C. J., Boyd, K., & Hamby, D. W. (1995). Family-oriented program models, help giving practices, and parental control appraisals. *Exceptional Children, 62*, 237–248.

Trivette, C. M., Dunst, C. J., & Hamby, D. W. (1996). Factors associated with perceived control appraisals in a family-centered early intervention program. *Journal of Early Intervention, 20*, 165–178.

Turnbull, A. P., & Ruef, M. (1997). Family perspectives on inclusive life style issues for people with problem behavior. *Exceptional Children, 63*, 211–227.

Turnbull, A. P., Summers, J. A., & Brotherson, M. J. (1984). *Working with families with disabled member: A family systems approach.* Lawrence: University of Kansas.

Turnbull, A. P., & Turnbull, H. R. (2001). *Families, professionals, and exceptionality: A special partnership* (4th ed.). Upper Saddle River, NJ: Merrill/Prentice Hall.

Turnbull, A. P., Turnbull, H. R., Erwin, E., & Soondak, L. (2006). *Families, professionals, and exceptionality: Positive outcomes through partnerships and trust* (5th ed.). Upper Saddle River, NJ: Merrill/Prentice Hall.

Turnbull, A. P., Turnbull, H. R., Summers, J. A., & Poston, D. (2008). Partnering with families of children with developmental disabilities to enhance family quality of life. In H. P. Parette & G. R. Peterson-Karlan (Eds.), *Research-based practices in developmental disabilities* (2nd ed., pp. 481–499). Austin, TX: Pro-Ed.

Turnbull, H. R., & Turnbull, A. P. (2000). *Free appropriate public education: The law and children with disabilities* (6th ed.). Denver, CO: Love.

Turnbull, H. R., Huerta, N., & Stowe, M. (2006). *The Individuals with Disabilities Education Act as amended in 2004.* Upper Saddle River, NJ: Prentice Hall.

U.S. Department of Education. (2002). *Evidence-based education.* Presented at the Student Achievement and School Accountability Conference. Retrieved from http://www.ed.gov/nclb/methods/whatworks/eb/edlite-slide003.html

Vacc, N. A., Vallecorsa, A. L., Parker, A., Bonner, S., Lester, C., Richardson, S., & Yates, C. (1985). Parents' and educators' participation in IEP conferences. *Education & Treatment of Children, 8*, 153–162.

Wang, M., Turnbull, A. P., Summers, J. A., Little, T. D., Poston, D. J., Mannan, H., et al. (2004). Severity of disability and income as predictors of parents' satisfaction with their family quality of life during early childhood years. *Research and Practice for Persons with Severe Disabilities, 29*, 82–94.

Wehmeyer, M. L. (1996). Student self-report measure of self-determination for students with cognitive disabilities. *Education and Training in Mental Retardation and Developmental Disabilities, 31*, 282–293.

Westling, D. L. (1996). What do parents of children with moderate and severe mental disabilities want? *Education and Training in Mental Retardation, 31*, 86–114.

Willoughby, J. C., & Glidden, L. M. (1995). Fathers helping out: Shared child care and marital satisfaction of parents of children with disabilities. *American Journal on Mental Retardation, 99*, 399–406.

Wolf, M. M. (1978). Social validity: The case for subjective measurement or how applied behavior analysis is finding its heart. *Journal of Applied Behavior Analysis, 11*, 203–214.

Wolfendale, S. (1983). *Parental participation in children's development and education.* New York: Gordon & Breach.

Xu, Y., & Filler, J. (2008). Facilitating family involvement and support for inclusive education. *The School Community Journal, 18*(2), 53–72.

Yau, M. K., & Li-Tsang, C. W. P. (1999). Adjustment and adaptation in parents of children with developmental disability in two-parent families: A review of the characteristics and attributes. *The British Journal of Developmental Disabilities, 45*, 38–51.

Yell, M. L., & Drasgow, E. (2007). The Individuals with Disabilities Education Improvement Act of 2004 and the 2006 regulations: Implications for assessment introduction to special series. *Assessment for Effective Intervention, 32*, 194–201.

Yell, M. L., Katsiyannis, A., Drasgow, E., & Herbst, M. (2003). Developing legally correct and educationally appropriate programs for students with autism spectrum disorders. *Focus on Autism and Other Developmental Disabilities, 18*, 182–191.

SECTION IV
Interrelated Disciplines in Autism

16

ENHANCING LANGUAGE AND COMMUNICATION DEVELOPMENT

Carol Alpern

PACE UNIVERSITY

Introduction

Early identification of children at risk for autism spectrum disorders (ASD) generally begins with parents' concerns about late language development in their child (Johnson, Myers, & the Council on Children with Disabilities, 2007; Wetherby, Prizant, & Hutchinson, 1998). Parents initially become concerned when speech does not develop by 15 to 18 months, although they may not discuss their concerns with their pediatrician for several months more (Johnson et al., 2007). Some parents of children later diagnosed with ASD express concerns when their child develops a few words age-appropriately but then loses them or fails to develop more (Lord, Shulman, & Dilavore, 2004). This delay in the acquisition of communication and language is one of the hallmarks of identifying the presence of ASD (Woods & Wetherby, 2003). Limited language ability is critical not only to the identification of ASD but is highly correlated with later outcomes. Higher verbal function is predictive of higher ratings for friendship, social competence, and academic achievement (Howlin, Mawhood, & Rutter, 2000; Sigman & Ruskin, 1999; Venter, Lord, & Schopler, 1992). Therefore, enhancing language and communication development is critical to effective intervention for children with ASD.

Several of the earlier chapters in this book have described approaches that have resulted in increased communication ability in children with ASD. While attention to intervention approaches is important, an understanding of the nature of communication disorders and the developmental factors that are predictive of a better prognosis for language acquisition is essential in order to set treatment priorities based on empirical findings (Bopp, Mirenda, & Zumbo, 2009). As Toth, Munson, Meltzoff, and Dawson (2006) state, "Given the critical importance of early language development for later prognosis, a better understanding of developmental factors that underlie, facilitate, and predict language acquisition in autism would shed light on the nature of the disorder and allow for the refinement of targeted early interventions" (p. 993). This chapter will therefore begin with a description of the language exhibited by children with autism at each stage of language acquisition. A discussion of the developmental factors that have been shown to predict language acquisition in autism will provide the basis for treatment goals throughout the lifespan. These goals follow from our understanding of the nature of language disorders in this population and the cognitive skills underlying the disorder. Although specific treatment goals may change as children age, the underlying core deficits that lead to the language disorder remain and must continue to be addressed. Goals at the prelinguistic, early childhood, and adolescent–adult stages will be described with attention to these underlying core deficits. Intervention approaches will be discussed from the perspective of applying evidence-based practice to the needs of children with varying communication profiles and to the very definition of successful language outcomes itself.

Language Disorders in ASD Throughout the Lifespan

Prelinguistic Stage

Communication versus Speech. It is important to stress that the deficits seen in individuals with ASD can best be characterized as deficits in communication rather than speech. Given this perspective, children at risk for ASD can be identified before speech fails to emerge. Developmental delays in many nonverbal functions have been shown to predict later language development. Joint attention and various forms of symbol use are two major areas of delay in prelinguistic children at risk for ASD. Joint attention deficits are reflected in difficulty shifting attention between people and objects. By 12 months, most typically developing infants share attention using alternating eye gaze, and follow the eye gaze or point of others (Toth et al., 2006). Absence of these behaviors can place a child at risk for delayed language development. Symbol use is essential for the development of conventional communication, both verbal and nonverbal (Wetherby, Prizant, & Schuler, 2000). Symbolic behaviors include the use of conventional gestures and pretend play. Play skills and language are related in that both require the ability to make one thing stand for another (Prizant, Wetherby, Rubin, & Laurent, 2003).

Wetherby et al. (1998) found that delays in both joint attention and symbol use differentiated children with ASD from children with other developmental delays (DD). The pattern of behaviors that distinguished them from children with other delays included both strengths and weaknesses. Children with ADS exhibited poorer scores on communicative functions, gestural communication, reciprocity, social–affective signaling, and symbolic play. However, they exhibited relative strengths in behavior regulation and constructive play.

Conventional hand symbols such as waving, showing, and pointing may be absent or late to develop. The observation that nonverbal children with ASD do not substitute gestural communication to compensate for speech deficits as do children with other communication disorders may be explained by this deficit in symbol use (Wetherby et al., 2000). Various forms of unconventional verbal and vocal behaviors such as echolalia and perseveration may also have their roots in symbol deficits (Wetherby et al., 2000; Woods & Wetherby, 2003). Echolalic utterances in the form of unanalyzed chunks of speech that represent a situation or event can be considered unconventional communicative symbols.

Predictors of Language Acquisition. Numerous studies have identified joint attention and symbolic behaviors as significant predictors of language acquisition (Anderson et al., 2007; Bono, Daley, & Sigman, 2004; Charman, et al., 2003; Smith, Mirenda, & Zaidman-Zait, 2007; Toth et al., 2006; Wetherby et al., 2004). Most recently, Bopp et al. (2009) found that children who were more attentive and socially responsive made greater gains in vocabulary and language. Another recent study (Shumway & Wetherby, 2009) found that rate of communicative acts and joint attention were the strongest predictors of verbal outcome at age 3, and Anderson et al. (2007) found that both joint attention and nonverbal IQ were strong positive predictors of later verbal outcome. Smith et al. (2007) found that vocabulary growth was associated with a greater number of gestures to initiate joint attention and with the demonstration of pretend play skills. Toth et al. state "Through joint attention interactions, infants begin to link words and sentences with objects and events" (2006, p. 994). It has been suggested that language deficits result because children are not tuned into the speech directed at them and therefore do not make relationships between verbal input and the context (Carpenter & Tomasello, 2000). Several studies have also identified imitation ability as predictive of later language development (Charmon et al., 2003; Toth et al., 2006; Yoder & Stone, 2006). Rogers and Bennetto (2001) hypothesize that deficits in imitation may interfere with the physical coordination required for social interactions. Therefore it is essential that speech assessments include evaluation of motor functioning.

Identifying Intervention Priorities at the Prelinguistic Stage. Knowing which behaviors facilitate language acquisition can guide clinicians in setting priorities for language intervention. There are a number of studies that document the effectiveness of targeting skills such as joint attention, play, and imitation. These behaviors have been successfully targeted in recent studies using a variety of intervention approaches (Ingersoll & Schreibman, 2006; Kasari, Freeman, & Paparella, 2006; Rocha, Schreibman, & Stahmer, 2007; Stahmer, 1999; Yoder & Stone, 2006). The Kasari et al. study targeted play skills in one group of subjects and joint attention in another group. Results were interesting in that targeting play skills were found to also improve joint attention.

Some evidence also suggests that the choice of an intervention approach may be guided by a child's prelinguistic status and may help us understand why some approaches work for some children and not for others (Bopp et al., 2009). For example, Yoder and Stone (2006) compared the efficacy of the picture exchange system (PECS) with responsive education and prelinguistic milieu teaching (RPMT) in 36 preschoolers with ASD. For children with a certain level of play skills, PECS training resulted in more rapid acquisition of nonimitative communicative acts. Children with lower object exploration skills responded better to RPMT, an approach which does target play skills. Bono et al. (2004) studied the effect of the amount of intervention on language development. They found that increased intervention was most effective for children with higher levels of response to bids for interventions. These results reinforce the principle that intervention approaches need to be highly individualized based on the profile of each child.

Early Childhood Stage

Although the onset of language is late in most children later diagnosed with ASD, a substantial number of these children subsequently develop some functional language. In 1997, Lord and Paul reported that approximately 50% of students with ASD in their study acquired functional use of language. This percentage contrasts with a later study (Seltzer et al., 2003) which found that approximately 70% of the individuals developed some functional speech. Seltzer et al. suggest that the intensive early intervention provided to their population may account for the improved language status of the individuals in their study.

The language of those children who develop functional speech is generally characterized by fewer disorders in the areas of syntax and phonology than in the areas of semantics and pragmatics. The speech and language of children with ASD is typically characterized by a limited verbal repertoire; reduced spontaneity; and poor conversational skills including topic initiation, maintenance, relevance; turn-taking, and taking the perspective of the listener (Paul, 2007). "Children with autism tend to talk less for the purpose of sharing or seeking information than for the purpose of expressing needs and wants" (Carpenter & Tomasello, 2000, p. 44). Echolalia, both immediate and delayed, is often demonstrated in the early stages of language acquisition by many children with ASD (Wetherby et al., 2000) and may continue throughout the child's life (Johnson et al, 2007). Paralinguistic deficits have also been noted. Sheinkopf, Mundy, Oller, and Steffens (2000) compared vocalizations of preschool children with ASD to those of children with other developmental delays and found significant differences in the vocalizations of the two groups. Those with ASD were differentiated from the other groups by production of a greater proportion of atypical vocalizations such as squeals, growls, and yells rather than by the proportion of well-formed consonant-vowel syllables.

Both echolalia and the use of memorized "verbal chunks" such as television advertisements or scripts from videos, may give the misleading impression of advanced language competence because of the sophisticated vocabulary, syntax, and articulation displayed (Johnson et al, 2007). These skills are in sharp contrast to the reduced receptive language skills often demonstrated. A child who may be able to label objects, colors, letters, or shapes may be unable to comprehend these terms in conversation or for academic tasks. Some develop "hyperlexia"; that is, advanced reading skills for decoding that coincide with poor reading comprehension (Nation, Clarke, Wright, & Williams, 2006; Newman et al., 2007).

Adolescent and Adult Stage

Although significant progress in language functioning occurs as individuals age, research following young children with autism into adolescence and adulthood demonstrates that language impairment continues to be "central to the disorder and might underlie many other areas of dysfunction" (Howlin et al., 2000, p. 572). Joint attention and symbolic abilities may improve but deficits continue to impact on communication (Tsatsanis, Foley, & Donebower, 2004). Conversational competence, for example, requires joint attention in order to be sensitive to the social context, to the interests of others, and to the previous knowledge of those involved. Higher levels of abstract language are required for understanding and using sarcasm, humor, and nonliteral language. The ability to understand and use nonverbal cues reflects symbolic behavior as well (Paul, Orlovski, Marcinko, & Volkmar, 2009; Rubin & Lennon, 2004).

Adolescents. A number of studies that compared the conversational skills of adolescents with and without ASD have found significant differences in the ability to manage topics and information appropriately in a conversation (Bellon-Harn & Harn, 2006; Brinton, Robinson, & Fujiki, 2004; Capps, Kehres, & Sigman, 1998; Paul et al., 2009). Language difficulties observed in these studies include staying on topic, extending topics with new, relevant, or sufficient information, and responding to nonverbal cues. Adolescent conversations are rapid, abstract, filled with figurative and nonliteral references, and dependent on the ability to take another's perspective. Even in high functioning individuals with ASD such advanced language skills may be limited (Brinton et al., 2004). In some studies of adolescents with Asperger syndrome (AS) inappropriate talkativeness was observed. A group of adolescents with AS studied by Adams, Green, Gilchrist, and Cox (2002) included a subset that was very garrulous and had a pedantic monologue style. Church, Alisanski, and Amanullah (2000) followed a group of children with AS over several years. In late elementary school, these children were described as communicating through long monologues on topics of their own choosing, frequently perseverating on these same topics. In spite of improvements in language over time, parents of these students reported that in adolescence, the lack of social-communication skills remained their greatest weakness.

Deficits in the vocal parameters of speech have also been described in this population. The subjects followed by Church et al. (2000) did not speak with appropriate volume and had difficulty with appropriate inflection. Similar speech and prosody errors were found in another study of adolescents diagnosed with high functioning autism (HFA) and Asperger's syndrome (AS; Shriberg et al., 2001). Not only were there more articulation errors in the ASD population than in the control group, but these students used inappropriate volume and pitch and demonstrated a greater frequency of disfluencies and word revisions. Vocal parameters intersected with pragmatic functioning because many of the subjects with ASD were unable to use stress patterns appropriately to convey old and new information nor were they able to recognize the meaning expressed by stress patterns in the voices of conversational partners.

Adults. Areas which remain problematic in adults with ASD have been described in several studies. Specifically, continued use of stereotyped utterances and inappropriate questions were found by Seltzer et al. (2003), and problems with the use of nonverbal communication such as eye contact were described by Howlin et al. (2000). Adults with AS have reported that their inability to understand idioms, double-meanings, and body language results in communicative misunderstandings with coworkers. Also reported were problems with making irrelevant comments and knowing when to ask questions in vocational settings (Hurlbutt & Chalmers, 2004). Analyses of the narratives of adults on the spectrum reveal a decreased use of personal pronouns, temporal expressions, referential expressions, and past tense (Colle, Baron-Cohen, Wheelwright, & van der Lely, 2008; Seung, 2007). Use of these linguistic forms is important for narrative cohesion because they provide the listener with information about the perspective from which the narrative is being told. Omission of these forms causes confusion in the listener.

Assessment and Intervention for Communication and Language Development

Assessment

Appropriate intervention goals for communication enhancement result from a complete evaluation of both prelinguistic and linguistic communicative strengths and weaknesses. Assessment of the prelinguistic child includes a description of gestural communication, the ability to respond to and initiate joint attention, the variety and frequency of communication intents, symbolic skills such as play and imitation of sounds, and response to verbal input. In the child who is demonstrating some verbal skills, the above skills are assessed in addition to the comprehension and production of conventional meanings at the word, sentence, and discourse level. A description of nonconventional communication strategies such as echolalia and maladaptive communicative strategies such as tantrums to express rejection should also be included (Paul, 2007; Wetherby et al., 2000). In adolescents and young adults, conversational skills and use of nonliteral language must be included in the speech–language evaluation.

Traditional forms of standardized, norm-referenced tests of receptive and expressive language cannot be relied upon to provide the information needed to assess communication in children with ASD. Most of these assessment instruments focus on the form of language, such as syntax and phonology. As pointed out above, communication deficits are evident at the prelinguistic stage of development in children with ASD, and therefore these instruments will be of limited usefulness in that age-group. Even for children who have developed verbal communication, such instruments do not typically assess the social-pragmatic functions of speech. For an authentic picture of a child's communicative competence, assessment should be carried out in natural contexts, in a variety of situations, and with a variety of conversational partners such as caregivers or peers. Assessment tools such as observational checklists, language samples, and caregiver interviews can provide a more accurate picture of the child's communication strengths and weaknesses (American Speech-Language-Hearing Association [ASHA], 2006; Tager-Flusberg et al., 2009; Wetherby et al., 2000).

Social-communicative functions in young children can be measured by a variety of instruments including the Communication and Symbolic Behavior Scales-Developmental Profile (CSBS-DP; Wetherby & Prizant, 2003); Early Social Communication Scales (ESCS; Mundy, Hogan, & Doerling, 1996); Assessing Linguistic Behavior (ALB; Olswang, Stoel-Gammon, Coggins, & Carpenter, 1987); and the MacArthur-Bates Communicative Development Inventories (Fenson, Marchman, Thal, Reznick, & Bates, 2007). These instruments have been used or recommended by a number of researchers (Aldred, Green, & Adams, 2004; Bono et al, 2004; Crais, 2006; Tager-Flusberg et al., 2009; Wetherby et al., 2004).

Reichow, Salamack, Paul, Volkmar, and Klin (2008) found that the comprehensive assessment of spoken language (CASL; Carrow-Woolfolk, 1999) could be used to identify the communication difficulties of children and adolescents with high functioning ASD. The CASL includes measures not only of language structure but also pragmatic functioning, figurative language, nonliteral language, and inferencing abilities. The test of language functioning (TLC; Wiig & Secord, 1985) was recommended (Paul & Sutherland, 2003) for assessing these areas as well.

An important component of the assessment process is to determine what supports might facilitate a decrease in nonstandard forms of communication such as tantrums and head banging. Using dynamic assessment and visual supports such as AAC or signing, for example, might be explored. Buchsbacher and Fox (2003) describe a process of functional assessment in which negative behaviors are analyzed to determine their communicative intent. Interventions can then be designed to replace these forms of communication with more positive behaviors. Assessment of interactions between the child and caregivers may also provide information about what facilitates or interferes with successful communication (ASHA, 2006; Prelock, Beatson, Botner, Broder, & Drucker, 2003).

Many children with ASD have motor planning deficits which result in apraxia of speech (Anzalone & Williamson, 2000; Rogers & Bennetto, 2000; Wetherby et al., 2000). It is important to determine if motor deficits underlie problems with speech development because if so, treatments such as the PROMPT approach may be effective. Rogers et al, (2006) conducted a small intervention study with five nonverbal children and found that four of the children developed some verbal communication after PROMPT treatment. Although PROMPT treatment has become very popular in the treatment of speech disorders in children with ASD, research supporting the use of this approach is limited.

Intervention

Historical Perspectives. Treatment approaches to communication disorders in ASD have changed over the years as a result of several factors: the increased understanding of underlying social–cognitive deficits; recognition of the differing learning styles of children with ASD; and appreciation of the role of the family in intervention. Understanding of the social–communicative deficits of children with ASD has resulted in a move away from traditional discrete trial approaches which focused on speech production (Lovaas, 1977) to more naturalistic, developmentally based programs which focus on social communication (Prizant, Wetherby, & Rydell, 2000; Woods & Wetherby, 2002). Recent advances in knowledge about the cognitive challenges of individuals with autism in areas such as executive functions, theory of mind, and social–emotional processing are reflected in contemporary approaches such as Winner's social thinking model (Winner, 2000). Rather than training scripted responses, this model attempts to teach the "why behind social skills" (Crooke, Hendrix, & Rachman, 2008, p. 583). Recognition of the visual learning style of many children with ASD (ASHA, 2006) has led to the use of approaches such as video modeling (Buggey, 2005; Charlop & Milstein, 1989; Maione & Mirenda, 2006; Sansosti & Powell-Smith, 2008) and alternative–augmentative systems such as PECS (Bondy & Frost, 1994). Family focused intervention, especially in the early years, has become a hallmark of effective intervention with ASD (Prelock et al., 2003). Parents are not only included in the planning process but have been effectively trained to carry out the interventions (Laski, Charlop, & Schreibman, 1988; Rocha et al., 2007; Schertz & Odom, 2007; Solomon, Necheles, Ferch, & Bruckman, 2007). In the following sections, research supporting the use of these approaches will be reviewed.

Intervention Approaches

Contemporary Behavioral Approaches. Some examples of behavioral approaches that recognize the need to teach more communicative verbal behaviors are pivotal response training (PRT; Koegel, Camarata, Koegel, Ben-Tall, & Smith, 1998); time delay (Charlop & Walsh, 1986); responsive education and prelinguistic milieu teaching (RPMT; Yoder & Stone, 2006); and the natural language paradigm (NLP; Koegel, O'Dell, & Koegel, 1987). These approaches have been used to teach a variety of linguistic skills. For example, PVT has been used to teach grammatical morphemes (Koegel, Carter, & Koegel, 2003), to improve speech intelligibility (Koegel et al., 1998), to increase complex social interactions (Pierce & Schreibman, 1995), and to develop symbolic play skills (Stahmer, 1999). Time delay has been used to increase spontaneous verbalizations (Charlop & Trasowech, 1991), to increase the use of requests (Charlop, Schreibman, & Thibodeau, 1985), and to facilitate use of question forms (Taylor & Harris, 1995). RPMT was effective in increasing turn taking and initiating joint attention (Yoder & Stone, 2006), and NLP trained parents to increase the frequency of their children's verbalizations (Laski et al., 1988).

Developmental Social–Cognitive Approaches. Interventions based on more developmental approaches are even more child-directed than the behavioral approaches described above. In these kinds of programs, the adult follows the child's lead, responds to all of the child's communicative attempts as if they were meaningful, and models more mature forms of communication. Communication is encouraged by strategies such as putting desired objects out of reach. Programs which utilize developmental, social, and pragmatic interventions include the floortime approach used in the DIR/Floortime model (Greenspan & Weider, 1997); the Hanen More Than Words program (McConoche, Randle, Hammal, & Le Couteur, 2005; Sussman, 1999), and the SCERTS model (Prizant et al., 2003). Children in a study by Solomon et al. (2007) demonstrated significant developmental progress in an 8- to 12-month DIR program administered by trained parents, and Ingersoll, Dvortcsak, Whalen, and Sikora (2005) demonstrated increases in spontaneous speech in a single-subject multiple baseline study of three children using a developmental social pragmatic (DSP) intervention based on the principles of the DIR, Hanen, and SCERTS models.

The emphasis on social-communication skills for older, higher functioning students is reflected in a continued shift away from the teaching of discrete skills to programs which reflect an understanding of the cognitive demands of social interactions which require rapid reading of continually changing contexts. For example, rather than teaching students to make eye contact, Winner's social thinking program (2000) teaches students to use their eyes to read the situation (Winner & Crooke, 2009). Crooke et al. (2008) demonstrated improved social behaviors using

Winner's model in a multiple baseline single–subject design study of six children diagnosed with either Asperger syndrome or high functioning autism. Continued research will be necessary to document the effectiveness of this new approach.

Family and Peer-Mediated Interventions. Models of intervention that recognize the impact of family and peer interaction differ from the traditional clinician–teacher directed format. A strength of both peer and parent mediation is that the intervention is provided by the communication partners with whom the child interacts daily in natural contexts. Peers have been trained successfully to serve as models and to interact with children with ASD in a number of studies (Kalyva & Avramidis, 2005; Pierce & Schreibman, 2005; Prenderville, Prelock, & Unwin, 2005). Parents have been trained to increase speech using the natural language paradigm (NLP; Laski et al., 1988) and to improve joint attention using both developmental (Scherz & Odom, 2007; Solomon et al., 2007) and behavioral models (Rocha et al., 2007). Training of parents is especially helpful because when children are not responsive, parents often become more didactic in their communication style. Parents need to be trained to become more sensitive and responsive to their child's communicative attempts because child-oriented and reciprocal styles of communication will usually increase communicative initiations from children with ASD (Aldred et al., 2004).

Visually Presented Methodologies. A number of studies have shown that social communicative skills can be taught by having the child watch a video that demonstrates individuals or himself engaging in appropriate social interactions (Buggey, 2005; Maione & Mirenda, 2006). For example, video modeling was used by Charlop-Christy and Daneshvar (2003) to teach perspective taking in children. More recently, Sansosti and Powell-Smith (2008) demonstrated increased rate of communication using video models of social-communication skills.

Use of the visual modality to develop communication has been especially successful for children who have not yet or cannot develop spoken communication. Augmentative/alternative communication (AAC) approaches include both unaided approaches such as sign language and aided approaches such as the use of pictures, symbols, or written cues. Voice output communication devices (VOCAs) are also aided approaches. A meta-analysis of studies using AAC concluded that most of these interventions were effective in producing positive behavioral change and generalization (Schlosser & Lee, 2000). More important, there is no evidence that the use of AAC impedes the later development of speech production. In fact, some studies have found that AAC actually results in increased vocalization in some children (Schlosser & Wendt, 2008). Mirenda (2003) points out that although numerous studies have supported the use of these approaches for children with ASD, decisions for which approach is best for a particular child must be measured in "specific contexts, with specific children, and to meet specific needs" (p. 212).

For children with ASD, the most frequently used AAC system is the picture exchange communication system (PECS; Bondy & Frost, 1994). PECS training results in more spontaneous communication because it teaches a variety of communicative functions rather than simply responses to adults' requests for labels. The earliest goal of the PECS program is to teach requesting behaviors. In the final stages, the program teaches the child to produce word combinations such as "I want_____." and to initiate and respond to a wider range of communicative functions. A number of benefits to the use of the PECS program have been documented. One benefit has been the emergence or increase in the use of spoken communication (Charlop-Christy, Carpenter, Le, LeBlanc, & Kellet, 2002; Ganz & Simpson, 2004). Although these studies addressed the benefits of AAC on speech development, AAC has also been shown to have a positive impact on communication, expressive and receptive language development, and behavior and emotional regulation (ASHA, 2006; Ganz & Simpson, 2004).

The use of scripts and social stories are strategies that also take advantage of visual strengths in children with ASD. Social stories have been used to help children with ASD who can read to initiate verbal communication and to engage in conversational exchanges with partners. A review of the empirical research literature on social stories (Reynhout & Carter, 2006) concluded that it is a promising approach but in need of further research to document efficacy of the various components of the methodology.

Issues in Research-Based Practice for ASD. A variety of teaching methodologies and approaches for language intervention in autism are supported by reviews of therapeutic practices (Goldstein, 2002; Hwang & Hughes, 2000; National Research Council, 2001; Odom et al., 2003; Rogers & Vismara, 2009). However, these reviews also highlight some limitations to the findings. Goldstein concluded that, although language development is a multidimensional, complex process, most studies are "designed to assess the effect of a restricted set of treatment components on certain aspects of language development" (p. 392). Hwang and Hughes (2000) concurred that many interventions targeted isolated behaviors in controlled settings.

Tager-Flushberg et al. (2009) point out that one of the problems with comparing outcomes of different intervention approaches is the lack of uniformity in defining successful language outcomes. The term *functional speech* is often used as the criterion for a positive outcome but the definition of "functional speech" is unclear. To address this problem, Tager-Flushberg et al. provide a detailed description of language development milestones that should be used as criteria for determining whether particular methodologies are facilitating age-appropriate language competencies. They maintain that using a similar set of milestones will allow comparisons to be made between intervention studies using different methodologies or research designs.

Effective Intervention for Communication Enhancement. In spite of these limitations, a number of conclusions can be drawn about effective interventions for developing social communication in children with ASD. Goals for communication should be based on the core challenges of ASD such as joint attention, related symbolic skills such as play, and communication skills for behavioral regulation and social interaction (Anderson et al., 2007; ASHA, 2006; Charman et al., 2003; Toth et al., 2006; Woods & Wetherby, 2003). These behaviors have been successfully targeted in recent studies using a variety of intervention approaches (Ingersoll & Schreibman, 2006; Kasari et al., 2006; Rocha et al., 2007; Yoder & Stone, 2006). Furthermore, specific goals addressing these core challenges must be adapted as communication abilities develop. ASHA (2006) and Prizant et al. (2003) provide sample goals to target core deficits in individuals at three stages of development: prior to the emergence of symbolic language, at emerging language stages, and at more advanced stages of conversational discourse. For example, a joint attention goal at the prelinguistic stage might be pairing communicative gestures with eye-gaze whereas a joint attention goal at the emerging language stage might be commenting to share enjoyment and interests. At the advanced language stage, a joint attention goal could be to consider the intentions and knowledge of others when sharing information about past and future events. A goal for symbolic behavior at the prelinguistic stage might be observing and imitating the functional use of objects. At the emerging language stage, a goal for symbol development would be understanding and using more sophisticated grammar, and at the advanced language stage, the goal might be to develop reading and writing skills. Effective programs must be embedded within the natural environment and therefore must address not just the skills or deficits of the child but also address communication within the family system (Woods & Wetherby, 2003).

Using parents as mediators of intervention was documented above. However, family centered principles also require that the families be included when selecting intervention approaches and goals. Respect for family values is required by law in early intervention and is recommended at all levels of practice (Prelock et al., 2003). Family beliefs, perceptions of autism, and needs may vary by culture (Wilder, Dyches, Obiakor, & Anzelone, 2004) and may affect choice of treatment approach (Wong, 2009). The value that parents place on early speech, talkativeness, and independence may affect rates of early identification and may be in conflict with therapeutic goals set by mainstream service providers (van Kleek, 1994).

Future Directions

Given the wide range of treatment approaches available and the variability in the response of children with ASD to these different approaches, an important goal for future research is to discover which factors predict the best approach for individual children. These factors may include not just the characteristics of the children but also their family, culture, and, community resources. Continued research into the cognitive, biological, and neurological underpinnings of the disorder may also have an effect on future programming for language intervention. Furthermore, while many approaches to treatment of younger children have a good deal of empirical support, a review of the literature finds limited evidence based support for intervention with older, higher functioning individuals. The needs of this older group are becoming increasingly evident to practitioners in the field and should be a focus of research.

Conclusions and Summary

In conclusion, communication interventions should target the ability to initiate spontaneous communication for a wide range of communicative functions in a variety of social contexts and with a range of age-appropriate conversational partners. Comprehension of both verbal and nonverbal cues in discourse is addressed in order to improve social communication, and both verbal and nonverbal means of expressive communication are appropriate options (ASHA, 2006; Woods & Wetherby, 2003). Goals must be individualized for children after carrying out an ecologically appropriate assessment of abilities. Ogletree (2007) states, "The most successful communication interventions for children with autism spectrum disorders (ASD) are implemented or coordinated by individuals who consider treatment options flexibly and apply a variety of approaches according to the needs of the child and family" (p. 190). The presence of fluent speech before the age of 5 is a significant predictor of both social and academic future functioning (Lord & Paul, 1997). Therefore, early and intensive attention to the development of communication is essential to helping all individuals with ASD achieve their potential.

References

Adams, C., Green, J., Gilchrist, A., & Cox, A. (2002). Conversational behavior of children with Asperger syndrome and conduct disorder. *Journal of Child Psychology and Psychiatry, 43,* 679–690. doi: 10.1111/1469-7610.00056

Aldred, C., Green, J., & Adams, C. (2004). A new social communication intervention for children with autism: Pilot randomized controlled treatment study suggesting effectiveness. *Journal of Child Psychology and Psychiatry, 45,* 1420–1430. doi: 10.1111/j.1469-7610.2004.00338.x

American Speech-Language-Hearing Association (ASHA). (2006). *Guidelines for speech-language pathologists in diagnosis, assessment, and treatment of autism spectrum disorders across the lifespan.* Retrieved from http://www. asha.org/policy

Anderson, D., Lord, C., Risi, S. Dilavore. P. S., Shulman, C., Thurm, A., ... Pickles, A. (2007). Patterns of growth in verbal abilities among children with autism spectrum disorder. *Journal of Counseling and Clinical Psychology, 75,* 594–604. doi: 10.1037/0022-006X.75.4.594

Anzalone, M. E., & Williamson, G. G. (2000). Sensory processing and motor performance in autism spectrum disorders. In A. M. Wetherby & B. M. Prizant (Eds.), *Autism spectrum disorders: A transactional developmental perspective* (pp. 143–166). Baltimore, MD: Brookes.

Bellon-Harn, M. L., & Harn, W. (2006). Profiles of social communicative competence in middle school children with Asperger syndrome: Two case studies. *Child Language Teaching and Therapy, 22*, 1–26. doi: 10.1191/0265659006ct295oa

Bondy, A. S., & Frost, L. (1994). The picture exchange communication system. *Focus on Autism and Other Developmental Disabilities. 9*, 1–19.

Bono, M., Daley, T. & Sigman, M. (2004). Relations among joint attention, amount of intervention and language gain in autism. *Journal of Autism and Developmental Disorders, 34*, 495–505. doi: 10.1007/s10803-004-2545-x

Bopp. K. D., Mirenda, P., & Zumbo, B. D. (2009). Behavior predictors of language development over 2 years in children with autism spectrum disorders. *Journal of Speech, Language, and Hearing Research, 52*, 1106–1120. doi: 10.1044/1092-4388(2009/07-0262)

Brinton, B., Robinson, L. A., & Fujiki, M. (2004). Description of a program for social language intervention: "If you can have a conversation, you can have a relationship." *Language, Speech, and Hearing Services in the Schools, 35*, 283–290. doi: 10.1044/0161-1461(2004/026)

Buggey, T. (2005). Video self-modeling applications with students with autism spectrum disorder in a small private school setting. *Focus on Autism and Developmental Disabilities, 20*, 52–63. doi: 10.1177/10883576050200010501

Buschbacher, P. W., & Fox, L. (2003). Understanding and intervening with the challenging behavior of young children with autism spectrum disorder. *Language, Speech and Hearing Services in the Schools, 34*, 217–227. doi: 10.1044/0161-1461(2003/018)

Capps, L, Kehres, J., & Sigman, M. (1998). Conversational abilities among children with autism and children with developmental delays. *Autism, 2*, 325–344. doi: 10.1177/1362361398024002

Carpenter, M., & Tomasello, M. (2000). Joint attention, cultural learning, and language acquisition: Implications for children with autism. In A. M. Wetherby & B. M. Prizant (Eds.), *Autism spectrum disorders: A transactional developmental perspective* (pp. 31–54). Baltimore, MD: Brookes.

Carrow-Woolfolk, E. (1999). *Comprehensive assessment of spoken language.* Circle Pines, MN: AGS.

Charlop, M. H., & Milstein, J. P. (1989). Teaching autistic children conversational speech using video modeling. *Journal of Applied Behavior Analysis, 22*, 275–285. doi: 10.1901/jaba.1989.22-275

Charlop, M. H., Schreibman, L., & Thibodeau, M. (1985). Increasing spontaneous verbal responding in autistic children using a time delay procedure. *Journal of Applied Behavior Analysis, 18*, 155–166. doi: 10.1901/jaba.1985.18-155

Charlop, M. H., & Trasowech, J. E. (1991). Increasing children's daily spontaneous speech. *Journal of Applied Behavior Analysis, 24*, 747–761. doi: 10.1901/jaba.1991.24-747

Charlop, M. H., & Walsh, M. E. (1986). Increasing children's spontaneous verbalization of affection: An assessment of time delay and peer modeling procedures. *Journal of Applied Behavioral Analysis, 19*, 307–314. doi: 10.1901/jaba.1986.19-307

Charlop-Christy, M., Carpenter, M., Le, L., LeBlanc, L., & Kellet, K. (2002). Using the picture exchange system (PECS) with children with autism: Assessment of PECS acquisition, speech, social-communicative behavior, and problem behavior. *Journal of Applied Behavior Analysis, 35*, 213–231. doi: 10.1901/jaba.2002.35-213

Charlop-Christy, M., & Daneshvar, S. (2003). Using video modeling to teach perspective taking to children with autism. *Journal of Positive Behavior Interventions, 5*, 12–21. doi: 10.1177/10983007030050010101

Charman, T., Baron-Cohen, S., Swettenham, J., Baird, G., Drew, A., & Cox, A. (2003). Predicting language outcome in infants with autism and pervasive developmental disorder. *International Journal of Language and Communication Disorders, 38*(3), 265–285. doi: 10.1080/136820310000104830

Church, C., Alisanski, S., & Amanullah, S. (2000). The social, behavioral, and academic experiences of children with Asperger syndrome. *Focus on Autism and Other Developmental Disabilities, 15*, 12–20. doi: 10.1177/108835760001500102

Colle, L., Baron-Cohen, S., Wheelwright, S., & van der Lely, H. (2008). Narrative discourse in adults with high-functioning autism or Asperger syndrome. *Journal of Autism and Developmental Disorders, 38*, 28–40. doi: 10.1007/s10803-007-0357-5

Crais, E. (2006, April). *Identifying infant/toddler behaviors that may lead to early diagnosis of autism.* Paper presented at the meeting of the New York State Speech-Language-Hearing Association, Saratoga Springs, NY.

Crooke, P. J., Hendrix, R. E., & Rachman, J. R. (2008). Brief report: Measuring the effectiveness of teaching social thinking to children with Asperger syndrome (AS) and high functioning autism (HFA). *Journal of Autism and Developmental Disorders, 38*, 581–591. doi: 10.1007/s10803-007-0466-1

Fenson, L., Marchman, V., Thal, D., Reznick. S., & Bates, E. (2007). *The MacArthur-Bates communicative development inventories: User's guide and technical manual* (2nd ed.). Baltimore, MD: Brookes.

Ganz, J. B., & Simpson, R. L. (2004). Effects on communicative requesting and speech development of the picture exchange communication system in children with characteristics of autism. *Journal of Autism and Developmental Disorders, 34*(4), 395–409. doi: 10.1023/B:JADD.0000037416.59095.d7

Goldstein, H. (2002). Communication intervention for children with autism: A review of treatment efficacy. *Journal of Autism and Developmental Disorders, 32*(3), 373–396. doi: 10.1023/A:1020589821992

Greenspan, S. I., & Weider, S. (1997). Developmental patterns and outcomes in infants and children with disorders in relating and communicating: A chart review of 200 cases of children with autistic spectrum diagnoses. *Journal of Developmental and Learning Disorders, 1,* 87–141.

Howlin, P., Mawhood, L., & Rutter, N. (2000). Autism and developmental receptive language disorder—A follow-up comparison in early adult life. II: Social, behavioral, and psychiatric outcomes. *Journal of Child Psychology and Psychiatry, 41*(5), 561–578. doi: 10.1111/1469-7610.00643

Hurlbutt, K., & Chalmers, L. (2004). Employment and adults with Asperger syndrome. *Focus on Autism and Other Developmental Disabilities, 19,* 215–222. doi: 10.1177/10883576040190040301

Hwang, B., & Hughes, C. (2000). The effects of social interactive training on early social communicative skills of children with autism. *Journal of Autism and Developmental Disorders, 30*(4), 331–343. doi: 10.1023/A:1005579317085

Ingersoll, B., Dvortcsak, A., Whalen, C., & Sikora, D. (2005). The effects of a developmental, social-pragmatic language intervention on rate of expressive language production in young children with autistic spectrum disorders. *Focus on Autism and Other Developmental Disabilities, 20,* 213–222. doi: 10.1177/10883576050200040301

Ingersoll, B., & Schreibman, L. (2006). Teaching reciprocal imitation skills to young children with autism using a naturalistic behavioral approach: Effects on language, pretend play, and joint attention. *Journal of Autism and Developmental Disorders, 36,* 487–505. doi: 10.1007/s10803-006-0089-y

Johnson, C. P., Myers, S. M., & The Council on Children with Disabilities. (2007). Identification and evaluation of children with autism spectrum disorders. *Pediatrics, 120,* 1183–1215. doi: 10.1542/peds.2007-2361

Kalyva, E., & Avramidis, E. (2005). Improving communication between children with autism and their peers through the "Circle of Friends": A small-scale intervention study. *Journal of Applied Research in Intellectual Disabilities, 18*(3), 253–261. doi: 10.1111/j.1468-3148.2005.00232.x

Kasari, C., Freeman, S., & Paparella, T. (2006). Joint attention and symbolic play in young children with autism: A randomized controlled intervention study. *Journal of Child Psychology and Psychiatry, 47*(6), 611–620. doi: 10.1111/j.1469-7610.2005.01567.x

Koegel, L. K., Carter, C., & Koegel, R.L. (2003). Teaching children with autism self-initiations as a pivotal response. *Topics in Language Disorders, 23*(2), 134–145.

Koegel, R., Camarata, S., Koegel, L. B., Ben-Tall, A., & Smith, A. (1998). Increasing speech intelligibility in children with autism. *Journal of Autism and Developmental Disorders, 28,* 241–251. doi: 10.1023/A:1026073522897

Koegel, R., O'Dell, M. C., & Koegel, L. K. (1987). A natural language paradigm for teaching nonverbal autistic children. *Journal of Autism and Developmental Disorders, 17,* 187–199. doi: 10.1007/BF01495055

Laski, K. E., Charlop, M., & Schreibman, L. (1988). Training parents to use the natural language paradigm to increase their autistic child's speech. *Journal of Applied Behavior Analysis, 21,* 391–400.

Lord, C., & Paul, R. (1997). Language and communication in autism. In D. Cohen & F. Volkmar (Eds.), *Handbook of autism and pervasive developmental disorders* (2nd ed., pp. 195–225). New York: Wiley.

Lord, C., Shulman, C., & Dilavore, P. (2004). Regression and word loss in autistic spectrum disorders. *Journal of Child Psychology and Psychiatry, 45*(5), 936–955. doi: 10.1111/j.1469-7610.2004.t01-1-00287.x

Lovaas, V. (1977). *The autistic child: Language development through behavior modification.* New York: Irvington Press.

Maione, L., & Mirenda, P. (2006). Effects of video modeling and video feedback on peer-directed social language skills of a child with autism. *Journal of Positive Behavior Interventions, 8*(2), 106–118. doi: 10.1177/10983007060080020201

McConachie, H., Randle, V., Hammal, D., & Le Couteur, A. (2005). A controlled trial of a training course for parents of children with suspected autism spectrum disorder. *The Journal of Pediatrics, 147*(3), 335–340.

Mirenda, P. (2003). Toward a functional augmentative and alternative communication for students with autism: Manual signs, graphic symbols, and voice output communication aids. *Language, Speech, and Hearing Services in the Schools, 34,* 203–216. doi: 10.1044/0161-1461(2003/017)

Mundy, P., Hogan, A., & Doelring, P. (1996). *A preliminary manual for the abridged early social communication scales.* Coral Gables, FL: University of Miami.

Nation, K., Clarke, P., Wright, B., & Williams, C. (2006). Patterns of reading ability in children with autism spectrum disorder. *Journal of Autism and Developmental Disorders, 36,* 911–919. doi: 10.1007/s10803-006-0130-1

National Research Council. (2001). *Educating children with autism* (Committee on Educational Interventions for Children with Autism, Division of Behavioral and Social Sciences and Education). Washington, DC: National Academy Press.

Newman, T. N., Macomber, D., Naples, A. J., Babitz, T., Volkmar, F., & Grigorenko, E. (2007). Hyperlexia in children with autism. *Journal of Autism and Developmental Disorders, 37,* 760–774. doi: 10.1007/s10803-006-0206-y

Odom, S, L., Brown, W. H., Frey, T., Karasu, N., Smith-Canter, L. L., & Strain, P. S. (2003)..Evidence-based practices for young children with autism: Contributions for single-subject design research. *Focus on Autism and Other Developmental Disabilities, 18*(3), 166–175. doi: 10.1177/10883576030180030401

Ogletree, B. T. (2007). In focus: What makes communication intervention successful with children with autism spectrum disorders? *Focus on Autism and Other Developmental Disabilities, 22,* 190–192. doi: 10.1177/10883576070220030601

Olswang, L., Stoel-Gammon, C., Coggins, T., & Carpenter, R. (1987). *Assessing prelinguistic and early linguistic behaviors in developmentally young children.* Seattle, WA: University of Washington Press.

Paul, R. (2007). *Language disorders from infancy through adolescents: Assessment and intervention* (3rd ed.). St. Louis, MO: Mosby Elsevier.

Paul, R., Orlovski, S. M., Marchinko, H. C., & Volkmer, R. (2009). Conversational behaviors in youth with high functioning ASD and Asperger syndrome. *Journal of Autism and Developmental Disorders, 39,* 115–125. doi: 10.1007/s10803-008-0607-1

Paul, R., & Sutherland, R. (2003). Asperger's syndrome: The role of speech–language pathologists in schools. *Perspectives on Language Learning and Education, 10*(3), 9–15.

Pierce, K., & Schreibman, L. (1995). Increasing complex social behaviors in children with autism: Effects of peer-implemented pivotal response training. *Journal of Applied Behavior Analysis, 23,* 265–295. doi: 10.1901/jaba.1995.28-285

Prelock, P., Beatson, J., Botner, B. Broder, C., & Drucker, A. (2003). Interdisciplinary assessment of young children with autism spectrum disorder. *Language, Speech, and Hearing Services in the Schools, 34,* 194–202. doi: 10.1044/0161-1461(2003/016)

Prenderville, J., Prelock, P. A., & Unwin, G. (2005). Peer play interventions to support the social competence of children with autism spectrum disorders (ASD). *Seminars in Speech and Language, 27*(1), 32–46. doi: 10.1055/s-2006-932437

Prizant, B. M., Wetherby, A. M., Rubin, E., & Laurent, A. C. (2003). The SCERTS model: A transactional, family centered, approach to enhancing communication and socioemotional abilities of children with autism spectrum disorder. *Infants and Young Children, 16*(4), 296–316.

Prizant, B. M., Wetherby, A. M., & Rydell, P. J. (2000). Communication intervention issues for children with autism spectrum disorders. In A. M. Wetherby & B. M. Prizant (Eds.), *Autism spectrum disorders: A transactional developmental perspective* (pp. 193–184). New York: Delmar.

Reichow, B., Salamack, S., Paul, R., Volkmar, F. R., & Klin, A, (2008). Pragmatic assessment in autism spectrum disorders. *Communication Disorders Quarterly, 29,* 169–176. doi: 10.1177/1525740108318697

Reynhout, G., & Carter, M. (2006). Social stories for children with disabilities. *Journal of Autism and Developmental Disorders, 36,* 445–469. doi: 10.1007/s10803-006-0086-1

Rocha, M., Schreibman, L., & Stahmer, A. (2007). Effectiveness of training parents to teach joint attention in children with autism. *Journal of Early Intervention, 29*(2), 154–172. doi: 10.1177/105381510702900207

Rogers, S. J., & Bennetto, L. (2000). Intersubjectivity in autism: The roles of imitation and executive function. In A. M. Wetherby & B. M. Prizant (Eds.), *Autism spectrum disorders: A transactional developmental perspective* (pp. 79–108). Baltimore, MD: Brookes.

Rogers, S. J., Hayden, D., Hepburn, S., Charlifue-Smith, R., Hall, T., & Hayes, A. (2006). Teaching young nonverbal children with autism useful speech: A pilot study of the Denver Model and PROMPT. *Journal of Autism and Developmental Disorders, 36,* 1007–1024. doi: 10.1007/s10803-006-0142-x

Rogers, S. J., & Vismara, L. A. (2008). Evidence-based comprehensive treatments for early autism. *Journal of Clinical Child and Adolescent Psychology, 37,* 8–38. doi: 10.1080/15374410701817808

Rubin, E., & Lennon, L. (2004). Challenges in social communication in Asperger syndrome and high-functioning autism. *Topics in Language Disorders, 24,* 271–285.

Sansosti, F. J., & Powell-Smith, K. A. (2008). Using computer-presented social stories and video models to increase the social communication skills of children with high-functioning autism spectrum disorders. *Journal of Positive Behavior Interventions, 10,* 162–178. doi:10.1177/1098300708316259

Schertz, H. H., & Odom, S. L. (2007). Promoting joint attention in toddlers with autism: A parent-mediated developmental model. *Journal of Autism and Developmental Disorders, 37,* 1562–1575. doi: 10.1007/s10803-006-0290-z

Schlosser, R. W., & Lee, D. L. (2000). Promoting generalization and maintenance in augmentative and alternative communication: A meta-analysis of 20 years of effectiveness research. *AAC: Augmentative and Alternative Communication, 16*(4), 208–226. doi: 10.1080/07434610012331279074

Schlosser, R. W., & Wendt, O. (2008). Effects of augmentative and alternative communication intervention on speech production in children with autism: A systematic review. *American Journal of Speech-Language Pathology, 17,* 212–230. doi: 10.1044/1058-0360(2008/021)

Seltzer, M. M., Krauss, M. W., Shattuck, P. T., Orsmond, G., Swe, A., & Lord, C. (2003). The symptoms of autism spectrum disorders in adolescence and adulthood. *Journal of Autism and Developmental Disorders, 33,* 565–581. doi:10.1023/B:JADD.0000005995.02453.0b

Seung, H. K. (2007). Linguistic characteristics of individuals with high functioning autism and Asperger syndrome. *Clinical Linguistics and Phonetics, 21,* 247–259. doi: 10.1080/02699200701195081

Sheinkopf, S., Mundy, P., Oller, D. K., & Steffens, M. (2000). Vocal atypicalities of preverbal autistic children. *Journal of Autism and Developmental Disorders, 28,* 15–23. doi: 10.1023/A:1005531501155

Shriberg, L. D., Paul, R., McSweeny, J. L. Klin, A., Cohen, D. J., & Volkmar, F. R. (2001). Speech and prosody characteristics of adolescents and adults with high-functioning autism and Asperger syndrome. *Journal of Speech, Language and Hearing Research, 44*, 1097–1115. doi: 10.1044/1092-4388(2001/087)

Shumway, S., & Wetherby, A. M. (2009). Communicative acts of children with autism spectrum disorders in the second year of life. *Journal of Speech, Language, and Hearing Research, 52*, 1139–1156. doi: 10.1044/1092-4388(2009/07-0280)

Sigman, M., & Ruskin, E. (1999). Continuity and change in the social competence of children with autism, Down syndrome, and developmental delays. *Monographs of the Society for Research in Child Development, 64*(1, Serial No. 256). doi: 10.1111/1540-5834.00001

Smith, V., Mirenda, P., & Zaidman-Zait, A. (2007). Predictors of expressive vocabulary growth in children with autism. *Journal of Speech-Language Hearing Research, 50*, 149–160. doi: 10.1044/1092-4388(2007/013)

Solomon, R., Necheles, J., Ferch, C., & Bruckman, D. (2007). Pilot study of a parent training program for young children with autism: The PLAY Project Home Consultation program. *Autism, 11*, 205–224. doi: 10.1177/1362361307076842

Stahmer, A. (1999). Using pivotal response training to facilitate appropriate play in children with autistic-spectrum disorders. *Child Language Teaching and Therapy, 15*(1), 29–40..doi: 10.1191/026565999672332808

Sussman, F. (1999). *More than words: Helping parents promote communication and social skills in children with autism spectrum disorders.* Toronto. Ontario: Hanen Centre.

Tager-Flusberg, H., Rogers, A., Cooper, J., Landa, R., Lord, C., Paul, R., ... Yoder, P. (2009). Defining spoken language benchmarks and selecting measures of expressive language development for young children with autism spectrum disorders. *Journal of Speech, Language, and Hearing Research. 52*, 643– 652. doi: 10.1044/1092-4388(2009/08-0136)

Taylor, B. A., & Harris, S. L. (1995). Teaching children with autism to seek information: Acquisition of novel information and generalization of responding. *Journal of Applied Behavior Analysis, 28*, 3–14. doi: 10.1901/jaba.1995.28-3

Toth, K., Munson, J., Meltzoff, A. N., & Dawson, G. (2006). Early predictors of communication development in young children with autism spectrum disorder: Joint attention, imitation, and toy play. *Journal of Autism and Developmental Disorders, 36*, 993–1005. doi: 10.1007/s10803-006-0137-7

Tsatsanis, K. D., Foley, D., & Donebower, C. (2004). Contemporary outcome research and programming guidelines for Asperger syndrome and high-functioning autism. *Topics in Language Disorders, 4*, 249–259.

van Kleek, A. (1994). Potential cultural bias in training parents as conversational partners with their children who have delays in language development. *American Journal of Speech-Language Pathology, 3*, 67–78.

Venter, A., Lord, C, & Schopler, E. (1992). A follow-up study of high-functioning autistic children. *Journal of Child Psychology and Psychiatry, 33*, 489–507. doi10.1111/j.1469-7610.1992.tb00887.x

Wetherby, A., & Prizant, B. (2003). *Communication and symbolic behavior scales—Developmental profiles.* Baltimore, MD: Brookes.

Wetherby, A. M.., Prizant, B. M.., & Hutchinson, T. (1998). Communicative, social-affective,and symbolic profiles of young children with autism and pervasive developmental disorder. *American Journal of Speech-Language Pathology, 7*, 79–91.

Wetherby, A. M., Prizant, B. M., & Schuler, A. L. (2000). Understanding the nature of communication and language impairments. In A. M. Wetherby & B. M. Prizant (Eds.), *Autism spectrum disorders: A transactional developmental perspective* (pp. 109–142). Baltimore, MD: Brookes.

Wetherby, A. M., Woods, J., Allen, L., Cleary, J., Dickinson, H., & Lord, C. (2004). Early indicators of autism spectrum disorders in the second year of life. *Journal of Autism and Developmental Disorders, 34*, 473– 493. doi: 10.1007/s10803-004-2544-y

Wiig, E., & Secord, W. (1989). *Test of language competence–Expanded edition.* San Antonio, TX: Harcourt Assessment.

Wilder, L. K., Dyches, T. T., Obiakor, F. E., & Anzelone, B. (2004). Multicultural perspectives on teaching students with autism. *Focus on Autism and Other Developmental Disabilities, 19*, 105–113. doi: 10.1177/10883576040190020601

Winner, M. G. (2000). *Inside out: What makes a person with social cognitive deficit tick?* San Jose, CA: Think Social.

Winner, M. G., & Crooke, P. J. (2009). Social thinking: A training paradigm for professionals and treatment approach for individuals with social learning/social pragmatic challenges. *Perspectives on Language Learning and Education, 16*, 62–69. Retrieved from http://div1perspectives.asha.org/cgi/content/abstract/16/2/62

Wong, V. C. N. (2009). Use of complementary and alternative medicine (CAM) in autism spectrum disorder (ASD): Comparison of Chinese and Western culture (Part A). *Journal of Autism and Developmental Disorders, 39*, 454–463. doi: 10.1007/s10803-008-0644-9

Woods, J. J., & Wetherby, A. M. (2003). Early identification of and intervention for infants and toddlers who are at risk for autism spectrum disorder. *Language, Speech, and Hearing Services in the Schools, 34*, 180–193. doi: 10.1044/0161-1461(2003/015)

Yoder, P., & Stone, W. L. (2006). Randomized comparison of two communication interventions for preschoolers with autism spectrum disorders. *Journal of Counseling and Clinical Psychology, 74*(5), 426–435. doi: 10.1037/0022-006X.74.3.426

17

ASSISTIVE TECHNOLOGY TO SUPPORT PEOPLE WITH AUTISM SPECTRUM DISORDERS

Kim Spence-Cochran and Cynthia Pearl

UNIVERSITY OF CENTRAL FLORIDA

In her book, *Thinking in Pictures and Other Reports from My Life with Autism*, Dr. Temple Grandin (1995), one of the most visible and outspoken people on the autism spectrum today, described how her brain processes information.

> I THINK IN PICTURES. Words are like a second language to me. I translate both spoken and written words into full-color movies, complete with sound, which run like a VCR tape in my head. (p. 19)

Grandin's description is particularly relevant given current trends in assistive technology (AT) implementation for individuals with autism spectrum disorders (ASD). The majority of technologies supporting students with ASD capitalize on their visual strengths (Ayres & Langone, 2008; Cafiero, 1998; Quill, 1997), translating and presenting spoken and written language in the form of visual images, including pictures (symbols and photographs), video clips, and multimedia presentations.

Innovation and research focused on specialized AT for individuals with ASD holds the key to communication, socialization, independent functioning, and the promise of full inclusion within their respective communities. Over the past decade, a proliferation of research has illustrated the potential of AT to address core impairments associated with ASD. Researchers have successfully demonstrated the power of technology-based supports for people with ASD to assist with communication (Ogletree & Harn, 2001), socialization (Bellini & Akullian, 2007; Cihak & Schrader, 2008; Corbett & Abdullah, 2005; Shukla-Mehta, Miller, & Callahan, 2010), and a variety of independent functioning skills (Shipley-Benamou, Lutzker, & Taubman, 2002).

In its definition on access, equal emphasis is placed by The Individuals with Disabilities Education Improvement Act (IDEA; 2004) on both "device" and "service." While rapid technological advances in AT hold great promise for individuals with ASD, innovations must be paired with appropriate services from qualified professionals with knowledge and skills to work collaboratively with others, including families, to assess needs, match those needs with specific evidence-based practices (EBPs), and ensure practices are implemented with fidelity. This chapter highlights past and current research in the AT field as it applies to effective practice and provides guidance for practitioners seeking to "increase, maintain, or improve functional capabilities" of individuals with ASD (Assistive Technology Act, 2004).

Historical Background

When the Individuals with Disabilities Education Act (IDEA) was first enacted in 1975, "supplementary aids and services" were the closest mention of technology support(s) for students with disabilities under the federal regulations. The Technology Related Assistance Act of 1988 (Tech Act) presented the first formal and legal definition for AT. Though this act was amended in 1994 and repealed and replaced by the Assistive Technology Act of 1998 (AT Act), the definition has remained consistent over time and has become the accepted definition used in all related legislation. According to the AT Act of 2004,

> The term "assistive technology" means technology designed to be utilized in an assistive technology device or assistive technology service.... The term "assistive technology device" means any item, piece of equipment, or product system, whether acquired commercially, modified, or customized, that is used to increase, maintain, or improve functional capabilities of individuals with disabilities.... The term "assistive technology service" means any service that directly assists an individual with a disability in the selection, acquisition, or use of an assistive technology device. (Sec. 3 Definitions (3)(4))

The IDEA 1990 Amendments (PL 105-471) adopted the AT Act definition and mandated that schools consider each student's need for AT devices and services during the IEP process (Zabala et al., 2000), putting in place the mechanism by which students who need technology might receive it. Unfortunately, federal mandates have not been sufficient to initiate the intended advances in the application and widespread use of technology in special education. Despite specialized marketplace innovations, a compelling AT research base is lacking (Gersten & Edyburn, 2007).

Assistive Technology Applications for Students with ASD

Over the past three decades, educators have endorsed the implementation of AT for their students with ASD in an effort to bolster instruction through the use of visual and auditory supports (Ayers & Langone, 2008). Historically, applied technology use for individuals with ASD has been most frequently implemented in the areas of visual representation systems, communication supports/systems, and computer assisted instruction (Mirenda, Wilk, & Carson, 2000; Pierangelo & Giuliani, 2008). With the advances within the field of technology, researchers have successfully demonstrated the power of AT use for students with ASD across a variety of settings, including schools, community-based settings, work environments, and specialized training programs (Ayers & Langone, 2008; Bellini & Akullian, 2007; Mechling, Gast, & Seid, 2009; Spence-Cochran & Pearl, 2009). Initial AT research, beyond investigations of its use to support communication needs of individuals with ASD, focused predominantly on skills of functionality (Ayres & Langone, 2008; Haring, Kennedy, Adams, & Pitts-Conway, 1987). More recent AT trends show increased emphasis on the use of social skills instructional tools (i.e., video modeling and video self-modeling; Bellini & Akullian; Cihak & Schrader, 2008; Shukla-Meht et al., 2010) and social skills interactive supports including prompting systems designed to facilitate specific interactions, and most recently, auditory and visual prompting systems for an assortment of people with ASD (Mechling, 2007; Mechling et al., 2009; Spence-Cochran & Pearl, 2009).

Communication-Based Treatments Using Technology. The impact of severe communication impairments on the inclusion of individuals with ASD in home, school, and community settings has led to a heavy focus on AT applications to support children with limited verbal abilities (Ticani & Boutot, 2005). Augmentative and alternative communication (AAC) systems have been implemented with people with ASD across several decades (Ogletree & Harn, 2001). According to Lloyd, Fuller, and Arvidson (1997), AAC is "the supplementation or replacement of natural speech and/or writing using aided and/or unaided symbols" (p. 524). Graphic symbols have been widely used to promote communication and language comprehension and production for individuals with ASD (Ogletree & Harn). Recognition of AAC as a practice dates back only as far as the 1970s (Zangari et al., 1994). While early applications focused on the use of tangible symbols, lexograms, manual signs, and traditional orthographic symbols, the use of visuospatial symbols, including photographs and line drawings, gained popularity in the 1980s. Voice output devices and computer software programs emerged as options for many individuals with ASD in the 1980s and 1990s (Mirenda & Erickson, 2000).

AT Applications Using Video-Based Technology. Video modeling (VM) and video self-modeling (VSM) have been determined as effective interventions for students with ASD (Bellini & Akullian, 2007; Cihak & Schrader, 2008). In some of the earliest research reviewing the use of video for instructional purposes with students with ASD, Haring et al. (1987) used videotapes to teach three students with ASD to locate an item in one store and then measured the generalization of these skills by the students to other stores in the community. This early work paved the way for modern day VM procedures by demonstrating that the applied use of VM (e.g., the use of a nondisabled peer in the video), coupled with direct instruction in a community-based setting, resulted in the acquisition of targeted skills and generalization of those skills by each of the study participants. In similar work, Alcantara (1994) used video to teach the location of items in a store to three children with ASD, which resulted in improved generalization skills across stores within the students' communities.

Use of Computers for Instruction. Computer assisted instruction (CAI) first emerged in educational literature in the mid-1970s (Okolo, Reith, & Bahr, 1989) and was widely touted as a means of revolutionizing education for all students. Originally this type of instruction was defined loosely as any instruction provided via a computer or computer screen (Chen & Bernard-Optiz, 1993; Okolo et al., 1989). In several early studies with students with ASD, researchers documented the benefits of CAI in providing a structured method of instruction for learners who struggled with stimulus overselectivity, language acquisition, and the need for predictability (Chen & Bernard-Optiz). Chen and Bernard-Opitz demonstrated that young children with ASD expressed more motivation and fewer aberrant behaviors during CAI than during instruction from a teacher, and Jordan (1988) illustrated the power of computers to provide often needed predictability and control over their individual learning environments for children with ASD.

Description and Overview

IDEIA (2004) mandates the consideration of equipment on a case-by-case basis, as well as the use of school-purchased assistive technology devices in a child's home or in other settings if these are deemed necessary and the child's IEP Team determines he/she needs access to those devices in order to receive FAPE. IDEIA further delineates the required school-aged technology intervention for students with disabilities as any service that assists a child with a disability in the selection, acquisition, or use of an assistive technology device (Bausch, Ault, Evmenova, & Behrmann, 2008).

Federal definitions place emphasis on the "compensatory" nature of AT (Parette & Peterson-Karlan, 2007) rather than specific guidelines for which types of services and supports should be provided to specific students. Consequently, educational professionals have a great deal of difficulty recognizing which types of devices or software would be most useful in helping students compensate for their individual deficits. These challenges are of particular concern given the wide range of AT available and the associated costs. AT applications fall on a continuum that ranges from low to high tech solutions. The implementation of AT for individuals with ASD predominately involves applications that support communication, independent living and job related skills, and social competence. Visual representation systems, such as communication boards, conversation books, and visual schedules are examples of low-tech AT widely used with individuals with ASD and are easy to implement in a variety of settings. In contrast, high-tech AT involves more complex electronic or computer driven technologies. Speech generating devices, computers, and video are examples of high-tech AT designed to increase the functional capabilities of individuals with ASD. In considering "each student's need for AT devices" (IDEA, 2004), teams must review the wide variety of AT options, both high- and low-tech, available to educators.

Increasingly, the field is recognizing the potential for AT for individuals with ASD. Students with ASD demonstrate strengths in their ability to respond to visual cues and information (Quill, 1997; Shah & Frith, 1983), and are considered by most observers to be highly visually oriented (Wetherby & Prizant, 2000). In addition, many show a clear ability to sustain attention for extended amounts of time (Buchsbaum et al., 1992; Garretson, Fein, & Waterhouse, 1990) over nonrelevant stimulus. Assistive technology offers a modality for instruction and engagement that capitalizes on the strengths and preferences of students with ASD. Recent studies have anecdotally illustrated that students with ASD appeared to enjoy using computers and technology versus traditional directed instruction (Chen & Bernard-Opitz, 1993; Hetzroni & Shalem, 2005). Promising research has illustrated that children with ASD attend with greater frequency to the provision of CAI, when provided with instruction from a teacher versus a computer screen (Moore and Calvert, 2000); and that they were better able to follow verbal directions from a computer screen versus a live human presentation (Shane & Douglas, 2002). In addition to these studies, researchers have strongly suggested the use of video-based instruction as a teaching tool because it can focus the instructional environment narrowly on a television screen or computer monitor (Ayers & Langone, 2007; Sherer et al., 2001).

The Research Base

The research to practice gap in AT implementation and services for students with ASD is well documented (Bauschet al., 2008; Van Laarhoven et al., 2008). More recently, the field has focused efforts on providing guidance to practitioners for what constitutes EBP in the area of AT for students with autism. Simpson (2005) identified AT and AAC as "Promising Practices" based on evidence that they have been widely used over time with few adverse outcomes and research indicating favorable responses and skill acquisition for children and youth with ASD. In interpreting Simpson's analysis, it is important to recognize that AT and AAC are umbrella terms covering a widely divergent set of practices. When AT and AAC interventions are viewed as a whole, his categorization is appropriate and provides guidance to practitioners by recognizing the potential for AT to support students with ASD and the importance of continued research. However, within the AT and AAC categories, discrete interventions and applications have emerged, each of which must be evaluated on its own merit to identify specific practices under the AT umbrella that have been found to be effective with students with ASD, through replicated research. Such efforts are seen in the work of The National Professional Development Center for Autism Spectrum Disorders, a multiuniversity center promoting the use of EBP for children and youth with ASD. The center adopted criteria for EBP (Horner et al., 2005; Nathan & Gorman, 2002; Odom et al., 2004; Rogers & Vismara, 2008) and to date has developed briefs for 24 identified EBPs. EBPs involving AT include computer assisted instruction (CAI), picture exchange communication system (PECS), speech generating devices/VOCA, video modeling, and visual supports.

Alternate and Augmentative Communication (AAC)

AAC is defined by the American Speech-Language-Hearing Association (ASHA; 2010) as "all forms of communication (other than oral speech) that are used to express thoughts, needs, wants, and ideas." Lloyd et al. (1997) more specifically defined AAC as the use of "a variety of symbols, strategies, and techniques to assist people who are unable to meet their communication needs through natural speech and/or writing" (p. 1). Mirenda (2003) described two types of AAC systems: *unaided*, which do not require equipment external to the body, and *aided*, which involve external devices. AT would include the latter. The range of aided communication systems runs from low-tech technologies, such as communication boards and books, to high-tech electronic devices that produce voice or written output (National Research Council, 2001). The picture exchange communication system (PECS; Bondy & Frost, 1994) and voice output communication aids (VOCA) are two AAC systems that have been successfully implemented with individuals with ASD (National Professional Development Center on Autism Spectrum Disorders, 2010).

In their review of the literature evaluating communication-based treatments for ASD, Brunner and Seung (2009) identified AAC as one of seven treatment categories with empirical support. Implementation of AAC with individuals with ASD is most likely to be effective if interventionists are flexible in their consideration of treatments and are willing to provide a variety of approaches based on the needs of the individual and his or her family (Ogletree, 2007). Consequently, teachers must be trained in a variety of technology choices for children with ASD (Hagiwara & Myles, 1999) and be prepared to provide technology services to assist families. Tincani and Boutot (2005) emphasized the need to address the family comfort level relative to the use of a technology device by involving the family in decision making; assessing sociocultural views and experiences with technology; and providing family members with training, access to devices, and ongoing support. Table 17.1 provides a sampling of the evidence for two popular AAC interventions (PECS and VOCA) with individuals with ASD.

Picture Exchange Communication System (PECS)

PECS (Bondy & Frost, 1994), which was developed at the Delaware Autistic Program, involves systematic application of visual symbols, and employs a six phase behavioral program to teach individuals who lack spoken language the skills necessary to enable them to communicate. This low-tech AAC application has been widely implemented with individuals with ASD (National Research Council, 2001). In a review of the literature, Sulzer-Azaroff, Hoffman, Horton, Bondy, and Frost (2009) identified 34 articles that included data and procedures representing the key features of PECS. The majority of study participants were children in special and regular schools who ranged in age from preschool to elementary school (Bondy & Frost, 1994; Ganz & Simpson, 2004; Yoder & Stone, 2006; Yokyama, Naoi, & Yamamoto, 2006). A limited number of studies demonstrated effectiveness with adolescents and adults (Lancioni et al., 2007; Lund &

TABLE 17.1 A Representative Sample of the Evidence for AAC (PECS and VOCA)

Study	Participants	Design	Dependent Variable(s)	Independent Variable(s)	Effects for Targeted Variables
Bondy & Frost (1994)	85 children with ASD, ages 3–7 years	Case Report	Number of pictures and number of spoken words used	PECS	Pictures alone (23%) Speech (48%) Speech & pictures (29%)
Charlop-Christy et al. (2002)	3 children with ASD, ages 3–12 years	Multiprobe across participants	Number of trials and time to mastery	PECS	All learned within 170 min. and 146 trials
Ganz & Simpson (2004)	3 children with ASD, ages 3–7	Changing criterion	Time to Mastery; number of sessions; number of trials	PECS	Word utterances and complexity of grammar increased in < 2 mo.
Parsons & La Sorte (1993)	6 children with ASD, ages 4–6	Changing conditions	Number of spontaneous utterances	VOCA	Number of spontaneous utterances increased
Olive et al. (2007)	4-year-old female with autism	Multiprobe across activities	Number of challenging behaviors; number of VOCA requests	Functional Communication Training with VOCA	Decreased challenging behavior and increased VOCA use
Schlosser et al. (2007)	5 children with autism	Alternating treatments	Number of requests	VOCA vs. nonelectronic systems	Frequent requesting during both conditions
Schepis et al. (1998)	4 children with autism, ages 3–5	Multiprobe across participants	Communication interactions	VOCA and naturalistic teaching	Increases in communicative interactions
Yoder & Stone (2006)	36 children with ASD, ages 1.5–5	Randomized group	Number of nonimitative verbalizations and words	PECS vs. responsive educational and prelinguistic milieu technology	PECS increased frequency of verbalizations and number of spoken words

Troha, 2008). Improvements in communication, specifically making requests, were found for the vast majority of these participants; and in comparison studies, PECS outperformed other methods. There was also some evidence associating the use of PECS with increases in verbalization and social approaches, and decreases in disruptive or dangerous behaviors (Frea, Arnold, Vittimberga, & Koegel, 2001).

Voice Output Communication Aids

Voice output communication aids (VOCA) are "portable computerized devices that produce synthetic or digitized speech output when activated" (Mirenda & Erickson, 2000, p. 5). The user may activate a device by pressing a button, typing on a keyboard, or touching a picture symbol (Tincani & Boutot, 2005). Types of VOCA range from single switch devices that deliver only one prerecorded message to more complex computerized systems that display combinations of letters, symbols, pictures, and words in various arrays on touch screens. Devices come in a variety of sizes and weights and can cost up to several thousand dollars. Challenges associated with VOCAs include issues with availability, portability, and maintenance of the device; as well as difficulties teaching the student to use the device (Scheuermann & Webber, 2002).

An examination of the evidence base supporting AAC interventions using VOCA reveals a limited number of studies specific to people with ASD (Miller, Light, & Schlosser, 2006; Schlosser & Blischak, 2001). Several investigations have been conducted with preschool and elementary aged children (Olive, Lang, & Davis, 2007; Parsons & La Sorte, 1993; Schepis, Reid, Behrmann, & Sutton, 1998; Schlosser et al., 2007). Skills targeted for intervention include making requests (Olive et al., 2007; Schlosser et al., 2007), spontaneous utterances (Parsons & La Sorte, 1993), and communication interactions (Schepis et al., 1998). Speech generating devices logically offer a viable solution when paired with the characteristics of people with ASD; however, while research suggests that VOCA can be effective with children who have limited or no verbal speech, the dearth of studies investigating the specific benefits for people with ASD underscores the need for continued and rigorous research.

Video-Based Instruction

In general, video instruction includes several techniques including VM, VSM, and point-of-view video modeling (PVM; Shukla-Mehta et al., 2010). According to Bellini and Akullian (2007), "Video modeling is a technique that involves demonstration of desired behaviors through video representation of the behavior" p. 266).Essentially, VM consists of showing a student a brief video clip or "model" of someone performing a targeted skill or behavior for instructional purposes. The video clip is prepared by instructional or intervention staff in an effort to specifically illustrate the essential behavior a student needs to attain. VSM is an application of VM in which the individual learns by imitating video clips, which also show his or her own successful performance of targeted behaviors (Ayres & Langone, 2007).

In contrast to VM and VSM and other forms of video-based instruction, PVM is defined by Shukla-Mehta et al. (2010) as, "the process of videotaping elements of the environment or activity context from the visual perspective or vantage point of the student who needs to acquire and/or master the target responses" (p. 24). Essentially, a videographer records steps for completing an activity or behavior by actually shooting video that would simulate what the student would be seeing while he or she is engaged in an activity or transition—making sure to keep the focus at the eye-level and perspective of the student. The use of PVM for individuals with ASD could potentially promote visual comprehension, increase familiarity with materials and settings, and could provide a clear picture of the completed process in an effort to reduce anxiety and increase predictability (Shukla-Mehta et al., 2010).

Table 17.2 depicts a representative sample of research studies investigating the effects of video-based instruction on individuals with ASD and demonstrating the effectiveness of an electronic medium to teach complex behaviors previously only taught via direct instruction. Positive outcomes for people with ASD are seen across the age span and spectrum for a variety of targeted dependent variables related to social, communication, functional living, and vocational skills (Apple, Billingsley, & Schwartz, 2005; Ayres & Langone, 2007; Ayres, Maguire, & McClimon, 2009; Bernad-Ripoll, 2007; Cihak & Schrader, 2008; Gena, Couloura, & Kymissis, 2005; Haring et al., 1987; Maione & Mirenda (2006); Nikopoulos & Keenan, 2004; Shipley-Benamou et al., 2002).

Research suggests video-based instruction is effective for teaching functional skills in a consistent manner without the need for repetitive lessons or time spent in or on alternate locations (Ayres & Langone, 2007; Bellini & Akullian, 2007; Cihak & Schrader, 2008; Shipley-Benamou et al., 2002). Teachers can produce permanent products for intervention, saving time and resources, and capitalizing on a consistent mode of instruction. Investigations in the area of social skills acquisition indicate video-based instruction is effective in teaching students with ASD to recognize and understand emotions (Bernad-Ripoll, 2007), improve social language during play (Maione & Mirenda, 2006), engage in compliment giving and imitation (Apple et al., 2005), and produce verbal responses (i.e., sympathy, appreciation, and disapproval) within social contexts (Gena et al., 2005).

The growing evidence base for video-based instruction is supported by two reviews in the area of social skills, social communication skills, and functional skills. Bellini and Akullian (2007) conducted a meta-analysis of VM and VSM interventions for children and adolescents with ASD. They reviewed 23 single-subject design studies, from 1987 through 2005, which included a total of 73 participants with ASD. Their synthesis indicated that VM and VSM were effective intervention strategies for addressing social-communication skills, behavioral functioning, and functional skills in children and adolescents with ASD, and promoting measurable skill acquisition.

Shukla-Mehta et al. (2010) conducted a literature review of video-based instruction (i.e., VM, VSM, and point of view video) related to individuals with ASD over the past three decades. They reviewed 26 studies focused on the acquisition of social and communication skills in learners with ASD. Their findings, like those of Bellini and Akullian, demonstrate the efficacy of video-based instruction for children and adolescents with ASD and illustrate several viable strategies for teachers that include (a) the use of a visually oriented instructional medium, (b) emphasis on fidelity of instruction, (c) precise management of instructional stimuli and contingencies, and (d) the provision of a consistent mode of instruction across settings with minimal teacher training.

Prompting Technologies

The use of self-prompting devices by students with ASD holds great promise for increasing an individual's independence while decreasing his or her reliance on teachers or instructional staff (Mechling, 2007; Mechling et al., 2009; Spence-Cochran & Pearl, 2009). Self-prompting technology includes any device or system capable of prompting a person through a task analysis, set of directions, or task to complete a designated task, assignment, or job without additional prompting by teachers or instructional staff. Palmtop personal computers are portable handheld systems that employ features of a touch screen for input and multimedia capabilities including

TABLE 17.2 A Representative Sample of the Evidence for Video-Based Instruction

Study	Participants	Design	Dependent Variable(s)	Independent Variable(s)	Effects for Targeted Variables
Apple et al. (2005)	2 children with ASD, age 5	Multiple baseline design across participants	Teaching compliment giving responses and initiations	VM with embedded, explicit rules for giving compliments	Effective in social skill acquisition of compliment giving via VM alone
Ayres & Langone (2007)	4 children with autism, ages 6–8	Adapted alternating treatments	Putting away groceries	First-person PVM vs. third-person PVM	All acquired skills in both models and generalized to natural environment
Ayres et al. (2009)	3 children with autism, ages 7–9	Multiple probe design across behaviors	Acquisition and generalization of targeted functional life skills	Computer-based simulation training of video of tasks using PVM	Mastered skills and generalized after 2 week follow-up
Cihak & Schrader (2008)	4 males with ASD, ages 16–21	Alternating treatments	Acquisition and maintenance of a vocational chain of tasks	VSM vs. video adult modeling	Both effective; 2 did better with VSM
Maione & Mirenda (2006)	Child with autism, age 5	Multiple baseline design across settings	Number of scripted and unscripted verbalizations and initiated responses	VM	Increase in social language in two of three activities
Nikopoulos & Keenan (2004)	3 children with autism, ages 6–7	Multiple baseline design across subjects	Social initiation, reciprocal play, imitative response, object engagement	VM	Enhanced social initiation skills, facilitated reciprocal play engagement and imitative responding
Shipley-Benamou et al. (2002)	3 children with autism, age 5	Multiple probe design	Skill acquisition of functional home-based tasks	VM from child's perspective	Effective in promoting skill acquisition and maintenance

the capability of producing text, sound, digital photographs, and video clips (Mechling, 2007) that can and have been used as prompting devices. *Personal digital assistant* (PDA) is a term used for any small, mobile hand-held device that provides customized computing and information storage and retrieval capabilities for personal or business use—the term *handheld* is frequently used to describe a PDA. PDAs are often used by the general population for keeping schedules, contact lists, and applications for reminders or recording formats. Self-prompting technology in relation to students with ASD has most frequently been studied with the use of a PDA.

Relatively few researchers have investigated the efficacy of prompting technologies specifically for students with ASD. Studies that have been conducted in an effort to systematically review the use of self-prompting devices with this particular population suggest this type of technology has the potential to improve daily living, behavior, vocational, and academic skills for learners with ASD (Cannella-Malone et al., 2006; Cihak, Wright, & Ayres, 2010; Mechling et al., 2009; Mechling & Gustafson, 2008; Myles, Ferguson, & Hagiwara, 2007; Spence-Cochran & Pearl, 2009; Taber, Seltzer, Heflin, & Alberto, 1999). Table 17. 3 illustrates evidence to support continued research and development in this area across a variety of settings.

As seen in Table 17.3, there is a positive correlation between video-based prompting systems and marked increases in designated life skills for students with ASD. Researchers have effectively demonstrated the use of prompting technology, specifically video-based prompting technology, to improve functional life skills such as cooking (Mechling et al., 2009; Mechling & Gustafson, 2008) and setting a table and putting groceries away (Cannella-Malone et al., 2006) for learners with ASD. Educators, agencies, and job coaches must ensure that people with ASD have ample opportunities to learn skills of independence in a variety of settings. In particular, efforts should be made to provide individuals with moderate to severe ASD with sound educational and learning opportunities to ensure the best possible postschool transition outcomes. In a comparison study, Spence-Cochran and Pearl (2009) demonstrated the use of hand-held computers for teaching high school students with ASD to acquire novel jobs in a community-based setting without direct instruction from instructional staff. Their findings represent elevated levels of independence and capability, which logically translate to individuals better prepared for real-world work experiences with reduced staff supports.

Studies that have included individuals with ASD using picture prompting systems or technology have frequently focused on schedules, transitioning, and skills of independence (Cihak et al., 2010); however, educators and parents alike agree there is a critical need to improve self-management skills of students with ASD in all school and community-based settings (Cihak et al., 2010; Mechling et al., 2009; Spence-Cochran & Pearl, 2009). A handful of existing studies illustrate the effectiveness of using PDA technology for the purpose of self-prompting for students with ASD within educational settings with the intention of self-monitoring (Cihak et al., 2010; Myles et al., 2007; Taber et al., 1999). Cihak et al. (2010) found the use of static picture prompts on a handheld computer device improved a student's engagement within his general education classroom and led to an increase in overall task engagement. The implications of this study are twofold, suggesting benefits for both teachers and students with ASD including: (a) Students who use handheld technology can operate in a more productive and independent fashion. (b) The need for the physical presence and attention of the teacher or educational staff is replaced with a socially valid method for learning and participating in all school locations.

Further illustrating the power of prompting technology in general educational settings for students with ASD, Myles et al. (2007) successfully demonstrated the use of a PDA with a young man with Asperger's syndrome in a middle school setting. As is typical in most secondary settings, this student was required to document his homework in a planner to assist him in being organized and completing homework. Researchers documented an increase of nearly 30% in

TABLE 17.3 A Representative Sample of the Evidence for Prompting Technology

Study	Participants	Design	Dependent Variable(s)	Independent Variable(s)	Effects for Targeted Variables
Cihak et al. (2010)	3 children with autism, ages 11–13	Multiple probe across settings	% of task engagement and number of teacher-directed verbal prompts	Self-monitoring and static self-model prompts via hand-held computer	Increase in task engagement and decrease in teacher directed prompts
Mechling et al. (2009)	3 male high school students with ASD	Multiple probe design	% of correct, independent steps for cooking recipes	PDA self-prompting device using video, auditory, and picture prompts	Improved performance for all students across all 3 recipes
Mechling & Gustafson, (2008)	6 high school students with autism, ages 17–21	Adapted alternating treatments design	% of cooking-related tasks completed independently	Comparison of static photographs and video prompting	Video prompting shown more effective
Myles et al. (2007)	17-year-old with Asperger's syndrome	Multiple baseline across settings	Correctly recording of academic assignments	PDA for assignment recording	Increase in independent homework recording with PDA
Spence-Cochran & Pearl (2009)	5 students with ASD, ages 15–19	Alternating Treatments	Number of prompts from staff required to complete novel job tasks	Hand-held prompting technology (PDA with video model) vs. staff model	Both were effective, hand-held required fewer prompts from staff
Taber et al. (1999)	12-year-old with autism and intellectual disability	Multiple probe across settings	Teacher prompts provided when student engaged in off-task behavior	Self-operated auditory prompting system	Decrease in off-task behavior and need for teacher prompting

recorded homework with the use of a PDA over the course of the study. This outcome exemplifies the potential of this type of technology for the purpose of supporting students with this most basic demand in an array of school settings.

Computer-Assisted Instruction (CAI)

People with ASD have a natural affinity for computers and the controlled environment or interactions provided by computers (Moore, Cheng, McGrath, & Powell, 2005), which supports the use of AT in an assortment of educational settings. The National Research Council (2001) defined CAI as something that "includes the use of computer delivered prompts, systematic learning programs, technology-based curricular adaptation, writing programs with word prediction, and virtual reality" (p. 63). Learners with ASD have made effective use of CAI in learning social skills (Bernard-Optiz, Sriram, & Sapuan, 2001; Golan & Baron-Cohen, 2006; Lacava, Golan, Baron-Cohen, Smith-Myles, 2007; Mancil, Haydon, & Whitby, 2009; Moore et al., 2005), identification of symbols (Chen & Bernard-Optiz, 1993; Hetzroni & Shalem, 2005), and for learning functional and standard curricula (Grynszpan, Martin, & Nadel, 2007). This demonstrates the potential that technology holds for the education of individuals with ASD. Computer-based technology offers educators a consistent and reliable format with which to provide instruction over a wide range of subjects and skills; and one that allows students with ASD to acquire skills and knowledge in situations and settings that may decrease the demand for social interaction and specific social behavioral expectations.

CAI has been proven to be an effective intervention for learners with ASD in the acquisition of vocabulary and word identification skills (Bosseler & Massaro, 2003; Hetzroni & Shalem, 2005; Moore & Calvert, 2000), improved behavioral skills (Mancil et al., 2009), social skills (Bernard-Optiz et al., 2001), and the recognition of facial expressions (Golan & Baron-Cohen, 2006; LaCava et al., 2007; Moore et al., 2005). This intervention category meets evidence-based practice criteria within preschool, elementary, middle/high school, and adult-aged groups for promoting an assortment of necessary and relevant skills for learners with ASD and includes studies conducted with learners ranging in age from 4 years to adulthood. Evidence exists to support the application of CAI in a variety of settings, strengthening the potential opportunities for learning across environments or promoting generalization across settings. Studies conducted in homes, schools, and specialized programs illustrate the opportunity to address specific areas of difficulty for learners with ASD (Bernard-Optiz et al., 2001; Bosseler & Massaro, 2003; Chen & Bernard-Optiz, 1993; Golan & Baron-Cohen, 2006; Hetzroni & Shalem, 2005; Lacava et al., 2007; Mancil et al., 2009; Moore & Calvert, 2000; Moore et al., 2005).

Golan and Baron-Cohen (2006) demonstrated the power of interactive media to successfully teach people with autism and Asperger's syndrome how to improve their ability to recognize complex emotions and mental states from both faces and voices by reviewing a specialized software program (*Mind Reading*) for 10 to 20 hours per week for 10 to 15 weeks. A group of individuals with ASD who utilized the interactive media were compared to another group who only received direct instruction in social skills over the same period of time. Results revealed that the group that received instruction with the specialized software demonstrated clear improvements versus the group who received a more traditional approach of direct instruction. In a similar study, LaCava et al. (2007) reviewed the use of comparable interactive media with eight children with Asperger's syndrome between the ages of 8 and 11 years of age with a similar outcome, all participants improved their ability to recognize basic and complex emotions in faces and voices after only 10 weeks of training. Further illustrating the positive outcomes of this type of innovative technology, Moore et al. (2005) reviewed the use of a specialized computer system utilizing avatar representations for four emotions: happy, sad, angry, and frightened with 34 children and youth (ages 7.8 to 16 years) with autism. Their findings indicated that over 90% of the participants demonstrated an ability to correctly interpret the avatars' representations of emotions. This result implies that this type of technology has the potential to effectively and correctly teach students with ASD essential emotional recognition skills across a variety of settings.

Future Directions for AT Applications

AT has the potential to increase and improve the quality of life of people with ASD by increasing the level and nature of possible learning opportunities across all settings and thereby supporting meaningful participation in all walks of society. However, while a variety of AT methodologies have been demonstrated to be effective for students with ASD, the practical issues related to using these types of intervention must be addressed and reviewed by future researchers. For example, in the case of VM and VSM, issues include access to technology, the amount of time it takes to develop intervention clips (tools), and the potential for single viewer usage which should be considered when copious amounts of time are required to create products that will be used with only one student in a classroom (Bellini & Akullian, 2007; Cihak & Schrader, 2008; Kimball & Smith, 2007; Shipley-Benamou et al., 2002). Cihak and Schrader (2008) reported that participants in their study indicated enjoyment with watching themselves on video and a preference for viewing VSM to learn tasks. In contrast, the support teachers in this particular study revealed they preferred to use VM over VSM since VM required less time and effort for development and editing of useful video clips and could be used with their students in a more expedient fashion (Cihak & Schrader, 2008).

While evidence exists to support the use of specialized software for the instruction and use of individuals with ASD in educational settings, there are also some significant issues with regard to the use of CAI with this population. A major concern is the general lack of research supporting specifically developed software programs for individuals with ASD. Other issues include pedagogical flaws such as distracting features, limited variety of reinforcers and instructional exemplars, and limited capacity for prompting and prompt fading in commercially available programs (Kimball & Smith, 2007).

A growing body of evidence indicates that teachers report insufficient training in AT and that teachers who are insecure about using technology are not likely to provide these types of supports for their students (Bausch et al., 2008; Van Laarhoven et al., 2008). It is critically important that teachers, therapists, and other support personnel be trained to use AT and the specific options available to all students. In particular, this need has been highlighted with respect to the importance of teacher training in implementation of a variety of AAC options for individuals with ASD (Hagiwara & Smith-Myles, 1999). To address issues of personnel preparation in the use of AT, a team at Northern Illinois University created a prototype DVD, *The Encyclopedia of Assistive Technology (EAT),* comprised of written video based tutorials for using various assistive technology software and devices. Research revealed EAT video tutorials were effective in increasing preservice teachers' familiarity, comfort level, and perceived effectiveness with using AT (Van Laarohoven et al., 2008).

Conclusion and Summary

This chapter has highlighted AT use for individuals with ASD, specifically evidence-based practices including AAC (PECS and VOCA), video-based instruction, prompting technology, and CAI. Research and literature reviews illustrate a range of viable intervention strategies for use with students ranging in age from preschool through high school and into adulthood. AT offers the promise of supporting students with ASD to overcome communication, learning, and social barriers by providing a means of advanced compensation that is consistent, reliable, and designed to meet the specific needs of the individual. Technology is a powerful tool for reducing functional limitations for students with ASD who experience difficulty in communication, social, and behaviorally based skills of independence.

References

Alcantara, P. R. (1994). Effects of videotape instructional package on purchasing skills of children with autism. *Exceptional Children, 61*, 40–55.

American Speech-Language-Hearing Association (ASHA). (2010). *Augmentative and alternative communication* (AAC). Retrieved from http://www.asha.org/public/speech/disorders/AAC/

Apple, A. L., Billingsley, F., & Schwartz, I. S. (2005). Effects of video modeling alone and with self-management on compliment giving behaviors of children with high functioning ASD. *Journal of Positive Behavior Interventions, 7*(1), 33–46.

Assistive Technology Act of 1998 (P.L. 105-394). Retrieved from http://www.nichcy.org/Laws/Other/Pages/AssistiveTechnologyAct.aspx

Ayres, K. M., & Langone, J. (2007). A comparison of video modeling perspectives for students with autism. *Journal of Special Education Technology, 22*(2), 15–30.

Ayres, K. M., & Langone, J. (2008). Video supports for teaching students with developmental disabilities and autism: Twenty-five years of research and development. *Journal of Special Education Technology, 23*(3), 1–8.

Ayres, K. M., Maguire, A., & McClimon, D. (2009). Acquisition and generalization of chained tasks taught with computer based video instruction to children with autism. *Education and Training in Developmental Disabilities, 44*(4), 493–508.

Bausch, M. E., Ault, M. J., Evmenova, A. S., & Behrmann, M. M. (2008). Going beyond AT devices: Are AT services being considered? *Journal of Special Education Technology, 23*(2), 1–16.

Bausch, M. E., & Hasselbring, T. S. (2004). Assistive technology: Are the necessary skills and knowledge being developed at the preservice and in service levels? *Teacher Education in Special Education, 27*, 97–104.

Bellini, S., & Akullian, J. (2007). A meta-analysis of video modeling and video self-modeling interventions for children and adolescents with autism spectrum disorder. *Exceptional Children, 73*, 264–287.

Bernad-Ripoll, S. (2007). Using a self-as-model video combined with social stories to help a child with Asperger syndrome understand emotions. *Focus on Autism and Other Developmental Disabilities, 22*(2), 100–106.

Bernard-Opitz, V., Sriram, N., & Nakhoda-Sapuan, S. (2001). Enhancing social problem solving in children with autism and normal children through computer assisted instruction. *Journal of Autism and Developmental Disorders, 31*(4), 377–384.

Bondy, A., & Frost, L. (1994). The picture exchange communication system. *Behavior Modification, 25*, 725–744.

Bosseler, A., & Massaro, D. W. (2003). Development and evaluation of a computer animated tutor for vocabulary and language learning in children with autism. *Journal of Autism & Developmental Disorders, 33*(6), 653–672.

Brunner, D. L., & Seung, H. (2009). Evaluation of the efficacy of communication-based treatments for autism spectrum disorders: A literature review. *Communication Disorders Quarterly, 31*, 15–41.

Buchsbaum, M. S., Siegel, B. V., Wu, J. C., Hazlett, E., Sicotte, N., Haier, R., ... Sabalesky, D. (1992). Attention performance in autism and regional brain metabolic rate assessed by positron emission tomography. *Journal of Autism and Developmental Disorders, 22*, 115–125.

Cafiero, J. (1998). Communication power for individuals with autism. *Focus on Autism and Other Developmental Disabilities, 13*, 113–121.

Cannella-Malone, H., O'Reilly, M., de la Cruz, B., Edrisinha, C., Sigafoos, J., & Lancioni, G. E. (2006). Comparing video prompting to video modeling for teaching daily living skills to six adults with developmental disabilities. *Education and Training in Developmental Disabilities, 41*(4), 344–356.

Charlop-Christy, M. H., Carpenter, M., Le, L., LeBlanc, L., & Kelley, K. (2002). Using the picture exchange communication system (PECS) with children with autism: Assessment of PECS acquisition, speech, social-communicative behavior, and problem behaviors. *Journal of Applied Behavior Analysis, 35*, 213–231.

Chen, S. H., & Bernard-Opitz, V. (1993). Comparison of personal and computer-assisted instruction for children with autism. *Mental Retardation, 31*(6), 368–376.

Cihak, D. F., & Schrader, L. (2008). Does the model matter? Comparing video self-modeling and video adult modeling for task acquisition and maintenance by adolescents with autism spectrum disorders. *Journal of Special Education Technology, 23*(3), 9–20.

Cihak, D. F., Wright, R., & Ayres, K. M. (2010). Use of self-modeling static-picture prompts via a handheld computer to facilitate self-monitoring in the general education classroom. *Education and Training in Autism and Developmental Disabilities, 45*(1), 136–149.

Corbett, B. A., & Abdullah, B. (2005). Video modeling: Why does it work for children with autism? *Journal of Early and Intensive Behavior Intervention 2*(1), 2–8.

Frea, W. D., Arnold, C. L., Vittimberga, G. L., & Koegel, R. L. (2001). A demonstration of the effects of augmentative communication on the extreme aggressive behavior of a child with autism within an integrated preschool setting. *Journal of Positive Behavior Interventions, 3*, 194–198.

Ganz, J., & Simpson, R. (2004). Effects on communicative requesting and speech development of the picture exchange communication system in children with characteristics of autism. *Journal of Autism and Developmental Disabilities, 34*, 395–409.

Garretson, H. B., Fein, D., & Waterhouse, L. (1990). Sustained attention in children with autism. *Journal of Autism and Developmental Disorders, 20*, 101–114.

Gena, A., Couloura, S., & Kymissis, E. (2005). Modifying the affective behavior of preschoolers with autism using in-vivo or video modeling and reinforcement contingencies. *Journal of Autism and Developmental Disorders, 35*(5), 545–556.

Gersten, R., & Edyburn, D. (2007). Defining quality indicators for special education technology research. *Journal of Special Education Technology, 22*(3), 3–18.

Golan, O., & Baron-Cohen, S. (2006). Systemizing empathy: Teaching adults with Asperger syndrome or high-functioning autism to recognize complex emotions using interactive media. *Developmental and Psychopathology, 18*, 591–617.

Grandin, T. (1995). *Thinking in pictures and other reports from my life with autism.* New York: Vintage Books.

Grynszpan, O., Martin, J. C., & Nadel, J. (2007). Exploring the influence of task assignment and output modalities on computerized training for autism. *Interaction Studies, 8*(2), 241–266.

Hagiwara, T., & Smith Myles, B. S. (1999). A multimedia social story intervention: Teaching skills to children with autism. *Focus on Autism and Other Developmental Disabilities, 14*, 82–95.

Haring, T. G., Kennedy, C. H., Adams, M. J., & Pitts-Conway, V. (1987). Teaching   generalization of purchasing skills across community settings to autistic youth using videotape modeling. *Journal of Applied Behavioral Analysis, 20*(1), 89–96.

Hetzroni, O. E., & Shalem, U. (2005). From logos to orthographic symbols: A multi-level fading computer program for teaching non-verbal children with autism to read. *Focus on Autism and Other Developmental Disabilities, 20*(4), 201–212.

Horner, R., Carr, E., Halle, J., McGee, G., Odom, S., & Wolery, M. (2005). The use of single subject research to identify evidence-based practice in special education. *Exceptional Children, 71*, 165–180.

Individuals with Disabilities Education Improvement Act of 2004., 20 U.S.C. § 1400 *et seq.* (2004).

Jordan, R. (1988). Computer assisted learning. In *Autism—Today & tomorrow: Congress report* (pp. 65–71). Hamburg, Germany: International Association Autism-Europe, Third European Congress.

Kimball, J. W., & Smith, K. (2007). Crossing the bridge: From best practices to software packages. *Focus on Autism and Other Developmental Disabilities, 22*(2), 131–134.

LaCava, P. G., Golan, O., Baron-Cohen, S., & Smith-Myles, B. (2007). Using assistive technology to teach emotion recognition to students with Asperger syndrome a pilot study. *Remedial and Special Education, 28*(3), 174–181.

Lancioni, G., O'Reilly, M. Cuvo, A., Singh, N., Sigafoos, J., & Didden, R. (2007). PECS and VOCAs to enable students with developmental disabilities to make requests: An overview of the literature. *Research in Developmental Disabilities, 28*, 468–488.

Lloyd, L. L., Fuller, D. R., & Arvidson, H. H. (Eds.). (1997). *Augmentative and alternative communication: A handbook of principles and practices.* Boston, MA: Allyn & Bacon.

Lund, S. K., & Troha, J. M. (2008). Teaching young people who are blind and have autism to make requests using a variation on the picture exchange communication system with tactile symbols: A preliminary investigation. *Journal of Autism and Developmental Disorders, 38*, 719–730.

Maione, L., & Mirenda, P. (2006). Effects of video modeling and video feedback on peer-directed social language skills of a child with autism. *Journal of Positive Behavioral Interventions, 8*(2), 106–118.

Mancil, G. R., Haydon, T., & Whitby, P. (2009). Differentiated effects of paper and computer-assisted social stories on inappropriate behavior in children with autism. *Focus on Autism and Other Developmental Disabilities, 24*(4), 205–215.

Mechling, L. C. (2007). Assistive technology as a self-management tool for prompting students with intellectual disabilities to initiate and complete daily tasks: A literature review. *Education and Training in Developmental Disabilities, 42*(3), 252–269.

Mechling, L. C., Gast, D. L., & Seid, N. H. (2009). Using a personal digital assistant to increase independent task completion by students with autism spectrum disorder. *Journal on Autism and Developmental Disorders, 39*, 1420–1434.

Mechling, L. C., & Gustafson, M. (2008). Comparison of static picture and video prompting on the performance of cooking-related tasks by students with autism. *Journal of Special Education Technology, 23*(3), 31–45.

Miller, D. C., Light, J. C., & Schlosser, R. W. (2006). The impact of augmentative and alternative communication intervention on the speech production of individuals with developmental disabilities: A research review. *Journal of Speech, Language & Hearing Research, 49,* 248–264.

Mirenda, P. (2003). Toward functional augmentative and alternative communication for students with autism: Manual signs, graphic symbols, and voice output communication aids. *Language, Speech, and Hearing Services in Schools, 34,* 203–216.

Mirenda, P., & Erickson, K. A. (2000). Augmentative communication and literacy. In A. M. Wetherby & B. M. Prizant (Eds.), *Autism spectrum disorders: A transactional approach* (pp. 333–369). Baltimore, MD: Brookes.

Mirenda, P., Wilk, D., & Carson, P. (2000). A retrospective analysis of technology use patterns of students with autism over a five-year period. *Journal of Special Education Technology, 15*(3), 5–15.

Moore, D., Cheng, Y., McGrath, P., & Powell, N.J. (2005). Collaborative virtual environment technology for people with autism. *Focus on Autism and Other Developmental Disabilities, 20*(4), 231–243.

Moore, N., & Calvert, S. (2000). Brief report: Vocabulary acquisition for children with autism: Teacher or computer instruction. *Journal of Autism and Developmental Disabilities, 30*(4), 359–362.

Myles, B. S., Ferguson, H., Hagiwara, T. (2007). Using a personal digital assistant to improve the recording of homework assignments by an adolescent with Asperger syndrome. *Focus on Autism and Other Developmental Disabilities, 22*(2), 96–99.

Nathan, P., & Gorman, J. M. (2002). *A guide to treatments that work.* New York: Oxford University Press.

National Professional Development Center on Autism Spectrum Disorders. (2010). *Evidence-based practice briefs.* Retrieved from http://autismpdc.fpg.unc.edu/content/briefs

National Research Council, Division of Behavioral and Social Sciences and Education. (2001). *Educating children with autism* (Committee on Educational Interventions for Children with Autism, C. Lord & J. P. McGee, Eds.). Washington, DC: National Academy Press.

Nikopoulos, C. K., & Keenan, M. (2004). Using video modeling to teach complex social sequences to children with autism. *Journal of Autism and Developmental Disorders, 37,* 678–693.

Odom, S. L., Brantlinger, E., Gersten, R., Horner, R. D., Thompson, B., & Harris, K. (2004). *Quality indicators for research in special education and guidelines for evidence-based practices: Executive summary.* Arlington, VA: Council for Exceptional Children Division for Research.

Ogletree, B. T. (2007). What makes communication intervention successful with children with autism spectrum disorders? *Focus on Autism and Other Developmental Disabilities, 22,* 190–192.

Ogletree, B. T., & Harn, W. E. (2001). Augmentative and alternative communication for persons with autism: History, issues, and unanswered questions. *Focus on Autism and Other Developmental Disabilities, 16,* 138–140.

Okolo, C. M., Reith, H. J., & Bahr, C. (1989). Microcomputer implementation in secondary special education programs: A study of special educators', mildly handicapped adolescents', and administrators' perspectives. *The Journal of Special Education, 23,* 107–117.

Olive, M., Lang, R., & Davis, T. (2007). An analysis of the effects of functional communication and a voice output communication aid for a child with autism spectrum disorder. *Research in Autism Spectrum Disorders, 2,* 223–236.

Parette, H. P., & Peterson-Karlan, G. R. (2007). Facilitating student achievement with assistive technology. *Education and Training in Developmental Disabilities, 42*(4), 387–397.

Parsons, C., & La Sorte, D. (1993). The effects of computers with synthesized speech and no speech on the spontaneous communication of children with autism. *Australian Journal of Human Communication Disorders, 21,* 12–31.

Pierangelo, R., & Giuliani, G. (2008).. *Teaching students with autism spectrum disorders: Assistive technology for children with ASD* (pp.135–164). Thousand Oaks, CA: Corwin Press.

Quill, K. A. (1997). Instructional consideration for young children with autism: The rationale. *Journal of Autism and Developmental Disorders, 27,* 697–714.

Rice, C. (2009). *Prevalence of autism spectrum disorders—Autism and developmental disabilities monitoring network, United States, 2006.* MMWR Surveillance Summaries, *58*(SS10), 1–20. Retrieved from http://www.cdc.gov/mmwr/preview/mmwrhtml/ss5810a1.htm

Rogers, S. J., & Vismara, L. A. (2008). Evidence based comprehensive treatments for early autism. *Journal of Clinical Child and Adolescent Psychology, 37*(1), 8–38.

Schepis, M. M., Reid, D. H., Behrmann, M. M., & Sutton, K. A. (1998). Increasing communicative interactions of young children with autism using a voice output communication aid and naturalistic teaching. *Journal of Applied Behavior Analysis, 31,* 561–578.

Scheuerman, B., & Webber, J. (2002). *Autism: Teaching does make a difference.* Belmont, CA: Wadsworth.

Schlosser, R. W., & Blischak, D. M., (2001). Is there a role for speech output in interventions for persons with autism? A review. *Focus on Autism and Other Developmental Disabilities, 16,* 170–178.

Schlosser, R. W., Sigafoos, J., Luiselli, J. K., Angermeier, K., Harasymowyz, U., Schooley, K., & Belfiore, P. J. (2007)

Effects of synthetic speech output on requesting and natural speech production in children with autism: A preliminary study. *Research in Autism Spectrum Disorders, 1,* 139–163.

Shah, A., & Frith, U. (1983). An islet of ability in autistic children: A research note. *Journal of Child Psychology and Psychiatry, 24,* 613–620.

Shane, H. C., & Albert, P. D. (2008). Electronic screen media for persons with autism spectrum disorders: Results of a survey. *Journal of Autism and Developmental Disorders, 38,* 1499–1508.

Shane, H. C., & Douglas, M. L. (2002). *Investigation into the use of intelligent agents in children evidencing autism.* Paper presented at the annual meeting of the American Speech-Language-Hearing Association, Chicago, IL.

Sherer, M., Pierce, K. L., Paredes, S., Kisacky, K. L., Ingersoll, B., & Schreibman, L. (2001). Enhancing conversation skills in children with autism via video technology: Which is better, "Self" or "Other" as a model? *Behavior Modification, 25,* 140–148.

Shipley-Benamou, R., Lutzker, J. R., & Taubman, M. (2002). Teaching daily living skills to children with autism through instructional video modeling. *Journal of Positive Behavior Interventions, 4*(3), 165–175.

Shukla-Mehta, S., Miller, T., & Callahan, K. J. (2010). Evaluating the effectiveness of video instruction on social and communication skills training for children with autism spectrum disorders: A review of the literature. *Focus on Autism and Other Developmental Disabilities, 25*(1), 23–36.

Simpson, R. L. (2005). Evidence-based practices and students with autism-spectrum disorders. *Focus on Autism and Other Developmental Disabilities, 20*(3), 140–149.

Spence-Cochran, K., & Pearl, C. (2009). A comparison of hand-held computer and staff model supports for high school students with autism and intellectual disabilities. In K. Spence-Cochran (Ed.), *Assistive technology and autism spectrum disorders: Research-based practice and innovation in the field.* Norman, IL: Special Education Assistive Technology Center at Illinois State University and Assistive Technology Industry Association.

Sulzer-Azaroff, B., Hoffman, A. O., Horton, C. B., Bondy, A., & Frost, L. (2009). The picture exchange communication system (PECS): What do the data say? *Focus on Autism and Other Developmental Disabilities, 24,* 89–103.

Taber, T. A., Seltzer, A., Heflin, J., & Alberto, P. A. (1999). Use of self-operated auditory prompts to decrease off-task behavior for a student with autism and moderate mental retardation. *Focus on Autism and Other Developmental Disabilities, 14*(3), 159–166.

Technology Related Assistance Act of 1988 (Tech Act) (P.L. 100-407). http://www.nichcy.org/Laws/Other/Pages/AssistiveTechnologyAct.aspx

Tincani, M., & Boutot, E. A. (2005). Technology and autism: Current practices and future directions. In D. Edyburn, K. Higgins, & R. Boone (Eds.), *Handbook of special education technology research and practice* (pp. 413–421). Whitefish Bay, WI: Knowledge by Design.

Van Laarhoven, T., Munk, D., Zurita, L., Lynch, K., Zurita, B., Smith, T., & Chandler, T. (2008). The effectiveness of video tutorials for teaching preservice educators to use assistive technologies. *Journal of Special Education Technology, 23*(4), 31–45.

Wetherby, A. M., & Prizant, B. M. (Eds.). (2000). *Autism spectrum disorders: A transactional approach.* Baltimore, MD: Brookes.

Yoder, P., & Stone, W. (2006). Randomized comparison of two communication interventions for preschoolers with autism spectrum disorders. *Journal of Consulting and Clinical Psychology, 74,* 426–435.

Yokoyama, K., Naoi, N., & Yamamoto, J. (2006). Teaching verbal behavior using the picture exchange communication system (PECS) with children with autism spectrum disorders. *Japanese Journal of Special Education, 43,* 485–503.

Zabala, J., Blunt, M., Carl, D., Davis, S., Deterding, C., Foss, T., … Reed, P. (2000). Quality indicators for assistive technology services in school settings. *Journal of Special Education Technology, 15*(4), 25–37.

Zangari, C., Lloyd, L. L., & Vicker, B. (1994). Augmentative and alternative communication: A historical perspective. *Augmentative and Alternative Communication, 10,* 27–59.

18

COLLABORATION AND COOPERATIVE TEACHING FOR SYSTEM-WIDE CHANGE

Jack Hourcade

BOISE STATE UNIVERSITY

Gardner Umbarger, III

SAGINAW VALLEY STATE UNIVERSITY

If a typical educator is asked to describe what a teacher does, the odds are good that he or she will respond with a description of a single adult in a classroom with a number of students seated at desks or tables. While there may be some individual variations in how many students are there, or what the physical surroundings look like, a near-constant component of this concept will be the presence of a sole adult in the room.

This teaching structure has remained little changed for over a century and a half. A teacher from the Civil War era would likely recognize most of the basic components of a typical contemporary elementary or secondary education classroom today, including 20 to 30 students at student desks or chairs at tables, books on shelves, a whiteboard or blackboard at the front of the room, and a teacher desk with a single teacher. While this classroom scene may have remained relatively unchanged over time, what has transformed dramatically over recent decades is the nature and range of student diversity in classrooms.

For example, during the second half of the 20th century, the nation's historically racially segregated schools were changing rapidly, dramatically altering their previous culturally homogeneous student characteristics. Skerrett and Hargreaves (2008) described the changes in one representative school during this period. In 1959 Sheldon High School had a 20% minority enrollment. Over the next two decades, district desegregation plans that included busing and the emergence of magnet schools led to an exodus of White students from the public schools. By 2005 enrollment at Sheldon High had changed to 61% African American students and 25% Hispanic students. Approximately two-thirds of the student body qualified for the free and reduced lunch program. Similarly dramatic shifts in the cultural, ethnic, and linguistic composition of classrooms were occurring throughout the nation.

This growth in racial, cultural, and economic diversity throughout the nation's schools has been accompanied by a parallel growth in diversity in student academic and behavioral characteristics. Up through the 1970s most students with disabilities were either completely excluded from participation in public school programs (e.g., Menzies & Falvey, 2008), or were educated in segregated special education programs (e.g., Smith, Polloway, Patton, & Dowdy, 2008). Historically, special education and general education functioned as independent and discrete systems. General educators had responsibility for typically developing learners and special educators maintained educational responsibility for students with disabilities (Simpson, de Boer-Ott, & Smith-Myles, 2003).

Throughout the 1970s and 1980s, however, students with disabilities increasingly began to attend general education schools instead of segregated special schools. In the aforementioned Sheldon High School, students with disabilities were essentially nonexistent in 1959, but by 2005 they accounted for 19% of the student population.

During this time the ways in which those programs were being provided was also rapidly changing, moving from segregated programs (e.g., separate classrooms in general education schools) to inclusive programs (e.g., placements in general education classrooms alongside typical peers; Connor & Ferri, 2007). In part due to federal legislative requirements that all students with disabilities be provided with access to the general education curriculum, by the year 2006 more than half of all students with disabilities were being educated in general education classrooms for 80% or more of the school day. Another quarter of these students were in general education classrooms for 40 to 80% of the school day (Fast facts, n.d.). This growing trend toward inclusion of students with disabilities in general education classrooms is also true for students with autism spectrum disorders (ASD; Simpson et al., 2003).

Not only are general educators increasingly being asked to take on primary educational responsibility for the education for students with disabilities, but the expectations for academic achievement for these students have risen dramatically in recent years. The increasing emphasis on educational accountability and the increasing standardization of curricular, instructional, and assessment practices for all students, with and without disabilities (e.g., Skerrett & Hargreaves, 2008), has only served to further exacerbate this situation.

Whatever historical utility the traditional structure of one autonomous teacher with responsibility for all students in a classroom might have had in the past, the present levels of student cultural, behavioral, and academic diversity make it unlikely that a single educator will or can possess the multitude of professional skills needed to develop and implement effective instruction for the diverse learners in the contemporary American classroom. At all grade levels, the range of student performance is widening (Winn & Blanton, 2005). What is required for the success of this heterogeneous student population is the combination of the diverse sets of professional competencies that multiple educators can bring to the general education classroom (e.g., Hourcade & Bauwens, 2003; Idol, 2006; Murawski, 2003). This combining and sharing of professional skill sets to enhance the education of diverse learners is at the heart of collaboration in the schools.

Historical Background of Collaboration in the Schools

General Education

The origins of collaboration between general and special educators have two distinct roots, one firmly based in each camp. In general education, team teaching was first widely advocated and emerged in the United States in the 1960s as a way to advance the overall quality of the nation's schools (Bair & Woodward, 1964). Team teaching features the presence of two educators in a classroom setting who share responsibility for the development, implementation, and evaluation of instructional services to students (e.g., Bauwens, Hourcade, & Friend, 1989; Welch, 1999). However, team teaching did not gain widespread support and implementation, although it did reemerge in the 1990s, especially at the middle school level (Pugach & Johnson, 2002).

Special Education

Historically, special educators have long incorporated consultation and collaboration into their professional roles, perceiving these functions as integral and fundamental to their work (e.g., Lilly, 1971; Pugach & Johnson, 2002). This perception may have evolved from special education's origins in the medical model (e.g., Fagan, 2000). In the medical field's use of consultation, an "expert" with particular expertise in an area (e.g., a cardiac surgeon) meets with someone who needs that information (e.g., a person with a heart issue). The expert seeks to identify and propose exactly what should be done.

In special education, the consultation structure emerged in the 1970s as a result of the struggles of students with disabilities when "mainstreamed" into unmodified general education classrooms. In such cases, the special educator often served as the "expert" on students with disabilities for the general educator, helping him or her to restructure general education classroom practices to instruct students with disabilities. Input from general educators on these issues was usually minimal, as the special educator was recognized by both as the "expert" on disability and special education (Pugach & Johnson, 2002). An issue with this consultation model is its fundamental professional asymmetry, with one person as "expert" having greater authority than the other who was seen as "in need" (Hourcade & Bauwens, 2003).

Growing concerns about these role issues in collaboration during the late 1970s and 1980s led to an evolution in terminology and practice. Increasingly the professional literature began to refer to collaboration and collaborative consultation to identify an evolving alternative to consultation. In these new approaches "specialists" (special educators) sought to work as equal partners with general educators in solving the issues associated with the education of students with disabilities in general education classrooms. The goal of these new models was for all involved service providers to come together as equal partners in seeking resolutions to specific problems (Idol, Paolucci-Whitcomb, & Nevin, 1986).

In a typical collaborative consultation situation, when an instructional or behavioral issue emerges in a general education classroom, the general educator seeks out a collaborative partner with some expertise in that issue. The two would then met outside the classroom, review the situation, and seek to jointly generate potential strategies. The general educator then returns to the classroom, implements and evaluates those solutions, and often reports back to the collaborative partner the success or lack thereof of their work (Hourcade & Bauwens, 2003).

Description and Overview of Collaboration in the Schools

The linguistic, intellectual, academic, behavioral, and social diversity of many elementary and secondary education classrooms today makes it difficult for any single educator to have the complete range of professional knowledge and skills to effectively respond to the needs of all students. Perhaps nowhere is the issue of growing student diversity in general education classrooms better exemplified than in the case of students with ASD, a group whose numbers have expanded dramatically over the last 20 years (White, Scahill, Klin, Koenig, & Volkmar, 2007) and who are increasingly being served in inclusive general education classrooms (Simpson, de Boer-Ott, & Smith-Myles, 2003). Their presence in general education classrooms often generates an array of challenging behavioral and learning issues, including significant differences in learning, social skills, behavior, and communication, any single one of which would tax many educators (Simpson et al., 2003).

Unfortunately, the trend toward the inclusion of students with ASD has not been accompanied by an equivalently substantial provision of proven instructional models and procedures that will facilitate the success of these learners in general education classrooms (Simpson et al., 2003). As a result, many skilled educators report that they consider themselves to be less than fully capable of competently providing the necessary education services to these students (Spears, Tollefson, & Simpson, 2001). Myles and Simpson (1989) found that 86% of general educators surveyed were willing to accept a student with a disability into their classrooms on a full-time basis if appropriate support and training were provided. Absent that support and training, less than 33% of the teachers were willing to accept the same student.

One promising approach that has emerged over the past two decades to provide that support seeks to combine the complementary sets of professional knowledge and skills that different education professionals (e.g., general educators and special educators) bring to their work. In so doing, the schools are able to provide to all students a maximally effective instructional package. Historically, general educators have particular expertise in large group instruction, grade level curricular expectations and standards, and class management strategies. Special educators possess in-depth knowledge about the learning characteristics of students with a variety of disabilities, and effective curricular and instructional adaptations (e.g., Rice & Zigmond, 2000).

In reviewing the published research on in-class professional collaboration between special and general educators, Weiss and Brigham (2000) reported that the special education teacher typically was responsible for modifying instruction, behavior management, and monitoring student progress. The general education teacher maintained primary responsibility for the content of instruction. Combining these two sets of skills in a general education setting maximizes the likelihood that diverse students, including students with ASD, will experience academic and social successes in these inclusive settings. To this end, in designing their ASD inclusion collaboration model to support general educators who assume responsibility for teaching students with autism, Simpson et al. (2003) based their approach on collaboration, emphasizing shared responsibilities and decision making among general educators, special educators, and support personnel.

In general, collaboration refers to the process of two (or more) professionals working together. Hourcade and Bauwens (2003) more specifically defined collaboration as:

> An ongoing style of professional interaction in which people voluntarily engage in shared program planning, implementation, evaluation, and overall program accountability. (p. 7)

Hourcade and Bauwens went on to note that collaboration is best conceptualized as a way for people to interact, not a process nor an end in and of itself. Collaboration is an overall way to think about and organize the shared planning and working relationships through which education professionals approach their work. Similarly, Friend (2005) stressed that collaboration refers not to what one is doing, but how one is doing it, specifically how one interacts with others.

Features of Collaboration

Effective and successful collaboration efforts are characterized by a number of basic features. These include the following.

Self-Examination and Commitment to Change.   Many teachers have only been taught to work in isolation. Even new teachers have well-established conceptions of what "teaching" is, based largely on their own experiences as students almost exclusively within the "one teacher–one group of students" structure. If collaboration is to be successful, participants must be prepared to reflect seriously regarding (a) how well they are able to meet the needs of their diverse students, and (b) how willing they are to make the substantial personal and professional changes in their lives that establishing true collaborative relationships with colleagues in the schools will require (Hourcade & Bauwens, 2003).

Sharing. At the most basic level, collaboration requires that the participants must share themselves and their work with each other. This involves a number of dimensions. Teachers who seek to collaborate in the schools must begin by sharing a common philosophy, a set of shared beliefs about schools, teaching and learning, and students. Absent this foundation, it is difficult to imagine a collaborative relationship being sustainable over the long term. In addition, schools that have a culture of shared beliefs are more likely to demonstrate higher levels of student achievement (e.g., Marzano, Waters, & McNulty, 2005).

Collaboration also features shared accountability and responsibility, with all students seen as the responsibility of all educators. This represents a significant shift from traditional structures of teacher responsibility, wherein each teacher was responsible for only one group of students. Shared accountability emerges from all participants contributing to the planning and implementation of interventions, and accepting responsibility for the outcomes of that work (Friend, 2005).

Unfortunately, at present this shared responsibility for the successful education of all students often does not exist. In a 2007 study of almost 500 first and second year teachers in four states, Kardos and Johnson reported that many new teachers do not believe their fellow teachers share a sense of collective responsibility for their students and for each other. This finding is especially of concern in that research consistently has suggested that in the most effective schools, teachers take collective and not just individual responsibility for student learning (e.g., Newmann & Wehlage, 1995, p. 3).

In true collaborative efforts, resources also are shared. These shared resources may include ideas, technical information and support, or time (Friend, 2005). For collaboration to succeed, each participant must contribute resources to the program.

Central to collaboration is the sharing of the many responsibilities that are required to provide quality education to all students. This sharing does not imply that the educational tasks and responsibilities always are equal. Indeed, at any given time there will likely be some imbalance, with one professional assuming relatively greater levels of responsibility. These decisions should be guided by specific program and student needs and by the unique competencies and strengths each professional brings to the work (Hourcade & Bauwens, 2003). However, inequities in structural roles that are long-lasting and are allowed to continue represent a major barrier to successful collaboration (Keefe, Moore, & Duff, 2004).

One of the most interesting indicators of the level of sharing that exists in a collaborative relationship between a general educator and a special educator is to listen to their vocabulary as they describe the students with whom they work. In the initial stages of collaboration, many special educators continue to speak of "my students" versus "her students" when talking about students with disabilities. The general educator often uses similar language when discussing students without disabilities. After the two teachers have moved more deeply into collaboration, including sharing, the language that both teachers use often shifts instead to "our students" (Bouck, 2007; Hourcade & Bauwens, 2003).

Volunteering. As any professional practice gains credibility in the field, it is understandable that it may be involuntarily imposed upon a school or system by administrators. The administrative temptation to unilaterally require that teachers "collaborate" is understandable, but the very social nature of collaboration requires a deep and voluntary commitment of the involved participants (e.g., Bouck, 2007; Scruggs, Mastropieri, & McDuffie, 2007; Walther-Thomas, Bryant, & Land, 1996). In the absence of this commitment, any resulting collaboration may be collaborative in name only, with the educational status quo remaining largely unchanged beneath a thin veneer. However, it may be possible nevertheless to generate an effective collaborative relationship even if initially the participation of both parties is not voluntary (Mastropieri et al., 2005).

Approaches to Collaboration

There are as many approaches to collaboration as there are collaborators. One can envision collaboration in the schools between two educators (e.g., a general educator and a special educator), between a teacher and another type of school professional (e.g., a special educator and a school counselor), or even between three or more school professionals (e.g., a special educator, an ESL teacher, and a general educator). For simplicity and for the purposes of enhancing the education of students with ASD in inclusive settings, this discussion primarily will emphasize two collaborators, often (but not necessarily) a special and general educator.

Collaborative efforts might be categorized as either indirect or direct collaboration (Bauwens & Hourcade, 1995; Hourcade & Bauwens, 2003). These two categories are distinguished by (a) how and where the collaborators meet and interact, and (b) what subsequently happens in the general education classroom.

In indirect collaboration, a consultation approach, the general educator meets with one or more "experts" or specialists outside the general education classroom, where they review issues identified by the general educator and develop educational plans and strategies that they anticipate may resolve the issues. However, only the general education teacher who is administratively assigned to that class returns to those students to directly provide educational services in the general education classroom. While this work is informed and guided by her interactions with the special educator, the special educator never actually teaches in the general educational classroom.

As an example of an indirect collaborative approach, a fifth grade elementary educator might recognize that she needs help to best meet the needs of a student with autism who has joined her class. To this end he or she might meet with one or more "experts" where she explains her specific concerns and asks for suggestions. Following this meeting, one of these expert colleagues (for example, the special educator) may come into the general education classroom to observe and gather information. The expert then provides the teacher with one or more suggestions, which the teacher on her own then attempts to implement for the targeted student(s).

Over the past 20 years, a variety of "consulting" models based on this indirect collaboration model have emerged, including the previously discussed collaborative consultation. In peer collaboration, two general educators collaborate by working through a four-step process to identify effective classroom interventions (Pugach & Johnson, 1988). In coaching, school colleagues with comparable levels of professional skills are paired as support for each other (Walther-Thomas, Korinek, McLaughlin, & Williams, 2000, p. 79). Teacher assistance teams represent one of the earliest approaches suggested to facilitate collaboration among educators (Chalfant, Pysh, & Moultrie, 1979). The teacher assistance team (TAT) approach uses a four-member team composed of three relatively permanent core members who are experienced master teachers elected to participate on the TAT by their colleagues at their school, and a fourth and changing member, an educator seeking help. The teacher brings to the TAT a student concern, the TAT then conducts a problem-solving and brainstorming meeting to identify possible solutions to the problem, with the educator then taking those ideas back to the classroom.

What is common to all these indirect collaboration models is that while the teacher receives advice, suggestions, and recommendations from others, ultimately that teacher returns to the classroom alone. Instructional responsibility and accountability remain largely or solely with that single teacher. Despite the assistance that is provided outside the classroom, indirect collaboration does not fundamentally change the essential nature of the "one teacher–one classroom" structure of traditional instruction in the schools.

In direct collaboration, two (or more) school professionals not only meet and plan beforehand, but also then go on to work together in the classroom, providing instruction to the whole group, small groups, or individual students. Direct collaboration is characterized by the simultaneous presence of two or more educators in the general education classroom for at least part of the instructional day, jointly sharing responsibilities for planning, instructing, and evaluating heterogeneous groups of students. Direct collaboration differs from indirect collaboration in a number of other ways.

Indirect collaboration often occurs episodically and "as needed." When a specific issue has been resolved, the collaboration vanishes. In direct collaboration, the relationship between the educators is ongoing and sustained over time (Hourcade & Bauwens, 2003).

Indirect collaboration is often characterized by professional asymmetry, wherein one partner is the "expert" and the other in need of assistance. In direct collaboration, the participants function as equals (Hourcade & Bauwens, 2003).

Over the past two decades, one particular approach to direct collaboration, cooperative teaching (or coteaching), has been widely implemented (Scruggs et al., 2007). In cooperative teaching, the special educator who is collaborating with the general educator is actually working simultaneously alongside the general educator in the classroom for at least part of the instructional day. The most distinctive feature of cooperative teaching, and the one that most differentiates it from the indirect approaches to collaboration, is this joint and simultaneous direct provision of instruction by two educators in the general education inclusive classroom. The relative roles of "expert" and "help-seeker" of the two vary constantly throughout the day, as each professional takes on those functions in which he or she has greater competence.

In 2003 Hourcade and Bauwens defined cooperative teaching as:

> direct collaboration in which a general educator and one or more support services providers voluntarily agree to work together in a co-active and coordinated fashion in the general education classroom. These educators, who possess distinct and complementary sets of skills, share roles, resources, and responsibilities in a sustained effort while working towards the common goal of school success for all students. (p. 41)

For students with autism who spend significant portions of the school day in inclusive general education classrooms, this might involve the special educator being in that room and actively teaching these and other students for some portion of the day. Alternatively, if the primary needs of the student with autism are behavioral, a school psychologist with special expertise in developing and implementing functional behavioral analyses and behavior intervention programs might work in that classroom alongside the general educator.

Cooperative teaching offers two distinct advantages over indirect approaches to collaboration. First, all students in these classrooms, both students with and without disabilities, have access to specialized and more individualized supports (e.g., Rice & Zigmond, 2000). Second, each educator can observe and begin to acquire and use the unique strategies and skills that the partner brings to the classroom. In their 2007 meta-analysis of qualitative research on cooperative teaching, Scruggs et al. (2007) determined that under cooperative teaching arrangements special educators acquire greater competence in content knowledge, while general educators attain greater skills in curricular adaptations.

Of course, it is not possible for every general education classroom with one or more students who have ASD to be staffed continuously with both a general and special educator. Hourcade and Bauwens (2003) noted that in a common cooperative teaching arrangement the special educator might join the general educator in the general education classroom for some limited period of time daily or every other day, perhaps at a point in the classroom schedule that is particularly challenging for the student with autism (e.g., transitions or social activities).

The implementation of direct collaboration does present unique challenges. Historically, special educators have administered programs in which students with special needs were removed from general education classrooms, and instead were provided services through separate pullout programs (e.g., resource rooms or self-contained special classes). If special educators instead work in general education classrooms alongside general educators who remain responsible for that program, the potential exists for the special educator to experience a loss of professional identity and autonomy. It is not uncommon to hear special educators say that they "feel like an aide" in the general education classroom (e.g., Bouck, 2007). The coordination of role responsibilities in a collaborative teaching relationship is a critical component in the success of that program (Simpson et al., 2003).

Resources Required for Successful Collaboration

In the past two decades certain themes have consistently emerged as practitioners have identified those resources necessary for successful collaboration, especially cooperative teaching. These include (a) administrative support, (b) planning time, (c) training and preparation, and (d) personal and professional compatibility.

Administrative Support. A near constant key to the success of collaborative efforts in the schools is the presence of administrative support. In successful collaboration programs, the presence of support from the school's principal is almost always identified as a major factor in that success (Idol, 2006). Positive principal attitudes, as well as administrative support for working with all students, including those with autism, are a prerequisite for optimal educational benefits of inclusive classrooms (Simpson et al., 2003). Administrative support can be expressed in a variety of ways, which include (a) identifying the vision of how the collaboration should look and function, (b) offering defense of the changes when needed, and (c) allocating such needed resources as time, space, and staff development (Hourcade & Bauwens, 2003). Perhaps most importantly, supportive administrators give their collaborative staff permission to try innovative practices, even if failure is a possible outcome.

Planning Time. Effective collaboration, especially cooperative teaching, does not take place just because two educators are present during instruction. For collaboration to be effective, substantial amounts of preparation are necessary. In terms of inclusion of students with autism, Simpson et al. (2003) noted that additional teacher planning time was critical to effectively individualize academic tasks, plan alternative or additional activities, and develop appropriate individualized instructional methods. Both Hazlett (2001) and Dieker (2001) reported that cooperative teaching partners received 40 to 45 minutes of planning time each week. However, that level of planning time usually was seen by participants as insufficient, with teachers stating the need for more frequent planning sessions totaling two to three times that amount.

Training and Preparation in Collaboration. It is not uncommon for both administrators and practitioners to initially discount the need for professional development in collaboration, thinking that "everyone has experience in working with others." However, the new and unique demands inherent when teachers share instructional responsibility for developing, implementing, and evaluating educational programs for diverse learners in inclusive classrooms almost always requires new sets of interpersonal and professional skills. Both special and general educators may require collaboration skill training to best prepare them for these new professional roles (Simpson et al., 2003). Scruggs et al. (2007) specifically noted the frequently stated need for specific training in collaborative skills reported by cooperative teaching partners.

Personal and Professional Compatibility.   One of the distinctive and unprecedented aspects of teachers moving from working by themselves in isolation to working side by side with another adult is that heretofore irrelevant adult interpersonal skills become paramount. Experienced cooperative teaching partners tend to be emphatic about the need for compatibility with partners (e.g., Scruggs et al., 2007). In a review of the research on cooperative teaching, Weiss (2004) concluded that the personalities or teaching styles of the teachers were particularly important in the success of their collaborative efforts. Bouck (2007) noted the importance of teachers being aware of and considering beforehand the interpersonal tensions that cooperative teaching can create. Teachers who consider moving into cooperative teaching should engage in specific preliminary discussions to determine their compatibility on such general issues as their individual autonomy and existing roles, mutual trust and respect; and on such specific issues as grading, student participation, behavior and classroom management, and instructional accommodations.

The Research Base for Collaboration and Cooperative Teaching

The practice of using collaboration to facilitate system change for children with ASD in the public schools is well documented in the professional literature and supported in practice. As noted and referenced below, a review of the literature finds that collaboration has been used to elicit change at the school level to facilitate the inclusion of children with autism and other disabilities in preschool and other settings, develop behavioral support systems, and coordinate the delivery of related and support services. Collaboration and consultation is also used extensively to deliver and enhance staff development, most often with paraprofessionals and related services personnel, and to involve parents in the educational planning process.

The ability to describe a practice as being evidence-based rests on both the number of studies that describe it as an effective intervention as well as the methodology used to collect the data on efficacy. In the case of the research base for collaboration and consultation, most of the reported data is anecdotal in nature, typically consisting of program reviews. As a result, the ability to generalize and anticipate outcomes based on a single report may be lacking. However, the early stage of the emergent evidence base on school collaboration should not preclude the use of collaboration as an effective practice for system change.

Using Collaboration and Consultation to Facilitate Inclusion of Students with Autism

In a multisite program evaluation study, Idol (2006) examined the effectiveness of collaborative practices and their impact on personnel attitudes and student outcomes to identify those practices that best facilitate the successful inclusion of students with ASD. Four elementary schools and four secondary schools incorporated collaboration practices to support success of these students in inclusive general education classrooms. The report concluded that these collaborative practices were successful, with students able to generalize learning across classroom settings. Even though teachers highly rated their ability to collaborate, they also believed that additional staff development in cooperative and consultative teaching was necessary for collaboration and consultation to be effective.

The selection of effective collaborative practices requires consideration of a variety of factors in order to achieve positive results. For example, Warger and Pugach (1996) suggested that collaboration among educators toward inclusion starts with a careful and critical examination of the general education curriculum when including students with mild disabilities. This same consideration of the nature of the general education classroom is equally necessary when planning for inclusion of students with ASD.

Using Collaboration to Develop Behavioral Support Plans

The increase in the number of students with autism who are receiving educational services in inclusive classrooms, with their often unique behavioral and social characteristics, has required general educators to more extensively support student behavioral needs. This has generated a variety of new collaborative models. Using the criterion of quantity of research as one indicator of an evidence-based practice, the effectiveness of collaboration in the development of behavioral support plans is supported by the research.

Chitiyo and Wheeler (2009) evaluated the treatment efficacy of a university-based behavioral consultation model. Participating teachers were surveyed on the social validity, acceptability, and effectiveness of the interventions in enhancing teacher compliance and participation in active collaboration in the school setting. Results indicated that teachers generally perceived this model as effective at addressing problem behaviors in school. However, the limited sample size and potential issues with the dependent variable measures in this study may limit its application as an evidence-based practice.

Another study by Marshall and Mirenda (2002) involved a case study involving a young student with autism where parent–professional collaboration was used to create a positive behavior support (PBS) system for the student and family. This study used a four phase process involving (a) building their collaborative relationship, (b) conducting a functional behavioral assessment (FBA), (c) developing a plan to improve the student's compliance with family routines, and (d) collaborating on the implementation and revision of the plan. Though limited, this report suggested that the processes involved with active collaboration can yield positive outcomes for students with autism in home settings.

A study by Moes and Frea (2002) involving three students with autism provided additional evidence for parents and school professionals collaboratively developing and implementing behavioral supports for students with ASD. Using a multiple baseline research design, they examined the challenging behaviors and functional communication of three children with autism across baseline, intervention, and follow-up phases. The students were monitored across all phases to evaluate changes in the dependent measures within training and generalization routines. The dependent variable measure was a self-report questionnaire that was administered intermittently to parents to determine if consideration of family context improved the "goodness of fit" of the functional communication training treatment packages across intervention phases. Their findings indicate that consideration of family context may contribute to the stability and durability of reductions in challenging behavior achieved with functional assessment and functional communication training procedures.

Staff Development and Coordination of Related and Support Services

A third area where a research basis for the support of collaboration as an evidence-based practice is evolving is in the area of staff development and coordination of services from related service providers and paraprofessionals. The complicated nature of effectively providing services for students with autism involves the planned coordination of services in the home, school, and community. The development and implementation of a transdisciplinary service delivery model to coordinate services and enhance the individual capacity of service providers is finding growing evidence-based support in the special education literature.

For example, the use of collaboration to provide staff development and coordinate school support has been studied with (a) paraprofessionals in special education settings (Carnahan, Williamson, Clarke, & Sorensen, 2009), (b) rehabilitation professionals in the transition process (Oertle & Trach, 2007), (c) mental health professionals (Perry, Dunne, McFadden, & Campbell, 2008), and (d) speech and language pathologists in consultation clinics (Cheseldine, Manders, & McGowan, 2005). In each case the implementation of collaboration in the process was concluded to have been efficacious.

Future Directions

Given that the philosophy and practice of inclusion of students with ASD in general education classrooms is well-established in the nation's schools, it seems reasonable to conclude that general educators will continue to require extensive support systems to most effectively help their diverse students experience success in both accessing the general education curricula as well as mastering their own unique individualized curricula. That support for general educators is likely to be provided, at least in part, through collaborative efforts, either through indirect collaboration (e.g., one of the various consultation models) or direct collaboration (e.g., cooperative teaching).

An often overlooked advantage to special educators working more with their general education colleagues in inclusive classrooms is that many of the strategies designed to enhance the success of students with disabilities that the special educator brings to that setting also benefit many other students who may not have disabilities (Idol, 2006). For example, instruction in social skills that a special educator develops for a student with autism in a general education classroom might also prove beneficial for other students in that classroom who also have social and interaction issues or needs.

Two relatively recent professional developments in the schools, collaboration and response to intervention (RTI), may have significant areas of overlap and convergence. RTI has emerged as a new way to address student struggles in school from the earliest indications of student concerns. In the common three-tiered approach to RTI, varying levels of supports are provided to students as appropriate. In Tier 1, targeting perhaps 80% of all students, high quality developmentally appropriate instruction is provided within general education classrooms. In Tier 2, perhaps 10 to 15% of a school's population receives more intensive services, often small-group instruction on the targeted area of concern. The goal of these services is to help these students achieve at levels commensurate with of grade level peers, or at least make adequate progress towards identified grade level expectations. In Tier 3, students receive even more intensive and individualized services designed as specific and direct interventions for specific needs. Tier 3 services are often seen as synonymous with traditional special education services (e.g., Mallard & Johnson, 2008).

Students with special needs who receive services at the Tier 2 level will likely access those services through a variety of school professionals. In these cases there must be clear collaborative coordination of professional roles between such providers as general educators, special educators, speech and language therapists, and school psychologists (Skokut, 2008).

While much early use of RTI emphasized the identification and provision of services to students with learning disabilities and related academic issues, the essential structural underpinnings of RTI can be applied to students with learning and behavioral characteristics consistent with those of autism. One can easily envision scenarios, for example in inclusive early childhood programs, where children who evidence behavioral, social, or linguistic issues associated with autism received increasingly intense services through an RTI-like intervention model with the aim that some of these students might be successfully maintained in subsequent inclusive settings with Tier 2 levels of services.

One intervention strategy for students with ASD that has conceptual similarities to RTI is the ecobehavioral approach (EBA; Carta & Greenwood, 1985). In EBA, much like in RTI, significant classroom variables are directly assessed, with the potential relationships of these variables to effective instruction collaboratively determined. EBA specifically seeks to identify and clarify the relationships between environmental and instructional factors (e.g., classroom settings, type of instruction, and teacher behaviors) and a student's response rates (Greenwood, Schulte, Kohler, Dinwiddie, & Carta, 1986). EBA has been found useful in analyzing the effectiveness of instructional practices for students with autism (Kamps, Leonard, Dugan, Boland, & Greenwood, 1991). Like RTI, EBA provides information that is essential to making decisions about the level, complexity, or intrusiveness of an intervention (Watson, Gable, & Greenwood, 2010).

For either RTI or EBA to effectively address instructional issues with students, the data that are collected must be comprehensive and come from multiple sources. This collaboratively generated cumulative data set provides the necessary information on student academic levels, student behavior, teacher behavior, and instructional environments (Burns, Jacob, & Wagner, 2008). Such a comprehensive data package can only be generated through the coordinated efforts of multiple collaborative education professionals in the schools (Skokut, 2008).

Murawski and Hughes (2009) concluded that for RTI to be successful, a wide array of stakeholders, including administrators, students, staff, the community, and all types of educators must be active participants. They proposed that collaboration is inherent in effective RTI implementation because this will assure that (a) diverse students, including those with autism, all have access to the general education curriculum, and (b) students at Tiers 2 and 3 will be able to receive intensive and specialized instruction in small groups. Programs for many students at Tier 2 should be cooperatively taught, as the ability to group students and have smaller teacher–student ratios are noted as advantages and benefits of both RTI and cooperative teaching. As RTI and such similar intervention strategies as EBA continue to be more widely incorporated in the daily structures and functions of schools to better support the needs of diverse students, the need for collaboration between multiple school professionals will only continue to grow.

As the use of collaborative practices to support the needs of students with autism grows in the schools, so does the need to continue establishing and extending the extant evidence base for these practices. Researchers who are studying collaboration in the schools must continue to identify and select research methodologies, measurements, and statistical analyses that will provide a high level of research rigor. Such efforts can further establish collaborative practices as evidence based, providing empirical guidance to educational personnel who seek to base their practice on such a foundation.

Conclusion and Summary

Over the past 20 years many articles and books on school collaboration in general, and on cooperative teaching in particular, have appeared in the professional educational literature. A review of these results leads to the perhaps inevitable conclusion that, as is often the case in education, much has been done while much remains to be done. Much of the published work on collaboration to date has focused on what it is and how to do it, essentially the logistics of collaboration (e.g., Hourcade & Bauwens, 2003). Other work has sought to explain how a collaboratively taught classroom might look and function (e.g., Zigmond, 2007). The types and amounts of resources required for collaborative teaching partners to develop and deliver instruction to diverse students has also received extensive coverage in the professional literature.

Much scholarly inquiry into cooperative teaching to date has looked at participant and administrative perceptions of the process. Much of that work has concluded that both teachers and principals who became involved with cooperative teaching liked it, and believed it to be beneficial to both students and teachers (e.g., Scruggs et al., 2007). However, some other perceptual conclusions by early participants may not be so positive.

Too often in cooperative teaching programs the special educator essentially operates as a guest in the general education classroom, with relatively little influence over the day-to-day operations of the class. Primary instructional and curricular decision-making responsibilities remain with the general educator. In these apparently frequent situations the role of special educator is fundamentally that of an assistant or an aide (e.g., Scruggs et al., 2007). This may be due to several reasons, including (a) the special educator is on the general educator's physical or professional "turf" (e.g., Hourcade & Bauwens, 2003), (b) the special educator may not have as much mastery of the general education content knowledge as the general educator, or (c) there are simply much greater numbers of students without disabilities than those with disabilities in general education classrooms (Scruggs et al., 2007). The mechanisms through which the professional role issues of the cooperatively teaching general and special educator might best be resolved are not clearly delineated at present.

While a significant amount of scholarly work on professional collaboration in the schools has focused on what is, how to do it, and how participants experience it, other significant questions remain largely unexplored. Since collaboration emerged largely as a response to inclusion of students with disabilities and other diverse characteristics in general education classrooms (e.g., Murawski & Hughes, 2009; Roach et al., 2009), additional examinations of the impact of inclusion and collaboration on educational outcomes for these students are necessary.

At the risk of oversimplification, there are two primary rationales typically offered for inclusion of students with disabilities, including those with ASD. These two positions are:

1. The ongoing segregation of students by ability (and disability) is ethically unjustifiable.
2. Students with disabilities, including students with ASD, will benefit more, both academically and behaviorally, in inclusive and collaboratively taught general education classrooms than in traditional segregated programs.

The first issue remains the source of considerable philosophical debate (e.g., Sailor & Roger, 2005; Zigmond, 2003). By its very nature the issue remains essentially irresolvable by objective data.

However, the second issue is a critical one, and does lend itself to some degree of empirical verification. Unfortunately, to date the data to support the instructional efficacy of cooperative teaching on bringing about academic and behavioral gains in students are largely weak or nonexistent.

In considering potential differences between education and other professions (e.g., the medical and legal professions), Watson et al. (2010) concluded that too often the education profession accepts standards of practice based more on their popularity with practitioners than on actual empirical research on student impact. This may especially be the case to date with collaboration and cooperative teaching, as the measurement of something as seemingly simple as the educational impact of educator collaboration quickly becomes complicated and difficult to unravel (Murawski, 2003).

For example, Weiss (2004) suggested that (a) the outcomes of cooperative teaching were typically reported in vague or subjective language, and (b) the amount of efficacy research on this collaborative model was limited. Bouck (2007) also concluded that not enough is known about the relationship between cooperatively taught classrooms and subsequent improvements in student outcomes.

Similarly, Zigmond (2007) acknowledged that research on the effectiveness of cooperative teaching was still in its infancy, but she suggested that to date cooperative teaching did not seem to be changing classrooms and instruction in ways that were likely to result in students with disabilities making greater academic gains. This conclusion was based in part on earlier work (Magiera & Zigmond, 2004; Zigmond, 2006) where cooperative teaching arrangements were not found to change basic components of instruction (e.g., smaller instructional groups, more time on task, greater student engagement).

So perhaps the next goal in the professional evolution of school collaboration and cooperative teaching is the rigorous examination of its empirical and verifiable impact upon academic skill acquisition, behavioral improvements, linguistic competence, and other measures relevant to students with autism in collaboratively taught inclusive classrooms (Simpson et al., 2003). While professional collaboration in the schools may maintain some desirability based on its appeal to its participants, in these days of enhanced educational accountability educators may learn that the resources necessary to initiate functional and productive collaborative relationships may not be available in the absence of an extensive empirical evidence base showing direct benefits to measurable student outcomes.

References

Bair, M., & Woodward, R. G. (1964). *Team teaching in action*. Boston, MA: Houghton Mifflin.

Bauwens, J., & Hourcade, J. J. (1995). *Cooperative teaching: Rebuilding the schoolhouse for all students*. Austin, TX: PRO-ED.

Bauwens, J., Hourcade, J. J., & Friend, M. (1989). Cooperative teaching: A model for general and special education integration. *Remedial and Special Education, 10,* 17–22.

Bouck, E. C. (2007). Co-teaching...not just a textbook term: Implications for practice. *Preventing School Failure, 51,* 46–51.

Burns, M. K., Jacob, S., & Wagner, A. R. (2008). Ethical and legal issues associated with using response-to-intervention to assess learning disabilities. *Journal of School Psychology, 46,* 263–279.

Carnahan, C., Williamson, P., Clarke, L., & Sorensen, R. (2009). A systematic approach for supporting paraeducators in educational settings. *Teaching Exceptional Children, 41,* 34–43.

Carta, J. J., & Greenwood, C. R. (1985). Ecobehavioral assessment: A methodology for examining the evaluation of early intervention programs. *Topics in Early Childhood Special Education, 5,* 88–104.

Chalfant, J. C., Pysh, M. V. D., & Moultrie, R. (1979). Teacher assistance teams: A model for within-building problem solving. *Learning Disability Quarter, 2,* 85–96.

Cheseldine, S., Manders, D., & McGowan, C. (2005). The role of consultation clinics in services for children and young people with learning disabilities and/or autism. *Child & Adolescent Mental Health, 10*(3), 140–142. doi:10.1111/j.1475-3588.2005.00351.x

Chitiyo, M., & Wheeler, J. (2009). Analyzing the treatment efficacy of a technical assistance model for providing behavioral consultation to schools. *Preventing School Failure, 53,* 85–88.

Connor, D. J., & Ferri, B. A. (2007). The conflict within: Resistance to inclusion and other paradoxes in special education. *Disability and Society, 22*(1), 63–77. doi: 10.1080/09687590601056717

Dieker, L. A. (2001). What are the characteristics of "effective" middle and high school co-taught teams for students with disabilities? *Preventing School Failure, 46,* 14–23.

Fagan, T. K. (2000). Practicing school psychology: A turn-of-the-century perspective. *The American Psychologist, 55,* 754–757.

Fast facts. (n.d.). Retrieved from http://nces.ed.gov/fastfacts/display.asp?id=59

Friend, M. (2005). *Special education: Contemporary perspectives for school professionals.* Boston, MA: Pearson.

Greenwood, C. R., Schulte, D., Kohler, F. W., Dinwiddie, G. I., & Carta, J. J. (1986). Assessment and analysis of ecobehavioral interaction in school settings. In R. J. Prinz (Ed.), *Advances in behavioral assessment of children and families* (Vol. 2, pp. 69–98). Baltimore, MD: JAI.

Hazlett, A. (2001). The co-teaching experience joint planning and delivery in the inclusive classroom. *Dissertation Abstracts International, 62*(12), 4064A. (UMI No. AAI3037002)

Hourcade, J. J., & Bauwens, J. (2003). *Cooperative teaching: Rebuilding and sharing the schoolhouse* (2nd ed.). Austin, TX: PRO-ED.

Idol, L. (2006). Toward inclusion of special education students in general education: A program evaluation of eight schools. *Remedial and Special Education, 27,* 77–94.

Idol, L., Paolucci-Whitcomb, P., & Nevin, A. (1986). *Collaborative consultation.* Austin, TX: PRO-ED.

Kamps, D., Leonard, B. R., Dugan, E. P., Boland, B., & Greenwood, C. R. (1991). The use of ecobehavioral assessment to identify naturally occurring effective procedures in classrooms serving students with autism and developmental disabilities. *Journal of Behavioral Education, 4,* 367–397.

Kardos, S. M., & Johnson, S. M. (2007). On their own and presumed expert: New teachers' experience with their colleagues. *Teachers College Record, 109,* 2083–2106.

Keefe, E. B., Moore, V., & Duff, F. (2004). The four "knows" of collaborative teaching. *Teaching Exceptional Children, 36,* 36–41.

Lilly, M. S. (1971). Forum: A training based model for special education. *Exceptional Children, 3,* 745–749.

Magiera, K., & Zigmond, N. (2004). Co-teaching in middle school classrooms under routine conditions: Does the instructional experience differ for students with disabilities in co-taught and solo-taught classes? *Learning Disabilities Research and Practice, 20,* 79–85.

Mallard, D. F., & Johnson, E. (2008). *RTI: A practitioner's guide to implementing response to intervention.* Thousand Oaks, CA: Corwin.

Marshall, J., & Mirenda, P. (2002). Parent–professional collaboration for positive behavior support in the home. *Focus on Autism & Other Developmental Disabilities, 17,* 216.

Marzano, R. J., Waters, T., & McNulty, B. A. (2005). *School leadership that works: From research to results.* Alexandria, VA: Association for Supervision and Curriculum Development.

Mastropieri, M., Scruggs, T. E., Graetz, J., Norland, J., Gardizi, W., & McDuffie, K. (2005). Case studies in co-teaching in the content areas: Successes, failures, and challenges. *Intervention in School & Clinic, 40,* 260–270.

Menzies, H., & Falvey, M. A. (2008). Inclusion of students with disabilities in general education. In T. Jiminez & V. Graf (Eds.), *Education for all: Critical issues in the education of children and youth* (pp. 71–100). Hoboken, NJ: Wiley.

Moes, D., & Frea, W. (2002). Contextualized behavioral support in early intervention for children with autism and their families. *Journal of Autism & Developmental Disorders, 32,* 519.

Murawski, W. W. (2003). School collaboration research: Successes and difficulties. *Academic Exchange Quarterly, 7,* 104–108.

Murawski, W. W., & Hughes, C. E. (2009). Response to intervention, collaboration and co-teaching: A logical combination for successful systemic change. *Preventing School Failure, 53,* 267–277.

Myles, S. B., & Simpson, R. L. (1989). Regular educators' modification preferences for mainstreaming mildly handicapped children. *Journal of Special Education, 22,* 479–492.

Newmann, F. M., & Wehlage, G. G. (1995). *Successful school restructuring: A report to the public and educators by the Center on Organization and Restructuring of Schools.* Madison, WI: Board of Regents of the University of Wisconsin System.

Oertle, K., & Trach, J. (2007). Interagency collaboration: The importance of rehabilitation professionals' involvement in transition. *Journal of Rehabilitation, 73,* 36–44.

Perry, D., Dunne, M., McFadden, L., & Campbell, D. (2008). Reducing the risk for preschool expulsion: Mental health consultation for young children with challenging behaviors. *Journal of Child & Family Studies, 17,* 44–54. doi:10.1007/s10826-007-9140-7

Pugach, M. C., & Johnson, L. J. (1988). Peer collaboration. *Teaching Exceptional Children, 20,* 75–77.

Pugach, M. C., & Johnson, L. J. (2002). *Collaborative practitioners, collaborative schools* (2nd ed.). Denver, CO: Love.

Rice, D., & Zigmond, N. (2000). Co-teaching in secondary schools. *Learning Disabilities Research and Practice, 15,* 190–197.

Roach, A. T., Chilungu, E. N., LaSalle, T. P., Talapatra, D., Vignieri, M. J., & Kurz, A. (2009). Opportunities and options for facilitating and evaluating access of the general education curriculum for students with disabilities. *Peabody Journal of Education, 84,* 511–528. doi: 10.1080/0161956090903240954

Sailor, S., & Roger, B. (2005). Rethinking inclusion: Schoolwide applications. *Phi Delta Kappan, 86,* 503–509.

Scruggs, T. E., Mastropieri, M. A., & McDuffie, K. A. (2007). Co-teaching in inclusive classrooms: A metasynthesis of qualitative research. *Exceptional Children, 73,* 392–416.

Simpson, R. L., de Boer-Ott, S. R., & Smith-Myles, B. (2003). Inclusion of learners with autism spectrum disorders in general education settings. *Topics in Language Disorders, 23,* 116–134.

Skerrett, A., & Hargreaves, A. (2008). Student diversity and secondary school change in a context of increasingly standardized reform. *American Educational Research Journal, 45,* 913–946.

Skokut, M. (2008). Promoting the social and cognitive competence of children with autism: Interventions at school. *California School Psychologist, 13,* 79–91.

Smith, T. E. C., Polloway, E., Patton, J. R., & Dowdy, C. A. (2008). *Teaching students with special needs in inclusive settings* (5th ed.). Boston, MA: Pearson.

Spears, R., Tollefson, N., & Simpson, R. (2001). Usefulness of different types of assessment data in diagnosing and planning for a student with high-functioning autism. *Behavioral Disorders, 26,* 227–242.

Walther-Thomas, C., Bryant, M., & Land, S. (1996). Planning for effective co-teaching: The key to successful inclusion. *Remedial and Special Education, 17,* 255–264.

Walther-Thomas, C., Korinek, L., McLaughlin, V. L., & Williams, B. T. (2000). *Collaboration for inclusive education: Developing successful programs.* Boston, MA: Allyn & Bacon.

Warger, C. L., & Pugach, M. C. (1996). Forming partnerships around curriculum. *Educational Leadership, 53*(5), 62–65.

Watson, S. M. R., Gable, R. A., & Greenwood, C. R. (2010). Combining ecobehavioral assessment, functional assessment, and response to intervention to promote more effective classroom instruction. *Remedial and Special Education.* OnlineFirst. doi:10.1177/0741932510362219

Weiss, M. P. (2004). Co-teaching as science in the schoolhouse: More questions than answers. *Journal of Learning Disabilities, 37,* 218–223.

Weiss, M. P., & Brigham, F. J. (2000). Co-teaching and the model of shared responsibility: What does the research support? In T. E. Scruggs & M. A. Mastropieri (Eds.), *Advances in learning and behavioral disabilities: Vol. 14. Educational interventions* (pp. 217–245). Oxford, England : Elsevier.

Welch, M. (1999). What's the score and game plan on teaming in schools? A review of the literature on team teaching and school-based problem-solving teams. *Remedial and Special Education, 20,* 36.

White, S. W., Scahill, L., Klin, A., Koenig, K., & Volkmar, F. R. (2007). Educational placements and service use patterns of individuals with autism spectrum disorders. *Journal of Autism and Developmental Disorders, 37,* 1403–1412.

Winn, J., & Blanton, L. (2005). The call for collaboration in teacher education. *Focus on Exceptional Children, 38*(2), 1–10.

Zigmond, N. (2003). Where should students with disabilities receive special education services? Is one place better than another? *Journal of Special Education, 37,* 193–199.

Zigmond, N. (2006). Reading and writing in co-taught secondary schools social studies classrooms: A reality check. *Reading and Writing Quarterly, 22,* 249–268.

Zigmond, N. (2007). Delivering special education is a two-person job: A call for unconventional thinking. In J. B. Crockett, M. M. Gerber, & T. J. Landrum (Eds.), *Achieving the radical reform of special education: Essays in honor of James M. Kauffman* (pp. 115–137). Mahwah, NJ: Erlbaum.

INDEX